IN GOOD COMPANY

Essays in Honor of Robert Detweiler

ÆR

American Academy of Religion
Studies in Religion

Editor
David E. Klemm

Number 71
IN GOOD COMPANY
Essays in Honor of Robert Detweiler
edited by
David Jasper
Mark Ledbetter

IN GOOD COMPANY

Essays in Honor of Robert Detweiler

edited by

David Jasper
Mark Ledbetter

Scholars Press
Atlanta, Georgia

IN GOOD COMPANY
Essays in Honor of Robert Detweiler

edited by
David Jasper
Mark Ledbetter

Design and production in Adobe Janson, compliments of
Darwin Melnyk
Cathedral Graphics
23250 NE Bald Peak Road
Hillsboro, OR 97123
(503) 537-9357

The sketch on the cover and page v. is by Jeanne Meinke, a free lance artist. She has done illustrations for many magazines including *The New Yorker, Bon Appetit* and others. She lives in St. Petersburg, Florida.

Library of Congress Cataloging in Publication Data

In Good Company : essays in honor of Robert Detweiler ; edited by
David Jasper, Mark Ledbetter.
      p.   cm. — (American Academy of Religion studies in religion ;
no. 71)
    Includes bibliographical references.
    ISBN 0-7885-0039-2 (alk. paper)
    1. Religion in literature. 2. Religion and literature.
3. Literature, Modern—History and criticism. I. Detweiler,
Robert. II. Jasper, David. III. Ledbetter, Mark. IV. Series: AAR
studies in religion ; no. 71.
PN98.R44I5   1994
809\.93382—dc20   94–33428
                                    CIP

Printed in the United States of America
on acid-free paper
∞

JEANNE

Contents

THEMES

TEXTS

CURRICULUM VITAE

ROBERT DETWEILER

EDUCATION

Eastern Mennonite College (Virginia): 1950-51.

University of Hamburg: Theologische Fakultät, 1955-57 (five semesters).

Goshen College (Indiana): Bachelor of Arts, major in English, 1959.

Goshen Biblical Seminary (Indiana): Bachelor of Divinity, 1959.

University of Florida: Master of Arts, major in English and minor in German, 1960.

University of Florida: Doctor of Philosophy, major in English and minor in German, 1962.

PROFESSIONAL BACKGROUND

Refugee rehabilitation work in Germany (Neuwied, Stuttgart, Lübeck, Hamburg, 1951-55).

Instructor in English, University of Florida, 1961-62.

Assistant Professor of English, University of Florida, 1963-65.

Assistant Professor of English, Hunter College of the City University of New York, 1965-66.

Associate Professor of Literature, Florida Presbyterian College, 1966-70.

Associate Professor of Liberal Arts/Comparative Literature, Emory University, 1970-74.

Professor of Liberal Arts/Comparative Literature, Emory University, 1974—.

Associate Faculty, Graduate Division of Religion, Emory University, 1973—.

Associate Director of the Graduate Institute of the Liberal Arts, Emory University, 1973.

Director of the Graduate Institute of the Liberal Arts, Emory University, 1974-82.

Director of Graduate Studies, Graduate Institute of the Liberal Arts, Emory University, 1987-89.

VISITING APPOINTMENTS

Fulbright Professor of American Literature and American Studies, University of Salzburg, 1971-72.

Visiting Professor of American Literature, University of Hamburg, 1976-77.

Visiting Professor of American Literature, University of Hamburg, 1981.

Visiting Chaired Professor of American Literature, University of Regensburg, 1983.

Fulbright Professor of American Literature, University of Regensburg, 1989.

American National Bank Chair Professor of Excellence in the Humanities, University of Tennessee at Chattanooga, 1990.

Fulbright Professor of American Literature, University of Copenhagen, 1993.

BOOKS

John Updike. Boston: G. K. Hall, 1972. Paperback edition, Indianapolis: Bobbs-Merrill, 1979. Revised, expanded edition, 1984. Compact disk version, 1989.

Story, Sign, and Self: Phenomenology and Structuralism as Literary Critical Methods. Philadelphia: Fortress Press, 1978. Second Printing, 1984.

Ed., with Glenn Meeter, *Faith and Fiction: The Modern Story.* Grand Rapids: Eerdmans, 1979. Author of "Afterword" and translator of two German stories.

Ed., Derrida and Biblical Studies. *Semeia* 23. Chico, CA: Scholars Press, 1982.

Ed., *Art/Literature/Religion: Life on the Borders.* Chico, CA: Scholars Press, 1983.

Ed., with Sara Putzell-Korab, *The Crisis in the Humanities: Interdisciplinary Responses.* Madrid: Studia Humanitatis, 1983.

Ed., Reader Response Approaches to Biblical and Secular Texts. *Semeia* 31. Atlanta: Scholars Press, 1985.

Breaking the Fall: Religious Readings of Contemporary Fiction. London: Macmillan, and San Francisco: Harper & Row, 1989.

Ed., with William G. Doty, *The Daemonic Imagination: Sacred Text and Secular Story.* Atlanta: Scholars Press, 1990.

MONOGRAPHS

Four Spiritual Crises in Mid-Century American Fiction. Gainesville, Florida: University of Florida Press, 1963. Reprinted in New York: Books for Libraries, 1970.

Saul Bellow. Grand Rapids: Eerdmans, 1967.

Iris Murdoch's The Unicorn. New York: Seabury Press, 1969.

ESSAYS (selected)

"Emerson and Zen," *American Quarterly* (Winter, 1963), 422-38.

"The Over-Rated Oversoul," *American Literature* (March, 1964), 65-8.

"Christ and the Christ Figure in American Fiction," *The Christian Scholar* (Summer, 1964), 111-24. Reprinted in Marty and Peerman, eds., *New Theology* No. 2 (New York: Macmillan, 1965), 297-316.

"American Fiction and the Loss of Faith," *Theology Today* (July, 1964), 161-73.

"Langer and Tillich: Two Backgrounds of Symbolic Thought," *The Personalist* (Spring, 1965), 171-92.

"The Curse of Christ in Flannery O'Connor's Fiction," *Comparative Literature Studies* (Special Issue No. 2, 1966), 235-45. Reprinted in George Panichas, ed., Mansions of the Spirit (New York: Hawthorn, 1967), 358-71.

"Speculations about Jakob: The Truth of Ambiguity," *Monatshefte* (Spring, 1966), 25-32.

"Patterns of Rebirth in Henderson the Rain King, " *Modern Fiction Studies* (Winter, 1966-67), 405-14.

"Literature and Christianity in the Twentieth Century," W. B. Fleischmann, ed., *Encyclopedia of World Literature in the Twentieth Century* (New York: Ungar, 1967), 227-30.

"Religion and Literature in Recent American Scholarship," *Midcontinent American Studies Journal* (Fall, 1968), 89-93.

"Religion in Modern American Fiction," *Salesian Studies* (Spring, 1969), 4-15.

"Updike's Couples: Eros Demythologized," *Twentieth Century Literature* (October, 1971), 235-46.

"The Moment of Death in Modern Fiction," *Contemporary Literature* (March, 1972), 269-94.

"Eudora Welty's Great Blazing Butterfly: The Dynamics of Response," *Language and Style* (Winter, 1973), 58-71.

"La critica literaria en los Estados Unidos," *El Urogallo* (May-August, 1974), 145-50.

"The Jesus Jokes: Religious Humor in the Age of Excess," *Cross Currents* (Spring, 1974), 55-74.

"Contemporary American Literary Criticism," *Sprachkunst* (1975), 115-22.

"Games and Play in Modern American Fiction," *Contemporary Literature* (1975), 45-62. Published as "Gry i zabawy we wspolczesnej literaturze amerykanskiej," in Zbigniew Lewicki.

"Response to Louis Marin," in Daniel Patte, ed., *Semiology and Parables* (Pittsburgh: Pickwick, 1976), 230-35.

"Theological Trends of Postmodern Fiction," *Journal of the American Academy of Religion* (June, 1976), 25-37.

"John Cheever's Bullet Park: A World beyond Madness," in Erwin Stürzl, ed., *Romantic Reassessment: Essays in Honor of Professor Tyrus* Hillway (Salzburg: University of Salzburg, 1977), 6-32.

"Spiele und Spielen in der modernen amerikanischen Erzählliteratur," in Hans Bungert, ed., *Die amerikanische Literatur der Gegenwart* (Stuttgart: Reclam, 1977), 154-75.

"Jüngste Entwicklungen in der amerikanischen Erzählliteratur," Bungert, ed., *Die amerikanische Literatur der Gegenwart*, 205-27.

"Generative Poetics as Science and Fiction," *Semeia: An Experimental Journal for Biblical Criticism*, 10 (1978), 137-50.

"Recent Religion and Literature Scholarship," *Religious Studies Review* (April, 1978), 107-17.

"European Criticism in America: Three New Approaches," in Sonja Bahn, et al., eds., *Forms of the American Imagination* (Innsbruck: University of Innsbruck, 1979), 25-40.

"'The Same Door': Unexpected Gifts," in David Thorborn and Howard Eiland, eds., *John Updike: A Collection of Critical Essays* (Englewood Cliffs, NJ: Prentice-Hall, 1979), 169-77.

"Updike's A Month of Sundays and the Language of the Unconscious," *Journal of the American Academy of Religion* (December, 1979), 609-25. Another version in James Hogg, ed., *Essays in Honor of Erwin Stürzl on His Sixtieth Birthday* (Salzburg: University of Salzburg, 1980), 76-100.

"Transcending Journalism: Olmsted's Literary Style in *The Cotton Kingdom*," in Dana E. White and Victor A. Kramer, eds., *Olmsted South* (Westport, CT: Greenwood, 1979), 67-80.

"Updike's Sermons," in Klaus Lanzinger, ed., *Americana-Austriaca V* (Vienna, 1980), 11-26.

"After the New Criticism: Contemporary Methods of Literary Interpretation," in Richard A. Spencer, ed., *Orientation by Disorientation: Studies in Literary Criticism and Biblical Literary Criticism* (Pittsburgh: Pickwick, 1980), 3-23.

"Mass Communications Technology, Postmodern Fiction, and Theological Considerations," *Union Seminary Quarterly Review* (Spring/Summer, 1980), 201-09. Another version in Konstantinovic, Kushäner, and Kopeczi, eds., *The Evolution of the Novel* (Innsbruck: Innsbrucker Beiträge zur Kulturwissenschaft, 1982), 489-95.

"What Is a Sacred Text?" *Semeia: An Experimental Journal for Biblical Criticism* (1985), 213-30.

"Sacred Space and the Built Environment," in Frederick Bonkovsky, ed., *The Built Environment: Present and Future Values* (Columbus: University Center Press, 1986), 32-40.

"Squabbles of Science and Narrative: Lyotard's The Postmodern Condition," *Art Papers* (January-February, 1986), 18-20.

"No Place to Start: Introducing Deconstruction," *Religion and Intellectual Life* (Winter, 1988), 7-21.

"Apocalyptic Fiction and the End(s) of Realism," in David Jasper and Colin Crowder, eds., *European Literature and Theology in the Twentieth Century* (London: Macmillan, 1990), 153-83.

"John Updike: 'The Music School'--A Quartet of Readings," in Klaus Lubbers, ed., *Die englische und amerikanische Kurzgeschichte* (Darmstadt: Wissenschaftliche Buchgesellschaft, 1990), 409-20.

"Parerga: Homely Details, Secret Intentions, Veiled Threats, *Literature and Theology*, (March, 1991), 1-10.

(With Vernon Robbins), "The Eclipse of Realism: Twentieth Century Hermeneutics," in Stephen Prickett, ed., *Reading the Text: Biblical Criticism and Literary Theory* (Oxford: Basil Blackwell, 1991), 225-80.

"Overliving," *Semeia: An Experimental Journal for Biblical Criticism* 54 (1991),239-55.

"Vexing the Text: The Politics of Literary-Religious Interpretation," *Christianity and Literature* (Autumn, 1991), 61-70.

"Torn by Desire: Sparagmos in Greek Tragedy and Recent Fiction," in David Jasper, ed., *Postmodernism and the Future of Theology* (London: Macmillan, 1993).

"Elementals: An Autobiography," in D. John Lee, ed., *Life and Story* (Westport, CT: Praeger, 1993), 221-45.

Preface

Then I'll hit the trail for that promising land;
May catch up with Wystan and Rex, my friend,
Go mad in good company, find a good country,
Make a clean sweep or make a clean end,
(C. Day Lewis, *The Magnetic Mountain*)

Dear Bob,

We know you too well, and have been friends for too long, to be doing this, but we know also that you will forgive us. The best things always in friendship, in art and in religion are left unspoken, governed by a doctrine of reserve. One knows best what one means by a sort of instinctive empathy. Yet you may allow us our celebration, our festival in your honor, and in the spirit of thanksgiving. (There's theology for you!)

The small company who have gathered to write this book represent not only your colleagues and friends, but also those very many people who have been and remain your students. We all share, it may be said, a common obsession with the business of literature and religion, and most of us (perhaps as a result), a recognition of the importance and sheer difficulty of sustaining in our modern or postmodern world the religious traditions which we have inherited. We all profess to be academics and teachers and it was a professor of theology who recently wrote of the academic life genuinely lived as "arguably more successful in producing courtesy, truthfulness, gentleness, amiability, a sense of justice than Christianity itself."

Those qualities characterize you for us. But we have not set out to embarrass you. What they represent for many of us who have, in your footsteps, engaged with so-called postmodern questions, are the profoundly ethical dimensions of our enquiry: a moral tenacity which never allows academic study in religion or literature to neglect the deep issues of power, violence and alienation (as well as love and humor) which confront our contemporary experience. From the earliest days of your career it was in the imaginative world of the modern novel that you were exploring these issues: in the 60s with Updike, Bellow, O'Connor and Murdoch. In never less than dramatic confrontation, you led us to reconsider the sense of spiritual crisis, the truth of ambiguity, the problem of reading religiously, and you continue to do so as you explore the frontiers of literature for us.

Yet we were always aware that this recognition of the importance of modern fiction rested upon a profound philosophical, hermeneutical and theological learning. Life on the borders is never easy, and demands that we are up with the best of them in our sense of the tradition and its intellectual roots. Schleiermacher, Heidegger, Bultmann and Gadamer continue to permeate your writing, while ten years ago your issue of *Semeia: Derrida and Biblical Studies* was (and remains) foundational reading for students of literature and the Bible. Nor will teachers among us fail to recognize the immense contribution of those essays which lead students through the thickets of terms and names—papers like "After the New Criticism" (1980) and "From New Criticism to Poststructuralism" (1991, with Vernon K. Robbins). That confusing field which lies between biblical scholarship and literary criticism and scholarship needs careful and measured voices and sure guides like yourself—writers who both know the field and can interpret it for others to walk in after them.

We sense from you, Bob, a restless sense of enquiry about the future. Why do we teach?—not simply for the aggregation of learning or the preservation of the past in the present. Nor do we wish to impose a program upon our students as if we knew something of which they were ignorant . From you we have learned that perhaps all we can do is show—as the poet put it, all one can do today is warn. Ours is never, therefore simply an intellectual game, for the stakes are too high for that. It may, indeed, be profoundly spiritual, and the imagination must be exercised in the drama of experience, so that we begin to recognize that if we are indeed living the unthinkable, our duty is all the more to address ourselves to thinking the unthinkable. The apocalyptic dimension of contemporary experience is an insistent note in your more recent writings (as in the work of other such distinguished observers of the times as Jacques Derrida), and the story must be told and read. As you yourself have written:

> One story underlies and threatens all others in the short history of human expression, and it is the story which all others resist. Its substance is that the world is out of control.[2]

This is precisely the reason why we must remain always conscious of the nature of the sacred text and the art of reading religiously, both constant themes in your teaching. This proper concern for the business of reading has led you in recent years to an extraordinary exchange with Mieke Bal, another excellent reader of the biblical text. Not only does this exchange demonstrate what we already knew—your ability to adapt your critical attention across a wide range of sympathies and modes of discourse—but also, and not least, your sense of humor which is a characteristic of your profound seriousness.

It is now some twenty years since you wrote an essay entitled "The Jesus Jokes: Religious Humor in the Age of Excess," in the journal *Cross Currents*. We select this piece since it continues to characterize your approach to religious and literary study: amused and amusing, yet profoundly serious in its insight into religious expression and sensibility; iconoclastic in the best sense of the word, cutting through humbug and pretence; combining deep learning with easy insight into popular culture and folklore. "The laughter," as you say, "is crucial. It can signal a welcome to chaos' rule, or it can mean the dismay of recognition, the insight into the self that impels us to change."[3]

We hope that each of these essays engages, directly or indirectly, with your own work and what it represents. Christopher Norris' commentary on the "Derrida in Cambridge" affair might well have been about you (not a bad comparison!), in its concern with ethics, the serious business of play, the art of good reading, and, perhaps above all, honesty. Playfulness is a key note, established early in David Miller's essay. Let us, in good company, learn to be brave and serious enough not to be so damned *serious*, especially about ourselves.

And so, Bob, we, your friends, offer you these papers in the hope that, as William Blake put it, "the road of excess leads to the palace of wisdom." We hope that you will read them religiously, as only you know how, and that they may carry forward somewhat your own thought and that of others in a creative community of reading and interpretation. Finally, to conclude with the Prologue which reminds us that even in tragedy there is sometimes an exquisite comedy of huge seriousness, remember that

> If we offend, it is with our good will.
> That you should think, we come not to offend,
> But with good will. To show our simple skill,
> That is the true beginning of our end.
> Consider then, we come but in despite.
> We do not come, as minding to content you,

Our true intent is. All for your delight
We are not here.
(Shakespeare, *A Midsummer-Night's Dream*)

With best wishes,
David Jasper and Mark Ledbetter

NOTES

1. Adrian Hastings, *The Times Educational Supplement* (7 September 1990).

2. Robert Detweiler, "From Chaos to legion to Chance: The Double Play of Apocalyptic and Mimesis," Robert Detweiler and William G. Doty eds., *The Daemonic Imagination: Biblical Text and Secular Story*. (Atlanta, 1990), p. 1.

3. Robert Detweiler, "The Jesus Jokes: Religious Humor in the Age of Excess," *Cross Currents* 24 (1974) p. 71.

Introduction

DAVID JASPER AND MARK LEDBETTER

T he community of writers represented in this volume, which celebrates the work of Robert Detweiler, is also, and perhaps primarily, a community of readers. All of us, in different ways, have learned something from Detweiler of the act of "reading religiously," and it is this act which binds together the diversity of essays in this book.

The notion of religious reading can easily slip over into something banal or dogmatic. In the recent writings of Detweiler it is neither of these things, but rather an activity which timelessly draws together the assiduously critical and the passionately celebratory. Neither of these qualities can long absent itself from the academic community without grievous moral or intellectual damage.

In his most recent book, *Breaking the Fall*, Detweiler promotes a notion of religious reading in which participants offer "gestures of friendship with each other across the erotic space of the text" (p. 34-5) in a ceaseless willingness to accommodate for differences and in celebration of the community of readership. In such an activity, we are not alone, but we are supported by a sympathetic collegiality, which is all too often lacking in the competitive world of the academy. We are not, of course, speaking in any particular religious context. Paradoxically, most of us would situate ourselves within a world which is felt to be deeply religious, but never merely confessional in the narrow sense.

Being within, and yet more than, our inherited communities of belief, our religious reading then becomes a festive act which is both participatory and also excessive: an engagement with metaphorical language, which attempts to control excess even while it participates in it (*Breaking the Fall*, p. 40). It is, therefore, a participation in (and perhaps the only genuine articulation of) pain and suffering, being an act on the margins, both excluded from and included in our strategies of power and authority.

This recognition of pain within the community confirms us also as a community of love, and, essentially, dare we say? a liturgical community, even if we have abandoned the traditional, referential activity of looking toward a divinity for the celebratory act of a community across the delightful eroticism of textuality.

Robert Detweiler has never eschewed the kind of bold language which we here use quite blatantly. As a Professor of Comparative Literature at Emory University in Atlanta, Georgia, he is specifically neither a literary critic nor a professor of religion or theology. He is both. For he is trained in theology, yet at the same time has maintained a central place in postmodern developments in literary and critical theory in the United States. His study on John Updike remains perhaps the most important critique of this central contemporary novelist and essayist. While his more recent work since *Story, Sign and Self* has charted some of the most profound philosophical changes in religious thought since the 1970's, as well as positioned him as perhaps the most articulate spokesperson of postmodern literary theory, certainly in the United States. His work at the Institute of the Liberal Arts of Emory University has produced generations of graduate students who are committed to interdisciplinarity as the crucial, if infinitely difficult, mode of their participation in discussions of literature and religion.

The essays in this book are offered in celebration of Detweiler's work both as a writer and a teacher. Celebration is never, properly speaking, a monologic activity. It is the unified act of a community which is diverse and richly manifold. In this spirit, these essays are offered and should be read. To drag them into a placid uniformity would be both unnatural, and an offence to the complexity of Detweiler's work. These essays are not only interdisciplinary, but also international and intercultural. They offer many voices and modulate different tones in a symphony which is at once deeply romantic within the the tradition of Western thought, yet also profoundly postmodern and dissonant. To hear their harmony, which is the harmony of a community of love and friendship, may require great effort, not only intellectually, but also emotionally and spiritually.

The essays are organized thematically into three sections: Theories, Themes, and Texts. After a prelude by the poet Peter Meinke, we begin the section on theory, "scared to death," with an essay by Mieke Bal, a feminist critic deep within the European tradition, with whom Detweiler has engaged in provocative and suitably naughty dialogue in their adventures in scholarship. David Miller, an American colleague, follows Bal with a quite serious exploration of the ludic quality of Detweiler's work with his own playful description of Detweiler as the critic who "naughts nothing." From these beginnings we enter into a complex philosophical defence of a major European voice, Jacques Derrida, in Christopher Norris' essay. The political dimensions of Derrida's ludicrous, and ultimately confirmatory exchange which Cambridge University, reflects, for us, the profoundly political implications of Detweiler's work.

Not least among the questions on this political agenda is that of gender, an issue taken up very insightfully by Mary Gerhart, in an essay whose equal commitment to literature and textuality is developed further by Gregory Bruce and his essay on textuality and community. The section on theory concludes with two very fine essays, David Pacini's discussion of how "symbolic narratives redistribute the space for cohesive living," and Bettina Detweiler-Blakely and Robert L. Blakely's essay on the intimate relation between narrative and the social sciences, in particular archaeology.

Section two of *In Good Company* falls under the heading of Themes. Gregory Salyer's essay begins this section by "Gambling with Ghosts" and reminds us that Native American voices have much to offer our contemporary understanding of postmodernism and the postmodern condition because Native American literature exists as a "legitimate voice in the noise of American culture both past and present." Salyer's essay is followed by Ann-Janine Morey's deeply personal and moving essay on the "Literary Physician," which reminds us that a quality of healing must remain a part of our literary and intellectual activity if that activity is to remain meaningful and significant. That is, we must never abandon a salvific note in our work in a postmodern world. And this theme is acknowledged and continued in Barbara DeConcini's essay on women's bodies, "Unspeakable Hungers and the Stratagems of Sacrifice," in which DeConcini is "tracing and re-tracing" the relationship of woman's body, food, and religious practice. The thematic section concludes with what Davis Perkins calls "a neglected factor in interpretation," publishing. Introducing "the missing link" into our narrative community, Perkins reminds us that publishing has a profound impact on how a literary text is brought to its audience and therefore plays a major role in accepted interpretation.

The final section of these essays in honor of Detweiler falls under the heading of Texts. Peter Meinke, again, is poetic prelude with the poem, "The True UFO Story." William Doty's essay, "The Winnebago Road of Life and Death and Rebirth," then takes us on a narrative journey into ritual studies by way of an extensive reading of the texts of Paul Radin in reference to Detweiler's methodology for "reading religiously" found in *Breaking the Fall.*

Thus begins several chapters of "reading texts." James Champion seeks "literary communion" and a more humane world in the work of George Eliot. David Klemm, in his careful explication of Tolstoy's *The Kreutzer Sonata*, reminds us that "real transformation of life depends on [the] capacity--conferred by narrative—to see oneself otherwise than one actually is." Irene Makarushka leads us through an ethical reading from a feminist perspective of Iris Murdoch's book, *The Book and the Brotherhood.* And Dan Noel takes us through a close reading of three of Russell Hoban's novels and celebrates the human being as member of a story reading community.

The section on texts concludes with essays by Carolyn Jones, Vernon Robbins and Gary Phillips. The text each uses is the biblical text. Jones does a powerful intertextual reading of the story of Moses and the people of Israel with Zora Neal Hurston's novel, *Moses, Man of the Mountain* and brings important insights to bear on the contemporary scene and concerns of power, oppression and freedom. Robbins, a New Testament scholar by training, explores biblical narratives from the perspective of a socio-rhetorical poetics and takes us through a creative reading of Mieke Bal's text, *Death & Dissymmetry.* Robbins suggests that the ritual we call reading must be prepared to engage "multiple readings of a text" in order to appreciate fully a text's interpretive potential. Phillips' essay continues Robbins' exploration of biblical texts and suggests that a postmodern reading of the Bible offers insight to what he describes as the "crises of modernity." Perhaps, suggests Phillips, in relation to the biblical text, the postmodern imagination may "enhance the prospects for seeing the face of the Other and becoming community."

In Good Company concludes with a personal encounter with Robert Detweiler. Sharon Greene conducts a personal and extensive conversation with him. These final pages are delightful. In his own playfully serious way, Detweiler tells us much about his fascination with story, narrative, community, erotica, sexuality, the body, and religion. He talks of the academic and personal influences on his work and life. He reveals to us an intimately personal side of himself that only a few persons have had the good fortune to know. Turn soon to these last few pages in this text, and you will discover why those of us who know Robert Detweiler are convinced that we are in good company.

We would be remiss as editors if we did not acknowledge the insight and encouragement of David Klemm. As the general editor of the American Academy of Religion Series, he has played a critical role in making this text possible. Also, a very special thanks goes to Greg Salyer, who played an invaluable role in this book's preparation. Without his computer "genius", his insightfully critical comments regarding this text, and more important, his friendship, we could not have completed our task so timely and with such good results.

Finally, while we have been in the good company of many persons who have assisted in the writing and editing of this text and whose suggestions have made marked improvement in its style and substance, we, the editors, take full responsibility for any errors of judgment and style, which readers may find.

Theories

Black Holes & Einstein

PETER MEINKE

First, they're marble-pale
as Venus, flicked in galactic flight
by the thumb of God (you can see a Thumbnail
creasing the curved sky on velvet nights).
Disbelieving the hole's odd behavior
Einstein bet—despite his thirty years'
failure to reconcile stone and star—
God wouldn't play dice with the universe.

He thought the holes too random: our sky
is no lunar love-nest or cosmic
jackpot where chips fall where they will. But why,
kaleidoscoping through charged fields like shots
lagged in the void, do stars collapse and die,
making a coffin of space so black and blocked

not even light can escape? Though now it seems
out of this darkest deck, this dense egg,
particles spin like roulette wheels—wild beams,
quarks, electrons—forming a spectral peg
reuniting the universe, fusing
supernova with atom, star with stone,
telling us there's a rule for everything
under the sun: and everything beyond.

Venus, green-eyed guide, dealer of hands, below
whose shaded light more dangerous than
x-rays we study the mysteries, if only
you would illumine--for us, for Einstein--
Zeus and zero-zero, blind luck, black holes;
and if God's a gambling man?

Scared To Death

Metaphor, Theory, and the Adventure of Scholarship

MIEKE BAL

Le métaphorique ancre l'invention conceptuelle dans la culture. Du fait de la métaphore, là où le neuf abonde, le passé surabonde. Judith Schlanger[1]

The notions of fetishism and ideology, in particular, cannot simply be appropriated as theoretical instruments for a surgical operation on the bourgeois "other." Their proper use depends on an understanding of them as "concrete concepts," historically situated figures that carry a political unconscious along with them. W.J.T. Mitchell[2]

When I say that I am scared to death that it is going to rain[3], I don't mean that literally. I am not even really afraid at all. I just want to emphasize my irritation about standard Dutch weather by the use of an expression usually called metaphor. Metaphors are forms of language use that are somehow special in terms of meaning. How exactly is a matter of debate. I do not wish to contribute to that debate.

When poets use metaphors, we assume they do so to say something new—or to "say the unsayable." That is how metaphors are cognitively stronger than "normal" language use. In her novel *Le vice-consul*[4] French author Marguerite Duras repeatedly uses metaphors to describe the crowd which populate the Vietnamese landscape, like the following:

Sur le talus s'égrènent, en files indiennes, des chapelets de gens aux mains nues. (175)

Roughly—as literally as possible—this means something like this: "On the mounds, one after another, walk rosaries of people, bare-handed." What a terrible translation! The verb "s'égrener" is used for picking berries as well as for praying with rosaries. Small, identical units, one by one, one after another. Prayers, murmuring, endless: those are, for me at least, the most immediate associations of the combination "s'égrener" and "chapelets." Rosaries of people: one sees it in one's imagination. Long queues; one after another; at equal distance; systematic, many, anonymous. This metaphoric use of language has doubtless semantic surplus value. Poetic metaphors can also have affective surplus value: they can be moving, aesthetically pleasing, they can even hurt one's feelings. Opinions vary about the cognitive surplus value. I don't feel like adding an opinion to this debate.[5] My concern lies elsewhere. I am not interested in the content or the adequacy of a theory, but in the question: "how to deal with theory?" In this endeavor I want to honor Robert Detweiler by pursuing the debate he so generously engaged me in earlier.[6]

Scared to Death of Theory

Just like the exchange with Detweiler, the following thoughts originated in a concrete situation of debate. An earlier version of this paper was presented as a lecture as part of a conference that took place in January 1993 at the Institute for Contemporary Arts Amsterdam. The conference was co-produced by the Belle van Zuylen Institute for Research on Gender and this cultural institution. The fact of that co-production had more than material meaning. The conference title is "The point of theory." Although the number of speakers scheduled suggested the opposite, the call for papers was received quite ambivalently by a considerable number of people. "What do I have to do with theory? / I am against theory / I don't know anything about theory" were three variations of the theme "no." And whereas the "no" was a constant element in these reactions, the alleged reasons were variable. "What do I have to do with theory" indicates that the speaker doesn't see "the point" of theory. According to our call for papers, this was a very good topic for a talk, but nevertheless "no"was the answer. "I don't know anything about theory" refers to a sense of personal qualification, esteemed unfit for the conference. And "I am against theory" implies that one knows about it, but after having considered "theory" one judged it negatively. These are three good reasons to say "yes" to our call, and many, fortunately, have done so.

One person alleged yet another motivation for his "no": "Theory scares me to death." I found that interesting, and pressed the person for more information. He found theory intimidating, and its practitioners "tough" and "scary." Theory is difficult, the theorist speaks jargon, theory sets rules and thus functions like religious fundamentalism. Hence, the conference topic was "scary" and the person concerned "scared to death." Fortunately, at the time we have been able to convince this person of the opposite: that his views and feelings were relevant, that we didn't mean that kind of theory, and that he should come to see. Which he did.

What is surprising about these responses is not their negativity but the taking for granted of a general notion of "theory," a generalization which the conference title promoted by not specifying theory, yet challenged by asking for theory's "point." Apparently there is a general sense of what "theory" is. For some, theory is the opposite—or "the other"—of empirical inquiry, for others, of practice; for yet others, of interpretation. In other words—if I interpret these "others" correctly—it is taken to be, respectively, free-floating, abstract, or objective. Yet none of the speakers at the conference spoke of theory in that way, and all of them argued in their theoretical discourse for some form or another of empirical analysis, practice, and interpretation.

Inge Boer and I, organizers of the conference and responsible for the unfortunate call for papers, did not mean by "theory" such an authoritarian, threatening regulation for how "real science" should behave. We meant something that Jonathan Culler calls "the most convenient designation," the nickname even, for a somewhat messy interplay of interdisciplinary perspectives coming from linguistics, literary studies, psychoanalysis, feminism, Marxism, structuralism, deconstruction, and I want to add theology, anthropology, sociology.[7] While literary studies *have* been more seriously interested than before in what their disciplines and theoretical perspectives had to offer, conversely, these disciplines have become more interested in what makes their discourses "literary."

The interaction amounts to more than, to something different from, a mutual borrowing of methods; its issue is a fundamentally different conception of scholarly discourses, including theory. Nicely looking symmetrical phrases like "the death of metaphor and the metaphor of death" or, to make it worse, "the rhetorical grammatization of semiology and the grammatical semiotization of rhetoric," to play on de Man's word play, do have serious methodological consequences. Rather than empty play they are meaningful elements whose apparent decorativeness sticks to them like a Kantian/Derridian parergon as Detweiler so pertinently interprets it.[8] In line with that interpretation, I would like to argue that the negative attitudes toward theory, understandable as they may be in terms of individual histories, are the result of a generalizing use of language which I call metaphorical—but in a "parergonic" interpretation of that term. This brings me back to the concept of metaphor which I will use here as a metaphor of theory-in-general.

Given the hybrid history of the field, the fact that metaphor is a favorite concept in literary theory can be seen as due to historical accident. It stems from classical rhetoric and it belongs as much to law, literature, linguistics, as to semiotics. This multidisciplinary background makes the concept of metaphor an appropriate metaphor for "theory" as Culler described it. For that same reason it has the potential as well as the problems of what Isabelle Stengers calls a "concept nomade." The word metaphor figures on moving vans in Greece. That fact makes us aware of its "literal" meaning of mobility and displacement, and reflects the position of the concept between the disciplines, usefully illuminated by the idea of moving household goods. I would like to exploit the historical accident that metaphor is the privileged concept of literary theory whereas elsewhere is "just used," to argue, on yet another level of metaphoricity, for the point of (literary) theory within the scientific and, to a certain extent, social, goings on at large.

To make myself clear: I understand by metaphor the substitution of one term by another. The new, metaphorical term establishes similarity between the two, on the basis of a difference that grounds the substitution. The substitution is somehow meaningful. Often, the new term brings to light new, unexpected meanings. But that is not necessarily the case. Duras' rosaries do that; the expression "scared to death" does not. Theories of metaphor differ in the delimitation and description of meanings which are replaced, added, and I want to add: obscured. For some, only words are replaced; for others, entire frames of reference. I want to make this a bit more specific and focus on *narratives* imported by metaphors.

The notion that metaphors yield some sort of gain cannot hold in general. Often metaphors are used out of intellectual laziness, or to other effects. The Dutch highschool jargon "cool" for everything positive relieves the speaker of the necessity to specify what is so positive. The gain is that the speaker indicates to belong to a certain group—a group within which the metaphor is immediately understood. Hence, its meaning is double: positive evaluation, and group identity. The "literal" meaning, say, a fresh temperature, recedes into oblivion.

Even abbreviations can be used like metaphors. Once upon a time I had to think before understanding "PC." Not even up to the use of the abbreviation for Personal Computer, my background in French studies always made me go through the detour of "Parti Communiste" before reaching "Politically Correct." Not that I don't *know* what it means; but I resist the group identity. I'd rather be into French than scared to death of PC. Yes, I know I am a bit behind. Not long ago—during the bulk of my American times—"politically correct" was a good thing; meaning that you take women and minorities into consideration when deciding things like appointments or the content of a course, the term had not yet been appropriated by the opponents of such considerations. In appreciation of Detweiler's total lack of fear, indeed, of great commitment to, "PC" in the old, positive sense, I would like to establish a connection between "theory," more specifically: theory of literature, the metaphorical expression "scared to death," and the problem of "PC." In other words: what do scholarship and society have to do with each other? And I want to build my argument around the concept of metaphor.

Metaphors As Narratives

A few yeas ago I had the privilege of collaborating briefly with physicist and philosopher of science Evelyn Fox Keller. Keller had made two studies of the connections between language and science. The first was about the way scientific inventions and ideas are presented to the larger public. The study focused on the word "secret" as in "the secret of life." The second study was about the language in which biology continues to build on evolutionary theory. A central concept in that work was the term "competition," traditionally related to "struggle for life" and "survival of the fittest." The price to pay for this attention to competition was a lack of attention to collaboration, an evidently indispensable element in the sexual reproduction of organisms. One doesn't need to be a biologist to see that this privileging of one term over another has potential consequences for the further development of the theory itself.

In the first study the issue was the use of metaphors which one can still maintain to be "innocent," "just language": rhetorical. But the second study demonstrated that language cannot really be dissociated from the scientific theory itself and that in that capacity it did influence the observations and manipulations the theory made possible. I will just concentrate on the first study. It concerned the discourse the developers of DNA used to present the importance of their research to the public. That discourse was filled with words carrying a long tradition. Thus the initial molecule was called mother-molecule, and nature was constantly referred to as a woman; the unknown that it was the project to understand was "the secret of life" which had to be found, if necessary by means of violence.[9] And Keller interpreted this discourse as follows:

> And if we ask, whose secret life has historically been, and from whom has it been secret, the answer is clear: Life has traditionally been seen as the secret of women, a secret *from* men. By virtue of their ability to bear children, it is women who have been perceived as holding the secret of life (4).

Here I limit myself to just one aspect of this discourse: the metaphorical one. I want to focus on the metaphor in that word secret, that sounds so common and ordinary. Whereas the word secret in combination with life or nature has indeed become quite usual—just as usual as the expression "scared to death"—the word is here, in fact, metaphorical. The difference between it and the equally common word "unknown" may be subtle, but it is relevant.

What is unknown, as the negating prefix suggests, can be known. The subject of that knowing is the researcher. What is secret can also be known. But here, the subject is not quite the researcher. The word "secret" implies an action, hence, a subject of withholding. If there is a secret, then somebody is keeping it. This fits into the network of gendered language in which nature and life are made feminine. And it implies a story in which secrecy is an act. "Secret" as metaphor for the unknown establishes an opposition between two subjects: the researcher who wants to know the secret and "woman" who withholds it. This opposition is easily turned into hostility, as the well-known metaphor of Francis Bacon shows, who wanted to put nature on the rack to torture her secrets out of her.[10]

But this gendering of the unknown comes with a second aspect of the word 'secret" which is of an altogether different nature. A secret that must be found out implies a process in which that finding out takes place. The series of events involved in that process can be considered a narrative. That narrative is "told" by the user of the metaphor. The narration is subjective in the precise sense of emanating from a subject. The word tells the narrative in the version—from the perspective of—the subject of "unknowing" who feels excluded by the lack of knowledge and experiences it as an action by an "insider," the subject of knowing and withholding. That subject is the narrator's opponent. This interpretation of metaphor as mini-narrative yields insight, not into what the speaker "means," but in what a cultural community considers acceptable interpretations; so acceptable that they are not considered metaphorical at all.[11]

Recently I ran into a comparable case in a special issue of the journal *Semeia* devoted to the connections between metaphors of war and women. Here, too, the inconspicuous metaphorical character of ordinary terms which carry a subjectivized narrative, remained unnoticed.[12] Since in this case the texts stem from an ancient culture, hence, different from our own, the authors were careful not to project anachronistically contemporary norms onto the past. The case is somewhat complex but deserves the necessary explanation because it concerns a dilemma we come across all the time. The issue is the question whether in the ancient Middle East something like just war was thinkable, and whether rape could be an acceptable practice therein.

The author, Susan Niditch, struggles with the difficulty that ethical norms differ according to time and place, whereas the language in which we write about other cultures is also time and place bound. In that context she raises the question whether "just war," in the biblical framework, "holy war," is possible and if so, if in such a war the practice we call rape can have a place. Thus she writes about the biblical book of Numbers:

> Of course, enslaving the enemy and forcing its women into marriage are the terms of an oppressive regime and difficult to imagine under the heading of that what is just (11).

The result of her reflection is not my point here. I am interested in, first, the notion "oppressive regime." The word "oppressive" is anachronistic in terms of the object under study—Numbers and the stake of the struggle described is hostility over land, not disagreement over human rights within the United Nations or something like that. The context in which Niditch's words were written makes the notion very much to the point: I read her paper during preparations for the gulf war, at a time when the description "oppressive regime" almost inevitably referred to Saddam Hussein. In other words, the description had a precise meaning including moral echoes and an imaginative and image-like resonance daily fed into on television—like a dream image. Without author and readers being aware of it the description thus becomes metaphorical. It becomes a metaphor by means of which the Western present with its norms and values collapses with the Middle Eastern past, and this happens in a paper, in the very sentence, in which an explicit attempt is made to avoid such anachronisms.

Yet, this is not my primary point. What concerns me in the sentence is that something, in the attempt, is carried over, a description, equally anachronistic by the way, of rape. The author wished to avoid that term because of its anachronism, and the concessive clause in which the description "oppressive regime" occurred was meant to help that avoidance. "Forcing its women into marriage" is Niditch's attempt to avoid the anachronism. She doesn't want to call the action rape, she argues, because in the culture under discussion, it was not perceived as such. Even if the war cannot be called just, the taking of women is culturally acceptable, and can therefore not be called rape. This is undeniably a sound argument. Except for one aspect.

In cultural anthropology this position would be called relativist; the not so felicitous alternative to ethnocentrism. This academic dilemma has been around for the better part of this century in the human and social sciences. It has a precise parallel in the social and political dilemma of moralism versus relativism (or "tolerance"); the imposition of one's own norms versus the acceptance of those of others, even if the latter are perceived as "oppressive." I would like to attempt to, at least, disturb that dilemma.

Niditch replaces "rape" with "forcing into marriage"; elsewhere, the action is called wife-stealing. As a cultural phenomenon it is in some cultures acceptable and ordinary, and is known in anthropological and historical studies. I agree with Niditch that "rape" is an obscuring term that fails to address the cultural status of the event. Also, it seems pointless to accuse the biblical culture, three thousand years after the fact, of a violation of human rights and feel better about our own behavior. Yet, the alternative is unacceptable to me. Rather, in the awareness and acknowledgment that the term is "ours"—and leads to a lot of disagreement in the culture I live in—I would like to take a closer look at the contested term, "rape." In other words, I want to *confront* the phenomenon through the word we *would* use if we were to speak "ethnocentrically," and see what happens. That confrontation, that collision, might be the most productive attitude toward the dilemma. It comes to what Gerald Graff, in his recent book about the American PC syndrome, calls "teaching the conflicts."[13]

The word "rape," then. That word is more often used as a noun than as a verb—which is my first worry. It is one of those nouns which imply a story.[14] Here, I want to argue that, first, the word "rape" itself is a metaphor that obscures the story it implies, and, second, that this obscuring locks us up in the dilemma that needs to be overcome.

Rape—the action for which we use that term: that of sexually appropriating another subject without her consent—has different meanings in different times and cultures. Its meaning depends on the status of, in particular, women in relation to men, and the status of the individual subject in relation to the community and its juridical organization. It is thinkable that the action concerned is interpreted as rape by a part of the culture at stake, and not at all by another part. Cultures which differ from "ours"—it becomes harder and harder to use "us" and "ours" in this context—tend to look more homogeneous and more coherent at a distance than they probably are. That deceptive vision is, precisely, the basis of ethnocentrism. Therefore, I assume that within each community, large or small, ancient or recent, far or close, differences increase as one's vision approaches. This, mind you, is an assumption modeled on my own culture, and could appear as ethnocentric; but is it a structural assumption, not a semantic one, and there lies the important difference. My assumption also holds for the meanings of words and notions. Rape implies an event, if not an entire story with a number of episodes. It is a word that, in the words of Barbara Johnson, contains a "difference within." [15]

Forging a noun out of a verb—nominalization makes the concept analyzable, discussible. That is a gain. There is also a loss. What gets lost from sight is the active character of the referent, the narrative of action including the subjectivities of the agents involved.[16] With the subject of action the responsibility for the action also disappears—with responsibility having a culture-specific meaning according to the status of the individual in it. Instead, the entire narrative remains an implication, skipped as it were, in the abbreviation that is the noun. The subject who uses the word is, say, the story's narrator. The subject whose vision is implied in the word is its focalizer. Then there are the actors. The process in which all these figures interact, the fabula, is dynamic: it brings about change. All this is lost when a noun is used instead of a verb which would necessitate their naming.

These aspects can be brought back into view by a narrative analysis of the noun. The narratological analysis of the term "rape" is not complicated, yet, not unambiguous. We have to appoint a narrator. The subject of action, the rapist, needs to be mentioned. Then, there is the subject into whose body the action is done, in whom it brings about change. Reflection on the nature and the extent of that change warrants an amount of attention not triggered by the noun. Then, who is the focalizer? Is it the rapist, who would be likely to call his action differently, or the raped one, the victim who experiences the action. Or is it the narrator, and if so, does this agent identify with either one of these two positions? The noun doesn't tell, and I don't want to answer the question in any general way. The point is in raising it. The realization of this narrative duplicity seems more productive than the unreflected choice for one of the possible answers. That, though, is what Niditch does by hastily adopting a description she considers more fitting for the ancient culture. That relativism is, in fact, condescendent. For if we take other cultures as seriously as our own, then the phenomenon in question deserves at least recognition as an event with "a difference within," an internal divisiveness which the quick narratological analysis clearly indicates.

"Rape," that seemingly simple and clear noun can thus be seen as a grammatical metaphor: a term that replaces another. It is a case of the metaphorization of grammar. Except that, just like Keller's "secret," it does not replace another term but an entire narrative. The item replaced and displaced, obscured, is a story with several agents, a variability of interpretation and a difference of experience. What is sex, or theft, or lawful appropriation for the one may still be a violation of the subjective integrity for another—whether culturally accepted or not; but who, then, *is* the culture? Such an analysis and recognition of the narratives and the subjective meanings they entail does, at least, disturb the academic as well as the social dilemma between ethnocentrism and relativism.

Comparing this case to the metaphor that represented people like rosaries, a striking difference appears. In the Duras passage the metaphor yielded many more meanings than any one "literal" description could convey. In the cases of "normal" words, the opposite happens. Here, too, a multiplicity of meanings is possible. But here the metaphor yields these meanings up only when it is considered as such. In other words, the *concept* of metaphor produces the insights. And this, then, brings us back to concepts, those theories in miniature.

The Concept of "Metaphor" and the Metaphor "Concept"

Metaphors are not vague, poetic oddities or decorations but fundamental forms of language use with an indispensable cognitive function. Let me first indicate why it makes sense to consider theoretical concepts as metaphors. Metaphors have three aspects to them. Firstly, they substitute something for something else. This substitution establishes similarity between two items. That is meaningful because the new term illuminates something in the meaning of the first term—or, to the contrary, obscures something. The second term must differ from the first, bringing a new, different element or perspective. At the same time the metaphor must be understandable, semiotically acceptable. One must be able to connect the new element or perspective to the old term. Hence, some degree of similarity is needed. This similarity does not have to lie in the meanings of the term itself but may be brought in by the respective contexts of the two terms. The combination of similarity and difference makes for the new, the creative, the informational surplus of metaphor. That surplus is crucially important for concepts, for through the use of concepts the scholar is supposed to learn something new about the objects.

Second, metaphors displace meanings, redirect them to something else, for example, from the events to the subject that gives them meaning in an implicit narrative. This directing makes metaphor a powerful heuristic tool. Through that mobility of the "lens" all kinds of unseen and unforeseen aspects of the first term come to the fore. This "reach" of metaphor is very important for concepts. It enables these to produce, in addition to a surplus of information, a contextual network for the object.[17]

Thirdly, metaphors offer a second discourse within which the first term can be placed. Seeing masses of people like rosaries imports a religious, in this case catholic, framework which raises all kinds of questions concerning poverty in Asia and the necessity to do something about it—as well as the way to do it, the issue of charity, so deeply religious a notion. Just as the expression "scared to death," but a bit less innocently, this metaphor brings two discourses and two frames of reference into collision. This aspect is best called framing. For concepts, especially those nomadic concepts that constitute the fragile foundation of interdisciplinary scholarship, this framing might well be crucial.

This standard theory of metaphor which, in its ambition to characterize concepts, becomes also an epistemology, is a kind of "searchlight theory." It is not so much meant to predict, explain, or generalize, but, to the contrary, to specify, analyze, get an eye for differences. Differences between objects, and differences between the aspects of the concept as metaphor: differences within. Concepts, according to philosopher of science Isabelle Stengers, serve the purpose of organizing a set of phenomena, determine the relevant questions to be asked about them, and determine the meaning of the possible observations concerning them.[18] In that sense concepts are theories and hence, may be evaluated like theories. According to the summary of standard procedures for the evaluation of scientific theories Thomas Kuhn provides in his paper "Objectivity, Value Judgment, and Theory Choice," such evaluation follows a standard set of norms. A useful theory is accurate, consistent, has a broad reach, is simple, and productive.[19] Not that these norms are unambiguous, but as rules of thumb they serve their purpose reasonably well. Concepts can be judged according to the same norms.

But, as I said before, concepts are not only theories but also metaphors. And metaphors can yield intellectual gain when they raise new questions and suggest new perspectives. They can also entail loss when they are thematically closing and semantically vague. That was the case with the metaphors "secret" and "rape," which required analysis to bring back their obscured meanings. The same can happen with concepts. These, too, are liable to either obscure or illuminate through their metaphoric work. Concepts are productive because, according to Stengers, they bring order and meaning to phenomena, and make these "askable." But concepts are limiting, sometimes vague, the opposite of specifying that is. Concepts are not only theories but much also be judged as metaphors if we are to bring these aspects to light.

An example is the grammatical category of "voice." The term refers to the speaker of an utterance, the implicit or explicit "I" supposed to speak, and the form in which this subject speaks. In the first instance the concept is helpful. For example, in the analysis of narratives it entices the analyst to address the question "who speaks." It is the question of responsibility for the meanings proposed to the reader or listener. Compared to classical structuralist semantics and narrative theories derived thereof, where meanings were seen as abstract units unrelated to, hence, unaffected by, the speaking subject, this is a good step ahead. The concept is also accurate, for there is indeed always a subject of speech, even if that subject is not alone and is internally divided. And the concept is productive, for it encourages asking further relevant questions. But it is also counter-productive. It is unhelpful when its metaphorical aspects are not perceived but still carried over: those "commonsense," self-evident meanings which produce dogmas. The concept of voice hangs together—is consistent—with a set of questions which have dogmatic status in the humanities. I would like to use the concept of voice to put that kind of dogmatism on the carpet.

Of course, with its connotation of bodiliness—embodiment—the term "voice" immediately brings to mind Derrida's critique of the preference for voice over writing. This preference, Derrida argues in *Of Grammatology*, partakes of a philosophy of language in which the illusion of immediacy as "pure" origin of language occupies central stage.[20] Here, I want to focus on the fact that the question of the subject—the productive yield of the concept—almost automatically entails the question of intention The issue of intention is so dogmatic that it seems almost impossible to circumvent it and raise questions that are not derived from it. And yet, intention is a psychological concept bound up with the modern West, and it surely does not have a universal, uniform meaning. In other words, as a concept it behaves like "rape." [21]

In a brilliant analysis of the rhetoric of a passage from Proust's *A la recherche du temps perdu* Paul de Man demonstrates the confusion between grammar and intention that the concept of voice entails. In the passage he analyzes, de Man reads—rightly, I think—a poetical statement representing Proust's literary vision. The passage consists of a series of correspondences between inside and outside which together suggest that metaphor is the best way of achieving the poetic effect sought. The text itself, however, is basically metonymic, de Man claims. I can only cite a fragment of the fragment here, but enough, I hope, to convey de Man's point:

> Cette obscure fraîcheur de ma chambre était au plein soleil de la rue ce que l'ombre est au rayon, c'est-à-dire aussi lumineuse que lui et offrait à mon imagination le spectacle total de l'été dont mes sens ... (The dark coolness of my room related to the full sunlight of the street as the shadow relates to the

ray of light, that is to say it was just as luminous and it gave my imagination the total spectacle of the summer, whereas my senses...)[22]

In terms of structure the imagery is more like the cliché "scared to death" than like the literary metaphor "rosaries of people." It is based on the complementarity of dark and light which, paradoxically, makes dark ore "illuminated", hence, more "enlightened," brilliant and wonderful to be in, than light itself. The juxtaposition of room and street, dark and light, inside and outside produces the meanings; not a similarity. Hence, the figuration is metonymical.

If we project the author's intention—his narrative as well as his argumentative "voice" onto the grammatical "voice," then we must conclude that Proust fails. His text does not do what he says it should. De Man writes about this passage:

> The term *voice*, even when used in a grammatical terminology as when we speak of the passive or interrogative voice, is, of course, a metaphor inferring by analogy the intent of the subject from the structure of the predicate. (18)

It would of course be absurd to conclude that Proust fails as a writer because the concept is frustrating, or because literature as an art is above and beyond theory, or because the choice to apply the concept of metaphor is only a "trial" that can demonstrate "error." But it would be absurd because the concept that raises the question of consistency between intent and practice is itself metaphorical. Hence, it cannot be "applied" as a dogmatically protected concept; what happens is a productive collision between two rhetorical figures, Proust's writing and the concept. The metaphor in the concept "voice," brought in unnoticed, collides with the metonymy through which metaphor is recommended.

The result of that collision is not a total loss. De Man draws attention to the paradox which he calls, with a good sense for metaphor, a "state of suspended ignorance." Proust can write beautifully, but in his argumentation he is wrong, and that only enhances the tension, the density, the richness of his text. The concept, too, survives the accident, but it is irremediably damaged. The damage, however, is therapeutic. The meaning "intention" must be amputated. In this case, and to open up yet another metaphoric discourse, the literary text has pronounced sentence over the concept.

And yet, the insight in the text, the capacity to assess and savor its incredible complexity fully, came about thanks to the half failed attempt to characterize it by means of this concept, not in spite of, but thanks to the uncontrollable metaphoric potential of the concept. This collision could be a model—a metaphor—of the effect of theory in all those disciplines and perspectives which Culler mentioned in his definition of "theory," and which I call for convenience the cultural disciplines. The violent metaphors I have used to describe this encounter serve a rhetorical purpose. I wanted to demonstrate the violence in the far-reaching effect of the concept "voice," which I was yet able to evaluate partly positively, thanks to the attempt to make explicit what its metaphoric baggage is. I could also have appealed to the register of the erotic to characterize the encounter between Proust's text and de Man's theory, and then we could all have gone home happy. But then again, clarity would have been sacrificed; insight into the elimination of aspects that conceptual metaphors entail would not have been driven home.

There are, of course, other views of theories and concepts. Views according to which concepts are conceived of as instruments which can only succeed or fail because their precise content is beyond discussion. Views according to which concepts must not be metaphorical because metaphors entails a margin of vagueness and ambiguity. Such a view makes it hard to notice the metaphoricity of concepts which, after careful screening, are judged acceptable. For example, the implication that grammatical voice and intention are conflated might remain obscured. I would, indeed, be scared to death of such a theory, wherein concepts remain out of critical reach and have no yield other than a paraphrase of what is already known. Proust would be admired for his metaphors: Because we already admired those, because he advocates them himself, and because the author is boss. Seemingly modest, put in the service of literature, such a concept is tyrannical, violent. Believing Proust at his word, such a concept overrules the words of the text Proust wrote.

Theory As Practice

Discussions of metaphor tend to be endless debates about which definition of metaphor is the most accurate; debates usually conducted through examples and counter-examples. In this paper I wish to stay far from such basically formalist detailing which I leave gladly to others, more expert than I. I am, instead, interested in the *effect* of the concept of metaphor, precisely, in its lack of clarity, its vagueness, its ambiguity; its undecidability; and, by extension, of all concepts to the extent that they are by definition metaphorical. So far, the attempt to "name" an expression, however unfinished and dubious the results, has produced insight. Duras' description of Vietnamese people has shown more aspects, has yielded a plurality of meanings, has become itself a rosary of polysemes. The struggle with banal clichés has demonstrated how "normal" language use carries stories along.

To understand language use we need concepts, and "metaphor" is such a concept. But concepts consist also of language, and their use is also language use. As my half-hearted attempts at analysis kept showing, a concept is not a ready-made mold, no matrix, model, pattern that yield automatically accurate descriptions of an object—here, language use. Most theoretical texts on metaphor present attempts to "fix" the concept in such a way. I want to advocate a different way of "doing theory"; one which I like to describe as "theoretical practice." In such a practice the confrontation between concept and object is a kind of robbing of two forms of language use against each other and which changes both. In that sense, too, concepts are always also metaphors.

If the examples I have discussed—"scared to death" and "rosaries of people," "rape" and "secret"—are any indication, metaphors are affectively as well as cognitively effective, and then effect is not limited to metaphorical signs themselves but also to the discourse within which these are embedded; the meanings both discourses, together, produce. This, in turn, affects the cultural/analytical dilemma: the question is not, whether "rape" is acceptable in one culture and not in another, but which subjects are obscured by such a term, what discourses these subjects evoke as soon as we analyze them into visibility.

Taking risks is the motto of an academic pursuit ready to face losing like a good sport. If anyone, Robert Detweiler knows this, and that is why I can so happily argue with him: neither of us fear defeat. This is, also, how Thomas Kuhn reasoned in his analysis of scientific practices. It seems appropriate, then, to end on one of *his* metaphors; one which entails gain and loss. Kuhn discusses the responses to his book *The Structure of Scientific Revolutions*. In that review he refers to the classical distinction between "context of discovery" and "context of justification." Decisions made during the scientific research program and which lead to results are totally different ones from those alleged to defend those results. Kuhn indicates how this distinction, in turn, mystifies yet another context, which he calls the "context of pedagogy," in other words, the teaching of science: history of science, methodologies, philosophy of science, teachings that occur in some form or another in any academic pedagogical program.

This context is characterized by a fargoing simplification in the representation of the process of research. Thus, examples in textbooks are not at all the cases which actually led to the discoveries they are alleged to illustrate, nor those used in defense of the result. The standard experiments hardly played any part in the decisions that led to the discoveries, nor in the formulation of theories about them. (Kuhn's examples are mainly from the sciences—like Foucault's pendulum, recently elevated to the status of overdetermined example in the humanities as well) .[23]

That the process of decision-making in the sciences is thus simplified doesn't bother Kuhn too much. But as a representation of the process of scientific decision-making such as the choice of theories, such a simplification does not provide a good basis for *analysis*. And here is his metaphor:

> these simplifications *emasculate* by making choice totally unproblematic.[24]

I wholeheartedly subscribe to Kuhn's protest against simplification. Simplification is something altogether different than simplicity, that criterion for the evaluation of theories. These two differ as much as, say, covering a lot and empirical content. Dutch poet Lucebert once used the notion of simplicity in a poetical statement in a poem:

> I try in poetic fashion/that is to say/simplicity's luminous waters/to bring to expression/the space of life in its entirety.[25]

Lucebert's poetic and poetical metaphor suggests that simplicity is illuminating and enlightening, as much as Proust's cool obscurity; simplification, in contrast, obscures. Instead of making more things, elements, aspects visible by illuminating complexities, simplifications render these things invisible. In this sense, "rape" is just such a simplification.

But "to emasculate" is a strong charge, bringing back, suddenly, the gender specific perspective, the semantic domain of violence, and fear. Would "scared to death," then, be the precise expression for something profoundly disturbing? The metaphor "to emasculate" for simplification can trigger many associations and questions. Given its usual metaphoric-semantic network it seems safe to assume that Kuhn is invoking impotence, powerlessness. Who, or what, loses its power? If the lack of problematicity is non-masculine, is it masculine to be problematic, to be, so to speak, in trouble? Is it masculine to find deciding difficult? And the overall question: what makes science so gender-specific? I give up answering these questions; it wasn't me who came up with the metaphor. Appealing to Kuhn's "voice," and his likely answer, that he didn't mean the metaphor to be taken so dead-seriously, don't seem satisfying to me. But I do hear in Kuhn's metaphor an appeal to a group identity which doesn't appeal to me.

But what I can say is this: these questions can only be asked if the metaphor is, just like a concept, unprotected, up for grabs; only if neither the self-evidence provided by their clichéishness, nor the invulnerability provided by their artistic potential, stand, to use a Dutch expression, like a pole above water: fixed, certain, obvious. "To do theory" is a commerce with theoretical concepts and objects; it is attempting to analyze the objects with the help of the concepts as well as the other way around, not by "applying" concepts like tools but by bringing them into touch with objects, if necessary, in collision. When an analysis fails, new insight can still emerge; more new insight than when a protected concept is routinely applied. De Man's confrontation with Proust's dark room made that clear.

What, then, does theory have to do with "scared to death," on the one hand, and the problem of PC, on the other? Gerald Graff, in his less than radical recent book on the subject advocates that we turn the problem PC into something productive by making the struggle into a starting point of academic teaching, including the structure of the curriculum. His description of theory is on the simplistic side, but not wrong:

> "Theory" . . . is what erupts when what was once silently agreed to in a community becomes disputed, forcing its members to formulate and defend assumptions that they previously did not even have to be aware of.[26]

Kuhn, I suppose, wouldn't mind this definition. At any rate, it does not at all refer to the kind of regulating with which austere methodologists of the kind I like to call "theo-theorists" tend to be obsessed, and of which others are "scared to death." In this sense, Graff's definition disarms the individual I staged at the beginning of this paper.

Graff's definition does not refer either to something that is often, but wrongly alleged to be equivalent to ideology, mostly by people who consider themselves as standing outside, or above, the clamors of PC-people. Those who are "against theory," in general, argue their position according to Graff, and Culler,—and I agree with that—by alleging that theory is ideological. But this resistance to theory is itself rather ideological. As Terry Eagleton formulated it:

> without some kind of theory, however unreflected and implicit, we would not know what a "literary work" was in the first place, or how we were to read it. Hostility to theory usually means opposition to other people's theories and an oblivion of one's own.[27]

Not, that theory is different from ideology in any absolute way. The two share a family likeness: both are metaphors. But whereas the former illuminates because it specifies, the latter obscures because it simplifies. And whatever else Kuhn's metaphor says about simplification, it sure does point at danger.

Those, finally, who find theory "too difficult," and themselves not knowledgeable enough, consider theory as something finished, complete, something you can succeed or fail to master, or speak, like a foreign language. I make that comparison on purpose, because theory is often perceived like "jargon," if not "a secret language"; an intimidating group language that can shut you out.

Once, not long ago, I gave a lecture for the American Association of Art Museum Directors, at the Association's request, on the potential contribution of theory for museum work. It went very well and the response was nice, the discussion productive. Hardly back home I received from one of the participants one of those priceless cartoons the *New York Times* produces to connect to people's obsessions, representing a woman at a social event saying to a man—note these cartoons tend to come in this gender distribution: "Oh, you're a terrorist; thank god, I understood 'theorist.'" Secret languages, apparently, scare, to death.

Of course, there are many theories, which get into use after the decisions Kuhn knows much more about than I; theories which you understand if they belong to your area of research, and not, if they are too far removed from what you know. Most theories in the sciences are totally incomprehensible to me; that seems both obvious and acceptable. But "theory" in general—theory as in "the point of theory"—is not a language, not a thing, not a whole. It is, rather, a way of interacting with objects. An interaction which does justice to the mission of the university to produce new knowledge and not just conserve traditions.

In that sense theory is a practice, a form of interpretation, not the pinnacle of objectivity as much as touching stone for subjectivity; not abstract but empirically anchored. This practice is neither politically correct, nor politically incorrect; it is not bound to party politics, not to specific ideological positions. Yet, in an important sense, theory can be called political. And that political meaning is, simultaneously, an academic, scholarly, scientific meaning. To end on a quotation of my favorite theorist, the American philosopher Charles Sanders Peirce, founder of semiotics:

> Conservatism, in the sense of a dread of consequences, is altogether out of place in science, which has, on the contrary, always been forewarned by radicals and radicalism.[28]

Risk: the readiness to face loss, to lose face, is indispensable in any academic pursuit. It is, perhaps, the most respectable feature an academic can sport. Robert Detweiler is one of those who do. As I have argued, that is a politically correct attitude in a very serious sense. Therefore, it is time to claim that notion back.

NOTES

1. Judith Schlanger, "La pensée inventive" 67-100 in Isabelle Stengers et Judith Schlanger, *Les concepts scientifiques: Invention et pouvoir* (Paris: Gallimard, 1991), p. 98.

2. W.J.T. Mitchell, *Iconology: Image, Text. Ideology* (Chicago: the University of Chicago Press, 1985), p. 204.

3. The Dutch expression badly translated is "als de dood," literally: "like death" or "as if death," a very common cliché which means "to be very afraid," but not necessarily seriously "scared."

4. Marguerite Duras, *Le vice-consul* (Paris: Gallimard, 1966). For an analysis of this novel see my book *On Story-Telling: Essays in Narratology* (Sonoma: Polebridge Press, 1991) pp. 174-196.

5. The literature on metaphor is enormous. One contrast: Paul Ricoeur, (*The Rule of Metaphor: Multi-disciplinary Studies of the Creation of Meaning in Language.* trans. by Robert Czerny with Kathleen McLaughlin and John Costello, (Toronto: The University of Toronto Press, 1979) over against Derrida's "White mythology," *New Literary History* 6, 5-74, (1974) or *De la grammatologie* (Paris: Editions de Minuit, 1967). See also Lakoff, George and Mark Johnson, *Metaphors We Live By*, (Chicago: the University of Chicago Press, 1980). A clear summary of various conceptions of metaphor is provided by Jonathan Culler in "The Turns of Metaphor," 188-209 in *The Pursuit of Signs. Semiotics. Literature, Deconstruction* (Ithaca: Cornell University Press, 1981).

6. First presented at a session of the Annual Convention of the American Society for Biblical Literature, Anaheim, 1989, and subsequently published in *Journal of Literature and Theology* 5, 1, (1991). Robert Detweiler, "Parerga: Homely Details, Secret Intentions, Veiled Threats," 1-10, and Mieke Bal, "Murder and Difference: Uncanny Sites in an Uncanny World."

7. See Jonathan Culler, *Framing the Sign: Criticism and Its Institutions* (Norman and London: University of Oklahoma Press, 1988), esp. "Literary Criticism and the American University" where he analyzes succinctly the developments and misunderstandings which have led in the U.S. to the "culture wars" (Gerald Graff's title) summarily indicated as "PC." More on this later.

8. See Detweiler, "Parerga," pp. 7-9.

9. See Evelyn Fox Keller, "From Secrets of Life to Secrets of Death," E. Fox Keller et al., *Three Cultures: Fifteen Lectures on the Confrontation of Academic Cultures* (The Hague: Universitaire Pers Rotterdam, 1989), pp. 3-16.

10. See on this Keller, *Reflections on Gender and Science*. (New Haven: Yale University Press, 1985).

11. The metaphor of secrecy has much more background than I can provide here. See Keller, "Making Gender Visible," *Feminist Studies/Critical Studies*, Teresa de Lauretis, ed. (Bloomington: Indiana University Press, 1986) and Eva Kittay, 'Womb Envy: An Explanatory Concept" pp. 94-128 in *Mothering*, Joyce Trebilcot, ed. (New York: Rowman and Allenheld, 1984).

12. Susan Niditch, "War, Women and Defilement in Numbers 31," in *Semeia* 61, 1993, Special Issue: "Women, War, and Metaphor: Language and Society in the Study of the Hebrew Bible." pp. 39-58.

13. Gerald Graff, *Beyond the Culture Wars: How Teaching the Conflicts Can Revitalize American Education*. (New York and London: W.W. Norton, 1992).

14. I have devoted a previous inaugural lecture to this issue. See my 1988 *Verkrachting verbeeld. Seksueel geweld in cultuur gebracht*. (Utrecht: Hes Publishers). The argument developed there appears in *Reading "Rembrandt": Beyond the Word-Image Opposition*. (New York and Cambridge: Cambridge University Press), pp. 60-93.

15. Barbara Johnson, *A World of Difference* (Baltimore: the Johns Hopkins University Press, 1987); also her paper "The Frame of Reference: Poe, Lacan, Derrida," in: *The Purloined Poe: Lacan*, Derrida & Psychoanalytic Reading, edited by John P. Muller and William J. Richardson, (Baltimore: the Johns Hopkins University Press, 1988), pp. 213-251.

16. This point was enthusiastically argued by Gunther Kress and Robert Hodge, *Language as Ideology*. (London: Routledge & Kegan Paul, 1979). l have gratefully used their views in *Death and Dissymmetry. The Politics of Coherence in the Book of Judges*. (Chicago: the University of Chicago Press, 1988).

17. For the creative, heuristic power of metaphors, see A. Koestler, *The Act of Creation* (New York: MacMillan).

18. Isabelle Stengers, ed. *D'une science à l'autre: des concepts nomades* (Paris: Editions du Seuil, 1987), p. 11: "Un tel concept a en effet pour vocation d'*organiser* un ensemble de phénomènes, de définir les questions pertinentes à son sujet et le sens des observations qui peuvent y être effectuées."

19. Thomas S. Kuhn, "Objectivity, Value Judgment, and Theory Choice," pp. 383-393 in Hazard Adams and Leroy Searle, eds. *Critical Theory Since 1965* (Tallahassee: University Presses of Florida, 1986) or in Thomas S. Kuhn, *The Essential Tension: Selected Studies in Scientific Tradition and Change*. (Chicago: The University of Chicago Press, 1977).

20. Derrida analyzes the philosophy of language of Jean-Jacques Rousseau in this context. See *De la grammatologie* (Paris: Editions de Minuit, 1967), esp. part 11: "Nature, culture, écriture." See also the useful introduction by Gayatri Chakravorty Spivak to the English translation, *Of Grammatology* translated and with an introduction by Gayatri Chakravorty Spivak, (Baltimore: The Johns Hopkins University Press, 1976).

21. See my article "Rape: Problems of Intention," pp. 367-371 in *Feminism and Psychoanalysis: A Critical Dictionary* edited by Elizabeth Wright (Oxford: Blackwell, 1992).

22. Paul de Man, "Semiology and Rhetoric" pp. 3-19 in *Allegories of Reading: Figural Language in Rousseau, Nietzsche, Rilke, and Proust* (New Haven: Yale University Press, 1979). The quotation, in de Man's translation is on pp. 13-14. For the Proust passage, see Edition de la Pléiade uitgave, Marcel Proust, *A la recherche du temps perdu* (Paris: Gallimard, 1954), p. 83.

23. Hardly recovered from Foucault's blow to the humanities as a power-free playground, students of postmodernism now had to face Umberto Eco's novel *Foucault's Pendulum*, too "serious" about itself to qualify for the label.

24. Thomas Kuhn, "Objectivity," p. 387; emphasis mine.

25. "Ik tracht op poetische wijze/ dat wil zeggen/ eenvouds verlichte waters/ de ruimte van het volledig leven/ tot uitdrukking te brengen." 47 in Lucebert, *Verzamelde gedicl1ten* C.W. van de Watering, ed. (Amsterdam: De Bezige Bij, 1974).

26. Gerald Graff, p. 53.

27. Terry Eagleton,*Literary Theory: An Introduction* (Minneapolis: University of Minnesota Press,1983), p. 7.

28. Charles S. Peirce, "The Scientific Attitude and Fallibilism," *Philosophical Writings*, J. Butchler, ed. (New York: Dover 1955), p. 58; quoted from Jonathan Culler, *Framing the Sign* , p. xvi.

Play Not

DAVID L. MILLER

Robert Detweiler's book, *Breaking the Fall: Religious Readings of Contemporary Fiction*, represents the advance guard of the Religion and Literature movement in North America simply because it stands as solitary exemplar in wrestling with the leading edge of literary theory. Detweiler leads the way into the postmodern deaths of author, subject, text, and god(s) while never abandoning the authors, subjects, texts and deities so important to the field of Religion and Literature. It is not a small feat. Therefore, all the more curious is the way Detweiler deals with "nothingness" in this award-winning book.

Detweiler naughts nothing. He asserts that "Christian myth attempts to answer Heidegger's question, 'why is there not nothing?', by narrating a case of a god born into human form, dying in that form and resurrected in a more exalted form."[1] This religious tradition, Detweiler believes, is one of the few to suggest that nothingness is not the primal condition nor the condition of human and worldly end. God's controlling presence was what it was before the beginning, always and already, and it therefore "counteracts nothingness."[2] "There is thus not *nothing* in the Judeo-Christian tradition," says Detweiler, "because we cannot image it."[3] The point is a Heideggerian one: namely, that giving image or idea to nothing already makes it into a something, like mistaking Being for a being, producing repression or forgetfulness in the manner typical of intellectualistic strategies within meta-physical traditions. Heidegger had written: "He who speaks of nothing does not know what he is doing. In speaking of nothing he makes it into a something. . . . Authentic speaking about nothing always remains extraordinary."[4]

Detweiler's point, however, is not philosophical. It is theological and literary. He is concerned to imagine and to demonstrate a religious

33

hermeneutic for these postmodern times. "Religious reading," he teaches his reader,

> is the deep play that reminds us how the text can never be completed, no more than can the author or reader. It is an effort that requires belief because we are always on the verge of being seduced by the (non-)vision of nothingness, the ultimate abstraction and the final goal of interpretation, and we need to recall, against that nihilism, the enduring inexpressibility of form that incessantly inspires our desire. [5]

I have already used the word "curious" to indicate this stance of Detweiler in relation to nothingness in Christianity and in literary theory. The resistance to nihilism is, to be sure, as admirable as it is crucial. But do the experience and the notion of nothingness ineluctably belong to and with nihilism? Are there not different nothings? And what of all of the void and nothingness of which much ado is made precisely in that theological tradition whose nothing Detweiler naughts? I am of course thinking of the concept of Yahweh as *en-sof* in the Jewish mysticism so well described by Gershom Scholem and Moshe Idel, and of the nothingness so affirmed and desired in Christian mysticisms (John Scotus Eriugena, Meister Eckhart, Nicholas of Cusa, St. John of the Cross, Angelus Silesius, Jacob Bohme, etc.) which is analyzed by Raoul Mortley in magisterial fashion.[6] Books by Thomas J. J. Altizer[7] and Michael Novak,[8] as well as articles by Robert Scharlemann[9] and Ray Hart,[10] are sufficient to explain why I might have found Detweiler's naughting nothing curious.

Further, the same plenitude of emptiness is experienced in the Western literary tradition, a tradition which—if Northrop Frye is to be believed, following upon Blake—can only be understood by utilizing the Bible, which Detweiler finds to be without nothing, as code. I have already alluded to Shakespeare, but there is also so much more: Baudelaire's "Gout du neant," Beckett's *Textes pour rien*, Borges' "From Someone to Nobody," Kafka's "Das Schweigen der Sirenen," Pinter's *Silence*, Creeley's "poem supreme addressed to emptiness," Rilke's "Hauch um nichts" (which is a breath within God), and Joan Didion's saying that she "knows what 'nothing' means, and keeps on playing." This litany is not exhaustive, of course; it is only indicative. It may indicate that literature is an answer to the Fool's question to Lear: "What can you do with nothing, Nuncle?" One can engage in "deep play" with it (to use Detweiler's phrase for literature and interpretation). Literature, and not unreligiously, could be felt as (again in Shakespeare's words) the "nothing [that] almost sees miracles."[11] So it is curious that Detweiler defends theologically against this nothing and identifies it with nihilism.

One might be tempted to think that "breaking the fall" is an attempt to break the fall of life and interpretation into the nothingness of religion and literature. The title image of Detweiler's book carries an allusion to Rilke who says, in Detweiler's translation:

> We all fall. This hand here falls. And look at others: it's in everyone.
> And yet there's one who holds this falling Infinitely gently in his hands .[12]

Is this an invocation of a Jewish and Christian God whom we hope will save us from nihilism? a theological stop-gap to brake the fall into literary nothingness? I think not, and in the pages which follow I should like to propose something about Detweiler's work which I believe is even more curious than this apparent brake against nihilism, curious by virtue of its being positive about nothingness!

Detweiler himself petitions words by Margaret Atwood at the beginning of his book's "Preface": " . . . but as you go on, the writing—if you follow it—will take you places you never intended to go and show you things you would never otherwise have seen."[13] I will try to argue that Detweiler's writing goes where he never intended it to have gone in relation to nothing, that it is indeed all about nothingness, but not in an unbiblical way, nor nihilistically. On the contrary, the work is, I believe, more in the spirit of the "fortunate fall" into nothingness of Percy's Barrett, about whom Detweiler feels there is the grace of eros and the energy of will. To be sure, the spirit of my own argument about Detweiler's not naughting of nothing intends to be the sort of deep play he holds as goal of our readings.

It may seem a bit oblique to the task of argument, but I believe the simplest way in which to make the point about nothingness in Religion and Literature studies is to review Detweiler's apparent naughting of nothing, his crucial "breaking the fall" of the *mise-en-abyme* in life and theory, with another work whose religious purpose in relation to literature is not dissimilar. At the same time that *Breaking the Fall* was being published, there was also in production a book edited by R. Melvin Keiser and Tony Stonebrunner. The books was called *The Way of Transfiguration: Religious Imagination as Theopoiesis*, and it contained essays by Stanley Romaine Hopper dating from 1951 to 1989. The books by Detweiler and Hopper shared hermeneutic purpose, but their stance on the naughting of nothing in the postmodern field of Religion and Literature was at odds, at least ostensibly so.

For a while, Hopper was perspectivally aligned with Detweiler on the theological importance of naughting nothing. In the fifties, Hopper was noting that modern poetry demonstrates the "manifold of inner nothingness"[14] and that modern poets "encounter the nothingness within when all the stabilities are gone."[15] He cited Edith Sitwell's poem on Nagasaki to the same nihilistic point that Detweiler had made: "Our final structure, the heart's ragged dress/That rose from Nothing, fell to Nothingness."[16] This is the nothingness to which at least the Christian tradition must say no.

But as early as the late sixties, Hopper began, as his essays show, to differentiate nothingness itself, indicating, for example, a distinction between the Romantic nothingness of Rilke and the mystical nothingness of Eliot. About the latter Hopper wrote that it was "a consecrated Nothingness in the pathos of a solitary though infinite longing."[17] Yet, between Romanticism and Mysticism—both marginal and somewhat suspect in Religion and Literature, not to mention in postmodern and deconstructive perspective—there must be a third way. Hopper found it in Wallace Stevens, first, and then in Japanese literature and religion.

Regarding Stevens' "illustered nothingness," Hopper wrote that "the poem is a 'fiction' fabricated by the imagination which, out of the nothing of its own inner-ness, creates a novel order and a 'meaning' where none was before."[18] In a time when for many "the gods come to nothing,"[19] Hopper finds that what he had earlier called a *via crucis* is a *descensus ad inferos*. Following Crispin's way in Stevens' "Comedian as the Letter C," Hopper writes that "our journeys today are journeys into nothingness, since the underworld [*inferos*] is an archaism."[20] There is nothing there, but that "there" is the goal of our vocation. As Kafka had said: "What is laid upon us is to accomplish the negative..."[21] Far from being wholly nihilistic, "it is as if nothingness," as Stevens had written, "contained a *metier*."[22]

In the seventies Hopper is still getting his hermeneutic and apophatically theological clue from Pascal's abysmal nothing, which is constituted by and in the "between" of the two infinites—the infinitely great and the infinitely small—where we mortals dwell. Literature artfully shows us our true nature and task, for, as Hopper put it, "poetry must go through the world of broken images in such a way as to bring into consciousness the nothingness on which we are striving to build."[23] But the tone changed in the eighties, and it is in Hopper's last writings where the apparent contrast with Detweiler seems strongest.

Perhaps it was first from Ezra Pound that Hopper learned that Archibald MacLeish was not being sufficiently radical and all too nihilistic when he complained that "suddenly gazing into nothing" is "nothing at all."[24] Or perhaps it was Meister Eckhart or Nietzsche who taught Hopper that one may have firmly to encounter nothing before giving birth to one's self as a dancing star.[25] Whatever the impetus, the expression came from the East. The insight from Chuang Tzu was likely crucial:

> The Yellow Emperor went wandering
> To the north of the Red Water
> To the Kwan Lun mountain.
> He looked around
> Over the edge of the world.
> On the way home
> He lost his night-colored pearl.
> He sent out Science to seek his pearl, and got nothing!
> He sent Analysis to look for his pearl, and got nothing!
> He sent out Logic to seek his pearl, and got nothing.
> Then he asked Nothingness, and Nothingness had it.
> The Yellow Emperor said:
> "Strange, indeed: Nothingness
> Who was not sent
> Who did no work to find it
> Had the night-colored pearl!"[26]

But if this was the impetus, it was the work of the Zen philosopher, Nishitani, who provided the hermeneutic which would enable Hopper to affirm the "nothing at the foundation of everything that is" and to make it possible for him, at the end of his work in Religion and Literature, to "rejoice in . . . the bloom of things out of the unfathomable no-thing-ness" which Wallace Stevens called "the dumb-foundering abyss."[27]

This is clearly a different reading of the nothingness with which modern and postmodern literatures must deal than the nihilistic one given by Detweiler. Perhaps the difference is that Hopper was dealing as a Christian critic mainly with poetry and drama, whereas Detweiler directed his attention mainly to the narrative traditions of novel and short fiction. Or perhaps the difference has to do with Hopper's psychological and ontological perspective as contrasted with Detweiler's sociological and political concerns. Whether Hopper's view of nothingness is finally in keeping with the biblical tradition is, as Detweiler notes without impugning Hopper, problematic. Suffice it to say that Hopper had in 1959 anticipated the problematic and the difference between his text and Detweiler's. He had written a mock conversation between Karl Barth, whom he called

"Protestant Theologian," and Søren Kierkegaard. This is a part of that dialogue:

> *Prot. Theo.*: But I begin from nothing other than God's revelation which has its ground within itself.
> *Kierkegaard*: Is that not from anything?
> *Prot. Theo.*: No, it is just the opposite. In this way everything is understood from *before* the beginning. . . .
> *Kierkegaard*: How shall I ever get over that difficulty—of your actually beginning without a beginning (though perhaps not in actuality). For I was about to say . . . that thou shalt *first* seek God's kingdom. But then in a certain sense it is nothing I shall do. Yes, certainly, in a certain sense it is nothing; thou shalt in the deepest sense make thyself nothing, become nothing before God, learn to keep silent; in this silence is the beginning, which is, *first* to seek God s kingdom.[28]

Is not the difference between Detweiler and Hopper precisely the difference between this fictionalized Protestant Theologian and Kierkegaard? So it would seem.

But things are not always what they seem. To be sure, Detweiler has affirmed, not only that there is not nothing in the biblical tradition because one cannot imagine it, but also that that same tradition affirms, like the fictionalized Barth above, that from before the beginning "there's one who holds this falling / Infinitely gently in his hands." Detweiler's book, in addition, compellingly presents literary evidence from contemporary fiction (Percy, Updike, Atwood, Hoban, Kafka, Dillard, and many more) which attests, not only to the fall into nothingness, but also, not unlike the biblical tradition, to the wondrous breaking of that fall in narrative community and in readerly *communitas*. All this seems testimony to the naughting of nothingness.

Surely there is indeed a naughting of nothingness in the nihilistic sense. Is this not the point of the titular image of Detweiler's book? But it is Hopper's point, too. So here there is no real difference, in spite of appearances. There is also more that does not appear. One might think of the saying that in a riddle whose answer is "a game of chess" the only phrase that is not permitted in the question of the riddle is precisely "a game of chess." Did not Heidegger, so often cited by Detweiler, point to the philosophical importance of the unsaid in discourse? Detweiler does not talk about nothing. Could it be that that is what his whole book is really about and that the only difference between him and Hopper is that in the latter's work it is explicit and in the former's there is a literalizing of

Kierkegaard's silence about silence? With this question in mind, consider the matter of "play."

Detweiler talks about play as much as he is silent about nothingness. From the epigraph on the book's first page to the very last page where he talks about Rilke's brake on the fall, there is a continual paean to play as clue to religious reading. The reader learns from Detweiler that the West has undervalued play (like its undervaluation of nothingness?) and has thereby lost its ludic quality. But "we manage to find in the gratuitousness of fiction, and of reading it, a relief from our labour and achievement oriented lives."[29] What Freud noted in the child concerning the well-known "*fort-da*" game, we carry on as adults in literature, namely, the ability to give imagination's shape and control to what is above and beyond us, i.e., the experience of nothingness.[30] So the "escape of language into the play of literature creates the conditions for new knowledge."[31] Very much as for Hopper, the literary journey into nothingness makes possible a sense of "meaning" where none was before.

This much may sound to some as a romanticizing perspective on play and reading, but Detweiler goes much further and much deeper. Not only is the reading of literature a ludic activity, but the hermeneutic act is responsibly playful in terms of community. Playing with the possibility of reading religiously in a secular age is indicative of a movement toward communities of play.[32] Detweiler's hermeneutic is broadened out of an incipient narcissism by petitioning the play-notion implicit in ritual studies of liminality and deep play (Victor Turner, Barbara Myerhoff, Mary Douglas, Arnold Van Gennep).[33] By viewing the hermeneutic of Religion and Literature as a ritual activity, Detweiler shows religious reading to be play in a double sense: reflective backing away from unconscious attachment to one's fixated feelings and thoughts, and a ritual activity that is constituted in love and through liturgy (*leitourgos* = "the work of the people").[34] In Detweiler's reading of Kundera's fiction, play becomes love's freedom, where free play is made possible by love and the freedom to love is made possible by the perspective of play.[35]

This is of course serious business. *Serio ludere!* It has to do with breaking the fall into nihilism for a people and a culture. "One reads," Detweiler testifies, "to engage in deep play, to enjoy the sensuality of the mind's possibilities, and especially to do so in the interactions of writing, reading and tracing that involve one with others."[36] It is, as Detweiler's first chapter title says, "playing for real," and it makes possible, as the author affirms on his last page, "crises [being] . . . deepened into the play of mystery."[37]

Some years ago there had been harbingers of this ludic hope in what was called the theology of play movement.[38] But Detweiler's deep play is not from that source; it is, rather, broadened by the social and political implications, not only of ritual studies, but also of postmodern meditations (e.g., Mikhail Bakhtin, Roland Barthes, Jean Baudrillard, Michel de Certeau, Gilles Deleuze, Jacques Derrida, and Jean-Francois Lyotard). This places Detweiler's perspective closer to the deconstructive theology of Mark C. Taylor, whose essays on play are apposite,[39] than it does to the theology of the theology and play movement. But it also raises another possibility: namely, that deep play is Detweiler's nothingness, as it is in fact for these other postmodern thinkers; that the book, so troped with and by play, is finally and actually about nothing, but not the nothing that the author naughts.

J. C. F. Schiller set the stage for play as non-nihilistic nothing. In his essay on *The Aesthetic Education of Man* he grappled postKantianly with the intellectual schizophrenia of so much of Occidental ideation concerning being and becoming. He re-imagined this *binarism as the* need to discharge energy (*Stofftrieb*) and the need to design experience (*Formtrieb*), what Nietzsche was to mythologize as Dionysos and Apollo.[40] Schiller, like Hans-Georg Gadamer after him (in *Wahrheit und Methode*), noted, however that there is a "third" drive or tendency which was termed *Spieltrieb*, the "drive to play." But this play is not a "third thing," a *tertium quid*. It is rather a *tertium non datur*, a "third which is not given," save in the interplay between the other instincts toward form and energy, being and becoming. It is a no-thing. Heidegger would call this the *Schwingungsbereich*, the "swing realm" in the "rift" (*Riss*), the experience of "nothingness" (*das Nichts*). This is hardly a nihilistic nothing. "Rather," as Heidegger put it, "it is the intimacy with which opponents belong to each other. This rift [and its play, like the 'play' in a bicycle wheel which makes movement possible] carries the opponents into the course of their unity by virtue of their common ground,"[41] and so produces the "swing" in which "mortals go to and fro slowly," the slowing down making possible a "ring" and resonance in life-experience in the direction of "space's throwing open" a "play of stillness."[42] Heidegger's deep play says: "Das Spiegel-spiel von Welt ist der Reigen des Ereignens . . . . Der Reigen ist der Ring, der ringt, indem er als das Spiegeln spielt." Here, in the no-thing-ness, play mirrors the world-play of being's meaning.

It is from Heidegger that Gadamer—and Derrida and others of the postmodern ilk after him—mapped the "clearing" (*Lichtung*) of play's no-thingness. And it is not without significance that Detweiler links his own notion of reading religiously to Heidegger's (and Eckhart's) notion of *Gelassenheit*.[43] For both Heidegger and Eckhart the notion of play and nothingness function as two sides of the same fundamental ontological coinage, with *Gelassenheit*, "letting be," being clue to both, and vice versa. For, as Detweiler appropriately says, the awareness of play (and no-thingness?) "provides a condition for letting *Gelassenheit* take over, through which nonchalance we can start to imagine how our stories of faith will proceed,"[44] since in the deep play of religious reading we learn "to merge suspense with *Gelassenheit*" and are thereupon "instructed in the value of mystery."[45] Detweiler could hardly have made a stronger case, without making it at all, for no-thing-ness, but, to be sure, not the nothingness of nihilism which he strongly naughted.

The importance of this nothingness which is neither being (a something) nor non-being (nihilism), but which is the play-between, cannot be stressed too much, especially in the current moment. Robert Scharlemann's title, "the no to nothing and the nothing to know," indicates the crux that is indeed felt as a *via crucis* by so many just now. I am referring to reports from those in the helping professions (teachers, clergy, counselors, physicians, therapists, etc.). It would seem that the present complaints, not only of individuals but also of whole communities, are not of classical description (hysteria, schizophrenia, Oedipal fixation, etc.). Our dis-ease in the moment is more often described as depression, low self-esteem, feelings of worthlessness and nothingness, all tired out and tired of being tired. The collective version of this hurt has to do with sensing persons of certain genders, races, and ages as worth nothing.

How can it be that certain religious traditions hold the achieving of nothingness to be an ideal of spirituality, whereas so many persons experience this very condition, not as salvation, but as suffering? Or are these nothings the same? And, if not the same, are they related, the one being symptom, parody, or condition of the other, the spiritual ideal being the depth dimension of the existential hurt? How can the nothingness one suffers, which is hardly ludic, be transformed into the Great Nothing of deep religious play?

Two things merit observation concerning this matter. The first has to do with the psychological and social fact that when a person or a community experiences what he, she, or it calls a feeling of nothingness it is not no-thing. That negative condition is felt by the one(s) making the complaint to be a serious some-thing. Nihilistic sensibility is a some-thing as much as being or God is a some-thing when either is taken to be a being. But perhaps psychologically, if not culturally, nihilism is the deep self's way of alerting the ego to what it really wants, namely, not nothing as something, but everything as un-thingified, unattached, unfixated, made less serious, more playful, in the deep play of religious readings which play for real. The nothing-ing even of nothing.

A second observation returns the matter to the Christian biblical and theological tradition where this essay began. Detweiler had affirmed that this religious tradition is one of the few to suggest that nothingness is not the primal condition nor the condition of human and worldly end. Meanwhile, this essay has argued that Detweiler actually meant a particular nothingness, the nihilistic sort, which, if the observation above has worth, may not be the authentic nothingness even Detweiler's book (unsayingly) seeks in deep play and religious reading. In fact, the Christian biblical tradition that, according to Detweiler, has no nihilistic nothing may have more to do with the negative nothing than one might at first imagine. That very religious tradition may bear directly on our time's pain. I am thinking of the image in Detweiler's title: the Fall. And I am thinking especially of the theologization of that image into the notion of '"original sin." Could it be that a shadow of the very Christian tradition which would soteriologically serve to break the fall into nothing has taught peoples and nations, in the name of humility, to feel like nothing in the negative sense (i. e., sinners)? Is there a tendency in the biblical perspective to valorize weakness, as Nietzsche complained, if not absolute worthlessness? Is the nothingness we feel, and that which we project scapegoat-fashion on others, actually an acting out of a Christian theologism? Does nothingness commended as religious ideal (humility) in the biblical perspective need precisely a Great Nothingness about which it refuses to speak?

If Great No-thingness as perspective is resisted, it is in part because it is confused with the nihilistic nothingness persons and communities experience. However it is also justly refused because, as Detweiler has said, speaking it makes it into something, idolatrously transforming nothing into something, something positive (being) or something negative (nihilistic anxiety or experience). This is the problem. It is the way in which Great Nothingness becomes nihilism, just as it is also the problem of idolatry in relation to other ideals—God, love, meaning, community, and so on.

But a refusal to speak nothing because of the problem of incipient idolatry may itself represent a fall into nihilism's nothingness. To imagine that imagining nothing makes it into something already carries the notion that an image is a some-thing, that imagination is referential to some real reality. Attempting to break the fall into nothingness may already be a fall into the onto-theological perspective which imagines everything, including its own imagining, to refer to some-thing.

Gaston Bachelard attempted to re-vision the matter imaginally, rather than meta-physically (turning "metas" into "physicals"), when he pointed out that imagination is not forming images (some-things) of something, but that it is rather the deformation of images of perception, as, for example, when I say "a cup of sorrow," having thereby de-constructed an apparently real perceptual image of my coffee cup.[46] The same point was made by James Hillman when he argued that a reason to utilize mythological images for psychological complexes and archetypal constructs is because everyone knows that myths are not real and yet they allow one to see reality in a new way. This helps to avoid committing idolatry on one's own concepts, thoughts, constructs, by taking them to be transparent to some "reality."[47] Jacques Derrida, following Heidegger, has called this imaginal nature of thinking, including the thinking about nothing, "traces [*éperons*]."[48] If we imagine that our imaginings about nothing are nothing, then it is no trick at all to avoid idolatry. Images of nothing are no-things; they are nothing but imaginal tracings. From the deep play of this perspective, it is not that we cannot imagine nothing; it is that we can never not imagine nothing. Everything is nothing, or, as Detweiler says, it is the fiction that makes narrative communities possible.

The point is the same with no-thing-ness as with the ideal of detachment in mystical perspective. Detachment, on the face of it, sounds amoral if not immoral. What spouse would wish of his or her wife or husband a love that was "detached"? Yet the point is missed by putting the matter this way. Most often our relationships are constituted by projections. "I want a gal just like the gal that married dear old Dad!" We don't relate to the other—the other person, the other nation, the other religion. Rather we relate to our own ideology concerning the other—male, female, African American, Southern European, Chinese, Latino, etc. The point of the ideal of detachment is to make conscious, to own, to withdraw and to detach from these projected ideas and ideologies of mind, sense, feeling and intuition. By detaching critically from individual and/or collective ego's privileged but unconsciously constructed fantasies, one may have a better chance at really relating to the real other. Detachment of a deep sort can make authentic attachment possible.

This is what Detweiler calls *communitas* and *eros*. And it is achieved, according to him, by a perspective of deep play concerning one's interpreting. It is what I am calling nothing, not the one to which we must say no, but the one we must all know and be called by and to before it is too late. "Breaking the fall," indeed!

NOTES

1. Robert Detweiler, *Breaking the Fall: Religious Readings of Contemporary Fiction* (San Francisco: Harper and Row, Publishers, 1989), p. 44.

2. Robert Detweiler, *Breaking the Fall.*

3. Robert Detweiler, *Breaking the Fall*, p.45.

4. Martin Heidegger, *An Introduction to Metaphysics*, tr. R. Manheim (Garden City: Doubleday and Co., Inc., 1961), pp. 19, 22.

5. Robert Detweiler, *Breaking the Fall*, p.45.

6. Raoul Mortley, *From Word to Silence* (Bonn: Hanstein, 1986), two volumes.

7. *Genesis and Apocalypse* (Louisville: Westminster/John Knox Press, 1991).

8. *The Experience of Nothingness* (New York: Harper and Row, 1970).

9. "The No to Nothing and the Nothing to Know," *Journal of the American Academy of Religion*, 55/1 (1987) pp. 57-74.

10. "To Be and Not to Be: Sit Autem sermo (Logos) vester, est, est; non, non . . .," *Journal of the American Academy of Religion*, 53/1 (1985) pp. 5-22.

11. *Kinq Lear*, 2.2. 165.

12. Robert Detweiler, *Breaking the Fall*, p.67; the reference is to Rilke, *Das Buch der Bilder, Samtliche Werke, I* (Wiesbaden: Insel Verlag, 1955), p. 400.

13. Robert Detweiler, *Breaking the Fall*, xi; the reference is to Margaret Atwood, *Second Words* (Boston: Beacon Press, 1984), p. 15.

14. Stanley R. Hopper, *The Way of Transfiguration: Religious Imagination as Theopoiesis*, eds. R. M. Keiser and T. Stonebrunner (Louisville: Westminster/John Knox Press, 1992), p. 19.

15. Stanley Hopper, *The Way of Transfiguration*, p. 23.

16. Stanley Hopper, *The Way of Transfiguration*, p. 25; the citation is from Edith Sitwell's *Canticle of the Rose.*

17. Stanley Hopper, *The Way of Transfiguration*, p. 32.

18. Stanley Hopper, *The Way of Transfiguration*, p. 73.

19. Stanley Hopper, *The Way of Transfiguration*, p. 91f.

20. Stanley Hopper, *The Way of Transfiguration*, p. 82.

21. Franz Kafka, *The Great Wall of China*, trs. Muir and Muir (New York: Schocken Books, 1970), p. 167.

22. The quotation is from Stevens' late poem, *The Rock*, and is invoked by Hopper in his discussion of "The Man with the Blue Guitar," wherein the nothingness of the sound-box of the musical instrument is responsible for our ability to hear the music. See Hopper, *The Way of Transfiguration*, p. 131.

23. Stanley Hopper, *The Way of Transfiguration*, p. 116.

24. Stanley Hopper, *The Way of Transfiguration*, p. 220.

25. Stanley Hopper, *The Way of Transfiguration*, p. 221.

26. Thomas Merton, *The Way of Chuang Tzu* (New York: New Directions, 1969), p. 74; see Hopper, *The Way of Transfiguration*, p. 222.

27. Stanley Hopper, *The Way of Transfiguration*, pp. 245, 251, 272.

28. Stanley Hopper, *The Way of Transfiguration*, p. 56.

29. Robert Detweiler, *Breaking the Fall*, p. 9.

30. Robert Detweiler, *Breaking the Fall*, p. 19.

31. Robert Detweiler, *Breaking the Fall*, p. 21.

32. Robert Detweiler, *Breaking the Fall*, p. 30.

33. Robert Detweiler, *Breaking the Fall*, p. 55.

34. Robert Detweiler, *Breaking the Fall*, p. 38.

35. Robert Detweiler, *Breaking the Fall*, p. 49.

36. Robert Detweiler, *Breaking the Fall*, p. 127.

37. Robert Detweiler, *Breaking the Fall*, p. 190.

38. For example: Karl Rahner, *Man at Play* (New York: Herder, 1967); Harvey Cox, *Feast of Fools* (Cambridge: Harvard, 1969); David Miller, *Gods and Games* (New York: World, 1969); Robert Neale, *In Praise of Play* (New York: Harper, 1969); Sam Keen, *Apology for Wonder* (New York: Harper, 1969); Jurgen Moltmann, *Die ersten Freigelassenen der Schöpfung* (Munich: Chr. Kaiser, 1971)); Gerhard Martin, '*Wir wollen hier auf Erden schon . . .' Das Recht auf Glück* (Stuttgart: Kohlhammer, 1970); Jean Jacques Wunenburger, *La fete, le jeu, et le sacré* (Paris: Editions Universitaires, 1977); David Miller, "From Leviathan to Lear: Shades of Play in Language and Literature," *Eranos 51-1982* (Frankfurt: Insg Verlag, 1983), pp. 59-109; etc.

39. Mark C. Taylor, *Tears* (Albany: SUNY Press, 1990), especially chap. 9, "Paralectics," and chap. 12, "How to Do Nothing with Words."

40. J. C. F. Schiller, *On the Aesthetic Education of Man*, tr. R. Snell (London: Routledge and Kegan Paul, 1965).

41. Martin Heidegger, *Unterwegs zur Sprache* (Pfullingen: Neske, 1975), pp. 108, 119.

42. Martin Heidegger, *Vorträge und Aufsätze*, Teil II (Pfullingen: Neske, 1967), pp. 53, 55.

43. Detweiler, *Breaking the Fall*, p. 35.

44. Detweiler, *Breaking the Fall*, p. 188.

45. Detweiler, *Breaking the Fall*, p. 183.

46. Gaston Bachelard, *L'Air et les songes* (Paris: Jose Corti, 1943), p. 7:

> On veut toujours que l'imagination soit la faculte de former des images. Or elle est plutot la faculté de deformer les images fournir par la perception, elle est surtout la faculté de nous liberer des images premiéres, de *chanqer* les images. S'il n'y a pas changement d'images, ... il n'y a pas imagination .... Si une image presente ne fait pas penser a une image absénte, si une image occasionelle ne determine pas ... une explosion des images, il n'y a pas imagination.

47. James Hillman, *Archetypal Psychology* (Dallas: Spring Publications, 1983), p. 19: "... by relying on myths as its primary rhetoric, archetypal psychology grounds itself in a fantasy that cannot be taken historically, physically, literally."

48. Jacques Derrida, *Spurs/Eperons* (Chicago: University of Chicago Press, 1979); and, Martin Heidegger, *Holzwege* (Frankfurt: Klostermann, 1972), pp. 250f: "Dichter sind die Sterblichen, die mit Ernst den Weingott singend, die Spur der entflohenen Götter spüren, auf deren Spur bleiben und so den verwandten Sterblichen den Weg spüren zur Wende.... Doch wer vermag es, solche Spur zu spüren? Spüren sind oft unscheinbar und immer die Hinterlassenschaft einer kaum geahnten Weisung. Dichter sein in dürftiger Zeit heisst: singend auf die Spur der enflohenen Götter achten."

Of An Apoplectic Tone Recently Adopted in Philosophy

CHRISTOPHER NORRIS

I

The recent rumpus at Cambridge over Derrida's honorary degree was on the whole such a lamentable episode—such a display of petty resentment and unthinking "philosophical" prejudice—that one's first response was to count the whole affair best forgotten as quickly as possible.[1] What is the use of engaging in dialogue with those whose idea of intellectual debate is represented by the kind of stock-in-trade insult and downright slanderous misrepresentation that appeared over various eminent signatures in the "quality" British presses? Why remark—yet again—on the willingness of so many otherwise reputable academics to go along with the bugbear image of "deconstruction" that has acquired currency on the chat-show circuit and in various organs of middlebrow cultural opinion? After all, there is little reason to hope that Derrida's opponents might yet be persuaded to *read* some of his work, rather than hold forth on its alleged demerits—its "irrationalism," "nihilism," "sophistry," "lack of intellectual rigour," etc.— whenever invited to do so by this or that hard-pressed journalist in search of a topical space-filler. Nor is Derrida likely to have lost much sleep over the intended snub, having known pretty well what to make of it from previous experience with their counterparts on the U.S. professional network.[2] All of which inclined me not to comment any further on this latest outbreak of professional *ressentiment* raised to a high point of principle by academics who lacked both the will and the competence to understand his work at anything like an adequate level of philosophic grasp. Better not dignify this

47

sorry display by treating it as if the opposing faction could muster even the semblance of an argued case against Derrida's candidature.

But to let it go at that—in the hope that at least a few readers will show more intelligence and capacity for independent judgment than a clutch of obtuse and ill-willed academics—would perhaps be unwise, given the extent to which the latter managed to impose their views on a duly scandalized (or easily diverted) public. So I will offer the following remarks by way of explaining first how the rumpus came about, second (more importantly) how the non-readers have got Derrida wrong, and third (less so) why Cambridge would have shown up in yet worse light had the anti-Derrida cabal triumphed and the vote gone against him as seemed very possible until the last moment. As I say it is a depressing little saga and one that must appear quite absurd to those overseas watchers of the British cultural scene with an eye to the special kinds of ingrown rancour that periodically surface to trouble the calm of our ancient universities. But since the issue had better not go by default let me run through just a few of the idiotic slogans that were canvassed under the name of "deconstruction" by those who (in virtue of their academic calling, not to mention the common intellectual and moral decencies) should have known better. The most that I can hope to do here is indicate just how wrong are these characterizations, and offer some corrective remarks for those in need of guidance through the minefield of obfuscating *idées recues*.

1) "All reading is misreading, all interpretation misinterpretation, all truths merely modes of error" (etc.). This idea has most often been imputed to Derrida by literary critics—sympathetic or hostile—who have little interest in philosophy and who suppose that deconstruction is just another name for the "anything goes" style of hermeneutic license that rejects all standards of interpretative truth or rational accountability. It bears no relation to Derrida's work, as should be plain to anyone who has read (for instance) his two early books on Husserl, his essay on Plato (in *Dissemination*), or the emphatic disavowals of any such creed to be found, e.g., in *Of Grammatology*.[3] Thus: "To recognize and respect all [the] classical exigencies is not easy and requires all the instruments of traditional criticism. Without this recognition and this respect, critical production would risk developing in any direction at all and authorize itself to say almost anything."[4]

Which is not of course to deny that textual close-reading of the kind that Derrida practices may often go against the intentionalist grain—or against what the author *consciously and explicitly* wanted to say—in response to anomalous or discrepant details which have hitherto escaped notice. So far as the appeal to intentions is concerned, "this indispensable guardrail has always only *protected*, it has never *opened*, a reading." And again, in perhaps his most succinct formulation: "[a deconstructive reading] must always aim at a certain relationship, unperceived by the writer, between what he commands and what he does not command of the patterns of the language that he uses."[5]

Of course these might be taken as mere passing gestures toward a high-toned ethic of "respect" and "recognition" which is elsewhere belied by Derrida's practice in the reading of philosophical or literary texts. After all (slogan 2), everyone knows that, according to Derrida, philosophy is just another "kind of writing," on a par with poems, novels, literary criticism, or any other sort of text you care to name. No matter that this phrase actually comes from the title of an essay by Richard Rorty who makes no bones about his own lack of interest in the more "philosophical" aspects of Derrida's work, and his desire to speed up the imminent demise of philosophy as an academic discipline by playing off "bad brother Jacques" against "honest uncle Kant" and all those other earnestly deluded seekers-after-truth.[6] Deconstruction thus figures as the sophist's revenge, as a handy set of rhetorical tricks for deflating philosophy's grandiose self-image, or again—in less provocative style—as a sensible adjustment to the pragmatist view of what's good in the way of belief. For Rorty indeed there can be no obligation to interpret Derrida aright, since notions like truth, right reading, argumentative rigour etc. are merely so many hungover symptoms of that same (now obsolete) "foundationalist" paradigm that has long exerted such a powerful and delusory appeal. One can see why this "strong revisionist" reading has enjoyed great favour with literary critics, few of whom possess much knowledge of philosophy beyond a vague sense of wounded self-esteem at having suffered an age-old history of arrogant put-downs, starting out with Socrates *versus* the poets, sophists and assorted rhetoricians, and carried on nowadays in numerous faculty disputes. More unfortunate is the fact that a good many philosophers have likewise given credit to the Rorty version, thus confirming all their preconceived ideas. For if this were anything like a fair rendition of Derrida's arguments then one could hardly blame the Cambridge Faculty of Philosophy for regarding him as a less than worthy recipient of its highest mark of esteem.

Hence (slogans 3, 4, and 5) the widespread idea that deconstruction heralds the "end of philosophy," or its demotion to the level of an undifferentiated textual "freeplay" where literary critics can claim the upper hand since they—unlike the philosophers—have long been aware that "all truths are fictions," that "all concepts are metaphors," and that interpretation (in Stanley Fish's phrase) goes "all the way down."[7] This message—or something very like it—has been doing the academic rounds for some time now, and was batted back and forth between journalists and philosophers during the Cambridge campaign. But even the most limited acquaintance with Derrida's work—for instance, with his essays in *Writing and Difference* or the superb deconstructive reading of Kant's third *Critique*—is enough to discountenance any such view of him as endorsing that facile "end-of-philosophy" rhetoric that Rorty so assiduously seeks to promote.[8] On the contrary, Derrida has often insisted that deconstruction has nothing whatever in common with those fashionable trends (postmodernism, post-humanism, post-Marxism etc.) which naively presume to turn the page on so-called "Western metaphysics" while failing to engage its problems and aporias with the requisite degree of analytical care. [9] One could multiply quotations to precisely this effect, all of them refuting the idea—the vulgar-deconstructionist doxa—that philosophy is just another "kind of writing," a literary genre whose concepts and truth-claims are so many sublimated metaphors, and whose stylistic resources (or periodic shifts of "final vocabulary") are its only contribution to the ongoing "cultural conversation of mankind."   Such may be Rorty's view of the matter, one shared by more than a few literary theorists with reasons of their own for adopting it. Still there is no question of Derrida's subscribing to any such wholesale irrationalist creed. See his classic essay "White Mythology: Metaphor in the Text of Philosophy" for a subtle and rigorous account of these issues that affords no excuse for the sloppy misreading put about by admirers and detractors alike.[10]

6) "If Derrida has anything worthwhile to say why say it in a style so willfully obscure, cryptic, mandarin, prolix, self-indulgent, allusive, repetitious, rhetorical, 'literary' (etc. etc.)?" And again: "why attempt to understand him if Derrida adopts such a range of sophistical techniques for baffling the good-willed reader?" On the rare occasions that this charge is backed up by reference to any specific text it is usually Derrida's notorious "response" to John Searle on the topic of Austinian speech-act theory.[11] Otherwise it seems to express little more than a resentment of the fact that he manages to write so much and a failure to grasp that his writings are "performative" in the sense of raising certain philosophic issues (e.g. the relation between concept and metaphor, or between constative and performative utterance) *in and through* the practice of a written style that self-consciously foregrounds those issues. One can see why such writing has caused great offense—if mainly through scandalized hearsay—to philosophers bred up on more orthodox ideas of what constitutes a decently

intelligible style. But it is yet another sign of ingrown professionalism when these latter are treated as the hallmark of genuine, "serious" philosophical work as opposed to mere "literary" dilettantism. Of course those who take this line will claim to be upholding the standards of argumentative rigour and truth against the blandishments of a pseudo-philosophical rhetoric which belongs (if anywhere) in departments of Comparative Literature, or maybe to some minor course-option in the history of ideas. Clear thought and fancy writing just don't mix, least of all the kind of writing that exploits certain fictive (as well as figural) devices by way of questioning the "law of genre" that would keep them firmly apart. What is thus ruled out—despite all the manifold counter-examples from Plato to Wittgenstein, Austin, Kripke, or Parfitt—is any notion that philosophy might stand to gain (to sharpen and refine its analytical insights) through a speculative but none the less rigorous reflection on the realms of metaphorical and fictive possibility. Otherwise there is simply no accounting for the view that Derrida's "style" goes beyond all the limits of genuine, competent or good-faith philosophical debate. For instances to the contrary see (e.g.) "Plato's Pharmacy," "The Double Session," "The Law of Genre" and—most strikingly—his essays on the tangled relationship between philosophy, fiction and psychoanalysis: "Coming Into One's Own" and "To Speculate—on 'Freud'."[12]

7) "How can Derrida see fit to complain that his work has been traduced, his texts misread, his arguments ignored or vulgarized etc., when he himself makes a regular practice of doing just this with whatever he reads?" Or, in similar *tu quoque* fashion: "why bother even trying to get Derrida right if, according to him, textuality rules and there is no appeal to the old ('logocentric') constraints of right reason, interpretive truth, authorial intention (etc.)?"[13] Again, this is just the kind of reflex response that "deconstruction" provokes among those who have avoided any contact with Derrida's work beyond a mere handful of phrases taken out of context and a firm conviction—on the authority of other non-readers—that the whole thing amounts to just a species of sophistical wordplay. It is hard to know what it would take to dislodge this deep-laid prejudice, backed up as it is by the guild mentality that equates "serious" philosophy with work in the Anglo-American analytical tradition, and which views the other ("Continental") line of descent after Kant as fit for consumption only by muddle-headed literary theorists. So the point needs making with maximum emphasis: that Derrida is an exemplary close-reader of philosophic texts whose keen eye for the marginal, the discrepant or the anomalous goes along with an equally exigent sense of the prime obligation—the ethical

imperative—to respect what is written and not let interpretation develop "in any direction at all." And this despite the fact—well attested in the latest round of polemics—that such reading may produce results which are counter-canonical (or counter-intuitive) to a degree that provokes outrage among mainstream commentators. But blanket dismissals are of course no substitute for what has so far been altogether lacking, that is to say, a critique of Derrida's claims that would engage them at anything like their own level of detailed textual exegesis. If he is able to run rings around an opponent like John Searle it is because Searle reads always with a view to confirming his own preconceptions, and thus fails to register the logical (as well as rhetorical) complications of Austin's, Derrida's and—not least—his own writing.[14]

Of course this is hugely annoying for Searle, as for others with the same understandable desire to ignore such bother-headed "textualist" puzzles and get straight on with the business of expounding a clear-cut, coherent and pragmatically useful speech-act theory. Hence (slogan 8) the idea of deconstruction as a set of geared-up sophistical techniques for "doing things with texts." But it remains the case—as I have argued at length elsewhere— that Derrida is by far the more attentive, scrupulous, and faithfully *Austinian* exponent of Austin's *How To Do Things With Words*.[15] Above all he is alert to those signs of categorical confusion which begin with the attempt to distinguish clearly between constative and performative speech-act modes, and which then create problems or, in Austin's phrase, "play old Harry" with the effort to sort out "serious" from "non-serious" instances, good-faith promises from promises uttered in jest, real-life from fictive or set-piece examples, "authentic" from "deviant" ("parasitical") cases, and so forth.[16] What is at issue is the relation between constative *theory* and performative *practice*, a relation which Searle thinks unproblematic— provided one adopts an orderly and disciplined approach—but which Derrida (and Austin) find subject to all manner of destabilizing ironies, doubts and complications. There are two crucial points to be made here, as against the standard view (standard at least in the Anglo-American "analytic" community) that Searle won the argument hands down and exposed Derrida as a charlatan bent upon creating deconstructive mischief. One is that Austin, had he lived to witness this exchange, would surely have acknowledged more affinity—more sense of a kindred philosophical spirit— with Derrida's "playful" than with Searle's ultra-"serious" way of reading his work. That is, he would have seen it as much more in keeping with his own willingness to suspend the requirements of "constructive" system and method when confronted with examples (jokes, anecdotes, "deviant" performatives, awkward bits of written or oral evidence) which failed to support his larger philosophical claims. And the second point—following from this—is that Austin, like Derrida, perceived no merit in the standard (implicitly ethical) equation between truth, seriousness, and the drive to assimilate marginal or non-standard cases. What unites these thinkers—and sets them at odds with a theorist like Searle—is an openness to the sheer variety of human needs, satisfactions, and sense-making gambits, and also a knowledge of the violence that can often lurk behind doctrinaire systematizing habits of thought.

That Derrida to some extent reads Austin against the grain is not—as Searle would have it—a willful misprision or an act of hermeneutic violence on his part. Rather it signals an awareness of the deep ambivalence in Austin's project, on the one hand his striving to articulate a systematic theory of (proper, authentic) speech-acts, and on the other his sense of the difficulties that arise to frustrate that ambition at every turn. A good deal has been written lately about the "ethics of deconstruction," some of it (e.g. Harpham, 1987 and Critchley, 1992) very much to the point while others (Miller, 1987) give plentiful scope for those who would maintain—slogan 9—that deconstruction celebrates the "death of the author," the dissolution of the subject (the knowing, willing, and judging subject) into so many radically "decentred" discourses or language-games, and hence the demise of any "ethics" worthy the name.[17] There are, I should allow, some few isolated passages in Derrida's (mostly early) work that lend themselves to a reading in line with this late-60s Nietzschean apocalyptic tone. They include the much-cited paragraph from "Structure, Sign and Play" where Derrida writes of the two "interpretations of interpretation," the one turned back nostalgically toward a Rousseauist ethos of origins, truth and presence, the other opening itself up to "the joyous affirmation of the play of the world and of the innocence of becoming, the affirmation of a world of signs without fault, without truth, and without origin which is offered to an active interpretation."[18] One can see—just about—why readers looking sharp for evidence of Derrida's profligate ways should have jumped at these seemingly extravagant pronouncements and felt themselves justified in avoiding any closer acquaintance with his work.

But such passages must always be read in context, like Derrida's equally notorious dictum that "there is nothing outside the text" (more accurately rendered, "no 'outside' to the text").[19] This statement has similarly been bandied about—item 10—as proof that deconstruction is just a species of last-ditch solipsism, a textualist variant of the sceptic's refusal to acknowledge any reality beyond the prison-house of ideas, sense-data, private imaginings, or whatever. But when restored to its original context in his reading of Rousseau the passage turns out to have no such dire or self-disabling implications. Derrida's point—familiar enough at least since Kant—is that we cannot have *direct or unmediated* access to the real, since our knowledge thereof is ineluctably structured by the forms of our sensory, perceptual, cognitive or linguistic grasp. To suppose otherwise is to confuse ontological with epistemological issues, and hence to find oneself driven—like Hume—into all sorts of fargone sceptical doubt. Textuality (or "writing," in Derrida's extended sense of that term) is best construed as a deconstructive metonym for the various culturally mediated structures of thought, knowledge and representation which alone make understanding possible. Thus is it nearer the mark to see Kant, not Hume, as the thinker who anticipates some of Derrida's most characteristic turns of argument. Of course one has to take account of the difference between Kant's transcendental (or strong universalist) claims as regards the *a priori* powers and limits of human understanding, and Derrida's much greater allowance for the various (culture-specific) constraints that play a role in thus establishing the "conditions of possibility" for thought and experience in general. Indeed, as Rodolphe Gasché has argued most convincingly, it is often with Derrida a matter of ascertaining the precise conditions of *im*possibility for anything like a Kantian transcendental deduction from first principles.[20] But these issues are raised—or these aporias located—through an enquiry into the structure, the logic and the grounding suppositions of Kantian thought which respects Kant's critical imperative to take nothing on trust but always to question what is offered in the name of self-evident (received, commonsense, or authoritative) truth. As with Austin, so here: Derrida's reading is more properly and rigorously "Kantian" than those orthodox accounts (or unswervingly "faithful" exegeses) that equate fidelity with a fideist acceptance of the standard interpretative line.

This is not to say of deconstruction (as Paul Ricoeur once remarked about structuralism) that it amounts to nothing more than "Kant minus the transcendental subject," or a replay of nineteenth-century idealist themes in an updated linguistic-textualist idiom.[21] Where such arguments all too easily conclude—as with Rorty—is by sinking the difference between philosophy and literature, viewing all texts (Kant's included) as so many optional "kinds of writing," and thus presenting the pragmatist upshot as an issue out of all our philosophical afflictions.[22] In fact Derrida's relation to Kant is both closer and more complicated than anything allowed for by Rorty's line of easygoing pragmatist adjustment. One has only to read an essay like "Perergon" (in *The Truth in Painting*) to appreciate how Derrida questions the "unthought axiomatics," i.e. the strictly unwarranted assumptions, pre-critical residues, *de jure* stipulations passed off as *de facto* truths, etc., which continue to characterize Kant's argument at certain crucial and problematic junctures in the three *Critiques*.[23] But this is—I repeat—no mere display of wire-drawn "textualist" ingenuity, or perverse demonstration of the pleasures to be had by pursuing out-of-the-way details (or odd turns of metaphor) with a view to undermining the entire edifice of Kantian critical thought. On the contrary, Derrida argues his case with meticulous attention to the logic (as well as the rhetoric) of Kant's text, despite what emerges in the course of his reading as the difficulty of maintaining any such clear-cut distinction. On one point at least his opponents are right: that deconstruction raises issues (or discovers complications) which are simply not there according to the mainstream interpretive view. Certainly one's reading of an essay like "Perergon" does nothing to facilitate—and much to problematize—one's reading of the three *Critiques*. Hence no doubt the quite extraordinary degree of resistance (including the downright refusal to read) which Derrida's texts have typically provoked among scholars of a more orthodox mind.

II

It is well to be clear what the charge amounts to if Derrida is to be counted a mischief-maker—or perverter of reason and truth—on the grounds that his writing presents such a challenge to received ideas of how Kant should properly be read. On this view it is the task of responsible commentary first so far as possible to elicit Kant's intentions, argumentative purposes, large-scale ("architectonic") designs, etc.; second, to relate these back at every point to the detailed exegesis of particular passages in his work; and third—where necessary—to adopt a principle of charity and apply certain techniques of "rational reconstruction" in order that his arguments be seen to comply with current (more refined or adequate) criteria of logic, consistency and truth. Such has been the standard approach of philosophers in the present-day analytic tradition. Undoubtedly it has yielded some impressive results and done much to elucidate matters of structure and detail. Moreover it is a project perfectly in keeping with the Kantian ethico-critical imperative, that which on the one hand enjoins a due respect for authorial intention (since otherwise one is at risk of treating texts, like persons, as a means to one's own interpretive end), but on the other upholds the right of philosophy to question doxastic truth-claims and beliefs in the interest of a better, more enlightened understanding. Thus the prime obligation is to *get things right*, whether right in the sense "warranted by appeal to the text in hand" or right as construed in keeping with alternative (currently prevailing) criteria of reason and truth.

Such commentary can of course take various forms according to the degree of interpretive latitude or—more often—the commentator's sense of what presently counts as a valid, cogent, or philosophically defensible reading. In some cases—as with Strawson's overtly "revisionist" approach—the aim is not so much to reconstruct Kant's intentions with maximum fidelity, nor yet to vindicate every detail of his argument, but rather to present a scaled-down ("descriptive" as opposed to "prescriptive") version of Kantian metaphysics which answers more readily to current ideas about philosophy's legitimate scope and limits.[24] All the same there are certain features that characterize the "analytic" approach despite and across these differences of view. They include a firm commitment to the principle of reason, a stress on the virtues of detailed and clear-headed conceptual exegesis, an acceptance of logical ground-rules (like the law of non-contradiction) whose abandonment would clearly spell the end of this enterprise, and—most importantly—a Kantian ethos that equates philosophical probity and truth with the quest for enlightened consensus on matters of shared disciplinary concern. Another main item, prominent in varying degrees, is the mistrust of writings that trade too much on their stylistic (or "literary") brilliance, and which thus—so it is argued—make a disreputable bid to sidestep the requirements of adequate professional scrutiny or informed peer-group review.[25] For there is simply no engaging in serious, constructive debate with philosophers who raise idiosyncracies of style to a high point of bafflement which they can then take as guard against any kind of reasoned counter-argument. In short there are certain minimal requirements—good faith, clarity, conceptual precision, the avoidance of willful misreadings, obscurantism, logical blunders, category-mistakes etc.—in the absence of which philosophy might as well yield up its every last argument, principle, or truth-claim.

It should be clear from what I have said above that Derrida is far from rejecting this approach in the name of some postmodern-textualist appeal to the infinitized "freeplay" of writing. Thus he acknowledges both the claims of authorial intent (that "indispensable guardrail," as he puts it, which prevents interpretation from running off "in any direction at all") and the critical requirement that reading should proceed in accordance with the best, most exacting criteria of logical accountability. It is simply a mistake—a polemical convenience—to suppose that "deconstruction" and "reconstruction" are flatly antithetical terms. But where Derrida *does* part company with commentators in the analytic school is in refusing to privilege those aspects of the Kantian text that conform most readily—or that offer least resistance—to a reading based on certain foregone assumptions about Kant's mode of argument, his philosophical priorities, conceptual resources, "transcendental" (as opposed to "metaphysical") claims, and so forth. What this amounts to is a *rigorous and principled* insistence that one read with an eye to certain "marginal" details— metaphors, footnotes, analogical devices, parenthetical remarks—which in fact play a more-than-marginal role in Kant's developing structure of argument. That such details scarcely register on other, more orthodox readings of the Kantian corpus—and that Kant may himself have had motives for according them a strictly ancillary status—is all the more reason to keep an open mind as to their possible function and significance. For in each case it is only natural, so to speak, that the devices in question will be marginalized—or treated as merely "parergonal"—in so far as they act (in Rodolphe Gasché's phrase) as "conditions of *im*possibility," that is, as enabling yet problematic grounds for the entire Kantian enterprise.

Small wonder that Kant scholarship has so far evinced a massive indifference to Derrida's reading, as also to other deconstructive essays (such as Paul de Man's "Phenomenality and Materiality in Kant") which likewise raise issues undreamt-of on the orthodox view.[26] But again I should wish to stress that the dividing-line here is *not* drawn up between (on the one hand) faithful, attentive, analytical readers of Kant who respect his argumentative purposes and (on the other) super-subtle deconstructors who despise those old-fashioned virtues. It is not just that Derrida reads with a fine (indeed unequalled) sensitivity to matters of textual detail. For this could still leave him open to the charge of exploiting such nuances for all they are worth, subjecting philosophy to the alien techniques of "literary" (i.e. rhetorical) exegesis, and thus—as Jürgen Habermas puts it— promiscuously levelling the "genre-distinction" between these two realms of discourse.[27] If such objections have a certain *prima facie* plausibility it no doubt results from Derrida's use of terms like "freeplay," "undecidability" and "dissemination," terms which suggest—on a cursory acquaintance— that to deconstruct a text is a matter of lifting all the usual normative criteria (logical, hermeneutic, historical, contextual or whatever), and extracting the maximum semantic yield without regard for those irksome constraints. And there are, to be sure, a good few literary critics—ranged on both sides of the current debate—who share this view of Derrida's work as a geared-up extension of the "old" New Criticism which merely substitutes its own, more adventurous rhetoric for the previous (rather homespun and routine) talk of "ambiguity," "irony," "paradox" and the rest. They are joined, as we have seen, by those ex- or anti-philosophers (Rorty chief among them) who find him a useful ally in the cause of cutting that discipline down to size by treating it as just another language-game, "final vocabulary," "kind of writing," etc.

All of which helps to explain—if not to justify—the latest round of hostilities. In so far as Derrida is to blame for his own reception-history one would have to agree with Habermas and the Cambridge opponents: that deconstruction is nothing more than a handy pretext for literary critics who want to romp freely over the philosophers' hitherto well-guarded textual preserve. These confusions have been worse confounded by the fact that Derrida's writings were first borne in upon the US literary scene by the same mid-70s wave of Francophile cultural fashion that heralded the advent of post-structuralist works like Roland Barthes's *S/Z*. What thus got around, very often in Derrida's name, was the notion—the strictly unintelligible notion—of a writing ("textuality" or *écriture*) that would throw off the bourgeois-realist constraints of truth, reference, origins, authorship etc., and henceforth revel in the prospects opened up by this utopian "freeplay" of the sign.[28] Then of course there was Derrida's well-known talk of "logocentrism" and the Western "metaphysics of presence," phrases which—cited out of context—acquired a kind of malign potency among zealots of the new textual dispensation. And so it came about that deconstruction suffered the kind of *deformation professionel* that has often been the fate of philosophical ideas when taken up by literary critics. If Derrida's writing offered no resistance, no counter-arguments or conceptual resources against this appropriative reading of his work, then philosophers would surely be justified in dismissing deconstruction as just another import from the wilder fringes of literary academe. But they do so resist, and most firmly with regard to the idea of deconstruction as a species of all-out hermeneutic license, a practice much akin to those modes of literary criticism that exploit the techniques of rhetorical close-reading in order to multiply semantic possibilities while showing no concern with language in its logical, propositional, or truth-functional aspect. Such ideas are completely wide of the mark, as Derrida has often had cause to complain.[29] For one thing they ignore his reiterated point that deconstruction has to do with the conceptual grammar (or logical syntax) of certain elements in the text, and not—as the commonplace account would have it—with the sheer multiplicity of meanings attached to this or that isolated key-word. Again I wouldn't deny that his writings can be thus construed—or plausibly nudged in this direction—by literary critics (Geoffrey Hartman among them) or revisionists like Rorty keen to play down their philosophical appurtenance.[30] But there does come a point with such readings—a point clearly signalled in Derrida's texts—where they overstep the limits of interpretive accountability and enter the realm of opportunist special pleading. It is all the more important that those limits be remarked when so many of the current misconceptions about Derrida's work derive from a hasty scanning of the secondary sources—most of them primers in literary theory—and a willingness to credit whatever is put around in the way of academic folk-wisdom.

There is no room here for an adequate address to this issue of truth-claims in deconstruction and the relation between logic, grammar and rhetoric as developed in Derrida's writing. All the same it is worth offering a few brief comments—with reference to the pertinent texts—since it is precisely on this question that opinion divides as to whether his work has any claim to philosophical standing or whether it is just a modish spin-off from the pseudo-discipline of literary theory. Some examples may help to clarify the issue for readers as yet uncommitted either way. Take for instance his discussion of the word *pharmakon* (= "poison" or "cure") in Plato's *Phaedrus*, a term whose ambivalence—or whose undecidability in each of its manifold occurrences—is shown to result from its logico-grammatical underdetermination, rather than from any vague piling-up of semantic (associative) meanings.[31] To call this a "literary" reading of the *Phaedrus* is fair comment if it is taken to signify a meticulous attention to matters of textual detail, a refusal to set aside complicating evidence in the interests of preserving the received (canonical) account, and an awareness of the conflicts that may always arise between, on the one hand, express philosophical truth-claims—in this case, claims about the relation between speech and writing, reason and rhetoric, philosophy and sophistics, spiritual and erotic love, paternal law and its bastard (unauthorized) offspring, etc.— and on the other hand the way that those claims are called into question through a reading alert to the manifold signs of a different, counter-canonical logic at work. But it is *not* fair comment when applied—as more often—in a sense that opposes "philosophy" and "literature" (or "concept" and "metaphor") with the aim of discrediting Derrida's enterprise by association with the sophists and other purveyors of a false rhetorical wisdom. For the fact is—and I make no apologies for putting it like this— that Derrida is a better reader of Plato, a more rigorous and faithful reader, than those who assuredly know in advance what the *Phaedrus* means or how the dialogue is certain to turn out, and who thus reproduce the Platonic order of priorities without the least sense of those complicating factors. If this is a case of "how to do things with texts"—the usual dismissive response—then what Derrida does with the *Phaedrus* is raise it to a level of philosophical interest and complexity unglimpsed by more orthodox commentators.

His reading of Rousseau in *Of Grammatology* is another impressive case in point. What Derrida locates is a curious and multiform "logic of supplementarity," a pattern of repeated chiasmic reversals that compel Rousseau—against his own express intent—to question the priority that standardly elevates speech above writing, nature above culture, presence above absence, the innocence of origins above the bad effects of civilized (decadent) "progress," and so forth. Again he is not simply discounting Rousseau's more explicit professions of intent, arguing (like the "old" New Critics) that intentions are inscrutable and in any case beside the point for exegetical purposes, or—least of all—endorsing that modish post-structuralist line for which the "death of the author" is a *fait accompli* and a cause for celebration among liberated readers. On the contrary: what Rousseau would wish to say (*voudrait dire*) is everywhere allowed due weight and prominence in Derrida's reading. But fidelity to the text doesn't stop at this point, since there is also a logic (more precisely: a chain of logico-grammatical-semantic entailment) that runs athwart Rousseau's overt statements of intent and generates aporias—moments of blindness to its own contradictory premises or implications—which cannot be contained by a straightforward appeal to what Rousseau self-evidently meant. Thus: "Rousseau's discourse lets itself be constrained by a complexity which always has the form of the supplement of or from the origin. . . . His declared intention is not annulled by this but rather *inscribed* within a system which it does not dominate."[32] And again: "[Rousseau] *declares* what he *wishes to say*, that is, that articulation and writing are a post-originary malady of language; he says or *describes* that which he *does not wish to say*: articulation and therefore the space of writing operates at the origin of language."[33]

Such is the "dangerous supplement"—or logic of supplementarity—which comes into play whenever Rousseau attempts to argue, narrate or theorize the relation between a good (natural) and a bad (highly cultivated or civilized) order of existence. It emerges across the whole range of his manifold concerns, from social anthropology to the origins and history of language, from civil institutions to music criticism and a nascent ethno-musicology, from educational theory and practice to the quest for self-knowledge and authentic autobiographical truth pursued with such unprecedented zeal in Rousseau's *Confessions*. In each case, as Derrida convincingly shows, there is a tension—at times a flat contradiction—between the level of overt (thematic) statement and the level at which such statements are subject to a complicating logic which cannot but call Rousseau's assumptions into doubt. What distinguishes this from a "literary reading"—in the usual (primarily interpretative) sense of that term—is its concern to articulate structures of logico-semantic entailment which characterize not only this or that passage, nor even some particular text of Rousseau, nor yet Rousseau's entire literary *oeuvre* treated as embodying distinctive attributes of consciousness, character, theme, or style. To be sure there is a sense—as Derrida acknowledges—in which *Grammatology* might well have been sub-titled "The Age of Rousseau." But this "age" is more an epoch, one that is defined—from Plato to latter-day self-professed Rousseauists like Saussure and Lévi-Strauss—by a set of deep-laid philosophical assumptions (call it "logocentrism" or the Western "metaphysics of presence") which Rousseau both upholds in exemplary fashion and nevertheless, perhaps unwittingly, works to undermine. Such claims would be worthless—portentous variations on a stock Heideggerian theme—were they not backed up, in Derrida's case, by textual close-reading and conceptual exegesis of the highest analytical order.

Then again, there is Derrida's deconstructive reading of Husserlian phenomenology through the effects of *différance* ("differing" and "deferral") as these impinge upon Husserl's attempted synthesis of the transcendental ego as source and guarantor of meaning.[34] Perhaps it is the case—as Derrida argues—that *différance* is not and cannot be a "concept," since any attempt to specify its meaning, logical function, truth-conditions etc. must ignore what his reading has set out to demonstrate, namely the impossibility of assigning it a definite (fixed or punctual) place in Husserl's rigorously argued account of thought, language and time-consciousness. But this doesn't mean—as the literary theorists and philosophical opponents are apt to conclude—that *différance* is therefore some kind of free-floating signifier, open to just about reading that suits the interpreter's fancy. What Derrida says of Husserl applies to his own work also: that the validity of a text, a reading or an argument is measured not so much by its adherence to preconceived (dogmatic) assumptions as by its readiness to acknowledge the problems that arise—the unlooked-for doubts and complications—in the process of detailed exegesis. Nor are these problems "merely" textual in the sense that they exploit certain localized symptoms of semantic instability or "Freeplay" with a view to levelling the difference between philosophy and literature, reducing philosophy to just another "kind of writing," or inverting the traditional (philosophic) order of priorities between logic and rhetoric. To deconstruct such differences and priorities is not simply to ignore, annul or even (in some notional Hegelian sense) to "transcend" them, as I hope will be evident from what I have written so far.

There are indeed some few passages in Derrida's work on Husserl where he might appear to endorse such a reading. Thus at one point in "Force and Signification" he invokes certain literary modernists (from Flaubert to Proust, Eliot and Woolf) as writers who implicitly questioned or problematized the axiomatics of Husserlian thought. These writers possessed what Derrida calls "a sure and certain consciousness, although in principle not a clear and distinct one, since there is not intuition of a thing involved."[35] And there is also—I should mention—the well-known passage in his introductory essay to Husserl's *The Origin of Geometry* where Derrida suggests that commentary confronts an ultimate choice between, on the one hand, a rigorous pursuit of essences, primordial intuitions, eidetic certainties, *a priori* concepts, univocal meanings etc., and on the other a "literary" (Joycean) openness to the greatest range of semantic possibility.[36] One could—rather feebly—account for such flourishes by recalling that this was the period when a good many French intellectuals—Barthes among them—extolled *Finnegans Wake* (by acquaintance or repute) as the "writerly" text *par excellence*, one whose transgression of the limits of bourgeois realism heralded an imminent "revolution of the word."[37] But this is to trivialize Derrida's long and intensive engagement with the question of philosophy and literature, one that started out with his abandoned doctoral thesis (on the "ideality of the literary object"), and which continued through numerous subsequent texts.[38] It was focused most sharply in his writings on Husserl since here, more than anywhere, the issue arose as to how far philosophy—a rigorous philosophy that deployed and refined all the critical resources of logocentric reason from Plato to Kant—could hope to render adequate account of language in its "literary" aspect. But what the term "literature" signifies in this context is not, as might be supposed, a domain of specialized rhetorical figures ("ambiguity," "polysemy," "paradox," "irony," the "writerly" as opposed to the "readerly" text, etc.) where questions of truth, logic and reference simply don't obtrude. Rather it is the name for whatever in language cannot be reduced to the Husserlian ideal of a pure, rigorously theorized yet unmediated *rapport-à-soi*, an "intellectual intuition"—so to speak—whose attainment would thus mark the passage beyond all the vexing antinomies of post-Kantian philosophical thought.

Derrida shows with exemplary precision how Husserl cannot but fail in this attempt; how his language everywhere betrays the effects of a *differance* (a movement of differing-deferral) which prevents it from achieving that punctual correspondence between word and object, concept and intuition, or articulated meaning and professed intent. But there is no question of Derrida's simply dismissing the entire project of transcendental phenomenology as a pointless or misconceived enterprise, one whose failure consigns it—as Rorty would argue—to the history of obsolete ideas. Nor does he suggest (like Rorty again) that if we *must* continue reading the great dead philosophers then we should read them not for any truths to be had— any valid arguments that might yet be sifted from the rubble—but rather for the sake of their story-telling interest, their offbeat metaphors, fictive excursions, stylistic idiosyncracies, etc. Of course there are some texts of Derrida (late texts mostly, *La Carte Postale* chief among them) which appear to lend credence to this view of him as a "literary" adept—brilliant or tedious according to taste—who couldn't care less about getting things right and who wishes only to frolic in the post-philosophical aftermath. So far as Rorty is concerned these are the writings that show Derrida at his best—as a gifted debunker of that boring old tradition—and which save one the trouble (the wasted effort) of engaging with his earlier, more "serious" productions. But this gets the order of priorities exactly back-to-front. The "Envois" section of *La Carte Postale* amounts to just a series of arcane, self-indulgent (and not very funny) jokes if one fails to perceive how it relates at every point to those various deconstructive topoi (speech/writing, presence/absence, Socrates/Plato, philosophy/literature and so forth) whose conceptual genealogy and structural logic are analysed with far greater depth and precision in works like *Margins of Philosophy* and *Of Grammatology*. This is, if you like, the "performative" pay-off—the fictive or literary *mise-en-scène*—of a project whose credentials have already been established (or whose claims to serious attention adequately earned) by the "considerable labour of conceptual exegesis" which makes up the bulk of Derrida's more analytic writings.

I borrow this sentence—slightly modified—from a remark of Paul de Man's *àpropos* the relation between constative and performative speech-act modalities in Nietzsche.[39] For it strikes me as yet more appropriate in Derrida's case, given his (decidedly un-Nietzschean) concern to remain faithful to the calling of philosophy—to its critical, pedagogical, and ethical imperatives—as against those varieties of postmodern scepticism which most often take Nietzsche as their tutelary spirit. And this despite Derrida's equal (but *not*, be it stressed, his opposed or contradictory) desire to question those grounding presuppositions—those "unthought axiomatics"—which have structured the discourse of philosophical critique from Kant to Husserl. "Who is more faithful to reason's call," he asks, "who hears it with a keener ear, . . . the one who offers questions in return and tries to think through the possibility of that summons, or the one who does not want to hear any question about the principle of reason?"[40] It is not hard to guess whom Derrida might have had in mind when framing this rhetorical question. On the one hand it evokes that long history of dogmatic rationalist thinking which flatly refuses to entertain doubts as to its own authoritative status, its possession of ultimate justifying grounds (a priori concepts, axioms of logic, clear and distinct ideas, truths self-evident to reason) the acceptance of which defines what it means to be a serious, good-faith, competent philosopher. On the other—more directly—the passage takes aim at those opponents of deconstruction who denounce its "irrationalist" or "nihilist" character without the least knowledge of Derrida's work.

The above-cited passage occurs in an essay ("The Principle of Reason") whose genre is that of a dialogue—unmarked but everywhere implicit—between a voice that upholds the philosophic values of reason, critique and enlightened debate and another, less assertive, more tonally modulated voice whose role is to question those values in the name of a Heideggerian "fundamental ontology." To this extent the essay is indeed a "literary" text, one that makes use of the dialogue form—along with various pronominal shifts, intertextual allusions, self-reflexive metaphors, passages of *oratio obliqua* and so forth—in order to maintain a certain calculated doubt with regard to the status (the enunciative modality) of its own statements and truth-claims. And there are other recent texts of Derrida—among them his *tour de force* in this mode, the essay "Of an Apocalyptic Tone Lately Adopted in Philosophy"—which likewise go elaborate ways around to forestall any reading that would allocate truth to some single voice in the dialogue.[41] All of which might seem to confirm the view that Derrida is a sophist, a wily rhetorician, or at best a canny "dialectical" thinker who will always shift ground (or simply switch language-games) when confronted with a strong counter-argument. How can one engage in serious, constructive debate with a writer who perpetually exploits such devices with the sole purpose—so it seems—of denying responsibility for his own words and twisting the words of others into all kinds of strange (unintended) relation? On this account "The Principle of Reason" would figure as a mere exercise in "literary" ventriloquism, a text whose occasional obligatory nods in a Kantian (or Leibnizian) direction are just the sort of tactic that Derrida deploys in order to pass himself off as a "philosopher" among readers of an ignorant or credulous disposition. Such is John Searle's exasperated response to Derrida, and such—with few exceptions—the Cambridge faculty line in so far as it achieved articulate form.

But this fails to take account of two main points, one with respect to Derrida's texts and the other concerning the role of "literary" devices (narrative, dialogue, irony, indirect discourse etc.) in thinkers whose work is generally acknowledged as having some claim to serious philosophical attention. The first point is made in "The Principle of Reason" by way of a sentence that evokes both the need for critique in the Kantian (enlightenment) sense and also for a thinking that would hold itself open to questions outside and beyond that established philosophical domain. Such thinking requires, in Derrida's words, "a double gesture, a double postulation: to ensure professional competence and the most serious tradition of the university even while going as far as possible, theoretically and practically, in the most directly underground thinking about the abyss beneath the university."[42] One should not be misled by the obvious Heideggerian allusions—to the "abyss" [*Abgrund*], the gulf that opens up beneath the "principle of reason"—into counting this merely a piece of irrationalist rhetoric, a mystified "jargon of authenticity" (in Adorno's telling phrase) which invalidates Derrida's dutiful talk of keeping faith with the values of enlightened critique. For despite his indebtedness in certain respects Derrida has always maintained a critical distance with regard to Heidegger's thinking, a distance that has become more explicit of late with the controversy surrounding Heidegger's allegiance to the politics of National Socialism.[43] His reserve is clearly marked in this essay by allowing the language of fundamental ontology to be questioned—summoned to account for itself—in the Kantian tribunal of reason. For in the end there is no dispensing with what Derrida calls the "desire for vigilance, for the lucid vigil, for elucidation, for critique and truth."[44]

Now of course it may be said that one displays great naiveté by taking such statements on trust; that after all this passage is cited from his essay "Of an Apocalyptic Tone," where nothing is what it seems since everything is subject to those invisible quote-marks which make it impossible to know for sure whether Derrida means what he says. But this leads on to my second point: that we shall misread Derrida if we take him to be merely playing off rival "positions" through a mode of intertextual ("literary") writing that subjects all truth-claims to a generalized undecidability equated with language in its rhetorical or performative aspect. For philosophy has shown itself to be not without resources when it comes to interpreting other (more or less canonical) thinkers—from Plato to Hume, Kierkegaard, Wittgenstein and Austin—who have likewise utilized the dialogue form or various techniques of indirection by way of communicating truths unamenable to straightforward constative treatment. That Derrida presses yet further in this direction—that he raises issues undreamt of by most thinkers in the mainstream analytic tradition—should at any rate not be taken as evidence that his work scarcely warrants serious attention. For there is a sense in which philosophy has always been engaged in a dialogue with that which exceeds its present powers of adequate conceptualization, its ability to offer reasons or justifying grounds on every question that is taken to fall within its proper remit. The history of philosophy is indeed in large part the history of just such unsettling encounters, from the "Eleatic Stranger" of Plato's *Sophist* to the puzzles and perplexities which regularly surface to trouble the thoughts of a Wittgenstein, an Austin or—as Derrida notes in passing—a thinker like Gilbert Ryle.[45] Only on the narrowest disciplinary conception of what counts as "competent" philosophical work—the professionalized ethos for which Searle is a prominent spokesman—could Derrida's writings be ruled out of court as not measuring up to the required (pre-established) standards.

Even then his critics would be missing the point in a manner inexcusable by their own professional lights. For with Derrida, as with Austin, that challenge takes the form of a constant readiness to question received ideas, among them the constative/performative distinction, the subordinate place of rhetoric (or "literary" style) as a mere adjunct to logic, and the assumption that genuine (rigorous) argument can have nothing to do with such frivolous "textualist" distractions. What they both bring out— Derrida more explicitly—is the extent to which the rigour of anything that calls itself "linguistic philosophy" must be a matter of reflecting on its own performance, noting the occurrence of anomalous or problematic details, and not (like Searle) brushing these aside in the interests of defending a speech-act theory immune to any challenge not licensed by its own self-authorizing precepts and principles. Thus:

> Even from the point of view of classical theory and of its necessary idealization in the construction of con-ceptual models, I objected to the series of exclusions practised by Searle. Inasmuch as it does not integrate the *possibility* of borderline cases, the *essential possibility* of those cases called "marginal," of accidents, anomalies, contaminations, parasitism, inasmuch as it does not account for how, *in* the ideal concept of a structure said to be 'normal', 'standard' etc. (for example, that of the promise), such a divergence is *possible*, it may be said that the formation of a general theory or of an ideal concept remains insufficient, weak, or empirical. In such a case, the idealization practised itself remains defective; it has not taken into account certain essential

predicates. It fails to render an account of that whose ideal concept it is seeking to construct.[46]

Again, this argument takes the Kantian form of an appeal to the *conditions of possibility* for any adequate (formalized) theory of speech-acts that would meet the requirement of covering all cases including—what Searle refuses to concede—those cases that deviate from the normative ideal, and which thus create problems for the standard account. More precisely, it involves a rigorous deduction of the conditions of *im*possibility that must apply to any such project (e.g., a generalized theory of performative utterance) in so far as there will always be problematic cases— "accidents," "anomalies," Austinian "misfires," etc.—which that theory will either take into account (thus perforce undermining its normative claims) or exclude by an act of unwarranted *de jure* stipulation (thus proving inadequate to the task). In the above passage—from his second-round response to Searle—Derrida puts the case in explicitly Kantian (constative or transcendental-deductive) terms, since he is concerned to counter Searle's idea of deconstruction as just a species of sophistical wordplay, a textualist ploy for evading the requirements of genuine (honestly-argued) philosophical debate. The approach is very different in *Limited Inc.* his previous rejoinder, where Derrida notoriously has great fun at Searle's expense by exploiting all manner of performative ("literary") tricks and devices in order to problematize Searle's confidently orthodox assumptions. But even here—despite all the textual high jinks—there is a cogent deconstructive critique of those assumptions conducted through a reading of Austin and Searle (more precisely: of Austin *contra* Searle) that brings out the latter's manifest failure to grasp the implications of Austin's thought.

III

Such is the "logic of supplementarity"—the questioning of preconceived truth-claims, values and priorities—that Derrida discovers everywhere at work in the texts of Western logocentric tradition. But he does so always as the upshot of a reading that respects both the intricate detail of the text (including those details that would appear "deviant" or "marginal" from an orthodox interpretive standpoint), and also the need for argumentative rigour in the strictest philosophical sense of that term. For it is an error—albeit a deeply-rooted error, one that goes back to the inaugural moment of Western philosophy in Plato's quarrel with the poets—to think that these are mutually exclusive activities, opposed along an axis that runs (roughly speaking) between logic and rhetoric, philosophy and literature, or a discourse accountable to reason and truth and a discourse of textual close-reading aware of its own rhetorical complications. This is why Derrida can claim Austin—outrageous though the claim must appear to a thinker like Searle—as a proto-deconstructionist *malgré lui*, one whose systematizing ambitions (or whose desire to come up with a workable *theory* of speech-acts) are subject to a kind of involuntary questioning at so many crucial points in his text. Of course this is not the view taken by most commentators in the Anglo-American "analytic" camp. For them (as for Searle) there is simply no question but that Derrida got Austin wrong, and that he did so either through sheer incompetence or out of a desire—a perverse, wrong-headed, typically "French" desire—to obfuscate the issues and cock a snook at the protocols of reasoned argumentative debate. To which one can only respond that in his reading of Austin—as also in his readings of Plato, Kant, Husserl, Heidegger and (not least) John Searle—Derrida achieves an order of jointly exegetical and philosophic rigour that his critics would do well to emulate.

So why has his work encountered such a degree of resistance, hostility and obdurate incomprehension? Adorno perhaps comes closest to the mark when he remarks how obsessional are the defences mounted by an unreflecting positivism when exposed to the kind of speculative thought that refuses to take language (or "style") for granted, and which demands—like Derrida—a vigilant awareness of the non-identity between word and concept.[47] Not that such awareness has been altogether lacking in the wider analytic tradition. I have already mentioned Wittgenstein and Ryle—together with Austin—as thinkers who maintained a lively awareness of the potential within language for creating problems with any simplified—non-self-reflective—account of meaning, reference, intentions, speech-act implicature and so forth. But in each case, especially with Wittgenstein and Austin, their texts underwent the kind of mainstream-orthodox appropriative reading which obscured those problems from view and produced on the one hand a consensus-based doctrine of "language-games" or cultural "forms of life," and on the other a wholesale systematic "theory" of performative utterance. And so it has come about that the cardinal texts of "ordinary language" philosophy have found their most subtle, intelligent, responsive and (yes) *rigorous* readers among those—not only Derrida but literary theorists like Shoshana Felman—whose powers of observation are not thus constrained by a pre-set philosophical agenda.[48]

This is (I repeat) very far from suggesting that deconstruction has no use for the "traditional" philosophic virtues of reasoned argument, careful exposition, and fidelity to the text in hand. For as Derrida remarks such thinking, "if it troubles all exclusion or simple opposition, should not capitulate to confusion, to vague approximations, to indistinction: it leads instead to an extreme complication, multiplication, explication of 'precise and rigorous distinctions'."[49] That his reading of Austin is dismissed out of hand by adherents to the orthodox (Searlian) view is not so much a genuine conflict of interpretations as a comment on the current boundary-dispute between philosophy and literary theory, or—as this quarrel is often represented—between genuine (analytic) philosophy and the "continental" sort that mostly finds a home in departments of comparative literature. Here it is worth recalling Derrida's observations, in "Limited Inc," on the complex network of debts, resistances and unwitting affinities that has marked the development of these two (supposedly quite distinct) lines of thought from Kant to the present day. Thus he asks at one point (with reference to the issue of intentionality in speech-act theory): "Isn't Searle ultimately more continental and Parisian than I am?"[50] And again, it strikes Derrida that this curious exchange "seems to be occurring—to take geographical bearings—in an area that disrupts all cartography, midway between California and Europe, a bit like the Channel, midway between Oxford and Paris."[51] To which he might have added Germany (or Frankfurt, Freiburg and Heidelberg), since the main point at issue is the complex relation that exists between linguistic philosophy in its Anglo-American (analytical) mode and the tradition of phenomenological thought whose chief exemplars are Husserl and Heidegger.

Gilbert Ryle is perhaps the most interesting figure for anyone attempting to figure out this tangled genealogy of influence. For it is a fact overlooked by most commentators that Ryle's early work included some lengthy and detailed (albeit highly critical) essays on Husserl and Heidegger, published at a time—the later 1930s—when as yet the lines of battle were not so clearly drawn up.[52] Indeed one could date that parting of the ways with some precision, at the point when Ryle concluded (wrongly as regards Husserl) that phenomenology was just a form of naive or uncritical "psychologism" dressed up in false (pseudo-transcendental) colours. All the same there is an interesting parallel to be remarked between Ryle's later work—in books like *Dilemmas* and *The Concept of Mind*—and Derrida's deconstructive reading of Husserl.[53] Both thinkers start out from a principled suspicion of the appeal to self-presence, to primordial intuitions or mentalist predicates as a means of securing indubitable truths. Moreover, both arrive at this position through a critique of certain deep-grained "metaphysical" ideas (for Ryle, the Cartesian mind/body dualism; for

Derrida, the priority of speech over writing, presence over absence, "expressive" as opposed to "indicative" signs, etc.) which are shown to deconstruct—or produce insoluble antinomies—when exposed to a rigorous conceptual exegesis. For Ryle and Derrida alike this involves a negative version of the Kantian argument from "conditions of possibility," i.e. a demonstration that it is *strictly impossible* to maintain such dualist or logocentric principles in so far as their logical grammar gives rise to inconsistent, aporetic or contradictory entailments.

Thus Ryle takes issue with the folk-psychology—the "commonsense" variant of Cartesian dualism—whose philosophic upshot is that notion of the "ghost in the machine" which thinkers since Descartes have vainly striven to exorcise. And he does so by invoking other, less systematically misleading instances and expressions from "ordinary language" which enable him—in Wittgensteinian fashion—to talk philosophy down from its heights of self-imposed metaphysical delusion. Such idioms suggest (for example) that we can manage without dualist or essentialist notions like "mind," "intelligence," disembodied "thought," etc. by replacing them with various adverbial modifiers, phrases on the pattern of "doing this or that thoughtfully, carefully, attentively, skillfully, with adequate concentration" and so forth.[54] Of course there is a difference—which I should not wish to minimize—between Ryle's very "Oxford" manner of appealing to the wisdom of ordinary language, as against the high gyrations of speculative thought, and Derrida's willingness (as commonly perceived) to pursue those gyrations to the giddy limit. But the commonplace perception is also prone to exaggerate this difference in keeping with the standard ("analytic" *versus* "continental") typology. For on the one hand Ryle—like Austin—could just as well be called an "*extraordinary* language" philosopher in so far as he discovers all kinds of problems with our established (commonsense) ways of talking and thinking. Such are the dilemmas or category-mistakes—the "aporias," in Derridean parlance—which may indeed follow with strict necessity from the dualist conception, but whose removal would require quite a mind-wrenching effort of linguistic reform. And on the other hand Derrida is *not* just concerned—as the received wisdom would have it—to deconstruct all our taken-for-granted beliefs about mind, language, expression, self-presence, speech-act commitment and so forth. What he does seek to question (in company with Ryle and also, be it noted, with Husserl) is the philosophers' habit of erecting those *de facto* commonsense-intuitive notions—natural and indeed indispensable in the conduct of our everyday lives—to a high point of *de jure* principle whereby they serve to exclude (to render "perverse" or illegitimate) any dealing with marginal or problematic cases. Such a gesture of exclusion indeed returns philosophy to the stage of a dogmatic (pre-critical) adherence to truths whose very questioning is taken to constitute an affront to reason and commonsense alike.

This is what enables Searle to construct his systematic theory of speech-acts supposedly derived from—and faithful to—Austin's way of treating these issues, but in fact ignoring all the counter-evidence that surfaces in Austin's texts. For it is precisely by considering such "deviant" or "anomalous" instances that philosophy can enable us to see (in Wittgenstein's phrase) how a certain language-game has hitherto "held us captive," whether through some piece of specialized (but obdurate) philosophic jargon or—just as often—some everyday, commonsense habit of talk. These are the cases that chiefly concern Derrida in *Limited Inc.*, that typify the various "dilemmas" examined by Ryle, and which crop up constantly in Austin's writing (not least in his footnotes, mock-casual parentheses, passing anecdotes etc.). To view them as lacking philosophical pertinence—or as offering no hold for rigorous analytic treatment—is an attitude complicit with the worst sorts of ingrained cultural prejudice, those that emerged with depressing regularity in the recent Cambridge "debate." Such counter-instances should at least give pause to anyone who thinks, like Searle, that the business of genuine (serious) philosophy is to beat the bounds between "normal" and "deviant" cases, between "ordinary" and "extraordinary" language, "analytic" and "continental" schools of thought, or again—as with Derrida—conceptual exegesis of the highest order and textual close-reading in the "literary" mode. For there is simply no reason—professional motives aside—to regard this rigid demarcation of realms as anything more than a curious fact of present-day intellectual life.

Derrida makes the point with admirable precision in the course of his "Afterword" to the exchange with Searle. The logic of deconstruction, he writes,

> can be "other" to the point of overturning a good many habits and comforts. It can lead us to complicate—distinctly—the logic of binary oppositions and a certain *use* of the value of distinction attached to it. The latter has indeed certain limits and a history, which I have precisely tried to question. But that leads neither to "illogic" nor to "indistinction" nor to "indeterminacy." This other logic does not authorize, in theoretical discourse *as such*, any kind of approximative statement. It never renounces, as Searle in the haste of a polemic seems to do and to advocate, clear and rigorous distinctions.[55]

This is not to deny that some "literary" readers—for instance, a poet-critic-theorist like Paul Valéry—may approach the source-texts of philosophy with a different kind of analytic rigour, one more keenly attuned to their tonal or stylistic qualities, their formal attributes and (very often) their blind-spots of "logocentric" prejudice. Even so, Derrida writes, "this elaboration would pass through the re-reading of all those texts. . . . It demands that one become engaged in it without endlessly circling around the form of those texts, that one decipher the law of their internal conflicts, of their contradictions, and that one not simply cast an aesthete's glance over philosophical discourse."[56] One could cite many passages to similar effect, each of them cautioning against the idea—the facile or vulgar-deconstructionist idea—that "philosophy" can be somehow played off the field by a "literary" reading that blithely disregards the requirements of logic and truth. This is where deconstruction parts company with New Criticism, post-structuralism and other such movements which elevate the rhetoric of multiple meaning (paradox, irony, intertextuality etc.) to a touchstone of literary value, an aesthetic ontology that finds no place for logic and its merely quotidian constraints. That the point was wholly lost upon Derrida's Cambridge antagonists—both philosophers and literary critics—says a good deal about what counts as "serious," "competent" debate among those whose voices were most loudly raised in defence of precisely such values.

Their petition chalked up more than ninety signatories, among them (according to a *Sunday Times* report) "Sir John Plumb, the eminent historian, Elizabeth Anscombe, the philosopher, and Derek Brewer, the distinguished Chaucer scholar."[57] It included the charge—unsupported (as usual) by any show of evidence or argument—that the main effect of Derrida's work had been "to deny and dissolve those standards of evidence and argument on which all academic disciplines are based." To which one can only respond that the charge comes back like a boomerang, whether upon those (like Miss Anscombe) who should have known better by professional avocation or those others (like Plumb and Brewer) whose competence to judge one may reasonably doubt. For as Derrida remarks in his "Afterword" there is an ethical as well as a "technical" aspect to this matter of simply *getting things right*—putting in the necessary homework—as regards deconstruction and its supposed "irrationalist" or "nihilist" character. What are we to think when so many (doubtless eminent and distinguished) authorities go on record with opinions that demonstrate only their ignorance of Derrida's work? More specifically:

> Why has the press (most often inspired by professors, when they themselves did not write directly) multiplied denials, lies, defamations, insinuations against deconstruction, without taking the time to read and inform itself, without ever

taking the trouble to find out for itself what "deconstructive" texts actually say, but instead caricaturing them in a stupid and dishonest manner? Why do such methods often so strikingly resemble what they claim to denounce but also begin to imitate (summary show-trials, falsification, incapacity to recognize what is said, done, written by those under attack and with whom accounts are to be settled, etc.)? Why so much fear, hate, and denial of deconstruction? Why so much resentment.[58]

Of course this was written before the latest Cambridge storm-in-a-teacup, an episode that Derrida has wisely let pass—so far as one can tell—with just a few good-humoured comments. But his questions still have a pointed relevance, all the more so when the same old charges get recycled in letters to the British press, very often over the signature of longtime opponents (among them the Halleck Professor of Philosophy at Yale) who appear to have devoted quite extraordinary amounts of time and energy during the past twenty years to this same single-minded (not to say obsessional) campaign.[59] If their characterization of Derrida's work bore the least semblance of truth—if he were *really* saying that rhetoric goes "all the way down," that philosophy is just a "kind of writing," that "all interpretation is misinterpretation," etc.—then one could understand their reasons for opposing deconstruction with the maximum vigour and the best, most decisive counter-arguments. But the vigour counts for nothing when the arguments are conducted at that level of baseless innuendo, of common-room intrigue and malicious hand-me-down gossip which has so far served as a substitute for reasoned debate. (The evidence is there in Derrida's "Afterword" for anyone who wishes to check out the depressing details.)

If one effect of Derrida's deconstructive readings—as likewise of Paul de Man's late essays—is to complicate the logic/rhetoric distinction, this is not for want of rigorous argument on their part, or out of some bother-headed "literary" desire to have done with reason, logic, and truth. "To empty rhetoric of its epistemological impact," de Man writes, "is possible only because its tropological, figural functions are being bypassed. It is as if rhetoric could be isolated from the generality that grammar and logic have in common and considered as a mere correlative of an illocutionary power."[60] Which is also to say that those commentators err who suppose deconstruction to be just a "rhetorical" bag of tricks on account of its extreme—and to their minds perverse—attentiveness to matters of textual detail. Thus deconstruction's "final insight may well concern rhetoric itself, the discovery that what is called 'rhetoric' is precisely the gap that becomes apparent in the pedagogical and philosophical history of the term. Considered as persuasion, rhetoric is performative but when considered as a system of tropes, it deconstructs its own performance."[61] Such statements would carry little weight—would indeed amount to so much empty rhetoric—were they not backed up by that level of sustained conceptual exegesis that one finds most impressively (if disconcertingly) displayed in de Man's essays on Pascal, Locke, and Kant.[62] And the debate is likely to become yet more heated as deconstruction approaches the source-texts of modern analytic philosophy, pointing out some of the unresolved problems—"aporias" in the strictest sense of that term—which accompanied Frege's strenuous attempt to demarcate the realm of logical truth from those of rhetoric, metaphor, ambiguity, and other such ills to which natural language was all too frequently prone. [63]

To be sure it is the case—as neither Derrida nor de Man would for a moment deny—that such claims are open to argued and cogent refutation; that they involve determinate values of truth and falsehood (as well as protocols of right reading) which set deconstruction firmly apart from its pseudo-deconstructive offshoots in literary criticism. But in order to demonstrate the falsity (or inaccuracy) of Derrida's or de Man's readings, one would need at least to match—and at certain points to surpass—the standards of interpretive rigour and probity established in their own best work. In some few cases the adversary discourse has achieved something like this level of sustained interrogative critique. Elsewhere—as in Gasché's exemplary essay on de Man—it has started out from a position of principled resistance, and then come around, as the argument proceeded, to a standpoint of grudging but compelled respect for the force and validity of his claims.[64] (Thus de Man: "[w]hat makes a reading more or less true is the necessity of its occurrence, regardless of the reader's or of the author's wishes. . . It depends, in other words, on the rigour of the reading as an argument . . . Reading is an argument . . . because it has to go against the grain of what one would want to happen in the name of what has to happen."[65]) But for the most part this whole "debate" has been characterized by the mixture of ignorance, prejudice and downright *failure to read* which stood plain to view in the Cambridge petition. No doubt it will provide fascinating material for some future cultural historian or latter-day Flaubert with a relish for such catalogues of pompous fatuity and clichéd common-room wisdom. Meanwhile Derrida's writings are there—well served in English translation—for those puzzled by the Cambridge charade and willing to read for themselves.

NOTES

1. Sufficient to recount that Derrida was nominated for an Honorary Doctorate at Cambridge; the proposal challenged by (among others) two members of the University who arose to declare *non placet* at the preliminary hearing; and the award eventually confirmed—after much agitated canvassing on both sides—by a sizable (nearly two-thirds) majority when the matter was put to the vote in May 1992.

2. See for instance the extraordinary episode that Derrida narrates in his footnote to *Limited Inc* (2nd ed., Evanston: Northwestern University Press, 1988), pp. 1588-9.

3. Jacques Derrida, *Edmund Husserl's 'Origin of Geometry': An Introduction*, trans. John P. Leavey (Pittsburgh: Duquesne University Press, 1978); *Speech and Phenomena and Other Essays on Husserl's Theory of Signs*, trans. David B. Allison (Evanston: Northwestern University Press, 1973); "Plato's Pharmacy," in *Dissemination*, trans. Barbara Johnson (London: Athlone Press, 1982), pp. 61-171; *Of Grammatology*, trans. Gayatri C. Spivak (Baltimore: Johns Hopkins University Press, 1975).

4. Jacques Derrida, *Of Grammatology*, p, 158.

5. Jacques Derrida, *Of Grammatology*, p. 158.

6. Richard Rorty, "Philosophy as a Kind of Writing," in *Consequences of Pragmatism* (Minneapolis: University of Minnesota Press, 1982), pp. 89-109.

7. See Stanley Fish, *Is There a Text in This Class? The Authority of Interpretive Communities* (Cambridge, MA: Harvard University Press, 1980).

8. Jacques Derrida, *Writing and Difference*, trans. Alan Bass (London: Routledge, 1978) and "Parergon," in *The Truth in Painting*, trans. Geoff Bennington and Ian McLeod (Chicago: University of Chicago Press, 1987), pp. 15-147.

9. See especially Derrida, *Margins of Philosophy*, trans. Alan Bass (Chicago: University of Chicago Press, 1982).

10. Jacques Derrida, *Margins of Philosophy*, pp. 207-71.

11. Jacques Derrida, *Limited Inc*, pp. 29-107.

12. Jacques Derrida, "Plato's Pharmacy" and "The Double Session," in *Dissemination*, pp. 173-286; "The Law of Genre," trans. Avital Ronell, *Critical Inquiry*, vol. VII, No. 1 (1980), pp. 55-81; "Coming Into One's Own," in Geoffrey Hartman ed., *Psychoanalysis and the Question of the Text* (Baltimore: Johns Hopkins University Press, 1978), pp. 114-48 and "To Speculate: on 'Freud,'" in *The Post Card: from Socrates to Freud and beyond*, trans. Alan Bass (Chicago: University of Chicago Press, 1987), pp. 292-409.

13. See for instance Jürgen Habermas, *The Philosophical Discourse of Modernity*, trans. Frederick Lawrence (Cambridge: Polity Press, 1987) and John R. Searle, "Reiterating the Differences: A Reply to Derrida," in *Glyph*, vol. I (1977), pp. 198-208; also John M. Ellis, *Against Deconstruction* (Princeton: Princeton University Press, 1989).

14. See Derrida, "Signature Event Context," *Glyph*, vol. I (1977), pp. 172-97 and *Limited Inc.*

15. Christopher Norris, *Jacques Derrida* (London: Fontana, 1987).

16. J. L. Austin, *How to Do Things with Words* (London: Oxford University Press, 1963).

17. Geoffrey Galt Harpham, *The Ascetic Imperative in Culture and Criticism* (Chicago: University of Chicago Press, 1987); Simon Critchley, *The Ethics of Deconstruction: Derrida and Levinas* (Oxford: Basic Blackwell, 1992); J. Hillis Miller, *The Ethics of Reading* (New York: Columbia University Press, 1987).

18. Jacques Derrida, "Structure, Sign and Play in the Discourse of the Human Sciences," *Writing and Difference*, pp. 178-93; p. 292.

19. Jacques Derrida, *Of Grammatology*, p. 55.

20. Rodolphe Gasché, *The Tain of the Mirror: Derrida and the Philosophy of Reflection* (Cambridge, MA: Harvard University Press, 1986).

21. See Paul Ricoeur, *The Conflict of Interpretations: Essays in Hermeneutics*, ed. D. Ihde (Evanston: Northwestern University Press, 1974).

22. See especially Richard Rorty, "Nineteenth-Century Idealism and Twentieth-Century Textualism," in *Consequences of Pragmatism*, pp. 138-59.

23. Jacques Derrida, "Parergon," in *The Truth in Painting*, pp. 15-147.

24. P.F. Strawson, *The Bounds of Sense* (London: Methuen, 1958) and *Individuals* (London: Methuen, 1963).

25. For an interesting variant on this cross-channel exchange of stereotypes, see Jacques Bouveress, "Why I Am So Very UnFrench," in Alan Montefiore ed., *Philosophy in France Today* (Cambridge: Cambridge University Press, 19983), pp. 9-33.

26. Paul de Man, "Phenomenality and Materiality in Kant," in Gary Shapiro and Alan Sica eds., *Hermeneutics: Questions and Prospects* (Amherst: University of Massachusetts Press, 1984), pp. 121-44. See also Derrida, "Economimesis," trans. Richard Klein, *Diacritics*, vol. XI, No. 1981), pp., 3-25 and *Mochlos, ou le conflit des facultés, Philosophie*, No. 2 (1984), pp. 21-53.

27. Jürgen Habermas, *The Philosophical Discourse of Modernity*.

28. Roland Barthes, *S/Z*, trans. Richard Miller (London: Jonathan Cape, 1975).

29. See for instance Derrida's "Afterword" to *Limited Inc*, pp. 111-54.

30. See Richard Rorty, "Philosophy as a Kind of Writing" and Geoffrey Hartman, *Saving the Text: Literature/Derrida/Philosophy* (Baltimore: Johns Hopkins University Press, 1981).

31. Jacques Derrida, "Plato's Pharmacy."

32. Jacques Derrida, *Of Grammatology*, p. 243.

33. Jacques Derrida, *Of Grammatology*, p. 229.

34. See Derrida, *Speech and Phenomena*.

35. Jacques Derrida, *Of Grammatology*, Derrida, "Force and Signification," in *Writing and Difference*, p. 46.

36. Jacques Derrida, *Of Grammatology*; Derrida, *Edmund Husserl's "Origin of Geometry"*: An Introduction, p. 46.

37. See for instance Roland Barthes, *S/Z* and Colin MacCabe, *James Joyce and the Revolution of the Word* (London: Macmillan, 1978).

38. See Derrida, "The Time of a Thesis," Alan Montefiore ed., *Philosophy in France Today* (op., cit.), pp. 34-50.

39. Paul de Man, *Allegories of Reading: Figural Language in Rousseau, Nietzsche, Rilke, and Proust* (New Haven: Yale University Press, 1979).

40. Jacques Derrida, *Of Grammatology*; Derrida, "The Principle of Reason: the University in the Eyes of its Pupils', *Diacritics*, vol. XIX (1983), pp. 3-20; p. 9.

41. Jacques Derrida, *Of Grammatology*; Derrida, "Of An Apocalyptic Tone Recently Adopted in Philosophy," trans. John P. Leavey, *The Oxford Literary Review*, vol. VI (1984), pp. 3-37.

42. Jacques Derrida, *Of Grammatology*; Derrida, "The Principle of Reason," p. 17.

43. See especially Derrida, *Of Spirit: Heidegger and the question*, trans. Geoff Bennington and Rachel Bowlby (Chicago: University of Chicago Press, 1989).

44. Jacques Derrida, "The Principle of Reason," p. 16.

45. See Derrida, *The Post Card*, p. 16.

46. Jacques Derrida, *Limited Inc*, pp. 118-9.

47. See for instance Theodor W. Adorno, *Against Epistemology: A Meta-critique*, trans. Willis Domingo (Oxford: Basil Blackwell, 1982) and *Negative Dialectics*, trans. E. B. Ashton (London: Routledge & Kegan Paul, 1973).

48. See Shoshana Felman, *The Literary Speech-Act: Don Juan with J. L. Austin, or Seduction in Two Languages*, trans. Catherine Porter (Ithaca, N.Y.: Cornell University Press, 1983) and Henry Slaten, *Wittgenstein and Derrida* (Lincoln, Nebr. & London: University of Nebraska Press, 1984).

49. Jacques Derrida, *Limited Inc*, p. 128.

50. Jacques Derrida, *Limited Inc*, p. 38.

51. Jacques Derrida, *Limited Inc*, p. 388.

52. See Gilbert Ryle, "Heidegger's *Sein und Zeit*" and "Review of Martin Farber's *The Foundations of Phenomenology*" in Ryle, *Collected Papers*, vol. I (London: Hutchinson, 1971), pp. 1997-214 and 215-24.

53. Gilbert Ryle, *The Concept of Mind* (London: Hutchinson, 1949) and *Dilemmas* (Cambridge: Cambridge University Press, 1953).

54. See also Ryle, *On Thinking* (Oxford: Basil Blackwell, 1979).

55. Jacques Derrida, *Limited Inc*, p. 127.

56. "Qual Quelle: Valery's sources," in *Margins of Philosophy*, pp. 273-306, p. 305.

57. "Cambridge Dons Declare War over Philosopher's Honorary Degree," *The Sunday Times*. 10 May 1992, p. 5.

58. Jacques Derrida, *Limited Inc*, p. 153.

59. See for instance the letter from Professor Ruth Barcan Marcus, addressed to the French Ministry of Research and Technology, and cited by Derrida—justifiably I think—as an example of the virulent campaign waged by opponents who manifestly lack any adequate knowledge of his work. The relevant passage appears in *Limited Inc*, pp. 158-9.

60. Paul de Man, *The Resistance to Theory* (Minneapolis: University of Minnesota Press, 1986), pp. 18-19.

61. Paul de Man, *Allegories of Reading*, p. 131.

62. Paul de Man, "Pascal's Allegory of Persuasion," in Stephen J. Greenblatt (ed.), *Allegory and Representation* (Baltimore: Johns Hopkins University Press, 1981); "The Epistemology of Metaphor," *Critical Inquiry*, vol. V, No. 1 (Autumn 1978), pp. 13-30; "Phenomenality and Materiality in Kant."

63. See for instance Ora Avni, *The Resistance to Reference: Linguistics, Philosophy, and the Literary Text* (Baltimore: Johns Hopkins University Press, 1990); Andrea Nye, *Words of Power: A Feminist Reading of the History of Logic* (London: Routledge, 1990); also Nye, "Frege's Metaphors," *Hypatia*, vol. VII, No. 2 (Spring 1992), pp. 18-39.

64. Rodolphe Gasché "Indifference to Philosophy," in Lindsay Waters (ed.), *Reading de Man Reading* (Minneapolis: University of Minnesota Press, 1989).

65. Paul de Man, Foreword to Carol Jacobs, *The Dissimulating Harmony* (Baltimore: Johns Hopkins University Press, 1978), pp. vii-xiii; p. xii.

Genre and Gender

Choices and Questions in Theology

MARY GERHART

There is a fairly well known story of a father and son, who while driving to a baseball game, were hit by a train at a railroad crossing. The father died but the son seriously injured was still alive and taken to a hospital in an ambulance. He was immediately wheeled into the emergency operating room, and the surgeon came in expecting a routine case. However, on seeing the boy, the surgeon blanched and muttered, "I can't operate on this boy. He's my son" (Hofstadter 136).

When I have told this story in classes and asked, "How could this be?" the answers over the years have been more varied than I expected: the father wasn't really the boy's father, the child was illegitimate, or the father was a priest. Most students enjoyed the story—whether or not they got the answer: namely, that the surgeon was the boy's mother. Once, however, two students who couldn't think of a plausible answer became annoyed and suspected the remainder of the class of tricking them. I noticed that the two students had not experienced, that is, had not read the story in the same genre as those who were intrigued by the story and the results of the telling. For the latter students, the story had been read as a cruel riddle or polemic.

I tell the story here to recall the intriguing and subtle relationships, between genre and gender, particularly on differing perceptions and receptions of those relationships. Since I will be applying my analysis of genre and gender explicitly to theology, I want to be clear that my goal is to enhance and to supplement theology as it is conventionally expressed and not to replace it with some other genre. With this statement of intention, I want also to pay tribute to Robert Detweiler for his wit and ingenuity in furthering what for this occasion may be called theology-with-a-difference—both singly and collaboratively, generously and perspicaciously.

By his writing and his person, he has made the field of religion and literature a richer and better place of abode.

Let me state my thesis straightforwardly: in order to be credible in our time, theology is in need of critical reflection on its understanding of genre and gender. By genre, I refer initially to that aspect of interpretation that treats of the framing of discourse, together with probable effects that specific frames have on specified readers. In this context, I am treating gender as a sub-set of genre in terms of three questions which can be raised across genres:[1] (1) what conventions are used to represent genders and how do these conventions both conceal and attend to certain segments of a population; (2) what values are attached to gender representations and what are the ways in which those values are both reinforced and called into question; (3) what contradictions persist with respect to gender values, and what generic strategies enable readers to avoid, appropriate and/or resolve those contradictions. By treating gender as a sub-set of genre, both regularities (patterns) and irregularities (breaking of patterns) in the relationships of genre and gender begin to appear. At the same time, the relationship between genre and gender becomes progressively complex as we move from considerations of fairness, to suggestions of how stereotypical values can be "transvaluated," to confrontation of the ways in which we ourselves embody the relationships we discover. In the background of this essay, then, is a moving viewpoint calling for awareness and discernment.

In the foreground, we will review the remarkable consensus among major theologians regarding the problem of the genre of modern theology. We will then recall the plurality of genres, especially with respect to some well known texts understood within the Christian tradition as theological and notice our surprise at the plurality of genders. Finally, we will consider one proposal for genre testing (with its gender implications) as one constructive means for more effective theological reflection.

The Problem: Modern Theology As A Genre

A remarkable consensus among some major theologians has recently emerged in Christian theology—namely, a consensus that the domination of theological discourse by the logical proposition and argument is not adequate to the contemporary work of understanding religious texts and experience. Hans Urs von Balthasar, for example, writes in the second volume of *Theo-Drama*, "Disciples and opponents alike . . . . have one thing in common. They all see theology stuck fast on the sandbank of rationalist abstraction and want to get it moving again" (25). Karl Barth, whose work is best known in its propositional form, himself turned to pre-modern realistic narrative, especially toward the end of *Church Dogmatics*. He did so for the purpose, as Robert Krieg noted as early as the mid-70s, of catalyzing the reader's "appropriation of the subject matter" (231). Bernard Lonergan moved from a highly rational argument for understanding God in chapter 19 of *Insight: A Study of Human Understanding* (1957) to a more meditative treatment of God, in his *Method in Theology* (1972), as the object of the dynamic state of being in love in an unrestricted manner. Karl Rahner presents a complex example of resistance to the domination of argument. Anyone familiar with Rahner's work has noticed his frequent asides in which he abjures the possibility of doing all the tasks he specifies as necessary in order properly to making an argument. Immediately following such asides, and often without further explanation, Rahner proceeds to make the argument anyway, in effect overruling his own objections.

One of the most elegant and, I think, persuasive arguments on this issue was one presented by David Tracy in his plenary address at the American Academy of Religion in November 1993. In his paper entitled "The End of Theism and the Naming of God," Tracy addressed the question of theological form in relation to thinking and naming God. He argued that "before further *arguments* on God occur, we need to rethink the relationship of all thinking God to naming God." That is, Tracy thought, "Any adequate naming and thinking God, . . . demands . . . attention to the . . . elusive and intricate relationship of form and content. Only attention to the myriad forms [here we could say, genres] of both naming and thinking God can suffice." Whatever belief has to gain from logical argument and proposition, belief understood *exclusively* in logical terms impoverishes our sensibility and mind by failing to take cognizance of the fullness of concrete reality.

Now many of the theologians above who have criticized the exclusive use of argument also have constructive proposals for addressing the problem as defined. Here, however, I want to pursue my own proposal which I have come to call genre and gender testing. I begin by recalling three contemporary ways by which we understand texts to "belong" to their genres.

In the first, the traditionalist view, genre theory is built on the tension between singularity and commonality, between individual and species. The traditionalists' major concern is to safeguard the uniqueness of the individual text, and in so doing to deny that the best texts are ever "just like" some other texts.

Ideological genre theory, a second approach, is built on the tension between texts and social contexts. "Ideological" here has the "relatively positive assessment" Paul Ricoeur gave the term with his differentiation among stages and functions of ideology.[2] In Ricoeur's sense, ideology in its primary stage is best located in the matrix of social identity and social action, which always remain at least partially unreflective. In this sense, everyone—including critics of ideology—is ideological. Although the best ideological critics typically select genres on the basis of their power to explain social privilege or oppression, they also object to the substitution of nonliterary explanations for the texts themselves.

Deconstructionist critics shift the focus of critique from social structures to the inter-textual/interdependent *language* of ideas, structures, and knowledge. In the deconstructionist view, texts and genres simultaneously betray one another, together with their users' stated intentions. In other words, deconstructionist critics illuminate the ways in which genres use authors and readers as well as the ways in which authors and readers use genres. My assumption is that most readers are not confined to one or another approach to genre but probably engage in all three approaches at different times.

All three approaches to genre afford ways of apprehending what is problematic with the domination of theology by argument and proposition. In his *At the Origins of Modern Atheism*, for example, Michael Buckley has shown the interdependence of atheism and theism. He attributes the rise of atheism at least in part to the separation of theism from experience. He shows the effects, moreover, of the turn theologians made during the Enlightenment to "nature"—away from human experience—expecting that nature could provide a more uncontroversial evidence or more universal basis for theistic argument. Inadequate rationalizations give rise to their denials, according to Buckley: theism gives rise to atheism because the *necessity* of the affirmation or denial of God appears only in a working context. To abstract the affirmation or denial from that context is to generate results not anticipated.

The -isms which for three hundred years have been endlessly debated—pantheism, deism, theism, atheism, agnosticism, panentheism—have led us to expect that such debates are what theology is all about. Even if we might expect to reach some minimal agreement that panentheism as the best "ism" wins—by virtue of such criteria as cognitive coherence, logical sense, and appropriateness to human experience (understood philosophically)—the debates seriously obscure an important fact: namely, that neither contemporary liturgy nor everyday conversation about God has been much affected by that victory.[3]

Where are today's attempts at a Summa, or even a Rahnerian foundations or Tillichian systematic—theologies which attempt grand synthesis of all we claim to know theologically, together with philosophical reflection on how we know what we claim to know? We don't attempt these arguments, perhaps because these forms have not had the sensitivity many like the later Barth (despite himself) and Von Balthasar are now beginning to have. Again, these latter theologians are not replacing argument but rethinking it, doing multiple readings of what a systematics or a systematic attempt would be.

Genres and Genders in Theology

A first step in systematics, therefore, might well be the recognition of a plurality of genres in Western theology. Consider the differences among the following texts. Anselm's *Proslogion*, for example, as a genre includes prayer, argument, and reflection. Anselm never named it the ontological *argument*. David Hume's *Dialogues Concerning Natural Religion* might be characterized as three characters in search of a fourth to say what is really the case. Karl Barth's *Romerbrief* is a commentary on Paul's Epistle, but as literary critics show, it is more like German expressivist work of its period than a typical commentary.[4] Rosemary Ruether's *Sexism and God-Talk: Toward a Feminist Theology*, the first feminist systematic theology, begins with a contemporary creation midrash and ends with the post-apocalyptic coming of the goddess. Søren Kierkegaard's pseudonymous disputations can be read as parodying both argument and arguer. Blaise Pascal's *Pensées* can be described as disorderly fragments in which certainty and uncertainty reciprocally undermine each other.[5]

Even if they would not agree with the foregoing descriptions, most readers could agree that there are diverse kinds of texts here. When we think of ourselves as doing theology, however, we are tempted to *treat* these texts primarily or even exclusively as argument, as an argument statable in terms of major and minor propositions. But is it sufficient to address only the argument of a text in order to arrive at a theological understanding? It was long assumed in theological practice, if not in theory that the answer to this question is yes. But we now can address questions that have been raised about this assumption. There are serious problems with decontextualizing and denaturalizing discourse in order to arrive at a set of abstract propositions. As Buckley said, "Propositions ripped from their context can never be more than an accumulation of opinions" (19).

What is seen when propositions are restored to their context? Within theology across the ages we find a number of genres: dialogues, apologias, catechisms, oaths, dictionaries, doctrines, liturgies, histories, summas, visions, narratives, poetry, parables, midrash, letters, genealogies, myths, hymns, prayers, eulogies, invocations. One might expect that these multiple genres function differently both intra- and inter-generically. How, for example, have interpreters moved from Paul's Epistle to the Romans in the genre "letter," to Karl Barth's *Romerbrief* in the genre "treatise"? The genre "letter" at one time suggested a communication of understanding accessible to both writer and reader. At the same time, the genre discloses the ambiguities, dichotomies, and obstacles incurred in addressing a dialogue partner who is both absent and present. The genre "letter" as theological displays an understanding from the perspective of an explicit subject horizon (indicated by the questions the author asks) and an explicit object horizon (the cognitive possibilities and constraints of what questions can be asked in a particular historical time and place).[6] By means of genre and gender analysis of letter, interpreters are empowered in a way not possible before and the crucial role of interpretation becomes visible.

Genre and Gender Testing in Theology

What difference would genre and gender analysis make for theology?

I have found Julia Kristeva's notion of a subject-in-process-on-trial[7] helpful in thinking about the larger project of constructive theology. If we think of "subject" in both of its traditional senses—as the subject of a text or conversation and as a human subject, we might expect to find a locus for moving theologically by engaging in what I have come to call genre and gender testing. Here I propose that genre and gender testing can first of all function as a corrective to the criticisms of modern theology noticed above, by heuristically bringing about an explicit affirmation of pluralism. Second, genre and gender testing can assist in the constructive task of theology by providing strategies for including other voices in theological discourse—the prophets, the mystics, the oppressed, the hysterics, the alienated, the dissenters, the artists—voices as both other and related.

Like the artists in the 18th century who taught us to see landscapes *as* landscapes, just to become aware of genres and genders is to enrich our vision and understanding. In the index to my book *Genre Choices, Gender Questions* , there are approximately 160 entries under the heading "kinds of genre" from adventure story and apocalypse to wasf (an Arabic genre found in "The Song of Songs") and wisdom literature. Under the heading "gender distinctions," there are 12 entries, including berdache (male gender-reversed sacred persons who act as shamans in several cultures, persons who are rarely discussed outside religious studies). These lists are intended as representative, rather than exhaustive, of both genre or gender.

Our attention to these two lists is interesting for different reasons. With respect to genre, we are not surprised at that there are so many. Moreover, we readily accept the fact that the genres we recognize are more numerous than the ones we reconstruct in our speaking, writing, or life-construction. Some recent research, for example, shows that Americans distinguish over thirty different genres of film, though few Americans are engaged in film production.

With respect to gender, our everyday expectations are challenged by the plurality of genders. We tend to assume the adequacy of thinking only in terms of two genders. One of the benefits of this dualism, of course, is to make evident the extent to which values—including economic values—have been assigned on the basis of gender differences. Thanks to semioticians like Julia Kristeva, we are also aware of the gendered function of language and signs and the fact that each individual orients or places her/himself within that, sometimes clear, often ambiguous network of language and artifacts. But our increasing awareness of gender differences far surpasses the naive expectation that of genders there are just two and that these two encompass what is worthwhile knowing about the issue.

However necessary the recognition of a plurality of genres and genders, the task of constructive theology does not leave that recognition a merely formal appreciation. How might genre and gender testing assist us in doing constructive theology?

Instead of the either/or expectations endemic to the genre of logical argument, genre and gender testing can assist in affirming a plurality of forms. To appropriate these resources for constructive theology, we can encourage the use of a multiplicity of genres to construct multiple readings of a text and to make explicit the gender implications in each reading. Such a practice would manifest both genre and gender as social constructs—genres as emplotted worlds and genders as embodied selves—presented in multiple cultural forms.

Which Genre, Whose Gender?

Neither the notion of reading a text seriously in terms of more than one genre nor the idea of reading a text in the light of more than one gender expectation has received wide acclamation. With respect to genre, however, Wayne Booth has shown how Jonathan Swift's "A Modest Proposal" requires readers to shift genres at a certain point within the text.[8] More to the point, in the course of arguing that genre makes a crucial difference in the meaning of a text Heather Dubrow cites the opening paragraph of a hypothetical text to show how the paragraph can be read as either that of a Bildungsroman or that of a mystery novel. Booth's and Dubrow's analyses are undisputed as far as I know, probably because the genre shifts to which they call attention require no special effort to understand. But the reader is seldom called upon to read the same text in different genres and is not likely to notice the phenomenon of shifting genres in the course of reading a particular text. Readers are like viewers who, confronted for the first time with visual conundrums—such as that of the duck and the rabbit or the lady and the wizened crone—discover, often only after repeated efforts, that each picture can be perceived equally well in two distinct ways. Most readers tend to adhere to one reading of a text until someone raises their expectations that there are other coherent readings.

Having been alerted to the possibility of reading a text in more than one genre, most readers do not question their ability to do so. But what would it mean to test the text in terms of gender? The very question "Whose gender?" alerts readers to the possibility that horizons of consciousness are affected by gender, race, and class. Gender-testing provides one means of recognizing structured inequities and oppression: readers become better readers as they are capable of imagining responses by persons of other genders, other races, other classes. Invitations to construe texts in terms of more than one gender abound, for example, in transcripts of job interviews in which "No-win" questions persist in being asked of women and minorities—notwithstanding legislation to the contrary. Feminists reproduce police transcripts of interviewing female victims of sexual molestation to show the gender-ladenness of certain kinds of incriminating remarks. Reversing the gender of characters in specific genres, such as biography or *Bildungsroman*, reveals to readers more impressively than general discussion, the immense dependence of gender expectations upon both traditional genres and texts.

Furthermore, the generation of multiple interpretations frequently generates the opportunity to arbitrate among contradictory interpretations. The interpretation of both contemporary and classical texts has the potential to give rise to an experienced need for arbitration. In her study of medieval spirituality, Caroline Walker Bynum, for example, finds above and beyond the misogyny of the period, a complexity regarding gender that challenges any simple or single interpretation. Bynum found that female imagery is referred to differently by male and female ascetics. Males are more apt to use female imagery dichotomously to express a reversal and conversion from their previous lives. By contrast, females say less about gender but speak more of interior motivation and continuity of self. Just how female imagery is being employed in any given text would seem to call for extensive genre and gender testing to elicit all likely interpretations.

The modern practice of interpretation assumed that that interpretation is best which accounts for the greatest number of elements in the text and which does so at the highest level of persuasion.[9] But the very engagement in arbitration would seem to preclude the expectation that there be only one adequate interpretation. Is one dominant interpretation in fact the best goal, as is often unreflectively presumed by the genre argument? Or is it better to expect that the text's silence on certain points gives rise to the practical inevitability of noticing our own assumptions about these silences? It is interesting to recall that there are two different theories about these silences. Wolfgang Iser calls the silences "gaps"—things which are missing from the text. Mieke Bal calls the silences "naturalized points"—things in the text which have avoided commentary in all conventional readings. Examples of Iser's denominated "gaps" can be found in Iris Murdoch's *The Sacred and Profane Love Machine*: in certain passages, the meaning of the text revolves around the indefinite pronoun "it"—which Murdoch leaves undefined. An example of Bal's "naturalized points" occurs in her analysis of the Book of Ruth in *Lethal Love*. Bal calls attention to a passage to which all Biblical critics had seemingly been oblivious—since they had not commented on it, nor had their readings of the text been informed by it. Bal cites Ruth 3:10, "The Lord has blessed you, my daughter. This last proof of your loyalty is greater than the first; you have not sought after any young man, rich or poor," as an unnoticed key to the character to Boaz. By not noticing or taking account of this passage, Biblical critics perpetuated the mutually exclusive beneficence of Boaz and neediness of Ruth—thus perpetuating male and female stereotypes, respectively, which are challenged in the story but reign unchallenged in the biblical commentaries Bal consulted.

With both theories of how "silences" occur in texts, we have another basis for expecting that a text can be oriented in more than one way, depending on how these silences are connected. We also have a basis for claiming that many of these different interpretations will not be idiosyncratic—rather that the appropriation of one or another interpretation can be integrative as well as liberating.

In any case, the awareness of such silences lead us to expect to have to try harder to hear differences among interpretations, given that different persons will notice different silences and will propose differing reconstructions of the text. Genre testing moves the conflict of interpretations from the work of understanding to the site of judgment, where we make claims for what is real based on our best interpretations. Confronted with the same text but within different frames, readers may pay attention to aspects of the text they hadn't noticed in previous readings.

Genre testing may also result in an experience of radical indeterminacy.[10] If the text is understood in terms of different, even contrasting frames, who can determine the best genre in which to interpret the test? For deconstructionists and some postmodernists, the indeterminacy of texts—traditional as well as contemporary—comes with their being written texts. In spoken language, such elements as demonstrative pronouns or genre can be accompanied and clarified by gestures, voice, and the situation at hand.[11] In written texts, however, ambiguity of reference can quickly mount into undecidability on the part of the reader. Ultimately the reader must choose either to remain in this state or to decide among different forms of intelligibility. Like faith, choosing a genre can be expressed either as an affirmation or negation of one form or many forms of intelligibility. Regardless, the reader takes a position in front of the text in order to be affected by it. Unless we are to be the Don Juan of the myths, as Paul Ricoeur wrote (1976)—courting them all in turn but appropriating none of them—the choice of genres ultimately resides in some kind of reader's choice.

Genre-testing forces one to reconstruct the text more than once, thus providing the opportunity to try out more than one understanding. To be able to reidentify the text is also to be able to reidentify different selves. During the process of testing, the self becomes one among several possibilities. In this sense, genre and gender testing makes possible a plurality of identities—of the text and of interpreters. Perhaps genre and gender testing also makes possible a live and growing tradition of readers— a tradition that is diverse and relatively unpolarized.

What has genre and gender testing to do with theology? One of the most telling anecdotes about what constitutes theology is the following:

> All theologians at some point, cry "Ah, mystery." But the difference between a good theologian and one less good is the point at which she cries, "Ah mystery."

It is interesting that no one ever asks, "Precisely what *makes* the difference? No one asks, perhaps because the unspoken in the saying is the presumption that theology consists of argument and propositions. Because of our familiarity with these genres and with traditional arguments, we presume that we will know how much of these two genres are sufficient. But just as we have come to accept that there is no presuppositionless theology, we are today becoming aware that good theology is not only argument and proposition. Theology is also genred in other ways and gendered in ways we have just begun to recognize.

My wager is that reflecting on these newly found differences can make a difference in the way we do theology.

NOTES

1. In *Genre Choices, Gender Questions*, gender has equal status with genre. In this essay, I subordinate gender to genre to maintain a single focus on theology.

2. See Paul Ricoeur, "Science and Ideology" in *Hermeneutics and the Human Sciences* (Fort Worth: Texas Christian UP, 1981), pp. 222-46.

3. See David Tracy, "The End of Theism and the Naming of God," Unpublished paper presented at the plenary session of 1992 American Academy of Religion Annual Meeting, 1992.

4. See Stephen H. Webb, *Re-figuring Theology* (Albany: SUNY Press, 1991), especially pp. 14-18.

5. According to Sara Melzer, there have been more than 150 editions of the *Pensées*, each trying to settle the question of disorder by still another new ordering of the fragments. Sara Melzer, *Discourses of the Fall: A Study of Pascal's Pensées* (Berkeley: U of California P, 1986).

6. See E.P. Sanders for an analysis of Paul's method of argument. E.P. Sanders, "Prooftexts, Theological Deduction and Revelation," unpublished paper presented at the U of Notre Dame, 1993.

7. See Julia Kristeva on the role of the analyst: "Help them, then, to speak and write themselves in unstable, open, undecidable spaces... to trigger a discourse where... emptiness and... out-of-placeness" become essential elements, indispensable "characters" if you will, of a *work in progress*." Julia Kristeva, *Tales of Love*, trans. Leon S. Rondiez (New York: Columbia UP, 1987), p. 380.

8. See Wayne Booth, *The Rhetoric of Irony* (Chicago: U of Chicago P, 1975), pp. 106-09.

9. Both critical and pedagogical practice often presume an agonistic relationship among conflicting interpretations. See Wayne Booth's list of theses used in articles interpreting Henry James' "The Turn of the Screw," and his arguing for one interpretation being best on the basis of the way the author constructed the text, in *Critical Understanding: The Powers and Limits of Pluralism* (Chicago: U of Chicago P, 1979), pp. 284-301. But see also Paul Ricoeur's discussion of the issue (1976) in terms of probability and agreement: "If it is true that there is always more than one way of construing a text, it is not true that all interpretations are equal. ... It is always possible to argue for or against an interpretation, to confront interpretations, to arbitrate between them and to seek agreement, *even if this agreement remains beyond our immediate reach*" (italics mine). Paul

Ricoeur, *Interpretation Theory: Discourse and the Surplus of Meaning* (Fort Worth: Texas Christian UP, 1976), p. 79.

10. See Robert Detweiler, "How to Read a Jaguar: A Response to Mary Gerhart, *Semeia* 43, Fall, 1988, pp. 45-51.

11. See Paul Ricoeur *Interpretation Theory*, pp. 25-44. See also Jacques Derrida, "The Law of Genre," *Glyph* 7, 1980, pp.176-232.

WORKS CITED

Balthasar, Hans Urs Von. *Theo-drama I: Theological Dramatic Theory.* San Francisco: Ignatius Press, 1989.

Booth, Wayne. *The Rhetoric of Irony.* Chicago: The University of Chicago Press, 1975.

Booth, Wayne. *Critical Understanding: The Powers and Limits of Pluralism.* Chicago: University of Chicago Press, 1979.

Buckley, Michael. *At the Origins of Modern Atheism.* New Haven: Yale University Press, 1987.

Bynum, Caroline Walker. "And Woman His Humanity": Female Imagery in the Religious Writing of the Later Middle Ages." In *Gender and Religion: On the Complexity of Symbols.* eds. Caroline Walker Bynum, Stevan Harrell and Paul Richman. Boston: Beacon Press, 1986.

Derrida, Jacques. "The Law of Genre," *Glyph* 7, 1980.

Detweiler, Robert. "How to Read a Jaguar: A Response to Mary Gerhart." *Semeia* 43 (Fall, 1988).

Dubrow, Heather. *Genre.* The Critical Idiom Series. London: Methuen, 1982.

Gerhart, Mary. *Genre Choices, Gender Questions.* Norman: University of Oklahoma Press, 1992.

Hofstadter, Douglas. *Metamagical Themes: Questing for the Essence of Mind and Pattern.* New York: Basic Books, 1985.

Iser, Wolfgang. *The Act of Reading: A Theory of Aesthetic Response.* Baltimore: Johns Hopkins Press, 1978.

Krieg, Robert. *The Theologian as Narrator: A Study of Karl Barth on Divine Perfection.* Notre Dame: Notre Dame Press, 1976.

Kristeva, Julia. *Tales of Love.* trans. by Leon S. Roudiez. New York: Columbia University Press, 1987.

Melzer, Sara E. *Discourses of the Fall: A Study of Pascal's Pensees.* Berkeley: University of California at Berkeley, 1986.

Ricoeur, Paul. *Interpretation Theory: Discourse and the Surplus of Meaning.* Fort Worth: Texas Christian University Press, 1976.

Ricoeur, Paul. "Science and Ideology" in *Hermeneutics and the Human Sciences*, pp. 222-46, 1981.

Ruether, Rosemary. *Sexism and God-Talk: Toward a Feminist Theology*. Boston: Beacon Press, 1983.

Sanders, E.P. "Proof-texts, Theological Deduction and Revelation." Unpublished paper presented at U. of Notre Dame, April 16, 1993.

Tracy, David. "The End of Theism and the Naming of God." Unpublished paper presented at plenary session of 1992 annual meeting of the American Academy of Religion. San Francisco.

Webb, Stephen H. *Re-figuring Theology: The Rhetoric of Karl Barth*. Albany: SUNY, 1991.

Textuality and Community

Giving Beyond Death

GREGORY C. BRUCE

Living/dying is like reading; reading is like dying or being called from the dead.[1] J. Hillis Miller

The basis of communication is not necessarily speech, or even the silence that is its foundation and punctuation, but exposure to death, no longer my own exposure, but someone else's, whose living and closest presence is already the eternal and unbearable absence, an absence that the travail of deepest mourning does not diminish.[2] Maurice Blanchot

One of the major tasks outlined by Robert Detweiler for the "religiously-reading community" is to seek out and interpret narratives dealing with pain and death.[3] Deciding *just how* to interpret such texts would seem to provide a key toward further explicating, and putting into practice, what Detweiler has in mind when he speaks—normatively—of community. The underlying challenge would be to expand *koinonia* beyond the kind of privatization that oftentimes is tradition, to thereby assist in Christianity's survival, by means of its own excess, within a larger "supplementing," postmodern world. That the postmodern condition constitutes a more expansive "world" (a more pervasive and influential textuality) is attested to by the fact that whereas it does not share the suppositions of realism behind Christian myth, the latter (which is to say latter-day-logocentric) world does now share in the revivified myths of postmodernism: *sparagmos*, Dionysus, Pygmalion, the Minotaur and the labyrinth, et al. That both worlds *are* mythic, moreover, is cause for further supplementing at the point where they are brought together. Here, myth is turned against myth, against itself *qua* myth, and deconstruction is shown to be not a "school of thought," but a biological drive, a matter of perpetuity.

If sacred texts are, as Detweiler holds, sacred by virtue of their excess, then it must be so because of an other-worldly extravagance, one always under erasure.[4] Evoking the Heideggerian *Durchkreuzung*, Detweiler ~~proclaims~~, ~~asserts~~, suggests that the crossing-out, the "X-pression," of faith is crucial to the religiously-reading community.[5] This is true for certain writers as well. John Updike, for example, invariably presents kerygma (which is tradition-bound) through the mouthpiece of an unreliable clergy (e.g., Reverend Eccles in *Rabbit Run*). This presentation alone makes Updike, as well as kerygma, in need of postmodern reconsideration, and it is perhaps the main reason why this prolific writer has habitually fascinated Detweiler; the dogged appearance of unreliability where reliability is so expected, as with theological authorities, forces the reader to construct his/her own "fiction" of religious reality instead of "merely" absorb an imitation of it."[6]

Such constructions are prime instances of what is so dearly cherished by Detweiler: "overliving," survival, to live above, to live again. The postmodern textuality of texts, the radical insistence on reading texts as worlds and worlds as texts in myriad and playful ways, "functions as an intensified negative capability: keeping on, living on as if we had a future."[7] The religiously-reading community follows the lead of postmodernism and the creation of unreliability by skipping or passing over traditional hermeneutics, which, in the final analysis, may not show enough respect for mystery.[8] In turn, those manifesting the sacrificial mark of awe before *absolute* mystery are spared a scion so to speak (as in the Passover); by passing over they are passed over, allowed to multiply in their name; they are given the law (*nomos*) and the preserved home (*oikos*) that defy objectivist interpretation or rationale. This GIFT, this positioning which is a bearing of the mark, requires nothing short of an ethical suspension of the teleological, to again reverse things, to reverse Kierkegaard. Anti-hermeneuts willingly enter a cycle of exchange, an economy, that *must be forgotten* in terms of its ends. According to Jacques Derrida, as soon as the gift delimits itself it is "prey to calculation and measure."[9] To forget God's gift (of life and of sparing, of new life and of sharing) is to allow it to be a gift; reciprocity must exceed itself. "The gift, if there is any [we cannot say, if we *have* forgotten], should overrun the border [between giver and recipient]. . . toward the measureless and the excessive; but it should also suspend its relation to the border and even its transgressive relation to the separable line or trait of a border."[10] The gift is, as Derrida maintains, another name of the impossible, but it is also the religiously-reading community's only possibility of living on.[11]

Writing "above" transgression, Derrida is looking for something more than, but not outside of, textuality; and Detweiler, writing "beyond" impossibility, is searching for the foundations of a textuality religiously aware of, and religiously capable of dealing with, all that is revealed by pain, by *Sein zum Tode*. Herein lies a telling religious supplement to Derrida; with prescience as to where deconstruction is moving, the above and beyond, Detweiler goes back—back to the *content* of play, lest it become a mere formal device. In the context of a religiously-reading community, play becomes a bit more serious under the guidance of *Gelassenheit*.[12] Pain, and the death that it foreshadows, exposes the necessity of "nonchalance," "abandonment," *and* "acceptance"; this creates a somewhat controlled ludic perspective, where the community of readers existentially in touch with the borders of suffering can look toward the *Geselligkeit* (sociability, communality) that the collective experience of the "gift" of pain elicits/solicits.[13]

For Detweiler, it is from pain (which, as he notes, is often erroneously conflated with evil[14]) that a community of readers can learn to "confess their need of a shared narrative"; and it is through pain, which biblically culminates in apocalypse, that this community can foster the literary energies of doubling, of aporia, and of paradox, forgetting and remembering life's "liminality and conclusion."[15] Just as *Dasein* anticipates its end, so too does *Mitsein*; this must be reiterated again and again in postmodern culture, and in the culture that traces beyond it.

Refusing the Economy of the Gift

Derrida's *Given Time: Counterfeit Money*, from which I have been drawing my preliminary conclusions about Derrida's beyond, employs the strategy, one favored by Detweiler, of reading a literary text "against" a philosophical line of exploration. Through a close reading—which for him is a reading at the margins—of a short text by Charles Baudelaire ("Counterfeit Money"), Derrida shows that the idea of the economy of the gift, its circularity, is problematized by the possibility of "taking back with one hand what the other hand has given."[16] In Baudelaire's vignette, two friends leave a tobacconist's and are immediately confronted by a beggar, whose eyes show to the "sensitive man" who can read them both humility and reproach, "like the tear-filled eyes of a dog being beaten." One of the two friend's offering to the poor man is much larger than that of the other, the narrator, who is disquieted by the "mute eloquence" of the beggar's eyes and is subsequently *given to* comment philosophically on the unexpectedness of the event: "Next to the pleasure of feeling surprise [that of the beggar], there is no greater than to cause surprise [in the act of his friend]." But, upon learning that his friend's gift was actually a counterfeit coin, the narrator's ruminations, bordered by his own displeasure, become more complex. Perhaps the gift of the counterfeit coin was excusable in the context of the intention to create an unanticipated event in the poor man's life. After all, this event might prove lucrative: the gift might multiply into real coins.

On the other hand, the event might just as easily lead to disaster: the beggar might land in prison for passing the *piéce fausse* himself. "And so," the narrator tells us, "my fancy went its course, lending wings to my friend's mind and drawing all possible deductions from all possible hypotheses." What ends the narrator's own logical flight is the sudden insight into the "stupidity" of his friend's calculations concerning the *dédoublement* of intention behind the gift. "I saw clearly," the narrator continues, "that his aim had been to do a good deed while at the same time making a good deal; to earn forty cents and the heart of God; to win paradise economically." But was the gift of counterfeit money a "clear and distinct" act of ineptitude (as in the maxim, one cannot fool an omniscient God), or was it that a) there was at least an intention to give, and/or b) there was at least an appearance of the gift as such to consciousness, and therefore c) the act was in fact pleasing to God? Under the scrutiny of a religious reading of texts, which would be attuned to any possible excess in "moral messages," we might indeed say that Baudelaire's narrative itself is counterfeit. That is to say that what can be "learned" from the plot with regard to charity (the respective gifts of the two friends), suffering (the beggar without a home), and law (does an intended or apparent good outweigh or at least equal a good as a *fait d'accompli*) is undermined by a surplus both at and exceeding the narrative border.

To put the central event of this story in this context (How was the act measured by God?) is to initiate an examination of it under the rubric of what Detweiler calls "fictions of kerygma," where an unreliable narration of moral precepts of Christianity is at work.[17] The narrator, who might be envisioned "preaching" to his foolish friend at a later date, is himself unreliable; he is not himself, not a friend to his friend, and hence beyond the text. What he perhaps fails to grasp is the fact that his friend has given him time, perhaps intentionally as a confessional provocation, given him *the* time to ponder in excess what it means to give. He offers the narrator the idea of a skepticism of economy, both in a specific sense (What is money anyway?) and in a general sense (What is the stuff of exchange if not time, time right now, *stigma*, time that does not allow the cycle of a "pay back," as in the case of the poor man's surprise unknown in its closure to the two friends).[18] The narrator's compensation to his friend is just as counterfeit as the *piéce fausse*. It is the endless "now" of rejection: "I will never forgive him," he says of his friend's alleged stupidity. The narrator comes to this condemnation by moving through a tendentious series of "nows" presented by an economy of philosophical reflection (the hermeneutical circle) that in actuality interprets his friend's act with a hard and fast forestructure of understanding. So inclined, the narrator misses the point of confession: not to impart knowledge, but to move toward forgiveness.[19] What is at stake, what is under "trial," as Derrida puts it, is much more than a single act. By giving himself to the narrator, by making a show of himself (*se donner en spectacle*), the giver of the counterfeit coin is, in essence, probing the heart of the narrator with regard to the economy of friendship. Any *pain* felt by the narrator's friend, then, is linked to the fictionalizing of kerygma, not in the sense, however, of an unreliable presentation of the Word (for the Word has not been spoken here, only alluded to in a most oblique way), but rather in the sense that it comes from a simulacrum of communion. And as Paul Ricoeur has suggested, kerygma is as perhaps as much a communion as anything else.[20] As the two friends, having left the beggar and the triadic confrontation he sparks, step off together, presumably returning to their tobacco and their "male-bonding," they do so without full trust and love.[21]

But let us not get too carried away here — with Derrida, with Derrida's beyond. First, male smoking partners, like male drinking partners, often do establish "friendships" solely within the economic excessiveness of these, and other, habits of luxury.[22] In this state of superfluousness, where communion may "go up in smoke," emotions might be seen as cutting against the grain of "maleness."[23] Perhaps looking for kerygmatic communion here is asking too much. Or is it? What does Baudelaire's story tell us about the "larger" question of the economy and its bearing on socially sanctioned activities. Second, the story would not count for Detweiler as a classical text of pain, which is to say there is no physical illness here (except perhaps in the case of the beggar) and hence no Heideggerian *Vorahnung* in the strong sense of the term. "Counterfeit Money" would at best constitute a borderline case of the textual premonition of death. On the other hand, this is why it is so interesting in the context of surplus.

Prosopopoeia and Christian Witness

Baudelaire's little text, read rather fancifully here before the imprimatur of Derrida, serves to challenge Detweiler's program and hence to focus it.

To wit, do all texts written within the Western literary tradition bear witness to Christian myth? In so far as (physical) pain is involved, Detweiler seems inclined to answer this question in the affirmative. Consider the following passage:

> The high valuation that our culture assigns to bodily pain . . . is not surprising in light of the stress on it in the Christian tradition. Close to the center of Christian myth and ritual is the passion of Christ, the mutilation, pain and suffering inflicted on his body in our stead, according to our theology of atonement: an inscription that we will read, Christian believers or not, in attitudes of guilt and awe. The pain of the crucifixion retains its power to affect us emotionally and is still at the heart of the Western sense of the sacred.[24]

But, again, Detweiler is here speaking of the "strong sense" of pain, of "illness [which is] above all an interpretation and as such constitutes a text."[25] So it is that the textuality of pain summons, to borrow from Umberto Eco, "the nebula of all possible archetypes: the puzzling identification among the sender (the divine Logos), the signifying message (words, Logoi), the content (the divine message), [and] the referent (Christ, the Logos)."[26] In other words, the overdetermination of the Word, so keenly focused by the sublimity of pain (the Sender sent his Son to die), provides a "Great Code" to assist in the interpretation of the body as text. But, of course, the textuality of pain is not limited to illness *qua* premonition; for pain is also written on the psyche, written as "the little death."

Little deaths are infinitely protean in kind and degree. A few can be found in Baudelaire's story: the death of not being forgiven, the death of economic exchange, the death of *philia*. But more than this, the story, read beyond its borders, exemplifies the trope of prosopopoeia, the "the trope of mourning", as J. Hillis Miller terms it.[27] The philosophical profundity of this figure of speech is realized in its comprehensive attempt to represent the absent other, in which case one feels that even the present other is always somehow absent—even in moments of intimacy. Prosopopoeia is an "invention of the other" (here, Miller draws from Derrida's influential *Psyche* essay) consequently inscribed with the unknown in that it takes/makes the other in absolute otherness as someone who is not me and may therefore leave me at any time. In this *counterfait-in-personation* (as classically termed) a disruptive *oikei mania* enters the cycle of exchange. That is to say that there is something markedly counterfeit, and hence enervating, about the gesture of speaking for the dead, or speaking beyond death. It is as if the dead, actual or anticipated, are thought to have no home, no *oikos*, and are therefore given one through invention; and, as Derrida maintains, "invention begins by being susceptible to reinscription and exploitation."[28] This creates a specific mania of double intention; for there is in the beginning of every act of prosopopoeia a desire to give, to give beyond death. But how does this intention end up? Can the giver bear to ponder the end?

The prosopopoeic mania involved in "Counterfeit Money" comes, perhaps paradoxically, in the form of a closed hermeneutical circle, an ending to the "feast of thinking" on the part of the narrator, a gift of time that is returned—"signed, sealed, and delivered"— and thus negated. It is a mania of solitude and finality. This is part of our Cartesian legacy; random, roaming thought ends in the *cogito*, which philosophically precedes God and the open-endedness of mystery. But what occurs when we (again) reopen the circle to a religious reading? Is an effraction of circularity possible? These questions are what lay beyond the *ergo sum* and are already presaged in the gambit of the *Meditations*. In this beyond, the circle becomes what Ricoeur calls "Descartes' loop."[29] Through establishing the clear and distinct quality of the *cogito*, Descartes has to set forth an order of reasons which admits of a "projection of the arrival point back onto the starting point."[30] The order is thus linear only at first sight; circularity assumes its role once the solitary self, plagued by hyperbolic doubt, considers God within a personal horizon of uncertainty. How might a deceitful God affect my feast of thinking? (And thus we are back to Baudelaire's story: the attempt to deceive God would rest on a reciprocal vision of His order as orderless, disconcerting, and clandestine.) *The upshot to the whole legacy of the hermeneutics of suspicion*, which takes its point of departure in Descartes' privatization of reflection, is that one can only break the (manic) circle through some form of loving-beyond-oneself: charity, trust, solicitude, friendship, etc.[31]

Love (forgives and) forgets. But what does this cliché mean within the context of a religious community? For one thing, love, in terms of a "prudence of solicitude" (to borrow again from Ricoeur), exceeds any strict order of reasons in that it is willing to deal with incommensurabilities arising from different perspectives on ethical events (Was the gift of the counterfeit coin intended to deceive God, or was it an intention to do good, or to provoke a deepened sense of *philia*, or to simply create a surprising set of circumstances?) If postmodernism is right in holding that the preconditions for *phronesis* do not necessarily exist, then there is an unmistakable call for surplus, for incommensurable yet compatible narrative expressions of the human condition.[32] One doubts, however, whether the mere recognition of the absence of preconditions is sufficient to move people toward a textual overliving. In this light, Detweiler would seem to be suggesting more than meets the eye when he posits pain as such a driving force; narratives of pain, by fomenting and fostering survival, can trigger a vast range of semiotic activity, part of which would inevitably touch upon what a prudent life in a postmodern world would be. Detweiler maintains that "the destiny of community is not merely to provide its members with a place to belong. It is also to give them a context where, and a structure how, they can constantly plot their lives."[33] The *story told* by this community, if it is to be told at all, must be told in the spirit of love, which is the flipside of pain, the "plotting" beyond pain.[34] But, here, an apparent contradiction comes to the fore: a community would seemingly not be a community without memory (e.g., solidarity comes, for Ricoeur, form the renewal of a communal past[35]); but a community of love must forget, forget in order to forgive the "historical source" of pain (others, God, the cosmos). A community of love must forget the gift of *Dasein* except as it is received in its nowness.

Detweiler betrays a specific form of nostalgia that is helpful in confronting this contradiction. In his return to "older storytelling communities" for guidance in delineating the religiously-reading community, he reveals the way he would approach forgetting.[36] What is called for here is not amnesia, but a reconsideration of the extent of the mimetic powers imputed to memory. The reconstruction of the past, a past permeated both by pain and giving, can no longer be a matter of "getting the story right," but, rather, must itself be viewed as an instance of prosopopoeia, recognized as an "invention" and thus something that is tentative, open to excess. To give a voice to the past is to create an aleatory chorus instead of an aria written out in advance. For the religiously-reading community, one assaying to invent its past as it bears upon its future, the central memory of Christ's sacrificial death must therefore be held in tension between "fable" and "reality."[37] It is the former in so far as the ramifications of the crucifixion have become doctrinaire (and, rendered literarily, those ramifications must therefore be submitted to unreliability); and it is the latter inasmuch as God's gift of His Son is experienced as a *stigma*, as an event that is an advent. With a eye trained only on the eventness of the event, the gift, it is possible for one personally to appropriate the *stigmata* of Christ, to give suffering an individualized voice within the context of a life in a given community. Collectively, the community in this way begins to interpret all pain (physical and psychological) against an ultimate boundary, which itself is a gift actually received by no one save Christ Himself, understood as an inscrutable Giver.

Given this, the kind of nonchalance valorized by Detweiler can only be borne along by a sociability that accepts the gift (of life, in its theological sense) in its nowness. As it originally appears in Meister Eckhart, *Gelassenheit*, acceptance, is yet another aspect of the gift.[38] Indeed, the contemplatives of the "negative way" may have it right here: the full taking-in of the gift is predicated on a refusal to name God as such, which is to say that one is "released" (the German term also carries this connotation) from the obligation, at the point of reception, to enter into an economy of debt. To whom does one address the debt if "God" has no name? Furthermore, what do I owe "God" for this gift? Nothing, for there is nothing I can do to compensate for (or earn in the first place) God's grace. This acceptance is tantamount, then, to "knowing God in His highest of names: charity."[39] On the other hand, narratives name, especially meta-narratives, and a communal acceptance of the gift, in order to transcend the merely personal, is forced to rely upon stories, perhaps in the mold of older transmissions of the Word. But, in the wake of Lyotardian incredulity toward larger narrative structures, their propensity for naming things once and for all, what would count for a postmodern Christian story, one heeding the call for "intensified negative capabilities?"[40] Jean-Luc Nancy provides some "food for the feast" here (despite the fact that he upbraids the "fable" of Christ to the point where the event is well-nigh forgotten); and in turning briefly to his thought, I would suggest that continuing to go the route of Continental poststructuralism is one of the more fruitful ways of supplementing Detweiler's *Textdenken*.

Beyond Mere Myth

It cannot be said that Detweiler conceals his hand with regard to the particular narrative structure of interest to him when he speaks of a religiously-reading community. His Christian roots are apparent, even if they become "rhizomatic" in his traffic with various anti-traditions.[41] On the one hand, he can be taken in the same company with, for instance, Robert Scharlemann, whose elucidation of the ecstasis mandated for true involvement with the gift—what the latter thinker calls the "reason of following"—is unmistakably Christocentric.[42] On the other hand, Detweiler, more so than Scharlemann (and other of their contemporaries), seems inclined to at least set the stage for not only cross-cultural analyses of the gift, but cross-disciplinary excursions as well. These latter dialogues most often appear to move Detweiler's thinking into the domain of negative or even a-theology, though this is clearly not where his heart rests. As for Nancy's (extreme) a-theological contributions to our understanding of a religiously-reading community, the place to start would be the surplus of thinking-on-community developed telescopically through Heidegger (in which case we already have some common ground here), Georges Bataille, Maurice Blanchot, and finally Nancy himself. The theme is one of ecstasis (so, though I will not do it in this study, one might also wish to usher Scharlemann into this foray); namely, we note a typical line from Bataille: "If it sees its fellow-being die, a living being can only subsist *outside* itself."[43] Nancy further stresses that this ecstatic moment provides the only point from which one can know community; *Dasein*, before it can harbor *Mitsein*, must first experience the impossibility of communion and immanence.[44]

Wishing to steer clear of the charges of privatization, Nancy argues that this experience obtains between/among at least two persons, a community of two, and through ecstasis, immediately overreaches itself to a much broader horizon, a community that in principle can be extended globally. Thus we sense, as with most poststructuralist thinkers, an apocalyptic tone to his call for communal awareness, which is concomitantly an awareness of possible ecological or nuclear destruction—notwithstanding the hackneyed voice warning against such. Nancy shifts Detweiler's focus on reading to the act of writing while remaining within the same vein of surplus and while defending what we might call, following Lyotard, the "unpresentability" of the divine aspects of community. He asserts that there is a need, felt in postmodernity more than in any other epoch, to *write the community*, to keep it in a critical sense "inoperative," that is, in a position to fully explore the negative capability that incessantly challenges authority.[45]

Our conception of community should emerge from a non-representational (which is to say non-mimetic) discourse escaping totalizing, epistemological schemes:

> Perhaps we should not seek a word or a concept for it [the community], but rather recognize in the thought of community a theoretical excess (or more precisely, an excess in relation to the theoretical) that would oblige us to adopt another *praxis* of discourse and community. But we should at least try to say this, because "language alone indicates, at the limit, the sovereign moment where it is no longer current." Which means here that only a discourse of community, exhausting itself, can indicate to the community of sovereignty of its sharing....An ethics and a politics of discourse and writing are evidently implied here.[46]

What stands in the way of such a *praxis*? For Nancy, it is myth and the regulative mechanisms indigenous to it. He views literature—particularly in the form of what he calls, somewhat misleadingly, "literary communism"—as the prime instrument in the undoing/interruption/dislocation of myth. Especially troublesome here, for Nancy, is what he finds in Christian myth in the way of an "opiate," as Marx termed it. Because it is ultimately unmanageable in terms of any one myth, and thus cannot in the long run be controlled or "sedated," literature stands as a prime revolutionary force. By *literarily* divesting Christianity of its mythic structure, short-circuiting its power-through-story, the inoperative community can begin to see the proper place of the divine in human activity: the sharing of voices *is* the divine.[47] This strategy extends to the negative-theological tradition as well in that it resists the "dialectical urge to turn sings of the withdrawal of the sacred into signs that would manifest the sacred as withdrawn."[48] Nancy, then, takes seriously the attempt to empty Heidegger's "being-to" of any divinity, as it is in essence, he suggests, a relation to no god (*pas de dieu*).[49]

The deconstructive force of writing does not end with the literary acts of humankind; God (or the gods), in so far as He writes human history (the Logos becoming agents of Logoi) is just as hard pressed to name us, our activities, proclivities, and mistakes, our "sins" against the community as divine:

> They thus have no names for each other. For the gods, man is unnameable, for there are no names in the language of the gods (it knows only the summons, the order, the expression of joy). And the name of God, among man, names only the lack of sacred names. But men and the gods find themselves brought together face to face in this way; unnameable, and perhaps absolutely intolerable to each other.[50]

For Nancy, this lack of toleration, made more intolerable by the act of writing-against-myth, evokes an *energeia* that keeps communal activities healthfully inoperative, in excess.

One need not probe any deeper into Nancy's analysis to see that two salient issues immediately come to the fore in relation to Detweiler's program. First, in the historical space created by the reciprocal inability/refusal to name, the "intolerable" act of mythologizing, the writer is faced with the task of discovering alternatives to myth. In Detweiler's monumental but sometimes overlooked study on Updike, such alternatives are explored. He argues that in Updike's *Couples*, and then more so in *Bech: A Book* and in *Rabbit Redux*, we find myth turning against itself; this sets the stage for a substitution for myth by a focus on world events and an "orchestration of images" detached from myth.[51] The imagistic montage created here is further removed from a typical (mythic) narrative line through the use of fantasy and "narrator tricks."[52] If the narrator at this point in Updike becomes a *trickster* (And if so would Updike still be in thrall to the mythic impulse?), it would seem to be because of a hermeneutical suspicion regarding the controlling force of myth. In light of this suspicion, Updike would again be in need of postmodern reconsideration; his strategy, in fact, is not too far removed from what Linda Hutcheon, under the category of her poetics of postmodernism, would term "historiographic metafiction," which partakes in the more purely metafictive "ironic contesting of myth as master narrative, where there is no consolation...of consensual belief."[53] Historiographic metafiction (paradigmatically represented by E. L. Doctorow's *Ragtime*) also assumes the postmodern objection to modernism's spurious location of itself outside of history *through myth*.[54] In contradistinction, this form of fiction firmly entrenches itself in the historical past while calling attention to the "fabular" aspects of writing and reading. Immersed in some detail in facts, dates, and historical personages, historiographic metafiction is nevertheless involved in a form of invention, thereby creating critical distance between text and world (or between text as world and world as text).

It is not the case that myth is jettisoned altogether in these instances of fiction, only that myth, where there is any, is cast in a *parodic* vein, as a "repetition...that allows ironic signaling of difference at the very heart of similarity."[55] In the context of the modern/postmodern debate, the a major object under parodic scrutiny would appear to be what Hutcheon, borrowing from David Gross, identifies as "the noble myths of capitalist exploitation."[56] Indeed, such a sentiment also undergirds much of Nancy's thinking (as it does much of contemporary French philosophy in general). Capitalist myth is, for him, the primary obstacle in the establishment of the inoperative community.[57] As he puts it: "Capital negates community because it places above it [in the form of a story] the identity and the generality of production and products: the operative communion and general communication of works."[58] Of course, not all critiques of modernity center on, or even wrestle with tangentially, the economic polemic; more often than this, one finds within postmodernism an attempt to extricate philosophy (as a "kind of writing") from the myth of Enlightenment reason. Yet one can hardly ignore the telling argument presented by Max Horkheimer and Theodor Adorno's *Dialectic of Enlightenment*: an Odyssean economy of "resourcefulness" looms behind any modern assumption regarding humanity being on the track toward an enlightened "progress."[59]

Since, in the wake of recent global events, it looks like capitalism in some form or another is here to stay, postmodern criticism has shifted toward an analysis of symptoms of the capitalist/technological myth. In this case, one does not *forget* the lessons of Horkheimer, Adorno, and the Frankfurt School, but rather one, à la Derrida, plays with the entire concept of economy. Detweiler, for his part, is sage to note how modern resourcefulness manifests itself in a society of the spectacle (as it was called by Guy Debord and the Situationists of the 1950s), a disposition or trend that has crept, despite the *détournement* of critical distancing, into the postmodern age. Specularity would thus be the second item raised in Nancy's philosophy of import to the religiously-reading community. Alluding to the capitalist foundations of specularity, Detweiler speaks of the impact of this disposition on the community:

> It seems to me that in our culture a technologically-enhanced and consumerist-driven voyeurism has become a way of life. Watching each other literally, and vicariously and representationally in films and videos, is now standard practice and is met with increasing exhibitionism. A challenge to poststructuralism...would be to develop the fascination with language into a more intense *regard* for the problems of compulsive visualizing in our society.[60]

Detweiler, perhaps following the lead of Hutcheon, seems here to recommend a parodic manipulation of "the look" in critical theory (which would include poststructuralism, postmodernism, et al.) such that it becomes self-reflexive, aware of its own vices. The controlling myth, then, for our societal scopophilia in need of deconstruction would be the story of Narcissus; for voyeurism in this instance is an attempt to privatize, to capture my reflection in the other, to bring the world into a solipsistic sphere of interpretation. In every act of the contemporary voyeur, there is a recuperation, a co-opting, of otherness under the exigence of sameness. This act is borne out either by myriad, disconnected individuals or by a Universal Subject of History, toward which all individuals must conform— in the privacy, to be sure, of a technologically-enhanced home. "The spectacle," to cite Debord, "is not [merely] a collection of images, but a social relation among people mediated by images."[61] Which is to say there is no relation at all. In other words, contemporary society, for whatever reason, has produced spectators who live a pseudo-communal life.

Here, one may, with Debord, experience the "impossibility of communion," but not that of *immanence*. Without the impact of the second impossibility, the economic circle still interferes with human relations, which, indeed, should be based on the notion that the shaping of voices is (in some sense) the divine. Again, the boundary profile of death, or pain as a premonition of death, or the boundary of the little death itself, must be experienced in order for specular privatization, "encircled" by a narcissistic economy, to be effectively broken, opened up. This increases the urgency of the role of the writer with regard to the trope of prosopopoeia, which becomes perhaps more important in its generality and scope than even Miller realizes. It is the writer who wields the initial power over the tropological structure of representing the absence tracing all immanences; he/she must construct the space for mourning death, now and in the anticipated future. The reader, on the other hand, has to then seize the opportunity forged within this space. After the writer "invents the other," the reader is enjoined not to exploit, with a reinscription of the gift of textuality, but to exceed this invention. The *nomos* of economy at this point is not to reciprocate the gift by interpretively giving back to the text *ad infinitum*, but to continue giving beyond the text, signaling the text's own death, for me now at this reading at this time. With prosopopoeia, the reader is given to act, given toward praxis.

As Miller points out, "this [praxis] happens in an act of reading that is a doing that does other things in its turn. But it is a doing that is not soundly based on clear and demonstrable knowledge. Moreover, the reader must even take responsibility for the arbitrary positioning of the "I" that affirms this doing."[62] Positioned ecstatically (as Nancy would say), this reader/doer does not know precisely the ground upon which he/she stands; for it is *unpresentable*. What the reader/doer does grasp within this space is the very "basis of communication," to recall Blanchot's epigraph, a *nomos* of dialogue grounded upon loss. But "to invent" also means "to reveal"; and so, what is uncovered for the reader is a textual encounter with death that frames all possible losses within his/her life-world.[63] As we have seen, this experience, which allows the effraction of the circle, carries a special meaning within the Christian community: the crucifixion (and no less the resurrection) of Christ figures into this framing, this *parergon*. But in order to find the Christ revealed within the frame, one must exercise a special kind of faith. One must again consider the economy of God's gift(s).

Derrida maintains that, at the heart of the general idea of the gift, there is a presupposition of faith, *some kind of belief* in the authority of accreditation.[64] What does this faith mean in the theological context of a forgetting of the gift? Very much or very little, depending. For the religious reader of the *Christian* community, this faith, at least momentarily, turns its attention away from the "fable"—Christ as portrayed throughout history:

via the church, the theologian, the economy of salvation—and embraces unencumbered the foci of each event of the experience of pain and death. Each event, in so far as it summons the boundary, is taken within the context of the gift: God gives us to be human as He gave himself through a Son. In their eventness, these two moments are inextricable and thus beyond the fable; they are to be met with a *Gelassenheit* now in a sense regulated by faith. What is more, this gift-event is survived *through* faith, which recognizes and affirms the surplus intrinsic to the boundary. I live on in the absence of others, and others will live on in my absence, just as the divine message lives on (as the gift of the Holy Spirit) in the earthly absence of Christ. The latter event, taken in pure acceptance (no questions are asked, as questions give something back hermeneutically), becomes the supreme object of faith for the Christian community of readers—readers of texts of pain.

Narratives of Action

Having been further specified, the question that once again surfaces in the context of the present discussion is, "How are we, then, to read texts of pain within the Christian community? The obvious answer has already been "revealed": we read texts of pain as texts of survival, as ways of plotting our lives in acceptance of the gift and with the hope for the coming of a plenary *communitas*. (Here, I am reminded of David Patterson, who, speaking of Mikhail Bakhtin's theology of the event, asserts that "outside of resurrection there is no signification."[65]) But there is more to it than this. Our individual and communal "plotting" should have direct effects here and now, as we act in accordance with what suffering illuminates in our personal lives and in our community writ large. Such a praxis is predicated upon how we view literature (the acts of writing and reading) *as art*, as an artifact in the world, and thus it requires a generalizable extrication of art from the cycle of economic exchange. What I am suggesting here is that the effractive power of pain may not be, and probably is not, strong enough in dealing with literature *qua* art in the context of our "consumerist-driven," specular society. If this is true, the inherent power of the boundary may need bolstering—bolstering in the way of a theoretically refigured praxis of art.

There is, of course, a whole range of debate concerning the precise role of theory in the practical realm, and I will leave it to various and capable meta-theorists (and anti-theorists) to settle the score on this matter. In proposing a theory of praxis, one that will be recognizable within this arena of contention, I will be falling without defense on the side of thinkers such as F. A. Hayek and G. B. Madison, inasmuch as I am assuming that theory is neither in command of praxis nor is it "inconsequential," as Stanley Fish might say.[66] To borrow a term directly from Hayek, I do not see anything unreasonable about maintaining that theory can aid practice in a "cultivating" capacity.[67] At any rate, the theory I wish briefly to consider, and extend/emend a bit with regard to Detweiler's program, is that of Hannah Arendt. I choose Arendt for three reasons. First, her thoughts on art are often neglected, in which case they may be thought of as "orphaned" alternatives; and in postmodern thinking, ideas left on the doorstep of theory are often found to be among the most illuminating, as they are not at the "center" of discussion and are thus in less need of deconstruction. Second, Arendt's ideas in some ways resonate both with contemporary Continental philosophy and the critical theory of the Frankfurt School; if these two strains sometimes merge, so much the better. Here, I endeavor to maintain some semblance of continuity in the line of thinking developed thus far.

The third, and most important, reason for turning to Arendt is that she notes a delicate differentiation between art and the sphere of *work* (the economy of making). To rehearse her tripartite scheme of the *vita activa*, work is set off first of all from *labor* in that the former corresponds to the unnaturalness of human existence.[68] Whereas labor is the activity of biological processes, growth, and the vital necessities surrounding such, work sets up an artificial world of things meant to augment and transcend what nature has provided.[69] Work makes a given biological being a being-in-the-world; it renders a world in which to dwell and prosper. *Action*, the third component of Arendt's scheme, is the only activity that goes on directly between humans without the intermediary of workaday things or present-on-hand matter; action is a response to the condition of plurality, the fact that others exist, and it bears itself out in terms of movements and signs, gestures and language.[70]

When language becomes art, however, it becomes a "work" of art constructing its own form of "housing" for human life. What becomes of this *oikos* of the work of art? Arendt holds that the way in which a given society treats art—economically—serves as an index to the respective hierarchical alignment of the three basic human activities within that society.[71] In Western industrial and then technological societies, art has been erroneously reduced to mere work, and this signals the triumph of economic reason, the rationality of work; for Arendt, this is an "unnatural" and "artificial" reduction.[72] Art, in its natural state, actually transcends and challenges the economic means-ends relationship characteristic of work. Art deals with "existence finalized toward appearance," and thus seems to be more properly linked with the sphere of action, with the direct (and sometimes subterranean, as in modern art) activity between human beings.[73] Art thereby also attempts to render lasting and meaningful the impermanent activities (experiences, thoughts, visions) of the life-world, the world of labor. Art is linked therefore with thinking (meaning) but not knowing (truth); and thinking, Arendt believes, is "useless" in that it does not, contrary to the "knowledgeable" world of work, pursue definite ends.[74]

Because of its uselessness and relative permanence, its undirected perseverance, art is especially vulnerable; it is in dire need of "a life willing to resurrect it," precisely at the moment that it is finalized.[75] Arendt cites two major phenomena, within the "rise of the social," which take advantage of this vulnerability in a way threatening the naturalness of art, making it just another commodity in the workplace: one, "an educated philistinism that transforms the work of art into a value, something useful to be exchanged"; and two, the "entertainment industry which metabolizes the work of art" and thus devours the life-world represented by it as another aspect of the workaday world.[76] In both instances, art becomes a manipulated object of specularity, a simulacrum stripped of its naturalness of form, its truck with daily activities and the "noncognitive," anti-utilitarian thinking arising therein—arising with the help of art.[77] This expurgation of the true function of art synecdochically represents, and is another symptom of, the general crisis of culture, which is a crisis of the economy. Put differently, and more in the language of Arendt, this crisis is "a consequence of the displacement of the fundamental characteristic of the life processes into the world of work."[78] Placing art back on the right track—in a theoretic way that cultivates praxis—is, to put it mildly, no easy task. This task is further problematized, given Arendt's scheme, due to the fact that art also seems contradictory, as an alternative to work, both to labor and action. Whereas labor is impermanent, art is, if resurrected, in some sense permanent; and whereas action comes without the intermediary of things or matter, art utilizes both, especially matter, or form. Perhaps this means that in the final analysis art has no "real home" within the dimensions of human activity, and hence that it will continue to be exploited. Or perhaps it means that art must be made, theoretically, to fit within one or both of these alternative dimensions, that is, if it (ever) is to be freed from its economic connotations.

In the context of Detweiler's religiously-reading community and the role of texts of pain and death, I would suggest the readjustment/rethinking of (specifically literary) art as a type of action per se, as an aspect of the *vita activa* that just may be event-ually capable of breaking the economic circle.

Moreover, on Detweiler's Christocentric development of the community of readers, an exemplary and basic *life* would be indexed in this undertaking, thus placing literary art in the sphere of labor as well. In other words, this particular labor would be the gift of life as an *imitatio Christi* in so far as the Son of God's worldly management of suffering provides a model for Christians brought to an awareness, through literary acts, of the philosophical import of the boundary. Here, one's efforts in the life-world would be aided, through faith, by an ultimate effractive potency. What would be called for, in giving beyond *this* gift, is nothing short of a cultivation of narratives of action proposing some form of resurrection of the tortured body (and/or mind) of the person "of faith." As to what the exact content of this faith would be, one cannot answer literarily or artistically; for the truth of this content, to recall Arendt's distinction, can be thought but not known (which is to say that it must be worked out for each individual in "fear and trembling" before the boundary).

A return to literature as art, in Arendt's sense, would accept the role of vehicle for an undirected, "useless" textuality of thinking. *As action*, literary energies would nevertheless proceed headlong toward a meaningful sociability understood as a communal plotting, with allowances for individual idiosyncrasy, that itself embraces the resurrection beyond the economy of the gift. Resurrection, as Detweiler argues, encompasses body, matter, and form[79]; these become the palpable objects of one's belief in a God that cannot be seen. Faith as labor, as a biological drive in creative tension with the drive to deconstruct, and as a means of *Überleben*, does then betray its own "replica" of content based on formal reality; this is a content realized via the stark, wordly givenness of form (as in Heidegger's question, "Why is there not nothing?"). For Detweiler, "to believe in Incarnation and Resurrection is to believe in the reality of form and its fundamental mystery."[80] By "narrating a case of a god born into human form, dying in that form, and resurrected in a more exalted form,"[81] Christian "myth" should be grounded exclusively in the event that is a recapitulation of the cosmogonic event of which Heidegger speaks. In the acceptance of this event as a gift with no possible compensation, any further mythic contourings of it are turned inside out, exposing the *stigma* beyond mythic imagination. Taken outside of the primacy of the event and its mystery, Christianity on the whole is indeed in danger of becoming a mere fable, and as such is open to a chaos of transmission; and as Detweiler notes, chaos is to be strictly set off from mystery precisely because it lacks content and focus.[82]

That the focus of Christian mystery is ultimately unpresentable to reason and the (artistic) imagination—in which case it becomes "sublime" in Kant's sense—is no cause for a further perpetuation of the fable. What this unpresentability calls for, rather, is an "intensity of form" approaching but never subsuming its mystery. Such intensification would be a chief goal of narratives of action dealing with pain; it would become part of its (anti-)mythic structure. Yet, in reading the metafiction characterized by Hutcheon, or in reading unreliable instances of kerygma, or in considering any other form of surplus solely on the basis that *there is* an excess, the community is not guaranteed progress toward a meaningful sociability. By valorizing surplus and unpresentability, Detweiler is not merely instructing us to the religious import of the *mysterium* of unlimited semiosis; he, rather, is at least implicitly involved in seeing to the survival of the Christian "myth" of the event; he thus guardedly creates his own sort of theoretic unreliability with respect to any dogmatic "knowledge" presupposed concerning its "true meaning" for humankind. We might even see Detweiler echoing Pascal here; if God's gift is a mystery, it must remain as such, remain a matter of faith (which, to be faith, must entertain doubt), and not a matter of reason.

Detweiler, furthermore, views the survival of Christianity to be always already bound up with the critical balancing that all manner of literary texts of pain provide in juxtaposition with THE TEXT, and with faith. The criterion for choosing among texts offering such a balancing would be whether they, through an intensity of form, an intensity of *the material*, give beyond death. This is where the reciprocal balancing of Christian faith emerges. The event of Christ foregrounds the fact that, in order to give of oneself communally, where one does not expect compensation, one must maturely handle the gift of one's own life, one's destiny, and one's death. Christ struggled with the weighty issue of His death at Gethsemane, and He emerged triumphant, able to frame his life meaningfully in terms of this "sense of an ending." As human, He could not "know" where the end would lead, yet his "thinking"—always pervaded by the life-world, by human labor—proceeded from the hope for resurrection (to again be with the Father). This hope, extended to all humanity, influenced the way he responded to the community, to those who had faith in Him and to those who did not. He offered the very possibility of all resurrection, or the resurrection of all. And He provided, to borrow again (unabashedly out of context) from Arendt, an "existence finalized toward appearance"; His actions and "art" (the Gospel) were embodied in a form that actually *reappeared* on the road to Emmaus.

With these thoughts in mind, a critical balancing of the event of Christ should come, ideally, from literature that speaks of resurrection while continuing to question any purported knowledge of the mystery of being, the mystery of form. It should come as well from the painstaking process of "locating, disseminating, and completing," as Detweiler says, literature establishing an intensity of form based on this tension.[83] *Jesus' Son*, a collection of stories by Denis Johnson, presents itself as a text to be reckoned with in the context of these further circumscriptions of the truely valuable, religiously speaking, text of pain.[84] Exemplifying a form of "counterfeit" narration common to postmodern literature, Johnson's latest volume utilizes a disjointed chronology. More accurately described as an "anti-novel," its eleven chapter-like sections are narrated by the same drifter who remains unnamed throughout. He is not named seemingly because of his "intolerable," as Nancy might say, existence before a world still containing God's promise of resurrection; yet it is a world (our, postmodern world) where there is a "lack of sacred names" expressing hope for the realization of resurrection. Johnson's title reflects this ambiguous promise, as it outlines a lineage of suffering examined through the hyperreal convolution of all linear sequences: bloodlines; the history of Christian witness (What do the notions of salvation and self-sacrifice mean *now*?); and the day-to-day task of a personal emplotment against a terrain of uncertainty.

Johnson's narrator, a heroin addict and a heavy drinker, leads the reader to believe that his problems stem to a large degree from his troubled upbringing. This inference is verified when his driftings lead him back to a bar named "The Vine" where he finds his favorite bartender, "the Nurse," still diligently tending to her "patients." "She poured doubles like an angel," he tells us, "right up to the lip of the cocktail glass... You had to go down to them like a hummingbird over a blossom." Swept away by a revealing nostalgia (before going to the bar, he had been thinking of his ex-wife), the narrator thinks to himself: "I'll never forget you [the bartender]. Your husband will beat you with an extension cord and the bus will pull away leaving you standing there in tears, but you were my mother." Here, we strongly sense, more specifically, that his problems with his wife were the result of a personal emplotment (his) ruled by the (perhaps distorted) archetype of the Great Earth Mother, the nuturing female spirit at once an angel of death.

The Cubist time line of *Jesus' Son* sets up a *mise-en-abyme* of the narrator's dysfunctional life; he is unable to create a "good story," unable, even, to keep facts and dates straight (in the third section, an acquaintance dies of a heroin overdose but is found in the fourth section smoking hashish and trying to aid a gunshot victim). This dual dysfunctionality creates a heightened state of unreliability made even more extreme by the narrator's habit of lying. The narration is self-reflexive in the sense that it is self-deprecating, and the latter tendency grows directly out of these prevarications. In lying to a girlfriend, he admits: "Nothing I could think up, no matter how dramatic or completely horrible, ever made her repent or love me the way she had at first, before she really knew me." His lying leads to other wrongdoings in the fifth section; he and his friend Wayne, also estranged from his wife, burglarize an abandoned house. Afterwards, however, they share an epiphany restoring somewhat their faith in the sacredness of women, who to be appreciated must be glimpsed from afar, through a certain detachment or nonchalance. Having ripped most of the wiring from the vacant house, they notice a speedboat coming up the river bordering its backyard: "This boat was pulling behind itself a tremendous triangular kite on a rope. From the kite, up in the air a hundred feet or so, a woman was suspended, belted in somehow. I would have guessed she had red hair. She was delicate and white, and naked except for her beautiful hair." Again nostalgic, the narrator realizes on the basis of this experience that his dependencies were solely to blame for his lifelong failure to detach from, to allow enough distance between (like that afforded by the kite string), himself and his various past lovers. In other words, he sees that his dependencies everywhere surround, and bleed into and out of, his "codependence" with the archetypal Female.

Not long after this Beatrice experience, we find Johnson's narrator on the long and provisional road to recovery. As "Jesus' son," he is ostensibly prepared to handle maturely the gift that is his life. Gaining our confidence under this archetype, he checks himself into a detoxification program, where he lands a part-time job writing for and editing the affiliated hospital's newsletter. He is especially intrigued at this time by a character named Bill, a newly arrived patient shot in the face "once by each wife, for a total of three bullets, making four holes, three ins and one out." Addressing his interviewee, whom we assume is also an addict, the narrator tries to comfort him with clichés, to which Bill responds: "Talk into here," pointing to a scar on his cheek... "Talk into my bullet hole. Tell me I'm fine." Such gallows humor adumbrates Johnson's own nonchalance (which is often taken by his readers as a Burroughsian "insensitivity") regarding the pathology of addiction and the general attitude of paranoid uncertainty that it causes. This uncertainty continues to haunt the drifter, as we find that the "Higher Power" (as it is called in Twelve-Step Programs) assisting in the narrator's recovery is not fully embraced even at the end of the novel. He accepts the initial gift of this power, but his interpretation of it is obfuscated by his distrust of the cultural fable of Jesus. Another of his unseemly habits reappears: his nighttime activity of peeping into windows to watch couples making love. He now seems a slave to this compulsion, and he continues to suffer (guilt) because of it. Moreover, the relationship that he begins at this point with a woman crippled by encephalitis augurs further codependency.

In *Jesus' Son*, Johnson echoes the need for a tension between religious faith and the interrogation of the myths neatly unpacking its mystery. He tells us that, in a world where pain is so ubiquitous, where its anatomy is so often misunderstood and simplified into categories, we are all progeny of the mysterious Christ of the cross—for better (as in the acceptance of the gift of possible resurrection), or for worse (as in the rejection of Christianity on the basis of its many paradoxes). The gift of life itself, because living is often painful, is placed under a microscope in Johnson's text. His continual allusions to wiring, belts, and strings collectively symbolize an umbilical cord, a *life-source*, detached from the Universal Feminine, and sometimes used against it locally as a weapon or a constraint. This parodic erosion of the "myth of the female" is a particularly unsettling form of the kind of myth-against-itself of interest to Detweiler: Is this erosion "in" society per se, or is it predominantly a textual creation? Is it something that feminists, for instance, should attack, or should they make use of its deconstructive potentialities? Obviously, other items found within Johnson's novel would be of particular interest to Detweiler and the community of Christian readers, and they might have some bearing on how we go about answering the above-mentioned questions. A list of these items would include: voyeurism and the debilitating cultural specularity of which it is a part; the "anti-novel" and the unreliability of narration, which would include any possible "fictions of kerygma" (Is the Word spoken in Johnson's text? Is it submitted to the Heideggerian *Durchkreuzung*?); the narrator's "drifting" and the surplus it engenders; the intensity of form achieved by the *mise-en-abyme*; the problematic of nostalgia; the bankruptcy of trust and love in contemporary society; and, to be sure, pain and the textual possibility of giving beyond death, the death of the soul through addiction.

But *does* Johnson's text give beyond death? Is resurrection, here, anything more than just a possibility? We may entertain hope for the full recovery of "Jesus' son," but that hope may fade when we consider how entirely irreversible the lineage of his self-destruction may be. Perhaps more than anything else, Johnson's novel highlights the difficult and even fear-inspiring project facing the religiously-reading community; taken as a narrative of (in)action, it compels the reader to focus almost exclusively on the postmodern life-world ruled by excess and doubt. Given the irreducible tension between faith and criticism, it may be the case that readers of novels such as Johnson's, novels with so much "negative capability," will find the prospects of living on within the literarily-influenced contexts of their own lives utterly unbearable. The praxis of personal emplotments drawing from "intensified" texts of pain might seem overwhelming, to say the least. At the heart—or on the outskirts—of textual surplus, one may in fact confront Thanatos, the Thanatos-wish, perhaps stronger now than ever before in its postmodern, mythic form. I should think that these considerations lead us to yet another "beyond." To survive the "post" in postmodern, which would here summon the "post" of post-mortem, one may have to outlast—even!— the literary impulse, the textuality of texts, *écriture*, life (and not, then, merely philosophy) "as a kind of writing." For the body is most fundamentally not a text but a thing; to affirm and claim the body that cannot be written is to exceed *this* fable, to emerge as well on the other side of the myth of death.

NOTES

1. J. Hillis Miller, *Versions of Pygmalion* (Cambridge, Massachusetts: Harvard University Press 1990), p. 200.

2. Maurice Blanchot, *The Unavowable Community*, trans. Pierre Joris (Barrytown, New York: Station Hill Press, 1988), p. 25.

3. Detweiler develops his notion of a religiously-reading community in *Breaking the Fall: Religious Readings of Contemporary Fiction* (San Francisco: Harper and Row Publishers, 1989). See pages 45-49 for his thoughts on texts of pain.

4. Robert Detweiler, "Overliving," in *Poststructuralism and Biblical Exegesis: Semeia*, eds. Stephen Moore and David Jobling, 1992. p. 242.

5. Robert Detweiler, "Overliving," pp. 254-55.

6. Robert Detweiler, *Breaking the Fall*, p. 114.

7. Robert Detweiler, "Overliving," p. 240.

8. Robert Detweiler, "Overliving," p. 244.

9. Jacques Derrida, *Given Time: I. Counterfeit Money*, trans. Peggy Kamuf (Chicago: University of Chicago Press, 1992), pp. 28, 91.

10. Jacques Derrida, *Given Time*, p. 91.

11. Jacques Derrida, *Given Time*, p. 29.

12. Robert Detweiler, *Breaking the Fall*, p. 35.

13. Robert Detweiler, *Breaking the Fall*.

14. Robert Detweiler, *Breaking the Fall*, pp. 105-113.

15. Robert Detweiler, *Breaking the Fall*, p. 190.

16. Jacques Derrida, *Given Time*, p. 98.

17. Robert Detweiler, *Breaking the Fall*, p. 114.

18. Jacques Derrida, *Given Time*, p. 122.

19. Jacques Derrida, *Given Time*, pp. 121, 168.

20. On this "suggestion," I am relying on S. H. Clark, *Paul Ricoeur* (London: Routledge, 1990), p. 9.

21. In chapter four of Derrida's *Given Time*, the intimation is made that Baudelaire's friends may have in fact been lovers, in which case, the whole notion of male-bonding may take on a parodic twist/tryst.

22. Jacques Derrida, *Given Time*, p. 103.

23. Jacques Derrida, *Given Time*, pp. 103-105.

24. Robert Detweiler, *Breaking the Fall*, p. 46.

25. This is actually anthropologist Michael Herzfeld's expression, quoted by Detweiler in *Breaking the Fall*, p. 48.

26. Umberto Eco, *The Limits of Interpretation* (Bloomington: Indiana University Press, 1990), p. 11.

27. J. Hillis Miller, *Versions of Pygmalion*, p. 4.

28. Jacques Derrida, "Psyche: Invention of the Other," in *Jacques Derrida: Acts of Literature*, ed. Derek Attridge (New York: Routledge, 1992), p. 316.

29. Paul Ricoeur, *Oneself as Another*, trans. Kathleen Blamey (Chicago: University of Chicago Press, 1992), p.10.

30. Paul Ricoeur, *Oneself as Another*.

31. The form of "getting outside," as I am calling it here, favored by Ricoeur is, in fact, solicitude. Drawing upon Aristotle, he shows how a *prudence* of solicitude, actually based on self-esteem, enables the self to exit solipsism and move toward a communal "concern" for the justice of all of one's fellow beings. He elucidates this notion in *Oneself as Another*, pp. 227-244.

32. For a helpful discussion of theoretic "incommensurabilities" and the possibilities of founding a workable *phronesis*, see Karey Harrison's review of Richard Berstein's *Beyond Objectivism and Relativism*, in *Telos* 63, (Spring, 1985), pp. 223-227.

33. Robert Detweiler, *Breaking the Fall*, p. 190.

34. Texts of love indeed play as important a role in Detweiler's thought as do texts of pain, perhaps more so. See his *Breaking the Fall*, pp. 49-54.

35. Paul Ricoeur, *Time and Narrative*, Volume III, trans. Kathleen McLaughlin and David Pellauer (Chicago: University of Chicago Press, 1987), p. 113.

36. See Detweiler's preface to *Breaking the Fall*, p. xiii. The rest of what I assume here on Detweiler's behalf is put together in a *bricolage* fashion. For more "hints" as to his position on history, see the "Overliving" essay, p. 241.

37. I extract my sense of the word "fable" here from Derrida, who in turn extracts it from Paul Valéry (e.g.,"In the beginning was the fable"); see Derrida's "Psyche: Inventions of the Other," p. 323.

38. Detweiler, in fact, refers to Eckhart in *Breaking the Fall*, p. 35.

39. Jean-Luc Marion, *God Without Being*, trans. Thomas A. Carlson (Chicago: University of Chicago Press, 1991), p. xxi. Marion's project of separating the acceptance of God's gift of love from the onto-theological tradition is in many ways concurrent with the line of thinking developed in the present study.

40. Jean-François Lyotard offers his critique of meta-narratives in *The Postmodern Condition: A Report on Knowledge*, trans. Geoff Bennington and Brian Massumui (Minneapolis: University of Minnesota Press, 1984). Detweiler, in turn, develops an insightful critique of this study in "Squabbles of Science and Narrative: Lyotard's *The Postmodern Condition*," *Art Papers*, 10/1 (January/Febuary, 1986), pp. 18-20. It is important to bear in mind here that I am following Lyotard's lead in linking mythic structures with the "controlling force" of reason, thus ascribing to myth more epistemological power than may sometimes be assumed.

41. Charles E. Winquist uses the image of the rhizome, an aleatory root/plant anti-system, to describe negative theology. See his thought-provoking *Epiphanies of Darkness: Deconstuction in Theology* (Philadelphia: Fortress Press, 1986).

42. See Robert Scharlemann's *The Reason of Following: Christology and the Ecstatic I* (Chicago: University of Chicago Press, 1991).

43. Bataille is quoted from Jean-Luc Nancy, *The Inoperative Community*, trans. Peter Conner (Minneapolis: University of Minnesota Press, 1991), p. xv.

44. Jean-Luc Nancy, *The Inoperative Community*, p.xv.

45. Jean-Luc Nancy, *The Inoperative Community*, p. xxv.

46. Jean-Luc Nancy, *The Inoperative Community*.

47. Jean-Luc Nancy, "Sharing Voices," in *Transforming the Hermeneutic Context: From Nietzsche to Nancy*, eds. Gayle Ormiston and Alan D. Schrift (Albany: State University of New York Press, 1990), p. 248.

48. Jean-Luc Nancy, *The Inoperative Community*, p. xxxiv.

49. Jean-Luc Nancy, *The Inoperative Community*, p. xxxiv.

50. Jean-Luc Nancy, *The Inoperative Community*, p. 142.

51. Robert Detweiler, *John Updike* (Boston: Twayne Publishers, 1984).

52. Robert Detweiler, *John Updike*, p. 126.

53. Linda Hutcheon, *A Poetics of Postmodernism: History, Theory, Fiction* (New York: Routledge, 1988), p. 50.

54. Linda Hutcheon, *A Poetics of Postmodernism*, p. 101.

55. Linda Hutcheon, *A Poetics of Postmodernism*, p. 26.

56. Linda Hutcheon, *A Poetics of Postmodernism*, p. 134.

57. Would it be the case here, then, that Christian myth is in concert with capitalist myth, or is it that the latter in fact exploits and distorts the true meaning of the former?

58. Jean-Luc Nancy, *The Inoperative Community*, p. 75.

59. Max Horkheimer and Theodor Adorno, *Dialectic of Enlightenment* (New York: Continuum, 1972).

60. Robert Detweiler, "Overliving," p. 254.

61. Debord is quoted from C. Carr " The Situationist Situation: What We Talk About When We Talk About the Avant-Garde," in *The Village Voice Literary Supplement*, #84 (April, 1990), p. 18.

62. J. Hillis Miller, *Versions Of Pygmalion*, p. 80.

63. Jacques Derrida, "Psyche," pp. 337-338.

64. Jacques Derrida, *Given Time*, p. 97.

65. David Patterson, "Bakhtin on Word and Spirit: The Religious Responsibility," in *Cross Currents: Religion and Intellectual Life*, 41/1 (Spring, 1991), p. 37.

66. On the praxis/theory debate, see G. B. Madison, "The Practice of Theory, The Theory Of Practice," in *Critical Review*, 5/2 (Spring, 1991), pp. 179-202.

67. G.B. Madison, "The Practice of Theory," p. 191.

68. Here, I rely on Bernard Flynn's lucid and detailed attempt to "salvage" the philosophy of art offered by Arendt. See his "The Places of the Work of Art in Arendt's Philosophy," in *Philosophy and Social Criticism*, 17/3 (1991), pp. 215-228. The specific idea expressed is this passage is on page 218.

69. Bernard Flynn, "The Place of the Work of Art," p. 215.

70. Bernard Flynn, "The Place of the Work of Art," p. 218.

71. Bernard Flynn, "The Place of the Work of Art," p. 223.

72. Bernard Flynn, "The Place of the Work of Art," p. 223.

73. Bernard Flynn, "The Place of the Work of Art," p. 219.

74. Bernard Flynn, "The Place of the Work of Art," p. 220.

75. Bernard Flynn, "The Place of the Work of Art," p. 220.

76. Bernard Flynn, "The Place of the Work of Art," p. 221.

77. Bernard Flynn, "The Place of the Work of Art," p. 220.

78. Bernard Flynn, "The Place of the Work of Art," p. 222.

79. Robert Detweiler, *Breaking the Fall*, pp. 44-45.

80. Robert Detweiler, *Breaking the Fall*, p. 44.

81. Robert Detweiler, *Breaking the Fall*, p. 49.

82. Robert Detweiler, *Breaking the Fall*, p. 55.

83. Robert Detweiler, *Breaking the Fall*, pp. 49-54.

84. I am greatly indebted to the review of *Jesus' Son* by James McManus appearing in *The New York Times Book Review* (December 27, 1992). In fact, the word "indebted" may not be strong enough here, as it occurs to me that I have cannibalized a great deal of his marvelous explication. Even the direct quotations he finds intersting seem to "fit my needs" quite well. Thus, rather than ferret them out, I refer the reader to McManus' review itself. The day on which this review appeared, coincidentally, is a day that I shall never forget, as I experienced the *un*anticipated "absence," and it now seems to be a rather permanent one, of a "presence" that I had always assumed would, barring death, stay with me.

Symbol Then and Now

Remembering and Connecting

DAVID S. PACINI

C ultural anthropology has taught us to think of religion as a system of symbols. And philosophy has instructed us to construe symbols as vehicles of conception. But we have yet to learn as distinctive a way to speak of Symbol—even though this arrangement of beliefs in condensed forms has played a formative role in the development of Christianity. In the absence of such a way of speaking, we have instead subsumed Symbol under the larger category of "symbol" or conflated it with the notion of "creed." So we tend to think of Symbol as pointing to and participating in a peculiar religious reality, or as a definitive set of knowledge claims about a religious reality that we are bound to regard as true.

Yet when it appeared among the practices of early Christians, the term *symbolum* referred to the practice of legitimately linking an individual to the larger Christian community. Hence, more than a summary conception of Christianity or its symbol system in miniature, Symbol functioned as an exchange between the community who challenged the individual with questions, and the individual who sought to claim rightful membership in the community through appropriate answers. Each of the questions the community addressed to the individual anticipated a response from him or her that would entail part of the narrative from the community's formulation of its beliefs.

This basic practice associated with Symbol is both informative and suggestive. It reminds us, at an elementary level, that the person to whom the community addressed its questions was seeking connection with the community. The knowledge of the community's belief narratives required for appropriate responses presupposed that the individual enjoyed a prior relation with the community. The questioning of the individual, in turn, implied some break in this tie with the community.

At another level, this practice of questioning and answering implies the joining together of two narratives: the narrative of the believing individual and the narrative of the believing community. Minimally, we know that the believing individual has become separated from the community, and that the one who is separated is now seeking connection. We know, too, that part of the experience of connecting with the community consists in speaking the narrative of the community's beliefs.

Let us provisionally consolidate these observations and speak of Symbol as a register of belief-practices. By the term, "register," I mean to invoke both the sense in which it means a record of acts, and the sense in which it refers to a range of voices. Symbol understood as register incorporates an array of practices, including interrogatories, responses, personal belief narratives, community belief narratives, gestures, and the resonances that inform the play among the practices. Such resonances, loosened from orbits of meaning, signal losses of understanding and the displacement of rationality.

We may summarize the distinctive character of Symbol as register by saying that in word and in deed, the avowal, "we believe in   . . ."marks the site of rupture, of what our rationality cannot fathom. We fill in the void left open with the narrative of the Symbol. Hence, we introduce through *saying* what our rationality can no longer *do*: the possibility of connecting what is fragmented, of using a narrative (in the absence of understanding) as a way of suggesting an itinerary for cohesive living.

As the sense of what a believing subject is alters, how do Symbolic narratives re-distribute the space for cohesive living? This is a central question for this essay; the observations we gather in the course of our inquiry will serve my larger aim of framing a distinctive way to speak of Symbol. Given the characteristic connection in Symbol between personal belief-narrative and community belief-narrative, it is appropriate that the materials I select for this exploration, and the ways in which I arrange them, should reflect turns in the course of my own thinking about Symbol, as well as narratives about Symbol. I shall therefore begin setting out some of the pertinent experiences that have informed my perspective.

The Course of My Thought: Connecting Subjectivity To The World of Shared Meanings

Death annihilated the child sprung from both of us. Now all my thinking figures, through writing, this loss about which I cannot speak. It is still the time of the empty room. Death whispers softly here. Senses strain to glean something that lingers from what is gone. As the setting sun soon vanishes, so also do times and places linked in grief's corridor transfix and then disappear from the mind's eye. At first, there were raging furies obliterating all that seemed to go so well, burying human hope near a tree. Shattered was the *pieta*: mother and child. Then came the immense void, bursting in the night, winter's bleak beach savaged by storms. With Spring's abundant flowerings, a regal tree predominated: more than this oak to which last year's dead leaves still tenaciously cling, the heart missed the sublime in April. In these and other images, Father, Mother find they no more know themselves than the dead know that they are dead.

To consent to live seems a betrayal of the dead, an apparent forgetfulness of a life once amongst us. An even greater outrage inhabits the thought that forgetting the dead for even a moment deprives their death of any hope for salvation. Abrogating the power of God with these thoughts, we either deny the godly powers their own course, or assign them to ourselves upon the presumption of their non-existence. Alongside these thoughts stand the declarations of the Symbol, affirming the resurrection of the dead, and the allied baptismal proclamation, "Christ's own forever." It is tempting to oppose these declarations to the thoughts of betrayal, as heart to mind. But matters of the heart are more easily converted into rational formulations than readily understood.

Attempting to live without betraying the dead or the heart, I have found myself thinking about Symbol by deviating from the rich store of generalizations with which our time abounds. I have put aside the idea that Symbol is "the rule of faith," just as I have suspended the notion that Symbol "gives intelligible expression to Christian faith." For I have grown wary of acquired rationalizations and their powerful centralizing strategies. So, rather than signifying some paradise of global history, Symbol now more nearly seems to me to designate a zone of silence—a lost, but great region of human experience.

To think about Symbol in this way is to make one's way around received formulations, probing tentatively and stepping cautiously in marginal areas. With such a sense of uneasy footing, my thinking about Symbol entails, as Michel de Certeau has deftly noted, a tacit acknowledgment of a lack of place.[1] In deviating from established taxonomies of knowledge that establish the boundaries and internal topographies of culture, I forsake the institutional sanction that locates my thinking with an established discipline (e.g., as *historical*).

Yet such exclusion is not without benefit. Freed in part from any particular cultural thought-code, my working with the words of the Symbol and their significances rearranges their social place. New resonances come into play. Images and concepts kaleidoscopically collide, mingle and merge, and then fall into distorted shapes. By forming and reforming, these shapes resist my adoption of any single stand-point. Hence, my thinking remains unsituated, a peripatetic signalling of the disquieting rupture of anamorphosis.

My thinking differed altogether when, as a boy, I was obliged to undergo catechetical instruction. I learned the Symbol by heart, and then only its length was daunting. Fortunately, its rhythms, progressions, and the sure knowledge that when I arrived at the section on the Holy Spirit, the Symbol's conclusion was imminent, rescued my efforts of recitation. In the particular reverie that comes with a child's exercises of memorization, I found my imagination wandering. It seemed that I was coming into possession of something of such importance that I should never forget it. And the spoken Symbol was of such apparent power that it could endow upon catechumens a special place: successful recitation of the Symbol meant not only passing the class, but also admission to the Table and (or so we were told) to the mystical body of Christ.

Years later, as a graduate student, I returned to the Symbol. I learned to regard it as a cultural artifact, and, in keeping with the Marxist sympathies of my teachers, to approach it as a product of socio-economic and political practices. Gone now was the transparency of the Creed, and in its place stood an opacity, resisting my domesticating intellectual efforts. Perhaps it was merely naïveté giving way to the curtain of critical thought, but this encounter with the Symbol diverted my thinking from universal claims to contingent facts. I busied myself more with the minute and less with overarching schemes, hoping that I could snatch from the swirl of incidentals some intimations of significance regarding the Symbol. Few of these have stayed with me, but one stands out. Somewhere in the fourth century, Christians began to employ the term *symbolum* for affirmations of belief, intimating an analogy with the passwords battle commanders imparted to their troops as a security measure. A challenged partisan established his legitimate connection with a battle force by answering interrogatories with the password. In similar fashion, Christians recited the Symbol in response to questions—oftentimes linked to the occasion of baptism—legitimizing their presence in the practices of the community with whom they were being united. The use of the term Symbol persisted in Christian parlance for centuries, doubtless owing to its connotative resonances assuring authentic place to believers. Near the end of the nineteenth century, the term (in this sense) disappeared as suddenly as it had appeared.

Perhaps the simplest observation I can make about these experiences is that they appear to reflect an increased awareness of Symbol's artful fashioning of human religious identity. Santayana tells us that they marked idiosyncracy of a religion is that it gives us ". . . another world to live in—whether we expect ever to pass wholly over into it or no."[2] Symbol shaped my childhood believing, as it introduced me to new vistas. Thinking critically about Symbol in my graduate years tempered my believing. I was reminded of the welter of common-sense experience from which the images of belief are hewn and to which the believer ineluctably returns. In death's shadow, Symbol became an affront, routing my beliefs that I might believe. For Symbol, though a token of another world, betokens the loss of place, the impossibility of living in that world as though it were the only one.

We believe ever more darkly. And our ways of thinking about believing and about Symbol would do well to reflect this. As Michael Baxandall has aptly observed, a description ". . . takes its meaning from reciprocal reference, a sharpening to-and-fro, between itself and the particular."[3] In other words, however much language may desire to refer us to reality, especially material reality, it is not the pointing of words to (elusive) things, but the playing among words and signs that imbues reality with its intelligibility, its range of tonalities, and its numerous significances. This playing always mobilizes the re-making of meaning. Yet we flee from the obvious: The infinite vibrations of Symbolic meaning prescind the immobility of our thought. We always think of Symbol differently from before.

The orthodox among us may insist that the course of my thinking is held captive to the tyranny of subjectivism. But something in my account prohibits them from reducing my sense of perambulating thought about Symbol to a psychologistic fate of my autobiography. I am mindful of the otherness of reality, which cannot be absorbed into language. I attempt as well to foreground the social character of language. By this I mean the embeddedness of language in social action and system of public signification, and the collective construction of language. Both foci devalue the exchange rate between "subjective" and "objective." The resistance I wish to note here, however, is not traceable to one or the other of these—reality or language. To be sure, language practices and reality are distinct—however muddy that distinction may be—and it would be wrong-headed to conflate the two. But they stand as well in a tenuous relation to one another that generates its own field of force. What is produced in this field partakes of the authority both of language practices and reality; any achieved identity, consequently, contains within itself the signs of this interplay. So the significance that attaches to my sense of Symbol as marking out a zone of silence is the product of bits and pieces of human experience, stitched together in loose but powerful associations, rhetorical patterns, and fundamental metaphors.

In the darkening of believing, we become aware that although Symbol holds before us the prospect of another world in which to live, it also indicates the untenability of living in that world as if it were the only one. This penumbral sentiment bespeaks a religious predicament larger than my own. It is comprised of shifts in the conception of the believing subject and in the belief-practices of the Symbol that have been mediated historically through language and social-structural processes. The fluidity of significance in Symbol today contrasts markedly with its totalizing, progressive, and integrative roles of yesterday. The tension between these two configurations of Symbol reflects combinations and permutations of thought that still permeate our modes of comprehension. How these changes play upon us predisposes us to widely differing ends and shadings of belief.

Sifting through some of these changes will bear upon the way in which we speak of Symbol. True, the questions that I ask of materials I explore are shaped by questions I ask myself, binding my experiences with those I study. But the shifts I discern in the perception of the real have shaped the materials as well as they have shaped me. So while certain facets of my experience have propelled me to encounter Symbol today in just the way I do—and I am bound to honor those experiences—I do not presume that what I see is unique to me. I hope only that the ways I forge to speak of Symbol and its role in rendering cohesive our religious predicament will cast some light upon what is already familiar to others.

My way of ascertaining the character of the shift in thinking embodies in our religious predicament will entail setting out two differing conceptions of the subject and the Symbol: the classical and the modern. While there is no such thing as a single explanation of this phenomenon of changing thought, except as an exercise in self-protection, reduction, and (thereby) control, I shall note an apparent set of governing conditions that informs the instances of the shift I examine here: first, a (political) crisis in faith, in which faith sundered from Creation combats scientific rationality, alternately winning and losing forays; second (as linguistic criticism and psychoanalytic theory have shown), faith so separated migrates with reason into language, by way of metaphor and metonomy; last, faith so constituted as a fashioning aspect of language articulates itself Symbolically not in terms of Nicaea, but of Westminster, with effects that need to be drawn out.

As my broader exposition of these governing conditions proceeds, an analytic discourse will unfold. What will simultaneously appear on the scene of this exploration, through the movement of this analytic discourse, is the contours of the "religious predicament" we are attempting to discern. These appear—or better, reappear—precisely because our thinking turns out to be a symptom of this predicament.

The Classical Subject and Symbol: An Historical Detour

The world "symbol" derives from the Greek, *syn* + *ballein*, "to throw together." Early Christian practices associated with the use of the term lent a different connotation: the questions put to believers prior to their baptism imply their separateness, and that what has been ruptured is seeking connection. The Augustinian reading of the Symbol of Nicaea turns upon this variant meaning of "symbol," and helped to consolidate its association with Symbol.

The Symbol of Nicaea triumphed at the Council of Constantinople in 381, marking the ascendancy of trinitarian doctrine. But its hold upon Western thought derives not so much from its Greek architects as from its Latin philosophical and theological interpreter, Augustine of Hippo. Virtually unlettered in Greek and only rudimentarily tutored in Hebrew, Augustine nonetheless possessed an independent and original mind. He devoted his intellectual energies to a massive literary corpus, while rigorously exercising the charge of his episcopacy. His way of casting philosophical and theological issues has remained formative in Western thought for fifteen centuries, and we must still reckon with him today.

Nonetheless, we hold little in common with Augustine. From a modern point of view, his outlook is dated: while it remains possible to believe in eternal forms and divine history, we no longer do so in the same way as Augustine. In any event, those with whom he quarreled have all but disappeared or been transformed. Manicheans no longer command a large religious following; Pelagians have been repeatedly discredited, if not routed; and Circumcellions no longer serve as "shock troops" for Donatists, who, moreover, no longer exist. The shattering of the Roman empire, so telling for the shape of Augustine's thought, is of such remove from us that it sparks little more than quaint interest.

What survives, however, is a portrait of the classical subject, its faith, and its relation to God, which has striking resonances with modern themes.

More instructive still are the portrait's differences from modernity that claims about its kinship tend to suppress.

"Scripture," Augustine tells us, "attracts us like children . . . but it is faith that speaks for us."[4] Everything begins and ends in faith for Augustine, although his construal of faith as the gateway to the understanding will be foreign to us who have been schooled in the critical arts of suspicion and disbelief.

Opposing Tertullian's notion of the absurdity and unreasonableness of faith, Augustine urged the view that faith is a necessary accompaniment to, and fulfillment of, reason. The move may seem modest enough, but its implications for the classic Christian conception of the subject are momentous.

Here is how Augustine puts the case. A subject exists, knows and wills—indeed, it knows that it exists, knows that it knows, and knows that it wills. The capacities of desire and memory, which enable the subject's self-knowing, are God's gift to the soul at the time of its creation. Desire animates the soul, while memory, which is the capacity of the mind to be present to itself (or, as Augustine frequently calls it, the "form of the minds"), guides it. In consequence of these gifts of creation, the protean adaptability of the subject seems inexhaustible as it directs its attention to every aspect of the world it desires, enjoying awareness (by memory) of what it attends to. In the tenth book of his *Confessions*, Augustine invokes the figural device of the inner and the outer man to describe the subject's experience of knowledge: "The inner part of man knows these things through the agency of the outer part. I, the inner man, know these things; I, the soul, know them through the senses of my body."[5]

The activity of reason is tantalizingly ambiguous. In a stanza of the *Confessions*, Augustine tells us, "I love a light of a certain kind, a voice, a perfume, a food, an embrace."[6] In the next stanza, Augustine qualifies this by adding, "but they are of a kind I love within myself when my soul is bathed in light that is not bound by space, when it listens to sound that never dies away, when it breathes fragrance that is not borne by the wind."[7] In short order, Augustine then asserts that "man, guided by reason . . . can question nature."[8] In rapid fashion, this follows: "To the man who merely looks . . . [nature] . . .says nothing, but to one who subjects it to inquiry while he looks . . . [nature] . . . gives an answer."[9] Still another turn in reason's course appears. Augustine maintains that the answer nature gives is ". . . only understood by those who compare the message it gives them through their senses with the truth that is in themselves.[10] The pattern of reason's activity unfolds roughly in this manner: reason is active in its inquiries (it seizes upon its thoughts); passive in its reflective judgments (its thoughts are brought under standards of judgement); and alternately active and passive in apprehending the principles of reflective truth (active in seeking them, passive as reason itself becomes the object of its own scrutiny).

These powerful, if ambiguous, movements of reason account for the knowledge a subject has of its own awareness, and set the stage for self-knowledge in the fullest sense. For though a subject may, through the spiralling movements of its own reason, achieve awareness of the sensations, affections, and thoughts it has, this does not amount to thinking about itself. Far from being picayune, this distinction between what may be called roughly self-awareness and self-knowledge (between cognition and re-cognition) carries considerable weight with Augustine. In order for a subject to think about itself, it must direct its attention toward itself by means of reflection. Reflection, in the Augustinian lexicon, refers to a complex mental activity entailing abstraction. Only by deliberately abstracting elements of awareness that are foreign to itself can a subject come into knowledge of itself. As is doubtless evident, the ambiguities that have bedeviled rational activity all along surface again here: if reason is to remove from thought all elements that are foreign to it, it must already know itself.

But this is just the point that Augustine wants us to grasp. Deliberation of this order is an act of will, in which desire, guided by memory, turns inward, abstracts sensational elements, and discovers what has been there all along—the form of memory. There is a certain errancy here for which Augustine has steadily prepared us in his tour of reason's configurations.

The introspective act does not grasp itself, but instead, what it takes to be itself: a thought of what the reflecting subject is. Hence introspection always misses its mark. All the subject really discovers is its own thoughts which bear the imprint of the form of the mind, not the form itself. It is in the light of the subject's general discovery, it seems to me, that we can advance the conclusion that memory is an enabling capacity of thought—not thought itself—which we apprehend in relation to particular thoughts. So while no thought can grasp memory in its entirety, the subject can glean knowledge from it fragmentary character.

This sensitivity to the incompleteness of thought, to the potentially deceptive turns of reason, and to the apprehensive flight of the subject from its own truth, is familiar to any reader of Augustine. It presses against our common-sense understanding of memory as a storehouse the mind builds for the gathering and holding of thoughts. It disturbs our belief that a subject develops its own memory. Contrary to our Cartesian cast of mind,

Augustine maintains that thinking does not give rise to existing. We can no more think memory into being than we can create ourselves. All measures that aim at self-knowledge falter, if they do not include the subject's cognizance of the fact that memory, and hence the basic life of the mind, is given to it. Expressed theologically, this amounts to saying that the subject only comes into knowledge of itself—in the wider sense—when it becomes cognizant of itself as created, as creature.

We must not, however, pass too quickly to a sense that in this intellectual apprehension, the subject may rest confident in its self-knowledge. Even here, Augustine discerns ways in which introspection may miss its mark. Simply being cognizant of the basic features of mental life does not render a subject knowledgeable to itself. For the subject, even though self-cognizant, is not thereby appreciative of itself: there is a vast gulf between being enlightened and acknowledging the light by which a subject knows. Such appreciation, thankfulness, or acknowledgement is not so much noetic as it is affective, yet it is only by virtue of this affection that cognition is completed. The subject re-sees or re-cognizes what it has already seen or cognized, but now differently from before, owing to the light of acknowledgment. At such a moment as this, the subject can still skirt the truth by withdrawing affection, even while simultaneously adopting the posture of self-knowledge: as the later Augustinian thinker, Kierkegaard, never tired of repeating, the pretense of self-knowledge is the perfect guise behind which a subject may hide—even from itself—its flight from itself.[11]

Critical interpretations of Augustine have been virtually unanimous in their acclaim for his perspicuity in the delineation of the subject's withdrawal of its affections from the truth. "Pride," Augustine writes elsewhere, "is the beginning of all sin; and the beginning of man's sin is a falling away from God."[12] Desiring the work of its own hand rather than that of the hand of God, the subject becomes absorbed in the delight of creaturely affections. So completely are the capacities of desire and affection intertwined that many have surmised that pride is the equivalent of self-love. Not only does this vilify self-love (as subsequent Christian thought and practice has borne out), it also weakly misreads the point. The intensity of the subject's attachment to creaturely affection arises in direct proportion to the absence of love that it feels for itself: "Yet though, in your sight, I despise myself and consider myself as mere dust and ashes . . . I do no know which temptations I can resist and which I cannot."[13]

To restore the capacity of the subject to love itself, a new, untainted love must present itself to the subject in the form of the creaturely. This, of course, is the doctrine of the Incarnation, the teaching of the eternal become temporal, the conviction that the universal unfolds itself without corruption in the particular. To Augustine, the incarnate one is the divine visitor who emancipates the subject's love from its bondage to despair by loving as a servant.

Warmed by this love, the subject may acknowledge the Word in the form of the servant: "Our milk is Christ in his humility; our meat, the self-same Christ equal with the Father."[14] Let us be clear: such love does not ameliorate the inescapable errancy of desire that seizes upon immediacy everywhere, not only in creation, but also in itself. Love of this magnitude does, however, open the prospect for the subject to see again in the mediacy of the creation, as well as in the mediacy of its own thoughts, the form of the eternal, the Creator, whom it has always known, but now assistance may recall, trust, and love. This awakened love of the subject by which it acknowledges the Creator through the mediator is faith.

What, we may now ask, is the relation of this conception of the subject to the symbol? And what is the significance of reciting the Symbol for the subject? The answer is two-fold, and we will discover it, in part, by summarizing thematically the foregoing remarks: the source of the being and unity of creation is at the same time the source of the being and unity of the mind of the subject. The subject who so directs its attention may discover through introspection the former principle of this being and unity. Having grasped this principle, the subject discovers its own nature only because it is in relation to the Author of its own being; the subject knows itself as created. Yet to acknowledge this relation, the subject must have its errant love redirected by the example of creator love manifest in the mediator, Jesus Christ, and continually renewed by the Holy Spirit.

In light of this summary, it becomes quickly evident that the Symbol's affirmations of God as "maker of heaven and earth, of all that is seen and unseen, of Christ as the mediator who "for us and for our salvation . . . came down from heaven," and of the Holy Spirit as "the giver of life," dovetail the structural features of the subject. So we may say first that the relation between subject and Symbol is one of conceptual recapitulation of a subject's knowledge of itself, its faith, and its place in the created order. In order words, the Symbol is the subject's profession in words of what it holds in its heart—even if at times its heart is faint. For the Symbol, above all else, sets forth in brief compass the work of the Creator, the Mediator, and the Holy Spirit, and excites the subject to love what it apprehends.

Second, the Symbol, insofar as it is a distinctive language, partakes of the power of language that defines, to various degrees, social arrangements from public body to social class. Augustine knew well this formative power: "When I learned language," he reports in the *Confessions*, "I entered into the stormy sea of society."[15] The labors of language not only birth rhetorics and shape new perspectives, but also marshall disciplines that secure the hard-won advances of language. Hence, language bedazzles, inciting inspiration, just as it belittles, enforcing conformity. Precisely because language is practice, it does not so much explain as arrange. And Symbol, as a configuration of language, is, as much as anything else, an arrangement.

In concentrating on the character of Symbol as arrangement, we can get at certain important qualities we might otherwise overlook. When Augustine sets out his view of Symbol as "faith . . . expressed in a few words . . . made known to . . . beginners and sucklings . . . that they may subject themselves to God,"[16] we can see more than mere credalism. Still more, we can divine something beyond Symbol as the product of sustained reflection, which recapitulates the (social) structure of the subject, its faith, and its relation to God. We now too can discern in Symbol a social presence that is itself a *producer* of social relations, capable both of aligning and altering the forces that brought its own production into being. This does not, as Augustine lamented, ameliorate the prospect that there will be those who ". . . under the color of the few words drawn up in the Symbol . . . will endeavor to conceal their poison."[17] History's nightmares of Christian domination attest to this, but do not obviate the equally compelling prospect that Symbol is a force for decency; this is the significance of the latter part of the Symbol, which affirms baptism for the forgiveness of sins; the historical character of the church as a medium of revelation and as an instrument to the fulfillment of knowledge; and the life of the world to come (of which the temporal recalling of the heart to the Eternal is a token).

The two-fold answer to our question about the relation of the subject to the Symbol deserves special emphasis. For Symbol is evidently a window to the soul of the classical subject, through which its gaze may fix not only upon itself, but also upon the ultimate ordering of the creation. What the subject apprehends, first, is the extent to which it is ruptured from itself and from the creation; and, second, how, though ruptured, both subject and creation seek connection. In light of this, we must note that Symbol is a strategic part of the events of a subject's self-knowing: Symbol is part of the subject, owing to its indispensability to self-knowing and believing, and the subject is part of the Symbol, owing to the subject's presence in the field of force that Symbol is.

One notable effect of this intertwining is that Symbol both is the subject and accords a sense of place to it. This explains, I think, a very odd quality of Augustine's writings on the Symbol, namely their mysterious passage from a kind a tedious pedantry to sonorous poetry. The laborious exposition of Symbol gives knowledgeable voice to the place Augustine had found and come to serve in his adult life; the poetic flights are Augustine's appreciative voice for the forming and transforming qualities of that place. Though we may note the differences between them, in Symbol these voices of faith are no longer opposed.

The Modern "Subject" and Symbol: A Detour From the Detour

If Symbol is a variable register of belief practices that introduces the possibility of connecting what is fragmented, or of intimating overflows of meaning that, despite our exhausted powers of rationality, exceed analysis and lend cohesiveness to life, how are we to speak of this in the modern context? The dizzying force of this question breaks in upon us as soon as we recognize that the method we have used to elucidate the central features of the classical subject and its relation to Symbol falters irretrievably with respect to the modern subject. For while it has been possible to draw predominantly upon a single theo-philosophical discourse to delineate the plight of the classical subject, the position of the modern subject obliges us to pursue a multi-discursive approach. Owing to the large scale transformations of social life that accompanied the emergence of the modern subject, only diverse ways of thinking and speaking accurately situate the dynamics of the modern subject. Among these constitutive discourses are the abstract and theoretical; others stress socially constituted interest. All of them elaborate aspects of human limitation. Yet none of these discourses grasps their own incompleteness. Hence, because no one discourse can legitimately claim predominance over any other, it remains more difficult for us to ascertain the precise sense of rupture Symbol addresses in the modern subject.

Comparing discourses with differing forms of rationality will help clarify what I mean by the "incompleteness" and intimate some of their debilitating interpretive consequences for our thinking about Symbol. The particular form of reason that is manifest in modern science shields the modern subject from its lost connection with (and its ensuing anxiety about) nature. By according certitude only to the principles of human rationality, modern science minimizes the modern subject's isolation. Rational discourses on ethics emphasize the will and the individuality of the modern subject; privileging the drive for autonomy and its concomitant utopian, speculative vision, these discourses reduce the constraints of society to the interests of a single class. If we take as our point of departure the heightened, critical awareness of "the transcendent" that rational religious discourses articulate we soon encounter the modern subjects ambivalence toward grace—or what is the same, to authority. What is beyond the ken of human reason is not authoritative for the modern subject; but the directives of its heart compel the modern subject to acknowledge dutifully the unknowability of grace as authoritative. In apparent opposition to the preceding discourses, we might take up the modern subject as it appears in the novel: here we encounter a revisionist trait of the subject that desires, through personal and psychological narratives, to re-establish an untainted and legitimate relationship with nature and to dissolve the complexities of society,

This disquieting incompleteness recurs in virtually every modern discourse, albeit in varying ways. The subject of which we speak when invoking modernity emerges at the points of convergence of these diverse, and often contradictory, ways of thinking and speaking. Far from embodying a homogeneous view, the modern subject is predisposed to widely differing ends. But even though the modern subject appears within a field of discourses who aims often conflict, it is nevertheless possible to form more than a muddled view of this subject, because the issues raised in one discourse recapitulate in others at different levels.[18]

One such uniting issue that surfaces in the discourse of physics, law, political theory, economics, ethics, metaphysics, the philosophy of religion and history is self-preservation. The figures who anchor these discourses are paradigmatic for modern thought: Newton, Grotius, Hobbes, Locke, Smith, Spinoza, Descartes, Rousseau, and Vico all ply the issue of self-preservation in differing ways. Yet despite these differences, the structural considerations of the notion of self-preservation are similar enough to help us sketch a coherent picture of the modern subject.[19] Such a sketch does not obviate the intractable differences among the discourses that define the modern subject, but serves instead to locate a point at which these differences conflict most sharply.

At its most elemental level, self-preservation assumes the following form: a force can act upon itself in a way that uniformly maintains its character. This idea is so familiar to us that we take it as self-evident and accord to it scant value.[20] Accordingly, we routinely overlook the radicality of this idea for Newton or Descartes, for Hobbes or Rousseau, or for numerous other thinkers in the early modern period. For them, the idea of self-preservation exhibited certain structural components that facilitated thinking in new ways about the terrestrial and celestial spheres. The idea was particularly useful in helping them to articulate their emerging sense of how individuals could relate not only to these spheres, but also to each other. The components they isolated were, first, a basic force or drive; second, a principle or code that governs for directs this drive; and third, a reflexive awareness that can thematize the components.

Before taking up some of the ways in which moderns mined the structural components of self-preservation to plot courses for a world-order, let us recall the historical context. Central events of British and European social history fueled and intensified the sense of urgency that pervades moderns' writings about self-preservation. The movements of the Continental Reformation, Henry VIII's break with Rome, and the contentious, separatist impulses of radical puritanism and Scottish Calvinism severely strained traditional religious sensibilities. Far-reaching shifts in political forms of association accompanied these strains. Evidences of this are far-flung, from Charles I's dissolution of Parliament and subsequent acknowledgement of the House of Commons, the revolt of the French nobles against Louis XIII and the ensuing peace initiatives of Cardinal Richelieu, to the Bohemian revolt against the emperor Ferdinand and the subsequent execution of leading rebels and expulsion of Protestant clergy. The wars between Sweden and Poland, Holland and Spain, England and Spain, the Huguenots and Louse XVI, and the Cavaliers and Roundheads in England eroded cultural values, despite attempts to create an inner focus of resistance. Deprived, consequently, of social and emotional security, great numbers of human beings feared that the fabric of society might soon tear apart. John Donne captured this sense of spiritual homelessness, alienation, and anomie in this poetic figuration:

'Tis all in pieces, all coherence gone;
All just supply and relation;
Prince, subject, father, son are things forgot.[21]

No lifting of a veil of childish illusion, this deep disquietude derives from the repressive uses of power and gives hints of the distinctively modern significance of "rupture." Grotius, Descartes, Spinoza, and Rousseau knew well the sting of ecclesial censure, just as they endured the lash of civil punishment; Hobbes suffered the hardships of political exile.

Inevitably, in turning from a catalogue of societal ruptures to a litany on self-preservation, our critical eye will be drawn to the stabilizing characteristics of this way of speaking. It appeals to an unaltering human inclination to belong to an easily identifiable group with a homogeneity of interests in the fundamental needs of food, shelter, security, and procreation. Yet, while there is much to commend this perspective, we had best not slight certain important features, which together form an intimate short-hand that qualifies its significance. Foremost among these features is a kind of *undoing of what has been done*, a quality of abjuration and detachment.[22] This feature has the effect not only of setting modern perspectives on self-preservation at a distance from what stands prior to them, but also of underscoring their presumed radical incommensurability with classical paradigms.

Consider, for example, Newton's formulation of the notion of self-preservation in the field of physics. Self-preservation, he tells us, is an impelling internal force that by itself maintains a body in its state of uniform motion. Beyond imputing to matter an innate force, Newton separated matter from space. The innate force of matter alone now accounted for movements of a body's position. No longer requiring recourse to an External Mover to explain changes in a body's position, Newton's novel theorem upended classical Aristotelian physics. The idea that a reciprocal relation between force and acceleration, between a drive and a principle that governs it, could be self-sufficient (inasmuch as force is both cause and consequence of acceleration) unhooked physical theory from its moorings in Aristotelian thought.

It was much the same for the other modern discourses that capitalized upon the notion of self-preservation. As a reflexive notion, implying the action of a force upon itself, self-preservation captured both the psychological and social ramifications of turning away from external authorities, whether ecclesial of civil, and seeking refuge within an inner sanctuary. In his writings on international jurisprudence, Grotius asserted the liberty of individuals to enter into contracts of their own choosing, in light of their consciousness of what is right. But when he tied that knowledgeable liberty to an individuals awareness for its own self-preservation, Grotius found a way both to affirm Protestant individualism and to sever effectively the Calvinist link between pre-ordained goals and virtuous self-expression. When Thomas Hobbes developed his notion of the political commonwealth as the union of wills, he construed this corporate will as nothing more than an amplification of the authority of the individual self-preserving will. By linking the interests of individual self-preservation to those of the political commonwealth, Hobbes dissolved the feudal connection between divinely sanctioned sovereignty and stable political association.

Concurrent with the kind of undoing I have just noted is a second feature: a re-alignment of thought toward conceptual rather than intuitive certitude. In the domain of metaphysical thought, Descartes pressed the notion of self-preservation in a direction that departed radically from the inherited canons of ontological argumentation. In his *Meditations*, reason— not faith—moves immediately from the concept of an unconditioned power of self-preservation (God) to the apprehension of the reality of God (power) that is disclosed through that concept. Thereby, Descartes initiated modern epistemology's eclipse of metaphysics. Ethical reasoning, too, as it achieved its modern paradigmatic formulation at the hands of Spinoza, enjoined the power of conceptual clarity to alter the bewilderment of the affections. Evidently, the Cartesian linking of the immensity of divine power to the immediate perception of God in our thoughts captivated Spinoza. For him, this connection signalled the prospect that the good toward which we direct our ethical conduct derives not from some external goal, but from an internal impetus of self-preservation to express our thoughts fully. Accordingly, the more fully and clearly an individual fashions its concepts— an activity of reason, not faith—the more God-like its character becomes.

What is haunting about these projects of self-preservation is a third feature: the perpetual reflexivity they demand, and with this reflexivity, perpetual self-estrangement. Rousseau, espying this feature in the background of his contemporaries' intellectual endeavors, showcased it in his own. He was committed to the blunt proposition that there was a distinction between apparent interest and appropriate interest of the individual. Of course, to strike such a distinction is to raise the prospect of identities other than, and unfulfilled by, those an individual is enacting, or worse, that the identity an individual preserves masks its essential identity.

No argument could convince Rousseau that private and public interest coincide, or that moral laws derive from the individual pursuit of happiness. Still less could he accede to the notion that an individual might surrender for the greater good what is essential to itself, and simultaneously maintain that it was preserving itself, as Hobbes seemed to be suggesting. Instead, the subject must have at its core not only the powerful capacity to reject and to detach from what is foreign to it, but also the powerful and inchoate counterforce of consent or obedience to what is essential to it. Deriving from the directives of conscience, this obedience impels the individual to will its own good, just as it precludes self-annihilation. Still more, this obedience subverts the cleverness of self-interested reason, because it foregrounds liberty as essential to the subject.

But what is it about Rousseau's notion of liberty that distinguishes it from those extolled by Rousseau's contemporaries? And how is it so differently poised that this notion of liberty escapes the very self-estranging prospects of self-preservation Rousseau denounced?

Rousseau's bedrock conviction that culture corrupts reason marks the avenue along which we may find answers to these questions. What culture teaches us, remarks Rousseau, is ". . . only to see men such as they have made themselves."[23] Rousseau instructs us to ". . . throw aside, therefore, all those scientific books . . . and contemplate the first and most simple operations of the human soul."[24] The tainted mediating power of reason, whether though cultural artifacts, political institutions, or even the church, becomes for Rousseau the very emblem of what is miserable and enslaving about society. The liberty of which he speaks is poised in the vast terrain of interiority, a terrain that all romanticism subsequent to Rousseau would continue to explore, precisely because it is independent from the estrangement of the outside world. Antecedent to reason, and therefore not susceptible to its poisoning, the liberty that issues forth from this domain pertains to the whole ordering life—not just to the selfish interests of the individual. To desire spontaneously one's own well-being is the hall-mark of all self-preservation; to discover this spontaneous announcement of desire for well-being is simultaneously the disclosure of universal life-ordering is liberating. For inasmuch as this principle of well-being regulates self-preserving conduct, it overcomes estrangement from what is essential to life, and this means that the good to which the directives of the heart commend us—to honor what protects a being and to love what seeks its good—is not an illusory end, but the real ordering of life (God or Freedom) in which we already participate. The expression of liberty can only enhance the individual's relation to the ordering of life.

If the immense difference in attitude toward conceptual reason that separates Rousseau from his contemporaries is veiled by his biting polemics, we can get at it more clearly by restating his insight from the perspective of one of his most ardent admirers: Kant. In his view, the configuration of reason that Rousseau criticizes is one that routinely oversteps its bounds. Rational concepts are nothing more than empty forms whose function is to organize thinking. The sensible content of our thoughts derives, to be sure, from nature, but it is always arranged by our concepts. The most that we can say of rational concepts without content is that they may serve our interests by enhancing the arrangement of our thought. Hence rational concepts may purport to represent totalities, but as mere forms, they are no more than parts imitating a whole: merely rational concepts are metonymic.

To be suspect of reasoning based upon concepts alone, especially when it presumes to lay bare our essential nature, is a justifiably laudable outcome of Rousseau's investigations.

With respect to Rousseau's case concerning the compelling directives of the heart, the Kantian perspective is more circumspect, finding Rousseau's argument far from clear. It is indubitable that we know ourselves as free by way of the directives of conscience, but it is contradictory to hold that we can reason directly about a liberty that is antecedent to reason without tainting it with the very interests of reason that Rousseau so roundly condemned. If such liberty derives from a domain of interiority, as Rousseau contends, but its effects are known in the external world, we can do no more than think of liberty metaphorically, and denote such metaphoric thinking as practical reason or faith. Self-preservation of what is essential to us is the maintenance in the social world of the force of such faith.

Aided by this Kantian gloss on Rousseau's conception of self-preservation, we may now note that in addition to the features of detachment, of realignment toward conceptual certitude, and of perpetual reflexivity and self-estrangement, modern discourses on self-preservation exhibit still a fourth feature: conceptual redefinition and transformation. Reason sundered from divine principles, from an external prime mover, or from heteronomously defined goals for existence, becomes increasingly circumspect and its concepts metonymous. Faith, denied access to the corridors of intuition, feeling and trust, becomes a foot-soldier to reason's principles (as Coleridge would soon note), commanded to express metaphorically what lies beyond the ken of reason.[25]

By now the number of entrées and accompanying qualifying descriptions on the modern menu of self-preservation may seem overwhelming—and this has been just a sampling. Like Cervantes' unfortunate misfit, companion, and alter-ego, Sancho Panza (who, thinking himself the governor of an island, and preparing to feast upon an array of dishes, finds his food repeatedly removed with the accompanying self-preserving admonition from the attending physician that he is to to eat only what is good for him, and be deprived of that which may do harm or injury), we may wonder if we shall ever find anything into which we may safely sink our teeth.

Should this be the effect of our labors to this point, our efforts have not been in vain. For it is precisely this frustration, this sense of unbridgeable chasms between discourses, and this foreshowing of the insolubility of modern life's riddles that recur to the plight of the modern subject. The peculiar features of modern discourses on self-preservation that we have been noting—detachment, realignment to conceptual certitude, perpetual reflexivity and self-estrangement, and conceptual redefinition—together form a short-hand that calls attention to its own frustrating processes that animate the subject.

The import of this short-hand of frustration deepens when we recall that the modern subject is a literary conceit—a figure of speech—that emerges out of the play of modern discursive practices.[26] The "subject" plays the role of the individual that it is not. Indeed, the conceit of the "subject" depends upon the reality of the individual and can be elaborated only upon the presumption that the powers of the individual accrue to the "subject." But while axiomatic, this presumption is nonetheless chimerical: a literary conceit can never be an individual expressing real power. Hence,t he frustration with which we are dealing cannot be imputed to some internal failing or transgression on the part of the individual that can be ameliorated through some corrective, whether human or divine. Rather, the frustration is coeval with and a defining feature of the dynamism of self-preservation that configures the "subject": apart from the inner antagonism between a basic force and a principle that limits or codifes it, no motion ensures. If it does not so much precipitate an evident disturbance in the everyday workings of the world, this frustration (which funds modern spheres of meaning and delineates the ordering within which various terms acquire their significance) erupts forcefully in the fictional figure of the "subject."[27]

Here we can point briefly to one site of this rupture. The modern "subject" is figured as a force that acts upon itself. Modern discourses inpute to this figure the capacity to grasp its own activity in reflective awareness, to thematize its components, and to authorize the maintenance of its life-conduct under the terms it has encountered within itself. Depicted as being in retreat from a hostile world that imperils it, the "subject" is said to discover that its interiority provides not merely sanctuary, but also resources for detaching from dictates pre-established by the so-called natural order. Yet the more success the "subject" enjoys in breaking away from the external world, the more this "subject" must draw even more deeply upon its own reflexive force to fund its endeavors. In casting about for ways to amplify its powers of self-stabilization, the "subject" looks increasingly to conceptual certitude as its anchor, while discounting intuition. Hence, the "subject" is portrayed as becoming more imaginatively absorbed in the claims of reason. But if through its thematic development of drives and codes into rational life forms, the "subject" seizes upon conceptual clarity to heighten its powers of self-preservation, so also does this very conceptual clarity turn back upon the "subject." What this exposes in the "subject" is its emptiness, its deceits, its self-estrangement, and its frustrated longing. And by the strength of this character of reasoning that has been inscribed in the "subject," an even greater frustration erupts: on the one hand, the "subject" (so characterized) discovers that the limitations of reason preclude it from the exploration of the deepest reaches of interiority; on the other hand, the "subject" (accordingly) cannot speak of this interiority that is essential to it apart from the rules of reason.

Circumscribed by these restrictions of reason, the "subject" betrays its chimerical cover, insofar as it is bound to speak hypothetically and metaphorically of the interior independence it claims as the touchstone of its identity and the ultimate identity of all life ordering. Hence the predicament of the fictive figure of the modern "subject" is a re-enactment of the bafflements of its reason: what it holds dearest is simultaneously that toward which it is most suspectly poised. So the modern "subject" is the locus/focus of a *foundational irony*: the life of liberty that the modern "subject" proclaims and craves inevitably and perpetually recedes into the distance of a timeless future. In the absence of cognitive access to this universal ordering of life, the "subject"—despite all the efforts ascribed to it—must acknowledge, in the end, that it has no more than an tenuous and increasingly disenchanted relation to such life-ordering and so to itself.

But if the modern "subject" cannot reach the paradise of freedom as its numerous authors ruefully conceded, the rich narratives that describe its purported strivings remain instructive. Redounding, as they do, with claims that are illusory, these discourses successfully disclose that the force of a *claim* about reality often has greater gravity than reality itself. For such claims introduce through *saying* what ratiocination cannot *do*: secure a measure of cohesiveness. And even if such claims are no more than what Paul de Man has called "linguistic complications," they do, nonetheless, animate structures of thought that defer, if not repress, the estrangements that continually threaten to surface in relation to the "subject's" belief.

Such cohesive "saying" that defers estrangement defines the relation of this figure of the modern subject to Symbol. Symbol is for the modern subject a language practice that enjoins freedom and opposes idolatry in any form. Hence, Symbol does not seek to establish hegemony for a single discourse and its social arrangements, but fosters diversity of expression and of social arrangements under a larger unifying theme. In this way, Symbol is a societal looking-glass, mirroring the qualifications that mark the (multi-discursive) identity of the figure of the modern subject—its detachment, its reflexivity, its reliance upon conceptual certainty, and its cognitive limitations.

What is compelling about modern Symbol is that it represents as alien (and therefore as capable provoking wonder) the ambivalence and disenchantment of the modern subject's faith—thereby defining the self-estrangement that threatens the subject's belief. For Symbol, while underscoring the vast gulf separating the immensity of the Godhead from the situations of the modern subject, now intimates that containment and ambivalence are marks of the *divine* identity.

All this is expressed the the Symbol of modern faith: the Westminster Confession.[29] Completed in 1646, a full century after the Reformation was established on the Continent, the Confession was the outcome of the Assembly that met in Westminster Abbey during the Puritan Revolution. Reflecting numerous theological traditions—including British Augustinianism, Puritan Covenant theology, Rhineland Reformed theology, and Calvinism—the Confession represented an effort to establish a new church order in England. These hopes faded in direct proportion to the successes Cromwell's "New Model" army enjoyed in 1646; only minimal parliamentary approval of the Confession was issued in 1648. Nevertheless, Presbyterians in Scotland and England adopted the Confession, as did Congregationalists in England and New England, and the Confession became the basis for Baptist creeds (1833, 1859, 1925), the London Confessions (1677, 1688, and the Philadelphia Confession (1742). We may trace the widespread influence of the Confession, in part, to its opposition to the hierarchical polity of William Laud, Charles I's Archbishop of Canterbury, and to Charles I's own volatile and arbitrary voice in matters of taxation and parliamentary procedure. In evident counterpoint, the Confession foregrounds, as no other creed does, the role of Holy Writ and places it in a new light, overshadowing voice. And in tacit re-enforcement of this, the form of the confession, extending over some thirty-eight chapters, virtually precludes recitation.

No longer does Scripture signal an eternal book that is never closed, a scroll that is never furled, as it did for Augustine. Now Scripture is the sole channel of God revelation, and, containing the whole counsel of God, displaces all other revelation—" . . . those former ways of God revealing his will unto his people being now ceased."[30] Indeed, nothing external, whether human traditions or revelations of the Holy Spirit, has any bearing upon the interpretation of Scripture. Even apocryphal literature is specifically excluded. So detached, Scripture itself becomes the grounds for its own interpretation. Consistent with this, and in obvious repudiation of the newly wide-spread availability of biblical translations, only the Hebrew and Greek Testaments, which God is said to have written, are deemed authoritative. This move, identifying the Word of God solely with Scripture, from which all else—God's eternal decree, providence, effectual calling, justification, sanctification, repentance unto life, and the like—follows, subtly infuses the modern temperament. It condenses the vast syntax of the divine ordering of life into the grammar of the Book. Self-contained and self-authorizing, then, the Book is saturated with presence—and absence. The work of God is now held to be fully contained in the written work, which not only privileges writing over speech, but also alters the mode of God's agency from performer of speech-acts to writer. The sense of this alterity is heightened by the claim of the Confession that the authoritative version of the Word is vested in a language foreign to most readers. But in claiming that Scripture is a finished work, and even greater transformation comes into play: the whole structure is represented as a stable system deriving is coherence from the Author's name. By this transformation, the indefinite work of writing and expressing ends, and a definite system of understanding begins: the Writer disappears, and the Author appears.[31] Hence, the Confession makes Scripture everything and nothing, a present work and a past (absent) experience, as befits the names of the Writer/Author-God: the Holy Spirit is a mere echo of the Author's former writing—no immanent, inward, illumination here—that reverberates through sentences of Holy Writ.

Just as the modern subject, in its calculating absence of detachment and through its system of understanding, is rendered incapable of expressing what is essential to itself, so also the Writer-God, in its absence (i.e., its displacement by the Author-God and the concomitant system of understanding) following upon the closure of the book, no longer expresses what is essential to itself: writing. Policed psychically and socially by the Author's detached and disenchanted character, the modern subject can obey its God because it can acknowledge the link between this God's imputed bad faith and its own.

Thinking About Symbol After Modernity: Memory and Healing

As the course of our thinking has made clear, Symbol was once a window into the subject's soul and its attachment to God. But modernity restaged Symbol and cast it as a looking glass, reflecting the glib detachment of the subject and that of its absent God. Similarly, Symbol once accorded place (catholicity) to the subject, but then came to signal its (geopolitical) displacement. And whereas Symbol was once sealed by appreciation, modernity secured it with suspicion, if not with bad faith.

To pursue, now, our aim of framing a distinctive way of speaking about Symbol, we might construe the outcomes of our thinking linearly. We could suggest that the explications of Symbol we have explored merely reflect their progressive initiation into differing laws of society and social bodies of knowledge. But this way of proceeding would do little more than camouflage, under the Enlightenment aegis of progressive demystification, the fundamental characteristic of Symbol: its rupturing kind of elucidation.

So we may more nearly succeed in framing a distinctive way to speak of Symbol if we take as our point of departure the experience of a shattered aesthetic. For this is the point at which we re-encounter, insofar as Symbol retains its power, the brief history I have been recounting. It is a history common to us all, embedded in each of our person histories through the patronage of language, though a protective religio-cultural amnesia may have led us to forget it.

When one's sense of beauty shatters, not only a particular pattern of life, but also the collective experience that transcends it, and completes its meaning, break. The shattering of beauty, the fissure of the sense of right relation, precipitates changes in the register of belief-practices and elicits memories of forgotten separations. As Michel de Certeau remarks, "Discourse about the past has the status of being discourse about the dead. The object circulating in it is only the absent, while its meaning is . . . shared . . . by living beings."[32] What Symbol was is never fully absent from what Symbol is today; or better: how Symbol was understood is never wholly removed from how we think of it today. But through confrontation with death, with the unsaid, received understandings break apart and ways of seeing sunder. Our fragmented perceptions and stammering diction oblige us to begin and to continue to think about Symbol. Beginnings on this order of thinking presuppose a lost object.

Thinking about the lost succeeds in nothing more than gathering snippets from the giddying whirl of images that have been scattered about the surfaces of the present and reckoning them as traces of the past—the gone—in an apparent attempt to resuscitate the dead. We are perhaps more alert to this process in the workings of our everyday lives than we are to its role in our intellectual pursuits. Mallarme lifted up a telling example from the everyday when he observed that he was bound constantly to bear in mind the thought of his lost son, lest his son be deprived of eternity.[33] Cast, in just this way, the sentiment is evident enough; less clear is its re-cast version in historical recollection. Yet is has been at work in the course of our thinking in the following manner: when we earlier spoke of the way in which, for the classical subject, Symbol participates in that to which it points (a window to the soul), we tacitly recalled to life a subject for whom such experience is actual. Or again, in our just concluded reflections upon the modern subject and its encounter with Symbol as a limit to thought (a mirror of societal arrangements), we have stealthily repristinated a subject that has experiences of this character. These transformations repress the absent. They have been functioning in our thinking, first, to avert our gaze from the textual staging that occupies the place of the dead; and, second, to re-direct it to the search for the places of these experiences and the subjects that inhabit them. However seductive this insinuation of the (revived) subject into our thinking may be, and however much it may (surreptitiously) govern the courses of our thought, it cannot outwit death. Such thinking therefore inevitably founders, as do all the archaeologies of knowledge that accompany it.

From the futility of this endeavor, as Mallarme apparently learned, blazes forth its deeper obligation: thinking about the lost is to pass away endlessly. It is always thought that moves between repression (transformation) and the lacuna or rupture repression creates with respect to a tradition and its images. Inasmuch as what has been repressed is forgotten and its content irretrievably lost, thinking about this relation cannot be translated into referential language. What has become unthinkable at a given moment is therefore excluded in the interest of what (at the same moment) counts as intelligibility. Thereby, intelligibility itself becomes a tactic of repression: claiming to save the repressed from oblivion, it produces a new understanding of the forgotten, the knowledge of which it substitutes for—and therewith hides—the real absence of the repressed. For this reason, all thinking about the lost is fictional. Conveying a tradition and its betrayals, this fictional thinking invariably repeats the repressive practices it sets out to correct. But now in the absence of the repressed, the practices to which it ineluctably recurs are exercised upon itself. Displacing itself, this thinking ceaselessly passes away. Symbol today is the acknowledgement of the region of the lost, of a chasm, which neither Revelation nor Scripture can fill in to create a sure space—save in a repressive and forestalling manner. Symbol is therefore the scene of mourning.

As did Mallarme, I have found my thinking about symbol concretized by death's cowardly thievery. "Baptism," the Sunday rector said, "is a sacrament for the end of the world." As I crossed the church yard, the first-fallen leaves of summer's end, still soft with life, muffled my step, while his words rang in my head. By mid-week, baptismal arrangements were in hand; at week's-end, baptism was said at the place where our son lay dead.

O'er his silent crib, a banner heralds: "Christ's own forever." A garden's fleeting flowering inscribe the silent law of his entombment, a figuring of the loss, omitted in the Psalmist's words—"Like a child at its mother's breast, my soul is quieted"—that likewise mark this site. As the seasons have turned, and as the leaves that bind a mother's milk-fevered breast wilt in their appointed task, the inexorable course of deathful thought has through such images pressed this sense upon me: to pass away endlessly is the graceful mourning that Symbol acknowledges by invoking the zone of silence.

Symbol thus binds us to the truth that we annul through the very practice of language. The language of Symbol is a metaphor of what it hides, bringing the repressed religious elements back in the form of fictions that haunt our post-modern dwelling place. But the uncanny familiarity of these fictions, the unspoken in which we no longer live, may be a small fragment of the truth by which the register of Symbol binds us to the truth of the dead, despite the displacements of the living. As I daily tend the garden, I feel so strongly the fullness of the silence that it becomes free, eternal, and here everywhere at once. With the touch of the earth, everything connects again.[33]

NOTES

(Thanks are due to Profs. Robert Detweiler and Paul Courtright for decisive encouragement and critical appreciation in the preparation of this essay—DSP).

1. Michel de Certeau, *The Practice of Everyday Life*, trans. Steven Rendall (Berkeley: University of California Press, 1984), p. 103.

2. George Santayana, *Reason in Religion* (New York: Charles Scribner's Sons, 1905), p. 6.

3. Michael Baxandall, *Patterns of Intention* (New Haven: Yale University Press, 1985). p. 11.

4. Augustine, *Confessions*, trans. R. S. Pine-Coffin (Harmondsworth: Penguin, 1961) XII, 14. Hereafter cited as *Confessions*.

5. Augustine, *Confessions*, X, 6.

6. Augustine, *Confessions*, X, 6.

7. Augustine, *Confessions*, X, 6.

8. Augustine, *Confessions*, X, 6.

9. Augustine, *Confessions*, X, 6.

10. Augustine, *Confessions*, X, 6.

11. Søren Kierkegaard, *The Sickness Unto Death*, trans. Walter Lowrie (Princeton: Princeton University Press, 1946).

12. Augustine, *In Joannine Evangelum: Nicene and Post-Nicene Fathers*, ed. Phillip Schaff (New York, 1900) XXV, 15.

13. Augustine, *Confessions*, X, 5.

14. Augustine, *In Epistolorum Joannine*, III, 1.

15. Augustine, *Confessions*, I, 8.

16. Augustine, *De Fide et Symbolo*, trans. John H. S. Burleigh (Library of Christian Classics, Vol VI, Philadelphia: Westminster, 1953) I, 1.

17. Augustine, *De Fide et Symbolo*, I, 1.

18. The course of my argument diverges significantly from that of Habermas, *The Philosophical Discourse of Modernity*, trans. Federick Lawrence (Cambridge: MIT Press, 1987) and of Blumenberg, *The Legitimacy of the Modern Age*, trans. Robert M. Wallace (Cambridge: MIT Press, 1985). Both seek to interpret modernity in terms of a single rational discourse or the normative dimension of rationality. Cascardi's *The Subject of Modernity* (Cambridge: Cambridge University Press, 1992) exploits the diversity of discourses that are formative of the modern subject, but fails to pursue the structures of these discourses far enough to discern the various levels at which themes sounded in one discourse, repete at different levels in others. Nonetheless, I have learned much from, and am indebted to, Cascardi's arguments and insights.

19. Here I will pursue a line of argument that Dilthey proposed in his essay, "Weltanschauung and Analyse des Menschen seit Renaissance und Reformation," *Gesammelte Schriften*, Vol. 2 (Leipzig: Teubner, 1914), p. 315. Dieter Henrich took up this line of argument again in three essays: "Die Grundstruktur der modernen Philosophie," "Uber Selbstbewusstein und Selbsterhaltung," and "Selbsterhaltung und Geschichtickheit," all in *Subjektivitat und Selbsterhaltung: Beitrage zur Diagnose der Modern* ed. H. Ebeling (Frankfurt am Main: Suhrkamp Verlag, 1976). My own study, *The Cunning of Modern Religious Thought* (Philadelphia: Fortress Press, 1987) has continued this trajectory of thought into the religious dimension. The argument I develop here differs from those I have previously held. What has become clear to me is the extent to which the discourses in which we participate commit us to a *symbolic ordering*, through which a *repressed* religious outlook shines.

20. This observation brings to mind Harold Bloom's instructive notion of "facticity"—a contingency that achieves such predominace that its novelty and distinctiveness are lost from view. For further discussion refer to Bloom, *Ruin the Sacred Truths* (Cambridge: Harvard University Press, 1989).

21. John Donne, "An Anatomy of the World," in *The Poems of John Donne*, ed. H. J. C. Grierson (Oxford: Oxford University Press, 1929). The context of this poem was the "untimely death" of a fifteen-year-old girl, whom Donne did not know, but these lines express a sentiment that pervades much of his metaphysical speculation about the tenor of his age, and is therefore, I think, aptly cited at this juncture of my essay.

22. Here I am following a concept of Freud, "ungeschehenmachen," from his 1926 essay, "Inhibitions, Symptom and Anxiety," as it pertains (and I think rightly) to the religious context. Sir Isaiah Berlin plumbed this notion in his interpretation of the "inward turn" in Western thought. Reissued in: *Against the Current: Essays in the History of Ideas*, ed. Henry Hardy (New York: Viking Press, 1980]. More recently, Stephen Greenblatt has exploited Freud's notion in his study, *Renaissance Self-fashioning: From More to Shakespeare* (Chicago: Chicago University Press, 1980).

23. Rousseau, *Discourse on the Origin of Inequality*, trans. G.D.H. Cole (London: J.M. Dent & Sons, 1973), p. 41.

24. Rousseau, *Discourse on the Origin of Inequality*, p. 41.

25. See: S.T. Coleridge, *Biographia Literaria*, ed. Shawcross (Oxford: Oxford University Press, 1950), XIII. Schleiermacher's emphasis on feeling as the locus of human religion might at first blush appear to run contrary to the Kantian limits upon rationality. But a closer reading of Schleiermacher reveals that he remains bound to Kant's strictures: we can never speak of the feeling of absolute dependence of the "Whence" in its own terms. but only as it affects empirical consciousness. See: *The Christian Faith*, (Edinburgh: T&T Clark, 1928), "Introduction," H.R. McIntosh and J.S. Stewart.

26. For important epistemological reasons, it is not appropriate to make the same claim about the classical subject. The classical subject has a sense of itself antecedent to language, owing largely to its ontological and epistemological connection with God. The modern subject has neither ontological nor epistemological links with the divine, and literally must "write itself," in order to bring a concept to bear upon experience that the subject would claim as its own.

27. For further discussion of the notion of "symbolic ordering," see especially, Julia Kristeva, *Desire and Language*, trans. Léon S. Roudiez (New York: Columbia University Press, 1983).

28. Paul de Man, "The Task of the Translator," in *The Resistance to Theory* (Manchester: Manchester University Press, 1986), p. 91.

29. "The Westminster Confession of Faith," in *Creeds of the Churches*, ed. John H. Leith (Atlanta: John Knox Press, 1963), pp. 193-230. For a more extended discussion of the Westminster Confession, I refer the reader to my essay, "Reading Holy Writ: The Locus of Modern Spirituality," in *Christian Spirituality*, Vol. III, eds. Louis Dupre and Don E. Saliers (New York: Cross Road, 1989), pp. 174-210.

30. "The Westminster Confession of Faith," I, 1.

31. For further discussion of the distinction between "writer" and "author," I refer the reader to an essay that has influenced me greatly: Roland Barthes, "Authors and Writers," in *Critical Essays* (Chicago: Northwestern University Press, 1972).

32. Michel de Certeau, *The Writing of History*, trans. Tom Conley (New York: Columbia University Press, 1988), p. 46.

33. What is now connected is *not a retrieval of origins*, but a subtraction. I am connected to a silence, an elipsis, which because full, cannot be regarded as static tradition, but instead as dynamic, incorporating all that stasis would marginalize. Hence I am bound by an *obligation of transference*, mobilized by energies of the silenced, to become a debtor

to the foreign place that "static tradition" refuses to claim: I am called to the interminable political labor of speaking in the name of the site of the excluded.

Narratives In Archaeology

BETTINA DETWEILER-BLAKELY

AND ROBERT L. BLAKELY

M any different approaches for interpreting archaeological data are emerging out of current debates on what constitutes archaeology. Fundamental questions that were asked in the past are being asked again. Is archaeology a natural science or a social science? To what extent can archaeological data be interpreted objectively, if at all? Most of the approaches within archaeology today can be characterized by philosophical underpinnings that put them into what is called either the processual or the postprocessual school of thought. Processualists tend to view archaeology as a positivistic, natural science, whereas postprocessualists view archaeology as a social science, with an emphasis on interpretation rather than on explanation of data. The narrative approach to interpreting archaeological data shares many postprocessual qualities. In this essay, following an adumbrative description of processual and postprocessual archaeology, we discuss some of the theoretical issues surrounding narrative interpretation in archaeology. We then offer suggestions for using the narrative approach to tell part of the macabre story behind the recent discovery of human skeletal remains in the basement of a nineteenth-century building on the grounds of the Medical College of Georgia in Augusta.

Processual and Postprocessual Archaeology

The answer to the question "What is archaeology?" has changed over time, and continues to change today. The changes reflect evolving philosophical positions in response to epistemological issues within the discipline. The processual archaeologists, for example, adopt the logical positivistic stance popularized by Lewis Binford in the 1960s in opposition to the traditional cultural idealism of the 1930s and 1940s (Muller 1991;

Preucel 1991a). The logical positivistic approach uses the scientific method for interpreting data, and involves developing hypotheses, analyzing data, testing hypotheses, and creating universal theories (Preucel 1991b).

Just as Binford is identified with logical positivism of processual archaeology, so Ian Hodder is identified with what is termed the contextual or interpretive archaeology of the postprocessualists. A major component of Hodder's interpretive archaeology is a hermeneutic methodology designed to attain an understanding of unobservable events—i.e., interpreting the past in the absence of direct observation (Johnsen and Olsen 1992; Preucel 1991b). Hodder (1991a) claims that, "On the whole, postprocessual archaeology...concern[s] power, negotiation, text, intertext, structure, ideology, agency and so on" (p. 8).

It is not surprising that processual and postprocessual archaeologists disagree on many philosophical issues, and are often so critical of the other's position that they create an illusion of diametrical opposition. Watson describes the dispute as a polarization between "...science versus history, ...explanation versus understanding, knowledge versus meaning, objectivity versus subjectivity..." (p. 269). And Preucel (1991a) points out the relativistic versus deterministic positions of the processualists and the postprocessualists, respectively. The dichotomy can be summarized by Watson's (1991) metaphoric description of "Binford [as the] personification of soulless method and Hodder of [the] methodless soul" (p. 270).

Often lost in the debate is the fact that variability in archaeological interpretation is so great that it does not fit comfortably into two schools of thought. Moreover, sometimes there is little in common among advocates of a particular school of thought. Hodder (1991b) contends that the differences between approaches of the postprocessualists are greater than the differences between the processualists and postprocessualists. He also points out that some processual archaeologists have adopted aspects of postprocessual archaeology and vice versa.

Within the diversity of archaeological approaches there is some agreement. Most, if not all, processual *and* postprocessual archaeologists contributing to Preucel's volume, *Processual and Postprocessual Archaeologies: Multiple Ways of Knowing the Past* (1991a), agree that archaeological data are the central focus around which competing interpretations revolve. This empirical view helps combat the pitfalls of relativism. Another possible area of agreement is suggested by processual and postprocessual archaeologists' deterministic bent, which is revealed through their methodologies that focus on finding patterns in the natural world (Watson 1991). And, increasingly, both sides are listening to each other. Hodder (1991b) believes that the issues raised by the postprocessualists are creating a healthy and necessary dialogue in the discipline.

Narratives

Narratives have long been used as a tool in many disciplines, and currently are finding a new niche in postprocessual archaeology. Polkinghorne, in a book entitled *Narrative Knowing and the Human Sciences* (1988), shows how and why narrative interpretation can contribute to knowledge in the social sciences. Narrative, as we use it in this essay, is defined by Polkinghorne (1988) as

> a scheme by means of which human beings give meaning to their experience of temporality and personal actions. Narrative meaning functions to give form to the understanding of a purpose to life and to join everyday actions and events into episodic units. It provides a framework for understanding the past events of one's life and planning future actions. It is the primary scheme by means of which human existence is rendered meaningful. Thus, the study of human beings by the human sciences needs to focus on the realm of meaning in general, and on narrative meaning in particular (p. 11).

We now turn to the qualities of narratives that are useful in social science research in general and in archaeological research in particular. All narratives have plots, and just as plots organize events into a central theme that develops a story, hermeneutics and dialectical reasoning guide and characterize human thoughts by fitting specific events into larger contexts. Because meaning—outside the logical positivistic model—cannot be verified or falsified, meaning for the same data set is often multiple. A different plot arrangement also changes a story.

According to Polkinghorne (1988), a plot organizes what would otherwise be just a chronological listing of disparate events into a meaningful story by relating the significance of events to each other and to the unfolding story. Polkinghorne (1988) also points out that "narrative is always controlled by the concept of time and by recognition that temporality is the primary dimension of human existence" (p. 20). Thus, the chronological order of events is important. It is through plots thus constructed that facts become understood (Gero 1991; Veyne 1971). Gero (1991) cites Veyne's notion that

> facts become intelligible by being endowed, by the (pre)historian, with a plot, a plot that is logical and compelling and that stays close to facts by always addressing the relations of events and facts to other events or facts. ...Thus, to

'explain more' is to narrate better (Veyne 1971: 93), associating more facts in a more compelling plot (p. 127).

In order to find a 'best fit' between events and facts that successfully explain a story, a process of dialectical reasoning locates the connections among and resistance between events (Polkinghorne 1988). Ian Hodder (1991a) cites a personal anecdote that illustrates the process of dialectic reasoning that is a major component of his brand of interpretive archaeology. When Hodder, who is British, thought he heard on American radio that "it was necessary to indoor suffering," it made little sense until he placed this phrase into the larger context of the radio program, which was about suffering in general, and applied that to what Hodder knew about North American culture. Only then did he realize that the word 'endure' had been pronounced to sound like 'indoor.' This process of fitting parts into a whole is an essential ingredient of hermeneutic interpretation and for creating narratives. Hodder (1991) says:

> We evaluate many arguments not so much by testing universal, general knowledge against data using universal, independent instruments of measurement but by interpreting general understanding or foreknowledge in relation to our understanding of particular contexts. We place the thing to be understood (in this case the sound 'indoor') more and more fully into its context, moving back and forth between 'their' and 'our' context until coherence is achieved... The emphasis is on part-whole relations. We try to fit the pieces into an interpretive whole at the same time as constructing the whole out of the pieces. We measure our success in this enmeshing of theory and data (our context and their context) in terms of how much of the data is accounted for by our hypothesis in comparison to other hypotheses (p. 8).

Even though little mention of language is made in this essay, as anthropologists we recognize the importance of language in organizing human thought. Polkinghorne (1988) contends that language plays a critical role in understanding meaning; that, "for human existence, linguistic forms are paramount, for they filter and organize information from the physical and cultural realms and transform it into the meanings that make up human knowledge and experience" (p. 158). He goes on to say that "human experience is hermeneutically organized according to the figures of linguistic production" (p. 159). Veyne (1971) takes the nominalist approach to narrative interpretation, which recognizes that language is used as a vehicle to label facts and events into categories upon which generalizations and theories are built. Discourse then revolves around the terminology (or jargon) of the discipline (Gero 1991).

Narrative interpretation accepts multiple explanations for the same set of events. Thus, Polkinghorne (1988) observes that "More than one plot can provide a meaningful constellation and integration for the same set of events, and different plot organizations change the meaning of the individual events as their roles are reinterpreted according to their functions in different plots" (p. 19). (Polkinghorne categorizes people's perception of reality into the material realm, the organic realm, and the meaning realm, which is the realm containing narrative meaning—a division we question because of its ethnocentric bias.) Similarly, Gero (1991) notes that "...we can take the same prehistoric facts carefully extracted from the archaeological record and, without ignoring any part of what we find or enhancing the associations between objects we recover, fit them to different forms of explanations" (p. 126). Veyne (1971) emphasizes that, since multiple explanations are possible, a narrative explanation is only a partial one. Hodder (1991a) asks rhetorically: "What is the boundary between an open multivocality where any interpretation is as good as another and legitimate dialogue between 'scientific' and American Indian, black, feminist, etc. interest?" (p. 9). Hodder's (1991a) own answer is that a hermeneutic interpretation must be made because

> The notion that truth and knowledge are contingent and multiple undermines the claims of subordinate groups. It disempowers them by alienating them from the reality they experience. Irony and relativism appear as intellectual possibilities for dominating groups at the point where the hegemony and universality of their views is being challenged (9).

Hodder argues that it is important to open up dialogue of the past and present to minority groups, and believes his brand of hermeneutic interpretation gives minorities the power and authority to do so. Many disciplines, including philosophy, sociology, ethnography, history, and literary criticism, use the hermeneutic approach in attempting to understand human thought and action, of course. The introduction of hermeneutics into archaeology was brought to the forefront by Hodder in the 1980s. Archaeology and hermeneutics have parallel goals that have been described by Johnsen and Olsen (1992) in the following way:

> Archaeology can be defined as a discipline in which archaeologists interpret past societies by reading the 'traces' or 'life expressions' those societies left behind. In a similar way, hermeneuticians are concerned with understanding or interpreting textual manifestations without the immediate presence of, or access to, the societies in which the texts originated (423).

Thus, hermeneutic interpretation is the thought process of the researcher as s/he seeks the meaning or intent of the creator(s) of a cultural artifact, whether written or material. The thought process entails the dialectic reasoning that relates parts to a whole—or places specific events into a larger context. Because the mental templates of the artisan are not directly observable, however, it is difficult to know whether we are imposing our own personal values on past events. Hodder claims to break out of this circularity by using 'guarded objectivity'. To support his claim, Hodder cites Ricoeur's (1990) contention that artifacts are "...distanced from its 'author'". Hodder (1991a) notes that "[material culture] is the product of meaningfully organized activity, and it is itself patterned by those activities. This patterned organization, distant from its original meanings, has an independence that can therefore confront our interpretations" (p. 12). In this way archaeologists can bridge the gap between material culture and the meanings implied by the artisans. Moreover, by interpreting the meaning of artifacts through 'guarded objectivity', minorities can empower themselves by claiming a right to the material artifacts as evidence of legitimacy of their own past.

Gero (1991) attempts to narrow the gap between archaeological materials and interpretation by sticking close to the data. She interprets findings from an archaeological site in Queyash, Peru, by using a narrative explanation. Gero does not believe that this particular interpretation is more truthful than any other; after all, "...neither the facts themselves nor the narrations linking the facts are scientifically 'tested'" (p. 138). She goes on to say that narrative plots "...are improved upon by being linearized into longer contingent strings of events ...[and by being]...constrained by the factual evidence ..." (p. 138). Gero also emphasizes that narrative interpretation of Queyash culture is only a partial explanation. And she adopts Veyne's (1971) position that categories should be broken down into specifics in order to base narrative explanations on the most basic events rather than on generalizations of those events, which themselves were created by the narratives.

Using a narrative approach to explain human actions has intrinsic problems common to all interpretions of meaning. Relativism is one concern. As we saw earlier, there is no way of knowing with certainty that our interpretations are anything but extensions of our own values imposed upon unobserved events and thought processes. This problem is particularly acute in archaeology since material objects produced by artisans in the past are separated from us by both time and culture. Hodder (1991b) believes that we shall always interpret the past through the present, but his 'guarded objectivity' is supposed to minimize this problem (p. 31). Because artifacts are products of meaningfully organized activity, function and meaning can be inferred—particularly as parts of contextual patterning. One could counter that the activity might be organized in a way that has no meaning for the researcher. Johnsen and Olsen (1992) present a similar argument against Hodder's 'guarded objectivity of the past'. They argue that if, as Hodder contends, "...'objectivity' of the data is hidden, in the sense that 'things are not what they seem' (Hodder, 1990: 307), [then] Hodder needs some transformation rules, e.g., a method." Johnsen and Olsen (1992) also point out that using 'guarded objectivity' to empower minority groups to gain access to their own past can backfire; it can be used to repress ethnic groups. If, for example, archaeological data revealed that an ethnic group was not among the original inhabitants of an area, that information could be cited as a reason to repress the later arrivals.

Medical College of Georgia Excavation

A brief description of our excavation and preliminary findings at the Medical College of Georgia follows in order to lay the groundwork from which a narrative interpretation can be developed to tell part of the untold story about the Medical College of Georgia. In 1989, construction workers renovating a nineteenth-century building on the grounds of the Medical College of Georgia unearthed human skeletal remains in the dirt floor of the basement. Construction was halted briefly to allow salvage archaeology by a team from Georgia State University. The construction crew subsequently screened the remaining unexcavated portion of the basement, resulting in the recovery of an estimated 90 percent of the skeletal material.

The old Medical College of Georgia building was built in 1837, and served as the institution's only teaching facility until 1912, when the campus was moved to its present location (Spalding 1987). During the Civil War the building was used for the treatment of injured and ill Confederate soldiers (Moores 1984). Throughout most of the nineteenth century, however, the building served as classroom and laboratory in which medical students dissected human cadavers as part of their training. Because dissection was illegal in Georgia until 1887 (Allen 1976), the practice had to be carried out surreptitiously. Cadavers were occasionally purchased from Baltimore, New York, and Savannah, but most seem to have been obtained locally (Allen 1976). A slave and later employee named Grandison Harris was charged with procuring the specimens for dissection. Harris, known locally as 'the resurrection man', would slip out under cover of darkness to remove fresh corpses from their graves in nearby cemeteries and cart them back to the college (Allen 1976). Harris apparently disposed of the dissected material in the basement of the college building.

The excavation uncovered hundreds of body parts—arms, legs, torsos, skulls. The bones are well-preserved, some with soft tissue still adhering to them. Most of the remains, it seems, had been tossed on the earthen floor, covered with a layer of dirt, then capped with quicklime to reduce the stench. Thus, as body parts accumulated, the floor slowly rose with the accretion of remains. Bones were found in all areas of the basement except a front room where a stairway had once ascended to the first floor. Perhaps the smell of decomposing flesh wafting up the stairwell was too much to take. A number of bones exhibit pathological conditions, and many show signs of postmortem amputation and dissection. Some had been autopsied, and a few had specimen numbers written on them with India ink. The remains include both genders and all ages from fetus to the elderly. Preliminary laboratory analysis indicates that the majority of the individuals were African-American (Harrington and Blakely 1993). One skeleton, found at the edge of the basement, was complete and interred in a metal container. Curiously, a dissected lower leg was also placed in the container. A latrine containing some dissected material was located in a corner of the building. A large, wooden vat—we found the metal bottom and stays—held dozens of articulated and disarticulated bones. Historic records mention a vat in which cadavers and body parts were preserved in whiskey (Allen 1976).

Hundreds of artifacts also were recovered in the course of excavation. These included ceramic jugs, scalpels, syringes, thermometers, coins, buttons, fabric (including coffin lining), belt buckles, shoes, remnants of a small furnace, and bottles used both for medicinal and domestic purposes. Some bottles contain residue of their original contents; one holds liquid preserving human organ tissue. Also found was a partial deer skeleton, a cockspur (from a fighting cock), and ubiquitous rat bones. Traces of peanut shells were scattered everywhere.

Most of the artifacts date to the nineteenth century and, together with the skeletons, hold important clues to activities undertaken in the basement, to nineteenth-century medical practices, and to the health and the nutrition of that segment of the population represented by the remains. The overarching goal of the Medical College of Georgia research is to illuminate aspects of covert medical practices and training in the nineteenth-century South.

Research Design

The research design is based on the clandestine nature of the subject and the wide ranging nature of the data available for study. We shall take a multidisciplinary approach that draws upon evidence from historic documents, archaeological inference, forensic anthropology, experimental anatomy, and interviews. A narrative interpretation—through interviews—is part of this research design. Narrative interpretation will help answer questions such as those below.

What preferences did anatomy professors and resurrectionists exercise in the procurement of bodies for dissection at the college? What procedures were followed in the dissection and disposal of specimens? How did the racist assumptions of southern physicians influence the treatment and dissection of African-American and European-American corpses? What were the social attitudes and medical knowledge of physicians at the college in the 1800s? What other activities took place in the basement and on the floors above? Was the basement more than a dumping ground? What stories—whether apocryphal or not—did Augusta's residents tell about clandestine activities at the college? What were the beliefs and attitudes of Blacks and Whites toward the college and its perceived activities? What resistance, if any, was there to grave robbing and dissection by folks traditionally viewed as passive victims of an oppressive society? What is the legacy left today by events in the 1800s that brought together in such a macabre way Augusta's citizens and the Medical College of Georgia?

Descriptive and Explanatory Narratives

Answers to these questions and others lie in research that conjoins natural science, humanities, and social science—including narrative investigation. Polkinghorne (1988) divides narrative investigation in social science into descriptive and explanatory types. The analysis of the Augusta interviews seems a likely candidate for both types. The descriptive approach to narrative research looks for narratives already in use by individuals and groups to provide an interpretation of the meaning of events in their lives. Descriptive research is evaluated by how accurately it represents the people's stories (Polkinghorne 1988).

The explanatory narratives use a narrative explication, instead of a scientific explication for example, to explain why an event involving human action occurred. The findings of explanatory research are based on extrapolations made from many different sources in support of the researcher's conclusions (Polkinghorne 1988). One of these sources, the interview, involves recollections of the past, which often change as time goes on. According to Polkinghorne (1988), "the reconstruction of past facts thus frequently resembles detective work, with several personal accounts together with partial written records needed to infer what actually has happened" (p. 174). Polkinghorne also compares plot building in narrative inquiry and hypothesis development in scientific inquiry. The objective of the explanatory narrative is to develop the plot—or to present events and their significance—in such a way that it leads to a reasoned outcome. These events are analyzed according to a hermeneutic procedure that selects and fits the original data into a story revealing underlying patterns.

Just as the scientist can 'rig' tests of hypotheses to yield the desired results, so too can researchers construct narrative plots to advance her or his own social or political agenda. The former is bad science; the latter is more often condoned. While we recognize the role of the researcher in plot development, as anthropologists we believe that, to the extent that the process subverts the meaning of the narrator's story, it diminishes the power of the narrative as a portrait of the past. Through self reflexivity both scientist and narrative researcher take responsibility for their interpretations.

For Polkinghorne (1988), narrative explanations always relate events to other events and acknowledge where human intervention or a different set of events would change the results. It is clear that this type of explanation uses teleological inference; that is, it makes the assumption that people act in ways they believe will help them to attain their goals. Their belief may be based on a false premise, of course, or on a premise different from that of the researcher. As a consequence of this and other caveats, the results of explanatory narratives cannot be proven to be true, predictable, or repeatable in the same way that scientific data can.

In this essay we do not develop the methods of ethnographic interview that we propose to use in the Medical College of Georgia research. (For a general treatment of the methods of ethnographic interview, see H. Russell Bernard's work, particularly *Research Methods in Cultural Anthropology* [1988].) We do adhere to Polkinghorne's (1988) characterization of the interview as a process of soliciting narratives from respondents. The interviewer acts as a guide for the narrator, who tells stories that often contain digressions and events out of sequence.

The complexity of the interview process is informed by discourse theory, which defines the parameters within which human discourse occurs. Polkinghorne points out that the interview process is effected by its environment. For instance, the interviewee may want to project a certain image in response to the interviewer and the story line that is chosen for study, while the interviewer may try to create a certain image of herself or himself through the story chosen. In order to reduce the need for interviewer and narrator to present themselves in socially prescribed ways, Paget (1983) suggests that they establish a relationship where both share important information about their lives and view each other as collaborators. We intend to follow this advice in the Medical College of Georgia research, and to take it one step further. Among our goals are (a) to become partners with the residents of Augusta in the dissemination of their heritage in both popular and scholarly outlets and (b) to offer them tools by which they can continue on their own to explore their past.

Conclusion

Page (1986) notes that "The narrator...is a human being who is likely to have prejudices and quirks which filter his memories and give a somewhat distorted perspective to his account" (p. 279). At least it is the narrator's perspective. Instead of seeing themselves through the alien eyes of the historian or archaeologist—the eyes of the dominant culture—narrative gives history back to people (Hastorf and Hodder 1991; Willson 1986). Although we can never rid ourselves of the researcher's imprint on interpretation, narrative counterbalances the tendency of social scientists to fit data to theory, thereby enclosing the past in ethnocentric biases (Hodder 1991a). Ethnohistory (or ethnoarchaeology [Brumbach and Jarvenpa 1990]), which often includes narratives, attempts to understand ethnic groups in and on their own terms. Accessing the past in this way means telling a story as well as testing formal hypotheses. Narration opens the past to public debate (Hodder 1991a).

WORKS CITED

Allen, Lane. "Grandison Harris, Sr.: Slave, Resurrectionist and Judge." *Bulletin of the Georgia Academy of Science* 34: 192-199, 1972.

Bernard, H. Russell. *Research Methods in Cultural Anthropology*. Sage Publications, Newbury Park: California, 1988.

Brumbach, Hetty Jo, and Robert Jarvenpa. "Archeologist-Ethnographer-Informant Relations: The Dynamics of Ethnoarcheology in the Field." *Powers of Observation: Alternative Views in Archeology*, ed. Sarah M. Nelson and Alice B. Kehoe, pp. 39-46. Archeological Papers of the American Anthropological Association No. 2, Washington, D.C., 1990.

Gero, Joan M. "Queyash, Peru." *Processual and Postprocessual Archaeologies: Multiple Ways of Knowing the Past*, ed. Robert W. Preucel, pp. 126-139. Occasional Papers No. 10. Center for Archaeological Investigations, Southern Illinois University, Carbondale, 1991.

Harrington, Judith M., and Robert L. Blakely. "Rich Man, Poor Man, Beggar Man, Thief: The Selectivity Exercised by Grave Robbers at the Medical College of Georgia, 1837-1887." Paper presented at the annual meeting of the American Association of Physical Anthropologists, Toronto, 1993.

Hastorf, Christine, and Ian Hodder. "Archaeology and the Other." *Archaeology and Indigenous Peoples: Ethical Issues and Questions*, ed. Kirsten D. White, pp. 1-11. Anthropology UCLA, Volume 18, Number 1. UCLA Anthropology Graduate Students Association, Los Angeles, 1991.

Hodder, Ian. *The Domestication of Europe*. Blackwell: Oxford, 1990.

Hodder, Ian. "Interpretive Archaeology and Its Role." *American Antiquity* 56: 7-18, 1991a.

Hodder, Ian. "Postprocessual Archaeology and the Current Debate." *Processual and Postprocessual Archaeologies: Multiple Ways of Knowing the Past*, ed. Robert W. Preucel, pp. 30-41. Occasional Papers No. 10. Center for Archaeological Investigations, Southern Illinois University, Carbondale, 1991b.

Johnsen, Harald, and Bjornar Olsen. "Hermeneutics and Archaeology: On the Philosophy of Contextual Archaeology." *American Antiquity* 57: 419-436, 1992.

Mascia-Lees, F., P. Sharpe, and C. B. Cohen. "The Postmodernist Turn in Anthropology." *Signs* 15: 7-33, 1989.

Moores, Russell R. "The Medical College of Georgia's Venerable Old Lady. *Ancestoring* 9: 16-28, 1984.

Muller, Jon. "The New Holy Family: A Polemic on Bourgeois Idealism in Archaeology." *Processual and Postprocessual Archaeologies: Multiple Ways of Knowing the Past*, ed. Robert W. Preucel, pp. 251-260. Occasional Papers No. 10. Center for Archaeological Investigations, Southern Illinois University, Carbondale, 1991.

Page, J. Bryan. "The Use of Reminiscences and Oral Tradition in the Study of Ethnohistory." *Ethnohistory: A Researcher's Guide*, ed. Dennis Wiedman, pp. 275-296. Studies in Third World Societies No. 35. Department of Anthropology, College of William and Mary, Williamsburg, Virginia, 1986.

Paget, M. A. "Experience and Knowledge." *Human Studies* 7:67-90, 1983.

Polkinghorne, Donald E. *Narrative Knowing and the Human Sciences*. State University of New York Press: Albany, 1988.

Preucel, Robert W. "Introduction." *Processual and Postprocessual Archaeologies: Multiple Ways of Knowing the Past*, ed. Robert W. Preucel, pp. 1-14. Occasional Papers No. 10. Center for Archaeological Investigations, Southern Illinois University, Carbondale, 1991a.

Preucel, Robert W. "The Philosophy of Archaeology." *Processual and Postprocessual Archaeologies: Multiple Ways of Knowing the Past*, ed. Robert W. Preucel, pp. 17-29. Occasional Papers No. 10. Center for Archaeological Investigations, Southern Illinois University, Carbondale, 1991b.

Ricoeur, P. "Hermeneutics and the Critique of Ideology." *The Hermeneutic Tradition*, ed. G. L. Ormiston and A. D. Schrift, pp. 298-334. State University of New York Press: Albany, 1990.

Spalding, Phinizy. *The History of the Medical College of Georgia*. University of Georgia Press: Athens, 1987.

Veyne, Paul. *Writing History*. Wesleyan University Press: Middletown, Connecticut, 1971.

Watson, Patty Jo. "Parochial Primer: The New Dissonance as Seen from the Midcontinental United States." *Processual and Postprocessual Archaeologies: Multiple Ways of Knowing the Past*, ed. Robert W. Preucel, pp. 126-139. Occasional Papers No. 10. Center for Archaeological Investigations, Southern Illinois University, Carbondale, 1991.

Willson, Margaret E. "Oral History Interviews: Some History and Practical Suggestions." *Ethnohistory: A Researcher's Guide*, ed. Dennis Wiedman, pp. 253-274. Studies in Third World Societies No. 35. Department of Anthropology, College of William and Mary, Williamsburg, Virginia, 1986.

Themes

Gambling With Ghosts

Native American Literature and Postmodernism

GREGORY SALYER

Postmodernism opens with the sense of *irrevocable* loss and *incurable* fault. This wound is inflicted by the overwhelming awareness of death—a death that "begins" with the death of God and "ends" with the death of our selves. We are in a time between times and a place which is no place. Here our reflection must "begin."—Mark C. Taylor

[Structuralism and other social science theories] are academic tropes to power rather than tribal stories in a language game. The postmodern pose is an invitation to liberation, a noetic mediation and communal discourse.—Gerald Vizenor

I take my title from a scene in the early part of *Tracks*, Louise Erdrich's third novel. The episode is instructive for non-native scholars like myself who would venture onto the sacred ground of Native American literature. As "outsiders" to this discourse, we risk finding ourselves in the position of the agent who goes into the woods that surround the home of Fleur Pillager, a medicine woman, to collect the allotment on Pillager land.

The Agent went out there, then got lost, spent a whole night following the moving lights and lamps of people who would not answer him, but talked and laughed among themselves. They only let him go at dawn because he was so stupid. Yet he asked Fleur again for money, and the next thing we heard he was living in the woods and eating roots, gambling with ghosts (9).

The applications of this parable-like passage are many, but for the purposes of this essay, I would like to apply its lessons to the topic at hand, the relationship between postmodernism and Native American literature. The "lostness" of the agent, who has clearly wandered into an unknown world, echoes the position of many who in the late twentieth-century have experienced the crumbling of the edifices of western thought broadly construed. The agent's lostness, moreover, derives not from a sense of discontinuity with everyday life but from conformity with the everyday requirements of "work" and "duty" as they are defined by the mythos of the culture. I believe, with Robert Detweiler, that this experience is one that is not predicated on reading Derrida, Foucault, or Fish or even Pynchon, Ballard, or DeLillo. The expressions of alienation and groundlessness that pervade much of contemporary life can be found in many and varied forms and are experienced in all sorts of contexts. We can point to many probable causes of this "postmodern condition," such as the corrosive influence of economic and social power, the disenchantment of nature arising from our successful completion of the Genesis edict to dominate and control it, and the inability of morality to keep pace with technology. But if we had to point the finger at just one source for these phenomena, the culprit may well be language, or at least our faith in language.

> [I]n our century language *per se*, not just literary language, has come increasingly under suspicion regarding its reliability as a conveyer of our ordinary-reality experience as well as of our scientifically discovered reality, so that the philosophy of our era has consisted in good part in dealing with the realization that language will not behave itself, will not function passively or tractably as an information-carrying vehicle, but even at its most innocuous always has its own agenda, its own hidden discourses, even—perhaps—its own reality (Detweiler, *Breaking the Fall*, 17).

This realization about the vagaries of language, it might be argued, was brought home brutally to Native Americans who trusted the words of the calvary officers and government agents who sought to deal with the "Indian problem." But such comparisons quickly become overwhelmingly complex, as we shall see. At the same time, I cannot ignore the fact that more and more of us who acknowledge our postmodern condition with regard to language and knowledge are turning to Native American literature out of some sense of recognition. It is equally clear that there is an interest in Native American culture that is developing if not flourishing in American (and even European) popular culture. Those of us who have become interested in this literature have to be careful that we do not consider it another body of work to be taxed by our various theories and agendas. Even as I revel in works by Erdrich, Silko, Vizenor, Welch, Allen and others, I must ask myself if I am not rehearsing the deeds of other whites who saw something in Native American culture, whether it be land or life, and said to themselves "I must have it." I make no claims to be above or beyond such trespasses, but as I continue to explore this subject I hope to do more listening than talking, more reading than writing, and, above all, to be more cautious.

The agent in Erdrich's story goes looking for money but finds ghosts instead, and his stupidity and single-mindedness keep him there. We need to read Native American literature with an openness to the unfamiliar that is born of respect for history and political struggle. This struggle has been well documented—but not necessarily widely read—in works such as *A Century of Dishonor, Bury My Heart at Wounded Knee, In the Spirit of Crazy Horse*, and *Lakota Woman*. As the concept of the canon expands to include more literature by and about Native Americans, those of us who did not participate in that struggle should be aware that we are gambling with ghosts, playing seriously with the cultural life of a people. We need to be cautious also because our past carelessness has reduced the prominent interpretations of this literature to either austere realism or baroque sentimentality. The former is in part a result of positivistic social science methodologies that produced most of the western interpretations of Native American cultures and the latter an effect of the co-option and commodification of things Native American in popular culture, one example being the rise of "Whiteshamanism" among certain new age movements.[1] In short there needs to be an ethics of reading Native American literature, especially by non-native scholars. This ethics can be derived from an interpretation of history and culture that privileges the voices of those who live the life of the literature. As Arnold Krupat notes in the introduction to his *The Voice in the Margin,*

> . . . [M]y own sense of the call to polyphony understands it as urging the refusal of imperial domination, and so of the West's claim legitimately to speak for all the Rest. Neither a formal theory nor a program, this call is, rather, an exhortation to proceed humbly and with care; it asks that we Westerners stop shouting, as it were, and that we speak with our ears open (7).

The question then turns to why we should read such literature at all. If we have trampled the rights and culture of native people for so long and in so many different ways, why should we even approach their literature? There are good reasons both practical and theoretical. More Native American literature is being read by the general public and more is being taught in college and university classrooms. As scholars it is incumbent upon us to be critical of attempts to treat literature by Native Americans as something that is "as good as American literature," as if that were the only source of legitimation. We should be equally loathe to allow this literature to remain under the aegis of the social sciences as if it contains merely archaeological or anthropological data of dead cultures.[2] In short if we are going to continue to read and teach this literature, then we should also be taught by it.

Another reason to make a conscious effort include this literature in our academic conversations—including those on postmodernism—is that it is part of American culture. Native American literature *is* American literature and exists as a legitimate voice in the noise of American culture both past and present. Krupat notes that ". . . American culture has had, has now, and will continue to have some relation to Native American culture—although that relation has most frequently been one of avoidance" (3). Accusations of political correctness notwithstanding, we can no longer pretend that American culture is a homogeneous entity or that one element is qualitatively superior to another. American culture is the mixture of tensions, recombinations, commodifications, and mythologies of all its cultures. In that sense Native American culture as an authentic voice and not a commodification of our convenient projections has yet to be fully heard.

Finally, and to the point of this essay, Native American literature has something to say about the "postmodern condition." The metaphysical structures of western thought that provided the impetus and rationale for the near total destruction of Native American cultures are under attack themselves. I do not need to rehearse this story here, for it will be well known by most. Suffice it to say that in the margins of our waning meta-narratives, concepts familiar to Native American life and literature are beginning to appear. Likewise, more and more Native American critics are beginning to turn to developments in recent theory to liberate their literature from the hegemony of social science and sentimental interpretation. The invitation to compare postmodernism and Native American literature seems to have come first from Native American critics themselves, and I will explore the work of one of these critics shortly. My aim here is to keep this conversation going and to maintain and advance the dialogue between Native American literature and postmodernism.

Why Native American literature and postmodernism and not Native Americanism or postmodern literature? This question deserves an answer. There is clearly no Native Americanism that can be compared to postmodernism. Native American scholars often feel obliged to point out from the beginning that there is no single thing that can be termed Native American culture, literature, or religion. There are only cultures, literatures, and religions, and any attempt to incorporate them into one system will serve only to desiccate them all. Native Americans typically do not engage in western rhetorical and philosophical strategies (such as those that cluster around various "isms"). Instead they articulate their understanding of themselves through what we can only analogously call art.[3] The world is not described so much as constituted through stories, ceremonies, and objects. Why not, then, compare Native American literature with postmodern literature? Such a project could be provocative to be sure, but for the purposes of this essay it is simply impractical. Postmodern literature remains engaged—intertextually, parodically, historiographically, and paradoxically—with the literature of the western tradition. To compare these two types of literature would require even more explanation than is necessary here with the topic I have chosen. Perhaps I should say that I am more interested in comparing the supertexts of postmodernism with the subtexts of Native American literature. Postmodern literature is so much about self-conscious technique and Native American literature so much about experience that I find a point by point comparison to be unfruitful if not unfair to one or both. Comparing the ideas that inform postmodern literature to the experiences described in Native American literature seems to have much more potential. Having said that, I also want to qualify it by adding that such a project can only begin to be sketched out in a short essay, but I do anticipate that this dialogue can continue in interesting forms and contexts.

Being cautious in treating Native American literature often means giving up our romance with categories and definitions. In this regard we can observe Brian Swann as he struggles with the question of defining Native American poetry in his introduction to a well-known anthology.[4] He notes that this literature is charged with historic witness and quotes Vine Deloria's remark that such literature can "tell you more about the Indian's travels in historical experience than all the books written and lectures given" (Introduction, xvii). Ultimately, he offers a loose yet powerful definition, one that I am willing to accept and use in this essay.

> If one says Native American poetry is poetry written by Native Americans the difficulty might appear to be solved. . . . The best way might be to say I'm not really interested in defining this poetry. Its full and generous presence . . . will *announce* what it is on its own terms, using its own names—"we wonder/whether anyone will ever hear/our own names for things/we do" (Gail Tremblay, "Indian Singing in 20th Century America).
> . . . The best definition I can arrive at is this: Native Americans are Native Americans if they say they are , if other Native Americans say they are and accept them, and (possibly) if the values that are held close and acted upon are the values upheld by the various native peoples who live in the Americas (xx).

Swann's struggle both to define and not to define poetry seems to be closer to the way such definitions are negotiated, if they are negotiated at all, in the critical authorship and readership of this literature.

Swann's definition may appear to some as a postmodern non-definition. Whether or not this is so, we can say that postmodernism is about such self-consciousness. I intend to use the term to describe in a general way the status of knowledge in late twentieth-century western culture. Knowledge is in fact a term left over from the modern and premodern worldview that postmodernism seeks to overcome. In a postmodern world there is only information flowing around and through human beings. Such a world has been brilliantly described in Don DeLillo's *White Noise*, a novel where academics and others seek to manipulate the flow of information as an attempt to stave off the death that it portends. For a provisional definition of postmodernism that captures this and other aspects of the phenomenon, I can do no better than Robert Detweiler's succinct articulation in a forthcoming encyclopedia article.

> Postmodernism, beginning in the early 1960s, recognizes the traumatic, estranged, and atomised nature of human existence but attempts to render it bearable and even affirmative by adopting attitudes and strategies such as irony, parody, anti-foundationalism, and play ("Postmodernism").

The postmodernism that especially interests me is found in the theoretical articulation of poststructuralist discourse. Here issues common to critical study in Native American literature come to bear in unique ways. Issues of language, signification, and the play of the trace are especially relevant. In the remainder of this essay, I want to examine the relationship between postmodernism and Native American literature by way of two concepts that contextualize Detweiler's sense of the "traumatic, estranged, and atomised nature of human existence." These concepts are speech and writing and the trickster sign.

Speech and Writing

Discussions of speech and writing figure prominently in poststructuralist discourse. The most obvious and provocative arguments coming out of the poststructuralist arena concern the attempt to overturn the privileging of phonocentrism over chirography or grammatology.[5] In attempting to reverse this hierarchy, Derrida argues that writing comes before speech both historically and logically. It is prior historically because the structure of writing, that is the play of difference between signifiers, is always already at work even in speech. This basic structure he terms arche-writing, and it is in arche-writing that writing logically precedes speech as well, for this structure of difference is a condition for speech and writing both (Derrida, *Of Grammatology* 56-7).

Other scholars who write about writing and speech, however, do not have the same theoretical axe to grind as Derrida. In fact Walter Ong's salient observations on the nature of orality and literacy problematize writing in ways that are similar to Derrida's problematization of speech. For Ong the spoken word operates much like Derrida's texts. The word is local and communal and conventionally constructed; its meaning is never fixed but fluctuates. Ong goes farther to say that speech is centered in the body. The scene of writing, on the other hand, is an artifact—paper or some other object external to the body. This tendency to interiority places the hearer within the center of the cosmos, for sound is all around us and we are able to be "in" it in a way that vision does not permit. Consistent with this notion is the appreciation for clarity in vision and harmony in sound. Vision is a divisive sense, separating things that are "here" from those that are "there." Sound seems to work holistically, taking in sensation as a unit that either exists or does not exist at any given moment; the character of speech is ephemeral. Sound exists only when it is going out of existence. By the time the "ence" in existence is heard the "exist" is already gone. Sound resists stasis; it is always fluid. The opposite is true of vision and thus writing, which are most efficient with the freezing of movement. To see an object or a text, both the object and the subject must remain still. The work of Marshall McLuhan is relevant here as well. He argues in *The Gutenberg Galaxy* that with the advent of print the human sensory field became dominated by vision to the degree that culture was hypnotized by print in the same way that an individual is hypnotized—by the exclusion of other senses due to the dominance of one. This divisive process also helped create and sustain the subject-object dichotomy that ascended with the rise of the sciences, since language, with writing and especially print, became encapsulated in an object instead of a subject. In this regard Ong notes:

> Writing separates the knower from the known and thus sets up conditions for "objectivity," in the sense of personal disengagement or distancing. The "objectivity" which Homer and other oral performers do have is that enforced by formulaic expression: the individual's reaction is not expressed as simply individual or "subjective" but rather as encased in the communal reaction, the communal "soul." Under the influence of writing, despite his protest against it, Plato had excluded the poets from his Republic, for studying them was essentially learning to react with "soul," to feel oneself identified with Achilles or Odysseus (*Orality and Literacy* 46).

Ong's emphasis on the communal nature of oral cultures is set against the context of solitude. He indicates that writing is a solitary activity as is reading, but speech is thoroughly communal with meaning being a function of a communal consensus that is more unconscious than conscious. The values and beliefs of the community thus create the reality of the community. As Ong remarks, "Oral cultures appropriate actuality in recurrent formulaic agglomerates, communally generated and shared" (*Interfaces of the Word* 19).

In an essay in a collection on Native American literature, Arnold Krupat brings issues of writing and speech to bear directly upon Native American studies. He recognizes that oral cultures have what we would call a postmodern approach to meaning while writing cultures have been obsessed with fixing meaning.

> What is curious to note is that from an historical point of view, such concern for fixed meanings seems not to have been typical of oral cultures at all; rather, it appears to arise only with the shift to literacy and to chirographic means of information storage, only to become emphasized later with the further shift from chirography to typography, from manuscripts to printed texts. So far as research has been able to determine, the audiences for oral performances—Native American or Yugoslav, a hundred years ago or today—are very little concerned with interpretive uniformity or agreement of any exactitude as to what a word or passage *meant*. These are the worries of manuscript and book cultures, pretty exclusively. Thus, it is probably not accidental, as Walter Ong has pointed out, that the post-structuralist insistence on interpretive openness and undecidable meaning coincides with the first moments of—this is Ong's phrase—"secondary orality" in the West, with a technological shift away from print to electronic information retrieval systems that are not exclusively or inviolably text based. . . . That post-structuralists in fact call this openness textuality rather than orality is a confusion bred of their relative lack of interest in historical detail ("Poststructuralism and Oral Literature" 118).

The distinction is an important one for Native American writers and critics. The oral traditions, according to many critics, are the source of almost all Native American literature. For Paula Gunn Allen the oral traditions are a force for resistance as well.

> The oral tradition, from which the contemporary poetry and fiction take their significance and authenticity, has, since contact with white people, been a major force in Indian resistance. It has kept the people conscious of their tribal identity, their spiritual traditions, and their connection to the land and her creatures. Contemporary poets and writers take their cue from the oral tradition, to which they return continuously for theme, symbol, structure, and

motivating impulse as well as for the philosophic bias that animates our work (53).

Understanding the importance and influence of an oral tradition is a difficult task for a literate mind, or a mind tempered by the technology of writing. Such a mind tends to think of the oral tradition in terms of writing, that is, as a record of various aspects of a culture including its evolution and its sustaining mythos. The oral tradition, however, is apparently much more than a record; it is a fluid, conflictual body that responds to its environment. It is therefore much like a person, able to maintain conflicting beliefs, able to adapt to different circumstances, able to change beliefs when necessary, and able to be changed by external elements.

> If the oral tradition is altered in certain subtle, fundamental ways, if elements alien to it are introduced so that its internal coherence is disturbed, it becomes the major instrument of colonization and oppression (Allen 224-5).

Orality in Native American cultures seems to bypass the problem of representation as we have come to know it. The signifier-signified-referent chain does not exist in many Native American languages. The word *is* the thing, the symbol *is* the symbolized. There is no *difference* between them. Again Paula Gunn Allen explains.

> Symbols in American Indian systems are not symbolic in the usual sense of the word. The words articulate reality—not "psychological" or imagined reality, not emotive reality captured metaphorically in an attempt to fuse thought and feeling, but that reality where thought and feeling are one, where objective and subjective are one, where speaker and listener are one, where sound and sense are one (71).

Joseph Epes Brown in *The Spiritual Legacy of the American Indian* echoes this same understanding of signification.

> What is named is therefore understood to be really present in the name in unitary manner, not as "symbol" with dualistic implication, as is generally the case with modern languages. An aspect of the sacred potency latent in words in primal tradition is the presiding understanding that words in their sounds are born in the breath of the being from whom they proceed, and since breath in these traditions is universally identified with the life principle, words are thus sacred and must be used with care and responsibility. Such quality of the spoken word is further enhanced by the understood close proximity of the source of breath, the lungs, with the heart, which is associated with the being's spiritual center (3).

The closest analog that postmodernism affords to such concepts is the French feminist concern with *l'écriture féminine* where "writing the body" brings a similar somatic aspect to language. Both Native American language and *l'écriture féminine* may be understood in opposition to "the violence of letter" that is associated with (phallocentric) writing and texts. Seeing language as centered in the body is a relatively new development in western thought, one that Robert Detweiler has been at the front edge of for some time. And yet the comparison to *l'écriture féminine* is only a door to understanding the bodily nature of language in Native American cultures. A century after Freud we remain at best uncertain about the function of the body in our interpretations of the world. As the body continues to be retouched and reshaped by cultural currents, we have in Native American cultures an example of what it might mean to have an articulate body so wedded to words that the two are almost indistinguishable in communal life. It is an understanding of language that is beyond and before poststructuralism and, Derrida notwithstanding, beyond and before writing.

The Trickster

Here we can bring to the discussion what is surely one of the most interesting and provocative proposals to come to light in recent discussions of postmodernism. In his book *Narrative Chance* Gerald Vizenor argues that what we have come to call the "postmodern turn" or "metafiction" is found in the structures of storytelling in oral cultures.

> . . . oral cultures have never been without a postmodern condition that enlivens stories and ceremonies, or without trickster signatures and discourse on narrative chance—a comic utterance and adventure to be heard or read (x).

Other essays in Vizenor's collection point out the similarity of interests in native aesthetics and contemporary theory. Robert Silberman notes that "Native American literature seems made to order for recent developments in literary criticism and critical theory." He goes on to say that one of the most important issues for Native American writers is an "obsessive" concern with the effects of speech and writing (102). It is Vizenor, however, who takes the issues to new heights of trickery. First of all, he sounds at times like Derrida speaking of arche-writing when he speaks of writing in Native American culture: "The printed word has no evolution in tribal literatures; the word is there, in trees, water, air, and printed on paper where it has been at all times" (x). Secondly, he offers a definition of the postmodern that is unique and thoroughly tribal. He states that the postmodern is "a situational pattern, not a historical template; an erudite riposte to tribal representations, not a disguise or formal grammar" (ii). The postmodern is a given in tribal culture. Tribal representations, on the other hand, are "modernist" relying on the tragic mode of social science rather than the comic mode that is the "postmodern" trickster. Vizenor, however, falls short of claiming that the postmodern is an articulated presence in Native American tribal life. It is instead "a noetic mediation that denies historicism and representation; in particular, it denies the kitschy speculation on the basic truth" (xii). According to Vizenor the context for Native American stories is a strange confluence of what theoreticians might identify as the orality theory of Walter Ong and the arche-writing of Derrida.

> Native American Indian stories are told and heard in motion, imagined and read over and over on a landscape that is never seen at once; words are heard in winter rivers, crows are written on the poplars, last words are never the end (xiii).

It is a strange confluence precisely because the presentation is Vizenor's, not Derrida's or Ong's, and thus it is a distinctly Native American "erudite riposte to tribal representations" of all kinds. It should be made clear then that Vizenor's claims for the trickster sign and tribal literatures in general are not simply an amalgam of elements of current literary theory but are trickster techniques themselves which are related strategically more than formally to some of the trickster interpretive strategies of poststructuralist discourse.

Clearly the most important sign in tribal narrative and Native American literature for Vizenor is that of the trickster. The trickster is not a person, as ethnological and mythographical studies have represented him, but a sign.

> The trickster is a communal sign in a comic narrative; the comic *holotrope* (the whole figuration) is a consonance in tribal discourse. Silence and separation, not monologues in social science methodologies, are the antitheses of trickster discourse (9).

In attempting to understand Vizenor's language we should understand first of all that the trickster is a sign. This is in opposition to traditional understandings of the trickster as a person in the tribe or in the tribe's mythology. Vizenor is clearly out to counter the representations of tribal cultures by social science and comparative religion methodologies. He displaces the word trickster, making it a semiotic category rather than an empirical one. One effect of this displacement is that the tribal narrative itself becomes open to literary interpretation. This is a move to rectify the fact that ". . . tribal narratives have been underread in criticism and overread in social science" (11). Once that door is opened many other significations become possible. Instead of the trickster being read as an artifact of a dead culture, it becomes a literary category and is freed from the dominating interpretation that circumscribes what the trickster can mean. In Vizenor's view the trickster can and does mean anything and everything. The trickster is a rip in the fabric of consciousness, it is the whole of meaning and the hole of meaning, it is a ludic character in a tragic story.

One of the other characteristics of Vizenor's trickster is that of chance, by which he means unpredictability and groundlessness, among other things.

> . . . the signifier in a trickster narrative, is signified in *chance*. The trickster is a semiotic sign, closer in connotation to an iconic sign than to the arbitrary symbolic signification or causal representation in semiotic theories. The trickster sign wanders between narrative voices and comic chance in oral presentations (189).

Living by chance is living without a solid foundation. In short, nothing is solid, and anything can change. This holds true for the sacred as well. Chance can be seen even more clearly when it is contrasted with Catholicism and other western religions where chance is something just short of chaos and needs to be controlled. The need to control chance initiates the various movements in Christian theology that attempt to align it to the "truths" of science and history. Left to chance religion becomes irrational and unpredictable and is thus unable to be made normative. An interesting aspect of the Christian attempt at control is the existence of missionaries. Motivated by the desire to eliminate the chance of that "primitives" might fall under God's judgement by their ignorance, missionaries brought the word of God to the natives. Anthropologists brought their own versions of order to Native American life that sought to elimate the idea of the inexplicable. Tricksters make fun of such serious attempts to control chance. Trickster signs disrupt and subvert attempts to provide order to tribal narratives.

Vizenor sounds like another trickster whose comic acts have been perpetrated upon the structures of literary interpretation—Jacques Derrida. For Vizenor the trickster is the deconstructor who denies presence and representation. "In trickster narratives the listeners and readers imagine their liberation; the trickster is a sign and the world is 'deconstructed' in a discourse" (194). The trickster is a deconstructor, or the sign that effaces itself as well as the discourse that it inhabits. As such it is comic, and the comedy it perpetrates is the denial of presence: "The trickster is not a presence or a real person but a semiotic sign in a language game, in a comic narrative that denies presence" (204).

With the emergence of postmodernism we are beginning to appreciate trickery again. It is better, postmodernism sees to say, to revel in the vagaries of language than to try to control it. Vizenor indicates that such an approach to language and life has long been a part of Native American culture, and that this understanding serves the community well by preventing it from taking itself and its words too seriously.

I would like to conclude by suggesting that there is a deeper connection between Native American literature and postmodernism than their ideas of writing and speech and signification. Postmodernism is surely many things, some of which have been discussed here, but it may also be seen as a rumination on things lost. We recall Mark C. Taylor's epigram to this essay that describes an "irrevocable loss and incurable fault." While we may begin with this sense of postmodernism, I do not believe we can ultimately live with it. This loss is not irrevocable nor incurable (at least we do not act as if it is), else the discussion of the loss would not continue. I do believe that postmodernism, while hacking away at the past, has some inclinations toward the future and future recoveries at that. One of the things it hopes to recover, I would suggest, is a sense of community that creates meaning without controlling it. While we struggle to imagine a world apart from foundational western concepts such as the subject, the object, and the truth, we do want to imagine it because the world that we have interpreted seems to be uninhabitable. In Native American literature we obtain glimpses of a world that can be lived in. It is certainly not a world that can serve as our most convenient and latest utopic vision. But it is a world where words are connected to the body, not to an abstract proposition. In this world trickery is acknowledged and affirmed and serves to keep one from the enervation of certitude.

The interface between the world of Native American literature and postmodernism may be approached by way of what Robert Detweiler calls "reading religiously." Here community becomes an important venue for meaning and for play.

Two German terms not easily translatable suggest what both religious and interpretive communities could strive for: *Gelassenheit* and *Geselligkeit*. *Gelassenheit*, a term already used by the fourteenth-century German mystic Meister Eckhart and developed by Heidegger, is sometimes rendered as "releasement" or "abandonment," but it also conveys relaxation, serenity and nonchalance, a condition of acceptance that is neither nihilistic nor fatalistic but the ability—and it may be a gift—to move gracefully through life's fortunes and accidents, or to wait out its calamities. *Geselligkeit* can be translated as "sociability," but the German term manages to impart a sense of closeness that is not cloying. If "togetherness" had not been ruined by encounter group psychology, it would be appropriate. "Communality" is also fitting. Religious reading might be *gelassen* and *gessellig*, balancing our dogged insistence on interpretation with a pleasurable interchange made valuable precisely by a refusal to simplify and manipulate the text into something else, another statement (*Breaking the Fall* 35).

This understanding of religious reading steers a course between the solitary interpreter and institutionally sanctioned interpretation. By emphasizing community and play, Detweiler captures elements found in both postmodernism and Native American literature. Here, I would suggest, is where our reflection can begin.

In that vein I want to give the last word in this essay to Gerald Vizenor whose writing evokes the interplay of speech and writing, of trace and track, and of the trickster.

> Holding forth at the spacious treelines with the bears and the crows, the best tellers in the tribes peel peel peel their words like oranges, down to the last navel, Mimicked in written forms over winter now, transposed in mythic metaphors, the interior glories from oral traditions burst in conversations and from old footprints on the trail . . . . The reader remembers footprints near the treeline, near the limits of understanding in written words, but the trail is never marked with printed words. The trail is made as a visual event between imaginative creators, tellers, and listeners: we hold our breath beneath the surface, the written word, but we know that respiration and transpiration are possible under water (*Earthdivers* 165-66).

NOTES

1. See Wendy Rose, "The Great Pretenders: Further Reflections on Whiteshamanism," in M. Annette Jaimes, ed. *The State of Native America: Genocide, Colonization, and Resistance* (Boston: South End Press, 1992).

2. In most of the chain bookstores Native American literature is often found not in the fiction or literature sections but in the social sciences or history sections, as if to indicate that potential readers might look here as if they were hunting arrowheads not literature. Something similar happens when "Americans" are puzzled as to why Native Americans object to elements of their cultures being treated as artifacts of a dead culture by various sports teams and their fans.

3. In many Native American languages, there are no separate words for concepts such as art, religion, the sacred, and even words.

4. This is Duane Niatum's *Harper's Anthology of Contemporary Native American Poetry.*

5. As in Jacques Derrida, *Of Grammatology,* trans. Gayatri Chakravorty Spivak (Baltimore: Johns Hopkins UP, 1976).

WORKS CITED

Allen, Paula Gunn. *The Sacred Hoop: Recovering the Feminine in American Indian Traditions.* Boston: Beacon Press, 1986.

Brown, Joseph Epes. *The Spiritual Legacy of the American Indian.* New York: Crossroad, 1982.

Derrida, Jacques. *Of Grammatology.* trans. Gayatri Chakravorty Spivak. Baltimore: Johns Hopkins UP, 1976.

Detweiler, Robert. *Breaking the Fall: Religious Readings of Contemporary Fiction.* San Francisco: Harper & Row, 1989.

Detweiler, Robert. "Postmodernism." Forthcoming encyclopedia article.

Erdrich, Louise. *Tracks.* New York: Harper & Row, 1988.

Krupat, Arnold. "Poststructuralism and Oral Literature." *Recovering the Word: Essays on Native American Literature.* ed. Brian Swann and Arnold Krupat. Berkeley: U of California P, 1987.

Krupat, Arnold. *The Voice in the Margin.* Berkeley: U of California P, 1989.

Ong, Walter. *Interfaces of the Word.* Ithaca and London: Cornell UP, 1977.

Ong, Walter. *Orality and Literacy: The Technologizing of the Word.* London and New York: Methuen, 1982.

Rose, Wendy. "The Great Pretenders: Further Reflections on Whiteshamanism." *The State of Native America: Genocide, Colonization, and Resistance.* ed. M. Annette Jaimes. Boston: South End Press, 1992.

Swann, Brian. "Introduction." *Harper's Anthology of 20th Century Native American Poetry.* ed. Duane Niatum. San Francisco: Harper Collins, 1988.

Taylor, Mark C. *Erring: A Postmodern A/theology.* Chicago: U of Chicago P, 1984.

Vizenor, Gerald. *Earthdivers.* Minneapolis: U of Minnesota P, 1981.

Vizenor, Gerald. ed. *Narrative Chance: Postmodern Discourse on Native American Indian Literatures.* Albuquerque: U of New Mexico P, 1989.

The Literary Physician

ANN-JANINE MOREY

I n some religious circles, Jesus functions rather like an imaginary playmate for grownups. His presence is calming and nurturing, and he is available twenty-four hours a day to protect and guide the believer. He is never sweaty, sick, whiney, distracted, greedy, lustful or grouchy. If he does have something reproachful to say, he always does so in a way that makes us grateful to hear it. He extends a healing, unconditional love to the heartsick petitioner, and his love is healing because he is the one who listens when all the world is deaf. That is, Jesus is both the perfect listener and the supreme healer, and these two activities are intrinsically linked together: listening and healing. When all human resources fail, healing is still available because Jesus hears our story, and his listening answers the plea of the suffering heart.

Jesus' identity as supreme listener is of a piece with the narrative genesis of Christian Word—creation by word and story, and a relationship between the divine and human by way of dialogue and response. "May I learn from you, who are Truth, and may I put close to your mouth the ear of my heart," says St. Augustine to God in a tenderly construed exchange of telling and listening (75). The heart, the "hidden mouth" that tastes the joy of the "rumination of your bread" (Augustine 114) is the instrument of reception, and in combining sensual metaphors of taste and sound, Augustine underlines the union of spiritual and physical activity in this hearing "as one hears in the heart" (150). Sometimes just knowing we have been heard is sufficient to bring comfort. At other times listening and hearing demand specific action as response. But without hearing "as one hears in the heart," there can be no appropriate response to the telling.

Listening is part of the narrative motion, and what I want to discuss in this essay is how efficacious listening is part of our ethical obligation as literary critics and scholars. I situate my interest in listening and hearing as part of a larger concern about the professional integrity of the humanities, and I use "listening" and "hearing" literally— that which we take in through the ears—and expansively—a quality of perception that engages all of our senses. To hear is to see, and to touch, and finally to understand. From such listening we are able to construct meaningful descriptions of human experience, narratives that stretch toward truth and the real in ways that encourage community and personal well being. Listening and narrative integrity are directly related to one another.

I am intrigued with listening as a literary-critical imperative because I am distressed by what seems to me a deficit in this dimension of the literary critical enterprise, if not in the human community at large. This deficit is visible in at least two dimensions, which may be related to one another. One is the distinctly un-human prose being emitted in some scholarly circles, and the other is the increasing fragmentation of the human community.

First, I have some uneasy sense that we (humanists in general; literature scholars in particular) have lost an intrinsic sense of purpose about the materials with which we work. In our writing, we make many claims to cultural and personal significance on behalf of narrative and our own words, but rarely are we in any danger of putting those claims on the line. Moreover, academic language sometimes gets so abstract, it is hard to tell we are speaking of anything human at all. We interrogate, privilege, subvert, elide or decenter texts, but when was the last time we read a good book and spoke about its contribution to human meaning in clear, vivid language? I take the convolution of our professional prose as a distress signal indicating a degradation of narrative skill that in turn implicates our inability to listen. Having heard nothing outside ourselves, it is possible that we have little to say, and so need many large words to cover up this deficit. My assumption is that beyond our own aesthetic and intellectual delight, we have an obligation as scholars and critics to address questions of human meaning through our materials, and to do so in such ways as to engage people beyond our immediate academic circles.

Second, I am concerned about doing justice to diverse voices while still affirming community and a sense of human commonality. In what is by now a scholarly cliché, feminist scholars have argued that the life-line stories of the "other" have been untold, repressed, and excluded from mainstream conversation. This is true, and women and minorities have every right to insist that difference matters and cannot be effaced by the dominance of "white" and "male." But I wonder: is there nothing at all we share as human beings?[1] And, *what if no one is listening?* Listening and really hearing something, after all, is a risky business, as Wayne Booth reminds us. When a well-told tale engages us, he says, it not only occupies our time, it occupies us. We are "colonized, occupied by a foreign, imaginary world," (Booth 139) and we can never be the same again. We are importuned on every side to hear the distinctive story of the other, but amidst the explosion of telling that has so energized the literary and theological world, who is listening? There has been so much emphasis on telling the story, but far less discussion of what it means to hear and to respond.

I have just leveled some generalized indictments at humanities scholarship, and in them I come uncomfortably close to joining the ranks of those who are making a career of criticizing the profession (Bloom, D'Souza). A good deal of intellectual-bashing issues forth from those who are protecting the traditional status of the humanities as a Eurocentric male preserve. But just because they are wrong in this attitude doesn't mean they are wrong about everything, and where we are vulnerable is in our failure to be vigilant and expressive about the meaningfulness of our pursuits. I do not scorn what we do as intellectuals, and where ideas are difficult to express, prose, too, must be challenging. Not everything we write must be for everyone. Nor do I think that intellectual life is somehow not as real as other forms of life. It is real because we are real people who love words and books and ideas, pursuits as real and as important as any other human occupation. My concern, however, is that while we reflexively insist that literature is a precious cultural resource, there is too little in the quality of our writing that invites and secures assent. Why do we do what we do, and when was the last time we made an effective case for the study of literature?

Obviously, I am not going to answer all these concerns in a single essay, but I have an intriguing resource to offer. I have turned to a writing community who values literature, and whose purposefulness is rarely in question, that of the literary physician. In this group I include psychiatrists, neurologists, surgeons and family practitioners who have written about their work in novels, short stories or nonfiction essays. These are writers who share our concerns about narrative, human meaning and professional integrity, and several of them are conscientious critics of their own profession. For them, narrative is not a game but a life resource, for, obviously, human lives depend upon their listening and narrative skills. But writing physicians also look beyond the diagnostic utility of narrative, for they believe that the goodness of life depends upon the exchange of telling and listening that comprises the narrative act. The narrative act, then, is a basic activity of human relationship. In telling and receiving a story, shared meanings and individual dignity are confirmed and renewed between persons, within community. That is why these literary physicians write, and perhaps their respect for narrative as a healing, moral activity can help refresh our own sense of purpose and meaning.

Although in this essay I am working with contemporary medical sources, the literary physician is not a recent literary novelty, and my resources are both aware of and obliged to their writing forbears. Rabelais, Chekhov, and William Carlos Williams all wrestled with how to "reveal the truth that lies hidden in the body" says surgeon Richard Selzer, "and that, too, is why I write" (15). For Selzer, the struggle to say and name is part of the "ritual of surgery," for practicing medicine demands a constant reflection on the intricate interlacing of pain, healing, and human love.

While Selzer celebrates the poet as the "only true doctor" (15), pediatrician Perri Klass approaches the relationship of healing and narrative from a different angle. She is interested in challenging the relationship between fiction and reality, and in her first novel, *Other Women's Children*,[2] she encourages us to reflect upon what constitutes a meaningful narrative and why we need stories at all. The narrator, Amelia Stern, is also a pediatrician and the mother of Alexander, who is a healthy, happy, white four year old. One of Amelia's patients is Darren Wilson, a black four year old dying of AIDS. Amelia tells us that she became a pediatrician because, unlike other populations, children are more likely to get well. AIDS, however, has changed all of that, and her professional life is increasingly consumed with struggling to comprehend the fatal distance between Alexander and Darren.

Amelia is an avid reader of nineteenth century women's fiction, and she retreats to the world of *Little Women*, *Rebecca of Sunnybrook Farm* and *Uncle Tom's Cabin* for relaxation. She takes comfort from the domesticity of the Alcotts, because "one of the qualities I envy is a sense of place, of propriety" (OWC 218). There is a universe of stability and coherent life order provided in *Little Women* and novels like it, and as Amelia's own marital crisis looms before her, she takes a trip to Orchard House, and finds the visit fulfilling and reassuring.

Like many readers, Amelia is not consistent about what she asks from her literary experience. She happily accepts the image of security, cheerful poverty and maternal omniscience portrayed in *Little Women*, yet she is furious with the portrayal of children's deaths in this same literature. "Dying children are the sweet creamy centers of literature; bite in and reach the dying child. . . goo and tooth decay. . . . Conjure up its endearing graces, the intensity of parental love which cannot protect it, the frail little limbs, the eyes, the smile—then kill the child off" (OWC 58, 81). Amelia is angry about two things relative to nineteenth century literature: that children are used as expedient plot devices to wring a sure response from an audience, and these authors cannot or will not tell the truth about death, but instead, they offer nonsense about heaven and angels and eternal consolation. Amelia wants resources for understanding both Darren's impending death *and* the unmerited safety of her own child, but the slow, torturous and technologically constructed death of a child barely visible in the mechanical glitter of a hospital finds no analog in the extravagant deathbed prose of the nineteenth century. The death of a child is "an unbearable thing. An impossible thing. I have a child and I cannot imagine it," (OWC 212) she says, and so she is angry at literature for not providing her with some realistic truths that will sustain her where medicine cannot.

Although *Other Women's Children* is filled with literary allusions, there is more emotional coherence than literary coherence to Amelia's musings. But Klass does want us to take the lives of children seriously, and in so doing, she urges us toward the dramatic question that structures her concern for children: how do we understand the difference between fiction and real life? The novel insists that there is a significant difference between dying, and writing about dying; between the reality of what a physician does and what a writer does. At one point, Amelia stops and addresses the audience directly about her writing strategy, inviting speculation about her narrative choices. Alexander is seriously ill; she could let him die—there are plausible medical situations available to the plot; the tragic outcome might play out thusly. But maybe she won't do this, and Alexander will thrive after all. In fact, what may be approaching acute morbidity is her marriage, not her son. And so, Alexander is spared, the marriage falters to its breaking point, and Darren will most certainly die.

In this brief, direct encounter with her gentle readers, the narrator calls our attention to the god-like author, who is making decisions in a plot about the god-like doctor. Look how powerful I am as an author and as a physician; yet look at the difference. What happens in a novel can be done, or undone, or done again. The same is not true for a doctor. The decisions made by Perri Klass the pediatrician are of a much different portent from the decisions made by Perri Klass the author.

This seems too obvious. Clearly, there is an immense difference between a fictional death and a real death, so much so the literary project appears hopelessly trivial in comparison. It is not my purpose, nor Klass's, to take cheap shots at academics and fiction writers, but is it my purpose to reflect upon the significance of what we do. Good stories *are* important;

they are the reason we do what we do, and they are not dispensable. This is clearly demonstrated in *Other Women's Children*. While Amelia protests the crushing gap between fiction and reality, she also returns to narrative and literary image as a resource for expressing and managing reality.

For example, given her complaints about the unrealistic deaths of children in nineteenth century fiction, we anticipate the death of Darren as the location where the narrator can set the story straight. And yet, Darren's death is easily as affecting as any of the nineteenth century scenes she complains about. One reason for this is that Amelia constructs the death through alternating images: the nineteenth century description contrasted with clinical language about the physiological process of death. Even though she stops periodically and tells you it didn't happen that way, the language of nineteenth century literary death becomes part of our experience in reading about Darren. Furthermore, despite the clinical structuring of Darren's death, Amelia adds the same heart-wrenching details any nineteenth century author might have noted: the tattered stuffed animal abandoned on the bed, the Grandmother sobbing on her knees, the little light body resting across his father's legs, the sure slowing of breath. All of these images are as plausible and truthful as the unadorned facts of bodily death, and so through Amelia, Klass, like her nineteenth century forebears, wrings from her audience willing tears, because no matter how you describe it, the death of a child is an unthinkable thing. Perhaps, then, nineteenth century novels do tell the truth about dying children. The emotions aroused are utterly appropriate to the subject, and such expression may be the only—and essential—consolation we have coming to us. Clearly, in constructing the narrative around the nineteenth century image, Amelia willingly draws upon that cathartic function, even while she cries out against its inadequacy.

Amelia concludes her narrative with her wish for her children, and imagines them healthy and whole, gamboling down the sterile hallways, warming the metallic rooms with shouts and laughter as they leave. Her vision is not simply narrative sentimentality; it is necessary for her well-being as a physician to be able to imagine a different ending, and to affirm her own work toward that ending, even if it doesn't always prevail. Amelia's relationship to narrative imagination as an essential, expressive access to the humanity of pain *and* possibility parallels any number of her real life counterparts who are my resources here: Perri Klass, Robert Coles, Oliver Sacks, Richard Selzer, William Carlos Williams.

My first point, then, recapitulates the agenda of *Other Women's Children*. It's time to get real about the difference between fiction and real life. Only then can we proclaim the genuine power of our professional materials and the contribution we have to make. Despite its human origin, scholarship suffers from its isolation from the concrete and vivid realities of human experience, and thus we find rather preposterous claims for the earth-shaking effects of literature and literary scholarship. Jane Flax makes this point in *Thinking Fragments*, using the postmodern notation of the disappearing self as an example. Postmodernist theory marks and even celebrates the decentered self, but Flax comments with both puzzlement and wonder that surely such an outlook takes for granted the essential wholeness of a sense of self, or else it would not be possible to anticipate the loss of self with such cheer and anticipation. Persons who actually suffer from clinical disorders in which the core self is so fragmented as to deform normal emotional and social relationships find nothing liberating about their decentered self (Flax 218-19). As a critic and scholar, perhaps Flax can tell her clients that they suffer from the postmodern condition, and to enjoy the playfulness and vertigo of their situation. But what can she offer as a therapist who understands the importance of a coherent sense of identity for human functioning?[3] About this aspect of postmodernism, then, Flax concludes that as a theory of knowledge and human meaning. . . "postmodernism in any existing form fails." We are not "two intersecting stories or texts in search of a temporarily mutually agreeable ending. I am not a scientist in a laboratory confronting a piece of a stream of "data" utterly other to and unaffected by me." What may be good-natured, experimental fun for the literary critic has serious consequences on other fronts, for "the analyst must be responsible to others in her work in ways that the literary critic is not" (131).

My second point is that in order to get some responsible perspective on ourselves, we need to recover meaningful language. The fascination of postmodernist theory with its own abstracted texts about texts is expressed in a dense, intricate wordiness that is brilliance to one reader and sheer techno-babble to another. But while this dazzling intellectual word play may well serve the needs of a small academic community, it offers little to the educated community at large. Slowly the humanity of the humanities disappears. It is something like this: "When the heart dies, we slip into wordy and doctrinaire caricatures of life. Our journals, our habits of talk become cluttered with jargon or the trivial. . . . As words grow longer and the concepts more intricate and tedious, human sorrows and temptations disappear, loves move away, envies and jealousies, revenge and terror dissolve. Gone are strong, sensible words with good meaning and the flavor of the real" (Coles, *Mind's Fate* 9).

This was Robert Coles, writing to his fellow psychiatrists in 1961, but his words are fully as urgent for his profession, and ours, as they were then. Physicians, like academics, have developed professional communication models that enhance their authority by creating a sense of distance and objectivity from the subject. Physicians write case histories in flat, formulaic prose that summarizes the patient as set of historical facts and presenting symptoms. One function of this professional prose is that the depersonalized case history gives the physician some breathing room. In *Other Women's Children* the narrative voice switches back and forth between first and third person, reminding us of the kind of emotional and imaginative shuttle necessitated by the physician's encounter with pain and despair. Sometimes you must stand outside yourself in order to preserve yourself. A physician has reason for distancing; no one could take the death of every child into themselves and still function.

Another function of the abstracted case history is that it presumably eliminates the subjectivity of the client narrative in favor of the objectivity of the physician's hearing. It assumes, in other words, a temporary, artificial certainty, where, in fact, there seldom is any (Hunter, *Doctor's Stories*) Medicine is not an exact science; much depends upon narrative guesswork and metaphoric leaps of imagination. Indeed, "clinical judgment is not so much a mathematical or logical ability of determining causes as a fundamentally interpretive one, a capacity for identifying and understanding the significant elements of multifactorial situations in the process of change. In narrative terms, it is the ability to discern a plot" (Hunter, *Doctor's Stories* 45). The clinical language of case study gives the physician a way to avoid overloading on painful human encounter, but it also insulates the physician from "ineradicable uncertainty" (Hunter, *Doctor's Stories* 81). Correspondingly, scholarly language functions much like case history language— it depersonalizes and in the deployment of weighty terms, achieves a "sounds like" sort of authority and certainty about what is, in fact, the "ineradicable uncertainty" of the human condition.

Robert Coles, like a number of writing physicians, links integrity of language with somatic, psychological and professional well-being. Coles suggests that theory, the source of so much abstracting and alienating medical language, in fact has its roots in concrete, visual experience, for the root means something like "I behold," as in what we do when we go to the theater. Theoretical language, then, addresses the human drama as an enlargement of our observations. Those observations, and that theory, then, should be rooted in the image, in concrete human experience, which we shape through the agency of narrative coherence.

Neurologist Oliver Sacks, who also defines the medical project in terms of narrative efficacy makes an important related point. Typical current diagnostic practice that is structured by categorical questioning from physicians reduces physical and metaphysical experience to mechanical terms. "How, what, when, where" physician directed questions that elicit primarily "yes," "no" and pointing answers foreclose on the possibility of learning something new, and in thwarting narrative information, "prevents the possibility of forming a picture, or pictures of what it is like to be as one is" (Sacks, *Awakenings* 25). It is the word pictures, the language of metaphor, image, symbol and narrative, that enables the physician to be a fellow traveler with the patient.

For Sacks, connection and communication occur most meaningfully in the concrete, not the abstract. Thus, the guiding philosophical principle of his case studies in *The Man Who Mistook His Wife for a Hat* is that case studies, or stories, perform the crucial function of restoring the human subject to the center, and like a number of other writing physicians, Sacks approaches this task with almost missionary zeal. *The Man Who Mistook His Wife for a Hat* begins with a medical parable about the soul-soullessness of radical abstraction brought on by an irreversible neurological deficit. The subject of the title essay, Dr. P, suffers from a profound visual agnosia, "in which all powers of representation and imagery, all sense of the concrete, all sense of reality were being destroyed" (17). Dr. P. sees like a computer, by means of key features and schematic relationships, and he recognizes people only if the presenting human can be identified within some schematic or paradigmatic relationship; hence, mistaking his wife for a hat atop a hat rack. Sacks, who is not known for understatement, turns this case study of severe neurological deficit into a warning about what happens to "a science which eschews the judgmental, the particular, the personal, and becomes entirely abstract and computational" (20). The cognitive sciences, he warns, suffer from the same kind of agnosia, and like Dr. P., are unaware of the horror of their deficit.

When Sacks argues that the life-saving capacity to connect appears most meaningfully in the realm of the concrete, not the abstract, he means nature, metaphor and symbolic language which create a personal, narrative weave. Sacks makes this point most dramatically with Rebecca, who is severely retarded. Rebecca falls apart under conceptual testing, but responds with grace and insight when offered the language of poetry and dance as forms of communication and expression. She is, Sacks says, alive and healthy as a narrative being, fully capable of appreciating the world and relating to other human beings. Poetry and dance are rich with image and metaphor and symbol, the embodied, figurative, connecting language that Sacks links with the concrete. "Concreteness is often seen by neurologists as a wretched thing, beneath consideration," but as far as Sacks is concerned,

> Narrative comes first, has spiritual priority. Very young children love and demand stories, and can understand complex matters presented as stories, when their powers of comprehending general concepts, paradigms are almost non-existent. It is this narrative of symbolic power which gives a *sense of the world*—a concrete reality in the imaginative form of symbol and story—when abstract thought can provide nothing at all (184, his emphasis).

In both *Awakenings* and *The Man Who Mistook His Wife for a Hat*, Sacks quotes his mentor, A.I. Luria, who wrote: "The power to describe, which was so common to the great nineteenth century psychiatrists, is almost gone" (viii). Luria is talking about the intrinsic power of right description to set one toward the truth. The power to vivify, make concrete, and render the nuances of human encounter in all its complexity is a descriptive, narrative power, integral to ethical reflection and healing. Philosopher Martha Nussbaum links the lucidity of literary perception with a quality of moral imagination that apprehends the intricacy and intimacy of human relations. Following the lead of Henry James, Nussbaum argues that through the refinement of our descriptive powers realized in literary vision, we are cultivating the "fine development of our human capabilities to see and feel and judge; an ability to miss less, to be responsible to more" (166), so that by "painful, vigilant effort, the intense scrutiny of particulars" we "make ourselves people 'on whom nothing is lost'" (148). Luria and Sacks lament the dearth of this descriptive ability in contemporary physicians. I suggest that we might well join this regret regarding our own profession as theologians and scholars, because where we fail to engage in the challenge of rich description, we impoverish our ability to function as moral beings.

Preceding description, however, is the hearing and listening, as is quite clear from Sacks's relationships with his patients. With Williams and Coles, he understands that "what you are hearing [from the patient] is to some considerable extent a function of *you*, hearing" (15, his emphasis). Indeed, when Robert Coles speaks of story, he is speaking about a process of reciprocity between the physician and the patient in which hearing is part of the story. That is, the primary teller of the story is the patient, but the primary listener is the physician, whose listening may hold the key to their very lives.

Here, then, is my third point. Not only must our language be regrounded in the concrete, but the power and meaningfulness of our descriptions depend upon the reciprocity of telling *and* listening in the human encounter through narrative. Coles's mentor, William Carlos Williams tells Coles that it's his job to be an all-day listener. "The people who come to see us bring their stories. They hope they tell them well enough so that we understand the truth of their lives. They hope we know how to interpret their stories correctly" (*Call* 7). This makes the physician sound more like a literary critic than a medical professional, and the young Coles is uncomfortable with the idea that a doctor is a reconstructor of stories. After all, he has been learning all this impressive medical and technological language, and so he argues with himself that medical jargon and procedure is just efficient shorthand. Characteristically, Williams retorts "Who's against shorthand? No one I know. Who wants to be shortchanged? No one I know" (*Call*, 29).

The ability to describe and see whole is predicated upon one's hearing and seeing—the extent to which we are genuinely open to another's reality. The kind of whole sense, whole self listening I am interested in here calls for an alarming intimacy and risk taking between audience and teller. Richard Selzer watches the diagnostic ministrations of Yeshi Dhonden, personal physician to the Dalai Lama. Dhonden, who is diagnosing an elderly woman, says little, but looks and touches. "I cannot see their hands joined in a correspondence that is exclusive, intimate, his fingertips receiving the voice of her sick body through the rhythm and throb she offers at her wrist. . . . All at once I am envious. . . . I want to be held like that, touched so, *received*. And I know that I, who has palpated a hundred thousand pulses, have not felt a single one" (34, his emphasis). Here, in the delicate touch of finger to pulse, Selzer translates a quality of hearing into such a profound acceptance of another as to constitute an embrace.

Indeed, even on a strictly literary plane the same kind of exchange of story is characterized by Mikhail Bakhtin as a highly intimate and erotic activity. What is heard is tasted upon the lips. According to David Patterson, Bakhtin's dialogic moves from mouth to mouth, not mouth to ear; "speaking and listening are simultaneous, not mutually exclusive. The organ by which we hear is the tongue; whether we are in the position of speaker or listener, we hear by responding" (35). When Janie in *Their Eyes Were Watching God* tells her story to Phoebe, Janie says "mah tongue is in mah friend's mouf" (17), articulating the same unblushingly intimate relationship between the teller and the hearer. To hear in this way is to take the story into oneself, and be forever changed in the transaction. No story can be complete without the graciousness and reciprocity of hearing, a hearing that responds with a full, open self, a self that risks touching and being touched. The kind of lucidity of perception called for by Martha Nussbaum and by the literary physicians quoted here, requires an attentiveness that can surely be described as moral in both its openness to the reality of the other, and in the necessary call to response elicited in the listening.

Not only is good listening a risky venture, its danger is compounded by the gender values placed upon listening. Traditionally women are the good listeners and good watchers, not the tellers of the tale, but compliant vessels waiting to be filled with the living word. Jane Flax addresses the gendered nature of the listening professions, commenting that although Freud called for psychoanalysis to be a flat, objective mirror, in fact the process is relational and intersubjective. But because openness and relationality are female defined and real work is instrumental and male defined, "look how threatening it would be to rethink psychoanalysis as relational: mothers relate, women relate—almost anyone could do this work; it is not scientific or skilled; no intrepid, objective, ruthless, heroic, skilled professional here" (Flax 87). Without belaboring the point, then, I suggest that one of the barriers to reciprocity is the way in which genuine listening is gender stigmatized. Women listen, men proclaim. Women receive, men inform. But who will listen to the listener?

Oliver Sacks tells two stories about Korsakov's syndrome, the profound amnesia usually brought on by alcoholism. In each case the victim is doomed to endless chatter whenever in the presence of other persons, because human encounter requires a self, and these men cannot remember a self to bring forth. Thus, their identity must be continually constructed in each present moment. So they talk, rehearsing the few fragments of the distant past still available to them, casting about for clues, raising voice against the psychological silence of no-self. Sacks comments that it is exhausting to be around these people, because there is certainly no exchange of self or ideas, and no rest for either party in this desperate kind of monologue. Without narrative memory, these people do not have enough self to allow them to stop talking. Sometimes we academics act like this too. We are all so eager to talk and be heard, and we've all been trapped in endless monosations (monologue masquerading as conversation) with self-absorbed intellectuals, who, if we are honest, are irritating to us because they don't have the good grace to shut up and let a real expert do the talking. How often are we secure enough in self to listen?

It is common to complain that doctors are cold and remote and think they are godlike, and medical schools have, to varying degrees, instituted courses in ethics, or literature and medicine, as a way to rehumanize the profession. Like physicians, perhaps we, too, should be looking to renew our sense of human commitment. I would like to see us work towards an ideal suggested by Robert Detweiler in *Breaking the Fall*. There he comments that although we (the scholarly community) give lip service to community and conversation, in fact we have been having monologues punctuated by long silences. Could we not, he asks, restore "the pleasures of trustful exchange based on principles of friendship rather than power?" (Detweiler 34), and in so doing, create the kind of sustaining narrative community that could respond to our uncertainty and hope?

The gifted physician writers I've used here look to literature and narrative, not to escape the responsibility of humanity, but to fulfill it. Sacks and Luria, Klass, Coles and Selzer all testify to the ethical imperative of medicine to rehumanize its habitat through a quality of narrative in which one human being strives to walk with the other, if only for a while. They urge their readers to know the whole, physical self as a hearing, healing instrument, to listen and hear "as one hears in the heart." Are we up to the challenge? What if we had to listen and write as if someone's life depended on our narrative and interpretive skills?

Finally, I think that this question of listening as moral, narrative activity has cultural urgency because of the erosion of cultural confidence in our divine listener. As I suggested at the beginning of the essay, Christendom is created by a living word, the narrative coherence of creation sustained by a supreme active listener, perhaps the only one who hears when all others are deaf. It is fair to note, however, that as our confidence in a divine listener recedes as cultural currency, we have, over the course of a century, seen secular models develop to fill that gap in the form of the counseling professions. Now, many of us pay someone to be a good listener, suggesting at the least, a breakdown in personal relations that surely signals a deeper crisis of human community, if not metaphysical community. Certainly both modernist and postmodernist fictions explore the frightening possibility that there is no such divine ear, leading to the desperate postmodern leap into the divine author's seat, as though we would be creator and teller, hearer and audience at the same time. I don't know what conclusion or reassurance may be available from this move, but the theological urgency of literary practice suggests at least one universal in this world of contending voices—our common terror that without being heard, we will perish.

NOTES

1. I am aware that many scholars still critique the idea of human universals as a method of suppressing difference in favor of a dominant group. I understand and share this concern in previous writings. Women and minorities must be granted the space and time in which to articulate their distinctive experience. After that, however, I find it hard to believe that we cannot responsibly speak of some shared human experiences, and do so without violating the dignity and distinctiveness of human diversity.

2. Perri Klass, *Other Women's Children* (New York: Random House, 1990). Hereafter cited as OWC with page number.

3. Flax is careful to distinguish between the idea of a unitary self, that postmodernism rightly critiques, and a core self. A core self is essential for human functioning, for it provides a basic sense of continuity from which to negotiate the world. See her discussion, pp. 218-219.

WORKS CITED

Augustine. *The Confessions of St. Augustine.* trans. Rex Warner. New York: NAL, 1963.

Bloom, Allan. *The Closing of the American Mind.* New York: Simon & Schuster, 1987.

Booth, Wayne. *The Company We Keep: An Ethics of Fiction.* Berkeley: University of California Press, 1988.

Coles, Robert. *The Mind's Fate: Ways of Seeing Psychiatry and Psychoanalysis.* Boston: Little, Brown and Company, 1975.

Coles, Robert. *The Call of Stories: Teaching and the Moral Imagination.* Boston: Houghton Mifflin 1989.

Detweiler, Robert. *Breaking the Fall: Religious Readings of Contemporary Fiction.* San Francisco: Harper & Row, 1989.

D'Souza, Dinesh. *Illiberal Education: The Politics of Race and Sex on Campus.* New York: Free Press, 1991.

Flax, Jane. *Thinking Fragments: Psychoanalysis, Feminism and Postmodernism in the Contemporary West.* Berkeley: University of California Press, 1990.

Hunter, Kathryn Montgomery. *Doctor's Stories: The Narrative Structure of Medical Knowledge.* Princeton: Princeton University Press, 1991.

Hurston, Zora Neale. *Their Eyes Were Watching God.* Urbana: University of Illinois Press, 1978.

Klass, Perri. *Other Women's Children.* New York: Random House, 1990.

Nussbaum, Martha. "'Finely Aware and Richly Responsible': Literature and the Moral Imagination." in *Love's Knowledge: Essays on Philosophy and Literature.* New York: Oxford University Press, 1990.

Patterson, David. "Bakhtin on Word and Spirit: the Religiosity of Responsibility." *Cross Currents* 41 (Spring): 33-51, 1991.

Sacks, Oliver. *The Man Who Mistook His Wife for a Hat*. New York: Harper & Row, 1985.

Sacks, Oliver. *Awakenings*. New York: HarperPerennial, 1990.

Selzer, Richard. *Mortal Lessons: Notes on the Art of Surgery*. New York: Simon and Schuster, 1976.

Unspeakable Hungers and the Strategems of Sacrifice

BARBARA DECONCINI

Introduction

Margaret Atwood's first novel, *The Edible Woman*, ends with a darkly comic gesture, a bizarre inversion of the Betty Crocker ethos of femininity. Marian, whose engagement to be married coincides with a progressively severe anorexia, bakes a cake to serve with tea to her fiancé. The cake is an effigy of herself, and she presents her confectionery double to him

> "carefully and with reverence, as though she was carrying something sacred in a procession, an icon. . . She knelt, setting the platter on the coffee–table in front of Peter.

> 'You've been trying to assimilate me. But I've made you a   substitute, something you'll like much better. . . I'll get you a fork" (EW 284).

Peter quickly loses his appetite—for Marian no less than the Marian confection. She is left alone to take tea and cake in her own image, to practice a Marian devotion in Proustian parody, a communion in which she is both consumer and consumed, sacred host and communicant. When her roommate, on discovering her, offers a horrified critical interpretation of this ritualized eating— "Marian, you're rejecting your femininity!"—, Marian "plunges her fork into the carcass, neatly severing the body from the head" (EW 286).

Anyone familiar with the Atwood corpus will recognize already in this earliest fiction, written when she was a graduate student and barely twenty–four, the contours of what must surely be her most perduring metaphoric and metonymic preoccupations: the "slippage" between and among the orders of the human and of nature, the separation of head from body, body as a site of psychological and cultural struggle, and the highly–ritualized sacred and sinful power of food and eating.

By my count, no less than eight of the ten stories in Atwood's most recent work, *Wilderness Tips*,[2] to some extent construct *their* dynamic of plot and meaning in terms of this nexus of food, eating, and the body. One of these stories, "Hairball," ends with a wildly grotesque evocation of the Marian devotion of *The Edible Woman*. Here the super–sophisticated, avant-garde career woman protagonist, Kat, ("as in KitKat,' she comments coyly to her soon–to–be lover, "That's a chocolate bar. Melts in your mouth" (WT 39)), later extricates herself emotionally from the vacuous affair that has ended badly through a ritualized food offering.

She sends—to her erstwhile business associate and lover and his wife with the freeze–framed hair—the same sort of box of designer chocolate truffles he sent her when she seduced him. ("The banality, the sweetness, the hunger to impress: that was Gerald," she thinks at the time (WT 40)). At the story's end, the now unnecessary and outmaneuvered Kat carefully flavors, dusts with chocolate, and wraps the grapefruit–sized ovarian cyst recently cut from her own body, nestles it among the other truffles, a queen among drones, and has it special–delivered to Gerald's cocktail party.

"Gerald, sorry I couldn't be with you," she notes on the card. "This is all the rage" (WT 47). The gift, she thinks, is distinctively her: valuable, dangerous. It is as well, she finally and painfully realizes, the thwarted fetus of their ungenerative affair. Kat ends where Marian ends, where virtually all of Atwood's characters and stories end: wiser, refusing the tempting role of female victim, poised for decision and change.

Marian's cake and Kat's hairball blur the boundaries between food and the body, outside and inside, making of food a fetish which gathers up, distills, and literalizes "all the rage," embodying in their offering gestures dark rituals of sacrifice and communion.

Part of what makes these sacrificial communions so disturbing, I think, is the way they press against and even exceed the boundaries of social acceptability. Indeed, there is about them—especially the latter—a whiff, if not the aroma, of cannibalism. It is intriguing in this connection to remind ourselves of the structuralists' work on food as a cultural category.

As anthropologist Marshall Sahlins demonstrates, we "practice a meaningful calculus of food preferences" in our "specific valuation of edibility and inedibility" (Sahlins 95). The operative criterion is the relation of the animal species to human society, i.e., whether the animal participates as "subject or object in the company of men" (97). (We do not, for example, eat dogs or cats). Inflected throughout by the principle of metonymy, our food (i.e., meat) system is a sustained metaphor on cannibalism (Sahlins 97). From another perspective, might we speculate that eating a particular species (in Atwood's case, women) can be understood as a way of objectifying; or, that offering oneself to be eaten might be interpreted as expressing one's sense of objectification?

In this essay I examine certain religio–cultural texts of women and food—networks of signifying practices that inscribe communion and sacrifice on women's bodies. I trace two separate food–inscribed codes which leave their traces in the Atwood passages cited above: the encodings of eating as religious practice and of femininity on women's bodies. In the spaces between these alimentary canals, I cleanse our palates with a tid–bit of French feminism, served up as *parler femme* and *écriture feminine*, themselves a "nourricriture," a nourishing and nurturing "writing (and speaking) the body" to feed resistance (Minh–ha 33, 38).

Let us begin with *cuisine as religious ritual*, allowing our thinking to be guided by some fascinating and suggestive work by a group of French anthropologists recently published in English as *The Cuisine of Sacrifice among the Greeks.*

Cuisine As Religious Ritual

As students of religion and religions, we do not need convincing about the power of food and, more exactly, of cuisine as signifying practice in the range of cultures, periods, and worldview systems. Indeed, we'd be hard pressed to name a religious tradition which does *not* take food seriously as *religious*, as part of the economy of signification which encompasses the always situational and relational categories of "sacred" and "profane" (Smith 1982, 46, 55). Whether we are considering dietary rules and food taboos in Buddhism, Islam, Jainism and the Indian religions, table rituals in Judaism and Christianity, the menstrual cuisines of Africa, or the entire self–definition of a people as food–related, as in the Hopi and other Native American tribes—food and its practices are pervasive religious phenomena. As Joyce Carol Oates wryly comments, God seems to care, and care mightily, not only *what* but also *how* we eat! (Oates 31).

Nor is this surprising, when we consider how important food is: how essential to life, how commonplace, how at once natural and cultural, culture–thick and culture–specific. Freud describes the obsession common to both neurosis and religion as "little preoccupations, performances, restrictions and arrangements in certain activities of everyday life" and "the tendency to displacement. . . which turns apparently trivial matters into those of great and utter importance" (Freud 9:117–127). As Jonathan Z. Smith comments, Freud's "remains the most telling description of a significant and perhaps even distinctive characteristic of religious activity" (39).

If religious ritual trades on the potentiality for significance in the commonplace, it is no wonder that food and its practices, so capable of bearing obsession, are a privileged site of religious activity (Smith 1989, 56). Even though religion scholars have devoted comparatively little of their attention to food per se, it is certainly not new to study the relations between religion and society through an inquiry focused on sacrificial meals, i.e., religious practices in which killing and eating animals are a way of maintaining relations with divine powers (Detienne & Vernant 1). As Marcel Detienne notes, such inquiry stretches from the Church Fathers to modern sociology and philosophy of culture in the work of Mauss and Durkheim, Cassirer and Girard.

Anthropologists have demonstrated the sacrificial meal's paradigmatic force for social hierarchy in Indo–European cultures (Smith, 1991), and in this the Greeks were no exception. On the one hand, participation in a political community authorized the sacrifice. On the other, the sacrifice confirmed the group's political cohesion by enacting the community's sense of itself with respect to the divine powers. If the importance of the sacrificial rites derives from their relation to political power (Detienne 14), it is because both are expressions of a cosmological order.

By and large women are excluded from the sacrificial meal, their absence signaling their peripheral location both politically and religiously. "As a general rule," writes Detienne, "by virtue of the homology between political power and sacrificial practice, the place reserved for women perfectly corresponds to the one they occupy—or rather, do *not* occupy—in the space of the city. Just as women are without the political rights reserved for male citizens, they are kept apart from the altars, meat, and blood" (131).

In other words, the Greek's cuisine of sacrifice is *gendered* space. Women tend to be excluded from this most commonplace and most significant politico–religious practice, and excluded precisely *because of* its significance. I want to propose as a thesis, however, that if *women* are absent from the food rite, *woman* is not. I want to argue that *woman* is present at each and every sacrificial event in the position of the *absent referent* of the rite. With the introduction of the notion of "absent referent" I am inserting into our discourse the Lacanian notion of the phallic signifier and its lack which makes its explicit entry below.

We turn now to the sacrifice's narrative context, for it is myth that provides the evidence for the religious justification of the rite's gendered character. My claim is that the myth's very inclusion of *woman* has explanatory force for the exclusion of *women* from both political and religious participation in the society.

The myth in question is that of Prometheus which, according to Jean-Pierre Vernant, "provides a valuable key to the mental system to which the (Greek sacrificial) ritual refers and the vast network of meanings that it bears" (21). In the story, the Titan Prometheus steals fire from the Olympians and makes a gift of it to man. He is punished for his perfidy by having his liver served up daily as dinner to Zeus' eagle–turned–ravenous-dog. But this is only the central episode in a sequence of events which together make up the plot of the myth as it appears in Hesiod's *Theogony*. As such, this event is embedded in a textual dynamics, a force–field of motives and consequences. Vernant claims that classical scholars have commonly ignored this narrative plotting and thus have misunderstood the relation of sequence to pattern in the story as a whole. His analysis shows how such inattention to the myth's narrative dynamics obscures its overall import.

Why did Zeus decide to deny humankind his fire in the first place? Because he "never forgets for an instant the trick Prometheus played on him" (Vernant 22) when, as chef–for–a–day, he slaughtered and cooked an ox, serving the humans the meaty portions and giving the Olympians the bones. Pawn in this rivalry between Titan and Olympian, man is denied fire precisely so that he will not be able to cook meat and prepare such a meal for himself; i.e., not abrogate to himself the powers of the gods. But Prometheus changes all that with his second deception, the gift of fire, whereby man is catapulted from nature to culture, from the raw to the cooked. Outwitted yet again by Prometheus, Zeus gets his revenge not only on the Titan but on the men too, this time making them a fraudulent gift— not unrelated to the gift of fire, as we shall see—a beautiful misfortune: the first *woman*. Thus do the *anthropoi*— human beings who are universal and sexually neuter though coded as male, who share not only the gods' table but their immortality as well—, thus do these anthropoi become *andres*— human beings now gendered either male or female, subject to procreation and death and separated from the gods' ambrosial table rituals. The joy of cooking, and the joy of sex to which it is related, come at a great price!

> "The trap closes on the anthropoi, who are forced into an ongoing confrontation and need to live with this 'half' of themselves created for them with the intention of making them what they are, andres; but they do not recognize themselves in her. Their indispensable complement, whom they

cannot live with or without, presents the dual aspect of unhappiness and attraction. In the eyes of humans, once only males, women are strange beings" (Vernant 62).

I propose that it is not simply the case that *woman* is the creation of the Olympian's anger, not even that *woman* can be used as a metaphor for what ails men. It is rather that *woman*—or more exactly *women*—literalize and embody *the* human problem. The Greeks, of course, have various ways of naming that problem—both for themselves and for us who are their cultural and philosophical heirs—estrangement from the gods, the pain of labor, the flesh and its appetites, mortality, death. But the whole tragic and problematic character of the human condition can be summed up in one word made flesh, and that word, that flesh, is *woman*.

Now one fruitful way of understanding religious ritual is as "an offensive against the objective world" (Smith 1982, 65). In their very control of the variables, however, religious rituals are *not* about compelling the world through manipulation but rather about expressing the realistic assessment that the world cannot be compelled. As an economy of signification, the sacrificial rite lifts up life's double–binds in order to memorialize them within the controlled ritual space, mediating beginnings and endings, estrangement and communion, presence and absence—all the undecidables of existence—through the food rite's dis–memberings and re–memberings. Fragmentation and swallowing are ingredient in the very logic of ritual communion.

Let me quote a passage from Vernant at some length to show how this logic of ritual works in the case at hand:

"The issue of food, so pronounced in the myth, has multiple echoes (in the) sacrifice. . . There is a religious intentionality to the meal. It aims to honor the gods by inviting them to take part in a feast. In this sense, as an alimentary rite, sacrifice. . . evokes the memory of the ancient commensality when, seated together, men and gods made merry day after day at shared meals. However, if in its intent sacrifice hearkens back to these far–off times of the golden age when, sharing the same food, men still lived "like gods," far from all evils, work, disease, old age, and women, it is no less true that sacrifice is a reminder that these blessed times when men and gods sat down together to feast are forever ended. . . By eating the edible pieces men, even as they reinvigorate their failing strength, recognize the inferiority of their mortal condition and confirm their complete submission to the Olympians whom the Titan believed he could dupe with impunity when he established the model of the first sacrifice. The alimentary rite that brings men into contact with the divine underscores the distance that separates them" (24–25).

Vernant grounds his claims in an intricate tissue of intertextuality which links a whole range of texts—from Homer to Herodotus, Pindar, Euripides, and Plato—both to one another and to the sacrificial event itself. I will refer here to just one of the elements in this web of intertextuality, because it is most germane to the line of argument about women and food that I am trying to develop. That element is the Greek term *gaster* or "belly" (Vernant 58 ff.).

In Prometheus' first act of trickery against the Olympians, he manages to get the meaty portions for men by wrapping them, by way of disguise, in the animal's belly, while the bones are covered with a thin layer of fat to make them look more appealing to the gods. Evidently, no Greek would question the effectiveness of such a ruse, precisely because they found that organ too repellent to eat.

Gaster not only means belly; it refers as well to the cooking pot in which the sacrificial animal is prepared. But what makes the *gaster* so appropriate as a deceptive wrapping in Hesiod's tale is its function in discourse as a synecdoche for the human condition, a rhetorical function that is precisely the result of the Promethean belly–disguise's very effectiveness. For the human condition is represented in its totality by the belly: in Homer's words, the ill–doing belly, the odious belly, the contemptible belly, the deadly belly, the belly that gives so much pain, that brings so many painful cares to mortals. In the *Odyssey*, the curse of the belly—the frightful need one suffers to eat in order to live and, in order to eat, to have food—is denounced with an obsessive force. To be human is to be a slave to the belly, for the belly represents the bestial, wild element, the animality that chains us to the need for food, thanks to the Olympian's punishment. According to Plato, it is this belly that makes us "a stranger to philosophy and the muses" (Vernant 1989, 60).

"The term *gaster*," notes Vernant, "is used throughout a long textual tradition to represent the one who, dominated by (the)

appetite for food, has no other horizon or mainspring than (the) belly. This voracious sensuality, this gluttonous greed is often found associated with sloth and lewdness, as if, according to the expression that Xenophon puts in the mouth of Socrates, one were slave all at once to 'the belly, sleep, and dissipation'" (60).

Now this triumvirate of evils—gluttony, sloth, and lewdness—is particularly projected onto women in the Hesiod myth. Women are the consumers, not the producers of food. Reiterating Zeus' phantom dog that eats Prometheus' liver, women are voracious bitches: "Is there anything more like a dog than a woman?" asks Agamemnon, mimicking Odysseus' "Is there anything more like a dog than the odious belly?" (Vernant 67). They stuff their bellies with the results of their husband's hard labor. What is more, in women food appetite seems easily to lead to sexual appetite, perhaps because the term *gaster* connotes not simply the woman's stomach but her uterus as well!

Woman is a ravenous belly who, in her double voraciousness for food and sex, to quote Hesiod, "no matter how vigorous her husband, grills him over the fire, dries him out. . . and sends him into premature old age" (Vernant 66). And, according to Palladas of Alexandria, "Woman is Zeus' anger; she was given to us to avenge fire, a fatal gift that is the counterfeit of fire. For she burns the man with cares, she consumes him" (Vernant 68).

And yet it is into this voracious belly, this cooking pot, that man must place the seed of life, just as he must bury seeds in the belly of the earth. "From the day that Zeus' will determined the existence of women, men, like wheat, no longer grow by themselves out of the ground. Men must put their seed in the belly of their wives so that. . .children who can extend their father's lineage will emerge from it" (Vernant 67).

Talk about a double–bind! Man's necessary complement, woman is also his negation, his double, his opposite, his other. Only she can give man one of life's greatest goods: a son like his father who will continue the line after his death, a son whom she feeds from her own body. But it is still the case that "she was made by Zeus as a feminine woman in such a way that all through life, in her and by her, misfortune will come to (offset) the good" (Vernant 63).

Thus is the exclusion of women from meat–eating, from the sacrificial rites, from virtually all aspects of political and religious life, given its justification in the narrative context of the rite itself. In an effective economy of signification linking knowledge and power, the human condition, with its myriad of problems, gets distilled into *woman* and, in order to deal with this now singular problem of *woman*, *women* get contained within a system which thrusts them to the margins of language and of society. This is what I mean when I claim that woman is encoded into the cuisine and discourse of sacrifice among the Greeks as the *absent referent*.

The obsessive force of this marginalizing testifies to a "Greek imagination hounded by the feminine" (Detienne 146) and may lead us to suspect that it is itself a reflection of woman's being "too much" for the system. Could *her* voraciousness be a projection of *his* terror? Such a suspicion is fed by other stories in the tradition which present a strange, exclusively female sacrificial activity in which animals are slain. In the *Bacchae*, for example, Pentheus is consumed by curiosity about such secret women's mysteries. He manages to hide himself and gaze upon them— sword-wielding, frenzied, stained with their victims' blood. Then, "all together, as if in response to an agreed upon signal, they leaped upon (the king and removed) the part of him that made him a male" (Detienne 130). Thus with a quick prick (of the knife, of the pen) is the king himself relegated to the *absent referent* side of the gender–equation! No wonder, this story seems to suggest, voracious females are excluded from the rites, in which butchering and eating behaviors are central religious and political practices, practices of power as well as knowledge.

Before leaving Greek religious cuisine, I want to add one more narrative to my recipe for *woman as absent referent* in these discourses of knowledge and power. Linking woman, food, the belly, and the god, this myth—like the Promethean—is from the *Theogony*. It too gives an account of an episode in the Olympians' long Titanomachia. And, like the story of the castrated king, it may well feed our suspicions about some hidden motives for women's erasure from Greek society, for in its reversal of the controlling discourse's female–gendering of ravenous eating and voracious belly, it seems to speak the unconscious.

"Zeus lusted after Metis the Titaness, who turned into many   shapes to escape him until she was caught at last and got with   child. An oracle of Mother Earth then declared that this would be a girl–child and that, if Metis conceived again, she would bear a son who was fated to depose Zeus, just as Zeus had deposed Cronus, and Cronus had deposed Uranus. Therefore, having coaxed Metis to a couch with honeyed words, Zeus suddenly opened his mouth and swallowed her, and that was the end of Metis, though he claimed afterwards that she gave him counsel from inside his belly" (Hesiod ll. 886–900).

Like man, Zeus can't seem to live with the woman or without her. Unable to control his lust or his gluttony, he consumes Metis, first raping, then eating—chewing her up, dismembering her—until, as the story says, "that was the end of Metis." As in the Upanishadic philosophy, it seems as if either you're the eater or you're eaten (Buckley). Is Zeus' belly now pregnant with her and the fetus she was carrying? Is containing these females—these ravenous womb–bellies—within his own belly an effective way of neutralizing the power of their voracious otherness? Could this be a clue to *woman's* absence from the ritual meal? Is she present not only as the encoding of "the human problem," but also in the sacrificial animal who is consumed as memento of a lost primal union, a time of unthwarted human desire, a time, that is, of the universal male, before and beyond desire, copulation and death?

And yet, and yet—the last word of the story is that dangerous supplement, that relative clause: "though he claimed afterwards that she gave him counsel from inside his belly." Having silenced female language, subsuming *it* with *her* into *absent referent*, Zeus takes counsel from the woman within! What are we to make of this absent presence and present absence, this return of the repressed, this woman who feeds male judgment and discourse? Denied her own voice, she now speaks from within the masculine; cannibalized as body and thrust out of sight—beyond representation—she is nonetheless *not* out of mind.

One is reminded of Adorno's criticism of Western idealism, "the belly turned mind" he calls it (23): that effort to comprehend reality, to wrap one's mind around it, which denies otherness, assimilating difference to the logic of the same. Or perhaps of Freud's insistence that conceptual thought has its origins in bodily phantasy. For Freud the ego is a bodily ego, derived from bodily sensations, and the oral is the oldest of instinctual impulses. Expressed in the language of the oral, judgment, that most rational of human activities, means, according to Freud, either "I should like to eat this, to take this into myself" or "I should like to spit this out." To swallow something in phantasy is to judge that it is true. So, too, in religious ritual, where (in the words of J. Z. Smith) "murder and eating are means of making something ours" (Smith 1982, 100).

Inter–Course: The Space of Woman in Poststructuralist Discourse

In my reading of these texts—the stories and the discourse of ritual eating to which they are related—I have been tracing certain homologies between *women's* absence from religio–political life and *woman's* presence within the discourse of sacrifice. In the Promethean myth, as well as the story of the castrated king, there is a logic (albeit a misogynist one) linking the "beautiful misfortune" which is *woman* to the exclusion of *women* from the community, though even here woman's undecidability leaves its traces. This undecidability is featured in the Zeus/Metis myth, greatly enhancing the story's hermeneutical potential for us.

Contemporary theory offers us strategies for reading Zeus' contradictory behavior, his cannibalizing of *women* which then embodies *woman* as (gendered–male) judgment. The text's indigestible oppositions open it to deconstructive play; and Zeus' consuming and co–opting of female voice invites a French feminist reading. The despised other becomes the same; the marginal assumes the space of interiority; Zeus, the very Law of the Father, engages in a parody of *parler femme*, speaking (as) woman in the patriarchal culture of which he is the quintessential embodiment.

Zeus' ingestion of Metis reiterates viscerally a gesture we have been tracing in these Greek texts: an eating at once violent and sacred codes the culture's efforts to contain the inflationary female. Poststructuralist theory both lifts up for scrutiny and inverts that transaction in theory: obsessively putting *woman* into discourse. It remains to be seen, however, whether and to what extent either the abundant release of *woman* into theory or *writing and speaking (as) woman* can offer *women* a new syntax of the symbolic, an escape from the position of universal predicate, a way out of the belly of the god.

It is not surprising that such a "putting of woman into discourse" is intrinsic to the poststructuralist project of searching for what has been hidden or denied articulation in Western systems of knowledge (36), since those systems' master narratives code absence or non–knowledge as feminine space. This feminization of theoretical discourse needs careful distinguishing from feminism, however; *woman* as those processes that disrupt symbolic structures is not *woman* as sexual identity.

What I like about *écriture feminine* and *parler femme* (commonly translated as *writing and speaking (as) woman* and virtually identifiable with *writing and speaking the body*) is precisely their multivocality and their disputatious character. For in their very oversupply of meanings, their very contra–diction, they are a fruitful site of one of the most intense debates within contemporary feminist thought. This debate centers on how poststructuralism's "theories of the feminine" relate to Anglo–American feminist theory's critique of ideology and ethico–political concern with women's status. Thinking about difference is poststructuralism's project, of course; what confronts poststructuralist feminism is finding ways to think about difference differently.

"Why is it," complains an American feminist, "that just at the moment when so many of us who have been silenced begin to demand the right to name ourselves, to act as subjects rather than objects of history, that just then the concept of subjectivity becomes problematic?" (Hartsock 163–164). To which, of course, French feminism responds that the status of women is determined not only at social and political levels but by the very logical and psychological processes through which meaning is produced (Jardine 44).

It is this poststructuralist insight that grounds so much of French feminism's fascination with Lacan. The Lacanian psychoanalytic/linguistic account of sexuality and subjectivity denaturalizes the human subject, disclosing it as *a logic* produced through language and the unconscious. Such an account, which uncovers language as a reaction–formation against the primacy of the mother, helps feminism bring the category of the "'the human' "down to earth and give it a pair of pants" by exposing "the male body of the allegedly transcendent western mind"—in the delightful phrasings of Susan Bordo (1990, 137) and Ann–Janine Morey (58).

But Lacan leaves woman outside language, in the pre–Oedipal imaginary, or, rather, inserts her into discourse not as a speaking/writing subject but as the defective male body, coded as *absent referent*, the body that has no–thing—predicated within the symbolic by (voyeuristic) speculation as lack, as nothing. *Ecriture feminine*, by contrast, is part of the effort to displace the phallic economy of desire by finding new configurations of desire outside the logic of substitution.

It advances a libidinal economy which figures *woman* not as lack and absence but as oversupply, polymorphous perversity, if you will. Just as the text is indeterminate thanks to its interplay with other texts, so *woman*—also a sign, a text—exceeds phallocentric identity as multiple otherness. French feminism disrupts the phallic signifier with an oral sexual paradigm. In Irigaray's phrase, "the sex which is *not* one' (i.e., which is defined as lacking a penis and therefore being defective) becomes "the sex which is not *one.*" "Woman," she writes in an often–quoted exuberance, "has sex organs just about everywhere" (Dallery 55).

Writing as coital penetration (with pen/is inscribing meaning into texts which are coded female) is to be dispersed by writing as touching, kissing, eating. If the belly has a mouth, so too does that other female belly, the womb. A new word, the child of female power, needs nurturing and bodying forth! In French feminism's new grids of writing and desire, lips of vulva and lips of mouth figure each other, as do speaking/eating/jouissance. "Texts," exclaims Helene Cixous, "I eat them, I suck them, I kiss them." And for Chantal Chawaf, writing is a form of feeding: "I offer [words] so that they may be touched and eaten . . . [may] comfort the body" (Marks 177).

Now this textual erotics unnerves not a few of us, including some feminists of a social/critical or political modification. "Jouissance" doesn't put bread on the table, nor does it give *women* a place of legitimacy or voice of authority at table rituals, whether religious, academic, or corporate.

Such feminists question whether poststructuralist theory fetishizes the body of the text not unlike the way women's bodies are fetishized by the culture. Indeed, some even suspect that the very language of *écriture feminine* is a not sufficiently reconstructed echo of that very fetishing of the female body. Can *écriture feminine* write *women* into a conversation linking the psychoanalysis of the repression of *woman* to the materialist analysis of historical forms of patriarchal control?

Others suspect that, for all its textuality, *writing the body* is a new version of biological essentialism, "the eternal feminine" coming around again, a rhetorically embarrassing if theoretically more sophisticated instance of what Monique Wittig calls "the myth of woman;" i.e., the "woman is wonderful" approach (Dallery 64).

I list these concerns as a way of foregrounding the problematic character of any feminist theory rooted in poststructuralism. Nevertheless, it does seem to me that the issues poststructuralism raises cannot go unthought, any more than feminist issues can. In particular, if on the one hand some version of *écriture feminine* is to survive the feminist critique, and on the other, political feminism is to contend with the power of the unconscious, then the relation of *woman* to *women* cannot go unthought.

Having uncovered traces of the articulation of woman/women in some of the earliest religious texts in our tradition, I want now to turn to a contemporary text which is, like the Greek, a discourse of practice. I want to see how the story of women and bodies and eating keeps on being told, how women's bodies are still being inscripted for and by them. How are contemporary women actually "writing the body?"

And so we shift from a textual erotics to what Toril Moi has called a sexual/textual politics, from *woman* as text to *women* being written and *women* writing themselves within a still phallocentric order. I am wagering, with cultural critics, that the template of gender can disclose aspects of culture and history previously concealed; and I am wagering, with the French feminists, that *écriture feminine* can be—indeed, may already be being—a *nourricriture*, cooking up some new and fruitful oralities for *women* and therefore for us all.

Women's Bodies As Cultural Texts

Last year filmmaker Henry Jaglom gathered together a few dozen actresses, provided a rudimentary plot about a birthday party, and "goaded them into revealing their most personal feelings about food, men, their bodies, and cake" (Hall). In the resulting film, titled *Eating: A Very Serious Comedy about Women and Food* and comprised largely of spontaneous monologues, the women describe food as "a lover," "the flow of life," "daddy approval," "a silent comfort," "protection" (Hall). All of them offer testimony to the power food has over them, the power to soothe and to savage. And all of them, no matter what they look like or what they have achieved, express the conviction that they are not good enough.

A darkly comic exploration of these women's disordered relations to food and to their own bodies, the film is, as well, an accurate reflection of the contemporary scene. The data on the technologies of diet, fitness, fashion, cosmetics, and cosmetic surgery and the multi–billion dollar industries built around them are too familiar to need rehearsing here, as are the studies demonstrating that women are spending more time, energy, money, and attention on the management of our bodies than ever before (Bordo 1989, 14). And yet, for all that, something like 90% of us have strongly negative feelings about our bodies, 80% of us think we're overweight, 40% of us *are*, while upwards of 10% are anorexic, and well over half of us are or have been bulimic.

Research suggests that concern with food is gender–disparate and gender–salient and that feeling discontent with one's body is normative for women in our culture (Basow 8). No wonder the contemporary obsession with diet and slenderness has become what philosopher Susan Bordo calls "the central torment of many women's lives" (Bordo 1989, 14).

As she points out, it is striking that this torment, as well as the exponential increase in eating disorders in the past 20 years, coincides not only with the emergence of the aesthetic ideal of hyperslenderness and hardness but also with the emergence of women into corporate, professional, and public arenas. What is more, *clinical eating disorders* fall on a continuum with *normal feminine eating practice* and typically develop from socially sanctioned behaviors (Bordo 1989, 23). Yet most of the professional and self–help literature continues to emphasize the disease model, focusing narrowly on eating pathologies, seeking their etiology in the individual patient, and reading the behavior in question exclusively as a body–language of the mind.

Traditional psychoanalysis, for example, reads the texts of women and food as a syntax of the unconscious, interpreting eating disorders as repressed erotic desires or oral impregnation phobias and emphasizing the compulsive eater's and anorectic's fear of sexual maturity. Other recent psychologies develop this Freudian plot of (female) disease in a variety of directions, depending on whether they foreground eating and non–eating on the one hand, or the resulting body configuration on the other. Thus, for example, compulsive eating may express women's inarticulate rage or compensate for women's loneliness; fasting may code the liberating triumph over unspeakable desires. Likewise, fat acts as a protective interpersonal barrier, while hyperslenderness reproduces the pre–pubescent, the androgynous, or the virile body.

Implicit in at least some of these theories is the recognition that the body is not simply a text of the mind, but also a text of culture. As historian Caroline Bynum puts it, the body "behaves as it does because of the categories in which it is conceptualized" (19). To discover what the body is saying, then, may mean deciphering the rules and hierarchies the culture inscribes on bodies and food. Feminist analysts argue, for example, that women's eating behaviors are not unrelated to our tradition's male–gendering of the mind, the will, and, indeed, "the human." They relate women's eating practices to the history of hunger's use as a potent cultural metaphor for female sexuality, power, and desire—a metaphor evident in a range of materials from Kali, the destructive earth mother, to the Greeks, as we have seen, to early Renaissance discourse on witches, to contemporary rock and rap lyrics (Bordo 1990, 101). They read eating pathologies as forms of "embodied protest–unconscious, inchoate, and counterproductive. . . but protest nonetheless", or, more exactly, as "protest and retreat in the same gesture" (Bordo 1989, 20).

Bordo uses the later Foucault in her feminist critique of contemporary food practices. Foucault has taught us that we misunderstand power if we continue to think of it on the model of binary opposition, one group against another. It is better understood as immanent in economic, social, sexual, and knowledge relations, and therefore as manifold and intentional but non–subjective. Power inheres in "a network of practices, institutions, and technologies that sustain positions of dominance and subordination within a particular domain" (Bordo 1989, 15). Bordo finds Foucault's analysis of how cultural codes construct and sustain power relations useful in showing how women's contemporary food practices are a political as well as psychological discourse.

She insists, for example, that to focus on *pathologies* of eating outside of a political discourse is to divert "recognition from a central means of the reproduction of gender" in our culture precisely because it "obscures the *normalizing* function of the technologies of diet and body management," the way, that is, these technologies construct what Foucault calls "docile bodies" (Bordo 1990, 85). Such a Foucauldian critique shows how female bodies are not merely biological, not even simply texts of culture; they are, as well, "a practical, direct locus of social control" (Bordo 1989, 13).

Like hysteria and agoraphobia before it, anorexia provides a paradigm for "protest and retreat in the same gesture" (Bordo 1989, 20), i.e., for protest utilized in the reproduction of the powers–that–be. Bordo describes a cultural transaction through which constraining and—in the case of anorexia—even fatal behaviors are experienced as liberating and life–giving by the women who practice them.

Just as hysteria (that quintessential female malady of the late 19th century) is the pathological repetition of such stereotypically feminine traits as passivity, delicacy, and emotionality, and agoraphobia, the 1950's parody of the female ideal of domesticity, so too does anorexia's "ingenious literalism" write itself on the female body as both collusion and resistance. In each instance, the disease's symptoms are crystallized from the language of femininity, inscribing the body with an ideological construction emblematic of the period (Bordo 1989, 16 ff.).

The control of the female appetite for food, indeed, the virtual erasure of that appetite, encodes the containment not only of female desire but even of the public space that the female body may occupy. At the same time, the ideal of hard slenderness and the technologies supporting it offer the illusion of having achieved the masculine virtues of self–control and mastery, values represented by the culture as propadeutic to entrance into the public domain.

Bordo documents the anorectic's equation of slenderness with power. "(It) was about power," an interviewee in the documentary *The Waist Land* explains, "that was the big thing. . .something I could throw in people's faces, and they would look at me and I'd only weigh this much, but I was strong and in control, and hey, you're sloppy" (Bordo 1989, 26). This note of moral superiority, with its suggestion that body size and shape indicate state of soul, is common in such testimonies and thematic in the diet and fitness industries. As Caroline Bynum, Rudolph Bell, and others have shown, it is a symbolism that informs medieval women's religious practice as well. According to Bynum, religious eatings and non–eatings, Eucharistic miracles, and mystical feedings on Christ tend to be female genres (122).

In a striking reiteration of the Greek lexicon on the female body, contemporary women's flab phobia focuses on the belly. Forthwith two characteristic published testimonies: "I don't see my whole body as fat. But I can tell the minute I eat certain things that my stomach blows up like a pig's. And it's disgusting." and "I like the way my body looks for exactly two days each month. Every other day, my breasts, my stomach—they're just awful lumps, bumps, bulges. My body can turn on me at any moment; it is an out–of–control mass of flesh" (Bordo 1990, 89).

Bordo reads female bodies as graphic cultural texts about gender, seeing anorexia as the graphic intersection of the traditional feminine ideal of the denial of desire with the new requirement that women embody the masculine values of mastery. Indeed, women's eating practices can be understood more generally as overdetermined and expressive of multiple double-binds. Here are a few examples: (1) Culturally coded as feeders, preparers of food, and nurturers, women are consistently seen as more feminine the less they eat. (2) Maternal femininity is itself counter-constructed as both frighteningly powerful in the mother–child dyad and utterly powerless in the socio–political hierarchy. (3) Women are acculturated to the strict management of their desires within an economic system dedicated to the proliferation of desirable commodities and thus to the proliferation of desire. The result is an agonistic personality structure and *a normative practice of eating disorder*, both of which iterate the contradictions in the cultural system itself. In such a system, bulimia, understood as a structure of unstable force relations, becomes the paradigmatic text of women and food (Bordo 1990, 97).

In this context, let me place before us an actual woman who is also *par excellence* a cultural construct and cultural icon: Diana, the princess of Wales—Lady Di, as we say, our very nickname for her marking her undecidability as mega–celebrity and ritual victim. No less than three of the ten books on the September 1992 *New York Times* best–seller list were biographies of Diana, the most popular of which tantalized with stories of her cheating husband, her repeated suicide attempts, her bulimia. Talk about the female body as cultural construct and practical direct locus of social control! The book is framed by two images: on the front is Diana in off–the–shoulder white—the goddess–princess, at once ethereal and sensual; on the back, Diana in black turtleneck, the beautiful boy, the androgyne (Paglia 23 ff.).

Does our obsession with Diana, our voyeuristic and consuming regard, figure something about the cultural construction of women? Could it be that there is—still, yet, and again—a cuisine of sacrifice being practiced in our culture? And if there is, how are *women writing the body* as a form of protest and resistance to it?

Narrative Hunger: A Conclusion

If women's hungers figure unspeakable desires for knowledge, sexuality, and power in a phallic economy of signification, then it is not surprising that women in the act of eating are conspicuously absent from the novel of realism (Michie). For fictional realism is a naturalizing stratagem, promoting the dominant culture's hierarchy and order in its representations and structures, making out of culture a sort of "second nature," as the Frankfurt School has shown us. As a structure of desire, the modern novel is ineluctably male in its ideological commitments (Boone 72). Indeed, a strong case has been made—by Nancy Miller, Joseph Allen Boone and others—that sexist values inhere in the very form of traditional fiction.

In his impressive study of narrative as the energetics of multiple desirings, Peter Brooks finds (male–coded) desire in fiction's paradigmatic themes, plots, and structures. The very acts of story–telling and story–following, as he analyzes them, are ejaculatory. For Brooks, the defining characteristic of the modern novel is that it makes (male–coded) *ambition* the vehicle and emblem of eros, that which *constitutes* the very readability of the narrative. Unfortunately, however, his description of the *female* plot of desire in the traditional novel warrants no more than an endnote and not a word of misgiving:

> "(T)he female plot (is) . . . what we might call an   'endurance': a waiting (and suffering) until the woman's desire can be a permitted response to the expression of male desire" (Brooks 330).

If we grant, on the one hand, fictional realism as a naturalizing discourse which universalizes maleness, and on the other, the coding of female desire as hunger, and the repression—even the erasure—of both from canonical fiction, then one feminist literary strategy we might well anticipate would be an eruption of eros and eating into writing. We have already seen how French feminists use the trope of orality in their call for a textual erotics. In her discussion of a feminist poetics of the body, Helena Michie charts contemporary feminist poetry's re–working and re–membering of the body in terms of food and eating, documenting an oftentimes juicy literary *jouissance*. And Alice Walker, the doyenne of African American literary feminism, foregrounds celebratory eating and the body in her now famous manifesto of the Black feminist or "womanist." The womanist is no slave to the cultural ideal of the docile body. Rather she is one who "loves music. Loves dance. Loves the moon. *Loves* the Spirit. Loves love and food and roundness" (xii).

Indeed, then, we can point to a contemporary feminist literature that signals newfound capacities to name and celebrate female hungers and satieties—thereby breaking the representational taboos of traditional realism, putting into imaginative discourse what has been marginalized and erased. But such literary affirmations are not the only type possible—and, I would argue—not terribly satisfying.

In the light of the discourse of practice we have been looking at, we might well expect in an *écriture féminine* that is both engaged and attuned to the unconscious a deferral of oral *jouissance* in deference, as it were, to women's bodies as "site(s) of struggle" (Bordo 1989, 28). Granted how women are actually managing their hungers today, when eating disorders, compulsive regimens of body improvement, obesity, and dissatisfaction concerning looks are all on the rise (Bordo 1989, 28), such an *écriture feminine* might practice resistance to the culture's *normalizing* inscriptions on women's bodies in and through its deconstruction of realism's *naturalizing* forms.

And in the light of geographically and historically persistent cuisines of sacrifice, we might well expect in an *écriture feminine* that is atuned to the unconscious a re–membering of women's bodies and desires that is also a moral recollection of suffering. Granted how sacrificial discourses of knowledge and power have claimed religious warrant for cultural judgments against women, such an *écriture feminine* might memorialize women's double–binds within a ritualized narrative space, tracing and re–tracing the multifarious inscriptions of women and food in the syntax of religious practices, the grammar of sacred and sinful and violent eatings.

Such a "writing the body" might ultimately be more complex and satisfying than *jouissance*, for it would formally embody the religious and cultural struggles we have been tracing—essaying the articulation of woman and women while eschewing the tempting totalizings of romantic feminism, the easy affirmations and easy victimizations of women, the easy vilifications of men. I began this essay with Margaret Atwood's fictions of protest in the comic mode precisely because I read them as instances of such literature. Hers is a body of work—pun intended—that enlarges the critical discourse about women and the rites of sacrifice. I regret that time does not allow further attention to her work here, but—after all—sacrifices must always be made!

NOTES

1. Margaret Atwood, *The Edible Woman* (New York: Bantam Books, 1990). Hereafter cited as EW with page numbers.

2. Margaret Atwood, *Wilderness Tips* (New York: Double Day, 1989). Hereafter cited as WT with page numbers.

WORKS CITED

Adams, Carol J. *The Sexual Politics of Meat*. New York: Continuum, 1990.

Adorno, Theodor. *Negative Dialectics.* New York: Seabury Press, 1973.

Atwood, Margaret. *The Edible Woman.* New York: Bantam Books, 1970.

Atwood, Margaret. "Hairball." *Wilderness Tips.* New York: Doubleday, 1989.

Basow, Susan. "What Is She Eating?: Women and Food." *Douglass Alumnae Bulletin,* Winter 1992.

Boone, Joseph Allen. *Tradition Counter Tradition.* Chicago: University of Chicago Press, 1987.

Bordo, Susan. "The Body and the Reproduction of Femininity: A Feminist Appropriation of Foucault." *Gender/Body/Knowledge,* eds. Alison Jagger and Susan Bordo. New Brunswick: Rutgers University Press, 1989.

Bordo, Susan. "Reading the Slender Body." *Body/Politics,* eds. Mary Jacobus, Evelyn Fox Keller, Sally Shuttleworth. New York: Routledge, 1990.

Brooks, Peter. *Reading for the Plot.* New York: Knopf, 1984.

Brumberg, Joan Jacobs. *Fasting Girls.* New York: Penguin Books, 1988.

Buckley, Jorunn Jacobson. "You Are What You Eat: The Meaning of Food in Christian Doctrines." Unpublished manuscript of public lecture, UNC, Greensboro, 1984.

Bynum, Caroline Walker. *Fragmentation and Redemption.* New York: Zone, 1991.

Chodorow, Nancy. "What is the Relation between Psychoanalytic Feminism and the Psychoanalytic Psychology of Women?" *Theoretical Perspectives on Sexual Difference,* ed. Deborah L. Rhode. New Haven: Yale University Press, 1990.

Dallery, Arleen B. "The Politics of Writing (the) Body: Ecriture Feminine." *Gender/Body/Knowledge,* see Bordo.

Detienne, Marcel and Vernant, Jean–Pierre. *The Cuisine of Sacrifice among the Greeks.* Chicago: University of Chicago Press, 1989.

Freud, Sigmund. "Obsessive Acts and Religious Practices," in J. Strachey, ed. *The Standard Edition of the Complete Psychological Works of Sigmund Freud.* London, 1959.

Hartsock, Nancy. "Foucault on Power: A Theory for Women?" *Feminism/Postmodernism,* ed. Linda J. Nicholson. New York: Routledge, 1990.

Hall, Trish. "New Movie Explores The 'Slaves' of Food." *The New York Times,* date unknown.

Hesiod. *Theogony.* trans. Apostolos Athanassakis. Baltimore: Johns Hopkins University Press, 1983.

Jardine, Alice A. *Gynesis: Configurations of Woman and Modernity.* Ithaca: Cornell University Press, 1985.

Marks, Elaine and de Courtivron, Isabelle, eds. *New French Feminisms.* New York: Schocken Books, 1980.

Michie, Helena. *The Flesh Made Word: Female Figures and Woman's Bodies.* New York: Oxford University Press, 1987.

Minh–ha, Trinh T. *Woman, Native, Other.* Bloomington: Indiana University Press, 1989.

Moi, Toril. *Sexual/Textual Politics*. London: Routledge, 1985.

Morey, Ann-Janine. "Feminist Perspectives on Arts, Literature and Religion." *Critical Review of Books in Religion*. Atlanta: Scholars Press, 1991.

Oates, Joyce Carol. *Not for Bread Alone*, ed. Daniel Halpern. Antaeus, Spring 1992.

Paglia, Camille. "The Diana Cult." *The New Republic*, August 3, 992.

Sahlins, Marshall. "Food as Symbolic Code." *Culture and Society*, eds. Jeffrey C. Alexander and Steven Seidman. Cambridge: Cambridge University Press, 1990.

Smith, Brian K. *Reflections on Resemblance*. Oxford: Oxford University Press, 1991.

Smith, Jonathan Z. *Imagining Religion*. Chicago: University of Chicago Press, 1982.

Walker, Alice. *In Search of Our Mothers' Gardens*. San Diego: Harcourt, Brace, Jovanovich, 1983 (1967).

The Place of Publishing:

A Neglected Factor in Interpretation

DAVIS PERKINS

Prologue: The Community of Bob

This essay is offered in homage of one of the most remarkable people I've been privileged to know. Robert Detweiler is a literary critic of extraordinary insight, a penetrating thinker of deep and varied thoughts, a colleague and friend who mentors and nurtures in marvelous ways, and a person who knows how to enjoy himself and the finer things in life.

He is well published and publishes well — that is, he knows the process of publication from many different angles: as a writer, volume editor, textbook writer/compiler, reader for numerous presses, dissertation advisor, and board-member facilitator. While he may not agree with the conclusions of this essay, he is certainly conversant with the issues discussed herein.

I first met Bob at an AAR/SBL Annual Meeting. We quickly discovered a mutual interest in a particular cultural period and Bob graciously offered advice about a grant opportunity. The grant didn't work out, but a couple years later I had occasion to facilitate a reissue of his important introduction to phenomenology, *Story, Sign, and Self,* from the publishing company for which I was working. Then yet a couple years later we became fast friends when I moved to Atlanta.

While in Atlanta together, Bob helped check (read, redo) a translation I prepared and we discussed the great metaphysical issues over good food, copious amounts of wine, and in the company of two wonderful women on many an occasion. I'll never forget the "goose jerky" Bob prepared one holiday, nor the image of Bob impersonating a walrus in a posh restaurant using his ever-present pocket pens as tusks.

I'm very pleased that my present publishing venue affords me the opportunity to work with Bob on a forthcoming major textbook, but most of all I'm pleased to have been part of the Detweiler *Kreis*. The community one experiences in Bob's presence is one to which it is most pleasant to belong.

The Missing Link

Contemporary interpretation has alternated between critical methods that investigate the author, the text itself, and, of late, the reader. Postmodern critics are very adept at esoteric ruminations on the multiple ways in which readers determine, over-determine, and distort meaning in the act of reading. Deconstructionists continue to belabor the point in ever more clever and disingenuous ways that there is no pristine kernel of meaning when the husk of a literary text is stripped away. And yet literary critics of any stripe have generally not, to the best of my knowledge, ever mined the obvious insight that I would like to advance and develop in this essay: that is, that the act of publishing has a pronounced impact on how a literary text is received (not to mention how it is produced).

It is true that certain Marxist theoreticians have made reference to the ways in which publishing serves as a conduit for particular ideologies, but critics have by and large overlooked publishing altogether. I am aware of the fact that postmodern critics are absolute (!) in their insistence that there is no such thing as absolute and fixed meaning and yet postmodern strategies of interpretation do not, I believe, undermine my point. Regardless of how criticism goes about its work — whether that is by focusing on the mind of the author, deconstructing the text, playfully highlighting intertextuality, sucking up signifiers or the lack thereof — critics have uncritically failed to regard publishing as worthy fodder for interpretation.[1]

Indeed, there is a sense of blissful ignorance on the part of interpretation when it considers the production of the text (author) and the reception of the text (reader) without giving a thought to the publication of the text (publisher) — that is, the very process by which authorship climaxes in readership. This ignorance is explicable by the fact that most literary critics are academics and academics are notorious for overlooking the obvious in order to mine the esoteric and insignificant.[2] The entire system of reward and retribution in the academy (a.k.a. tenure and promotion) is predicated upon the discovery of an insignificant point as if it were the most neglected factor in a particular field of inquiry, as if the explication of this point is capable of revolutionizing the discipline (my current point about the oversight of publishing notwithstanding).

The blissful ignorance in the academy as regards the importance of publishing for the interpretive enterprise springs from another academic misapprehension, however. And that concerns the naive notion that publishing operates according to an absolute and universal law. This law legislates that if an author produces a "good" book, it will be published. Experienced writers who have received rejection letters from publishers invariably recognize this law to be false, but even so, many of them believe (as a coping mechanism or as a form of denial) that there is something wrong with the publisher. Authors who devote a large amount of their time and energy to producing a book-length manuscript almost invariably believe the merits of the work will be so compelling to a publisher that a publishing agreement will be issued and the book will be scheduled for publication forthwith. Such a view is absurd of course and no self-respecting academic would admit to holding it, but I assure you that it is latent in many a rejected author's unwillingness to believe "that this work does not fit our publishing needs at present," "that we already have extensive commitments in this area which preclude our expressing further interest in your work," "that despite the obvious merits of your argument, we are unable to envision a sufficiently broad readership to support publication," etc. Authors always want to believe that there is room for one more good book like theirs in a publishing program. Suffice it to say that most academics don't understand the dynamics of publishing all that clearly. I hope to make a small effort to dispel some of this ignorance in this essay.

Academic literary critics are similarly obtuse in general when it comes to publishing as the missing link in interpretation. Otherwise sophisticated and astute literary critics will blithely assume that a text springs full blown from the pen/word processor of the author directly to the reader[3] and that the process of publication which makes this possible is of negligible import for interpretive purposes. They will expostulate at length on the myriad ways in which deep structures and similarly mystifying realities impinge obliquely upon the hermeneutical machinery while overlooking the obvious ways in which the publishing predetermines reception, conveys meaning and serves as a spoke in the wheel of understanding.

To ask the question rhetorically, is it not the case that publishing a book constitutes an important moment in the life of a literary work? Granted, the production of the text by the author and the reception of the text by the reader are the primary poles between which literary criticism does and should operate. And yet the publication process influences both of these poles profoundly and stands as an indispensable point of mediation between the author and the reader. *Any act of interpretation of a published work that does not close the loop by examining the act of publication itself will not succeed in producing the full measure of explanatory power.* A literary text is the result of an author, a publisher, and a reader.[4]

I would like to pursue this contentious thesis in two ways. First, I would like to reflect upon *why* something is published in the first place. (The ontological question of why is something published and not nothing holds little interest for me.) Second, I would like to discuss some of the ways in which *how* a text is published affects the reception and interpretation of that text.

I offer this essay as a self-reflective apologetic for my profession. I intend to advance certain formal claims about the publishing enterprise which will bolster the case for including publication in the work of interpretation. In addition, I hope to convey some basic information about publishing itself en route.

Why?

Axiomatic to my thesis is that a literary text is most fully available for interpretation when it is published. I do not mean simply that more people can read a text when it is published; privately circulated texts could easily have a larger audience than many published books. (And of course a text does not require publication in order to be interpreted.) Rather I mean that something decisive happens when a text is "published" (actually many things decisive happen).

The very term "publication" indicates that the text is in the process of being made *public* — and this is determinative for the text, its reception, and should be for interpretation. Consider the difference between public and private as suggested by Milan Kundera in *Immortality*.[5] Kundera skillfully draws out the difference by invoking the dilemma of a man who is given the choice of either sleeping with a world-famous beauty and not being able to tell a soul or not sleeping with this woman and yet being able to convey the public impression that they are sexually intimate. Kundera properly insinuates that most men would choose the latter option, since making something public is usually preferable to maintaining a private reality.

Transferred to the subject at hand, this means that a published book is generally regarded as having greater significance than an unpublished work. Canons of elitism notwithstanding, most writers do not write out of a private impulse for self-expression and most readers vest published texts with a measure of authoritativeness that they do not similarly accord to unpublished texts. One of the purest and most poignant coincidence of the private/public polarity in this regard occurs when an author's work is published posthumously to great public acclaim.

But my point here is that publication profoundly affects the reception a literary text receives. An unpublished literary text approaches the reader in a different way from a published text. A host of important but oftentimes unrecognized assumptions accompany a published text as it makes its way to the reader. The most obvious and undervalued assumption has to do with the implicit conviction on the part of the reader that *someone* thinks this text is worth reading. The act of publication invests the text with an authority that indicates to the reader that something of value is resident in this work. A cynical version of this insight would maintain that the perception of value (as guaranteed by publication) is more significant that the reality of value (in an unpublished text). Nevertheless, it is obvious that the benefit of doubt as far as the value of a literary text is concerned does not accrue to the unpublished work (unless a reverse snobbery is at work).

Everyone knows publishers publish bad books and that publication itself is no assurance that something of value is resident in the work, but yet the sheer facticity of publication predisposes the reader to open the first page of a book or examine the dust jacket with a predilection to find meaning (or experience the text as worthy of deconstruction). The question of *why* a book is published is unconsciously answered for the reader by the facticity of publication.

The fact of publication suggests that someone beside the author has found the work worth reading and of course publishers typically do not rely upon their own judgment in reaching this conclusion. They frequently rely upon outside readers for substantive evaluations and/or upon editorial and marketing colleagues in the publishing house. Academic publishers are generally ruthlessly scrupulous about soliciting evaluations from outside advisers who are specialists in the particular field.

Outside evaluators must be chosen with care, however, since a particular reader may have an ideological ax to grind with the author's method or may harbor an antipathy to the subject matter of the work itself. Editors may also predetermine the course of the evaluation by turning to former teachers, friends, or scholars (theirs or the author's) with self-interest in a particular field or method of inquiry. In the best of all possible worlds, it is to be expected that objective reader reports would drive the publishing decision fairly toward its proper conclusion. This being an imperfect world, however, publishers generally feel the need of multiple reader reports as a check against any single report and the prejudices of the editorial staff.

A Typological Prelude

In thinking about the theme of this volume in connection with the subject of this essay, it is appropriate to raise the question of community and to ask *whose* story gets told in the act of publishing and how the act of publishing facilitates a community in the first place. Since publishers facilitate various communities of discourse with various books and create various communities of authors on their publishing lists, let me offer a typology based upon my limited experience with several publishers in the religious-academic arena as a way of examining this complex of issues.

In each case, the publishers identified in the following typology are caricatures of real publishers. None of them are Platonic ideals of their type and all of them bear the marks *more or less* of their type. And yet each typology implies a particular type of critical community; I hope to enumerate some of the characteristics of these communities at each turn in the typology.

Type A - Vanity Publisher

By the term "vanity publisher" I do not mean simply those publishers who serve as production agents for an author who is willing to pay in order to have a work published. I also mean to include those publishers who abrogate editorial responsibility and ignore marketing considerations. Thus the fact of having a manuscript refereed is no guarantee that a publisher is not a vanity publisher. The question then is *whose vanity is being served* in the decision to publish a manuscript.

A publisher may place a high premium on the evaluations of outside readers who are specialists in the field and still be a vanity publisher by failing to exercise editorial oversight of a book in terms of its content and its fit with other titles on the publisher's list. By ceding responsibility to an outside agent (whether author or specialist readers) for the basic decision to publish, the publisher forfeits the right to define the character of the publishing program (a basic publishing function). Moreover, the Type A publisher is asserting that this book should be published irrespective of the prospective audience for the book because the specialist advisers said it should. The author, the learned society, or the university-subsidized press will end up paying the production costs.

For example, if Type A publisher publishes a book that was vetted by a series editor or specialist readers on behalf of a learned society (possibly at the expense of the learned society as well) without the authority to make the final publishing decision and determine whether there is indeed a readership for the work in the first place, I would submit that this publisher is functioning as a vanity press. In this case, the vanity served is that of the learned society.

Type A publishers render a valuable service by publishing works of technical scholarship that would not typically be of interest to "the trade."[6] In addition, Publisher A often makes an important contribution to the cause of publication by providing value-added production capabilities (e.g., ability to typeset arcane languages, produce critical editions with an elaborate scholarly apparatus, and so forth). Individual readers and scholars in the field are the customary beneficiaries of this type of publishing.

So it is relatively easy to delineate the sort of critical community this type of publishing creates. The specialist who is conducting specific research in a given area is the most likely community member for a Type A publication. Library data bases and certain institute bibliographies will be the primary advertising vehicles for a Type A work beyond the publisher's direct-mail catalogue. The author, sponsoring agency, and thesis-writing student constitute the heart of the critical community for a Type A publisher.

I can easily imagine being taken to task for defining Type A publisher as a vanity publisher. I am admittedly construing the typology rather narrowly at this point. I am assuming, however, that the act of publication itself entails a relationship with a *public* and that by bracketing virtually *all* marketing considerations (about who would use the book, how they would use the book, how they would become aware of the book, etc.) the publisher is catering perniciously to the interests of the author or an institution to the exclusion of the interests of the reader.

I do not mean to suggest that the fact of a financial subvention (from any quarter) alone constitutes vanity publishing. One can easily imagine a subsidy for a specialized, technical work enhancing the availability of an important text for a circumscribed audience. My main point here is that a vanity press exhibits little or no concern about the intended audience for the book. Thus, as with all typologies, it is difficult to identify a "pure" instantiation of this type of publisher. To the extent that a publisher abrogates the basic publishing responsibility to maintain a partnership with the reader, any and every publisher may accurately be characterized as a vanity press (regardless of who pays), in this view.

Am I saying that certain texts should not be published *as books* if only a handful of readers will benefit from access to the text? Basically, yes. I am not saying that the data or the text should not be made available to the scholars with interest in the material; I am saying that perhaps it should not be transmitted via a traditional book publication where a particular sort of relationship between author (editorial responsibility) and reader (market considerations) is implied. After all, what are journals, learned society meetings, private correspondence, and photocopy machines for?

The basic question for Type A publishers is "Who's *Paying*?"

Type B - Market-Driven Publisher

Type B publisher is at the other extreme; this type publisher places extraordinary emphasis on the reader and orients the publication process in favor of the "end consumer" to the detriment of the author and the work itself on occasion. Type B publisher will not publish a book unless a market large enough to justify publication can be envisioned. Publisher B will often solicit outside evaluative reports and attend to the recommendation of members of the editorial staff, but in the final analysis the marketing department will have the last word in whether or not the book is published.

The publisher will usually endeavor to quantify the market for the book by comparing the work in question with sales of comparable books on the publisher's backlist, with sales of other books by the same author, by calling several of the publisher's key accounts to see if this is the sort of book they would order in bulk, by querying members of the sales force, etc. Oftentimes, an effort will be made to identify the major market segments for the work in advance and to project what percentage of the print run will be sold through particular channels (e.g., 50% to the trade via sales force, 20% to direct mail/retail customers, 10% to jobbers, 10% to chain bookstores, 10% to foreign distributors). It is not uncommon for production estimates to accompany the publishing proposal so the publisher may determine at what point the initial investment will be recovered in all likelihood.

According to the internal structure of the Type B publishing house, the marketing department will either have a veto vote over the editorial department in terms of whether a book is published or a product manager from the marketing department will actually be assigned to develop the work for publication with the editor and will serve as an advocate for the project when publication is proposed. Revisions will always be requested in order to expand the market for the work, not simply to strengthen the internal structure of the work (though these two types of revisions are not mutually exclusive).

This type of publisher enjoys the obvious advantage of relative certainty about whether there is indeed a market for the book. So the publisher is essentially serving the marketplace by providing readers with books that they need (or think they need). Books published by Type B publishers typically appeal to a well-defined audience which can be successfully reached through a well-orchestrated marketing campaign. Strong emphasis is placed upon the design of the cover, endorsements from respected figures, and a competitive retail price.

The well-defined audience which is the object of Type B publisher's marketing effort is not a small one typically. The critical community is one in which a book is perceived as meeting an existential need. Self-help manuals, inspirational works, edifying autobiographies, and volumes offering moral guidance in turbulent times are the staples of this sort of community. In fact, the community will often gather to read and discuss the book from Type B publisher collectively. Type B publishers will often create temporary communities through promotional events such as autograph parties in bookstores, radio/television interviews with authors, and newspaper reviews. Communities of two or three will spring up as readers of mystery novels, romance novels, and/or thrillers discover each other at 30,000 feet across the aisle of an airplane or on adjacent beach blankets at water's edge.

Book purists would prefer to disassociate themselves on occasion from Type B publishers, but in point of fact there is a bit of Type B in all successful publishing companies who traffic in the mainstream of trade publishing (as opposed to specialty, niche publishing). All publishers (excluding Type A publishers of course) are market-driven to some extent; otherwise they would soon run out of operating capital. Structurally, Publisher B tends to be well-defined and to be preoccupied with corporate reorganizations that will facilitate market-sensitive publishing decisions. The dynamics of the publishing operations in a Type B house are deliberate as a rule; the process itself (from manuscript editing to copyediting to book design within and without to pricing to production scheduling to advertising and beyond) is designed to proceed methodically and to minimize mistakes that could jeopardize sales revenue. Depending on one's perspective, this type of publishing is either the most responsible or the most boring — or both.

The downside to the Type B publisher has to with the methodology employed by market analysis and the effect it has on the totality of the publishing program. Market research will identify a need and then a book can be developed to meet that need. Essentially, Type B is practicing "safe" publishing.

Yes, the publisher is providing a useful service but there is a certain price to be paid. Market-driven publishers are generally reactive rather than progressive. They often cast a cold eye upon cutting-edge works that might be controversial but that might not open up (large enough) new communities of discourse. Original books that don't fit neatly within preexisting and easily identifiable markets may never find their way into Publisher B's program. Of course I am generalizing at this point, but then that's what a typology allows one to do.

The basic question for Type B publishers is *"Who* Cares?"*

Type C - Editorially Driven Publisher

In Type C, the editorial staff rules the roost. Marketing personnel may be consulted now and again, but the editorial recommendation with attached positive reader reports will usually suffice to provoke a positive publishing decision.

In most every publishing house, the editor does not possess unilateral authority to make a publishing commitment. So even in Type C, editorial authority is lodged in an editorial-department hegemony. Editors may band together in loose alliance to support each other's projects — or nix them — and they may enlist marketing support at the time of sales estimates, establishing pricing thresholds, etc. But basically editors have the definitive voice in publishing decisions in Type C.

Editors are usually academically trained in one of the disciplines in which the publisher publishes, and so they presumably have a command of the subject matter of the books. Moreover, they are generally well-read individuals who make an effort to keep up with new developments in their field. Frequently, they wear their knowledge conspicuously on their sleeve and cultivate an air of superiority which is off-putting to their publishing colleagues in other departments. Editors in Type C shops may encourage the notion that there is a publishing *gnosis* which only the initiated and experienced editor possesses. Marketing personnel who don't understand a book are sometimes made to feel like hulking peasants in the feudal publishing society.

Apart from the internal staff dynamics in Type C companies, though, it is easy to discern how and why editors would favor original books that may be difficult to market successfully. When editors call the shots, "important" books supplant "saleable" books on the publisher's lists — and this is a two-edged sword (upon which many an editor falls). There is always the danger that the editorially driven publisher may lose sight of the prospective reader and verge into the Type-A-publisher arena.

On the one hand, the importance of a book may not be recognized by more than a handful of readers and then the publisher is left with a financial loss which must be made up for by other titles. On the other hand, truly seminal works may be published to critical acclaim *and* enjoy unexpectedly broad sales. Publishing lore is replete with tales of "sleepers" which awoke to mass market sales and put the publisher's bottom line awash in black ink (e.g., *The Road Less Traveled*).

Editorially driven publishing houses fall short of fulfilling their publishing responsibilities, in my opinion, by privatizing the publishing process and disregarding the responsibility publishers have to the reading public (but unlike the Type A publisher, the Publisher C editor does posit a reading public). By generalizing from their own interests, editors in Type C publishers may envision an audience for a book that simply does not exist. The argument for publication of a particular book in an editorial meeting may run as follows:

'I realize there are not a lot of people currently interested in the hermeneutical implications of the psychoanalytic turn to the de-centered self as defined by primitive cultures and embodied in Incan mythology. But this book is important nevertheless, and we should do it in order to advance the discussion among those thoughtful readers on the fringes of several disciplines.' When asked by the marketing manager who those people are and how they will become aware of the book, the editor may respond by saying, 'Well, of course they are the open-minded anthropologists, historians of ancient civilizations, iconoclastic shrinks, postmodern lit-crit jocks, and the literate *generalist* who reads the *New York Times Book Review* section. If only the publicist will get on the stick and secure a review there, I'm sure this book will become a cult classic and enjoy strong sales life-of-title.'

Naturally, the marketing department doesn't want to stand in the way of the next cult classic and doesn't have the (hard?) data to counter the editor's rather positive (read: "ridiculously unfounded") assessment of the expansive market for the work.

My characterization of Type C publisher has been overly severe in certain ways, and yet the community fostered by this type of publisher is probably the one with which most readers of this essay would choose to identify.

The critical community created by Type C publishers is different from the one created by Type A publishers in that this community generally regards book-reading as an important intellectual activity that is part and parcel of ordinary living — and not just as a means to an academic end. Whereas Type A readers use Type A publisher's books more or less as research tools, Type C readers use Type C publisher's books as vehicles for mental stimulation, pleasure-reading (but not escape), a means of satisfying an intellectual curiosity, or as a cultural act.

The Type C community will, for example, take its marching orders from the *New York Times Book Review* section and will browse in mom-and-pop bookshops or superstores rather than mall chain stores or rather than order highly technical works from mail-order publishers. The reading done by this community is intentional without being directive or focused in narrow ways. Expressed positively, this community forms the literate subculture of the society at large in which shared knowledge is valued as the *lingua franca*.

This community is more inclined to read translated works, biographical studies, commentaries, historical surveys, critiques of cultural movements, and poetry. One is more likely to hear the stock question "So what are you reading these days?" as part of ordinary conversation in this community than in any of the others spawned by the publishers in this typology.

Type C publishers' sales revenues are generally erratic, but these publishing houses are typically interesting places to work — despite or rather because of the tension between editorial and marketing. Authors are very fond of this type publisher because they feel their work is taken seriously and they come to trust their editor as a genuine partner in their intellectual labor. In the mind of the author, the editor is the one person who understands the author's work most fully. If the book does well sales-wise, the editor and author will exult together in its success, and if it falls short of expectation, they will console themselves with the sure knowledge that the market was just not ready for such an original work or that, yes, the marketing department did regrettably drop the ball now and again.

Given the editorial insistence upon an original argument or a fresh interpretation, the basic question the Type C publisher asks of a project is "*So What?*"

The Use And Abuse of Typologies

No one publisher in this typology is superior to another (though Type B and C have an edge over A in my mind); all three of them are caricatures and have distinctive contributions to make. Each and every publishing house has its own corporate culture and these emphasize particular features of the publishing enterprise in specific ways. Holding marketing and editorial in a balanced tension is extremely difficult, but surely produces the best type of publishing.

In conclusion to the typology discussion, I would like to return to an earlier point and reassert that the type of publisher associated with a book most decidedly influences the reception the book receives. In the mind of the discerning reader (and in many cases the undiscerning reader when the physical features of the book are taken into account) a book from Publisher A, Publisher B, and Publisher C will be approached in distinctly different ways. An interpretive bias will subjectively influence the way the book is read and the work is interpreted based upon the (perceived) identity of the publisher.

For example, Oxford University Press enjoys a certain cachet among academics which it has earned by virtue of several centuries of publication of well-refereed, handsomely produced, if not over-priced, monographs. The OUP backlist is quite impressive. By contrast, there are a number of publishers who are willing to publish almost anything within a matter of months upon receiving author-generated camera-ready copy and the only requirement this publisher has of the author is that he or she purchase a certain number of copies of the book and not complain when the publisher fails to advertise the work. Anyone who bothers to notice the publisher's imprint on the spines of books, pays attention to publisher's ads in journals, or studies publisher's catalogues will appreciate the myriad and complex ways in which a publisher's identity determines the reception of texts.

How?

But *how* a book is published also affects the meaning a reader finds and hence is an appropriate subject of inquiry for literary criticism. Even the physical features of a book may have a profound meaning upon the reception by the reader. The binding (cloth or paper), the trim size, the typography (style and size), the advertising copy, the interior paper stock, the colors on the cover, the use of graphic images, etc. all influence the way in which the reader receives the text.

The use of the Helvetica typeface as opposed to Times Roman will suggest to the reader that a book be construed in a certain way.[7] Traditional typography and design will reinforce a predisposition on the part of the reader to find a conventional argument, whereas an avant garde typeface (this is an actual brand-name) will suggest a book with more radical contents. Meaning is definitely resident in book design. Other factors such as the retail price, the place of purchase, the publisher's imprint, and so on will also determine the meaning of the work for the reader in particular and decisive ways.

Desktop-publishing technologies are revolutionizing the publishing industry in profound ways at the moment — and yet not altogether. It is routine for authors to submit manuscripts electronically now and exempt publishers from the need to pay typesetters to re-key the text. But publishers must still administer copyediting conventions and facilitate a cogent internal text design. Whether the publisher is able to recover the keystrokes or not, though, it is becoming more commonplace for publishers to send diskettes of the cover and the text to the printer in lieu of camera-ready copy. The printer then outputs directly to film and several steps in the traditional production process are obviated, saving time and money presumably.

But even if computers have altered the *means* by which a book is produced, the *end* remains virtually the same: a printed, bound, portable book. While many publishers are touting CD ROM, data-base publishing, video accompaniments, books-on-tape audio products, etc., few are predicting the demise of the printed book as we know it. Interactive, user-friendly, hand-held high-resolution readers may prove this prediction wrong, but barring a major technological breakthrough or a cognitive shift on the part of readers, I would tentatively but boldly forecast the continued existence of the book as we know it. But of course dinosaurs probably didn't see their demise coming either.

How Specifically?

So *how specifically* does publishing influence — or should it influence — the understandings that might emerge in the critical process? This is not a question I am able to answer adequately inasmuch as a) I am not a literary critic, and b) I indicated at the outset that I wished to proffer *formal* claims. Nevertheless, let me make a few feeble efforts to answer this question.

In the case of Robert Detweiler's *Breaking the Fall*, I assume that the British reader-critic would immediately note the price of the book. A retail price of 35£ would suggest that this is not a trifling work meant to appeal to the tastes of a mass market. The clothbound, series format will intimate that this is a work for the specialist, for the reader-critic who is already familiar with the literature being discussed and contemporary interpretive methods. The physical features of the book and the retail price will convey the impression that this is high-powered literary criticism that will demand a certain measure of erudition on the part of the reader-critic. The ideal prospective reader-critic would possess certain attributes associated with a George Steiner.

The fact of the British publisher of record's series "housing" will direct the reader-critic's attention to the other titles in the Studies in Literature and Religion series and will indicate that a community of discourse is being created that finds value in relating religion and literature. Given the listing of other authors and titles in the series, the reader will know that this community is an international one and that the conversation fostered by this community is a transatlantic one.

The Macmillan imprint denotes a solidity of substance and content and affirms that this work has been refereed and meets certain exacting scholarly standards. The Foreword by Series Editor David Jasper successfully imparts to the reader-critic a sense of the importance of the project.

Upon plunging into the text, the reader will be cheered by the lucid structure of the work (as indicated by the straightforward table of contents) and the readability of the text (thanks to an elegant but simple typographical design, replete with helpful running heads at the top of the pages). The reader will know immediately that the author does not traffic in unnecessary obscurities and that the discourse is pitched toward the general reader of literature and/or the person interested in the religion-literature intersection. It will quickly become manifest that Detweiler does not intend the community of discourse created by his work to be a private one.

The American reader-critic of *Breaking the Fall* approaches the North American edition with a different set of assumptions. Thanks to the extensive marketing operation of HarperCollins, the American reader-critic is more likely to find *Breaking the Fall* in a university or general bookstore than in a direct-mail catalogue or a library (as with the UK edition). This will bespeak more accurately than is the case with the British edition the true nature of the work and imply a more accurate image of the intended audience for the work.

Moreover, the reader-critic will instantly be struck by the beauty and appropriateness of the Chagall graphic on the dust jacket. This multicolored, glossy piece of art by a well-known contemporary artist will predispose the reader-critic to find within the covers a contemporary treatment of traditional religious themes. The reader-critic will know this is a precious book after paying $24.95, but will not feel shortchanged after learning from the publisher's back ad copy that this work comes "from the premier exponent of theology-based literary criticism."

After learning that *Breaking the Fall* won the American Academy of Religion's Book Award in 1990, the reader-critic will rejoice to discover that "the experts" also appreciated the merits of this book and its import for the study of religion. The reader-critic who happens upon advertising from the North American publisher in 1992 or who attempts to use the book in a class as a text thereafter, however, will be disappointed to learn that the North American edition has been "remaindered" and will soon be out of print. The member of the *Breaking-the-Fall* community who has come to value this book as a friendly thought-provoking dialogue partner, who is empowered to read literature religiously and to understand the significance of literary texts in fresh ways, and who is cognizant of publishing-world machinations will feel slighted at this precipitous action on the part of the publisher. This awareness will lead the reader-critic to question the publisher's commitment to scholarship of this sort in the first place (more about marketing considerations below) and to subconsciously experience a fragmented sense of community.

A Marketing Interlude

Straddling the question of *why* a book is published and *how* a book is published is the issue of marketing. The area of marketing and promotion in book publishing is certainly the most mysterious to many outsiders and the one which is subject to the most misunderstandings.

Many authors seem to regard the marketing of books as a tainted activity. Since marketing in book publishing utilizes marketing techniques from the larger world of commerce, book marketing is a bit suspect in the mind of certain academics. Indeed, many book purists within and without the industry decry the recent trend of many publishers (of the Type B genre) to move the marketing function up into the editorial arena by having "product development teams."

Nevertheless, the notion of product development does capture an important truth about book publishing and that is that marketing considerations are ultimately inseparable from editorial judgments about content. Just as literary criticism has realized that interpretive truth is not self-contained within the text itself or the mind of the author, so product development in book publishing owns up to the fact that form and content are integrally related and that the publisher had better be intentional at every turn in the publishing process in order to reach the intended audience for the work.

Whether a publisher operates with a product-development paradigm or not, most publishers do ask marketing questions at the time of making a publishing decision — and properly so. Nothing is more tragic in book publishing that issuing an important and original work that everyone on the publishing house staff "believes in," only to have the stock collect dust in the publisher's warehouse (warehouses are notoriously dusty; it is a publishing law that they be so dusty). The publisher is frustrated at not recovering the expense involved in producing the book and the author is likewise presumably unhappy at not being taken seriously in the marketplace. This situation can easily lead to recriminations postpublication.

The publisher recalls how the author resisted editorial advice that might have opened up the argument for a larger community of readers and feels the author should be grateful to them for taking on the book in the first place. The author by contrast feels that the publisher has killed the book through promotional neglect and actually conspired to keep the book a secret by not advertising it in the obvious media. Both parties may have a legitimate complaint; which suggests that it is not inappropriate for the publisher to be self-conscious about marketing issues during the evaluation process.

In the best of all possible worlds (in a hyper-literate society) the publisher would not need to introduce marketing considerations in the evaluation process and indeed many authors believe the originality of their thesis alone should compel the publisher to undertake publication. And when publishers are independently wealthy and/or authors only care about being able to list a publication on the resume without regard for a readership, this paradigm works fine. But most serious publishing demands that the publisher and the author come clean on the issue of market at the outset.

Much unhappiness and frustration can be avoided if both parties share a common understanding about the market for the work. Since both parties presumably have the same goal for the book, it is actually a good thing for the publisher to endeavor to quantify the intended market at the time of the publishing decision. Discussions of the maximum length for a work of this sort, the optimum retail price, the right binding, the available distribution channels, the cost of appropriate advertising, the possibility of key publicity events, and so forth, should occur before a publishing partnership is established. The author who has produced a work for a "general" audience with untranslated foreign terms, unexplained technical jargon, and more footnotes than text on any given page needs to be disabused of some cherished and precious assumptions. Publishers are frequently called upon to cite marketing considerations as part of a reality check with authors.

Authors sometimes become queasy at the thought that their intellectual work would be subjected to this sort of marketing scrutiny and yet no one is well-served if marketing considerations are pushed to the side and the book is published and immediately languishes. It is simply the case that some books do not fit in a publisher's program, that a particular publisher does not have access to a certain market, that the book under question would be anomalous to the other books on the publisher's backlist, that the cost of promoting the book properly would be greater than the publisher could comfortably afford.

Publishers frequently praise the content of a work to the author in a letter of rejection while citing marketing considerations as determinative in the decision — and authors predictably don't appreciate this news. But in the larger scheme of things, both parties are better off if marketing considerations are faced honestly.

At this point I would like to introduce a distinction which is basic to the publishing industry and is helpful in understanding how different publishers go about reaching a particular market. The distinction I refer to is between a "trade" publisher and a "direct mail/retail" publisher.

A "trade" publisher is one who sells — in the first instance — to the trade, that is to bookstores who stock the publisher's books. Trade publishers usually employ sales representatives to call on bookstore accounts in order to determine whether the store will carry the publisher's books. Trade publishers reach the final consumer (the retail customer) indirectly via the bookstore.

Direct mail/retail publishers often publish more specialized works with limited trade appeal. It doesn't really matter if books from this sort of press are in bookstores or not, because the consumer is a specialist in the field in all likelihood who has probably seen an advertisement for the book in question and ordered a single copy directly from the publisher. The astute literary critic will take account of the type of publisher when interpreting a book.

Obviously the trade publisher incurs greater expense in promoting books, so it is not surprising to realize that trade publishers need to envision larger audiences for their titles than do direct-mail publishers. A direct-mail publisher may, for example, publish a technical monograph and reach the majority of the audience for that particular work through a few well-placed space ads in key journals in the field. By contrast, the trade publisher must support sales representatives while they travel (typically 40+ weeks per year) and call upon bookstores in order to present new titles. The trade selling season varies from publisher to publisher, but in most cases the majority of selling activity occurs in advance of publication. So a large (one hopes!) percentage of the print run is sold before the first copy comes off press and he publisher may know prepublication how the book will fare sales-wise. Books which "sell at a stately pace" prepub may enjoy a nice enlivening boost when reviews begin to appear (the publisher finds consolation in this possibility), but in large measure the most important moment in the life of a trade book occurs as the sales rep utilizes the seasonal catalogue, the cover design, and galleys to solicit orders from *bookstores* before the publication date. In publishing as in other areas of life, timing is everything.

Trade publishers are on occasion berated for not publishing heavy academic tomes and yet they have little chance of selling the truly specialized monograph to a large enough number of bookstores to justify the sales representation effort. Moreover, the bookstore *may return unsold copies of books for credit within 12 months usually*, so there is little incentive for the trade publisher to sponsor those really specialized academic works. In addition, the direct mail publisher will typically price books with the retail consumer in mind and will offer the bookseller only a modest discount, leaving the retail establishment with little or no profit margin with which to work (unless they are willing to charge *more* than the publisher's retail price.)

Most authors and most book buyers do not realize all the machinations that transpire in the commerce between trade publisher and bookseller. Large amounts of money are spent on advertising, promotions, sales forces, special catalogues, imprinted brochures, shipping, "receiving," and other activities geared strictly toward the trade market. (*Publishers Weekly* is the primary news medium for this business. A perusal of *Publishers Weekly* will give one a feel for the complexity of trade publishing.) Given the numbers of copies that must be sold to support this sort of marketing infrastructure and the deeper (40% - 50%+) discounts that prevail, it is small wonder that trade publishers find it necessary to publish books in larger quantities (or not at all).

The marketing of a book, then, is a significant factor interpretatively in *the reception of the text*. To be sure, the interplay between author-text-reader is paramount in the interpretive process, but I also think it is naive to assume that the marketing a publisher undertakes on behalf of a book is unworthy of consideration. In subtle and direct ways, the way a book is presented to the market influences the reception of the text.

A Financial Coda

A brief word about the finances of publishing is in order here since marketing issues come more sharply into focus when the finances of publishing are understood.

Publishing is not the best business in which to make a lot of money. In fact, publishing is one of the most retrogressive business activities in the contemporary world of commerce. Hypothetically, a publisher may spend $2.50 per copy in producing a book (manuscript editing, copyediting, designing, typesetting, printing, binding, shipping, warehousing) plus overhead for administration, advertising and promotion, and accounting plus royalties. The book may carry a suggested retail price of $14.99, but the publisher will generally sell copies to the trade bookstores at a discount of 40% - 50%, depending upon the number of copies purchased. So the publisher has only 50% to 60% of the retail price to pay the direct costs associated with producing the book and the indirect costs of maintaining a viable publishing company to support the books promotionally, including paying salaries and the direct expenses involved in advertising. Moreover, bookstores reserve the right to return unsold copies of the book to the publisher within 12 months after purchase for partial or full credit, if they do not sell! So the publisher very definitely is forced to operate within narrow parameters when it comes to profit margins.

This thumbnail sketch of publishing finances is not meant to elicit sympathy for those who work in publishing, but to clarify in part why publishers are forced to set the sort of prices they do. Every author wants his or her book to cost next to nothing so everyone will be able to afford it, and yet every author also wants to publisher to spend a lot of money in promoting the book and then pay a handsome royalty to boot. Unless the publishing staff is willing to donate their time or to cut out the profit for the retailer (this is called "short discounting" in which the publisher says the retailer will only receive a 20%-25% discount), there is not much room to maneuver in the financial arena of publishing.

Quite obviously the finances of publishing impact the reception a text receives in rather immediate ways and yet complaining about book prices is near the top of everyone's list of pet peeves (right behind gripes about the IRS, lawyers, crooked politicians and other unpleasant subjects). To lay the blame for book prices squarely on the publisher alone, though, is a bit like holding Boris Yeltsin solely responsible for the Russian economy.

Conclusion

Publishing, if it is considered at all, is the subject of many misconceptions. For example, it is frequently assumed that editors incur chronic eye strain from reading manuscripts all day long when the fact of the matter is they are more prone to chronic boredom as a result of having to attend seemingly endless meetings ("where minutes are taken and hours are lost"). Likewise, it is assumed that bookstore managers derive great personal satisfaction from being around books all day; as if they had time to look up from their inventory reports, their purchase orders, or their point-of-sale cash register long enough to appreciate their surroundings. Or, at the other extreme, it is assumed that book publishing is simply commerce applied to intellectual properties — a slightly less naive view than the one that regards publishing as a "gentleman's" profession in which overly educated fellows with little or no business acumen dabble.

And yet like all subcultures, the world of publishing operates according to a complex and discrete set of dynamics. There are always polarities to be held in tension (e.g., between marketing and editorial, between the desire to meet market "needs" and to be on the cutting edge), and there are always publishers who will succumb to one side of any given polarity. Moreover, there are different sets of publishing environments. Publishers of bodice-ripping romance novels are as different from publishers of religious-academic books as are publishers of statistical data.

Nevertheless, publishing as it is usually and generically practiced involves a complex set of relationships and is, I would like to suggest, a suitable subject for disciplined inquiry.

I am not suggesting a sociology of publishing, an archaeology of desktop publishing technologies, or statistical reports on publishing data (these do exist) as prerequisites for interpretation. I would like to suggest simply that otherwise intelligent and sophisticated people (academics) frequently cultivate a second naiveté about publishing matters and this is deleterious to the cause of the interpretation of literary texts.

Perhaps it is because they are more comfortable speculating on metaphysical matters like "the mind of the author," "the implied reader," or "the intertextuality of whatever." Perhaps it is because a serious study of the ways in which publishing impacts interpretation could require a bit of empirical research in addition to the proffering of generalities, unsubstantiated conclusions, or silly word games. I suspect there is a self-cultivated ignorance about publishing which is rooted in one or both of two fallacies.

According to the first fallacy, publishing is an ordered set of mechanical learned procedures, and according to the second fallacy editorial judgment and publishing discernment cannot be taught or learned, but only be cultivated. For most laborers in the publishing vineyard, the truth lies somewhere in between: it's neither environment nor genetics, but both. But attention to both the *why* and the *how*, together with an understanding of the dynamics operative in the publishing-industrial complex, will cast light on the meaning of a literary text.

To focus on the writer, the writing, and the reader without also taking account of the publisher is silly at best and irresponsible at worst. The reception of the text is a dynamic process that proceeds by way of publication in most instances. Interpretation that overlooks this moment in the literary event is not fully adequate.

NOTES

1. I can imagine a negative hermeneutic or a postmodern interpretive strategy in which what publishing *conceals* is reputed to be more consequential than what publishing *reveals*. But I cannot imagine publishing receiving no attention whatsoever.

2. "The recent boom of the criticism industry in universities has turned the modest mounds of trash that literature left behind into veritable Himalayas of refuse." Octavio Paz, *The Other Voice: Essays on Modern Poetry*, trans. Helen Lane (New York: Harcourt Brace Jovanovich, 1991), p. 87.

3. This is not even true in the case of electronic publishing. The medium certainly renders the text more immediate to the reader, but even here the act of publication functions as a decisive intermediary step. For example, the software and the machinery by which the text is transmitted affect the nature of the experience of reception.

4. Of course there are literary texts that are not "published" per se. Throughout this essay I am defining literary texts as those put forward by a publisher for public consumption. Obviously one can have a literary text with only an author; a publisher and a reader are not strictly necessary. By way of nuanced qualification, I do not want to get involved in a logical quagmire over whether a text must have a publisher and/or a reader in order to qualify as a text; clearly, in a self-referential way the author may function as the publisher in the act of writing and the implied reader as the text is self-objectified. Such ruminations, though, are akin to the Berkeleyan tree-in-the-forest quandary. Such questions as "if a writer wrote, and a publisher published, but no reader read, would a literary text exist?" may best be left to those literary critics without enough real texts to interpret. The correct answer to the above question is "yes," but who cares. I am construing literary texts in the plain sense of a published work that is printed (in type) and distributed.

5. Milan Kundera, *Immortality*, trans. Peter Kussi (New York: Grove Weidenfeld, 1991), p. 331.

6. A "trade" publisher is a publisher who sells books to trade accounts (bookstores), usually via sales representatives, as opposed to directly to the retail consumer, usually reached via direct mail. Trade publishers will usually sell to the trade at a discount of 40-48% in order to give the retail outlet a profit margin. More about this below.

7. It is impossible to avoid the assumption that there are certain universal constants in the world of human perception such that a sans serif typeface will inform the manner in which the text is received in a particular way (given the presence of a well-defined

culture with a historical tradition). I suppose this insight could foster a (Jungian) archetypal scheme of typography or at least give rise to the recognition that typography is culture-specific (but not an individualistically relative matter).

Texts

The True Ufo Story

PETER MEINKE

Here's what they say: I was abducted
at two a.m. by small grey creatures
with huge eyes who inserted hairlike
probes into my brain . . .

Well, why not? These are honest people—
hordes of them! And yet we doubt. No-one
likes to be conned and what are these times
if not one long disgraceful scam? Therefore

I have been chosen to explain,
given this voice and this vision,
this gift from a far height. There's
nothing you can do. So here

is the true story: An unmarked star
probing eastward like a Siberian tiger
beyond the cold Plutonion wastes of time
has come around to us. Its languid citizens

feed entirely on brain cells, vast fields
of brain shuddering in the yellow air
like Greek sponges under water. This crop,
delicate as the anemone, needs constant

weeding, pruning, grafting of new life,
new brainbuds on the ancient stock or else
it withers from repetition, flushing
stale images through collapsing chambers,

the language of loyalty oaths
and insurance policies bloating
the cerebra like ads for light beer, staining
its cavities with darkling liver spots.

For millennia uncounted they've raided
planet and satellite till only the dregs
of intelligence remain, namely us.
This is how they do it: a detector,

pure selenium, scans the earth searching
for original thought. On their screen
our world's a Sahara, blank and bland
as a dean. But here and there, pinpricks

of purple pick up a living brain, and
they zero in. They know existence is
electric: matter, mind, and dream are all
the Idea of God at different frequencies

and God Itself is variable, modulating
from deities of weasels, mice, and corn
to Cronus, Maya, Shango. They zero in,
brushing every pulse, the ox, the falcon,

and the poor patient oyster, where it sleeps
within its pearly house. There are no little men:
only projections injected on our nerves
like silkscreen anesthesia, while they perform

long-distance biopsy, visiting our beds
the way Selene flew to Endymion each night.
Painlessly they take their little samples,
leaving these scooplike scars, and we are left

a little more foolish than before, while they
retreat in shadow like titanic forms
carrying our finest thoughts to reanimate
their brainfields. Their victims rub their eyes,

and try to tell their stories: I was floating
over trees, naked and unafraid. We laugh,
uneasily and unbelieving, as Zeus laughed
when Pluto stole Persephone forever.

The Winnebago Road of Life
and Death and Rebirth
Reading a Ritual Drama Religiously

WILLIAM G. DOTY

Ajo ajo,	Journey journey,
Ajo mi re.	This is my journey.
Kini l'awa o?	What are we?
Ajo ajo.	Journey journey.[1]

ANCESTOR-HOST: All who are standing here, I greet you. When I sit down and begin I will be reenacting what Earthmaker himself did.

EAST: The great Island-Anchorer in the east, whose impersonator I am, took four steps as he traveled toward the Creation-Lodge. . . . He who travels on the Road he laid down, never will he stumble or fall; death will not come to him.

ANCESTOR-HOST: Earthmaker gave us this life of the Rite. It is truly the only kind of life that exists (Radin 1973:251, 267, 278).

For most Native Americans, life unfolds in the midst of a landscape endowed with the symbolic significance that provides orientation and direction. The mountains, the cardinal directions, the celestial bodies, and many other natural features commonly reflect complex religious symbolism. The cycle of human life, the journey from birth to death, is brought into line with cosmology by being depicted as a process of movement within the landscape. Life is a road one travels, and the proper course for that road is often defined through cosmic symbolism (Gill 83).

A number of modes of approach hover.[2] I could utilize one or several of the metacritical approaches that Robert Detweiler has pioneered (and I've reviewed). But I focus here upon the second chapter of *Breaking the Fall*, where Detweiler suggests a methodology for "reading religiously." I do not take that phrase to stipulate exhaustive parameters but rather additions to our existing hermeneutics. "Reading religiously" elicits some *supplements* to the corpus of interpretations, perhaps even some *applications*, in the context of the three traditional hermeneutical modes of: *exegesis*—elucidating the details of the text itself, its historical climate and sociological setting, *interpretation*, the ways the text before us was sited and transmitted within the communities that passed it on, and *application*—making-real, making-contemporary (*Vergegenwärtigung*) that would not have been evident before this approach was promulgated in this insightful book.

Hence: agreement with the basic walking-through. Agreement that mythological/fictive materials share a trajectory of fictiveness/reality that spans from the most far-out extrapolations of meanings projected forward to the most mundane data laden recovery of the everyday. I won't worry the *fictio-/facere/*constructed/fiction/factory linguistic net since it has been noted repeatedly and it seems unnecessary in terms of the Winnebago materials I'll treat.[3] On the other hand I will try to incarnate here ways by which Detweiler's reading religiously sends us toward texts/rituals/experiences that we might otherwise treat like overly-cooked oatmeal. If the newest hermeneutical guidelines do not stimulate *new* readings (exegesis and interpretation), if they do not stimulate revisionings (applications), they do not earn the price of comprehending them. But Detweiler's contributions take us to a new plane, a new level of insighting texts within communities that may well need categories like his to sanctify or accredit their anti-traditional readings. The hinge-making readings often derive from another continent, especially from Europe: consequently I am enchanted by the fact that Detweiler's depend upon no dictional jawbreakers other than a few traditional German locutions.

There *are* anti-traditional elements here, let us not blink the issue. Even though within the contemporary "religion and the arts" context, Detweiler seldom names particular religious orientations or choices, his approach is not that of conservative adherents of any contemporary religious institution. Herein lies dynamite, as the hermeneutical frames simultaneously (1) respect/refract the faithfulness to the Christian tradition that Robert's own Mennonite background contributes (he and I were in Germany simultaneously, in the late 1950s—he as a conscientious objector, working in the refugee camps that I, as an undergraduate at Die Freie Universität Berlin, only visited) and (2) educt a secular hermeneutics of some sophistication, built out from some of the important critical schools of our period, but especially from the work of the individualistic Paul Ricoeur.

The retrieve is that of *communitas*, the idealized community familiar from the work of Victor Turner (but also prior works by Percival and Paul Goodman, and others) as well as the Pauline longing for *koinonia*. Of course the Freudian hermeneutic helps us realize the status of *koinonia* as an unattained "impossible possibility" that Paul must reiterate hopefully if not realistically (in the light of the many subsequent "splinterings," heretical ways of being Christian). Such an idealized community might recover a sense of myths-working-in-society, pretty much along the lines of what Mircea Eliade recovered of the sense of the ancient-sacred by looking at what contemporary fiction is able to accomplish (see selections in Part I, Beane and Doty). Others have sought continuities in literary genres that would help us comprehend our psychoactive addictions to particular modes of story. Can the legends of sports heroes in *Sports Illustrated* be compared generically to the lives of the saints?—earlier generations thought that their narrative contributions met similar psychological needs. Can we think in terms of a universal literary apparatus that unites humankind's fabulous curiosities, appearing now in this, now in that literary manifestation and increasingly in cinematic transformations?—Borges's and Eco's universal libraries extend the necessary shelf space.

The framework Detweiler quickens in his concept of "reading religiously" supports such questions; it seeks to determine how narratives operate within communities, even within the curious reader-responsive communities of contemporary secular criticism. Detweiler's criticism *explicates religiously in non-religious modes*: few modules of his critical program might be identified with a particular religious orientation, except perhaps that of the timeless-liberal, but a Mennonite won't be liberal-Jewish in the ways of upbeat Manhattan. Detweiler believes in the human ability to confront chaos (Camus's plague) in ways that provide an existentialist resume for provisional meaning—even if sometimes we discern a cloaked Christian-existentialism. The writers he has been discussing at one point in *Breaking the Fall* "probe the painful points of their characters' lives not as a prelude to presenting resolutions but for the opposite reason: to portray humanity always held in the tension of suffering and health, yet to encourage the imagination's play of *Gelassenheit* with this elemental condition as a strategy for making meaning and wholeness on the way to death" (113).

And sometimes we recognize even more clearly the face of the non-religious religious person today: belief in *the power of narrative* comes through repeatedly, as in: "it is very hard, if not impossible, for us not to tell stories, and even if these stories plot our lives of disorientation, their very telling is at least an impulse toward reaching an *other* and occasionally even a gesture of community" (Detweiler 118). That community/*communitas* /*koinonia*, I repeat, is an ideal, a gesture; it does not stem from living in contemporary America wherein currently more private than public police are employed, or where one in four African American males are incarcerated or on probation or parole. It does not derive from any idealized version of the academic world, where one's peers are only too happy to masticate proposals for change. And it does not derive from any experience in driving on a contemporary highway, on which one's survival comes only from the most defensive driving skills imaginable: sealed in the private space for spending, drivers fragment any semblance of communal safety, let alone courtesy (read J. G. Ballard's *Crash* and *Concrete Island* for examples of the ways that space can be fictionalized in postmodern expression).

But Robert Detweiler believes that there are ways in which contemporary personhood, the multi-complected selves of our being-in-the-sight-of-god, are yet yoked, tied-together in the *religare* of our common lives, ways that implicate "religious" readings of experience, whether the immediate experience of lover-beloved or that of the sacred text by which we've found significances in our lives. I'll emphasize six elements of Robert's "reading religiously" framework:

(1) Contemplation of texts rather than domination of them by means of particular religious or hermeneutical perspectives; conversation with texts as they become means of opening us to what we have not considered previously. "Religious reading might be *gelassen* and *gesellig*, balancing our dogged insistence on interpretation with a pleasurable interchange made valuable precisely by a refusal to simplify and manipulate the text into something else, another statement" (Detweiler 35).[4]

(2) Certain privileged fictions resist the seduction of chaos, which is synonymous with a meaningless cosmos. Fictions are unreal in the sense of being super-real, surreal, rather than non-sensical, but as they are probes of possible or provisional meanings. Interpretations, theologies, handbooks of logarithmic functions: all are "fictional" (fiction, datum, fact—what is given/made) in terms of being arbitrarily established . Yet as yoking

elements (yogas, religions) myths and scriptures enable seizures of at least temporary meaning, selective collocations of significances that let us breathe in spite of the lung-constricting challenges of chaos that have been there since, according to Western mythologies, a deity first relinquished the usual Ancient Near Eastern potter's wheel in order more empathically to kiss/breathe life into that lump of adamic clay.

(3) Festive engagement with texts leads to playful realizations of them; belief systems represent agreements that certain forms are irreducibly important (and most likely to be embodied ritually). At the same time, any important belief system will recognize the limitations of formal organizations of experience, and recognize that humans can remain within the particular framework only momentarily (*Gelassenheit*), no matter how the ritual frameworks delight us by promising more when they become just one more ideologizing component of the social whole (see Bell).

(4) Important narratives/fictions/ritualizations/myths model ways our multiple selves may be instantiated into now this, now that shaping of being. Our choice of important narratives and enacted dramas identifies our significances as cultures, since we are the stories we tell; we represent as stories of "good news" (*euangelia*) only those versions that shed insights across what we take to be the central landscapes of our histories. The range of hero/ine stories maps the various probes by which a society calculates maturity and achievement; we deal with pain and its aftermath by means of the metaphoring/embodied figures that subplot our relative significance within the orders of being (and today, alas, only an occasional "ecological" sensitivity will be acknowledged before we annihilate the organon upon which we have had our short-term existence).

(5) Presence marks absence; we learn through attention to the absent just what the present might realize. Likewise the future is marked already by the insufficiencies of the past and the present. Otherwise there would be no market for science fiction, which in contrast to the works produced according to academic creative-writing-school standards now dominates the publishing market for fiction.[5] And just as the imagery of endings (*Endzeit*) mirrors that of beginnings (*Urzeit*), so as a nation we can hardly rest on our laurels when we haven't yet managed a reasoned politics of multicultural coexistence, for all the sham of American melting-pot idealism in which the old racism has merely been cloned by the more subtle new "social" racism.

(6) Mystery remains. The infinite overplus marks/mars the liminal or borderline cases that we screen out in all our IQ and achievement tests, although Howard Gardner protests. Where the genius actually resides, we are never certain, or fear to acknowledge. How to decide between the

rational and the irrational, choose who inhabits the White House and who sleeps on the street gratings only two blocks away—such distinctions arise today from communal framings of meaning, whether political or religious. "Religious reading" seems less the desiderata of the elite than the prophetic challenge to the ordinary. "Deep play," truly ludic and supportive of structure-threatening communitas: this reads against the ordinary grain, *for the disenfranchised*. But precisely here I situate the deeply moral element of Detweiler's framework: the ideal community ought to provide positive models, and it ought to discern vigorously among the voices of the culture, in order to indicate the limitations but at the same time, the possibilities, of the era.

As the first of two ways of running with Detweiler's proposed "reading religiously"[6], I will illustrate Radin's Winnebago text (1973) for a non-religious audience that yet "reads religiously." The "ritual drama" of Radin's title, echoed in my own, is to be taken seriously, especially in light of Ronald Grimes's devastating critique of the theologically-motivated narrative criticism that has given such priority to narrative that embodied enactments have been ignored entirely, when not trivialized behind a limited ethnocentrism whose stories recited are granted absolute priority over dramas and rituals (Grimes, Chapter 7). I emphasize more appropriately the enritualization of the Winnebago worldview represented in *Road*.[7]

We confront all sorts of contemporary sensitivities in treating such materials: speaking others' words for them, presuming to comprehend worldviews we barely understand, failing to crosscheck with informants' own contemporaries, even daring to blunder into a sacred cosmos the very narration of which was considered by older tribal members to represent a "mortal" sin—the political and ideological issues surrounding this text fascinate me, and I will return to them more than once. Something of a safeguard to my overreaching is that I do not attempt to reveal the true Winnebago meanings, but rather to explore how a ritual text might be opened up as it comes to us now as a work of Western literature. Recently reissued in a paperback series, Mythos: The Princeton/Bollingen Series in World Mythology, it now carries two authoritative imprimaturs—that of Princeton University Press and the financial support of the Bollingen Series. And also we ought to remember that the material was collected under the governmental auspices of the Bureau of American Ethnology (Radin 1973:ix). The text itself sets off Radin's long Introduction (35-77) and notes (335-45) from The Medicine Rite itself, which alternates between text and frequent italicized rubrics (81-334) and begins with a Prologue situating its place in Winnebago ritual (1-33).[8]

If on the one hand I own up to my hesitations about interpreting materials from what is not my own culture of birth, I am also worried about the problem of allegorizing: I don't want to substitute Detweiler's interpretive categories for units of the Winnebago ritualization. But using those categories has helped me find several layers of meaning to which I was not formerly attentive, so I will share my "reading religiously" approach to this ritual drama and hope that self-consciousness about these problematic elements will provide some checks on arbitrary substitution of my meaning for those of either the Winnebago or Detweiler. Even with Grimes' cautions about overvaluing narrative in mind, we recall the statement by Detweiler already cited: "it is very hard, if not impossible, for us not to tell stories, and . . . their very telling is at least an impulse toward reaching an *other* and occasionally even a gesture of community." Or in Margaret Atwood's stunning nod to the claims of the narrativists, "because I'm telling you this story I will your existence. I tell, therefore you are" (344).

Whether or not we extract moral interpretations from narrativity itself, since now such essentialist claims seem suspect, we are doubtless at a stage in narratological interpretation where interest in *how stories/myths function*, the technical markers of their composition and delivery, is being supplemented by interest in *what they perform*, how they influence the contexts in which they are told, how their contents shape the tellers themselves. We ask practical questions about *eutropic stories—the anastrophic* as opposed to the *katastrophic* that has typified our contemporary fiction. We seek stories that might support change, that might rescue us from the maladaptive patterns by which we have endangered our planet. Hence Detweiler remarks:

> Our behavior that corresponds to *this* sense of an ending—that we permit this wholly irrational drift toward catastrophe [in our toleration of the destruction of our environment]—is uncanny in the fullest sense of the term; if novels such as these can make us feel the madness of this behavior, through the shocking depictions of its probable results, and help us will to change it, they can become actual fictions of survival (189).

And Suzi Gablik attacking the Modernist separation of the "high arts" from everyday life, as she works toward a more participatory aesthetics, proposes that: "If modern aesthetics was inherently isolationist, aimed at disengagement and purity, my sense is that what we will be seeing over the next few decades is art that is essentially social and purposeful, art that rejects the myths of neutrality and autonomy" (4).

In contrast to the postmodernist stress upon the death of the *gran recít*, Gablik emphasizes one we may not relinquish lest we perish: "Ecology (and the relational, total-field model of `ecosophy') is a new cultural force we can no longer escape—it is the only effective challenge to the long-term priorities of the present economic order" (27). Aware of challenges to such a view, Gablik notes that "the sacredness of both life and art does not have to mean something cosmic or otherworldly—it emerges quite naturally when we cultivate compassionate, responsive modes of relating to the world and to each other" (181). She returns repeatedly to the example of Dominique Mazeaud's project begun in Santa Fé in 1987, "The Great Cleansing of the Rio Grande River," a ritual return every month to clean up debris. In contrast to the famous earth artists whom Gablik criticizes for their brutalizing of the earth's surface with tractors and earth-movers, Mazeaud's enterprise takes on mythical overtones not of Prometheus or Faust but of Isis: "The human debris she gathers are the dismembered parts of the murdered Osiris (garbage being a wonderful cipher for how we are dismembered by our technologies). Through her worry and care, Mazeaud resurrects Osiris's body, ensuring the renewed fertility of the vegetable kingdom in the crescent of the river" (122).

The Winnebago Road text also speaks of shattering (being shot by sacred shell projectiles, a fairly common motif in shamanic initiations) and rebirth/resurrection: the Winnebago initiate stands up shortly after being ritually "killed" in order to portray in advance the future rebirth to which the Rite leads. The literary record of the ritual (Radin variously refers to it as a ritual drama, a medicine rite, and a medicine dance), *The Road of Life and Death* [and Rebirth!], took shape over several years of Paul Radin's career: his initial paper about it was published in 1911, only two years after recording the ceremony (and in the middle of his work with the Winnebago, 1908-13). Radin refers to it in a number of his works, and gives it its own chapter in his *The Winnebago Tribe* (1990), as well as discussing associated myth texts (1950) and his informants (1983). The ritual text was dictated and translated along with an interpreter, although other texts were written directly in the Winnebago syllabary, including the legend of the giving of the Rite.

What we mean by "literary record" is something different today from what it was in the first decade of the century, and Radin's attempt to differentiate data from interpretation would today be treated with a suspicion that members of the Boasian school would have found odd.

Crashing Thunder, the first full-fledged Indian autobiography, has been critiqued several times in the extensive material on Indian autobiographies (perhaps most accessibly in Krupat's additions to the reprint of 1983 and Brumble's essay of 1987). My concern here cannot be with the literary aspects, even given the growing recognition of the Native materials *as literature* —at last!, I'd say, after a period reaching back to Margot Astrov's *The Winged Serpent* (1946), a work whose significance in this regard was only excelled by Jerome Rothenberg's compendium, *Shaking the Pumpkin* (1972). Rothenberg's work is briskly dismissed by some professional anthropologists, but I am not now concerned with the question of ethnographic authenticity so much as with the *literary* qualities, and I find both Astrov and Rothenberg unsurpassed and proleptic of what we are beginning to appreciate.

No matter how we judge technically the ethnographic dimensions of the literary text, *Road* is a stunning, sprawling record of a five night, six day ceremonial that combines an extraordinary number of ritual features. It has to do with immortality and facing death, with facing life crises; it records ritual performances and liturgical texts along with associated ritual elements such as sacrifice and the vapor lodge (sweat bath); it reflects the Winnebago cosmology and hermeneutics, its attitudes toward social change, its use of herbal medicines, and its teachings concerning ethico-moral values; it reflects Winnebago secular as well as sacred society, and their shamanistic specialists[9]; and it imbricates mythical materials, specifically the origin myth that is linked, as in other Native cultures, with the etiology of this ritual and the salvific figures of Winnebago religion such as "He-whom-we-call-our-nephew," Hare, who "trampled under foot all the evil spirits" (161). Various portions of the Rite may be purchased in incremental stages, over a long period of time, just as shamanistic instruction is transmitted in many societies.

Given so many features (in a book of almost 350 pages, and with parallels elsewhere so that Radin published more than 500 pages on this rite alone), it is not possible to treat the Rite extensively, and I shall restrict my scope to three aspects: first I will summarize the Rite; then I will mention some of the main themes; and third, in the next section of this essay I will demonstrate how Detweiler's characteristics of "reading religiously" might approach this complex work and how other approaches to the journey/tao motif complexify and elucidate *Road*.

Initiation into the lodge—which is the central focus of this ritual—may take place early in life (as was the case with the informant Blowsnake, at thirteen) or not, but initiation only begins a life-long observance of the

Rite, during which one may work one's way up to purchase of many particular ritual perquisites: the right to sing particular songs, to lead portions of the Rite, to hold ritual paraphernalia in particular postures, or to cross the ritual temenos in a particular direction. Radin (or his informant) divides *The Rite* into five components, *The Ritual* (in each case) *of Tears, Purification, Expectations, Rewards*, and *Life, Death and Rebirth* (these names are not immediately justified in the text or annotations).

A specially purified ground becomes the temenos for a ritual lodge built specifically for the occasion from canvas stretched over poles (faint photographs in Radin 1990), and what follows transpires within this space, except for the sixth-day initiation itself, which is held in a secret place "in the bush." Preliminary materials speak of the etiology of the Rite—it was founded by Hare, at the end of the period treated in the Origin Myths; over the four preliminary evenings, the historico-legendary origins of the Rite and its moral tenets are related, and the initiate is prohibited from sleeping (a fairly common ritual feature of initiatory ceremonials). Simultaneous with the preparation of the initiate, each of the six ritual subgroups (Ancestor-Host's Band, plus those of East, North, West, Ghost, and South) undergoes four nights of preparation. Forming the bulk of the Rite account, the highly repetitive texts for each evening stress being prepared for the ceremonial to follow; they bring the six subgroups into a state of religious preparedness that I would compare to a contemporary non-Indian sorority or fraternity practicing its ritualistic set-speeches and performances, or the reading- and then dress-rehearsals of a dramatic troupe. These evenings of preparation help the confraternity to recall important mythico-scriptural passages, ritual actions, and legendary accounts.

Purification introduces the steam bath for all concerned, and leads to the central "shooting" that characterizes *Road*: death and rebirth are symbolized/enacted repeatedly when magical shamanic shells (*migis*) are projected into participants—who fall to the ground in apparent death, only to rise immediately to demonstrate their having conquered death's strictures. The almost Calvinistic *Rewards* segment features the moralistic sermonizing that is characteristic (so far as I can tell) of Winnebago formal materials (cf. the instructions to youths, in Radin 1990). Something of an anti-climax, *Life, Death and Rebirth* repeats some of the moral preachments, but it articulates the "shooting" of the initiate and others for which we have been well prepared all along.

The particular ritual segments/sequences alone do not give us much of a sense of the importance of the Rite and the explicit texts of the ritual units need to be supplemented by a thematic overview. From what I can tell, the revelation of important themes is not necessarily successive or additive— i.e., the placement within the Rite doesn't seem to determine the importance of the specific material transmitted. But what we find included thematically may seem astonishing to those who think of the Native American Indians in terms of primitive bows and arrows (now increasingly imported from Taiwan) sold in tourist shops, or in terms of the sorts of categories used even by the sophisticated ethnologist Radin, such as "primordial," "nature people," and the like.

In fact there is a sophistication of thought comparable to Taoism, on the one hand, in terms of the elevation of the Path of Life motif to a delicately-balanced motif of moral teaching, and on the other to (Asian) Indian religious thought, with its careful considerations of reincarnative performances that may or may not lead one to come back as a cockroach or hamster. Likewise there is a sophistication similar to the Indian system of ashramas (archetypally repeated stages of life) that realistically differentiates accomplishments: only as one gains in secular stature can one afford the perquisites of high ritual stature.

Certainly the central emphasis (to the Winnebago, to Radin, and to me) is the theme of immortality. But this theme divides into various ways, not only into the almost-Hindu emphasis upon reincarnation, but likewise into the moralistic shapings of "how to live to old age/long life" which seems to be the Winnebago focus. They regard the Rite as a means by which certain people may more adequately face life crises:

> The purpose of the Medicine Dance is in part the desire to attain a long life, a safe journey to the next world, and the possibility of a return to this life again, preferably in human shape. All these benefits may be obtained by taking an active part in the ceremony, and by performing to the best of one's ability all the duties of a member. Although it is essential to participate in the entire ritual in order to obtain these benefits to the fullest extent, nevertheless the phenomena of shooting and being shot at play an especially important role in this connection.
>
> Long life means essentially the life consisting of a normal length of years, with all the possessions of wealth, social and intellectual distinction, that would naturally be included.
>
> When in the Medicine Dance [the Winnebago] pray for long life, what they mean is the ability to surmount the crises of life. Whatever may be the nature of these crises,—whether they relate to family disasters, sickness, old age, etc.,—it is expected that they will be overcome by membership and active participation in the society (Radin 1911:194).

Like the invocation of the life-giving spirits through ritual tobacco smoking, part of the preliminary segments of the Rite are directed toward forcing an extension of the allotted span of human years (1973:151), precisely what is referred to as a miraculous gift, "reincarnation, the shedding of our skin" in the same evening's proceedings (154). Such a gift both is and is not a feature of another life. On the one hand the referent is the future—Earthmaker "will permit you to be born into the world of men again whenever and wherever you wish" (264)—and on the other hand, "living a second life" refers to entering a moral path that leads to health and happiness: "Thus have the members of the Rite always encouraged one another to act and behave so that they will attain to the good life as long as the world lasts" (264). The Rite is said to enable the initiate "to live to a normal old age" (257) or to "obtain life, to live to extreme old age" (306).

The extended series of reincarnations is no longer possible as it was in the mythical beginnings (169), and the contemporary experience of the rewards of the Rite seem less oriented toward future lives than toward what most religions speak of as the narrow path of righteousness:

> This is the Road laid out by He-whom-we-call-our-nephew, and the initiate cannot fail to stay in it. For him there will be neither falling nor standing, illness nor death. The spirits created this Road for us and He-for-whom-we-seek-life will stand in it firmly, will step into it, into life, firmly, today. He who travels along this Road, if he has lived properly and if he has been virtuous, will discover that our grandmother, Earth, has been observing him and that she will extend her broad breasts to him and to us. What I tell you is absolutely true, dependent, however, upon whether the spirits have seen you leading a virtuous existence.
>
> Try then, I beg of you, to act virtuously in your travels along the Road upon which you are now to enter. If you walk along it properly it will benefit you greatly (250-51).

How does "religious reading" open this ritual text to us, help us to insight it with the perspective of deep play? Well hopefully by something more than just what we bring ordinarily to texts even in a liberal reading that favors *the other*, the almost prophetic stance that recognizes the dangers of monocultural hegemony, of simple-sighting what ought to remain complex and manifold. And hence we might hear here a familiar concept (such as reincarnation or—why not?—incarnation) in an unfamiliar setting, the North American Indian context. Doesn't "long life" in this context, just as much as the reincarnational cycles (up to eight, in the Winnebago context, Radin 1973:114) provide unintended and serendipitous glances at the Eleusinian promises of the Homeric Hymn to Demeter or Sophokles ("thrice blessed are those among men who, after beholding these rites, go down to Hades. Only for them is there life; all the rest will suffer an evil lot"): were those folks *really* concerned primarily with the afterlife, or were they not just like the Winnebago concerned at once with the future and the present? "It is said that no matter how long ago it is that a person has been dead, if he had performed this Rite of our ancestors well, when he was alive, *he will remain happy* " (104, my emphasis).

Such a statement ought to remind us of the use of the early Christian ostraca—bits of Scripture written on small pottery fragments, treated as magical purveyors of divine protection. Or to reexamine the *Bardol Thödol* (the Tibetan Book of the Dead): are those words read to the dying persons really for *them*? or aren't they just as important to the *survivors* who like to feel *some* control over where the loved ones go and who want to know that they (the survivors) have met their last ritual duties faithfully, making an appropriately clean break with the deceased? (I deduce this from the experience of having had such a rite performed for a departing friend of several decades—whatever the benefit to my friend, telling me the story of what had been done for her on her deathbed was enormously important to her husband.) And such an approach would emphasize the community's self-representation, as it glances at their own social ordering through this sacred history/mythology.

The frame such an approach determines is not mechanistic or arbitrary in the ways so many contemporary types of arbitrary codings and allegorizings lead to simplistic books and lectures on the popular lecture circuits, but it asks for *sympathetic and empathetic hearing* . What the text meant for "them," what it means for "us," even as the categories of themness and us-ness shrink across the postmodern planes of our everyday existence. Here we go beyond "scientific" and "impartial" analyses into a hermeneutics that exceeds Marxian demystification by honoring *the mysteries*, the left-overs excluded from most rationalistic criticism today.

And we might come to refract "their" use of sacred materials through the lenses of our own ritualizations, while simultaneously adapting their view of us: do we discover different aspects of ourselves as we pretend/imagine ourselves performing these rites? Can we converse with these Winnebago observed so scientifically by the Boas-trained Radin, whose social constructions of reality we can only guess at, since additional materials are lacking, following the nation's geographical and social division between Wisconsin and Nebraska moieties? Where is the linking to the meaning of this material that even a non-religious person may find so affecting? It is important to recognize how even such a person is strongly influenced by the cultural determinations of particular groups, such as the dominant Protestantism of most of American history, which has bequeathed such a heritage—note well!—of anti-ritualism.

Several other aspects of the content or message of the Rite ought to be explicated before we return to Detweiler's hermeneutical hexagon. I want to mention the emic/native references to the significance of the Rite, the role of moral instruction in it, and various aspects of the ritualization. The Rite is "a ceremony of great significance" (Radin 1973:104) that must be attended even if the participant is ill—"participation in the Rite will cure him." "Never has a renegade been heard of. Never must anyone drop out of the Rite after he has once joined it. At all times must we try to perform this ceremony correctly and with sincerity" (168). Normally the participant will increase his supply of ritual techniques gradually by buying them from others: that may sound "commercial" to a generation trained in a "spiritual *versus* material" religiosity, but the Winnebago share the common Native American understanding that such techniques, or songs, or stories, are the property of the individual with whom they originate, and that individuality ought not be compromised by copying or stealing another's possessions.

Paul has to reprimand early Christians for mishandling the Eucharist. He argues in 1 Cor 11:29-30 that taking the sacramental elements as merely so much food to gobble down, without respecting their religious, symbolical significations, causes weakness, illness, and premature death. Such a sense of magical power in the religious ritualization is found in the Winnebago warning not to try to obtain too much or inappropriate power, lest it kill one (175). And it surrounds the very mention of the Rite:

> Never tell anyone about this Rite. Keep it absolutely secret. If you disclose it the world will come to an end. We will all die. [When Paul Radin's father died after Radin began the recording, the death was taken by the informant as a confirmation of the importance of this proscription.] Earthmaker himself assured us that happiness and good fortune will come to us only if we keep silent about these matters. Into the very bowels of our Grandmother, Earth, must we project this information, so that by no possible chance can it ever emerge into daylight. So secret must this be kept. Forever and ever must this be done (265).

The ritual was disclosed only when it seemed evident that the Winnebago tribe was being overwhelmed, and the peyote ceremony was replacing traditional rites—I will discuss this important social context of the narrative text below.

The moral teaching of the Rite are repeated any number of times in the long moralistic speeches of instruction and admonition that we see also in the education of a young Winnebago man (in Radin 1990). Such a person chosen for initiation into the Rite will be "virtuous, . . . kind-hearted, . . . very wise, . . . accustomed to wisdom and slightly beyond middle age"(85). The moral aspects provide the "real world" counterpart to the elevated sacralization of the Rite itself: in the middle of the initiation one of the initiators is reminded: "What I am going to tell you now is nothing really unusual. . . . If you will abide in every respect by what I am now going to speak about to you, you will enable the initiate to live to a normal old age," (257) and then an extended, moralistic and allegorical explication of the road/tao of life follows (257-64). Likewise a table of six commandments encompasses "true living," which avoids doing evil, stealing, lying, and fighting, and stipulates how males should respect women (88). Other ethical stipulations from Earthmaker add loving everyone, and taking care of one's own people and one's own self so that one might live a long life (279).

The initiate is enjoined "to act virtuously in your travels along the Road upon which you are now to enter. If you walk along it properly it will benefit you greatly" (250-51), and the members repeatedly emphasize the connection between the ritualization and existential meaning. Addressing the Ancestors who have transmitted the Rite, an officiant states: "You have passed on to me the means-of-thankfulness; you have passed onto me life; you have made me realize that I had been brought into connection with life. . . . You have made me realize what life really is. As far back as one can go, from that distant time, my relatives have made new life come to me" (206). Likewise: "Earthmaker gave us this life of the Rite. It is truly the only kind of life that exists" (278), a form of existence that Earthmaker imagines or intends from the beginning of the planet (17).

Finally I want to indicate some of the ritualization features of this text.[10] The Rite is one of the life crisis rituals: performed for this initiate when he was 13 (although the stated ideal of the ritual text is the middle-aged male), it is related to the vision quest as well as to the mourning ("tear-pouring") service for the dead. And it is one of the ritualizations that connects the past (hence it is prefaced by Creation Myths) with the present ("just as the Rite members do today, so did [Wolf] make the circuit of the lodge," 83). While the repetition of the aboriginal never has quite the same power as the original, as we are reminded several times (e.g., "We are indeed only imitators. But we will try our best, in a pitiable, humble fashion" (94), there is a sense of ritual compulsion (*do ut des*): "No matter how poorly we sing it our ancestors will deign to accept it" (98).

A priestly-lay distinction is emphasized. Not only must the initiate anticipate being at the low end of the spectrum of respect for a long time, but she or he will have to learn many meanings accruing to the most apparently simple items, as she or he learns both the ritual acts and their significance. Hence Radin's professional frustration: while "obtaining the text itself took two and a half months, working six hours a day seven days a week" (45), the final translation and interpretation took much longer. Ritual language is highly valorized language whose referents and expressions are seldom monophonic; hence "this interweaving of the concrete and the symbolic and mystical led to a double, at times even a triple, set of significances for every action and word and which, occasionally, reached incredible heights of complication, intricacy and subtlety" (72). This is, after all, the record of a secret ritual society, whose contents are themselves ritually proscribed in the strongest terms: "Never tell anyone about this Rite. Keep it absolutely secret. If you disclose it the world will come to an end. We will all die" (265).

In selecting out a few aspects of this complex text, I must omit here discussion of the sweat lodge ceremony—elaborately presented, because of its importance: "In entering the Creation-Lodge I am in the presence of something utterly real and true. I greet its blessing. . . . Now I know what it is to be endowed with life!" (214). Likewise I omit discussion of the shamanistic elements, as in the close relationship to the Ojibwa Midewiwin emphasized by Radin (1911:165), and all the accoutrement of the Rite itself (rubrics on how to move within the ritual space, the sacred chemical peyote, sacrifices and offerings and their meanings, censing, the drum and other musical instruments, and others, but perhaps I will stimulate study by others.

I note in conclusion some of the ways Detweiler's six categories (now summarized in my own words, italicized) provide us with entrees into the ritual text of *Road*. Obviously one does not undertake such a project as I have undertaken here without some sense of comfortable fit between intentions, and I'll not play innocent observer. I move here to a shorthand-like diction because the conclusions seem obvious, even redundant. The hermeneutic Detweiler proposes provides a means of recovery of originative energies from Native American contexts that we might otherwise bypass in the traditional perspecting of NAI materials as primordial, *scil* . primitive (inferior, not-yet-developed into the rationalistic perspectives that have led to banal culture as well as to Belsen and Auschwitz).

(1) *Contemplation/conversation with the texts in place of hegemonic domination*. Reincarnation strikes the average contemporary Westerner as nonsense: what can we learn from texts in which it is verbalized? What other aspects of the mystery of texts need to be sheltered, given ou

society's usual opposition between the moral, religious, or artistic and the scientific, technological, or commercial? Might not aspects of the text come to be regarded as more significant if we relax before them, instead of demanding that they be shaped to meet our techno-generic expectations? I cannot help but wonder about the missing song-texts, as I indicated in an earlier note. The element of repetition is important across the range of Native American religio-artistic materials, although almost all pre-contemporary collections simply added admonitions such as "repeat refrain" endlessly, usually citing only the first line of a song, followed by that command. But the song itself is part of a ritualization that ought not be presumptively summarized and shortened. And furthermore, it is characteristic of traditional Native American songs to be brief in diction: "the song is very short because we understand so much" (Maria Chona, a Papago woman, quoted in Beck 44) and closely related to the historical context in which it originated or to which it refers. Allowing a passivity toward these elements helps us comprehend the dynamics of the ritualization and to look for other dynamics we may be ignorant of as we regard only printed versions.[11]

(2) *Some privileged fictions resist chaos by religiously linking and selecting meanings* . The several instances of moral preachments already noted help us to see some of the ways any moral road provides a survival mode that must be inculcated before it can be followed; the link between the Rite and reincarnation = the good life provides in this case a strong psychological motivation for adhering to Winnebago moral teaching. As the centering of the participants' consciousness, the Rite facilitates interpersonal relations and prepares one to face life transitions equitably. The element of "privileged" fictions implicates the ideological aspect, an aspect I'd like Detweiler to discuss further, and one I'll address at the conclusion of this section. It also raises questions about the priestly-lay distinction, clearly supposed in the Winnebago material, but perhaps still a sticking point in the Protestant Reformed traditions as it is not, apparently, in the Winnebago.

(3) *Celebration and signification of what seems at the same time ineluctable and irreducible and yet provisional.* Certainly the Rite we have looked at helps one recognize one's limits. Death comes to the good and the bad; participation in the Rite provides an answer, but not for everyone. What is signified results in the patterning by which these given parameters of existence can be accepted and lived through. And the living-through is now done in the name of the ritual community, a community that understands itself as both transmitting and shaping: a participant would understand

"herself as part of a community engaged in simultaneously recognizing, criticizing, and reshaping the myths and rituals it lives by" (Detweiler 38). The individual is transcended by the community; the present is subsumed into generic time, and we begin to see something of Detweiler's textual erotics: pulling the individual into a shared community of celebrants, its attracting one to the confrontational and con-celebratory "conflict of interpretations" by which we model open-ended polysemy in a festivaling of the "surplus of meaning that reading [and ritualizing] supplies" (39; cf. also 33, 40).

(4) *Important fictions mythicize the everyday by providing models* ("probes," 13) *of possible enactments of selfhood and one's relationship to society, as through its language.* The importance of the language—"life-engendering greetings" in the Rite—is marked by its ritual frames, including dance as a form of song ("In a moment I shall start up a minor dance-song. That will be my speech," Radin 1973:238). The element of mystery surrounds the recital of creation myths no less than the magical "shooting" of sacred projectile shells that do and do not kill. It is there in the acknowledgment of the mysterious aspects of the afterlife, even though the admonitions of the Rite form a bulkhead against chaos. Selfhood is ethically shaped, as we've seen repeatedly above, just as the communal is revalued constantly:

> It is through [the members of the Rite] that I live; it is they who endeavored to make me live. It is good.
> The leaders of the Medicine Rite used to say that if once you are blessed and if once you emulate the words and actions of those of long ago, then those who blessed you will see you following just behind them. They will see you walking and falling along the Road (318).

(5) *Presence marks absence; the present is qualified by the past and the future.* The incorporation of the Origin Myth that forms a preface to the Rite itself operates just as such a myth often prefaces healing and other rites among other Native American Indian groups. It is difficult to avoid use of Eliade's technical term for the special condition of recalling and re-enacting the primal times, *in illo tempore*, or to question (in this instance) his emphasis upon the priority of the cosmogonic myth (see Beane and Doty 1976:passim). The special Winnebago ceremonial lodge is termed the Creation-Lodge (108), and the Ancestors present in it from the beginning will "cool your face" as the participants march around the lodge, dancing, drumming, and singing (240). The awareness of the cosmic powers being invoked is very clear at the beginning of the penultimate section of the Rite when a leader remarks that "when I sit down and begin I will be reenacting

what Earthmaker himself did" (251). This comment is followed by the section of the Origin Myth in which human beings are created (52-55) and we may note also the explicit parallels between Creation times when Trickster and Hare did magical acts and the time of the Rite in the present (281, 287). I have tried in an earlier essay (Doty 1990a) to show how the fictive projects tenuous connections (religion, yoga) between portions of our experiences; Detweiler's approach expands the purview of what we may regard as "religious," even if approached or treated in an entirely non-religious manner.

(6) *Deep play: prophetic reading on behalf of the disenfranchised and what may yet be possible impossibilities for communal sharing.* How myths and rituals are related as prototypes for the societies in which they appear can be simplistically understood à la the old socio-functionalism, but it can also be more subtly understood, as is increasingly the case in contemporary anthropology (see Doty n.d., where I refer to the updating perspectives reported by Eisenstadt 1990 and Lévi-Strauss 1976, when the sociohistorical is brought into conjunction with the logico-imaginative). Clearly the Rite reflects and establishes social orderings within traditional Winnebago society; it models possible accomplishments—in fact the ultimate, that of overcoming "death." And it provides for its own self-maintenance while recording for posterity the details of the ritual.

But just that last provision is what has not been voiced so far in this essay, and leads me to suggest that the Winnebago *Road* text provides us with an instance wherein Detweiler's approach might be developed somewhat. Several aspects of the ideology of the Winnebago are expressed through (and constituted by) the Rite, and I'd like to see Detweiler develop his "prophetic reading" along the lines of the critique of the ideological functioning of texts that has been developed recently in various schools of critical feminism and in crossdisciplinary cultural studies. Analysts following such approaches ask about who determines canonical texts and their proper interpretations; they stress the need for oppositional readings that operate alongside normative interpretations and texts; and they recognize the mystifications of one's own cultural productions. While sketching such ideological criticism here would take me too far afield, I can at least note Catherine Bell's important contribution to ritual studies (her influence is strong on Doty n.d.-b) in which she shows how important it will be to incorporate some of the leading theories into ritual studies, and refer to the massive reader, *Cultural Studies* (Grossberg) that encompasses the cultural studies field that now increasingly replaces earlier narrowly-conceived ethnographies.

Greater awareness of the ideological dimensions of the contexts in which texts are produced would have led Radin to be more aware of the blinders of his own late-Victorian ethnographic principles, as well as to appreciate more extensively and sensitively the curious fact that the Rite was recorded as an aggressive act of one Winnebago religionist against others (likewise three other peyote followers dictated the Origin Myth earlier, Radin 1973:38). The informant, Jasper Blowsnake, having decided that precisely this sacred ritual was no longer valid, had become a peyotist, and after dictating the Rite to Radin, "Blowsnake was ostracized for half a year by [the traditionalists], many of whom were his relatives and former colleagues in the old rituals. It was not a pleasant experience but the opinions of [the traditionalists] had come to mean very little to him by that time [because of his recent conversion to peyote] and he was steeled to any fate" (45). We learn, indeed, that some of his visionary experiences with peyote had convinced him that he ought to share the Rite with Radin; subsequent personal experiences convinced him that "*the telling and the translation of the Medicine Rite is my mission in life and I am willing to tell all to the full extent of my knowledge* " (49, Radin's italics). The last celebration of the *Road* was given about the time of World War 2 (Lurie 701); we wonder how much Radin recognized of the split into traditionalist, mission-Christian, and Peyote factions (Lurie 701, 704) that transpired shortly after he recorded the Rite.

It would be irresponsible to accuse the editor of a text originally published in 1945 (Radin 1973) but discussed already in a 1911 publication, of lacking psychological sophistication, since the relevant psychosocial and psychohistorical tools were not available then. No matter how one longs for more information, one finds only:

> Into all these fascinating psychological questions I shall not enter here. The only important thing which we have to remember is that a multitude of factors were involved in [Blowsnake's] final acquiescence to do something fundamentally quite repugnant to him.
>
> We must regard this acquiescence, in short, as in the nature of a conversion of the same type as his conversion to the peyote (49).

This sort of restraint is common in most of the crucial early accounts of Native American culture, and the whole question of how ethnography can be configured between the person presenting and the person reporting information is now hotly debated.[12] A sensitive psychological criticism might find any number of ways in which this account of the Rite portrays Blowsnake's own ambivalences and his doubts about the future. It might even be argued that his emphasis upon the linking of the primordial and his own experience derived not from a Winnebago norm but from the fear that that link was shattered by the adoption of the new (non-traditional) religious forms.

Beyond the question of the Blowsnake informants and their particular roles in the Winnebago religious transition to twentieth-century forms,[13] we might inquire also about Radin's own attitudes toward having left behind his native Poland and undergoing the initiation of anthropological fieldwork and writing. The sorts of religious communities he participated in are never indicated, although such information would help us to appreciate his contributions in this text, since we now recognize, as we learn from Detweiler with respect to the importance of recognizing theological differences between groups of writers/informants, that it is important to respect informants' secrecy about mysteries that are not mysterious to us. Or the importance of recognizing how particular figures are figured in a particular tradition in ways quite opposed to those with which we may be familiar—here one example is the Winnebago Rite's Trickster, who is not the usual Native American human-aiding figure but one who is inimical to humans (59). Or possessing significations that might never occur to us— here the example is the sacred Twins: "Their adventures constitute real happenings and not, what one might have supposed far-off divine events, for one simple reason, namely, their resting-place is on earth and they, and this resting-place, have actually been seen by the fathers of present-day Indians" (in Radin's sketch of Winnebago mythological figures, 54). But was this interest in historicity Radin's or the Winnebago's? Reading dated texts such as Radin's is extremely instructive in terms of revealing just how contemporary collecting (or collaboration, increasingly the dominant situation) has developed sensitivities toward emic tenets and ideological prior-understandings that were simply not in the awareness of earlier ethnographers.

We might also ask about the Winnebago reactions to the social crisis constituted by contacts with Euroamerican culture, and about how this Rite and others changed during the confrontation. And in a more extended intellectual context we might ask about the marked interest of sociologists and anthropologists in men's societies that began already toward the end of the eighteenth century. Indeed we might ask beyond the immediate exploration of the text to just some of the crosscultural comparisons I've long hoped to compile in terms of the journey/way/road motif: not only do we need to discuss further the explicit parallels to the Tao that cannot be named, but the Christian Way or Path (*hodos*; already present in Mark as a way of justifying Jesus' death, developed in Luke and the later canonical materials as a pattern for a distinctive Christian ethics, and at its height in medieval labyrinthine floor mosaics meant for slow walking-meditation), the Australian Walkabout, or the graphic representations of participants' feet in ritual paintings in both Middle America and Navajo ceremonials. Here I can but point in these wider directions, and recommend a delightful charting of a number of the associated images and metaphors, in Northrop Frye's essay, "The Journey as Metaphor" (212-26).

"Reading religiously" helps us recognize the ways a text constitutes its sacred functioning within a specific community. It clarifies how a particular ritualization brought about and reflected a particular worldview. And it enables us to recognize just how a community of readers determines the specific parameters of its own social constructions of significant reality. That *Road's* role in its religious community was replaced by the newer peyote way just as it was recorded remains ironic if not tragic. But perhaps the Winnebago text, even if it is no longer sacred for most of that tribe, can remain non-religiously "sacred" for any careful reader today, if read religiously according to Detweiler's expansion of our interpretive discipline.

NOTES

1. A Shango song from Trinidad, Courlander 1976:xxi.

2. I am delighted to contribute to Robert Detweiler's honorific Festschrift, although as he approaches the Wise Old Man archetype I anticipate that his contributions will only begin to explode in new directions and creativity, instead of tapering off. Hence what I say here will most likely need proofing anew very soon. Our association over the last decade has been one of the delights of my academic career, and trekking to Emory to be adjunct faculty at the ILA on doctoral committees has invariably been made more pleasurable by the thought of good conversations with him.

3. Arnold Krupat notes that we are dealing with the issue of "textualization" of the "facts" (see Radin, 1983:xiv), as the ethnographers have helped us all to respect more clearly what is "made up" and what "collected." But already Radin ought to have been of assistance. In *The Winnebago Tribe* (1990.236), he treats the theme from the context of "personal or impersonal":

> It is because we Europeans do insist that the presence or absence of corporeality is the test of reality or unreality that we have been led to make the classification into personal and impersonal. But the Winnebago apparently does not insist that existence depends upon sense perceptions alone. He claims that what is thought of, what is felt, and what is spoken, in fact, anything that is brought before his consciousness, is a sufficient indication of its existence and it is the question of the existence and reality of these spirits in which he is

interested. The question of their corporeality is of comparative unimportance and most of the questions connected with the personal or impersonal nature of the spirits do not exist.

The now-classical essay by Claude Lévi-Strauss on four Winnebago myths (1976) is helpful for recognizing how the structuralist's algebraic abstractions could be useful in analysis that was not necessarily adequate to the historical contours of the texts themselves, a judgment to which I will return at the end of this essay.

4. I have long been impressed by Susan Sontag's concept of the erotics of interpretation, or as Lash (1989:176) calls it, an aesthetics of sensation, which I find similar to Detweiler's position here. Lash shows how Jean-François Lyotard provides theoretical development of such a position.

5. Kakutani 1992 creatively relates what she finds to be new, but has been around for some time, the "futuristic novel," to recent meditation on the end of the millenium.

6. The second will be "Reading Religiously in a Non-Religious Age," in terms of engaging the allegorical questions raised across the critical theory spectrum today, Mieke Bal's attention to reading for the gaps, and various feminist modes of attending to texts.

7. Or "the Rite"—I'll use both as abbreviations for the ritual or the book, Paul Radin, *The Road of Life and Death: A Ritual Drama of the American Indians*, Radin 1973. Originally published in 1945, it was dictated to Radin by a wisdom person (traditionally, "medicine man"), Jasper Blowsnake, in 1908.

I have been teaching Native American materials critically for too long to remain passive before asseverations such as Radin's conclusion to an "Editor's Note" (ix), that "The songs are not included. Most of the rather complete collection I possessed was destroyed. Owing to technical difficulties it would, however, have been quite impossible to translate them, even had they not been destroyed." Such mystifications can only irritate a contemporary reader: how "destroyed"? what "technical difficulties"? One characteristic of pre-mid-20th-century collecting was the Noble White Man's Burden assumption of gentlepersons' collusion: of course one would trust the collector and excuse the problems created by difficulties of collection in what seemed to the EuroAmerican a savage and foreign land within our own continent: Radin speaks more than once of the "promordial." But when he mentions that the literal meaning of "to sing the songs" is "to make one's breath visible in the form of song or speech," a ritualistic circumlocution for song (1990:423), or when Radin mentions that songs were considered "our life-engendering greetings" (1973:101), that the singing of a song by a sorcerer leads to death (119), or that song is a form of speech (238), just as "the songs will obtain for you whatever it is you have in your mind" (95), we cannot but wonder just how much we have missed by not having the songs in the ritual text.

Likewise I have trouble interpreting the origins of the rubrics of the ritual: are these "portions that are purely descriptive" entirely, as Radin implies from the narration of his informant (ix), or are they his own descriptive interpolations? An example: "*In the distance a line of men and women can now be discerned walking slowly* " (9). Some passages give me flashbacks to naive days in a pre-Masonic fraternity, rituals replete with archaisms such as those renderings of Radin's like "O you who sit in the east where-the-sun-comes-from, you who impersonate the spirit who first sat in that position when He-whom-we-call-our-nephew, Hare, first established this Rite . . . " (10). Or stage directions such as *Greeting, singing and dancing as before* (11) and *Ancester-Host sits down and East now rises to speak* (13): I can't imagine anyone freely dictating a crucial sacred ritual using such diction, and have to suspect that we are facing the sort of phenomenon familiar to the pre-contemporary editions of Native poetry in which the repeated refrains, in a culture where the very repetition has sacredly compelling significance, got watered down to the command to *Repeat the refrain.*. Perhaps just such sensitivity led to Radin's shortening the title of this ritual drama, clipping off the last phrase that might have alienated White readers: in the text (12) it is referred to as "the Road of life, of death *and of rebirth*" (my emphasis)! Why Road is hypostatized, one can only guess—no linguistic evidence is presented, any more than explanation why the term sometimes appears in lower-case (for example, 13 ff.).

There have been various critical views of Radin's collecting of Winnebago materials, but some of his versions are still important, and while there are studies of Radin's involvement in the production of *Crashing Thunder* (Krupat, in Radin 1983 [1926] and Brumble 1987), I have not located any secondary studies on this particular ritual text, although I have consulted experts such as Christopher Vecsey and Sam Gill.

8. Elsewhere the ritual is named the Medicine *Dance*, i.e., in Chapter 14 dedicated to it in Radin 1990 and in Radin 1911. In Radin 1950 it is referred to as the Medicine Rite.

9. Although it does so perhaps less positively than we might today, when the fundamental character of the shaman as a religious specialist along with many other types is simply taken for granted. See for instance Lurie's (1978) article.

10. I am aware of the problems with treating a text dictated in a non-ritual setting as an accurate account of the ritual itself, but that does not keep me from reflecting on several aspects that *are* clearly indicated. I use "ritualization" to avoid the essentializing "ritual"; the term includes an emphasis upon the interpersonal and contextual shapings of the performances/enactments. In another essay (Doty 1992) I suggest that ritualizations are physical embodiments of meaning-finding that indicate appropriate relationships between the lone ego and the society. Rituals are politics enacted and are formative of society as they name and define its contours, providing knowledges not otherwise accessible, including its praxis in the production of individual and social meaning.

11. But overcoming this barrier for the classroom may be another matter. When *Road* became available in paperback, I thought to use it in my Native American Religion course, but I and an independent studies student both agreed that contemporary college students would find the text so repetitious—not only of the same words, but of the same ritual units—that it would not be possible to entice them to read the long text through to the end.

12. As I've demonstrated in Doty 1990b. Oddly enough, it was Radin himself who was one of the first to stress variation across a culture in terms of religious tenets and mythological versions presented by various raconteurs in different settings—see Radin 1915, especially "over and above the precise form in which he obtains a myth stands [the raconteur's] relationship as an artist to the dramatic situations contained in it and to his audience" (47).

13. In his Appendix to Radin 1983:205 Krupat notes that at times Radin apparently confused materials given by Sam and by Jasper.

WORKS CITED

Astrov, Margot, ed. *American Indian Prose and Poetry (The Winged Serpent)*. New York: Capricorn, 1946.

Atwood, Margaret. *The Handmaid's Tale*. New York: Fawcett Crest, 1985.

Beane, Wendell C., and William G. Doty, eds. *Myths, Rites, and Symbols: A Mircea Eliade Reader*. New York: Harper and Row; 2 vols, 1976.

Beck, Peggy V., and A. L. Walters. *The Sacred: Ways of Knowledge, Sources of Life*. Tsaile: Navajo Community College P, 1977.

Bell, Catherine. *Ritual Theory, Ritual Practice*. New York: Oxford UP, 1992.

Brumble, H. David III. "Sam Blowsnake's Confessions: *Crashing Thunder* and the History of American Indian Autobiography." In Brian Swann and Arnold Krupat, eds. *Recovering the Word: Essays on Native American Literature*. Berkeley: U California P; 537-51, 1987.

Courlander, Harold. *A Treasury of Afro-American Folklore*. New York: Crown, 1976.

Detweiler, Robert. *Breaking the Fall: Religious Readings of Contemporary Fiction*. San Francisco: HarperCollins, 1989.

Doty, William G. "Contextual Fictions that Bridge Our Worlds: `A whole new poetry'." *Journal of Literature and Theology* 4/1: 104-29, 1990.

Doty, William G. "Writing the Blurred Genres of Postmodern Ethnography." *Annals of Scholarship: Studies of the Humanities and Social Sciences* 6/2&3: 267-87, 1990.

Doty, William G. "Wild Transgressions and Tame Celebrations: Contemporary Construals of Ritualization." *Journal of Ritual Studies* 6/2: 115-30, 1992.

Doty, William G. "From the Traditional Monomythic Hero to the Contemporary Polymythic Hero/ine." In Robert W. Funk Festschrift issue of *Foundations and Facets Forum*, eds. Bernard Scot and John L. White, n. d.

Eisenstadt, S. N. "Functional Analysis in Anthropology and Sociology: An Interpretive Essay." *Annual Review of Anthropology* 19: 243-60, 1990.

Fish, Stanley. *Is There a Text in This Class? The Authority of Interpretive Communities*. Cambridge: Harvard UP, 1980.

Frye, Northrop. *Myth and Metaphor: Selected Essays, 1974-1988*. ed. Robert D. Denham. Charlottesville: UP Virginia, 1990.

Gablik, Suzi. *The Reenchantment of Art*. New York: Thames and Hudson, 1991.

Gill, Sam D. *Native American Religions: An Introduction*. The Relig. Life of Man Ser. Belmont: Wadsworth, 1982.

Grimes, Ronald. *Ritual Criticism: Case Studies in Its Practice, Essays on Its Theory*. Stud. in Compar. Relig. Columbia: U South Carolina P, 1990.

Grossberg, Lawrence; Cary Nelson; and Paula A. Treichler, eds. *Cultural Studies*. New York: Routledge, 1992.

Kakutani, Michiko. "Novelists Make a Literary Lunge into the Future." *The New York Times* Living Arts section, 21 February:B1, B6, 1992.

Lash, Scott. *Sociology of Postmodernism*. International Library of Sociology. New York Routledge, 1989.

Lévi-Strauss, Claude. "Four Winnebago Myths." *Structural Anthropology*. trans. Monique Layton. New York: Basic; vol. 2: 198-210, 1976.

Lurie, Nancy Oestreich. "Winnebago." *Handbook of North American Indians* vol. 15: 690-707, 1978.

Radin, Paul. "The Ritual and Significance of the Winnebago Medicine Dance." *The Journal of American Folk-Lore* 24/42: 149-208, 1911.

Radin, Paul. *Literary Aspects of North American Mythology*. Canada Dept. of Mines, Geol Survey, Mus. Bull. No. 16, Anthro. Ser. No. 6. Ottawa: Government Priniting Bureau (#1535), 1915.

Radin, Paul. *The Origin Myth of the Medicine Rite: Three Versions. The Historical Origins of the Medicine Rite*. Indiana U Publ. in Anthropology and Linguistics; Memoir 3 of *International Journal of American Linguistics*, and Special Publ. of Bollingen Foundation, 2. Baltimore: Waverly P, 1950.

Radin, Paul. *The Road of Life and Death: A Ritual Drama of the American Indians*. Bollingen Ser. V. Princeton: Princeton UP (reprint 1991 in Mythos: The Princeton/Bolligen Series in World Mythology), 1973 [1945].

Radin, Paul, ed. *Crashing Thunder: The Autobiography of an American Indian*. Lincoln: U Nebraska P, 1983 [1926].

Radin, Paul. *The Winnebago Tribe*. Lincoln: U Nebraska P.

Rothenberg, Jerome, ed. 1972. *Shaking the Pumpkin: Traditional Poetry of the Indian North Americas*. New York: Doubleday, 1990 [1923].

George Eliot's Daniel Deronda

Imaginative Communion and the Critical Imperative

JAMES CHAMPION

All meanings, we know, depend on the key of interpretation. George Eliot,
Daniel Deronda

It all comes under the main heading of "Fucking Around With the Reader."
My father thinks there's an orderly contract between writer and reader.
Martin Amis, Interview in *Rolling Stone*

What today is atheism tomorrow will be religion.
Ludwig Feuerbach, *The Essence of Christianity*

Those who celebrate or call for a "decentered" self seem self-deceptively naive
and unaware of the basic cohesion within themselves that makes the
fragmentation of experiences something other than a terrifying slide into
psychosis.
Jane Flax, *Thinking Fragments*[1]

Poor Marian Evans (1819-80). Limited by nineteenth-century logocentrism, she naively believed she was writing "realistic" fiction. Today we know that "realism" is nothing of the kind. It is actually a construct, a discursive practice entwined in the aesthetic delusions and politics of nineteenth-century culture. Despite some formal innovations and feminist insights stemming from her liberal humanist ideology, "George Eliot's" fictional practice failed to problematize the representation of reality. Her texts are, finally, complicit in the dominant symbolic order of Victorian patriarchy.

These remarks briefly reiterate a current view of George Eliot. It has become a commonplace critical "take" on her work, largely replacing a former assessment widespread in the 1960's. That formerly dominant view, which was more inclined to take literary representation at its word, arose through distinctive stages. F. R. Leavis's rehabilitation of Eliot's reputation in *The Great Tradition* (1948) was a major step. Thereafter, Eliot's novels were increasingly rendered fit for inclusion in English Department canons. This transition was perhaps best signaled on the literary critical front by Barbara Hardy's study, *The Novels of George Eliot* (1959). Such positive appraisals established a connection—the key connection required by the strictures of New Criticism—between Eliot's moral interpretation of life and the formal coherence of her narrative techniques.[2]

From New Criticism to new historicism, studies of George Eliot have proliferated. They would appear to be reaching critical mass on library shelves. As for the novels, high school students today may still have to read *Silas Marner*. In college, English majors may still encounter *Middlemarch*. By brushing up against the trustworthy "values" one finds in Eliot's novels, young persons may somehow be made better, it is supposed. Or, in adherence to a different kind of didactic impulse—this one more appropriate for graduate schools—Eliot may be read because her overly "authoritative" novels need to be dismantled and exposed for the rhetorical stratagems they really are.

Whatever the uses to which Marian Evans's novels may be put, the possibility of interpreting them remains. Notwithstanding the Eliot industry, a work such as *Daniel Deronda* can be an arresting read. Bring the most sophisticated dismissals to it, you may then find the novel highly capable, at unanticipated junctures, of placing interpretative torque upon your reflections as they are (you grudgingly acknowledge) provoked. In other words, however much this novel may be explained and its machinations laid bare, there is a richness of signification in the text that persists in tandem with a reader's concern to understand. Understanding, itself a theme within the story, is elicited and "occurs" through open engagement with the work. Admittedly, such engagement must be ventured in the face of the contemporary terror of appearing naive by momentarily heeding the power of the author's voice. Engagement must also be ventured in the face of the novel's assorted failings. In Eliot's day, one half of the novel—the entire "Jewish" section—was considered a "flaw," or, at least, a lapse in good taste. For many contemporary readers, the social world represented in such a work amounts to a deficiency of a different sort. As in most novels "before Freud," Victorian novels in particular, the social world depicted is impossibly contrary to our own. It is exasperating, say these readers, to watch characters forever bent upon doing the very opposite of what they most desire to do. Further, the fictional world in *Daniel Deronda* is marred by an omniscient narrator whose melodramatic asides prove distracting. "Poor Gwendolen," the narrator is liable to sigh after insisting too much on her heroine's delusions.

Whether inscribed through the compositional craft of "George Eliot" or in spite of Marian Evans's conscious control, *Daniel Deronda* reaches into life beyond the range of melodramatic codes.[3] In spite of Victorian conventions and the limitations of realist fiction, there is a depth of complexity dived for in this text, a depth that is religious in the widest sense. To explore that dimension of depth, as Robert Detweiler's premier work in literature and religion has so effectively shown, we must attend to contexts. In Eliot's case, we must attend to the author's historical situation, clearly, but no less, to the aesthetic setting of her narrative project overall.[4] With a view to such contexts, the following discussion traces two aspects of the religious in *Daniel Deronda*: the sacramental and the prophetic.[5]

These broad facets of the religious take decidedly secular shape in Eliot's works, for, as is well known, the author experienced a profound loss of traditional faith. Her honesty in witnessing to that loss led her to discard theistic belief and theological creeds—but not a preoccupation with religious matters. Influenced by Ludwig Feuerbach's efforts to translate the language of Christianity into secular terms, the sacramental returns in Eliot's writings, after belief. It returns as a transcendent space within the secular religion she adopts. This "space" is highly relational and its rituals inexact, for it is found, strangely enough to our ears, in the bonds of imaginative sympathy sustained between narrator, text, and reader.

The prophetic facet appears concurrently. Through satirical indictments against sexism, religious prejudice, and the wealthy elite, this side of the novel amounts to an attack on social injustice. That, of course, is how the prophetic generally takes shape, and no less so today. The contemporary prophetic style tends to include severe attacks on the cultural blind spots and the false steps taken by previous prophetic critics, such as Marian Evans. It is worth recalling, on occasion, that such figures helped to break the ground of our own critical freedom. They might also be the ones who reveal to us the ambivalence bound up in our Casaubon-like illusions that we have found, or will find, the key to all ideologies.

Imaginative Bonds

Daniel Deronda begins *in medias res*. This is necessary, the authorial voice tells us, since origins cannot be reached: "No retrospect will take us to the true beginning." On the other hand, we must jump in somewhere, since humans, apparently, "can do nothing without the make-believe of a beginning" (35). This sense of the arbitrary nature of story-telling shows a surprisingly modern recognition (antedating Frank Kermode) of the artificiality of time as a way of ordering experience.[6]

With some coordinates provided by the narrator, albeit in a (make-believe) quoted epigraph, the reader plunges in. The scene opens upon the protagonist, an attractive young woman, gambling at a pseudo-aristocratic Mediterranean resort. We see Gwendolen Harleth, at the roulette-table, momentarily a goddess of luck in the midst of a fashionable crowd of empty, masked faces. The light is on Gwendolen, determined, seeking admiration, there "not because of passion, but in search of it" (45). Gwendolen: somewhat narcissistic, with "a certain dynamic quality in her glance," yet suddenly feeling judged as inferior by a young man who is watching her. Apprehended by the sight of "this problematic sylph," Deronda enters as one who meets her gaze, who ignites her defiance, and who seems to send her at that moment into a losing spiral.

With its unusual beginning, *Daniel Deronda* is, at least initially, an experiment with the narrative use of time. In its opening descriptions of a gambling casino in Leubronn, it is also an indictment of the vacuous ruling class at its "well-fed leisure." Simultaneously, the novel is a love story that begins with the ambiguous desires of two people caught up in social constraints and self-deceptions, two characters on their way to transformation. Yet this love story, while predominant, turns out to be one story-line in a multi-plot novel. In attempting as much, Eliot tries to convey, in a relevant format, a life-like panorama. She gambles on achieving wholeness through a conjunction of aesthetic, psychological, and historical concerns, while evoking the rich particularity of social background.

In a letter of 1876, the year of *Daniel Deronda's* publication, Eliot speaks forthrightly of her holistic aim: "I meant everything in the book to be related to everything else there."[7] To the postmodern mind, this is perhaps a quaintly naive remark hailing from an age when culture still required content. Obviously, so the argument goes, Eliot is reaching for cohesion in order to counter a perceived threat. While on the one hand she is known for her intellectual embrace of progress, scientific discoveries, and the higher criticism of biblical belief, on the other hand she recognizes warily that the divine foundations of human community are slipping away. In response, she labors in her writings to maintain an integrated sense of life and to situate what is essentially human in relation to a principle of unified content. Towards those ends she draws on the resources of Victorian fiction.

Eliot draws in particular on a mode of fictional writing that is strongest in the middle decades of the nineteenth century. As Virginia Woolf observes (from the vantage point of our own century), the fiction of this bygone era is characterized by "the sense of an audience."[8] Its diverse practitioners, including Charles Dickens, William Thackeray, Anthony Trollope, Elizabeth Gaskell, and Charlotte Bronte, assume a sort of "contract" between writer and reader. Their fictions, at mid-century, tend to unfold in the public space of print culture where they serve to highlight the narrative relations between the configuring author and the refiguring public.

Such works show an inherent confidence in the possibility of imaginative communion between popular novelist and reading public. Of course, confidence of this sort does not rise out of an aesthetic vacuum. In many respects, it is derived from the legacy of the Romantic writers and their earlier endorsements of the power of sympathetic imagination.[9] With a view to rendering the world substantially, accurately, and ethically, the Victorians extend the phenomenon of sympathetic imagination to suit their own purposes. As Janice Carlisle notes, the result in the realm of fiction is the production of novels marked by "faith in the reader's innate capacity to feel with and for the characters."[10] Through direct addresses to the common reader, and through a variety of mediating techniques, authors of such works strive especially for moments of alignment of the perspectives of narrator, reader, and character. Eliot, in one of her earlier essays, describes the overarching goal of such story-telling: "Art is the nearest thing to life; it is a mode of amplifying experience and extending our contact with our fellowmen beyond the bounds of our personal lot."[11]

Eliot complicates this view over the course of her career. In part, she refines it by addressing in her own novels issues concerning the reading and writing of fiction. For example, in Deronda we find a character acutely affected by his reading experiences (at an early age, no less). These, the narrator implies, have been catalysts in the development of the man's signature trait: his capacity for "thinking . . . imaginatively into the experience of others" (570). In Gwendolen's case, on the other hand, detached and "uncontrolled reading" of an anemic kind of realism fails to "prepare" her for a particularly trying "encounter with reality" (193). A narrator who considers reading to be so formative not surprisingly finds an occasion to declare what the teller of tales should be trying to do: namely, "thread the hidden pathways of feeling and thought which lead up to every moment of action, and to those moments of intense suffering which take the quality of action" (202).

In devising such action and its undercurrents, the authorial voice of *Daniel Deronda* becomes highly controlling—overly so at times. The narrator reflects this control in the effort to oversee a reader's imagination. It is deemed "good" to conjure up dignified scenes—"Imagine [Mirah] with her dark hair brushed from her temples . . . " (422). Sometimes the narrator also seems bound by some undefined "good" to explain a character for the audience—"Hans Meyrick's nature was not one in which love could strike . . . deep roots" (709)—even after we have become familiar with the character's traits through action and dialogue. Yet on other occasions the narrator carefully conserves information that would reveal and explain. For example, when Deronda and Grandcourt are first brought together, we are told only that their relation hinges "on circumstances which have yet to be made known" (198).

The ambitions of the narrator eventually to make all essentials known for the sake of "completeness" (202) clash with a concurrent need to restrain the story's burgeoning implications. It is this need for restraint that generates the novel's periodic, moralizing intrusions. These are the moments in *Daniel Deronda* when the narrator offers up maxims. "The truth is something different from the habitual lazy combinations begotten by our wishes" (280), is typical of such asides. These sentiments, a staple of mid-century fiction, are invariably right as far as middle-class morality goes, but their correctness overrides the unruliness of the "hidden pathways" that the narrator also declares important. Late in the novel, for instance, in Deronda's wrenching interviews with Leonora Charisi, his lost mother, an array of repressed feelings surfaces in each character, and the emotions are profoundly examined. But the forcefulness of these encounters is diluted when the narrator concludes them with a little lesson for the reader: "[Deronda] had gone through a tragic experience which must for ever solemnize his life, and deepen the significance of the acts by which he bound himself to others" (731).

But in spite of such instances of compulsive moralizing, events unfold in *Daniel Deronda* that insinuate themselves into the reader's unsupervised imagination. In other words, however driven the narrator may be to illustrate values and to represent human fulfillment, attempts at closure are unsettled by unresolved conflicts and by the sheer variety of utterances that come and go. Omniscient tallies of the moral balance fail to hold up because the range of voices in this novel—an instance of the polyphony intrinsic to the genre of the novel—destabilizes such reckoning. In Mikhail Bakhtin's terms, something of the "heteroglot" world inevitably breaks through. It happens even in a novel by George Eliot, who is nothing if not monological in her story-telling instincts.[12]

"Novelness," in Bakhtin's sense, may be the main factor working to undercut the artificial constraints in *Daniel Deronda*. However, I want to explore another (and perhaps related) possibility here: namely, that it is a religious incentive in Eliot's thought and artistry that generates multiplicity and moves the novel beyond one-dimensional moralizing. This is an aspect of Eliot often slighted by commentators who rush to point up her "atheist" allegiances.[13] In other words, the influence of Feuerbach and Auguste Comte on Eliot tends to get noticed; what she calls her "yearning affection towards the great religions of the world"[14] does not. Yet Eliot can speak of such "yearning" because the religious for her does not reduce to a conception of "theism" standing over against "atheism." And she is hardly a public propounder of the impossibility of belief. Like a number of Victorian poets negotiating the period's crisis of faith, she tries first to show the spiritual predicament. At strategic moments, she points out absences—in particular, "the gap between positive parroted institutional doctrine and private religious experience in process."[15] Her awareness of the dangers of that gap, along with her extensive reading in contemporary philosophy and theology, sometimes leads her to venture new spiritual formulations. Most often, though, her religious impulse finds a secular outlet in fictive inventions—in the character of Deronda, for one, who serves as a secular priest to other characters over the course of her final novel.

Eliot's attention to the potential of humane religious life is coupled with her high regard for the advancement of science. It is not always easy to distinguish the two. Consider the following remark from a letter of 1876:

> My writing is simply a set of experiments in life—an endeavor to see what our thought and emotion may be capable of—what stores of motive . . . give promise of a better after which we may strive—what gains from past revelations and discipline we must strive to keep hold of as something more sure than shifting theory.[16]

Here Eliot poses as a scientist of sorts. But if a scientist, she is an odd one, for her "experiments" make ethical and religious questions the primary "object" for study. The statement just quoted begins with an air of detachment, but the last words show that something more than research is at stake. Empirical observation, successful execution of realist technique, the reader's assent to little moral truths—these are not ultimate matters for the author.

Rather, Eliot's religious concern finds expression in the imaginative connections she sustains through her fiction. Beyond the requisite contract, she forges bonds among author, character, and reader that take on a covenantal quality. Her highly serious view of a text as entwined in, and mediated by, a community of readers may be a remnant of her evangelical youth, but it reflects as well the strong influence of David Strauss (whom she translated in her early adult years). As E. S. Shaffer notes, it is from Strauss that Eliot derives the notion that a text's unity is explicitly linked to "the religious experience of a community."[17] An eminent "history," like Ernest Renan's *The Life of Jesus*, can serve as such a text. But, for Eliot, so can a work of fiction. Her comment on *The Life of Jesus* throws some light on her own aims in writing fictional narratives: "Such books . . . have their value in helping the popular imagination to feel that the sacred past is of one woof with that human present which ought to be sacred too."[18]

In *Daniel Deronda*, Eliot incorporates the notion of the "sacred" into the complete world she is at pains to convey. For instance, at an emotionally intense moment towards the end of the tale, Daniel speaks of "the foundations of sacredness for all men." In this metaphorical evocation of "something stronger, with deeper, farther-spreading roots" (727), or in the narrator's extended talk of an "Invisible Power" (875), it is hard not to hear Eliot behind the scenes. Such talk embodies the author's hope of "resurrecting religious culture"[19] into contemporary secular spheres. If we stay within the novel, on the other hand, these references to the sacred work to suggest that there is something universal in life underlying the vastly different destinies unfolding in the double plot. Intimations of unity are further corroborated by Daniel's development over time. We follow his shift from isolated individual to community as he gradually discovers his Jewish identity. Like the novel's circular structure, his new "sense of communion" (416) correlates with the author's stated purpose of making "everything" in the story relate to "everything else." The unifying movement also provides the reader with a purview of a manifold, interconnected world.

Hardly a detached experimenter, then, Eliot writes as if narrative were urgently involved in actually constituting reality. She composes the world of her text, "something more sure than shifting theory," with the express intent of extending sympathy. The "experiential realism"[20] that results requires the author's trust in the reader's emotional clairvoyance. At the same time, the reader must trust in the author's intention to be more orienting than disorienting. This imaginative pact can generate what Eliot calls the "truth" of fiction, a phenomenon that cuts through one-dimensional perspectives—including those of conspicuously authoritative narrators. We see the process in *Daniel Deronda* at moments when the narrative digresses from recreating and assessing the behavior of the characters to contemplation at the level of the human soul. When reflecting at this level, the narrator is less prone to moralize and more inclined to mention "the mysteries of our human lot" (673). Here it is recognized as a mystery that "our consciences are not all of the same pattern, an inner deliverance of fixed laws: they are the voice of sensibilities as various as our memories" (570). It is at this level too that the narrator points out the mediocrity of certain upstanding men, like the rector, Mr. Gascoigne, "some of [whose] experience had petrified into maxims" (195). It is also at this level that readerly consciousness is invited to contemplate the surprising bonds that can form between very different psyches. On the occasion of a meeting between Daniel and Mordecai, for instance, we are told that Daniel "felt nothing that could be called belief in the validity of Mordecai's impressions . . . what he felt was a profound sensibility to a cry from the depths of another soul" (553).

When the reader cuts through surface layers, contradictions in the soul come into sharper focus. Human ambivalence looms large as the narrator strives to tell how things really are. In proffering the characters' experiences as touchstones for living readers, in other words, the unconscious side of human subjectivity is inevitably brought into view. It is not openly trumpeted, though. The unconscious is insinuated subtly. It is depicted as an extensive "unmapped country within us" (321). It appears on the periphery of scenes, yet in a way that is meant to inform. With Gwendolen, for instance, we first see her restless energy, her egoism, and desire for control as prominent traits in the opening scene at the gaming table. But her words and actions soon reveal fears that form the underside of her urge to power. The reader notices ties between Gwendolen's "disposition to vague terror" (616) and her wishes as they take shape "in the dark seed-growths of consciousness" (337). Layers of personality appear, yet not in order to perplex; they make intelligible the gradual emergence of this woman's whole self out of a welter of self-deceptions. The slow process of maturation (signaled by altering mirror imagery) runs through many stages. We move from "The Spoiled Child" phase of Book One—in which Gwendolen's plan is "to do what pleases me" (100)—through a jarring "vision of herself on the common level" (306), to eventual recognition of her state of ignorance. The healing that follows is also processive; in includes the growth of "a root of conscience" (733), the discovery of responsibility, and articulation to another of her state of self-enclosure.

Deronda's responsive words to Gwendolen—"you know more of the way in which your life presses on others, and their life on yours" (508)—form another key articulation along the way. Yet these words also point in the direction of the audience. The discovery of human interdependence, at the level of feelings and not only of ideas, may be a telling event in the reader's own story.

For the engaged reader—the one, that is, who sustains the analogy between the characters' lives and the reader's experience of them—the ambivalence grows deeper. With Gwendolen we have found a lack of sympathy concealing subconscious dread. In Daniel's case, on the other hand, an excessive (and sometimes incapacitating) sympathy for others turns out to hide the anxiety of abandonment.[21] After first hinting at such a complex, the narrator eventually speculates on Daniel's tendency to seek out "difficulty and struggle." These

> elements of life . . . had a predominant attraction for his sympathy, due perhaps to his early pain in dwelling on the conjectured story of his own existence. Persons attracted him . . . in proportion to the possibility of his defending them, rescuing them, telling upon their lives with some sort of redeeming influence. (369)

The upshot of these ruminations is that Daniel's efforts to help others are duplicitous in part. Over the course of the novel, his need to enact rescue fantasies proves to be a distortion of an unconscious desire to rescue himself.

Deronda's rescue fantasies are sexually ambivalent as well. He fools himself about his own sexual attraction while playing the knight-errant in his liaison with Gwendolen. This form of self-deception is then repeated with Mirah—at least, at the outset when he discovers her destitute and alone. The forlorn scene stirs in him "a fibre that lay close to his deepest interest in the fates of women—'perhaps my mother was like this one'" (231). The suggestion that Mirah is a mother substitute in part, various comments on Daniel's "fascination" with Gwendolen's "womanhood" (370), Sir Hugo's words about "playing with fire" (510)—such references reflect the author's concern to infuse sexual undercurrents and motivations into the novel, (a theme Eliot derives from Feuerbachian philosophy).[22] However, it is not exactly sexual realism that we get. Without relinquishing omniscience, the narrator relies on minor characters to divulge the erotic sublimation going on. Hans Meyrick, for instance, debunks the idealized image of Deronda by lightly mocking his friend's "supreme reasonableness and self-nullification" (706).[23] On the occasion of a party at Lady

Mallinger's, it is also Hans who exposes Daniel's sexual jealousy by pointing out that Daniel's ernest talk with Gwendolen looks to bystanders rather more like a lovers' "quarrel" (625).

Daniel's reluctance to admit what is going on reveals a split self. But that, of course, is a condition the author believes can be healed. Towards the end of the tale, when Daniel confesses to Gwendolen and faces his duplicity, an I-Thou bond forms between them. Recovery and self-understanding do arrive. Yet such developments do not simply override the ambivalence we have seen throughout, nor nullify the emphasis the narrator has repeatedly placed upon the obdurate power of self-deception: "what construction of another's mind is not strong wishing equal to?" (388). Still, with Deronda, the stronger emphasis falls upon the possibility of coming into one's whole self. Differently put, we are a long ways in this text from the completely alienated self of literary modernism or the multiple selves of postmodernism. That does not mean that Eliot, by contrast, treats the self as some sort of substance. Personality unfolds, but in ways that can make it cohere. It is a process, "the transmutation of self" which is "happening every day" (523).

When the self transmutes toward self-understanding and maturity, it also enters into relation to community and covenant. Eliot's belief is that she can involve her audience in such a process by reenacting it in a humane context of common feeling in her novel. Hence, when Deronda receives a letter from his absent mother and begins to emplot an identity and vocation out of his shrouded origins, the narrator has good reason for calling it "a sacramental moment" (676).

Prophetic Regeneration

Sacramental moments are interwoven with pertinent prophetic criticism in *Daniel Deronda*. In other words, Eliot attempts to forge imaginative bonds with readers also in the hope of regenerating peoples' values and consecrating social change. Three areas in particular are targeted for criticism: deep-seated anti-Semitism, the abusive powers of the ruling classes, and the subjugated position of women. The way each of these is dealt with in the novel could be the subject of an extended study. Here I will touch upon key points.

The "Jewish portion," as it is sometimes called, comprises almost one-half of *Daniel Deronda*. It is that part of the work some have thought should simply have been left out in favor of a narrative focused upon Gwendolen Harleth.[24] Yet the story of Mordecai, Mirah, and their marginalized world is not only intricately woven into the structure of the tale; it carries an element of prophetic concern that Eliot will not conveniently extricate. In this part of the text, Eliot goes beyond the formal impulse to embellish her novel with bemusing flourishes of social satire. Her cultural criticism is substantial, not decorative. While the novel's portrayal of the Jewish community in London is idealized in some respects, the act of intercultural recognition that underlies the author's attack on anti-Semitism is momentous.

The placement of a Jewish character at the center of this Victorian novel introduces a host of complexities. Above all, it provides a means by which to criticize the Christian chauvinism endemic to English society. Such intentions are stated forthrightly in Eliot's letter of 1876 to Harriet Beecher Stowe:

> Because I felt that the usual attitude of Christians towards Jews is—I hardly know whether to say more impious or more stupid when viewed in the light of their professed principles, I therefore felt urged to treat Jews with such sympathy and understanding as my nature and knowledge could attain to. Moreover, not only towards the Jews, but towards all oriental peoples with whom we English come in contact, a spirit of arrogance and contemptuous dictorialness is observable which has become a national disgrace to us. There is nothing I should more care to do, if it were possible, than to rouse the imagination of men and women to a vision of human claims in those races of their fellow—men who most differ from them in customs and beliefs.[25]

With *Daniel Deronda*, then, Eliot is attempting to wake up an ostensibly Christian society to awareness of the culture that was once Christianity's "enabling milieu" and is now a living remnant suppressed in Christendom's midst.[26] This clarion call follows upon Eliot's extensive research into the history of the Diaspora. Her research happens to include a visit to the synagogue in Frankfurt, Germany (in 1873). There, among other observations, she takes note of Samuel Raphael Hirsch's ideas concerning the Jewish national vocation[27]—ideas that then turn up in the novel in Mordecai's talk of reviving "the organic centre" (592) and of "a new Jewish polity" (594). In short, Eliot uses her research to present contemporary patterns of Jewish life and thought as authentically as possible. At the same time, she aims to depict the denigration of Judaism pervasive in the highest cultural circles, where respectable organizations like the "Society for the Conversion of the Jews" (267) conduct business as usual. We also hear less pernicious formulations of prejudice in *Daniel Deronda*, as when Mrs. Meyrick's expresses her hope "that the intensity of Mirah's feeling about Judaism would slowly subside" (628). Deronda himself, through the device of dramatic irony, serves to make the ubiquitous nature of bigotry abundantly clear. For "knowing hardly anything about modern Judaism or the inner Jewish history," he grows up, "like his neighbors," regarding Judaism "as a sort of eccentric fossilized form" (411).

It is Mordecai who refutes the reduction of Judaism to a dead form. His evocation of "prophetic consciousness" (588) and his visions of a higher ethical reality form an interpretation of Israel's life that exposes the ignorance of both popular and high cultural dismissals of "the Jews." Yet Mordecai's reference to "the breath of social justice" (588) functions in the novel in another way as well: it names the criterion by which dehumanization is constantly measured and made known.

Making dehumanization known is one of the author's imperatives. Throughout the novel, it is shown to stem particularly from the inbred world of the controlling classes. It is a world debunked outright at times through the voice of the narrator, who points out the casual cruelty of the elite's penchant for taking an operatic perspective on things: "What horrors of damp huts, where human beings languish, may not become picaresque through aerial distance!" (193). On other occasions, it may be a minor figure (such as Catherine Arrowpoint) who divulges the "ridiculous mish-mash of superannuated customs and false ambitions" (290) that suffuses the lives of the affluent, ruling families. Above all, though, it is in the portrayal of Henliegh Grandcourt—truly a master of "aerial distance"—that Eliot's attack on social injustice is most forcefully wrought.

Grandcourt's personality is, first and foremost, authoritarian. He is consistently depicted, with little resort to caricature, as enjoying unlimited power over dependents. His compulsive drive to turn Gwendolen into property presents the reader with stark evidence that there are "those who prefer command to love" (646). In one of Eliot's finer strokes, Grandcourt's exploitative drives are also shown to be analogous to features of the culture at large. For example, following upon an earlier reference in the novel to atrocities inflicted on various peoples in the far-off land of Jamaica (in October, 1865[28]) Grandcourt's "delight in dominating" (389) is linked explicitly to the techniques of colonialism:

> If this white-handed man with the perpendicular profile had been sent to govern a difficult colony, he might have won reputation among his contemporaries. He had certainly ability, would have understood that it is safer to exterminate than to cajole superseded proprietors, and would not have flinched from making things safe that way. (655)

The association made here between inhuman policies and the mystification surrounding an esteemed authority has the effect of questioning the seeming naturalness of a range of social institutions upheld by the landed estate.

Grandcourt's "delight in dominating" pertains to women above all. Gwendolen, in an attempt to escape "subjection to an oppressive lot" (373), enters a mercenary marriage with him, but as a wife she is turned into one more item of the man's "outward equipment" (458). Initiated by the tale of Lydia Glasher into female experience—"'I am a woman's life'" (190)—Gwendolen becomes increasingly terrorized within her husband's "empire of fear" (479). This latter expression mimics references to the larger Empire often made at gatherings of the well-to-do. The effect of the double usage is to suggest ties between the ideology that bolsters "the conditions of colonial property and banking" (94) and sexism. The conditions of sexism are no less the focus of Eliot's critique.

Through ironic narrative commentary and dramatic evidence, we see several women in *Daniel Deronda* trapped by economic, educational, and legal constraints. Gwendolen in particular is caught in a series of double binds, as the novel's images of handcuffs and fetters also attest. Despite her spirit of rebellion, she has little chance in combating a process of socialization and gender stereotyping epitomized by Gascoigne's refrain: "Marriage is the only true and satisfying sphere of a woman" (180). Such attitudes determine the aura of domestic appearances, while also ensuring the sexual plight of women, whether through mismating, marital prostitution, sexual deprivation, or renunciation. Eliot, before Freud, seems to have recognized that hysteria is one symptom that results from this paucity of possibilities for women. Gwendolen's "disposition to vague terror" (616), the "hysterical violence" (407) of her screams when Grandcourt enters the room after she has read Lydia's letter, ongoing "visitations"—aside from vague hints, these moods and startling moments are never fully explained. The frustration and anger suppressed beneath them, however, is given voice by another woman on at least one occasion. When Leonora Charisi finally tells her story to Deronda we hear explosive anger about "wives and daughters" who are turned into "slaves." She identifies outright men who "would rule the world if they could," but who, out of impotence, "throw all the weight of their will on the necks and souls of women" (694). These words accuse Leonora's family, and on a broader scale they indict patriarchal religion. For it is her own Jewish tradition which she implicates above all as a system of coercive customs perpetuating male dominance and her own exclusion. At this late stage in the novel, then, we learn that the religious heritage that has enabled Deronda to find a core identity and communal purpose "has been experienced only as bondage by his mother."[29]

The insight into women's bondage that comes through Leonora's story retains an element of ambiguity, for like every character in the novel, she is not without her own capacity for self-deception. This ambiguous note, constant as it is in Eliot's novels, leads modern critics into numerous debates about the author's feminist sympathies. I do not wish to rehearse those debates here.[30] In closing, though, I want to make one claim counter to those who would write off Eliot's feminism as severely limited.

Eliot's feminist stance is marked by tension between a strong interest in women's rights, problems of gender, and issues of women's work and marriage, and, on the other hand, a hesitation to become an active worker in "the Cause."[31] Her position is also limited by her attachment to ethical universals, which sometimes disguise historically discrete interests. For example, her incessant earnestness about moral choice depends on an unwavering commitment to the idea of the centered human subject. While she does not represent the subject as a fixed substance, she fails to examine many of its culturally constructed aspects, those "truths" of personal experience that are actually determined by the self's embedment in decentering structures of discourse and power. To say as much, however, is in part to disregard Eliot's historical constraints. It is to notice that neither Eliot's idea of personhood nor her feminism is informed by a reading of Michel Foucault, and that insight has limitations of its own.

Whatever her blind spots, Eliot's view of the human subject is open to complexity—enough so, I think, to provide an antidote to the postmodernist tendency to dissolve the subject by reducing it to nothing more than an arbitrary and groundless creation of the modern episteme. In contrast to that tendency, Jane Flax (a contemporary feminist thinker well versed in poststructuralism) has raised a number of critical questions concerning theories that simply equate any notion of self or subjectivity with "humanist myth." As Flax puts it, "I am deeply suspicious of the motives of those who would counsel such a position at the same time as women have just begun to re-member their selves and to claim an agentic subjectivity . . . ."[32] Flax makes a related point in regard to resisting patriarchal powers: in order for struggle against domination to be carried out in the first place, "something must exist within and among persons that is not merely an effect of the dominating discourse."[33]

To fathom that "something," one could do worse than to read George Eliot. If we avoid turning Eliot into another logocentric scapegoat, her perspective on selfhood may prove in some respects instructively "other" to the predominant one today. If we have only replaced the predictable Victorian word "duty" with the predictable contemporary word "play," something else is needed. If what is wanting today is not simply a dissolution of the human subject but rather its richer comprehension—a renegotiation, so to speak, of the relation between subject and object—Eliot's explorations of the self and its "basic cohesion" warrant consideration. For to say, with Eliot, that the self can have cohesion is not to make claims for a monadic, always actualized, total unity of experience. It is to suggest, rather, that there are purposive moments in the life of the self when centering does occur, moments of remembering and choosing which enable participation with others in their various stories. To read *Daniel Deronda* is to observe closely the intricacies of such moments (and, incidentally, the special role that the human face plays in mediating them). It is also to recognize the dynamics of self-deception and mutual incomprehension, those staples of human relations Eliot is especially skilled at delineating. To reflect on this novel, then, is not necessarily to be manipulated by a disciplinary apparatus.[34] More likely, it means entering into a world of nuanced emotion—what the narrator calls "the subtler possibilities of feeling" (72)—and a certain daring of ethical saying. In the time required to read and to reflect within such a world, "the wonderful mixtures of our nature" (683) have a chance to appear.

I wish to conclude by briefly summarizing two basic orientations of thought woven together in *Daniel Deronda*. What I have called the sacramental side of Eliot's thought is evident in the relation she sustains with her readers—and with her congregating guests. For Eliot, it is worth mentioning, made it a regular Sunday event to meet with some of her readers. I concur with George Levine when he says that "the image" of Eliot on such an occasion, "bending forward, listening . . . with selfless and disciplined attention to her admiring visitors, corresponds precisely to the moral and intellectual ideal that informs her novels."[35] I would add that the ideal has a religious dimension also, one that consistently extends the range of the imaginative power around which Eliot seeks to create community.

Conditions for literary communion may be in place—at least, for middle-class readers—throughout the middle decades of the nineteenth century. But fragmenting historical developments soon leave the foundations for realist aesthetics behind. By the early decades of the twentieth century, novelists such as Joseph Conrad and James Joyce are working against the conventions of the tradition of imaginative sympathy.[36] They parody its ulterior motives and effectively exploit its ironic capacities. That does not mean, however, that even from our own standpoint late in the century, writers such as Kingsley Amis cannot see themselves as maintaining an "orderly contract" with their modern readers. But the covenantal quality of the unifying arrangement vital to Eliot's venture is not there. For covenants get profaned. With bleak hilarity in their postmodern novels, writers such as Martin Amis, son of Kingsley, bring vigor to the task.

Though she draws upon Feuerbach's work, Eliot herself develops views on the process of profanization. But her understanding of another religious phenomenon, idolatry, is almost traditional. It is implicit in her own criticism of social evils, a stance that constitutes a second fundamental orientation in her thought. In her novels, that stance may surface in an attack on the Philistinism of the declining elite. In *The Impressions of Theophrastus Such*, to give a different example, we find it in the prophetic naming of "an idolatrous Christianity,"[37] which in arrogant equation of itself with truth is denying justice to an outside group. In the end, Eliot's notion of social justice does not, in the manner of her character Mordecai, rely on a coming "Messianic time" (598). Yet it carries the potency of expecting something beyond "the established order of things" (279). It looks simply to what can appear now—to what, in another context, Martha Nussbaum has called "a more compassionate, subtler, more responsive, more richly humane world."[38]

NOTES

1. George Eliot, *Daniel Deronda*, ed. Barbara Hardy (Harmondsworth: Penguin, 1967), p. 88. Subsequent references to this edition are cited parenthetically by page numbers in the text. Martin Amis, "The Wit and Fury of Martin Amis," interview by Susan Morrison, *Rolling Stone*, no. 578 (May 17th, 1990), p. 98. Ludwig Feuerbach, *The Essence of Christianity*, trans. George Eliot (New York: Harper & Brothers, 1957). p. 32. Jane Flax, *Thinking Fragments: Psychoanalysis, Feminism, and Postmodernism in the Contemporary West* (Berkeley: University of California Press, 1990), p. 218.

2. For a helpful overview of the literary critical reception of George Eliot's writings, see K. M. Newton, "Introduction," *George Eliot*, ed. K. M. Newton (New York: Longman, 1991). This volume collects a number of essays on Eliot revolving around poststructuralist and new historicist standards of interpretation. For a representative attack on Eliot's realism see, Colin McCabe, "The End of a Metalanguage: From George Eliot to Dubliners," pp. 156-68. According to McCabe, "George Eliot's texts are devoted to repressing the operations of the signifier by positing a metalanguage which exists outside of materiality and production. The multitude of objects which appear in her texts do not bear witness to the activity of signification, to the constitutive reality of absence..." (p. 168).

3. In this essay, I follow literary critical practice in citing the pseudonym "George Eliot." It should be pointed out, however, that the usage is problematic, for it leaves Marian

Evans (or Mary Ann Evans) wearing the mask of a man. This situation is highly ironic, given the boldness of Evans's battle against the systematic "exclusion of women from the realm of intellect and effective power" Jennifer Uglow, *George Eliot*,(London: Virago, 1987), p. 80. J. Hillis Miller tries to deal with the dilemma by highlighting Eliot's mask. In a discussion of *Adam Bede*, for example, Miller refers to Eliot with masculine pronouns. Here is Miller: "I say 'his' to remind the reader that the putative speaker... is not Mary Ann Evans... but a fictive personage, 'George Eliot', who narrates the story and who is given a male gender" *The Ethics of Reading*, (New York: Columbia University Press, 1987), p. 66. While this sounds right in theory, it seems to ease the critic more than it serves Evans. The gender of the narrator remains enigmatic.

4. In myriad ways, I am profoundly indebted to Bob Detweiler's outstanding studies in the field of literature and religion. Like many for whom Detweiler has consistently opened new doors over the years, I have found his inquiries into the nature of narrative and his treatments of narrative community especially rich.

Detweiler offers some provocative insights into George Eliot's realism in *The Daemonic Imagination: Biblical Text and Secular Story* (Atlanta: Scholars, 1990). In his Introduction to this volume, "From Chaos to Legion to Chance: The Double Play of Apocalyptic and Mimesis," Detweiler highlights the strong "apocalyptic strain" in Eliot's novels. I attempt to approach the religious side of Eliot's art from another angle in the present essay by examining sacramental and prophetic elements instead.

For contextual understanding, I am also indebted to Anne E. Patrick's study, "George Eliot's Final Experiment: Power and Responsibility in *Daniel Deronda*," in *Morphologies of Faith: Essays in Religion and Culture in Honor of Nathan A. Scott*, Jr., eds. Mary Gerhart and Anthony C. Yu (Atlanta: Scholars Press, 1990), pp. 319-42.

5. These broad terms refer to polar elements in living religion. The prophetic has the character of profound critique; it is evident in every attack upon present conditions in the name of future justice. The sacramental, on the other hand, is defined by an experience of the presence of the divine, especially in the consecration of certain objects or actions.

Whether properly religious, or in a secularized form, the prophetic and the sacramental can also be viewed as fundamental dispositions. In one direction, we find a radical questioning of symbols beyond the biases of priests and cultural authorities. In the other direction, we find an awareness of present meaning mediated through symbols and the priestly function. Priestly function and prophetic protest: both may be carried out by artists, however indirectly.

6. I refer to Frank Kermode's well-known discussion in *The Sense of an Ending*. According to Kermode, human life transpires 'in the middest': "to make sense of their span [men and poets] need fictive concords with origins and ends, such as give meaning to lives and to poems." See *The Sense of an Ending* (New York: Oxford University Press, 1968), p. 7.

7. Letter to Madame Bodichon (October 2, 1876), *Selections from George Eliot's Letters*, ed. Gordon S. Haight (New Haven: Yale University Press, 1985), p. 475.

8. *The Letters of Virginia Woolf*, ed. Nigel Nicolson and Joanne Trautmann (New York Harcourt Brace Jovanovich, 1979), 5: 334.

9. Numerous commentators on Victorian literature have pointed to this Romantic influence. On the topic of mid-nineteen-century authorship and the ideal of imaginative sympathy, I am indebted to Janice Carlisle, *The Sense of an Audience: Dickens, Thackeray, and George Eliot at Mid-Century* (Athens: University of Georgia Press, 1981).

10. Janice Carlisle, *The Sense of an Audience*, p. 5.

11. *Essays of George Eliot*, ed. Thomas Pinney (London: Routledge & Kegan Paul, 1968), p. 170-71. Eliot's views on realist art undergo many changes. In a well-known excursus in Chapter 17 of *Adam Bede*, she espouses what one might call "empirical" realism, with its adherence to "the faithful representing of commonplace things" *Adam Bede* (San Francisco: Rinehart, 1948), p. 182). This is not merely referential literalism, as is sometimes implied by critics of the early Eliot. Yet by the time Eliot writes *Daniel Deronda* she has considerably complicated these early notions by placing greater emphasis on the capacity of the imagination to open up new perspectives on the real. John P. McGowan provides a fine overview of "The Development of George Eliot's Realism," in *Representation and Revelation: Victorian Realism from Carlyle to Yeats* (Columbia: University of Missouri Press, 1986), pp. 132-57. For a new historicist critique of Eliot's theory of literary representation, see Catherine Gallagher, *The Industrial Reformation of English Fiction: Social Discourse and Narrative Form, 1832-1867*, pp. 219-33.

12. Mikhail Bakhtin discusses these aspects of the genre of the novel in his essay, "Discourse in the Novel," *The Dialogic Imagination*, ed. Michael Holquist, trans. Caryl Emerson and Michael Holquist (Austin: University of Texas Press, 1981). With its unusual beginning (*in medias res*) and an equivocal ending that qualifies the happy Victorian standard, *Daniel Deronda* proves to have, in some measure at least, that unique capacity to which Bakhtin refers: the "ability of the novel to criticize itself," p. 6.

13. Patrick, for one, stands against this tendency of critics to reduce and to pigeon-hole Eliot's ideas on religion. As Patrick points out, "no less than William James was George Eliot investigating the nature and varieties of religious experience." See "Rosamond Rescued: George Eliot's Critique of Sexism in *Middlemarch*," *Journal of Religion* 67 (April 1987), p. 221.

14. George Eliot, Letter to Clifford Albutt (August 1868), *The Letters of George Eliot*, ed. Gordon S. Haight (6 vols., London, 1955), Vol. 4, p. 472.

15. E. S. Shaffer, *'Kubla Khan' and The Fall of Jerusalem: The Mythological School in Biblical Criticism and Secular Literature, 1770-1880* (Cambridge: Cambridge University Press, 1980), p. 242. I am indebted to this fine study, one of the few which does justice to the sophistication of Eliot's theological concerns.

16. Letter to Joseph Frank Payne (January 25, 1876), *Selections from George Eliot's Letters*, p. 466.

17. E. S. Shaffer, *'Kubla Khan' and The Fall of Jerusalem*, p. 237.

18. George Eliot, "Letter to Mrs. Peter Alfred Taylor" (July 30, 1863), *Letters*, Vol. 4, p. 95.

19. The phrase is Shaffer's. See *'Kubla Khan' and The Fall of Jerusalem*, p. 290. Eliot's theological interest is also reflected in *Daniel Deronda* in the narrator's recommendation of "a religion... which is something else than a private consolation" (876). Patrick

discusses this important passage in "George Eliot's Final Experiment: Power and Responsibility in *Daniel Deronda*," (p. 341-42). A further declaration of Eliot's own perspective is perhaps echoed in one of the narrator's descriptions of Deronda: "It was his characteristic bias to shrink from the moral stupidity of valuing lightly what had come close to him, and of missing blindly in his own life of to-day the crises which he recognized as momentous and sacred in the historic life of men" (567).

20. The term is Robert Alter's. He describes this type of realism in *The Pleasures of Reading in an Ideological Age* (New York: Simon & Schuster, 1989): "The character's pulse beats and perceptions and shifting emotions are caught in the full tide of living from moment to moment, while at the same time the narrator who renders this immediacy retains the freedom to ironize, analyze, and judge what is going on in the character," p. 185.

21. Deronda's self-sabotaging disposition is remarked upon, sometimes humorously, by other characters. As Sir Hugo says to Daniel, "It will not do to give yourself to be melted down for the benefit of the tallow-trade," p. 224.

22. Feuerbach's analysis of the sexual constitution of humans has a strong impact on Eliot's thought. According to Shaffer, "For George Eliot, exposure and espousal of the sexual sources of religious feeling and action was explicitly demanded by her Feuerbachian formula," *'Kubla Khan' and The Fall of Jerusalem*, p. 276.

23. Cynthia Chase argues that Hans' parody of Daniel's seriousness, especially in his long letter to Daniel in Book Seven, virtually "deconstructs" the novel. See "The Decomposition of the Elephants: Double-Reading *Daniel Deronda*," *George Eliot*, ed. K. M. Newton, pp. 198-217.

24. Henry James and F. R. Leavis, for example, both disparage the "Jewish" sections. Though he would eventually repudiate the idea, Leavis argues in his most influential book that *Daniel Deronda* should be severely edited—and even renamed. See *The Great Tradition* (Garden City, N.Y.: Doubleday, 1954), pp. 150-54.

25. "Letter to Mrs. Harriet Beecher Stowe" (October 29, 1876), *Selections from George Eliot's Letters*, p. 476.

26. E. S. Shaffer, *'Kubla Khan' and The Fall of Jerusalem*, p. 235.

27. The impact of Hirsch's Neo-orthodox and Zionist views on Eliot are discussed by Barbara Hardy in her "Notes" to Book Four (Penguin edition), p. 893. That Eliot's engaged study of Judaism and her efforts to portray Jewish life in *Daniel Deronda* were received with much gratitude by a number of Jewish people deserves wider recognition. On the novel's inspiring effect for Jews, see Ruth Levitt, *George Eliot: The Jewish Connection* (Jerusalem: Massada, 1975).

28. This historical reference to atrocity committed on a Jamaican plantation is made by the "Voltairian" figure, Miller, during the "Jewish night" of open debate at the Hand and Banner where Deronda goes with Mordecai. See Hardy's "Notes," p. 898.

29. The point is made by Patrick, "George Eliot's Final Experiment: Power and Responsibility in *Daniel Deronda*," p. 333. Carlisle also remarks on the force of Charisi's testimony: "Deronda's mother dismisses as nonsense his claims that his imagination allows him to participate in her suffering," *The Sense of an Audience*, p. 217.

30. Even a cursory comment on these debates must point out that critics' views on Eliot's brand of feminism greatly vary, not to mention the question of whether she can even be regarded as a feminist author. In *The Madwoman in the Attic: The Woman Writer and the Nineteenth-Century Imagination*, Sandra M. Gilbert and Susan Gubar find throughout Eliot's novels a scenario in which submissive women repeatedly battle against oppressive men (New Haven: Yale University Press, 1979), Chapter 14. More recently, in an essay on *Silas Marner*, Gilbert emphasizes Eliot's ambivalence in regard to feminism: Eliot attempts to undermine patriarchal ideology while simultaneously apologizing for it. (See "Life's Empty Pack: Notes toward a Literary Daughteronomy," *George Eliot*, ed. K. M. Newton, pp. 99-130.) For a strong defense of Eliot's feminism, on the other hand, see Gillian Beer, *George Eliot* (Brighton: Harvester Press, 1986).

A number of articles specifically on *Daniel Deronda* discuss the question of whether Deronda advises Gwendolen merely to acquiesce to her oppressive marriage conditions, and, if so, whether Eliot's perspective is to be identified with Deronda's. See Joanne Long Demaria, "The Wondrous Marriages of *Daniel Deronda*: Gender, Work, and Love," *Studies in the Novel* 22 (Winter 1990): 403-17, and Nancy Pell, "The Fathers' Daughters in *Daniel Deronda*," NCF 36 (1982): 424-51. For a less suspicious reading of Eliot's feminist perspective in *Daniel Deronda*, see the essays by Patrick and Shaffer.

31. Some commentators see this reluctance as an outright contradiction rather than as a tension—proof, in short, of Eliot's desire to side with an ethic of renunciation despite her other impulse in the direction of autonomy. For an insightful evaluation of this issue, see Uglow, *George Eliot*, pp. 1-11 and 65-81.

32. Jane Flax, *Thinking Fragments: Psychoanalysis, Feminism, and Postmodernism in the Contemporary West*, p. 221. Though less directly stated, Janet Todd makes a similar point in her *Feminist Literary Theory* (New York: Routledge, 1988), p. 84.

33. Jane Flax, *Thinking Fragments*, p. 231.

34. Daniel Cottom argues that Eliot (with the monstrous force of liberal humanism behind her) was "devoted to the maintenance of a certain order no less than were the London police," *Social Figures: George Eliot, Social History, and Literary Representation* [Minneapolis: University of Minnesota Press, 1987), p. 27.

35. George Levine, "George Eliot's Hypothesis of Reality," *Nineteenth-Century Fiction* 35 (June 1980):1-28, p. 1.

36. See Carlisle, *The Sense of an Audience*, pp. 214-26.

37. George Eliot, *The Impressions of Theophrastus Such* (Edinburgh: William Blackwood & Sons, 1878), p. 327.

38. Martha C. Nussbaum, *Love's Knowledge: Essays in Philosophy and Literature* (New York: Oxford University Press, 1990), p. 379.

Refiguring The Self in Fiction:

Narrative Identity and the Text of Tolstoy's
The Kreutzer Sonata (1889)

DAVID E. KLEMM

According to Ricoeur, human beings answer the question of identity—Who?—formally by naming the individual or community in question and substantially by telling a story about the one named. The story shows the identity of the "who" as an agent over time; it confers a "narrative identity" on that individual or community. In Ricoeur's words, "Individual and community are constituted in their identity by taking up narratives that become for them their actual history."[1]

Moreover, fictional texts play a special role in the task of narrative self-understanding: texts of fiction project a redescribed world for the reader, a world in which the I of any reader can project itself in its own genuine possibilities to be, there to undergo the purgative and clarificatory effects of the plot. In reading or telling narratives, one learns how to act and to suffer as do the characters in the world projected in the text. Real transformation of life depends on this capacity—conferred by narrative—to see oneself otherwise than one actually is. For Ricoeur, one sees oneself as another by responding to the call of the voice of a character in its narrative identity.

In this paper I shall attempt in part one to present Ricoeur's concept of narrative identity and to propose that it be supplemented with Robert Scharlemann's notion of the textuality of texts.[2] I shall attempt in part two to use the corrected notion of narrative identity to interpret the infamous and marginalized novella by Tolstoy, *The Kreutzer Sonata*.[3] I will ask of the narrative: Who speaks in this story? How does it ask the reader to refigure the self through fiction? How does it form a narrative community? I hope to demonstrate how the corrected notion of narrative identity can contribute to the interpretation of literature with religious import, especially insofar as such literature might enable a religious refiguring of the self.

Narrative Identity and the Text

In *Being and Time*, Heidegger argued that care is the being of the self or *Dasein*. Care names the act of combining the universal meant by "I" with a particular location on the grounds that in all of my intentional acts, I am always relating to what is here in care. Moreover, the meaning of Dasein's being is *time*: in projecting my being as finite possibility to be, I project my being temporally, against the horizon of time. In *Time and Narrative*, Ricoeur argues that narrative is the privileged place for understanding the meaning of human being as time. The thesis of *Time and Narrative* is that "Time becomes human time to the extent that it is organized after the manner of a narrative; narrative, in turn, is meaningful to the extent that it portrays the features of temporal existence."[4] How so? What does this double claim mean?

Consider the first statement: "Time becomes human time to the extent that it is organized after the manner of a narrative." According to Ricoeur, reflection on the question "What is time?" reaches an aporia. On one side, following Aristotle, reflection construes time as a mere succession of "now" points—that is, an objectively given and measured chronological or cosmic time. On the other side, following Augustine, reflection comprehends time as a "present" in which past, present, and future are grasped together in and for the subject—that is, as a nonchronological or psychological time. No speculative resolution of the aporia is possible—we cannot think the unity of the two, nor derive one from the other—and hence the attempt to form a concept of time is shattered at its center.

Narrative activity responds to the aporia of time, however, with a poetic solution to the speculative paradox, thus saving human time from meaninglessness. The key to the poetic solution lies in the plot, or, better, emplotment, as the structural principle of narrative. Plot mediates in the distinct medium of language between a succession of now points given as a manifold of particular events or episodes and the present intelligible whole or "thought."[5] Emplotment of events is a synthesis of the heterogeneous, a submitting of discordant events to a principle of temporal order or concordance. A story is followable when a reader understands how and why the successive episodes lead to its conclusion.[6] The followability of narrative bridges the speculative fault between cosmic time and lived time, rendering the fragile mix Ricoeur calls "human time" as "narrated time."

Consider now the second statement that narrative is meaningful to the extent that it portrays the temporal features of existence. According to Ricoeur, narrative texts, whether historical or fictional, specifically refer to the temporal character of human experience for the sake of refiguring it. Historical narratives aim to recount the lived time of past events against cosmic time and owe a specific obligation to the memory of the dead, an obligation that makes history accountable to the documentary archives. Fictional narratives, by contrast, are freed from the documentary trace of the past to invent imaginative variations on the theme of the fault separating the two perspectives on time: personal lived time and apersonal cosmic time.[7] Fictional works in particular have the capacity to present a fundamental fictive experience of time and thereby to become "tales about time."

Tales about time have, according to Ricoeur, a "reflexive temporal structure" that plays with a universal feature of all narrating, namely, that the act of story-telling divides in the nature of the case into two moments: the narrative both utters what happens and reflects on what happens.[8] Grasped temporally, these two moments are the *narrated time* (the chronological time of the narrated episodes inscribed and frequently dated within the story) and the *time of narrating* (the nonchronological time of the narrator's direct address to the reader).[9] Narratives become tales about time by placing the two moments into dialectical play with each other, so that the story both narrates (times) events and comments on its timing of narrated events. The controlled play between narrated time and time of narrating refers the reader to an implied fundamental fictive experience with time, without its being considered directly as a theme.[10]

The fictive experience of time enables the literary work to escape its own structural closure and directs the reader into the mode of being proposed by the work against the background of open possibility.[11] Fictional exploration of possible being through imaginative variations on the temporalization of time has, according to Ricoeur, the experiential value of eternity when human time opens to and is infused with the eternal.[12] In the act of reading, the world of the text and the fictive experience of time at stake in it intersect with the world of the reader and his or her temporalizing of time. Self-critical appropriation of a mode of timing inscribed in the text can be both revelatory and transforming: a matter of refiguring the self in the temporal meaning of its being. Narrative refiguring of the self results in what Ricoeur calls a "narrative identity," or that sort of identity to which a human being has access thanks to the mediation of the narrative function.[13]

Let me now point out an unnecessary limitation in Ricoeur's theory. Ricoeur restricts the refiguring of the self to the reader's response to the narrative identity of a *character* in the fiction. Ricoeur constructs the identity of a character in a narrative in strict correlation to the plot in its structure of concordant-discordance. He says in *Oneself as Another*, "The identity of the character is comprehensible through the transfer to the character of the operation of emplotment. Characters are themselves plots," that is, structures of concordant discordances.[14] Thus the narrative constructs the identity of the character, his or her narrative identity, in constructing the story told.[15] Character is the correlate of plot: if you understand the plot, you understand the central character of the fiction.

Consequently, just as one continuous narrative as emplotted divides into two poles of time of narrating and narrated time, a single character's selfhood divides into the poles of character and fidelity. By *character*, Ricoeur means those relatively stable distinctive marks by which one can reidentify an individual, "the set of lasting dispositions by which a person is recognized," such as habits and acquired identifications.[16] By *fidelity*, Ricoeur means the quality of keeping one's word, remaining loyal to some intended meaning. Fidelity is the more changeable element: one retains a character in shifting loyalties more readily than the reverse. Character is the what of the who, fidelity is the who of the what. Narrative identity mediates between the two poles, joining and disjoining them in time.

So constructed, Ricoeur's hermeneutics of literary narrative is both richly suggestive and yet strangely impoverished. If we ask of a work of fiction, Who goes there?, Ricoeur gives us sophisticated means for interpreting the narrative identity of the character through analysis of plot. However, Ricoeur does not conceive of the possibility that the structure of the plot might have another voice than that of a central character as its correlate. Ricoeur does not provide the systematic possibility for interpreting the voice of the text as an embodied whole. To achieve this possibility, we turn to Robert Scharlemann's notion of the "textuality of the text."

According to Scharlemann, a text as text is not merely a written means for conveying meanings from writer to reader, as Ricoeur has it, but is itself an intelligible entity, an "inscribed self-understanding," which is "there too with" us in the world. The other human being in its being is, as I am, a combining of pure subjectivity with location in time and space; so too is a text. But whereas a human being combines universal subjectivity—the I—with a particular physical and psychic structure called the human body, the text combines universal subjectivity with a particular linguistic structure, fo example, what Ricoeur calls a narrative configuration. Both text and human being are embodied subjectivities endowed with voice, but they are differently embodied.

Scharlemann's understanding of text in its specific quality of textuality means that a reader can respond to the voice of the text as an embodied I, which is systematically distinguishable from the voice of a character, or that of the narrator or implied author, for that matter. The capacity to hear this voice is dependent on the capacity "to redo in one's own self, the dynamic which has structured the text that is there, or to understand the voice that is inscribed in it."[17] So as not to leave things too abstract, I turn now to a work of fiction that exhibits such an irreducible voice of the text.

Tolstoy's The Kreutzer Sonata (1889)

I choose this story by Tolstoy not only because it is a masterpiece of fiction that has been badly misunderstood and needs reevaluation, but also because the narrative configuration of this tale about time rules out identifying the voice of the text with the voice of the character, and thus exposes the limitation in Ricoeur's hermeneutics from the side of fiction. This text calls for a refiguring of the self not in response to its central character, but in response to a distinct voice of the text. Let me review the frame of the story before interpreting its complex structure all too briefly and inadequately.

Like the Beethoven composition from which it is named, Tolstoy's story is divided into three movements with a slow introduction preceding them. The timing of each section corresponds to Beethoven's sonata: *adagio* for the introduction, *presto* for the first movement, *andante con variazioni* for the second movement, and *presto* returning to the *adagio* of the introduction for the third movement.[18]

The introduction to the story sets the stage: it is a first person narration of the beginnings of a railway journey. Various passengers gather in a carriage, including the narrator himself who is a character in the novella. As the train departs, a dispute about the question of divorce breaks out among the passengers. An old tradesman asserts that divorce occurs because people today are too well educated and women are no longer made to fear their husbands. This remark infuriates a lady passenger who replies that forced marriages among those who do not love each other are to blame for divorce: "Marriage without love is not marriage," she says, "for love alone sanctifies marriage," and "real marriage is only such as is sanctified by love."

The argument is interrupted by the broken laugh or sob emitted by a nervous man who had previously been quiet. He asks the lady to say what she means by "true love," which she defines as "an exclusive preference for one above everybody else." The man does not dispute the definition but raises the question of *time*: "Preference for how long?" The lady and her lawyer companion try to explain that time is not the issue; the question is only whether the marriage is based on love as spiritual affinity—an identity of timeless ideals—for only spiritual affinity makes a marriage morally binding.

The nervous man retorts, "Spiritual affinity! Identity of ideals! ... But in that case why go to bed together?" He claims that every man experiences what the lady calls love for every pretty woman, and that the only difference between loves—or better, lusts—is time. In marriages, he asserts, people deceive and are deceived, they coerce and are coerced, until they take to drink, and kill or poison themselves or one another.

The narrator (who is a passenger on the train) tells how this man grows increasingly agitated until he abruptly stands and announces, "I see you have found out who I am!" The words astonish all who hear them, in fact no one has a clue as to his identity. "I am that Pozdnyshev," the one who killed his wife, was jailed, tried, acquitted, and turned loose. None of the fellow passengers know what to say; all fall silent. Just as abruptly, the irritable Pozdnyshev falls silent. At the next station, the dumbstruck passengers discretely abandon his carriage, with the exception of the narrator, who remains. So ends the introduction.

The heart of the remainder of the novella is a long-term, retrospective, confessional narrative told in the first-person by Pozdnyshev. But Pozdnyshev's narrating is itself embedded in the narrator's narrating of Pozdnyshev's narrating. Pozdnyshev's narrative retrieves times past, a narrated time of a former self caught in the vice grip of dissoluteness and sexual passion. It does so from the standpoint of a kind of present time and a new self, the time of the train ride as a time of narrating. The two times are divided by an event, which Pozdnyshev calls "that episode" through which "my eyes have been opened and I have seen everything in quite a different light. Everything reversed! Everything reversed!" Pozdnyshev professes now to know the truth about himself, a truth which was previously hidden and has now been revealed. But the narrative structure, and the voice speaking through it, which is not his voice, belie his claim.

Pozdnyshev makes his narrative confession to his nameless partner on the journey, who sits knee-to-knee with him, drinking a potent tea which brings them both to increasing intoxication. This person is none other than the narrator, who narrates Pozdnyshev's present time of narrating as itself past narrated time. The narrator's present time of narrating is a time quit affected by the encounter with Pozdnyshev, a time of engagement with Pozdnyshev and not of merely neutral observation. The narrator intrudes on Pozdnyshev's story with questions, descriptions of Pozdnyshev's odd mannerisms, and the like, which give physical and psychic presence to Pozdnyshev. The narrator's narration also shows how the narrator gets caught up and dominated by both Pozdnyshev's story and story-teller himself.

Notice the interesting and significant narrative structure here: We have Pozdnyshev's narrating of an emplotted story and the narrator's narrating of that narrating as a slightly different emplotted story. There is a difference in temporal structure: Pozdnyshev's time of narrating past events become the narrator's narrated time in a new time of narrating. There is a difference in plot: the narrator's narrating shows how he, the narrator, becomes affected by Pozdnyshev. And there is a difference in character: Pozdnyshev's construction of his own narrative identity, an identity which ostensibly involves a transformation from old to new self in correlation to the emplotted divided time between then and now, is reconstructed by the narrator and put into dialectical play with the narrative identity the narrator constructs of himself as he recounts how he is drawn into Pozdnyshev's story and becomes grasped and dominated by it. Here is how Pozdnyshev's story comes out as a story whose meaning is belied by the narrator's narrating of it.

In the first movement, in *presto*, the narrator recounts Pozdnyshev's story of "how and why I married, and the kind of man I was before my marriage." It tells how Pozdnyshev fell into the concerns and views of his social class and the time of everyday self-forgetfulness. In brief, the world around him said "Seek sex!" and he did so; at the same time this world said "Honor matrimony" and he did so. As a consequence, he says, "I weltered in a mire of debauchery and at the same time was on the lookout for a girl pure enough to be worthy of me." Pozdnyshev's narrating is interrupted throughout by the narrator's narrating of Pozdnyshev's odd mannerisms in his telling: the odd laughing or sobbing noises of Pozdnyshev punctuate the story, striking the time of narrated events with the present time of the narrating.

From his purported present standpoint of truth, Pozdnyshev sees social life as all of one piece. From the brothel to the rituals of proper courtship, wedding, and honeymoon, Pozdnyshev in retrospect finds "nothing but a systematic excitement of desire." Men reduce women to instruments of unnatural and horrid sexual pleasure, and women respond by enslaving men through "those adornments of the body directly evoking sensuality." People deceive themselves into thinking they marry for shared ideals or poetic love and that so married they live in a moral world, says Pozdnyshev. In reality people marry out of lust— marriage is itself licensed prostitution.

The second movement, in *andante con variazioni*, recounts episodes of Pozdnyshev's married life as one of increasing disappointment, agitation, irritation, and jealousy. Husband and wife contend with each other in alternating bouts of an animal passion that they called "love" and venomous hostility. These alternating bouts exposed "the abyss that really existed between us." Purportedly a happily married couple, they were in fact "two egotists quite alien to each other who wished to get as much pleasure as possible each from the other." Although it was unrecognized at the time, Pozdnyshev now sees that the animosity which followed love was "nothing but the protest of our human nature against the animal nature that overpowered it." Again, the narrator reminds the reader of his presence to Pozdnyshev by recounting a sense of Pozdnyshev's agitation in telling his story.

The anticipated blessing of children turned out to be "a torment and nothing else." Husband and wife used the children as weapons of their strife; they lived in a fog, blind to their position. When the doctors told his wife she could bear no more children, "the last excuse for our swinish life— children—was then taken away, and life became viler than ever."

In the third movement, *Presto*, the narrator tells how Pozdnyshev nervously rises and sits in alternation as Pozdnyshev describes how his wife comes to awaken from the nightmare of marriage and to dream of some other, clean, new love through music (she was a pianist). In no time a real musician appears, a violinist named Trukhachevski, as if in answer to the dream. Pozdnyshev, the libertine, was suspicious from the first of the violinist, because he could see into the soul of a fellow libertine. Nonetheless he encouraged his wife to play piano accompaniment to Trukhachevski's violin, and the two developed a musical friendship. Pozdnyshev, however, increasingly observed the electric current established between them through the music, and he alternated between jealous rage at the couple and suffocating fear that his wife would leave him. Music brought the violinist and his wife together, and music made Pozdnyshev increasingly jealous. The narrator shows how passionately Pozdnyshev delivers his descriptions of the presumed passion between his wife and Trukhachevski.

At a recital the pair played Beethoven's Kreutzer Sonata, and Pozdnyshev noticed the strange effect produced by it: "Music makes me forget myself, my real position; it transports me to some other position not my own. Under the influence of music it seems to me that I feel what I do not really feel, that I understand what I do not understand, and that I can do what I cannot do." When the sonata was over, the mad beast of jealousy was entirely on the prowl; Pozdnyshev knew that the end was nigh. He could tolerate his wife's presumed affair no longer.

Again Pozdnyshev's narration is interrupted by the narrator, who describes the conductor replenishing their candle in the train carriage, while Pozdnyshev's voice grows more excited and full of suffering. Pozdnyshev continues: Following the recital, he reluctantly made a business trip to Moscow, conscious and tormented that his crisis was at hand, and returned early unannounced to his home, where he found the couple in the drawing-room. In a rage, he took a Damascus dagger off the wall, and silently stalked his wife. The sonata returns to the *adagio* of the beginning; time slows down. The more frenzied he became, the more brightly the light of consciousness burnt in him, and, against all pleas, he plunged the knife into her body with extraordinary clarity about his deed. Now in the train he narrates how, as she lay dying, "for the first time I forgot myself, my rights, my pride, and for the first time saw a human being in her." "Forgive me," I said. "Forgive! That's all rubbish. Only not to die," she cried.

Pozdnyshev's wife died shortly afterward. On the third day after his arrest for murder, Pozdnyshev was taken to see his dead wife, and only "when I saw her dead face did I understand all that I had done. I realized that I, I, had killed her; that it was my doing that she, living, moving, warm, had now become motionless, waxen, and cold, and that this could never, anywhere, or by any means, be remedied." This recognition of guilt and responsibility provoked moral change in Pozdnyshev. It changed him absolutely, according to his testimony. Henceforth he could see as a solitary I his past profligacy under a universal and necessary "moral law which avenges itself when it is violated" (184).

The story telling finally concludes with Pozdnyshev sobbing and trembling. The combined affect of the story and Pozdnyshev's presence leaves the narrator utterly without words. Pozdnyshev confesses: "Had I then known what I know now, everything would have been different. Nothing would have induced me to marry her.... I should not have married at all." He lies down and covers himself with the blanket. The two sit together in silence. At the next station, the narrator must get off the train. But before doing so, he touches Pozdnyshev with his hand and says good bye. The narrator says, "he gave me his and smiled slightly, but so piteously that I felt ready to weep." "Yes, forgive me..." said Pozdnyshev. These concluding words, "Forgive me," are the most important words of the text. Who speaks them? What do they mean?

If narrative identity gives poetic solution to the question "Who am I?", as Ricoeur claims, it does so neither unintrusively nor unambiguously in the case of Tolstoy's Pozdnyshev. As a pirated copy of the tale spread around Russia, a community of avid readers formed. Groups gathered together to recite the story aloud. In the larger public, the reception of the tale was divided and controversies broke out.[19] Some people found Tolstoy guilty of corrupting the youth with his lurid prose, of unmasking the noble sentiment of love, and of titillating his readers with the seductive wiles of sexual desire.[20] Others found fault with the uncompromising moral message from the reformed Pozdnyshev that absolute chastity alone is acceptable, that physical love in itself is a brutish and shameful act, and that sex is the single most pernicious obstacle for humans to achieve their goal of goodness, righteousness, and love.[21]

Among English-language critics, judgment of the novel has been harshly negative, on the grounds that it is confused: Donald Davie could not make out whether the work is a novel or a didactic tract, and thus he labeled it a contrived and grossly imperfect work.[22] The charge stuck, and it has been amplified by succeeding critical reviews. Critics commonly judge the work as that of a divided mind, uncertain whether it is an aesthetically seductive novel of sexual and murderous intrigue or an ethically rigorous polemic advocating virginity and purity.

Oddly, the critics following Davie have put their collective finger on the problem—namely, the conflict between the *aesthetic relation* to the other, in which one forgets oneself, and, seeking pleasure, is drawn into another's world; and the *ethical relation* to the other, in which one remembers oneself along with the bindingness of the moral law, and treats the other with respect. The critics following Davie do not realize, however, that what they view as a structural flaw of the text is in fact a structural feature of the text demanding interpretation. The voice of the text, speaking through the split relation, asks the reader: Who are you? An ethical human being who lives for the sake of what is good in itself, or an aesthete who lives for the sake of the pleasure of the moment? My question is: Who asks this question of the reader? Who is the voice of the text uttering it? And how does it ask the reader to refigure the self?

Let us first consider what the text is about at the level of its emplotment by articulating the fundamental fictive experience with time indicated in the dialectic between the time of narrating and narrated time. Perhaps then we can decide whose is the voice of the text. On the surface of things,

Pozdnyshev's narrative is divided simply into a past narrated time of aesthetic identity shrouded in darkness and driven by the pursuit of pleasure, and a present time of narrating, a time of ethical identity marked by illumination and pursuit of the good under the moral law. But this superficial impression, which corresponds to what Pozdnyshev says of himself, is falsified by the underlying narrative structure, which shows an alternation on each side of the opposition between time temporalized under a principle of seeking pleasure and time temporalized under a principle of seeking the good. The narrative structure shows that time is not merely divided between a past time of immoral indulgence and a present time of moral rigor, as Pozdnyshev presents it. Why?

During the time of so-called libertinism, Pozdnyshev alternates between a dominant time of animal passion and a subordinate time of irritation, which is the time of the protest of his human and therefore moral nature against its domination by appetite. Hence in the past narrated time of profligacy, moral good was hidden for the most part but not altogether absent: the good was dimly intended but misidentified. Likewise, after his moral awakening, Pozdnyshev oscillates in his present time of narrating between pontificating on the truth and persuading his listener by telling a story to seduce the narrator with his own narrated music, his own version of *The Kreutzer Sonata*. Hence in the present time of narrating, the pleasures of seduction are supposedly suppressed but in fact partially indulged.

The underlying structure therefore points to the fundamental fictive experience of time as a quantitative alternation between actions directed toward pleasure and actions directed toward the good. Pozdnyshev's life story is one in which alternations between opposites are found both in the time of profligacy and in the time of purity. Pozdnyshev invokes the moral law as truth in the domain of practical reason and believes he has converted his life to that law, but the structure of the text shows that he has failed to do so. In fact, Pozdnyshev alternates between the impulse for pleasure and respect for the moral law, without finding a unity between them.

The voice of the text, speaking through the structure of the text, in this way detaches itself from Pozdnyshev's voice and discloses his narrative identity as hopelessly divided, and hence guilty. The voice of the text says in effect to Pozdnyshev, "You claim to have undergone a conversion and to have unified your life around the one truth (of the moral law), but your life is in fact an oscillation between the two principles." At the same time, the voice of the text insists that it should not be so. Why? Under what principle should we live? According to the voice of the text, human beings are answerable in every moment of their lives *not* to the principle of personal desire alone (else they lose their humanity, as Pozdnyshev knows), *nor* to the principle of universal morality alone (for they continue to be creatures of desire even following a moral conversion, something which Pozdnyshev does not know), but rather to the principle of the individualized unity of the universal law and particular desire. Guilt, requiring forgiveness, is not merely a matter of failure under the moral law but of separating one's being into a duality of sensual existence on one side and moral accountability on the other. Nothing less than wholeness is required.

We are able to hear the voice of the text quite independently of Pozdnyshev's own voice because of the reflexive temporal structure. The narrator's narrating of Pozdnyshev's narration in a separate time of narrating enables the reader to understand Pozdnyshev quite differently than he understands himself. The narrator, although unobtrusive, is not a mere passive observer. He constructs an image of Pozdnyshev quite different from the one the reader would have had without the inclusion of the narrator in Pozdnyshev's story as his traveling partner. The reader cannot help but see the pathetic excesses and dissemblances of the reformed Pozdnyshev's self-constructed narrative identity.

At the same time that the reader sees through Pozdnyshev by virtue of acquiring the distance of the narrator's standpoint, the reader cannot overlook the pathos of the narrator's own position *vis-à-vis* Pozdnyshev. The narrator too oscillates from an ethical relationship with Pozdnyshev on meeting him to an aesthetic relationship as Pozdnyshev transports him into his world. The narrator then returns to tell the story truthfully to the reader, whom he hopes to draw into the pleasure of the text. Pozdnyshev and narrator relativize one another's voices, and the voice of the text exposes and judges them both harshly, for the narrator just as much as Pozdnyshev lives in a time of divided alternation.

The reader too is exposed by the voice of the text: the reader is drawn into the story by the lure of promised pleasure in the text, not knowing for the sake of what, and is hence identified as divided when the moral law is invoked by Pozdnyshev. The reader hears the sounds of *The Kreutzer Sonata* and is transported into a world of desire, there to be exposed. What alternative does the reader have? What alternative does anyone have? Should we give up reading and become blind, deaf-mutes? Should Pozdnyshev and the narrator cease telling stories? Can we give up desire any more than we can give up moral consciousness? Pleasures and responsibilities would come in dreams and images as unwanted guests, even if we willed them away.

Here we expose the human dilemma posed by the text: The moral law commands practical reason unconditionally; but under the finite conditions of space and time, human thinking is necessarily codetermined by irrational particularity through the organic desires of sensing, perceiving, and feeling. Hence the moral law given voice by the text is both uncompromisingly binding and impossible to fulfill—unless, of course, soul and body become one such that organic desires become desires for what is right under the law, and the intellectual function judges by a moral standard given as desirable in organic existence (and not merely in thought).

Whose is the disturbing voice of the text? Is it Tolstoy's? In a sense, yes, because Tolstoy's art has allowed the voice unifying the moral law and the desire for pleasure to be heard. But in a more emphatic sense, the answer is no. Why? The reason is that Tolstoy's *art* has inscribed the voice of the text within the body of the text, and the voice of the text exposes Tolstoy's art as well. Tolstoy could have written a tract on the moral calling of life with a minimum of rhetoric; or he could have written a lurid story arousing physical desires. However, he did neither, yet in a sense he did both. In truth he wrote a story with enormous capacity both to overpower its readers with the pleasure of the text and to precipitate in the reader a moral consciousness. The story is written so that the reader alternates in consciousness between a time lived for pleasure and a time lived for the sake of the good. Tolstoy indulges in the desire to play enchanting music, to take us far away from a world governed by obedience to the moral law, only to bring us back to that law, judged guilty by it. Thus Tolstoy's voice is one of alternation, but the voice of the text he constructed asks the reader to reject the life of alternation, and therefore to reject Tolstoy just as Tolstoy rejects Tolstoy.[23]

True, Tolstoy believes that he himself transformed the aims of his art from art for the sake of pleasure to art for the sake of the good. But this art is still not art as the unity of pleasure and goodness, but a divided, guilty art. Tolstoy's subordination of art to ethics is a dangerous path, as he knows, in which the good end justifies the means of pleasure. Under such a principle, can't one use violence to supposedly good ends? For example, could not Pozdnyshev draw the Damascus dagger on the narrator to force from him a confession of moral laxity? In principle is that not what Pozdnyshev does do to the narrator, and what Tolstoy does to the reader? The alternative for Tolstoy would be to give up art, music, story-telling as well as sex and murder, for we can see that moral purity is unattainable. But the voice of the text convicts us all, Tolstoy included.

So what should we do? How should we live? Who should I be? Interestingly the voice of the text provides the answer in the words of Pozdnyshev: "Forgive me." The words are uttered by Pozdnyshev to his dying wife and to the narrator at their parting. Appearing in both narratives, those of Pozdnyshev and the narrator, the words embody a voice that speaks to the reader from the structure of the text itself. Uttered by Pozdnyshev, the words refer to the murder of his wife; uttered by the voice of the text they refer to the human ontological condition of living in alternation between principles. The words "Forgive me" answer the dilemma by expressing the desire for justification under the moral law. They thereby enable a mode of being in which one becomes whole by accepting the necessity of both parts, thus overcoming the conflict between the polarized aspects, no longer subjecting either side to the domination of the other side. This mode of being actually occurs when one acts in the world for the sake of the good, while desiring the good (as is the case in asking forgiveness). At the same time, the action of seeking forgiveness is itself reflexive. In uttering "Forgive me!" one both momentarily embodies a unity and acknowledges that one cannot achieve the demanded unity.

As Tolstoy has written this text, he has constructed it as an embodied I with a voice that is not his own, not that of his story's main character, nor that of the narrator, but that of the God of Leo Tolstoy. Tolstoy's God is not a fully transcendent being (e.g., author of the moral law) nor a fully immanent being (e.g., the body of desire) but a being embodying the unity of the two: spirit made flesh.

What is astonishing about this voice is that it imparts what no human voice can impart—for the words "Forgive me" heard in *The Kreutzer Sonata* grant the reality they request. They confer forgiveness—and with it, a sense of the unity of the ethical and aesthetical—on the reader, the narrator, Pozdnyshev, and Tolstoy himself. They confer the reality of forgiveness and thus *make* a future possibility actual, putting guilt in the past. These words can do so, because they issue not from Tolstoy or Tolstoy's character (Pozdnyshev), but from the unity of the aesthetic and ethical principles. "Forgive me"—these words have a musical and poetic power to transport us in their appeal for the respect for the moral law, yet the content of the words deny the actual separation of that power from the desired good.

In 1889, in Russia, when copies of the banned story by Tolstoy circulated in pirated form, people reportedly no longer asked each other "How do you do?" when they met on the street. Instead they asked, "Have you read *The Kreutzer Sonata*?" In so doing, the readers formed a kind of community in response to the voice of the text. We can see from the voice of the text that the proper answer to the question is "Yes, forgive me." The voice of the text asks its readers to refigure themselves and to time their activities as though guilty under the moral law yet forgiven nonetheless by dwelling in the words "Forgive me."[24]

NOTES

1. Ricoeur has developed the concept of narrative identity in *Time and Narrative*, 3 vols., trans. Kathleen McLaughlin (vol. 1 and 2; Kathleen Blamey in vol. 3) and David Pellauer (Chicago and London: University of Chicago Press, 1984, 1985, 1988), especially in vol. 3, pp. 244-249, and in *Oneself as Another*, trans. Kathleen Blamey (Chicago and London: University of Chicago Press, 1992), pp. 113-68. This quotation is from *Time and Narrative* 3:247. In a series of articles, Ricoeur condenses his reflections in the three-volume *Time and Narrative*. Most helpful are "The Human Experience of Time and Narrative," *Research in Phenomenology* 9 (1979), pp. 17-34; "Narrative Time," *Critical Inquiry* 7, 1 (Autumn, 1980), pp. 169-190; "Narrativity and Hermeneutics," in *Essays on Aesthetics*, ed. John Fischer (Philadelphia, Pa: Temple University Press, 1983), pp. 149-60; "Narrated Time," trans. Robert Sweeney, *Philosophy Today* (Winter, 1985), pp. 259-71; "Narrative Identity," trans. Mark S. Muldoon, *Philosophy Today* (Spring 1991), pp. 73-80.

2. See Robert P. Scharlemann, "The Textuality of Texts" in *Meanings in Thought and Action: Questioning Paul Ricoeur*, ed. David E. Klemm and William Schweiker (Charlottesville, Virginia: the University Press of Virginia, 1993), pp. 13-25. See also Robert P. Scharlemann, *The Reason of Following: Christology and the Ecstatic I* (Chicago and London: The University of Chicago Press, 1991), pp. 170-88.

3. Leo Tolstoy, *The Kreutzer Sonata*, trans. Aylmer Maude, in *The Death of Ivan Ilych and Other Stories* (New York: New American Library), pp. 157-240. The story was begun in 1887 by Tolstoy, sent through nine drafts in which the author made drastic revisions, finished and censored under imperial edict in 1889 by Tsar Aleksander III. The ban was lifted in 1891, when the Tsar gave permission to Tolstoy's wife to publish *The Kreutzer Sonata* in the collected works of Leo Tolstoy.

4. Paul Ricoeur, *Time and Narrative* 1, p. 3.

5. The episodic dimension of the narrative draws on the linear representation of time in many ways: 1) the sequence displays a relation of exteriority among episodes, 2) the episodes constitute an open-ended series, 3) the episodes follow one another irreversibly in the manner of physical events. The configurational dimension of the narrative draws on nonlinear representation of time: 1) it makes the succession into a whole that is the correlative of an act of conceiving the many under one thought, 2) the plot provides a "sense of an ending" enabling the reader to apprehend the end in the beginning, and 3) the retelling of narrative enables the reader to read time backward, Paul Ricoeur, "Narrative and Hermeneutics," pp. 153-4.

6. Paul Ricoeur, "Narrative and Hermeneutics," pp. 153-54.

7. Paul Ricoeur, "Narrated Time," pp. 268-9.

8. Paul Ricoeur, *Time and Narrative* 3, p. 100; see also p. 61.

9. Paul Ricoeur, *Time and Narrative* 3, p. 68. Ricoeur discusses how sometimes the use of different verbal tenses signals the division between direct narration and commentary. Preterite, imperfect, pluperfect, and conditional tenses belong to the narrated world and present, compound past, and future tenses belong to the commented world. The tenses signify either that this is commentary or this is narrative. Tense-identification only illustrates the shift, however, it does not infallibly accompany it.

10. Paul Ricoeur, *Time and Narrative* 3, pp. 80-81.

11. Paul Ricoeur, *Time and Narrative* 3, p. 84.

12. Paul Ricoeur, "Narrated Time," p. 269.

13. Paul Ricoeur, "Narrative Identity," p. 73.

14. Paul Ricoeur, *Oneself as Another*, p. 143. The narrative structure as a whole joins together two processes of emplotment, that of *action* and that of *character*, for telling a story is not merely linking discrete episodes into the sequence of the story, but telling *who* did what and *how* with whom and to whom. Action is always interaction among humans who are both actors and sufferers.

15. Paul Ricoeur, *Oneself as Another*, p. 148. The identity of the narrative as plot makes the identity of the character by emplotting the character's identity as concordant-discordance.

16. Paul Ricoeur, *Oneself as Another*, p. 121.

17. Robert Scharlemann, *The Reason of Following*, p. 181.

18. R.F. Christian, in *Tolstoy: An Introduction to His Writings*, p. 233, cites Dorothy Green's work on the structural parallels between Tolstoy's and Beethoven's sonatas in *The Kreutzer Sonata*: Tolstoy and Beethoven," in *Melbourne Slavonic Studies* 1 (1967).

19. People were reported no longer to ask "How do you do?" when they met, but rather "Have you read *The Kreutzer Sonata*?" See the monograph on the controversy in historical context by Peter Ulf Moeller, *Postlude to The Kreutzer Sonata: Tolstoi and the Debate on Sexual Morality in Russian Literature in the 1890s*, trans. John Kendal (Leiden, New York, Copenhagen, and Cologne: E. J. Brill, 1988).

20. The Archbishop of Kherson pronounced anathema on Tolstoy, and Tsar Aleksander III banned the sale and distribution of *The Kreutzer Sonata*. See David McDuff, "Translator's Introduction," in Leo Tolstoy, *The Kreutzer Sonata and Other Stories* (London: Penguin, 1985) p. 17.

21. See Ernest J. Simmons, *Introduction to Tolstoy's Writings* (Chicago and London: The University of Chicago Press, 1968), pp. 157-158, and Moeller, *Postlude to The Kreutzer Sonata*, p. 17.

22. Donald Davie, "Tolstoy, Lermontov, and Others" (1965) in Donald Davie, ed. *Russian Literature and Modern English Fiction: A Collection of Critical Essays* (Chicago and London: The University of Chicago Press, 1965). p. 164; picked up by J. M. Coetzee, "Confession and Double Thoughts: Tolstoy, Rousseau, Dostoevsky" *Comparative Literature* 37, 3 (1985), p. 199; Renato Poggioli, "Tolstoy as Man and Artist" in Ralph E. Matlaw, ed. *Tolstoy: A Collection of Critical essays* (Englewood Cliffs, N.J.: Prentice-Hall,

Inc., 1967) p. 25; Gary Saul Morison, "The Reader as Voyeur: Tolstoy and the Poetics of Didactic Fiction" in Harold Bloom, ed., *Leo Tolstoy: Modern Critical Views* (New York: Chelsea House Publishers, 1986), pp. 188-189; E. B. Greenwood, *Tolstoi: The Comprehensive Vision* (New York: St. Martin's Press, 1975). See also Louise Smoluchowski, *Lev and Sonya: The Story of the Tolstoy Marriage* (New York: G. P. Putnam's Sons, 1987), pp. 138140; R. F. Christian, *Tolstoy: A Critical Introduction* (Cambridge: At the University Press, 1969), pp. 230-232. The mother of all negative criticisms is Isabel Hapgood, "Tolstoi's Kreutzer Sonata," originally published in *Nation* 50 (17 April, 1890), pp. 313-315, and reprinted in Edward Wasiolek, *Critical Essays on Tolstoy* (Boston: G. K. Hall & Co., 1986), pp. 162-68.

23. I refer to Tolstoy's rejection of all his work prior to the religious conversion, including the greater masterpieces, *War and Peace* and *Anna Karenina*.

24. I wish to thank Gary L. Bailey and Lyone Fein, graduate assistants at the University of Iowa, for helpful comments and conversations about this paper and *The Kreutzer Sonata*..

Reclaiming 'The Fall'

Grandmother's Spells and The Decline of Patriarchy in Iris Murdoch's The Book and the Brotherhood

IRENA MAKARUSHKA

Introduction: Religious Reading and a Feminist Re-Writing of a Moral Life

In *The Book and the Brotherhood*[1] Iris Murdoch turns her attention to a group of old friends whose lives are enmeshed through a variety of choices, accidents and coincidences. They gather for the midsummer ball at Oxford where they met more than two decades ago. The narrative unfolds over a nine month period of moral crises, renegotiations of relationships and reassessments of allegiances. Murdoch describes lives connected by love, jealousy, hatred, envy, fear and empathy experienced on different levels of intellectual, spiritual and moral consciousness. The midsummer ball, perhaps an allusion to the magical unpredictability and danger of *A Midsummer Night's Dream*, is attended by Rose Curtland and Gerard Hernshaw and Duncan and Jean Cambus. Surrounded by an assortment of friends and acquaintances including Lily Boyne escorted by Crimond, Gerard's niece Tamar, her mother Violet partnered reluctantly by Gulliver and Jenkin Riderhood, they recollect their past and contend with its aftermath in the present.

At issue for this cohort of friends facing middle-age is the desire to live a moral life at a time when the old order of things appears to have lost its sustaining and nurturing power. A sense of exhaustion and limpness marks their growing awareness that the icons that defined moral life in their youth have lost their brilliance and that inevitable and unpredictable changes have altered their friendships and intellectual commitments. Even their desire to believe in the decision to support Crimond in his intellectual endeavor to write 'the book' and their sense of being a community of readers have begun to fade.

Such times of transition and moral crises have been variously assessed. In "Ash Wednesday," echoing the words of Ezekiel who grieves the meaninglessness and faithlessness of his age, Eliot asks, "Shall these bones live?" Unlike Eliot, in *The Book and the Brotherhood*, Murdoch asks, *should* these bones live? What can the dry bones of the past contribute to the creation of a moral community in the future? What constitutes a moral life at a time of transition?

Murdoch's concern with the possibility of living a moral life not only informs her fiction but shapes her philosophy. In "The Idea of Perfection,"[2] the first of three essays in *The Sovereignty of Good*, she offers an alternative to what she describes as the existentialist-behaviorist view of the moral life which has its roots in empiricism and analytical philosophy. Objecting to the claim that moral life is judged "from the outside in,"—that the moral life is the observable manifestation of the will's alignment with moral laws (SG 22), Murdoch suggests that a moral life is lived from the inside out. A moral life is both an inner struggle to be loving and just toward the other and the activity that follows from the struggle. As activity, a moral life is the ongoing effort to live "in the light of the command, 'Be ye therefore perfect' . . ." (SG 30). She points out that "Innumerable novels contain accounts of what such struggles are like" (SG 22). Undoubtedly, her own novels count among these since they too are primarily concerned with the struggle to live a moral life.

Both as a moral philosopher and as a novelist Murdoch explores the contingencies, ambiguities and coincidences that collectively collaborate to keep human experience slightly off balance and unpredictable. She describes the resistance of experience to categorization, definition, conclusion and closure as she explores the conditions necessary for living a moral life. With an abiding care for her characters and without condemning their efforts, Murdoch patiently describes their struggles to live morally in relation to the community. Her attitude toward her characters as well as her insights into the state of culture in the late twentieth century resonates with Detweiler's description of religious reading in *Breaking the Fall*.[3] Explaining the rationale for religious reading as an interpretative strategy, Detweiler states that it begins "with the premise that writing and reading fiction are activities . . . through which we seek to replace whatever satisfactions were provided by . . . storytelling communities" (BF 30). Further, he observes that a text invites religious reading by "its very openness to others; its willingness to accommodate and adapt; its readiness to entertain the new, the invention, while honouring the old, the convention; its celebration of . . . possibilities rather than delimiting them" (BF 35). As a reader and writer Murdoch vivifies the qualities Detweiler's associates with religious reading and writing of culture and fiction. Her novels and her philosophical essays are expansive in their attitude and augment the range of possible interpretations of experience.

Following Detweiler, I propose a religious reading from a feminist perspective of Murdoch's religious reading and writing of late twentieth century culture in *The Book and the Brotherhood*. I suggest that this novel is framed by Murdoch's implicitly feminist ethics. She treats moral questions within a larger cultural context and focuses on the transition from a dominant patriarchal culture to an emergent feminist one. As Detweiler observes, religious reading, and, by extension, religious writing, is "engaged in simultaneously recognizing and reshaping the myths and rituals we live by" (BF 38). There is evidence of such reshaping in *The Book and the Brotherhood* with regard to the status of 'the Fall', the consequent concern with salvation and the possibility of living a moral life. Murdoch's exploration of 'the Fall' and of the efficaciousness of rituals that reenact a sense of connectedness with the past is continuous with the themes of her previous novels. In a tone that is always sympathetic, she describes well-meaning but oftentimes befuddled individuals who try to make sense of their lives in spite of their various vices and virtues. In her renarration of the human frailty, the traditional patriarchal interpretation of 'the Fall' which emphasizes 'original sin' and human depravity appears to be an overstatement of the case.

In my reading of *The Book and the Brotherhood*, I begin by exploring a series of events, including a double suicide attempt and an accidental death, that signify fallenness and alienation. Murdoch's concern with the process of coming to terms with one's finitude is informed by her belief that an inner sense of how a moral life is lived is more instructive than are external laws. Her characters create elaborate illusions as a means of sustaining their fragile sense of self. For those who choose to live just, loving and humble lives, moral and spiritual transformation is possible. Next I argue that Murdoch's focus on the death of the father, whether it be as parent or as an intellectual and spiritual mentor, signifies the inadequacy of the traditional patriarchal interpretation of human nature as fallen. Not only do fathers fail their sons by their silence, their lack of affection, their lies, but the sons carry this ineffectualness to its logical conclusion. They remain childless whether by choice or chance, thereby bringing the cycle of impotence to its inevitable end. I conclude by suggesting that in reconfiguring the contours of the moral landscape in the wake of the demise of the patriarchal order, Murdoch celebrates women as healers and agents of moral transformation. 'The fall' is reclaimed as a signifier of the ambiguity of human experience lived in freedom and self-knowledge. Not fathers, but grandmothers who embody the wisdom of the tradition of witches become the source of spiritual and moral energy. In the spells and potions of witches Murdoch recovers the possibility of a moral life lived as a struggle to develop and sustain a loving and just attitude toward others that emerges out of an inner desire to be humble, caring and attentive.

Murdoch's turn from an ethics determined by external moral laws to an ethics of interiority wherein a moral life lived in freedom and humility is a life attentive to the reality of the other reflects a feminist ethical consciousness.[4] Although Murdoch does not engage in an explicit critique of patriarchy, *The Sovereignty of Good* can be interpreted as a refusal of the normative assumptions about values, virtue and justice that have traditionally been associated with logocentrism and the law of the Father. Murdoch's position is shared by many feminist ethicists for whom a moral dilemma constitutes a conflict of responsibilities rather than a conflict of rights or entitlements. Solutions are directed toward strengthening relational bonds. There is less of an appeal to abstract rules and principles and more of an appeal to love and compassion that tries to negotiate between justice and care. Whereas male-biased ethics functions ideologically to delegitimate the interests of women and subordinate them to the interests of men, feminist ethics recognizes women as moral agents countering the traditional stereotypes of women as less-than, child-like, close-to-nature.[5]

Murdoch's high regard for women as moral agents is evident in "The Idea of Perfection." As a model of exemplary moral reasoning, she chooses the often maligned and caricatured mother-in-law as a moral agent who struggles to arrive at a more loving and just attitude toward her daughter-in-law. Her choice challenges the assumptions of traditional masculinist philosophical models of normative attitudes and behaviors and legitimates the experience of women. The determination to reclaim the significance of the "ordinary and everyday" (SG 17) allows her to move beyond the dry bones of the claims of objectivity by analytical and linguistic philosophers whose discourse on ethics is unrelentingly abstract and dissociated from lived practice. Murdoch's ethics implicitly engage questions of gender and power and the cultural myths that have traditionally functioned to sustain the privileged order. In both her moral philosophy and in her fiction she acknowledges that men and women are differently situated and, therefore, do not have equal access to power. She sees individual actions within a broader cultural and historical context which provides for a more nuanced interpretation.[6]

In *The Book and the Brotherhood* Murdoch describes the struggles of women and men exploring the values and assumptions that sustain their lives as an exercise of the will trying "to see a particular object more clearly" (SG 23). The processes she describes emerge out of the reshaped contours of ethical discourse that privilege interiority, attention and care. Adumbrating the task of feminist ethics outlined by contemporary philosophers such as Jaggar,[7] Murdoch subtly challenges the subordination of women by representing their experience and their inner lives as significant elements of a moral life that is worthy of respect. In her reading and writing of late twentieth century culture, the value and significance of women's private, domestic and public lives becomes a legitimate subject for philosophical discourse and for the literary imagination.

'The Fall' and Other Vicissitudes

With Duncan's fall into the river at the Commem Ball at Oxford, Murdoch begins her exploration of the sense of fallenness and alienation experienced by a group of old friends whose lives are on the verge of unraveling. Duncan falls as a result of being pushed by Crimond whose appearance at the ball signals his desire to reclaim the love of Duncan's wife, Jean. This event recalls a fight many years earlier when Duncan found Jean and Crimond in bed in their home in Ireland. This event ended with Duncan's loss of vision in one eye and the first break up of their marriage. Impaired vision and alcoholism signify the constraints upon Duncan's struggle to continue to believe in the possibility of love and a moral life. By pushing Duncan, Crimond appears to assert his superiority over Duncan and affirms his hold over Jean. Or does he? asks Murdoch as she sets the narrative within a larger framework that questions the traditional models of male power, dominance and violence and looks toward the possibility of more just and caring relationships based on selfless love and compassion.

In *The Book and the Brotherhood* Murdoch retells and reconfigures the meaning of 'the Fall'. Rejecting the notion that it is a transgression against the law of the Father, Murdoch reclaims 'the Fall' as descriptive of human failings that are part of the muddle and ordinariness of experience. As an alternative to the traditional interpretation of 'the Fall' that includes the loss of Eden and punishment for disobedience leading to a life of pain and suffering, Murdoch's approach is to interpret 'the Fall' as descriptive of the condition of finitude that is normative for human experience. No longer viewed as punishment for wrong-doing that requires expiation, 'the Fall' becomes an invitation to live a moral life in spite of the ambiguities and paradoxes embedded in experience. In the flawed marriage of Duncan and Jean Cambus which includes betrayal and alienation, Murdoch offers a case study of the possibility of forgiveness and self-transcendence that emerges as a result of an inner moral struggle rather than a compliance with external laws.

The appearance of Crimond once again poses a threat to the marriage of Duncan and Jean which becomes the concern if not the obsession of their friends, their friend's friends, family and acquaintances. Murdoch weaves together the complex lives of these characters with a breathtaking flourish. The range of plots and sub-plots, texts and sub-texts concerning lives connected across more than two decades of change can only be suggested rather than retold. Crimond, Duncan, Gerard and Jenkin were all at Oxford where Gerard met and fell in love with Sinclair who died in a glider accident while still a student. At Oxford, Gerard also met Rose, Sinclair's sister who fell in love with him and who is still perceived as 'belonging to Gerard' (5). After Sinclair's death, Gerard fell in love with Duncan before he married Jean Kowitz, Rose's school friend and Oxford intellectual. During their university days these friends identified themselves with various Marxist and leftist causes that, for the most part, have lost their attraction. Of this Oxford 'brotherhood' Crimond remains a recognized authority on British Marxism (5) and Jenkin believes in the possibility of a New Theology that emerges out of the interface of religion and Marxism (15). Consequently, he values Crimond's leftist politics and his endeavor to write 'the book' for which 'the brotherhood', as part of their memorial to Sinclair's memory, continues to provide financial support (99).

The reappearance of Crimond who after nearly two decades has still not completed the promised book and who again threatens the Cambus marriage generates a climate of distrust and concern among the brotherhood (103). Whether directly, indirectly or by default, Crimond's return sets into motion a series of events that lead to an attempted double suicide, an accidental death and an abortion. Designated as the outsider, Crimond elicits a range of responses from the extreme of Jean's nearly pathological self-denying love, to Lily's romantic love, Gerard's grudging respect, Jenkin's admiration, Conrad's idolization, Rose's fear and Duncan's hatred. As a Scot who wears his Macpherson tartan kilt to the Commem Ball, and who comes from a working class family and remains committed to leftist activism, Crimond is the 'other'. Among the things he shares with Jean, a Jewish leftist intellectual who writes about issues concerning women's rights, is the sense of otherness. The brotherhood—including Rose who wanted to be a priest (16) but settles for playing the role of caretaker—are insiders whose lives reflect their upper class roots. Duncan is a retired diplomat, Gerard, a retired government official. Jenkin, a schoolmaster, fits in although he comes from a working class family because he does not appear to be burdened by his class identity. Rather than living as an outsider, Jenkin feels related to the entire human community. The narrative reveals Murdoch's belief that alienation and suffering are afflictions common to all regardless of social status. She describes degrees of alienation that range from despair to doubt, from self-destructive impulses to grief and sadness.

Is Crimond the romantic hero, utopian thinker, fanatic, ascetic and *l'âme damnée* (as Jenkin suggests) or is he the terrorist, charlatan, self-obsessed theorist and dangerous tyrant who thrives on dramas and ordeals (as Gerard believes him to be) (128-30)? The novel's conflicting interpretations deflect the possibility of a simple answer. Arguably Crimond is none of the above and all of the above. In contrast to descriptions of Crimond offered by Gerard, Rose and others that are marked by their jealousies, fears, doubts or hatreds, Jenkin's reading is more about Crimond than it is about himself which allows him to see the complexity of Crimond's character. He observes,

> The thing about the man is that he's a puritan, he's a fanatic, his ancestors were Scottish Calvinists, so he's got a huge sense of sin and a death-wish, he believes in hell but he's a perfectionist, a utopian, he believes in instant salvation, he thinks the good society is very close, very possible, if only all the atoms could shift, all the molecules change, just very slightly—maybe this could happen, maybe it won't, everything is changing, deeply, terribly, like never before, and maybe it's *hell* ahead, but he thinks it is his job to say it's possible to accept all and sacrifice almost everything and somehow make the new thing into a good thing . . . (249).

His belief in Crimond's moral rectitude, however, errs on the positive side as Gerard's errs on the negative. The suicide pact Crimond makes with Jean suggests that he doesn't possess the level of moral certitude and power that either Jean or Jenkin attribute to him, nor does he possess the awful Shiva-like power that Gerard sees and fears (36). Murdoch suggests that in the end Crimond's sense of despair drives him both to write 'the book' and propels him toward the edges of darkness because he lacks the inner strength to live the ordinariness of life. Crimond hides from the messiness of life behind books in a basement room where he is isolated and protected from anyone who would make intellectual or emotional demands on him. In this he is similar to Gerard who also evades every opportunity to live fully in the world.

Conflicting interpretations of Crimond reflect the differences between Jenkin and Gerard as well as Murdoch's claim that a moral life is both struggle and activity. An exchange between Jenkin and Gerard as they walk in the freezing night air during the traditional midwinter get-together of the brotherhood for a week of reading and communing at Rose's country estate—the Boyars—is significant and revelatory. They rehearse the same argument they have had for years accusing one another of being religious. The irony (or perhaps comedy) implicit in their insistence that the other has erred on the side of religion, is that the difference between them is not whether one is or is not religious, but how one lives one's life as part of the human community. In their dispute Murdoch forefronts the limits of conceptual categories when it comes to attaining a deeper (or higher) level of understanding about living a moral life. Gerard accuses Jenkin of being religious because he is concerned with feeding the poor (250). Jenkin accuses Gerard of being religious because he wants to believe in the adequacy of the Platonic world of ideas yet believes that "*up there* it just looks like death" (251). Jenkin observes, "Yes, as we keep telling each other, we do see life differently. I see it as a journey along a dark foggy road with a lot of other chaps. You see it as a solitary climb up a mountain, you don't believe you'll get to the top, but you feel that because you *think* of it you've done it. That's the idea that takes *you* all the way" (250-1)! For Gerard, their difference lies in the fact that he believes in goodness whereas Jenkin believes in justice, though neither believe in an ideal society.

The critical difference voiced by Jenkin illustrates Murdoch's commitment to the practice or activity of a moral life. Bringing their debate to closure he notes, "I feel I *live* in society, you don't—I think you don't *notice* it" (251). Whereas Jenkin embraces life with all of its vicissitudes, Gerard idealizes it and failing in that attempt, he holds life at arm's length. Like Crimond, he is haunted by a sense of the fallenness of humanity. However, whereas Gerard protects himself from the messiness of life by refusing to engage it fully, Crimond tries to stave off the horrors he fears by thinking and writing for the future. Arguing with Gerard about the significance and meaning of the book he is writing under the patronage of the brotherhood, Crimond professes, "*That's* what's worth doing, and it's the *only thing* that's worth doing now, to *look* at the future and to make sense of it and *touch* it" (299). His rhetoric does little to temper the sense of despair and fallenness he feels and which he plays out as high drama in the suicide pact with Jean.

When Jean returns to him after the ball, Crimond says, "If you come to me you must do what I want" (117). Agreeing, she says, "This is real. Isn't it" (117)? For Murdoch the question is, Is it? And if it is, why is it? And if it isn't, why isn't it? What elements are necessary for a relationship to real, to be about the lived messiness of human life? Crimond tells Jean, "You are the only woman I have ever wanted or ever will or could want" (177). He sees their love as "entirely necessary and entirely impossible" (177). Rebuked by Jean that their being together proves that love is not impossible, Crimond concludes that like God, "it exists necessarily " (177) suggesting a higher order of things that can evade the ordinariness of experience. The difference between the love of Crimond and Jean and that of Duncan and Jean reflects Murdoch's concerns about the nature of love, moral judgment and virtue. Jean and Crimond are related by pain, escape, need, despair and finally death; whereas Jean and Duncan are connected by suffering, failure, desire, patience, forgiveness and ultimately the depths of love. Whereas Crimond 'wants' Jean, Duncan loves Jean. This difference becomes critical at the moment Jean decides not to do what Crimond wants and chooses life over death—effectively a refusal of possession, patriarchal power and external laws. Her decision vivifies Murdoch's view that present-mindedness and reflection grounded in a deep internal commitment to a moral life and to doing the right thing for its own sake is preferable to living according to externally imposed rules and laws.

When he completes 'the book' (342), Crimond becomes depressed. Finding it impossible to sleep and ultimately to live, he invites Jean to enter into a suicide pact with him. Despite her initial disbelief and fear, she agrees to his proposal that in order for their love to last forever, they should kill themselves by driving their cars toward one another creating a deadly head-on collision (355ff). At the agreed upon time, having said their goodbyes, as she begins to accelerate, thoughts crowd her mind, thoughts of Crimond's desires, wants and needs. "[T]he book was finished, and were they not perfectly happy, was not this, what she was doing now as an instrument of Crimond's will, perfect happiness" (381)? Obsessed with the notion that the suicide pact is only Crimond's way of testing her courage, as the cars speed toward one another, Jean suddenly realizes that she cannot kill her lover and that "it isn't a test, it's the real thing, it's the end" (382).

The instant she turns the wheel of the car avoiding the collision by crashing her car into the woods, she acts out of her own inner sense of the wrongness of their pact denying Crimond his power over her. In the aftermath, she suffers Crimond's wrath and rejection. Her failure to obey his wishes, ends their relationship. He tells her, "Don't come near me again, now or tomorrow or in any future time. You are nothing to me now, nothing. Go away, take your freedom, *take your chance*" (385). Crimond ascribes Jean's 'fall' from his grace and love to her disobedience constituted as the freedom to choose life over death. Murdoch's irony is apparent in the shift from Jean's perception that her love for Crimond is a "a *complete* removal of (her) being, a *complete* change . . . . It's a meeting with an absolute"(308), to her inability to believe that indeed Crimond meant them to be together in death rather than in life. Not unlike the suffering of Eve, the first woman to choose freedom and knowledge over blind obedience to the law of the father, Jean's journey of recovery, healing and return to Duncan is painful and deeply felt. In both instances real life with its pain and pleasures is affirmed over against the illusion of an Eden that requires the absolute subordination.

Jean decision to reclaim life, though she initially assumed it would be with Crimond, reflects the inner tension she experiences between wanting to please and desiring to live as a thoughtful independent woman in a relationship based on mutual understanding. In this tension Murdoch locates the feelings of failure and limitation experienced as an element of the inner negotiations that are part of the process of living a moral life. Though Jean idolizes Crimond, accepts being his "little falcon" (169) and tries to embrace his asceticism, she claims her independence by occasionally going on her own to a gallery or shop. Jean is equally conflicted with regard to her father, Joel, who values her intellect though wishes she had children. She sees herself as failing on both counts being neither a productive intellectual nor a mother. She experiences a similar sense of failure in relation to Duncan owing to her infidelity and their childlessness. Ironically, she considers her decision to leave Duncan for Crimond as an expression of her freedom.

Jean's relationships with women are equally ambiguous. She desires to mother or even adopt Tamar, Gerard's niece, yet she fails to understand the depth of her distress. With regard to Rose, Jean sets aside their friendship in order to satisfy Crimond's possessiveness, but turns to her when she needs solace after the suicide attempt. With Jean as with other women in this narrative, Murdoch focuses on their struggle to live a moral life not on their conformity to external moral laws nor on the measure of their success. Though at times they appear to lose ground, or in Tamar's case exchange one form of external authority for another, the struggle, *per se*, brings them to greater self-understanding and a greater empathy for others.

The choice Jean makes to save herself becomes the occasion of her reconciliation with Duncan which is negotiated by their friends: Rose,

Gerard and Jenkin. If Crimond tried to control her, Duncan sets her free by his unconditional forgiveness. Coming to see her at Rose's where she is recuperating, Duncan simply asks, "Do you want to be with me again, Jean" (402). Her equally simple yes is enough to settle the matter. The strange look on his face, Murdoch writes, "had been his attempt to control his agonizing tenderness and pity . . ." (402). Duncan's patient, hopeful love is selfless and forgiving in part because he did not allow himself to be defined by the views of their friends, (94). Rather, it is grounded in some deep inner sense of its rightness, its reality and its merit. He believed Jean would one day be able to see and value it too. Jean leaves and returns to Duncan twice and each time he accepts her as she is, not requiring that she become someone else, nor punishing her for the pain she caused him. He does not require surrender, only her desire that they be together (98, 403ff). Their relationship survives the pain they cause one another because each is willing to see the other as real, possessing both strengths and weaknesses. Yet, Murdoch casts their reconciliation as part reality and part illusion implying that life is indeed after 'the Fall' and therefore resists absolutes. In order to come to terms with the past they retreat to a "determined hedonism"(427) permitting themselves to celebrate the survival of their marriage yet engaging in selective forgetfulness in order to escape their weighty emotional baggage.

The opportunity to indulge their need to protect one another from further chaos surfaces when Duncan is summoned by Crimond to resolve their unresolved differences and when Tamar tells Jean about her brief affair with Duncan which results in her pregnancy and subsequent abortion. In these two instances Murdoch locates the tension between external law and the internal struggle which is shaped by fate. The desire to control experience is held in check by contingency which for Murdoch becomes the occasion for responsible moral action. In Tamar's case, the opportunity for self-determination is lost when she decides to become a Christian and to align herself with patriarchy in the guise of Father McAlister (455ff). Duncan, on the other hand, having accidentally shot and killed Jenkin who walked into the middle of his duel with Crimond, manages to salvage something "out of an unimaginable terrible, horrible catastrophe . . . by swift intelligent action" (472).

Tamar, an illegitimate child carrying the name of the Biblical daughter of King David who is raped by her brother, Amnon, and disregarded by her father (II Samuel 13:1-22), is the embodiment of the sins of the fathers. The result of a casual affair between her mother and a forgotten sailor, she is told that she exists only "because Violet could not afford an abortion " (10,

108). Violet is also illegitimate. Her mother was abandoned by Gerard's uncle Benjamin leaving her on the margins of the Hernshaw family who regard her with a mixture of guilt and pity. Tamar is defined by her sense of being abandoned by her father and controlled by her mother who refuses to allow her to return to Oxford to continue her studies (105). Tamar copes with her sense of loss and hopelessness by seeking out others who can provide some degree of affirmation. She loves and admires her uncle Gerard (160ff), has a crush on Jean (163), falls in love with Duncan (219), seeks advice and support from Lily when she decides to have an abortion (326), finds comfort and understanding in Jenkin (368) and in the end turns to Father McAlister, an Anglican priest, who promises salvation in the name of Jesus (286). In Murdoch's view of cosmic order, Tamar remains a victim whose moral life is determined by external laws and the powerful voices of others in the patriarchal and Christian tradition (455, 492ff, 514ff).

Not having a sense of self, not speaking in her own voice, not thinking her own thoughts, having internalized her mother's sense of being a victim, following Violet's example, Tamar blames others for her choices. Duncan is blamed for their liaison (349), Lily for the abortion (348) and Jean for creating the occasion for her to love Duncan (327; 447). Though Rose and Jenkin try to help her, Tamar is overwhelmed by pain and self-hatred which is somatized as anorexia. Seeking to find her lost father in her relationships with men, she remains child-like, spoken for and incapable of making an adult decision. When she confronts Jean with her confession, she does so to further punish Jean in an effort to find peace for herself (447). Jean's response is to salvage something from the horror. Believing that they now have a chance to live in a loving and mutually supportive marriage, she decides not to tell Duncan what Tamar has told her (456). The moral order of things, Murdoch seems to suggest, is sustained by the various secrets that are kept as an act of love to protect others from harm (525). The inevitable ambiguity of secrets is that they also isolate and protect the keeper from the wrath of others. In certain instances the greater good outweighs selfish motives (457, 525ff).

Duncan keeps secrets from Jean. He doesn't tell her about Tamar, nor does he tell her that he killed Jenkin. Jenkin's accidental death is suggestive of Murdoch's belief that ordinary lives are determined by contingencies, coincidences and fate rather than controlled by divine providence bent on punishing the sons and daughters of Adam and Eve. Duncan goes to Crimond's house at his behest in order to fight a duel which he later discovers was staged to assure Crimond's death. Jean discovers Crimond's note in Duncan's desk and calls Jenkin to intervene by going to Crimond's n order to protect both men. He succeeds but pays with his life. As Duncan turns the gun always from Crimond toward the target hanging on the door and squeezes the trigger, Jenkin open the door and dies from a bullet in his head.

With Jenkin's death, Murdoch brings his life as the 'other' full circle. He is Murdoch's humble man, who like Christ dies for no good reason.[8] Lauding his selflessness Murdoch writes, "Jenkin seems to lack any strong sense of individuality and was generally unable to 'give an account of himself'" (123). An intensely private man Jenkin belongs to the brotherhood in a characteristically personal and, therefore, somewhat marginal way. He lives a solitary and ascetic life that allows him to be attentive to the lives and needs of others such as Gerard, who loves him and proposes that they live together, and Tamar who needs him to suffer with her through her pain. His life and his choices emerge from a deep and abiding sense of what is right and good. Less interested in the well-meaning gossip about the others, his attention is focused on living for others in a quiet and unassuming way. His love for Gerard is not reduced to sexual passion since "a great love involves the whole person and Jenkin's attachment was perhaps in the true sense Platonic" (137) which becomes a model of a love that allows the other to be free and, therefore, is represented by Murdoch as worthy of emulation.

Jenkin's life is based on the idea that moral action is good for its own sake. Unlike Gerard who believes the "(n)ovels are over, they're finished" (124) and who equates happiness with hedonism, Jenkin believes that fiction and happiness are important elements of human experience. Jenkin trusts others to do what they believe is right, Gerard distrusts others and thinks that knowing 'what really happened' will make enigmatic individuals like Duncan, more understandable (131). Gerard hates God, loves the fog and wants to know the truth about people's lives. Jenkin cares deeply for those whose lives are defined by oppression and injustice, he notes the ambiguity of evil imaged in the whiteness of the Berlin Wall (132-3) and connectedness of all humanity. Whereas Gerard is focused on universals and sees the other as exotic, Jenkin focuses on particulars—"on little events or encounters" (135) and sees the other as ordinary. He observes,

> Sometimes sitting at home, Jenkin imagined individual other people, people he had never met, these were always lonely people, a girl in a bed-sitter with her cat and potted plant, an elderly man washing his shirt, a man in a turban walking along a dusty road, a man lost in the snow. Sometimes he dreamed about such people or was one himself. Once he thought so intensely about a tramp at a railway terminus that he actually set off late in the evening to

Paddington to see if the tramp was there. The tramp was not there, but a variety of solitary persons were there, waiting for Jenkin (135).

Jenkin's life is not defined by hatred, attachment to the past or desire to control the future. Whereas Gerard is haunted by God, his father, his dead parrot and his friends' lives, Jenkin lives his life fully in the present respecting the past, his parents, their religiosity, their goodness without being defined by the past (135). In an epiphanous self-transcending moment Jenkin observes, "I'm a slug . . . I move altogether if I move at all, I only stretch myself out a little, a very little" (136). Like Father McAlister, Jenkin is a reader of hearts (286). However, the priest makes a secret of his loss of faith in God, Jesus and the Church in order to live the life he loves (522ff) saving the souls of the fallen. Jenkin's life is the inner struggle to be true to his faith in humanity in spite of its moral ambivalence.

Dead Fathers, Lost Parrots and the Irretrievable Past

In Rose's exclamation: "How you men do live in the past!" (18), Murdoch inscribes her concern about the moral life, the power of memory and the freedom to desire. Determined by patriarchy, the past privileges a moral economy that is not responsive to the reality of the late twentieth century. In *The Book and the Brotherhood* Murdoch not only reshapes the significance of 'the Fall', she also reflects on the decline of the power of patriarchy—the law of the father—and its implications for the future. The book and the brotherhood, *per se*, are emblematic of the failure of patriarchy and of the traditional assumptions that power is located in the revealed Word, the wisdom of the Patriarchs, the law of the Fathers, the classics of Western thought, the literary canon as well as in the cult of the religious and intellectual priesthood. Logocentrism and absolute truth-claims provided those in power with a sense of security and assurance of salvation. Crimond's distinctly private book, Gerard's unwritten book, Jean's unpublished book, Rose's unread books all bear witness to the failure of logocentrism to speak to the real and ordinary in human experience. Books become surrogate offsprings, the brotherhood, a surrogate family and community. In the end neither offers adequate insights into the nature of moral activity. Murdoch's rereading of these traditional assumptions deflates the pretense of privilege, resists the comfort of nostalgia, rejects patriarchy and creates the conditions for a more inclusive, just and caring world. For some the fear of change is paralyzing and masquerades as veneration of the past with its illusory innocence. For Murdoch, the past must be grieved for as a condition for the possibility of the future.

The icon of the dead, lost or absent father—whether biological, spiritual or intellectual—represents the haunting of the present by an ideology in decline. Through the lives of her characters Murdoch probes the models of hierarchy and power including the father as head of the family, the master-student relationship, the philosopher-scholar and the brotherhood. She suggests that these models are sustained by a nostalgia for the absolute and require external rather than internal validation making them morally suspect. Several characters are defined by the presence or absence of their fathers including Gerard, Tamar, Violet and Crimond. However, Murdoch's detailed exploration of the death of Gerard's father and its effect on Gerard is particularly instructive. In addition, her introduction of Gerard's beloved parrot, Grey, which together with the image of the father and son is suggestive of a transfigured or transmuted Trinity invites speculation. Is the father/Gerard/Grey Trinity a parody of the Christian symbol or is it an example of Murdoch's reshaping of a failed symbol of absolute power and perfect unity? Does the experience of grieving the loss of both his father and Grey allow Gerard to recover their importance without being determined by the power he ascribes to them?

While attending the Commem Ball, Gerard is told of his father's death by his sister Patricia who calls him at the rooms of Levquist, his former Classics Professor (54). The connection between his real father and his intellectual father is telling. Both men connect Gerard to the past to which he chooses to be bound. Part of the tradition of the Ball is a visit to Levquist's rooms where the "old traditional liturgy" (23) of their mentor-student days is reenacted. Levquist tests Gerard's recollection of Latin and Greek, admonishes him for not doing something with his life and recites his views on history, philosophy and politics. As he touches Levquist's books, Gerard is overcome with an "agonizing sense of the past. It's gone, he thought, the past, it is irrevocable and beyond mending and far away, and yet it is here, blowing at one like the wind." (25). The presence of the past haunts Gerard's life. In Murdoch's moral landscape Gerard's anguish, his clinging to old familiar patterns, his acceptance of external laws, his resistance to change betrays his unwillingness to disengage from a patriarchal ideology whose value and significance are in decline.

Murdoch marks the end of patriarchy by the absence of biological and intellectual descendants. Gerard's father dies without a grandson to continue the family name. Similarly, Levquist, who is among the last of his generation of classics scholars, dies without passing the tradition to the next generation ((582). Neither Gerard not Jenkin follow in his footsteps. Similarly, Crimond never marries and remains childless, as does Jenkin.

With Duncan's case Murdoch rehearses the ironies of human life. Duncan grieves his childless marriage with Jean oblivious of Tamar's decision to abort the fetus he fathered (456-7). If children signify continuity, their absence marks the end of business as usual. The future is glimpsed as a mere thought in the minds of Lily Boyne and Gulliver Ashe who consider the possibility of children as they prepare for their wedding (599). Their marriage, however, is blessed by the magic spells of Lily's grandmother who practiced witchcraft (607).

Gerard's grief for his father is compromised by the unexpressed anger, guilt and love he feels toward him. As he sits looking at the face of his dead father, he is overcome with remorse for all the things he hadn't said and hadn't resolved (58). At the heart of the matter is his anger at his father for having lied to him about the death of his beloved parrot, Grey, which joined their household when he was eleven. Gerard shared the care of Grey with his father since neither his mother nor sister found the parrot as compelling as he did. Returning from boarding school, Gerard is told that Grey has been sold to a pet store which in turn sold him to "some very nice people" (62). As his mother and sister recount this story, his father's discomfort marked by silence and averted eyes leaves Gerard convinced that Grey is dead and that his father didn't protect the parrot from the women. The matter was never spoken of again. Although his mother thought that the Grey incident was over, his father felt that his betrayal of Gerard was unforgivable and experienced Gerard's anger as an "indelible icy line" (62) embedded in his every act of kindness. Both father and son, articulating neither remorse not anger, choose to allow the death of Grey to remain an irreconcilable difference between them.

Gerard's inner life is absorbed by his attachment to the unforgiven pain of the past. The conspiracy of silence and secrecy that Gerard and his father tacitly accept as the condition of their relationship leaves them both bereaved. By choosing to be determined by the past—which in Gerard' case is his emotional life at the age of eleven—the reality of the present is deferred. His life-long obsession with Grey, his inability to forgive either his father for lying or himself for still caring prevent him from engaging fully with those he loves. If his father was ineffectual in preventing the death of Grey and in seeking to be reconciled with his son, Gerard's sense of having been betrayed leaves him equally ineffectual and incapable of passion whether sexual, intellectual or spiritual. Accusing him of indifference, Crimond tells Gerard, "You've never really cared for anything except for your parrot" (298).

The grief Gerard experiences over the loss of Grey and the death of his father becomes a meditation on the sense of loss he feels about his own life, its ordinariness and its loneliness. Healing comes but gradually, shaped by sorrow. He begins to see the unreality of his desire for unconditional love which allows him to overcome his initial resistance to owning his grief and feeling its profound effect on his life. Reflecting Murdoch's belief that freedom "is a function of the progressive attempt to see a particular object clearly" (SG 23), like Murdoch's exemplary mother-in-law who tries to see her daughter-in-law as she really is (SG 23), Gerard begins to see his father in a different light. Insofar as his starting point is unresolved anger and a sense of betrayal, he moves at first to the other extreme. He awakens from a dream about his father in which he hands Gerard something wrapped in a newspaper "with the words, 'It's dead' (276)," and is overwhelmed by the sense of missing "his father's absolute love" (277). Absolute love, however, presupposes a god-like nature which places unrealistic and self-defeating expectations on an imperfect human father. Before he allows himself to abandon his nostalgic desire for the absolute, Gerard is shaken to the depth of his being by the death of Jenkin (487ff). Having risked loving Jenkin and suggesting that they live together, his death brings Gerard to the edges of despair. He displaces onto this death other long-denied sorrows including his feelings about the loss Grey and his father as well as of Sinclair, the love of his youth. To complete the circle of loss, Gerard is informed by Duncan about the death of Levquist, "who had also been his father" (583).

Confrontation with death and the recognition of his own mortality (584) and the intensity of his grief brings Gerard to a new—if temporary— level of self-understanding. His epiphany begins as he recalls the distinction Levquist once made between Jenkin and himself, a distinction informed by Murdoch's own vision of virtue and living a moral life. Levquist values Jenkin because he "walks the path, he exists where he is" (585). Gerard's meditation sustains this image as he recalls that indeed,

Jenkin always walked the path, with others, wholly engaged in wherever he happened to be, fully existing, fully real at every point, looking about him with friendly curiosity. Whereas I have always felt reality was elsewhere, exalted and indifferent and alone, upon some misty mountain peak which I, among the very few, could actually see, though of course never reach . . . while I enjoyed my superior vision, my consciousness of height and distance, the gulf below, the height above, and a sense of pleasurable unworthiness shared only by the elect—self-satisfied Platonism, Augustinian masochism, Levquist called it . . . . Now . . . I *feel* at last alone—and the mountain peak, that hanging on, that looking up, was it all an illusion (585)?

Recognizing the hubris implicit in his construction of an absolute reality that protects him from messiness of ordinary life, Gerard begins to let go of the need for absolutes—whether Platonic or patriarchal—and to rethink his relationship with his father whom he sees in a more just and caring light.

Images of a father who either betrayed his love and trust or who loved absolutely and unconditionally are supplanted by images of an ordinary man. Gerard "began to think about his father, and what a gentle, kind, patient, good man he had been, and how he had given way, out of love, to his wife sacrificing not only his wishes but sometimes even his own principles. All that must have caused him pain, and his children too, never quite in tune with him, must have grieved him . . ." (589). Forgiving his father, he also forgives himself for his ordinariness and begins to think that his love for Rose is real and worthy of attention (589).

Gerard's transformation is problematized by his refusal to accept the priority of the real and by his retreat to the ideal. Once again his sorrow over the death of Grey returns him to his child-like need for the security of the absolute. He decides, "I've got to go on, or rather . . . *up*, because I am not going to abandon my life-image, not for Levquist, not even for Jenkin. *It is* up there, solemn, changeless and alone, indifferent, pure . . . how separate from my corrupt being" (590). In images suggestive of mystical union, Gerard sees himself "shrivel before . . . an indifferent flame" to which he responds that he will indeed write "the book" (590). Murdoch, with more than a hint of parody, leaves Gerard dreaming of Grey and the reader with a sense that nostalgia for the absolute may be in decline but for some remains a powerful source of comfort and security. Exhausted by grief and spiritual renewal, Gerard dreams that he is "standing on the mountainside holding an open book upon whose page was written *Dominus Illuminatio Mea*—and from far far above an angel was descending in the form of a great grey parrot with loving clever eyes and the parrot perched upon the book and spread out its grey and scarlet wings and the parrot was the book" (591). Allowing his inner life to be consumed by a narcissistic focus on the self, Gerard remains in a dream living by the book.

Gerard's struggle to live a moral life speaks of Murdoch's attentiveness to the ambiguities and ambivalences of experience. Just as he wants to glue together the pieces of the porcelain Staffordshire dog he accidentally broke (583, 590), he also wants to put the pieces of his own life together so that it can once again resemble the tradition into which he was born and which he desires to perpetuate. His surrender to the traditional models of patriarchal power neither denies the value of his struggle—regardless of his choice to privilege the absolute over the real—nor does it deny the significance of enkin's choice to live fully in the present. Murdoch doesn't condemn Gerard for his inability to transcend the past. Rather, she offsets his fears and self-doubts by the lives of others for whom patriarchy is not only in decline but exorcised from their lives.

Conclusion: Of Snails, Witches and a Moral Life

In *Breaking the Fall*, responding to Eagleton's comment that "women will tend to have a more inward, bodily relationship to script," Detweiler writes, "If this is so, the Western societies gradually overcoming patriarchy may look to women's texts as *embodying* what is nothing less than an extended sacred moment in our history: our passage from the violence of male domination in our sexual politics to the equanimity of compassion that can come through authentic female-male partnership" (54). *The Book and the Brotherhood* is representative of the kind of text Detweiler describes. In the process of reclaiming the Fall and reflecting on the waning power of patriarchy, Murdoch recovers the power of women who reenact spells learned from their witch-grandmothers in order to bring about authentic partnerships.

All of Murdoch's characters are engaged in the struggle to live a moral life and succeed in various degrees. Jenkin perhaps comes closest to her image of the humble man whose self-less respect for reality allows him to be loving and just toward others (SG 95). Gerard, on the other hand, resists reality and, despite his well-intentioned efforts, remains in a metaphysical fog. Duncan and Crimond make peace with their limits and live somewhat compromised lives that respect reality from a safe distance. For Duncan this means a house in France and a loving marriage with Jean sustained by secrets and mutual guilt (525). For Crimond it means remaining socially isolated but intellectually engaged (565). Jean and Rose also choose marginally satisfying lives that assure security, provide companionship and imperfect love. Jean returns to Duncan, accepts his forgiving love and departs for France putting some distance between herself and her guilt (525). Rose reinvests her energies as healer and enabler in Gerard who pledges his love and invites her to live with him and act as his research assistant (573ff). Murdoch's representation of the relationships between Duncan and Jean, Gerard and Rose illustrates the tension implicit in moments of cultural transition. All four reflect a strong connection with tradition and the value system that informs it while at the same time recognizing that things are changing. Murdoch leaves it to the outsiders, Lily Boyne and Gulliver Ashe, to set the agenda for the next generation. Somewhat younger than the brotherhood and only marginally connected to the traditions of Oxford, Lily and Gull (conceivably an analog to the sainted parrot, Grey) with whose marriage Murdoch ends the story, reanimate the traditional moral of the story with magic spells and mystical snails.

If Lily and Gull are to 'live happily ever after', their anticipated future together is informed by their awareness that they are both similar to and different from the generation of the brotherhood. Their marriage signifies a recognition of social conventions and celebrates their participation in them on their own terms based on their own inner sense of the rightness of things. Their lives reflect both the dominance of patriarchy in sexual politics as well as their attempt to create a relationship that speaks of compassion, care and love. Murdoch's characterization of Lily and Gull is both whimsical and wise. Their struggles lead to an assortment of misjudgments and provide opportunities to fall back on habitual behaviors that rehearse the past. In the end they choose to risk, to trust their inner voices and to move forward with their lives. Murdoch situates their hope within the framework of the maligned and marginalized history of women's power and women's morality. Therefore, like other feminists, she "does not offer a program or dogma, a new Law for the future, but she does offer a new vision of human nature, reality and the socio-political arrangement." Her vision concerns the priority of the inner life that is actively engaged in becoming attentive, just and loving toward others.

Lily—a feminist, an eccentric, a witch—is connected with the brotherhood through Jean, who fell in love with her during their women's lib and yoga days (31), and through Rose, who thought she was common but admired her being "tough and imagined her to be 'worldly' in ways which remained, for Rose, mysterious and obscure" (31). Lily inherits her husband's money in an out-of-court settlement with his family after he died in an accident. Squandering some, investing some, she manages to indulge her expensive taste and help others. Gull is an unemployed London University graduate who is trying to reconcile his assumption about class privilege and entitlement with the realization that he needs a job. As part of his attempt to discover himself, in his younger days he frequented leather and chain gay bars where he had originally heard of but had not met Gerard. His connection with the brotherhood is through Gerard whom he meets when Gerard is invited to financially rescue "a little *avant-garde* theater" with which Gull had been connected. Gerard subsequently invited Gull to be part of the committee concerned with Crimond's book. Gull's flirtatious feelings toward him, however, are not reciprocated. If the Commem Ball is an occasion of Duncan's fall, it is also occasion of Gull's dancing with and falling for Lily who comes to the ball with Crimond but leaves without him (38).

Both Lily and Gull feel that they are the exotic 'other', the misfit. At first, thinking that Gull was still part of Gerard's circle, Lily sees Gull as "a social asset" (146) and enjoys his company. Only gradually does she fall in love with him. Since their relationship starts off as a friendship it allows them to freely exchange stories about their dreadful childhoods, abusive parents and efforts to escape (146). Lily's father abandoned her, her mother—a Roman Catholic who lived in fear of hell—was an alcoholic and foisted the responsibility of raising her onto her grandmother who was a witch (146). Lily, in turn, felt guilty for having abandoned her dying mother (207). In her characterization of Lily's grandmother, Murdoch reclaims part of the repressed history of women's power. Witchcraft, as Lily instructs Gull, "is an old religion, far older than Christianity, it's about power" (143). Her grandmother's ancestry is unclear. All Lily remembers is that she hated Christianity, the religion of her parents and represented herself as either a gypsy or as Jewish, thereby magnifying her difference. Grandmother was an exceedingly well-read wise woman, a mid-wife, an herbalist, a healer and rainmaker. She was as feared as she was needed. Although Gull remains skeptical about her powers, Lily assumes their reality.

In the nine months period (suggestive of gestation) between the Commem Ball and their wedding, both Lily and Gull experience a number of crises through which they reconcile themselves with the past and with the unmet expectations of present and begin to imagine the future. For Gull, the crisis of joblessness is resolved as a result of his encounter with a snail at King's Cross station; for Lily, her determination to be truthful with Crimond about her love for him leads to freedom from illusion. In each case Murdoch celebrates their growing sense of self-worth, their ability to see the significance of others and accept that "[o]ther people are . . . mysterious" (606).

Lily goes to see Crimond the day before her marriage to Gull in order to confess her long years of love for him and her desire to be his slave (597). Her secret infatuation began before her first marriage when she heard Crimond give a public lecture. During the years of her depression following her husband's death, "Crimond played for her . . . the role of God. Here was one relationship that required of her only the best . . . . It was also . . . a source of fear" (152). Lily's conflicted response to Crimond is emblematic of Murdoch's perception that relationships require a clarity of vision which emerges out of years of struggle. Her final visit to Crimond is defined by fear and a clinging to the illusions and dreams of the past. She sees herself as "a little worthless person" (597) whose life is entirely contingent on Crimond's acceptance of her. Telling her that she is neither little nor worthless and that he neither shares her affection, nor does he have something to give her, Crimond sends her off to be happy in the real world with Gull (598-9). In Lily's confession and Crimond's absolution, Murdoch sees the possibility of freedom. Absolved of her desire to be defined by 'God', Lily is ready to continue to plan their wedding, define herself and their 'real' life together (601, 606-7).

Gull's intended trip to Newcastle to find a job—to which Lily had objected—turned out differently than he had anticipated and he feels he owes Lily the truth before their wedding. At King's Cross while awaiting the train he finds a snail that changes his life (603). Developing an instant personal attachment to the snail, Gull decides that he can't just leave it there, nor can he keep it in a hotel room, so he sets off to find it a home in Hyde Park. In process of locating a safe place for the snail, he encounters Justin Byng who not only listens to the whole snail story, he helps Gull provide it with a safe haven and, after hearing about Gull's state of unemployment, offers him a job in a stage design studio (603). Gull wonders at the sheer chance that determines life, whereas Lily wonders "[i]f it *was* chance" (605).

Underscoring the difference between fantasy and imagination, between secrets that sustain dreams and those that are the necessary condition for love, Murdoch reaffirms the power of magic spells and the ancient rituals of women's power. Thinking about Gull's confession about the snail, Lily remembers that during one of her visits to Rose's estate, she too found a snail sitting on her dressing table. "As she took it out into the garden, worrying about Gull, she had mumbled to it some words from an old snail-charm which her grandmother used to recite" (607). Marveling at the coincidence and at the mystery of life, Lily decides not to tell Gull about her own encounter with a snail because, given "the vicissitudes of family life, a little extra secret power might come in handy . . . and as her grandmother has told her, power depends on silence. I'm a witch! I'm a witch! thought Lily—grandma did say it was hereditary" (607). Lily's magic, like that of Murdoch, works because it is motivated by love.

NOTES

1. Iris Murdoch, *The Book and the Brotherhood* (New York: Viking Press, 1988). Parenthetical references refer to page numbers.

2. Iris Murdoch, "The Idea of Perfection," *The Sovereignty of Good* (London: Routledge & Kegan Paul, 1970). Hereafter cited as SG with page number.

3. Robert Detweiler, *Breaking the Fall: Religious Readings of Contemporary Fiction* (San Francisco: Harper & Row Publishers, 1989). Hereafter cited as BF with page number.

4. Allison M. Jaggar, "Feminist Ethics: Projects, Problems, Prospects," Claudia Card, ed., *Feminist Ethics* (Lawrence, KS: University Press of Kansas, 1991), pp.78-105. Jaggar cites Iris Murdoch along with Simone Weil and Edith Stein as philosophers, albeit noncanonical, whose works lead into feminists ethical theory (78). See also, Marilyn French, *Beyond Power: On Women, Men, and Morals* (New York: Ballantine Books, 1985).

5. Allison M. Jaggar, "Feminist Ethics."

6. Allison M. Jaggar, "Feminist Ethics." pp. 97-98.

7. Allison M. Jaggar, "Feminist Ethics."

8. Iris Murdoch, "The Sovereignty of Good Over Other Concepts," in *The Sovereignty of Good*, (London: Routledge & Kegan Paul, 1970), p. 102ff.

9. Marilyn French, *Beyond Power*, p. 536.

"A Mighty Fortress Is Our Something"

The Gaining of Loss in Russell Hoban's Creative Hermeneutics

DANIEL C. NOEL

A s I have recounted in an earlier essay,[1] it was in late May of 1983 that I stood before a wall painting in Canterbury Cathedral and had a middle-aged Englishwoman, a stranger, sidle over to me and ask, in a whisper, "Are you here because of *Riddley Walker*?"

Riddley Walker, Russell Hoban's 1980 novel about a post-nuclear dystopia of the far future in the Kentish countryside around Canterbury, England, had indeed brought me there to the cathedral to help form this little community of two. Such is the power of a fictive narrative like Hoban's that it can foster actions and attitudes in the factual lives of its readers, feeding their need for meaning in a time widely believed to be bereft of it. This is a rough magic that I should like to call, in Hoban's case, "creative hermeneutics," a term I borrow from the historian of religions Mircea Eliade and employ so as to celebrate the sort of heterodox historiography into which his novels implicate us as a story-reading community, attentive to the relations between Hoban's characters and *their* (fictive) communities. Although I shall need to allude occasionally to his earlier novels, I want to concentrate upon his three most recent: *Riddley Walker* (1980), *Pilgermann* (1983), and *The Medusa Frequency* (1987).[2] A major reason for my selecting this focus is that I can thereby take as my point of departure Robert Detweiler's discussion of *Riddley Walker* in the final chapter of his *Breaking the Fall*, where he treats it along with Margaret Atwood's *The Handmaid's Tale* in/to a "religious reading."[3]

While *Riddley Walker*'s creative hermeneutics led me and an English stranger to the Canterbury wall painting, it was conversely the image-idea presented by this painting, Hoban has said, that brought the world of the novel into being through him. In his Acknowledgments he recalls: "On

March 14th, 1974 I visited Canterbury Cathedral for the first time and saw Dr. E.W. Tristram's reconstruction of the fifteenth-century wall painting *The Legend of Saint Eustace*." He began the novel two months later and completed it five-and-a-half years thereafter. More particularly, he informs us in an interview that, as he puts it, "when I saw this painting, I think the thing jumped into my head pretty well complete: that of a time when our civilization is gone, our technology is gone, and the inheritors of the wasteland that has been created have a traveling puppet show to carry on the state religion, such as it is."[4]

The state religion of *Riddley Walker*'s remote future is, understandably, a subject of Detweiler's religious reading. He engages its myths and rituals in the context of a culture that has survived, with bleakly reduced means, a nuclear apocalypse two millennia earlier in our late-twentieth-century present. This is an apocalypse dimly understood and inaccurately, if evocatively, conveyed in "The Eusa Story," a mythic account in thirty-three verses which is ritually enacted by the puppet performances. These are then interpreted by the shamanic "connexion men" at each settlement, and one of these shamans is the novel's twelve-year-old narrator-protagonist, the Riddley Walker of the title.

Riddley is Russell Hoban's mouthpiece for a language so far from standard written English that the reader is virtually forced to sound out the strange but generally phonetic spellings of the words on the page. Detweiler notes the "deceleration" that Riddley's narration imposes on the reading process, and sees a benefit: "It enables one to enter into the fiction of a regressed future society, whereby the very ponderousness of puzzling out the dialect provides a parallel to the confused conceptualizing of the characters themselves."[5]

This is certainly true in my own slow reading of the text, but the phonetic factor points to a further advantage of Hoban's language: sounding out the bizarrely-written sentences replicates to some degree the oral-aural communication of the storytelling community that, Detweiler points out, fiction-writing and -reading lacks and attempts to restore. Hoban has told his interviewer "I'm a big sounds person. I often walk about making sounds aloud and listening to them."[6] This still seems quite privatized; nevertheless, the potential for a kind of community exists for readers of *Riddley Walker* in greater measure, I believe, because of its defamiliarizing phonetic orthography. Indeed, in teaching the novel I ask students to take turns reading aloud, for example by each reading a verse of The Eusa Story as we go around the room. In a small class it is uncanny how, after two or three turns, students will become more proficient oral readers as they are also, so they report, drawn more deeply into Riddley's religious world. The students who read aloud teach one another, in the hearing, how to do so, and our experience of the novel begins to simulate—if not constitute—participation in a mythic ritual while it adumbrates what a believing community might feel like.

Of course, *what* a community believes is also a factor to consider in a religious reading. Detweiler rightly indicates that in *Riddley Walker* the ritual recitation and acting-out of The Eusa Story comprise as much a politically repressive maneuver as a genuine effort to tell the mystery of the society's nuclear origins. What is needed is what Detweiler calls "corrective stories," and these young Riddley tries to provide as the narrative concludes. Still, The Eusa Story can be an implicit corrective for *us* as a reading community to whom nuclear holocaust is a doom yet impending. This garbled creation narrative recycles the imagery of the Canterbury wall painting of St. Eustace (Eusa) in order to grope for an historical explanation of the "Bad Time," when technology in the service of war-making destroyed itself and triggered the devolution that Riddley and his cohorts have inherited in the fourth millennium CE. Since the Bad Time following the nuclear cataclysm in the novel took place in our present or immediate future, The Eusa Story becomes a cautionary lesson for our own current history together, well worth pondering as we learn what the dark side of "the new world order" might be.

But it is not only our present that this futuristic novel informs. The centrality of The Eusa Story in Hoban's narrative can also shape our sense of the past, our community of memory. Here the confused account of two thousand-year-old events implies that *our* interpretations of two thousand-year-old events—including the historico-mythic events of the biblical past—may be similarly flawed. In this inference by the religious reader the ideal of representation and its supposed successes are slyly deconstructed. With this reading experience we take to heart just how creative Hoban's hermeneutics of history can be—not only in The Eusa Story's fabrications woven around the hagiography of St. Eustace but also in the egregiously misconstrued reading one of the characters gives to the caption of the Canterbury wall painting, the only written document in twentieth-century English in the novel.

Reflecting upon a phrase from the caption, the character Goodparley says "Any how I wer reading over this here Legend like I use to do some times and I come to 'the figure of the crucified Saviour'." Recalling a New Testament reference (though none of its provenance or context) which he expresses as "A littl salting and no saver," Goodparley conflates "saver" (savor) with "Saviour" and then confuses "Crucified" with the "cruciboal" used in the society's primitive attempts at "chemistery." In one of these blundering insights he constructs a meaning for the standard-English phrase. As he concludes for Riddley, "so 'the figure of the crucified Saviour', is the number of the salt de vydit in 2 parts in the cruciboal and radiating lite coming acrost on it. The salt and the saver. 1ce [once] youve got that salt youre on your way to the woal chemistery and fizzics of it" (128-29).

This, says Detweiler, borrowing the novel's terminology, "[is] 'terpitation' with a vengeance, in which any explanation, no matter how far-fetched, is better than none at all. . . ." And while he recognizes that "all this may be a more than faint parody of the manner in which reckless exegetes exploit religious texts toward any conclusion,"[7] he may not be reckoning sufficiently with how broad an indictment of *all* biblical exegesis Hoban's hermeneutic amounts to—how de(con)structive it can be in creating an alternative viewpoint and vision, particularly as it decenters received pretentions to historical representation.

Riddley Walker even casts aspersions upon our confident sense of where we are right now historically between what we think has happened and what we expect may or may not happen in times to come. Another member of the community Hoban's novel has created, the English Jungian psychoanalyst and essayist David Holt, extrapolates startlingly but persuasively from the novel's revisionist historiography: there must be events *already* in the history of Western thought and culture, he suggests, that are tantamount to the nuclear holocaust we fear from the future. Holt pursues this radical ramification of *Riddley Walker* by speculating on possibly fateful developments in alchemical symbology and its aspirations, in the Christian theology of the Eucharist, or in the modern philosophy of science as glossed by Whitehead.[8] He comes to no settled position concerning such possibilities, for this is "deep play" of the sort Detweiler recommends—perhaps deep *dark* play in Holt's case—and it interacts with a polyvalent text that conveys, as Detweiler expresses it, "an ingenuous drive to *believe* and interpret in the absence of real comprehension."[9] The larger implication of this religious reading is that through such play fresh insights on besetting cultural issues, including provocative re-arrangements of our accustomed *Heilsgeschichte*, have been made available to a community of readers called into being by its reading.

In 1982 Hoban was asked if *Riddley Walker* had become the cult book it had been predicted to become. He first pleaded that it was too early to tell, then granting that "the amount of feedback I've got indicates that I've made a breakthrough in the United States in that its got a lot of attention and a lot of good reviews. . . . A whole lot of attention, so that now I'm known there where I wasn't before." This has led, he added, to a communal impact few novelists can claim: "I had a letter from a Methodist minister in Montana with an adopted child. He and his wife named it Riddley Walker O'Connell. So I'm quite moved by that. I sent him the first pages of the first draft." [10]

Russell Hoban is like his young hero who walks in riddles with a kind of post-apocalyptic negative capability—what Detweiler, following Heidegger, terms *Gelassenheit*, or releasement.[11] The novelist, too, is a "connexion man," very much a social role today as in Riddley's future world, and one Hoban has publicly applied to himself: "I always feel as if the novelist is a shaman who is functioning for his tribe, he's offering his experience for the use of the rest of the tribe."[12]

I am most pleased to be a member of his tribe and to learn from his releasement, but the foregoing is a mere beginning of what might qualify as a religious reading of Hoban's most recent novels, little more than a supplement to Detweiler's discussion of *Riddley Walker*. What he calls for in such a reading is a "ludic interactive response" producing "participatory interpretations" both "*gelassen* and *gesellig*"—the latter term indicating the communality so central to this approach—and these together countering any *oppositional* interpretations with "a pleasurable interchange made valuable precisely by a refusal to simplify and manipulate the text into something else, another statement."[13] By conversing with *Pilgermann* and *The Medusa Frequency* at some length I would hope to extend Detweiler's process in an experimental fashion, because I see these two texts offering as much to an understanding of the history of our religions as a religious or theological discourse has to offer in illuminating the novels. Within this more even-handed and relaxed interplay of reader and text, however, Hoban's two latest narratives proffer pleasures and perspectives not entirely anticipated by readings of *Riddley Walker*.

Like the latter, *Pilgermann* is also named for its narrator. Actually, "Pilgermann," or pilgrim, is a somewhat arbitrary name for a ghostly collection of waves and particles who narrates from roughly the present the story of his life "in the shape of a man," a Jew, in the eleventh century, in a Mediterranean town (11). Where *Riddley Walker* dealt primarily with the future, Hoban's next novel explores the past. Where the religious world of the earlier novel was magical, animistic, pagan (notwithstanding its dealings with St. Eustace and Canterbury Cathedral), and occasionally mystical, the later one thrusts us into the world of the Crusades, with the three "religions of the Book" in deadly contention for the sacred spaces of the Middle East.

In his comparison of *Riddley Walker* to Atwood's *Handmaid's Tale* Robert Detweiler decides that "they are narratives of and about the impossibility of narrative in a world that refuses to acknowledge its own apocalyptic mode."[14] Comparing *Riddley Walker* to Hoban's own later novels reveals other aspects of this apocalypse of narrative, starting with a text that should be most hospitable to a religious reading. *Pilgermann* not only originated with its author's visit to the ruined Crusader's stronghold of Montfort in Galilee, but it takes as its three epigraphs verses from the Hebrew Bible, the New Testament, and the Quran. More enigmatic is Hoban's acknowledgment here that "*Riddley Walker* left me in a place where there was further action pending and this further action was waiting for the element that would precipitate it into the time and place of its own story"(9). Apparently the visit to Montfort provided this element. But what is the "further action" pending from *Riddley Walker*? And how does *Pilgermann* continue such action in a time and place so far removed from post-apocalyptic England? Can a religious reading concerned with communities of faith respond to such questions in a spirit of deep play?

It turns out that the term "action" turns up rather often in Hoban's novels, usually in contexts laden with metaphysical purport. On the first page of *Pilgermann* the ghostly narrator tries to tell us what has become of his existence since the death of his body some 900 years earlier:

> Ah! the flickering in the darkness, the passage of what is called time!
> I don't know what I am now. A whispering out of the dust. Dried blood on a sword and the sword has crumbled into rust and the wind has blown the rust away but still I am, still I am, still I am of the world, still I have something to say, how could it be otherwise, nothing comes to an end, the action never stops, it only changes, the ringing of the steel is sung in the stillness of the stone (11).

Several things can be inferred in conversation with this early passage: the narrator's skepticism about the reality of time, at least the profane time of duration, and his self-conscious uncertainty about his own state along with his sense of what could be understood as the conservation of energy, the bio-cosmic action that never stops. Additionally, the reference to something going on "in the stillness of the stone" is another Hobanesque crotchet. Several novels and interviews allude to the relation between stillness and motion, a dynamic he imagines in terms of gender but more often conveys in the imagery of, loosely speaking, modern physics: the particles moving in the stone (which latter usually serves the portrayal of duration), or, in the words of The Eusa Story's mad scientist Mr Clevver: "Yu mus fyn the wud in the hart uv the stoan & yu wil fyn it by the dansing in the stoan & thay partickler traks" (30)—where "hart" generates in turn the imagery of the stag hunt that I have discussed in some detail in my aforementioned article.[15]

A few pages later, as Pilgermann moves into the story of his life as a Jew during the Crusades, describing his assignation with the wife of the Christian tax collector in his town, he pauses for a further metaphysical observation: "That this man should have the management of such a woman is absolutely scientific in its manifestation of that asymmetry without which there would be no motion in the universe. Yes, such a coupling imparts spin to the cosmos, it creates action, it utterly negates stasis" (14). Not only is such universal action produced by/manifested in unlikely marriages, however. It also shows through in the darker interactions between Christians—particularly German Christians—and Jews. Despite its Mediterranean setting Pilgermann (itself a German name) frequently employs German to designate people and things Christian. Our Jewish narrator's tryst takes place, for instance, on Keinjudenstrasse in the Christian quarter. The tax-collector's wife, on the other hand, though certainly Christian, is named Sophia, as if Christian women offer Jewish men mystical gnosis as much as anti-Semitic threat.

Here an autobiographical factor cannot be ignored: Hoban is a Jew, religiously non-observant, in a second marriage to a German Christian woman named Gundel. This is reflected in another variation on the theme of relationships between Jewish men and German Christian women. In *The Lion of Boaz-Jachin and Jachin-Boaz*, a 1973 novel, Gretel, the Jewish mapmaker Jachin-Boaz's second wife (in London, where Hoban moved in 1969 and met Gundel), ponders how she met him:

> Here's another one. Perhaps we could have lunch one day soon. Yes, let's have lunch. My people killed six million of you. He had brought her a single rose. A yellow one that day, red ones later. . . . Now his haunted face awoke beside her every morning. A mighty fortress, sang Gretel in her mind, imposing her will on the choir. . . . I knew that I'd be happy with him, unhappy with him—everything, and more of everything than ever before in my life. Something there is that won't die. A mighty fortress is our something (117).

Gretel's Lutheran version of the unending "action" of the universe sounds libidinal as well as theistic, perhaps giving the last laugh to that "Godless Jew," Freud. Meanwhile, Pilgermann, the Mediterranean Jew with a German name, has endured the stillness in the garden at the foot of the ladder, then climbed up to find his Wisdom in bed with Christian Sophia: "The centre of time is, as I have said, the waiting. This is now off the center, this is the motion of everything, the action of the universe, the destined world-line of the soul, the living heart of the mystery" (16).

The cost of Pilgermann's sexual fulfillment of a mystical quest is high. He loses his sex the next morning when a Christian mob castrates him on his way back from No-Jew Street. Sexless in a second circumcision, a painful new covenant, he nevertheless continues his quest and has more to do with mystery. Indeed, his mystical experience is heightened, beginning with a vision, as he lies bleeding on the cobblestones, of high-flying storks, "circling like those intersecting circles of tiny writing sometimes done by copyists with texts of the Holy Scriptures" (19). This metaphor of celestial inscription serves to remind us of the three scriptural quotations preceding the novel's main text. The one from the Hebrew Bible, Jeremiah 8:7, exclaims that "Yes, the stork in the heaven/Knoweth her appointed times;/ . . . But My people know not/The ordinance of the LORD," while the New Testament verses if Luke 17:20-21, Jesus's response to the Pharisees' question of when the kingdom will come: ". . . behold for the kingdom of God/within you is." Surah 96:6-7 then balances this with a condemnation of humans' prideful self-sufficiency. The drift of the three passages chosen is that expectation of the divine presence must be mystically perennial rather than millennially time-bound, but it should not be tied literalistically to human merit or psychospiritual heroics.

But all this is only prelude to our play with *Pilgermann*. After calling out, somewhat cynically, to the God of Israel and receiving no reply, Pilgermann has a vision of Christ with the eyes of a lion (lions being prominent among Hoban's important animal images):

> He was no one in whom I had any belief but there he was and there was no mistaking who he was.
>
> I looked at him and listened to his silence for awhile. When I was able to speak I said, "You're not the one I was calling."
>
> He said, "I'm the one who came through. I'm the one you'll talk to from now on." . . .
>
> "Until now I've dealt with your father."
>
> He said, "Until now you've dealt with no one and no one's dealt with you."
>
> I said, "Is this the Day of Reckoning then?"
>
> He said, "Every day is the Day of Reckoning" (20-21).

This communication, which could be called serio-comic, is far from clear-cut. It continues for seven pages and harbors many a metaphysical nuance, including the theological message that God is an It, not a He—or a Father—and is gone if not dead. Noteworthy in this regard is the return of the term "action": Christ says that "'after me it's the straight action and no more dressing up,'" and to the question of whether there will be a Last Judgment there is a similarly arcane reply: "'The straight action *is* the last judgment. . .'"(21).

Avoiding any temptation to oppose Hoban's multivocal text with a monocentric interpretation, we are still entitled to ask what this *might* mean. Eliade offers one possibility for construing "the straight action." He writes that for the Christian, "the greatest of all miracles having been, in fact, the Incarnation itself, all that *which was clearly manifested as miraculous before* Jesus Christ is of no further use or meaning *after* his coming." Eliade also notes suggestively that for every Christian "the paradise regained—may be attained *from this moment. The time to come* announced by the Christ is already accessible, and for him who has regained it, history ceases to be."[16] We have to do here, it seems, with the immediate and direct heirophany of Christ's saving and judging power, and an escape for every Christian from 'the terror of history."

Except, of course, that Pilgermann is not even a devout Jew, let alone a believing Christian. On the other hand, such religious ambivalence probably accords with and helps to consolidate the community reading his story (while complexifying or suggesting an alternative to Eliade's formulae).

In the midst of his vision, walking with Jesus through the Jewish quarter where the Christian mob has recently rampaged, Pilgermann sees on the blood-stained cobbles, as he voices it, "patterns I have not noticed before: there are twisting serpents, shifting pyramids, I see the face of a lion that comes and goes" (21-22). This is not the last time a lion's face will appear in "patterns" that become another part of Hoban's preoccupation with issues of stillness, motion, and the action of being. And it is almost as if, in this novel, he shifts back and forth between a quite abstract gnosticism remote from earthier biblical concerns and a prophetic voice of Jewish survival and indignation.

For the reading community, I imagine, this can sometimes be an uneasy alternation of elements that blend more seamlessly in *Riddley Walker*. To be sure, there is no obviously Jewish voice in the earlier novel, but Riddley's occasional mysticism is rendered through the thickness of "particklers" and a diction that is concrete where it is not scatological. Even gnostic sentiments have their lion imagery in *Riddley Walker*, as with its epigraph from the *Gospel of Thomas*. Logion 7:

Jesus has said: Blessed is the lion that the man will devour, and the lion will become man. And loathsome is the man that the lion will devour, and the lion will become man.

It may be that Pilgermann's post-theistic messiah is the lion become man. But what is the lion? His vision continues: "Jesus is the great dead Lion of the World," who holds in his mouth "the live black body of Christ Radiant"; conversely, "The great live Lion of the World" holds in his mouth "the tiny dead golden body of Christ" (23). This heterodox Christology is neither elaborated nor explained before Pilgermann goes on to rage at the Christ for betraying his people, letting them be slaughtered in his name. He is, however, unmoved: "'Whatever I am,' says Jesus, 'I'm the one you talk to from now on.'" Pilgermann's prayers to the God of Israel are unavailing: "'There was no answer when the knife was on your flesh and there'll be no answer now'" (24). Moreover, Jesus refuses to heal his castration and even says that Pilgermann had wished for it. This is understandably denied, but Jesus says he wished it in order to be "'tuned to me.'" Again Pilgermann resists and again Jesus persists:

> Jesus said, "Life moves by exchanges; loss is the price of gain. Some pay with one thing, some with another; whatever is most dear, that is my price."
> I said, "Why is that your price?"
> Jesus said, "What is dear is what is held dear, and there can be no holding by those who go my road; there can be no holding by those who will be here with me and gone with me" (25).

Coming in a section of the novel that is replete with religiosity but refractory to any conventionally religious reading, this last passage—along with Jesus's additional remark: "'the only wholeness is in letting go, and I am the letting go'"(26)—echoes an important revelation that comes to Riddley Walker: "I cud feel some thing growing in me it wer like a gran sea surging in me it wer saying, LOSE IT. Saying, LET GO. Saying, THE ONLYES POWER IS NO POWER" (167). Later Riddley refines this insight: "It aint that its *no* Power. Its not sturgling for Power thats where the Power is. Its in jus letting your self be where it is" (197). Detweiler says of this development that "Riddley . . . has already absorbed the lesson of *Gelassenheit.* . . ."17

Still, such "alert nonchalance"—as Detweiler also calls this state—is easier said than done for Pilgermann, notwithstanding the endorsement of it by his hermetic Christ. His vision over, his wound healing, he sets out for Jerusalem on a quest that might be thought to take him even farther than Riddley, participating as he does in that "further action pending" from the previous novel. In this pilgrimage of the Pilgrim Man there is a significant motive stemming from what he feels is a better understanding of Jesus's words puzzled over earlier:

> Now I knew what Jesus had meant when he said, "After me it's the straight action and no more dressing up." God was already gone from us. How much longer would Jesus be with us? . . . the world is full of mysterious, unseen, fragile temples; it was in these many temples that God used to dwell among us. . . . How many temples between us and Christ's last day, between us and the eternal face-less action of God as It? Quickly, quickly must something be done before all the temples were gone. Now I understood why everyone was rushing to Jerusalem, now I knew why this was a time unique in history. . . . all of us were now hurrying to Jerusalem to make with the gathered power of our hearts' desire a church of all souls craving Jesus, a place of rebirth in the place of holy sepulchre and resurrection (32-33).

Although Pilgermann realizes that the Pope's call for a Crusade was the more immediate impetus for this mass pilgrimage, he stands by his analysis of its deeper causes, and thereby raises a question.

While he refers to this time in the Middle Ages as unique in history, much of his narrated experience and philosophizing in the text proclaims the unreality of time and history, as when he encounters on his journey the headless corpse of Sophia's husband, the Christian tax-collector, and sees "the light of the total Now" (47). This again recalls, as it interrogates, Eliade's discussions of the seemingly paradoxical theme of the abolition of history in Judaism and Christianity within those traditions' commitment to the actualities of historical embodiment. Not only does this conundrum play into the novel's problematic alternation between the abstract-transcendental and the concrete-immanental (or incarnational), it also calls into question the entire idea of story itself—and this in turn implicates the style of the novel.

The narrative, it must be said, is sometimes so meditative as to be plotless: a point both Pilgermann and Hoban himself acknowledge, although not as a fault. The ghost-narrator admits that "my perceptions are uneven, my understanding patchy but I have action; I go. I can't tell this as a story because it isn't a story; a story is what remains when you leave out most of the action . . ."(38). It is not necessary to agree with the narrator's assessment of storytelling, and the "action" of the novel is often interior, disembodied, the action of ideas, or even the frequent ideas about action, as already noted. Nevertheless, in this matter the novelist supports his narrator; he at least argues for the necessity, if not the virtue, of departing from a strong narrative line. Interviewed before writing his most recent novel, *The Medusa Frequency*, Hoban has said:

> *Riddley Walker*, I think, is my most successfully put-together book in terms of the story going from its beginning to the place where it lets the reader out and all the ideas inte- grating themselves with the story. Now *Pilgermann* is, I think, much less integrated in that way. . . . I think I'm drifting in the direction of improvisation. I care more about going wherever the thing takes me and letting it branch out into little odd spaces where perhaps one mightn't think anything was happening in terms of story.[18]

Hoban goes even further in another interview, conceding that *Pilgermann* isn't a novel, that "maybe the thought material is more important than the narrative. It could well be a progression of fragmentary essays rather than a novel. . . ."[19]

These "essays," or attempts, at expressing elusive metaphysical perceptions may indeed dominate *Pilgermann*: Hoban has an avowed investment in certain notions of this sort that we will want to return to. Once more, however, we need not agree with this anti-narrative reading of his (quasi-) novel. There may be something of a story-line here even though Hoban was personally more interested in pursuing ideas or "thought-clusters"[20] for their philosophical appeal than in incarnating them into the texture of the narrative. Like many a postmodernizing novelist, Hoban can be accused of writing theory upon occasion, and such forays are not without value. Referring to the apple in Eden, Pilgermann maintains that "God did not make it resistible, it must be eaten so that a mystery will be perpetuated, the mystery of the gaining of loss. . . . What if Adam and Eve hadn't eaten of the fruit of the tree, what then? No Holy Scriptures, no story to tell" (31). So Hoban's narrator's speculations can extend provocatively to the sources of story. This suggestive self-consciousness will be a factor to consider in conversing with *The Medusa Frequency*. But I would think that the greater contribution of Hoban's writing lies not in his ideas about it or his ideas about religious realities but in his praxis, the execution of what we in fact receive as novels.

In *Pilgermann*'s (and Pilgermann's) case we do, despite thought-provoking diversions, want to know what will happen next. However strange and spasmodic it is, the story carries us forward on the pilgrimage. As our storyteller himself asserts: "When I had my proper parts I must have been blind and deaf, the world had not come alive for me, I had never talked with Christ, had never put my feet into the footsteps of my road away, had never, alone in a dark wood, seen the light of Now. So, Pilgermann, let your heart have balls, and on to Jerusalem"(55).

Thus we move through a forbidding territory of bizarre encounters with figures corporeal and otherwise (notably Death in the guise of Bruder Pfortner the Gatekeeper), then to Pilgermann's capture by pirates and on to his purchase in the Tripoli slave market by a like-minded Muslin Turk named, because Hoban liked the sound,[21] Bembel Rudzuk. Rudzuk frees Pilgermann, but he decides to travel with the Turk, ending up not in Jerusalem but in Muslim Antioch, where a siege is soon mounted by an army of Frankish Christians. There Pilgermann supervises for Rudzuk the designing and building of a large and intricately-tiled plaza floor, patterned so as to reveal figures he had foreseen in his vision of the Christ: twisting serpents, shifting pyramids, and the face of a lion.

The design is called "Hidden Lion," and its interpretation as a pattern "contiguous with infinity" (124) is a major concern in and of the novel. We can also take it almost for granted that it is Hoban's simulacrum of how exegetes will construe *Pilgermann*:

> "One of the virtues of this simple but at the same time complex design," said Bembel Rudzuk, "this design in which we see the continually reciprocating action of unity and multiplicity, is that it suits its apparent action to the mind of the viewer: those who look outward see the outward preeminent; those who look inward see the inward" (139).

Inwardly or outwardly seen, Bembel Rudzuk's perspective as interpreter—another embodiment of Hoban's creative hermeneutics—is iconoclastic: as a Muslim he opposes images as idolatrous:

> "Although serpents, pyramids, and lions seem to appear in the pattern, that is only because the human mind will make images out of anything; the pattern is in actuality abstract, it represents nothing and asserts no images. It offers itself modestly and reverently to the Unseen and the Unseen takes pleasure in it" (146).

Clearly Pilgermann shares Rudzuk's perspective, having already recounted the idolatry of his Jewish ancestors in words that reverberate with the condemnations of the prophets of Israel:

> . . . He had chosen them to be the ark of the idea of Him and of It, the idea of the Unseen, the Ungraspable, the Unknowable, the idea never to be contained by the mind that is contained by it. He had chosen them to be mind-heroes, to open their minds to the idea that could not be held by any mind, and what did they do? They fouled themselves, they rolled in the dung and degradation of

the seeable, the knowable, the ordinary. They said to stocks and stones, "Be thou our God" (94).

Such prophetic iconoclasm serves a hunger for the occult that *Pilgermann* richly fulfills. Whether Hoban finds his Jewishness fed by the arcana that crowd his book, storytelling finally, if atypically, prevails. Nor does condemnation of images, however awkward it may be for literary description, need to foreclose on narrative as a properly religious mode of communication. There can be tales of idolatry, tales against idolatry. More important for a religious reading is to ask the kind of questions Robert Detweiler has put to *Riddley Walker*.

It is hard to believe that *Pilgermann* could foster the breadth of communal attraction the earlier novel seems to have produced. Its surrealistic style and—at the very least—digressive plot surely offer obstacles to many readers. Yet for those who find its elusive narrative thread the benefits are real. Hoban does enlist such a reader into a community of yearning, a community of those who can teach us possible truths about our entwisted Western legacy of desert faiths. In particular it pulls us into the memory of a member of the Jewish past who searches the history of three religions for the origins of a Holocaust that was always, apparently, about to happen and then, in our time, did. Most of all this novel plays on the peripheries of story, taking us, as readers, into the precincts of mystery.

The story continues on its complex way through the siege of Antioch, to Pilgermann and Rudzuk's realization that the Hidden Lion was also idolatrous, to the fall of Antioch, to the death of Rudzuk and, finally, to the death of Pilgermann himself—who, as narrator, has been dead from the first page. Truly no summary is adequate since so much that transpires is profession: ruminative, hortatory, vatic. Nonetheless, the novel (and it is a novel) enfolds all of this, impressing us in its telling with what Bembel Rudzuk calls the first lesson: "'the heart of the mystery is meant to remain a mystery'" (142).

There is no acknowledgment in *The Medusa Frequency* that it continues the action of *Pilgermann* as the latter says it does the action of *Riddley Walker*. However, there is one slight hint of the continuity between Russell Hoban's two most recent novels. Midway through *Pilgermann* the Governor of Antioch climbs the observation tower in the center of the plaza to view the Hidden Lion tiles. Pilgermann narrates:

> Not a breath of air stirred his white burnous, the blue sky was utterly without a sign of any-thing. At just such an unheralded moment, I thought, might marvels appear to a watcher on a tower: the earth opening up; the kraken rising

to the surface of the sea; the mountain lifting itself into the air over the city. It occurred to me that the Unseen might at any moment make use of any pair of eyes to see everything in an al-together different way, a way never thought of before (155-56).

The Medusa Frequency deals with one of these marvels, and does so in a way never thought of before. The setting and the style of this novel are altogether different from *Pilgermann*, although it shares some of the latter's concerns. This is to be expected in view of Hoban's own statement as a "connexion man" of contemporary fiction-writing: "I get obsessed with images, with things I see or things that come into my mind, connections between one thing and another. I have a whole series of revolving obsessions that keep surfacing in all of my books."[22] Surfacing like the Kraken, great ocean cephalopod, whose message materializes in the green-light letters on Herman Orff's computer screen, late at night as he struggles with his writer's block. Like Hoban, Orff works at his word processor with the short-wave radio crackling songs in untranslated languages over far-away frequencies. Unlike Hoban, this writer-as-hero has a name derived from two figures prominent in Greek mythology, and also prominent in the novel, along with Persephone, the Medusa, and especially Eurydice, who, "at three o'clock in the morning . . . is bound to come into it"(9).

Seized by his automatic word-processing, Orff channels these mythic figures and forces: the gial Kraken, coeval with the terror of creation, mostly head and writhing tentacles, who shares an identity with the head of Orpheus, undying singer, son of Hermes, here-and-gone, in this account, and also Eurydice, lost to the Kraken and to Orpheus, who shares an identity with two mortal women in Orff's London and with Vermeer's painting *Head of a Young Girl*. This painting was also referred to in *Pilgermann* (97), and seems to have been as important to the genesis of *The Medusa Frequency* as the Canterbury wall painting was to the origins of *Riddley Walker*. Hoban, we know, was an illustrator—as well as a prolific and successful children's book author—before turning to "adult novels"; he is keenly attuned to visual-arts imagery and the imploded narratives it may be broadcasting. He also confesses to suffering, like Orff (though less chronically), from bouts of writer's block—which he calls, out of superstitious paranoia and/or word-playfulness, "blighter's rock." This he discusses in a 1991 article where he also talks about the Vermeer painting:

> if you follow your mind into the look with which that girl looks at you, you come to Thing-in-Itself and the terror at the back of her eyes. You come to what waits in the blank paper: the ungraspableisness of what is. In trying to take hold of it the mind finds only the incomprehensibility of itself and the

original terror of Creation, the bursting into being of something out of nothing. . . . When it comes at you out of the blank paper, it's difficult to sort out what wants to be put into words, and it isn't always possible to look straight at it; that's why any blighter can find himself or herself rocked from time to time. But with patience, blank paper of the right kind, and a favoring road from Hermes, one gets unrocked enough to make it worth the bother.[23]

The right kind of paper, by the way, for both Russell Hoban and Herman Orff, is 80-gram A4 (four being a number, says Hoban, associated with Hermes[24]). In *Kleinzeit*, from 1974, there was not only an important bit of the Orpheus and Eurydice myth, but a character named "yellow paper" who at one point becomes a roaring lion (147, 108).

Revolving obsessions indeed, and they all come around again in *The Medusa Frequency*. When Orff receives a flyer from Istvan Fallok at Hermes Soundways about a machine for curing writer's block, the flyer is typed on yellow paper, the same kind he uses. "HEAD FOR IT?" (16) asks the announcement, and once he finds Fallok's offices he undergoes the EEG device that promises to get him to places in his head he hasn't been able to get to on his own.

When the electrodes are attached and the machine is turned on, Orff enters an olive tree he and Luise von Himmelbett (heavenbed) had seen on the Greek island of Paxos, "an entrance to the underworld, a Persephone door" (26), and has a vision of the vast head of the Kraken at the bottom of the sea. As he rises with the head it metamorphoses into the head of Orpheus, bobbing on the surface of the ocean and bellowing the name of Eurydice. This then elicits the faces of Orff's significant female others—his lost love Luise, his new possibility Melanie Falsepercy (Persephone), and the Vermeer girl—until he finds himself on the Underground, wires dangling from his head and no jacket against the November chill. He makes his way home and collapses into sleep, but the next morning he is up early walking by the Thames near Putney Bridge when a voice begins to sing in his head: "'Eurydice!' . . . It was an eyeless and bloated human head, sodden, covered with green slime and heavy with barnacles" (30-31).

It is the Orpheus head again, but this time "he" and Orff have a conversation; Orpheus begins to tell his story, a story that is central to the novel. It is partly about Orff's vocation as a (blocked) storyteller, partly about storytelling itself. Having been told Orff's name, the head exclaims:

"I am the first of your line. I am the first singer, the one who invented the lyre, the one to whom Hermes brought Eurydice and perpetual guilt. I am your progenitor, I am the endlessly voyaging sorrow that is always in you, I am that astonish- ment from which you write in those brief moments when you can write. . . . I'm manifesting myself to you as a rotting head but there's no picture for what I am: I am that which sings the world, I am the response that never dies. Fidelity is what's wanted" (33).

Orpheus's appearance in Hoban's narrative provides a self-consciously postmodernizing text and its postmodernized community—artists, would-be artists, watchers of artists (us)—with the kind of mythos that might be said to survive the demystification of master narratives and a fidelity that lies beyond a no-longer-possible totalizing trust. The recurrence of "the Orphic voice" has been scrutinized by Elizabeth Sewell and many others in recent decades, but seldom has it sounded through such a hip, reflexive, sardonic narration that at the same time allows for the arrival in our midst, in this presence-less present, of something akin to perceived mystery.

Likewise, the kind of faith that Orpheus's head countenances in *The Medusa Frequency* is without appeal to traditions that have come to seem discredited:

"Fidelity is a matter of perception; nobody is unfaithful to the sea or to mountains or to death; once recognized they fill the heart. In love or in terror or in loathing one responds to them with the true self; fidelity is not an act of the will: the soul is compelled by recognitions" (63).

If this all sounds somewhat "archetypal," it is. Not, however, in the essentialist mode of standard Jungianism such as Christine Wilkie falls into in her 1989 study of Hoban's fiction, *Through the Narrow Gate*, where she sees the "contemporary myth" represented by *The Medusa Frequency* as "the process by which psychic contents, that are the archetypes, are named as characters on the outer projection plane."[25] This fails to play deeply, fluidly enough with Hoban's brand of Orphism.

More to the point is the psychological faith of a post-Jungian like Noel Cobb, who makes a challenging statement about the creative hermeneutics put forward by this novel: "The head proposes a way of looking at myth which is based on the image, a way that is not linear or narrational but rather simultaneous."[26] If this is indeed the Orphic mythography in force in *The Medusa Frequency* we have come 180 degrees from the religious iconoclasm of Bembel Rudzuk and Pilgermann. For Cobb the interchanges on story which continue intermittently throughout Hoban's story interrogate it, perhaps discredit it. As the head begins to tell Orff his story, starting with his birth to Hermes and Calliope and how he killed the tortoise to make the first lyre, he recalls his encounter with Aristaeus:

"'You are the story of yourself,' he said. With his finger he traced figures in the air.

"'What's that you're doing?' I said.
"'Your name. You are the story of Orpheus.'
"'How can I be a story? I'm a man, a live person.'
"'You're a story.'
"'Not a story,' I said. I began to run . . . .'"

As is the habit with story-hearers, Orff wants to know more:

"What happened next?" I said after a reasonable interval.
"My story is not a sequence of events like knots on a string," said the head;
"I could have started with the loss of Eurydice and ended with the killing of the
tortoise—all of it happens at once and it goes on happening; all of it is
happening now and any part of it contains the whole of it, the pictures needn't
be looked at in any particular order" (38-39).

In line with his "imaginalist" deconstruction of narrative, Noel Cobb
quotes this paragraph approvingly, adding, in his note, "or, as archetypal
[post-Jungian] psychology would say: 'Myths never happen; they always
are.'"[27] I wonder. If this is true even in our present how can Hoban keep on
storying? Has he outlived story's usefulness as a guiding fictive category or
hermeneutical construct? Surely he has laid bare some of the contingencies
at the source of story, both with his practice (moreso in *Pilgermann*) and his
preachments (moreso in *The Medusa Frequency*). As a compromise perhaps
post-Jungians like Cobb would accept the adjectival notion of an
"archetypal telling," [28] a sense of the perennial survival of the seeds of story
in even the least promising ground. The idea implied by Robert Detweiler
that the single images of paintings constitute an "implosion of narrative"
seems a no-less-hopeful affirmation of what that proto-postmodernist
Wallace Stevens somewhere calls "the fecund minimum."
For Detweiler the psychodynamic of desire and release explains the
"teasing" power of a painting—and presumably any single image of the sort
Cobb privileges—to trigger "the dissemination of meaning by which we
survive."[29] Thus may the seeds of story be strewn by a process that is as
primally sexual as it is primally imaginal (archetypal): which is to say, as
mysterious. Life goes on, outdoing itself, and a religious reading might be
well-adapted to give discourse to that coursing.
The boon of a creative hermeneut like Hoban may be to offer his own
(revisionist) religious reading to critics implicated in embattled
communities of religious belief, helping to transform their crisis into a
liminal passage promising a revitalized *communitas*. The story Hoban's
Herman Orff hears from the head of Orpheus may only be a hallucinatory
result of having his own head re-scrambled by Istvan Fallok's machine; what
we as readers visit, in other words, may be a new place in Orff's head rather

han ancient Greece restoring and re-storying itself in contemporary London.

On the other hand, Hoban is not above re-sequencing history, as we noted in connection with *Riddley Walker* and *Pilgermann*, just as the Orpheus head suggests the scrambling that—what? Life? Being? Mystery?—can do to the linearity of narrative. Can communities of Christians and Jews surviving today, for instance, afford to ignore the kind of question raised by Pilgermann's ghost, hovering over history from the Crusades to the Holocaust? "Might it even be possible," he asks, "that God, in his Hebrew aspect writing from right to left, writes first the slaughter of X [the Jews] and later the crucifixion for which they are slaughtered? If we look at it in that way we might see the slaughter as cause and the crucifixion is effect: the sin of the slaughter being heavy on the sinners, there comes the redeemer to offer his innocence for their guilt, the one for the many." And this speculation is further fueled by another consideration: ". . . speaking as a witness to what has been done to six million or so X not too very far from here in what is called time . . . I begin to think that it may be with him even as with some lowly mortal novelist who, having written a tremendous later scene, must perforce go back to insert an earlier one to account for it" (39-40).

Moreover, just as God and demi-gods like Orpheus are entangled in the creation and fate of story, so also in Hoban's hermeneutics do they both authorize *loss* as crucial to that process of time and narrative. With Pilgermann's Hebrew author-God we lose the Garden and gain a flawed story called "Salvation History" or "Western Civ." With Herman Orff's progenitor we lose Eurydice and gain a reflexive myth called "Text" or "Western Lit." "'Hold a pomegranate in your hand,' the head challenges Orff, "'and tell me where is the beginning of it and where is the end. The name of this pomegranate is Loss: the loss of Eurydice was in me before I ever met her and the loss of me was in her the same'" (39).

It turns out that Istvan Fallok had had similar interactions with the Orpheus head, as he later tells Orff, when he was experimenting with his own machine. As a musician he had tried to capture Orpheus's singing until he ended up in hospital with a heart attack (poor exchanges with the head give Orff, too, episodes of angina). Fallok had then gotten the head onto Orff to spare himself, so he cancels the charge for the brain-machine treatment. When Orff says that the head has begun to tell him its story, Fallok replies "'Ah, it would do, wouldn't it. Music with me and a story with you. Well, good luck with it.' . . ."(45).

Orff's pursuit of "Orphic action" in London continues; conspiracies and synchronicities abound as he follows his intuitions to the Cheshire Chees pub near Tower Bridge (the head had already appeared as an Edam cheese and back to Putney Bridge. The head fails to show up in these places however, so he asks Fallok for another jolt from the brain machine. Fallok refuses, but the Kraken comes through for a chat on his computer monitor annoyed with Orff's preoccupation with Orpheus's head, which then reappears as "the thinking man's cabbage head" (60) that Orff buys from a fruit and vegetable vendor.

The head narrates more of his story of losing Eurydice, of how she had said to him "'Be the world-child with me'" (62), a puzzling motif that recurs in several conversations. More significant than this transmission may be Orff's revealing, as narrator, that "I spent the rest of the day typing up everything so far which brought me to this page" (63), calling attention very pointedly to the process of narration. Gosta Kraken, a modish film-maker who has had his own dealings with the head of Orpheus, adds to this postmodernist action by way of his film *Code-name Orpheus*, which Melanie Falspercy finds reviewed in *Sight and Sound*: "'Sylvestre Lyzee wrote the piece; he said that it worked on the deconstructionist level but he had a little trouble with the reality-frame'" (66). Clearly Hoban is having a good romp with this quest, and yet it is no less serious for all that—and this mixed message, I suspect, makes for a peculiarly postmodern community of readers.

When the head materializes in Orff's refrigerator we are given still another angle on the problematics of story. The head tells of its early love-making with Eurydice, then of its fear: "'I felt myself becoming story and was afraid'" (69). In reading Orff's story, or Hoban's, we have to wait to find out the reason for this fear.

First there is Orff's brief affair with Ms. Falspercy to hear about, in the process of which he scarcely neglects his story about the story of Orpheus. As Orff says to her,

> "I think we're all in this together, you and I and the head of Orpheus."
> "In what?"
> I was about to say, "This story," then I decided not to. "I don't know."
> "For a moment I thought you were going to say, 'This story.' I'm glad you didn't."
> "So am I" (74).

And then there is Orff's somewhat abortive trip to a museum in The Hague to see Vermeer's original of *Head of a Young Girl*. The painting is on loan in America; he finds instead Gosta Kraken in the flesh, also there to see the Vermeer girl. The two seekers joust about Kraken's films—Orff snaps "'Don't you come the deconstructionist with me, you ponce'" (86-87)—and about Luise von Himmelbett, who had left Orff for Kraken. She was later lost to Kraken as well, however, qualifying her to be an avatar of Eurydice and prompting a reflection from the ontological film-maker on one of Russell Hoban's revolving obsessions: "'Being is not a steady state but an occulting one: we are all of us a succession of stillnesses blurring into motion with the revolving of the wheel of action, and it is in those spaces of black between the pictures that we experience the heart of the mystery in which we are never allowed to rest'" (87). Not bad for a rather pretentious "flickerer" who ends the conversation with an egotistical snub: "'I'm disappearing now,' he said, 'but you will continue to think of me,' and he withdrew" (89).

Immediately thereafter, contemplating another painting, one by Franz Post of an island called Taramaca shown in the middle distance, Orff has a vision of Luise, then someone else:

> Out of the pinky dawn water, naked and shining in the dawn, rose Luise, quivering like a mirage between the beach and the island seen across the water. Quivering, shimmering, her body becoming, becoming, becoming a face loosely grinning, with hissing snakes writhing round it in the shining dawn. Around me ceased the sounds of the day; the stone of me cracked and I came out of myself quite clean, like a snake out of an egg, nothing obscuring my sight or my hearing. The Gorgon's head, the face of Medusa, shimmered luminous in a silence that crackled with its brilliance. Her mouth was moving.
>
> What? I said. What are you saying?
>
> You have found me, she said. I trust you with the idea of me (89-90).

Very early in the novel and years earlier in his life Orff had found a note from a departed Luise von Himmelbett: "I trusted you with the idea of me and you lost it" (16). Even earlier, in *Riddley Walker*, indeed in The Eusa Story, this notion comes in when Eusa asks the Littl Shynin Man the Addom "Wut is the idear uv me? The Littl Man sed, That we doan no til yuv gon thru aul yur Chaynjis" (136).

It is the Orpheus head that adds the ingredient in *The Medusa Frequency* that "'when people fall in love they entrust to each other the idea of themselves. . . . the essential idea of them that they don't even know themselves'" (70), thus explaining Luise's note. But now Herman Orff has found his Medusa frequency, tuning in to the idea of one who entrusts that idea to him. Lest this be taken too statically, though, we must remember that changes, motion, also enter the equation—leading, it may be, from finding to loss, and from an epiphany of presence back to the ambiguities of narrative. This is strongly suggested in Orff's final discussion with Orpheus.

He is talking to Orpheus's brain, exposed in a grapefruit half, learning more of the story of Eurydice's leaving. The brain says "'I think it was the story that finally did it. When there was love and happiness there was no story, what there was could not be contained by words. With the death of love came the story and the story found words for it'" (118). Orff asks for specifics and the brain continues:

> "We'd made up names for ourselves and those were the names we were known by. Then one night we came to a place and people said to me, 'Sing about Orpheus and Eurydice.'
> "'Who are Orpheus and Eurydice?' I said.
> "'Lovers in a story,' they said. 'Eurydice died of a snakebite and Orpheus went to underworld to bring her back but he turned around to look at her too soon and he lost her.'. . ."
> "'Orpheus,' she said to me sadly, 'now the story has found us, now we have become story and I must leave you.'
> "'Why?' I said. 'Why must you leave me?'. . ."
> "'That's the story of us and there's nothing to be done about it'" (118-19).

Here is the fearsome negative side of narrative, and *a fortiori* of sacred narrative or myth: its mystifying, ideologically oppressive influence, archetype as stereotype. But if the fruits of story can be deterministic its roots are in any case, says *The Medusa Frequency*, entangled in loss, and this colloquy with the brain of Orpheus expresses the proposition most eloquently. It was Eurydice, the brain recounts, who first realized it:

> "'You will sing better than ever,' she said. 'Art is a celebration of loss, of beauty passing, passing, not to be held. Now that I am lost you will perceive me fully and you will find me in your song; now that underworld is closed to you the memory of the good dark will be with you always in your song. Now you are empty like the tortoise shell, like the world-child betrayed, and your song will be filled with what is lost to you'" (119).

The Orpheus brain gets the last word, though, or at least *his* last word (Orff soon absent-mindedly eats the half-grapefruit) by telling Orff an end to his story. Orff finds it an unsatisfying end, but the brain elaborates:

> "You must do the best with what you've got," said the brain. "Eurydice is lost to you but Medusa trusts you with the idea of her." . . .
> I'd said that I'd never lose the idea of Medusa but I wasn't at all sure that I knew what the idea was. The head had said "Behind Medusa lie wisdom and the dark womb hidden like a secret cave behind a waterfall. Behind Medusa lies

Eurydice unlost." "Let it lie," I'd said, "you're wording it to death." It was a mystery and I hadn't wanted it explained to me (120-21).

It isn't explained to him—or to us. For Orff, Orpheus is gone, Medusa now speaks through his word-processor, and the Kraken comes up with a story, "The Seeker from Nexo Vollma," that Orff uses to unblock his writing career, selling it to a publisher of "deep comics" to appear as a serial on the back of bran flakes boxes. Near the end of *The Medusa Frequency*, Orff (and, it is hard not to infer, Hoban) expresses his hope for the novel he has described himself as writing, the novel about his not being able to write:

> I hope that this little volume may be a *vade mecum* not so much for the specialist as for others like me—the general struggler and straggler, the person for whom the whole sweep of consciousness is often too much (134).

A *vade mecum*, a "go-with-you" book, or constant companion, for the community of strugglers and stragglers suffering from (and reveling in?) the postmodern condition: this is Orff's ambition for his work and Hoban's achievement with *The Medusa Frequency*. The latter novelist has called himself "a religious writer," saying "I keep going because I really feel that all the ideas and words and special effects that are in the air want us to be the organs of perception that perceive them. It wants to be done. It's my religion."[30]

We keep going with him, reading religiously his writer's expressions of a religion that may be unique to him. He has found a frequency in his latest novel that accords with his rationale for being a religious writer: ". . . you tune into some main line that's moving through the air and some things branch off from it and attach on to it and you wind up with all kinds of references that will fit into systems that you know nothing of."[31] Hence critics wrongly take such systems as part of Hoban's intentions or reduce the meaning of his novels to one of them. This can be a danger for a religious reading as for any reading that derives from so-called extrinsic concerns or programs. Accordingly, if unfashionably, I have attempted to remain quite close to the texts of his two recent novels after my brief discussion of *Riddley Walker*.

This also follows Robert Detweiler's practice with the latter, which he treats as if it were the account of an actual historical culture, thus allowing it to "speak . . . more expansively"[32] than the other texts he treats in *Breaking the Fall*. My own motive for a close reading of *Pilgermann* and *The Medusa Frequency* is somewhat different: it is to avoid imposing any sort of standardized version of religious meaning upon Hoban's own idiosyncratic novelistically-embodied version—and to emulate, thereby, the subtlety of Detweiler's idea of a "religious reading."

It is felicitous, to my way of thinking, that the religion in his readings is far from obvious. He is schooled sufficiently in the incredulities of poststructuralist theory to proceed with extreme reticence in applying religious priorities and perspectives to contemporary fiction. Consequently, we find these limited to a few broad, though important, considerations. Detweiler speaks of "nurtur[ing] a respect for the incomprehensibility of form and a reverence for mystery;"[33] he invokes his book's title to emphasize the West's late-twentieth-century involvement in "the mythology of the Fall," whereby a religious reading "seeks in its fictions to brake/break the fall into meaninglessness and death;"[34] he attends to "the prophetic potential of fiction;"[35] he is concerned religiously to foster community, *Geselligkeit*;[36] and he favors "the spirit of *Gelassenheit* and of deep play"[37] both substantively (one might almost say theologically) and methodologically as means or modes with/in which to engage texts. Such critical presuppositions are therefore "religious" in the least narrow or "dogmatic" senses. Generally biblical and Western, they are finally quite pertinently and unobjectionably *human* and, as I have said, well-suited to mesh with postmodernist perceptions and presumptions.

In extending Detweiler's strategies experimentally I have perhaps been even more reticent about the religion in my reading of a small body of recent narrative fiction by a single author, and/because I may be more intent upon having a writer like Hoban and his characters inform *my* understanding of just what late-twentieth-century religion as well as late-twentieth-century narrative could be. I have tried to adduce only those biblical and Western themes that provide Hoban's "creative hermeneutics" with something to act upon, inform, conceivably re-invigorate—which is to say I have focused on only those religious themes *he* has chosen to explore through his fiction.

In borrowing Professor Eliade's term, I must acknowledge the extent to which I have departed from his usage. For him "creative hermeneutics" seems to be a way to describe the mission of his history of religions discipline, as he understands it, to sustain interpretations of religious phenomena that support their culture-creating function, protecting it from reductionistic demystifications. Indeed, he has called for "demystification in reverse," as he puts it: "we have to 'demystify' the apparently profane worlds and languages of literature, plastic arts, and cinema in order to disclose their 'sacred' elements. . . ."[38]

Eliade's quest was a distinctly modernist (even if anti-modernist) one: to rehabilitate the sacred sources of Western culture as they exist(ed) in traditional societies. But Russell Hoban's world is just as distinctly postmodern and postmodernist. His texts therefore offer, with their alternative history of religions, an alternative hermeneutic, one whose interpretations create meanings that explicitly or implicitly suggest religious attitudes and a religious community in positive dialogue with a world in which unmasking the camouflaged sacred may be beside the point.

My conversation with Hoban's novels wants, then, to listen very closely for *his* interpretations, *his* proffered meanings, and *his* writer's religion of makeshift mysticism. This entails, in turn, attending to the problematics of narrative which, as a member of our postmodern community, he is intent upon foregrounding in the narratives he writes. The meanings he creates with the interpretive action his narratives convey are never far from these problematics. And probably the major occasion for conversing critically with this set of issues in a religious reading, it seems to me, is Hoban's handling of the relation of loss and gain, or finding, to story.

In his 1975 novel *Turtle Diary* one of the two main characters wakes up on a dreary Monday morning with a sense of defeat. "Things would always be the way they were," laments William G. "Why struggle." He is reminded of a line from Eliot's *East Coker*, takes the *Four Quartets* off the shelf and finds the line, then reads another section near the end of the poem:

> There is only the fight to recover
>   what has been lost
> And found and lost again: and now,
>   under conditions
> That seem unpropitious. But perhaps
>   neither gain nor loss.
> For us, there is only the trying. The
>   rest is not our business (179).

This verse seems to cohere with Orff's statement that he has told his story for a company of strugglers and stragglers, those who are constantly trying but usually losing ground, falling behind. The novels do sometimes reflect such an ethos of struggle, coming from an existentialist sensibility of weary resignation if not downright desperation. But this modernist posture hardly describes the whole of Russell Hoban's complex postmodernist outlook. For him, unlike Eliot, "the rest" is manifestly his business.

We have seen, for instance, that losing and finding, falling and restoration, are inspected, interrogated, parodied, and pondered in the

novels. More than that, loss is held up as the wellspring of story, eve
(implicitly) by Pilgermann's Jesus, as though Detweiler's Fall int
meaninglessness and death is also/rather a lapse into narrative—for bette
and for worse. To play deeply with Hoban's writing is to be entertained int
entertaining religious meanings that are unorthodox if not aberrant, bu
also provocatively innovative (perhaps most when they manipulate ancien
traditions or archetypal inclinations). His reversals of historical sequenc
and reflexive self-awareness of his own storytelling process call creativel
into question not only the received orthodoxies of Western religion but th
received scholarship about it as well, whether from biblically-derive
theologies or more covertly Judeo-Christian methodologies like the histor
of religions school.

On the other hand, it must be stressed that Hoban does not simpl
disengage from the religious legacy of the West. Whether it is th
scriptures of the three desert faiths or the pagan polytheism of Greece o
the shamanistic inheritance of northern Europe and the British Isles,
religious reading, interpreted *by* its receptive interactions with his texts (a
well as trying out its own tentative interpretations of them), has much t
offer because it has much to learn, in these times, from such a writer'
stories.

These are, after all, times in which we have loss in good supply
Turning the millennium and losing hold, in a sense, of a thousand years o
history ought to point this up. And yet we are also, I think, asked by ou
calendar and our condition to let go of that history—at least in the terms w
have habitually understood it—and to practice *Gelassenheit* as a complicit
with mystery and an alternative to struggling as we straggle into the nev
century. "Its the not sturgling for Power thats where the Power is" (197
says Riddley, siding with the Eliot who could write "Shantih," so that los
and trying may be only half the story of story.

Orff survives story as Orpheus doesn't: with Medusa he begins agair
begins anew, maybe begins a *new* story. Instead of turning to stone stillnes
at the sight of her, this male in Hoban's mostly male-oriented narratives i
set in motion, unblocked. Still, religiously, falling in love most often seem
in Hoban's hermeneutics, to be falling out of Fallenness, fulfilling desir
re-finding the Garden but *losing* story—though not for long. Because in th
meantime (or after love is lost), there are stories of survival that help u
survive our falling-out with what we can then only desire, erotically an
eschatologically. So we should be buoyed with Hoban when, like th
Kraken, story breaks through our surfaces to float upon an ocean of loss

heading our way like Orpheus, but singing of happenstance as though it were happy ending.

NOTES

1. Daniel C. Noel, "The Nuclear Horror and the Hounding of Nature: Listening to Images," *Soundings*, LXX, 3-4 (Fall-Winter 1987), p. 290.

2. The novels I will cite (with parenthetical page references in my text) are *The Lion of Boaz-Jachin and Jachin-Boaz*(London: Picador, 1973/74); *Kleinzeit* (New York: VikingPress, 1974/83); *Turtle Diary* (New York: Random House,1975); *Riddley Walker* (New York: Washington SquarePress, 1980-82); *Pilgermann* (New York: Summit Books,1983); *The Medusa Frequency* (London: Jonathan Cape,1987).

3. Robert Detweiler, *Breaking the Fall: Religious Readings of Contemporary Fiction* (San Francisco: Harper & Row, 1989),pp. 159-91.

4. Interview in Christine Wilkie, *Through the Narrow Gate: The Mythological Consciousness of Russell Hoban* (London andToronto: Associated University Presses, 1989), p. 99.

5. Robert Detweiler, *Breaking the Fall*, p. 161.

6. Christine Wilkie, *Through the Narrow Gate*, p. 113.

7. Robert Detweiler, *Breaking the Fall*, p. 170.

8. David Holt, "Riddley Walker and Greenham Common: Further Thoughts on Alchemy, Christianity and the Work Against Nature," *Harvest*, 29 (1983), pp. 29-54.

9. Robert Detweiler, *Breaking the Fall*, p. 163.

10. Christine Wilkie, *Through the Narrow Gate*, p. 108.

11. Robert Detweiler, *Breaking the Fall*, pp. xiii, xvi, 35.

12. Christine Wilkie, *Through the Narrow Gate*, p. 121, n. 26.

13. Robert Detweiler, *Breaking the Fall*, pp. 34, 35.

14. Robert Detweiler, *Breaking the Fall*, pp. 189-90.

15. Daniel C. Noel, "The Nuclear Horror."

16. Mircea Eliade, *Images and Symbols: Studies in Religious Symbolism*, trans. P. Mairet New York: Sheedand Ward, 1969), pp. 170, 171. Emphasis in the original.

17. Robert Detweiler, *Breaking the Fall*, p. 186.

18. Christine Wilkie, *Through the Narrow Gate*, pp. 103-104.

19. Christine Wilkie, *Through the Narrow Gate*, p. 123, n. 5.

20. Christine Wilkie, *Through the Narrow Gate*, p. 122, n. 5

21. Christine Wilkie, *Through the Narrow Gate*, p. 113.

22. Russell Hoban, ". . . excerpts from a talk at San Diego State University," transcribed and ed. A. Allison, *Poets &Writers Magazine* (July/August 1992), p. 32.

23. Russell Hoban, "Blighter's Rock," reprinted in *Poets & Writers Magazine* (July/August 1992), p. 31.

24. Russell Hoban, "Blighter's Rock," p. 29.

25. Christine Wilkie, *Through the Narrow Gate*, p. 79.

26. Noel Cobb, *Archetypal Imagination: Glimpses of the Gods in Life and Art* (Hudson, NY: Lindisfarne Press, 1992), p. 256.

27. Noel Cobb, *Archetypal Imagination*, pp. 256, 286, n. 76.

28. Daniel C. Noel, "Joseph Campbell: Tuning in to Archetypal Telling,"*San Francisco Jung Institute Library Journal*, 9, 2(1990) pp. 51-66.

29. Robert Detweiler, "Overliving," in D. Jobling and S. Moore, eds. *Poststructuralism and Biblical Exegesis*, Semeia, 54, 1992, p. 250.

30. Hoban, ". . . excerpts," p. 36.

31. Hoban, ". . . excerpts," p. 36.

32. Robert Detweiler, *Breaking the Fall*, p., xvi.

33. Robert Detweiler, *Breaking the Fall*, p. xiv.

34. Robert Detweiler, *Breaking the Fall*, p. xv.

35. Robert Detweiler, *Breaking the Fall*, p. xvi.

36. Robert Detweiler, *Breaking the Fall*, p. xiii.

37. Robert Detweiler, *Breaking the Fall*, p. xvi.

38. Eliade, *The Quest: History and Meaning in Religion* (Chicago: The University of Chicago Press, 1959), p. 38.

Moses

Identity and Community in Exodus

CAROLYN M. JONES

On April 3, 1968, Martin Luther King, Jr., one day away from death, made his last speech. His final words were:

> I don't know what will happen now. We've got some difficult days ahead. But it doesn't matter with me now. Because I've been to the mountaintop. And I don't mind. Like anybody, I would like to live a long life. Longevity has its place. But I'm not concerned about that now. I just want to do God. And He's allowed me to go to the mountaintop. And I've looked over. And I've seen the promised land. I may not get there with you. But I want you to know tonight, that we, as a people will get to the promised land.[1]

In his final words, King reaches into the texts and metaphors of his culture to express a message both about his people, journeying to freedom, and about himself as leader, as Moses, the man who has brought them to this point but who will not be able to take them home. From the Mayflower Compact of 1620 whose swearers pledged to "Covenant and combine"[2] themselves into a body politic; to John Winthrop's "A Modell of Christian Charity" of 1630 in which the American colony is described as a "Citty upon a Hill" that, echoing "that exhortaction of Moses that faithfull servant of the Lord in his last farewell to Israell [in] Deut. 30,"[3] will be blessed if it follow God's ordinances and cursed if it does not; to Harriet Tubman who was a woman called Moses; and to Jose Arcadio's attempt to lead his people into the modern world in *A Hundred Years of Solitude*, the story of Moses informs and shapes the experience of peoples in the Americas. It is an essential plank in the foundation of that American mythos that Whitman, in "Democratic Vistas," called a "New World metaphysics."

The story of Moses and the people of Israel is particularly suited to and indicative of the new world experience. It is a story of pilgrimage and of flight. It is the story of an exemplary human who articulates the deepest longings of a people and who forms them into a community by giving them their own story. It is also a story about a God who intervenes in and shapes history to found a nation. This journey, this person, this story, and this God are important for their significations on the meaning of power and identity. Moses, as the liberator of Israel, redefines the meaning of power in the political realm, bringing the sacred into the political, and he redefines the meaning of power in human relationships, creating a new identity for the human being in relationship to "others" in the world.

Moses' tools for making this definition and this relationship are his right hand which, raised to God, makes Moses a center of power connecting God to human and which indicates the importance of human action; his staff which is pilgrim's staff and magician's wand, as well as a symbol of fructification; and, despite his protests, his voice, which is the vehicle of his translation and transmission of God's will. Moses binds love to power and creates a society based on the revelation of a creative justice in the laws and in the human being. Moses can do this because as the hero, he is a hinge,[4] standing on the boundary between God and human, power and weakness, free and slave, Hebrew and Egyptian. If we think of the story of Moses as epic, in the Hegelian sense, the issue of the relationship of the Hebrews to God in the Promised Land—the identity of Israel—cannot be resolved until the question of the meaning of Moses' life is resolved. In the course of the journey towards that resolution, Moses redefines the terms of the dialectics which he represents, particularly that of freedom and slavery, in his own person and in the structure of the Covenant. Michael Walzer argues in *Exodus and Revolution* that the Exodus is a political event cut to a human scale,[5] and I want to argue that that human scale is Moses. Liberator, scholar, judge, prophet, priest, law-giver, teacher, and charismatic leader,[6] Moses is the man whose force of character allows him to lead the Hebrews out of bondage and to forge them into the nation of Israel.

I want to work intertextually with the Exodus myth and the Moses figure. Intertextuality, as Henry Louis Gates says in *The Signifying Monkey*, represents a process of repetition and revision in which the text becomes "double voiced."[7] That is, the text retains its original meaning while revealing secondary meanings for the new reader:

> The audience of a double-voiced word is therefore meant to hear both a version of the original unnterance as the embodiment of its speaker's point of

view (or"semantic position") and the second speaker's evaluation of the utterance from a different point of view.[8]

I want to use the biblical text and Zora Neale Hurston's novel *Moses, Man of the Mountain* as the focus of this paper. I will also use other readings of the myth to elucidate the meaning and importance of Moses for the modern human being. The other interpretations include: Martin Buber's theological, literary critical, and historical reading of the book of *Exodus*, called *Moses: The Revelation and the Covenant*; Latin American "liberation" theologian Gustavo Gutierrez's *A Theology of Liberation*; and, finally, passages from Jewish legend. Hurston's *Moses, Man of the Mountain* is a significant text because it not only looks at the black American experience and its relationship to Exodus, but, written in 1939, the novel also explores the problem of Nazism. As Deborah Mc Dowell says in her introduction:

> That Hurston was concerned with questions of racial purity in a novel published in 1939 gains significance when we consider that this was the year that Hitler ordered the attack on Poland and led Germany into a world war [and into a practice] of racial improvement through selective breeding. The shadow of Nazism is cast from the beginning of *Moses, Man of the Mountain*, which opens on the process of marking Hebrew male babies for extinction...The coordinates of the novel's typology seem clearly drawn: Jewish oppression in Egypt prefigures black oppression in American, which parallels Jewish oppression under Hitler.[9]

Hurston's figural reading of the myth points to my critical concerns: the escape from power and oppression and the meaning of freedom, community, and identity in a "promised land."

The biblical text juxtaposes two images of force as it begins the story of Moses. First, seeing an Egyptian beating a Hebrew, Moses deliberates and acts: "He looked this way and that, and seeing no one he killed the Egyptian and hid him in the sand" (Exodus 2:12). The next day, however, Moses discourages the same kind of action between one Hebrew and another: "When he went out the next day, behold two Hebrews were struggling together; and he said to the man who did the wrong, 'Why do you strike your fellow?'" (Exodus 2:13). One of the Hebrews, either having seen himself or having heard about Moses' killing the Egyptian, makes it clear that he knows about the murder and asks, "'Who has made you a prince and a judge over us?'" (Exodus 2:14). The Hebrew is asking two questions. First, "What is the difference between what you did and what I did?" In other words, he is arguing that force is force. Zora Neale Hurston, in *Moses, Man of the Mountain*, says of Pharoah that "Force was his juices and force was his meat."[10] The Hebrews have learned that lesson well: that the only power that matters is the power which can crush the "other." The unnamed Hebrew, who represents the people, also questions Moses' identity: "Who are you to tell me what to do?" Moses will have to respond to both these questions in forming his identity and Israel's: Who is he to be the leader, and, in a nation in which God is the leader, what is the meaning of human power?

Moses stands on the boundary between Israel and Egypt. He is born a Hebrew but reared an Egyptian, and that fact means that he is uniquely qualified to lead the Hebrews out of bondage. Martin Buber, in his *Moses: The Revelation and the Covenant*, puts it this way:

> In the biblical narrative of the saving of the boy Moses the meaning is obvious: in order that the one appointed to liberate his nation should grow up to be the liberator—and of all analogous legends this is the only one containing this historical element of liberating a nation—he has to be introduced into the stronghold of the aliens, into that royal court by which Israel has been enslaved; and he must grow up there. This is a kind of liberation which cannot be brought about by anyone who grew up as a slave, nor yet by anyone who is not connected with the slaves; but only by one of the latter who has been brought up in the midst of the aliens and has received an education equipping him with all their wisdoms and powers, and [who] thereafter "goes forth to his brethren and observes their burdens."[11]

In order to become the liberator, Moses, endowed with the privilege of power, has to give up the safety of his identity as an Egyptian and begin to redefine himself as a Hebrew, as one of the powerless. He begins his rite of passage with a paradoxical act of force that deprivileges him. He kills the Egyptian, "one of his own," to save a Hebrew, "one of his own." Identity in question and crisis, he flees Egypt for Midian, "moving Godward" (MM,103), leaving behind all that he is.

Hurston, in the rhythm of a sermon, uses the metaphor of "crossing over" to indicate Moses' entering the limen. He crosses the Red Sea across which he will lead the Hebrews later as they begin their rite of passage. The river is also a baptismal image, cleansing Moses; he is reborn. Hurston says,

> So he walked out with clean feet on the other side [of the Red Sea]. Moses had crossed over. He was not in Egypt.He had crossed over and now he was not an Egyptian.He had crossed over. . . He had crossed over so he was not of the house of Pharoah.He did not own a palace because he had crossed over. He did not have an Ethiopian Princess for a wife. He had crossed over. . . He had crossed over. He felt as empty as a posthole for he was not of the things he

once had been. He was a man sitting on a rock. He had crossed over (MM, 103-104).

On the other side of the river, Moses begins the construction of a new identity. Moses moves from from city to tribe, and, there, he is a shepherd, a husband, and a father. He turns from the use of force he saw in the cities of the Egyptians. Yet, he is destined to combine the peace that he finds, this relation of the tribe and of the family, with the political action of the city and of the state to create another kind of power.

The source and symbol of this power is the mountain. There, Moses, having left his Egyptian ancestors behind, finds his "ultimate ancestor," to use Alice Walker's phrase. Hurston is clear that Moses is the "man of the mountain" in the sense that he partakes of its essence. Jethro affirms Moses' identity:

> "The great I AM took the soul of the world and wrapped some flesh around it and that made you. You are the one being waited for on this mountain . . . You are the son of the mountain. The mountain has waited for the man" (MM, 137).

The mountain's power finds its instrument: Moses. The god of the mountain is a god of power, and he transforms Moses into an image of that power. The god of the mountain is also a god of wonder, and it is wonder that brings Moses into the god's service: "And the angel of the LORD appeared to him in a flame of fire out of the midst of a bush; and he looked, and lo, the bush was burning, yet it was not consumed" (Exodus 3:2).

Jewish legend says that the bush was a thorn bush burning with celestial fire "that has three peculiar qualities: it produces blossoms, it does not consume the object around which it plays, and it is black of color."[12] The thorn bush is the lowliest of all species, yet it can lacerate the wings of any bird that lights upon it. So Israel in its exile is the least powerful of all nations, yet those that subjugate Israel will be punished while Israel will flower as God promised in the Covenant with Abraham. The bush is also a symbol of God's modesty and of God's willingness to suffer with Israel.[13] Seeing this wonder, Moses is startled and thinks: "I will turn aside and see this great sight, why the bush is not burnt. When the Lord saw that he had turned aside to see, God called to him out of the bush, "Moses, Moses!" And he said, "Here am I" (Exodus 3:2-4).

The breaking of the sacred into the profane is a site of absolute potential in which transformation can occur. Here, in this moment and in this place, Moses and God exchange names. By doing so, they begin to redefine power, not as force, but as reciprocity; that is, Moses partakes of

the name of God, and God partakes of the name of Moses. This passage i
one of dislocation, relocation, and revelation on Moses' part and on God's.

When God calls Moses' name, Moses as shepherd, father, and husband
is undone. When Moses answers, "'Here am I'" (Exodus 3:4), he is both
verifying his name and his present location in the world and opening
himself to recreation. Moses is relocated in time and space: he learns that he
is Hebrew and that this God who is the God of his father (Exodus 3:6) i
also the God of the patriarchs (Exodus 3:6). Moses' identity—both religiou
and personal—is revealed to him, and the wanderer is located in a human
family and in a people's history.

Then, Moses is dislocated; he learns that that location brings with it a
responsibility: he must lead his people out of bondage. He becomes an
instrument of God's will, and in that relationship, in that vocation, his
identity as one of God's people must be defined. In Moses' answer to God's
call, Moses begins his movement towards his full humanity and identity. Yet
Moses naturally hesitates, especially since the call means that he must
return to Egypt.

> [H]is first question is: "Who am I that I should go to Pharoah, and bring the
> sons of Israel out of Egypt?" In a moment of what we must presume to be fear,
> self-doubt, and uncertainty, Moses asks, "Who am I?"...Notice how the
> dialogue has changed. His response to his name was "Here am I." Now, his
> response to his call is "Who am I?"[14]

The call is both an affirmation and a destruction of identity. Hurston's
Moses, after the burning bush, is identified and identifies himself again and
again as "a man who has been called" (MM, 163-165, 173, 312). He will
work both to define his identity as a man called and to struggle for
liberation. Located in the history of the Hebrews, Moses is called to
continue the work that God began at the creation. Gustavo Gutierrez
explains:

> By working, transforming the world, breaking out of servitude, building a just
> society, and assuming his destiny in history, man forges himself...To work, to
> transform this world, is to become a man and to build the human
> community.[15]

Identity, community, and religious meaning are defined as Moses carries
out his vocation.

But Moses, I think, is not the only one transformed in the call, for the
call is reciprocal. Interdependence means that the response changes the
caller as well as the called. God as God of the mountain and of the burning

bush, of nature, too, is undone. Moses, resisting the call, asks God's name, asks for verification of power, and in giving both, God is transformed. God gives up a part of Godself[16] and enters into a process of defining God's identity with Moses and with the Hebrews. God enters history. Just as the fire does not consume the bush, however, the giving of the name does not consume God. Rather, God defines Godself as pure being which is outside the process of history while participating in it.

These qualities of God, his purity and his participation, are to be Moses' sign to both the Hebrews.

> Then Moses said to God, "If I come to the people of Israel and say to them, 'The God of your fathers has sent me to you,' and they ask me, 'What is his name?' what shall I say to them?" God said to Moses, "I AM WHO I AM" (Exodus 3:13-14).

God's answer, "I AM WHO I AM" is an act of deconstruction and reconstruction, doing two things. God is saying a thing that can be spoken: that when questioned, Moses should assert Moses' own identity as the agent of God, "I am who I am." God is also saying a thing that cannot be spoken: the name of God which indicates, not a historically bodied being, but a process and a promise. "I AM WHO I AM" can also be translated in other ways, including:

"I am who am"
"I am he who will be"
"I am what I am"
"I will be what I will be"
and
"I am he who is being."[17]

Though God provides a name, God's identity is not fixed and finished. Like the vocation of Moses, the name of God is a revelation that connects the past, the creation and the promise to Abraham, to the future, the Exodus, the Covenant, and the Promised Land.

The name of God is also a sign of power that is, at the same time, a transformation of power. The name of God is a symbol that begins to answer the unnamed Hebrew's first question to Moses: "What is the difference between what you did and what I did?" Though the nature and necessity of violence is always risky to judge, one can say that what Moses makes in striking the Hebrew is an act that breaks through both the overt and covert violence of the unjust social system in Egypt.[18] Professor Jose Miguez-Bonino says that the question of violence must be judged always in particular terms:

An ethic of revolution cannot avoid discussion of the use and justification of violence. This question, nevertheless, needs to be placed in its proper perspective as a subordinate and relative question. It is *subordinate* because it has to do with the "cost" of desired change—the question of the legitimacy of revolution is not decided on the basis of the legitimacy of violence and vice versa. Violence is a cost that must be estimated and pondered in relation to a paraticular revolutionary situation. It is *relative* because in most revolutionary situations—at least those with which we are concerned—violence is already a fact constitutive of the situation. Injustice, slave-labor, hunger, exploitation are forms of violence that must be weighed against the cost of revolutionary violence.[19]

Seen as revolutionary violence, Moses' murder of the Egyptian is a "No!" to the violence that the Hebrews have suffered. It is a human action, almost an invitation, creating an opening through which God can enter and can begin to operate in the life of Moses and in Hebrew history. When Hurston's Moses faces the Hebrews, he says of God that "'His sign is power'" and that the name "I am what I am" is a "'great answer'" that "takes in the whole world and the firmaments of heaven'" (MM, 174-175). In other words, Moses' paradoxical act indicates that there is something other than Pharoah's brute political force. There exists, he is saying, universal justice, power tempered by love. Thus, Moses abdicates patriarchal political power, with its absolute claims and structures, and becomes a leader, one showing Israel how to be in relationship to God. As the charismatic leader, his power is always in question.[20] Thus, Hurston indicates, his role is forever in formation, and he must call on all his creative powers to maintain the people's recognition of his authority:

> [Moses] thought and led. He prayed and led . . . even when he knew that he would have been better loved as a King and more popular as a politician. But he chose to be a leader and he was. He stood in his high, lonely place and led (MM, 303).

In the name and the call, then, the Hebrew slave's second question, "Who are you to tell me what to do?" also begins to be answered. The answer is two-fold: Moses is the messenger of "I AM," and that role legitimates him. But Moses is also only Moses, and, ultimately, he cannot tell the Hebrews what to do. I hope to make that clear, presently.

The meaning of God's power and Moses' vocation is made clear in Moses' duel with Pharoah for the people of Israel. The source of power of Moses as leader is a foil to the sources of power of Pharoah as political leader. Martin Buber illustrates the contrast this way: "..the 'theo-political' idea of Moses; namely, his conception of the relation between YHVH and srael, which could not be other than political in its realistic character,... tarts from the God and not from the nation in the political indication of goal and way."[21] Thus, the order of power is reversed, making Moses a different kind of leader than Pharoah:

> [Moses] himself possesses the power, but his power is a doubtful one. He is the leader who demands no dominion for himself, and evidently by reason of a sentiment in which different motives converge.... [The most important of those motives] is the passionate wish to make a serious political issue of the faith in the earthly dominion of the god...The stern and deep realism of Moses, which could not bear that, as elsewhere, a sacred symbolism should replace or supplant the factual realization of his faith, determines the type, the order of power.[22]

This is clear in the way in which the two men approach the duel.

In *Moses, Man of the Mountain*, while the young Pharoah Ta-Phar (who in the biblical text is not named, making him a symbol of all oppressive power) dreams of monuments and riches for his own honor, the young Moses is tutored by Mentu, a Hebrew wise man, about the origins of the world and the power of God. Mentu tells Moses stories that "did not die. They were stronger and more enduring than men" (MM, 55). Mentu, clearly a play on Telemachus' Mentor, forms Moses' soul while the young prince Moses learns the Egyptian arts of religious ritual and the skills of the military. The differences in the boys' characters are apparent when the two collide as adults. Where Moses performs miracles, transformations of matter that alter and inform the consciousness and the imagination, Pharoah sees magic, manipulation of matter for power. Self-centered, the Pharoah, faced with Moses' power, cannot open his heart to the wonder of God, and he, thus, dooms his people to the very curse that he put on the Hebrews.

In Exodus1, Pharoah proclaimed, "'When you serve as midwife to the Hebrew women, and see them upon the birthstool, if it is a son you shall kill him; but if it is a daughter, she shall live'" (Exodus 1:16-17). The spirit of God, angered by this threat, turns it on Egypt: "And you shall say to Pharoah, 'Thus says the Lord, Israel is my first-born son, and I say to you, Let my son go that he may serve me; if you refuse to let him go, behold I will slay your first-born son'" (Exodus 4: 22-23). God becomes the murderous midwife destroying "the first-born in the land of Egypt, from the first-born of Pharoah who sat on his throne to the first born of the captive who was in the dungeon, and all the first-born of the cattle" (Exodus 12: 29-30).

In the Passover, we are presented with another passage. As God's spirit "crosses over," identity for the Egyptians is destroyed in a fundamental way:

> Darkness balanced up on midnight looking both ways for day. Then the great cry arose in Egypt. They cried and died in Egypt. It was the great cry that had issued first from the throat of Israel years before and spread to the rim bones of the world and come back again . . . Egypt cried out at the death of the first-born. Every house in Egypt was bloody. Blood outside the door in Goshen, blood inside every house in Egypt (MM, 220-221).

As Hurston indicates, God destructively levels power, making every Egyptian from the leader to the criminal to the animal the same. In making the Covenant, God will also level power, but in terms of love and justice God also inverts the terms of power. To be "inside" is to be "outside," unprotected and open to destruction. God's anger is a universal sign to those whose pride causes them to thwart God's will. God can engage in the reciprocity of power in order to punish, and God does so here. Pharoah's heart hardened to wonder, can respond only to pain, to the demonic and destructive force of God. God makes Moses step aside and acts Godself, using that same power that tried to kill the uncircumsized Moses (Exodus 4: 24-26). Power is the only language that Pharoah can understand, and God unleashes its full fury on the Pharoah and on his nation. Forced by God to undergo what they had forced the Hebrews to undergo, Pharoah and Egypt are made to experience and to understand powerlessness and defeat. They cry, but there is no response. Beaten on his own terms and rejected by his people, Pharoah lets the Hebrews go.

The crossing of the Red Sea in Exodus 14: 21-30 is the transition between slavery and freedom. The parted sea is a kind of aisle down which the Hebrews move, indicating a rite-of-passage from one life to another, from servitude in Egypt to a "marriage" with God. Like Moses, who "crossed over" leaving his Egyptian identity behind, the Hebrews also "cross over," leaving behind their identities as slaves. The passage establishes Moses as the chosen one, the conduit of God's power. God could part and close the waters, but God chooses to have Moses stretch out his hand and become the medium. In these actions, parting the waters and choosing his leader, God shows God's dominance over nature and over culture. Indeed, when the waters flood the Egyptians, we feel that their era of importance in history is over. The Hebrews, despite their murmurings in the wilderness and their desire for Egypt, have nothing to return to; they must go forward.

Moses, the liberator, must now become Moses the founder of a nation. The vehicle for that formation is the Covenant. The liberation of the people and the Covenant are different aspects of the same movement leading to an encounter with God. The movement is from "despoilation and misery" to the beginning of "the construction of a just and fraternal society. It is the suppression of disorder and the creation of a new order."[23] The wilderness is the place where that new order is created; the wilderness, for the Hebrews, as it was for Moses, is a "school of the soul."[24] There are, however, really two wilderness experiences in the narrative: the first ending with the episode of the Golden Calf and, after that episode, the second ending with the entry into the land.

Slavery has made the Hebrews weak. Hurston describes the first wilderness experience as a struggle between service in Egypt and service at Sinai. The Hebrews in Egypt have no responsibility for themselves; they merely do what they are told and, at least, as they tell Moses, they are fed. In Egypt, they are people without a god, without a story, and, therefore, without any sense of identity. Sinai, in contrast, represents the gift of God, story, and identity, but earned through choice, acceptance, and responsibility. Like Moses, who is called to be the liberator, the Hebrews are called to become Israelites. The Hebrews who leave Egypt, however, cannot take on that responsibility.

To illustrate the Egypt/Sinai contrast, Hurston uses the metaphor of hunger, contrasting the hunger of the body for sustenance to the hunger of the spirit for freedom, tying Eden to the Covenant. The Covenant potentially redeems Adam's Fall, should human beings choose proper food. The murmurings of the Hebrews are about bodily needs which they want Moses to fill. Faced with the murmurings, Moses invokes the metaphor of the hunger for freedom:

> "I had the idea all along that you came out here hunting freedom. I didn't know you were hunting a barbecue. Freedom looks like the biggest thing that God ever made to me, and being a little hungry for the sake of it ought not to stop you" (MM, 252).

The purpose of the Sinai experience is to give the Hebrews a taste of what freedom means, to feed the Hebrews what food bondage took out:

> Now they acted like they knew they were free by ear but they couldn't conceive of it. They did not believe they could take on any responsibility for themselves at all. They kept clamoring for somebody to act for them (MM, 248).

Freedom, Hurston argues, is more than release from bondage. It is the capacity to act as a person. Moses cannot act for any other individual. Though Moses is the intermediary between God and the community, the Covenant essentially displaces Moses as it calls each person to act for himself or herself. Thus, as I suggested earlier, ultimately, Moses is nobody to tell the Hebrews what to do.

The present generation of Hebrews, however, cannot act for its own freedom as is illustrated in the incident of the Golden Calf. The Calf is not only like an Egyptian god and, therefore, a symbol of the past and of slavery; it is also the symbol of the murmurings: it is deified food. Finally, it represents the greatest struggle between Egypt and Sinai—that between the idol and the law. Making the Golden Calf is an external symbol of an internal condition. Left alone, these people cannot be a nation, so God calls for their destruction. Hurston's God says to Moses,

> "They have betrayed me. They have betrayed you, and most of all they have dirtied their souls by betraying themselves . . . The people that you have brought out of Egypt have soiled themselves and tempted me to destroy them" (MM, 288).

Thus, the Hebrews are doomed either to die—as Moses, in his one act of force, imitates the God of the Passover, slaughtering those who "break loose" (Exodus 32: 25) like wild animals; or to wander—as Moses, in this pitiless act, imposes penance on these domesticated beings, driving them further into the wilderness which is a sign of spiritual homelessness.

> To wander and to fall down and to die in strange places where nobody lived and where nobody would live again for thousands of years. The Voice had said to take a nation across the Jordan, and the generation which he had brought out of Egypt had failed him. "The third generation will feel free and noble. Then I can mold a nation. Forty years is a long, long time,...but the Voice commanded me to lead." And Moses was very sad (MM, 317).

The desert, as a symbol of homelessness, however, is also a solitary and silent place where the Hebrews can learn about their true home. As Eric Voegelin puts it, the Hebrews must learn that Egypt is the real desert and that the silence of the wilderness, in contrast, is filled with the voice of God. Once they hear God's voice and accept God's command, they become capable of moving forward to the Promised Land.[25]

Forty years bring a different group of Hebrews to Sinai, a group that can choose, as individuals, to form a nation through the Covenant. The Covenant that Moses wants to establish is a founding document and a founding act. As a document, it contains law, ritual, and tribal stories about the history of the people, binding the religious, the ethical, and the political. It is a site of memory—particularly the memory of slavery—and fuel for the imagination of the nation:

> "When your son asks you in time to come, 'What is the meaning of the testimonies and the statutes and the ordinances which the LORD our God has commanded you?'then you shall say to your son. 'We were Pharoah's slaves in Egypt; and the LORD brought us out of Egypt with a mighty hand; and the LORD showed signs and wonders,great and grievous, against Egypt and against Pharoah and all his household before your eyes; and he brought us out from there, that he might bring us in and give us the land which he swore to give to our fathers. And the LORD commanded us to do all these statutes, to fear the LORD our God, for our good always, that he might preserve us alive, as at this day.And it will be righteousness for us, if we are careful to do all this commandment before the LORD our God, as he commanded us'" (Deuteronomy 6: 20-25).

The Covenant requires the free people that God demands, for, as Walzer says, these are people who must choose to bind themselves to the Covenant and, thus, to God, to each other, and to memory, creating both an individual and a national consciousness: "the individuals who commit themselves are moral equals. 'There is,' in the words of a modern biblical scholar, 'a fundamental equality of status so far as Yahweh is concerned, or put things right way around, an equality of responsibility.'"[26]

The acceptance of this responsibility transforms the Hebrews into Israelites, from a disorganized and unrelated group of individuals into a people. The acceptance of responsibility also underscores the point that the Promised Land is never completely possessed but is always a promise.[27] The Covenant is double-voiced. It is a document that requires action, symbolizing that freedom is a quality of the integrated individual and is bound to the capacity to exercise the creative and ethical imagination.[28] As each generation makes its vow to the laws and remembers the stories, those laws and those stories will be transformed, gaining new meaning and new power, as members of the community interact with one another. The Promised Land may be a physical place, but it also, as the Jewish people later proved in exile, a structure of the imagination and a symbol of hope for a just and perfect society.

Moses stands as the transitional figure between Egypt/Hebrew and Israel. The reciprocity of power of Egypt, illustrated in Pharoah and in the unnamed Hebrew who strikes his fellow and asks Moses, "Who are you to tell me how to behave?" is a world in which blow is traded for blow and in which force is the victor. The reciprocity of justice that Moses brings is Israel: a land in which individuals are bound to one another in love under the law of a powerful God who requires fairness and freedom—"the blessing of being responsible for [one's] own" (MM, 346). The love of both self and "other," human and holy, is the foundation of community. "'Anyhow, chief,'" says Joshua in *Moses, Man of the Mountain*, "'we ain't the same folks we was when we viewed the Jordan last time. We're a people now'" (MM, 338).

The Covenant is made. Moses gives Israel the structures for identity and community, but he can take them only to the threshold. They must step into the land themselves and build it in their own image, answer God's call with their own voices. Hurston's metaphor is the addition of words to the music that Moses gives them: "[Moses] had given Israel back the notes to songs. The words would be according to their own dreams, but they could sing. They had songs and singers" (MM, 346).

The hero's job is done. Joshua, with his military might tempered by what he has learned as Moses' disciple, will lead the people into the Promised Land. Aaron and Miriam, who represent the cultic force of the Hebrews in Egypt and in the wilderness are dead; their power is not proper for life in Canaan. If they and Moses are brothers and sister, their deaths indicate that Yahweh is not the god of a family, related by blood, but the god of a nation, human beings related by the Covenant. Israel is a reality, and God approves the community.

What of Moses? Is his importance diminished because he cannot enter the land? Moses answered, "Here am I" and asked "Who am I?" Finally, how can we assess Moses in relationship to his own responses?

Moses is, above all, a man—an exemplary human being who, though fearful and unsure, accepts his calling and who, in making himself humble and responsible to the will of God, brings the *possibility* of freedom, dignity, and identity to a people. Hurston struggles in her novel with that qualifier: possibility. The leader/master, she concludes, cannot make the follower/disciple free; if he or she tries to, those roles become rigid and another form of slavery emerges. The hero only can point the way. Hurston's Moses, standing on Mount Nebo, thinks:

> He had meant to make a perfect people, free and just, noble and strong, that should be a light for all the world and for time and eternity. And he wasn't sure he had succeeded. He had found that no man may make another free. Freedom was something internal . . . All you could do was give the opportunity for freedom and the man himself must make his own emancipation (MM, 344-345).

Moses, who offers this possibility, is an image of its fulfillment: a man with radical freedom achieved through accepting the burden of radical responsibility, through exercising radical thought, and through making radical action. He embodies and resolves the action of the epic. As Martin Buber explains:

> [This] constitutes his idea and his task: the realization of the unity of religious and social life in the community of Israel, the substantiation of a ruling by God that shall not be culturally restricted but shall comprehend the entire existence of the nation, the theo-political principle; all this has penetrated to the deeps of his personality, it has raised his person above the compartmental system of typology, it has mingled the elements of his soul into a most rare unity.[29]

This "rare unity" is preserved as Moses is not allowed to cross into the Promised Land.

> And the LORD said to him, "This is the land of which I swore to Abraham, to Isaac, and to Jacob, 'I will give it to your descendants.' I have let you see it with your eyes, but you shall not go over there." So, Moses the servant of the LORD died there in the land of Moab, according to the word of the LORD, and he buried him in the valley in the land of Moab opposite Bethpeor; but no man knows the place of his burial to this day (Deuteronomy 34: 4-6).

What seems a cruel punishment, a failure, for a man who has worked so hard is, in fact, a triumph, a gift, and a way of honoring his unique character. In this denial, God grants Moses his freedom, for the spirit of Moses should and could never be confined in the robes either of kingship or of the priesthood. Moses is that "homeless spirit"[30] that demonic (in the Tillichian sense), creative power, that Yahweh is, loves, and honors.

For the modern person, particularly for colonized peoples of the new world, Moses' role as homeless spirit represents the promise of liberation and of justice. This story, his story, illustrates the power of signification by the powerless. That is, the Exodus story is the symbol of the master's trope's being used to undermine the master's power. The Exodus myth, that central myth of the West, also makes a critique of its most terrible acts. It is the story within what Toni Morrison calls "the master narrative," the ideological script of the West, that, again and again, has been used to symbolize and to encourage the flight of people from and the fight of people against oppression and terror. It is a cry from within: a reminder and a cultural conscience.

Moses, finally, is both center and hinge, the one connected to God who can clear a path to freedom for his community. This sense of Moses' special connection to God is beautifully illustrated in the Jewish legend of Moses' death which God, along with the archangels Michael, Gabriel, and Zagzagel, attends. God stands at Moses' head while the angels stand at his hands and feet. Moses' soul is God's daughter who is reluctant to leave Moses' body because she loves it. Moses, learning that his soul will return to God, urges her to leave him, and she consents: "Moses...permitted his soul to leave him, saying to her: "Return unto thy rest, O my soul; for the Lord hath dealt bountifully with thee." God thereupon took Moses' soul by kissing him upon the mouth.[31]   That great soul exists in eternity to be reborn in time in all those who fight for human dignity and for freedom.

Moses never becomes an Israelite. He is not of a nation; he remains a sojourner in a foreign land. He is Moses: a free and pure individual, "whom the LORD knew face to face" (Deuteronomy 34:10), and who, because his body is never found, never really dies. Ultimately, Moses' majesty, wisdom, and beauty are fleeting, yet eternal, and he is like the Promised Land—a space in time and a wish.

NOTES

1. Martin Luther King, Jr. "I See the Promised Land," in *The Essential Writings and Speeches of Martin Luther King, Jr.*, ed. James M. Washington (San Francisco: Harper San Francisco, 1986), p. 286.

2. Mayflower Compact" in Giles Gunn, ed. *New World Metaphysics* (New York: Oxford University Press, 1981), p. 48.

3. John Winthrop, "A Modell of Christian Charity," in Gunn, pp. 53-54.

4. See James M. Redfield, *Nature and Culture in the Iliad : The Tragedy of Hector* (Chicago: The University of Chicago Press, 1975), pp. 99-127 for this kind of language on the hero.

5. Michael Walzer, *Exodus and Revolution* (New York: Basic Books, 1985), pp. 12, 17.

6. For a good and brief summary of Moses' various roles, see Elias Auerbach, *Moses* (Detroit: Wayne State University, 1975), pp. 215-216. He concludes that Moses was "the artist who saw in the rough block not only the hidden, the perfect form; impatiently and patiently, he struck it out of the stone with a heavy hammer and smoothing chisel. He was a man in his fullness, one in a thousand years."

7. Henry Louis Gates, Jr., *The Signifying Monkey: A Theory of African-American Literary Criticism* (New York: Oxford University Press, 1988), pp. 22, 60.

8. Quoted in Gates, p. 50.

9. Deborah McDowell, "Lines of Descent/Dissenting Lines," Foreword to *Moses Man of the Mountain* (New York: Harper Collins, 1991), pp. xiv, xvi.

10. Zora Neale Hurston, *Moses, Man of the Mountain* (Chicago: University of Illinois Press, 1984), p. 52. Hereafter, quotations from this text will be parenthetically, MM and the page number.

11. Martin Buber, *Moses: The Revelation and the Covenant* (New York: Harper Torchbooks, 1958), p. 35.

12. Louis Ginzberg, *The Legends of the Jews*, Vol. II, trans. Henrietta Szold (Philadelphia: The Jewish Publication Society of America, 1969), p. 303.

13. Louis Ginzberg, *The Legends of the Jews*, pp. 303-304.

14. Cecil Eubanks, "The Flaming Presence," Unpublished paper.

15. Gustavo Gutierrez, *A Theology of Liberation: History, Politics, and Salvation*, trans. and ed., Sister Caridad Inda and John Eagleson (Maryknoll, N.Y.: Orbis Press, 1973), p. 159.

16. I recognize the inelegant quality of this word, but I use it to avoid gendering God.

17. See Gutierrez, pp. 165ff. and *The Oxford Annotated Bible*, notes to Exodus 4:14.

18. See Robert McAfee Brown, *Religion and Violence* (Philadelphia: Westminster Press, 1987), pp.34-37 on the problem of structural violence.

19. Jose Miguez-Bonino, *The Development Apocalypse*, p. 108, quoted in McAfee Brown, p. 32.

20. Max Weber, *From Max Weber: Essays in Sociology*, trans. and ed., H. H. Gerth and C. Wright Mills (New York: Oxford University Press, 1946), p. 246: "[The charismatic leader's] claim breaks down if his mission is not recognized by those to whom he feels he has been sent." Weber sets the charismatic against the patriarchal. I wonder if we might argue, following Weber and using, as I will later, the idea that Moses' soul is feminine, that the feminine is that charismatic power that arises at certain historical moments to check and transform masculine, patriarchal power.

21. Martin Buber, p. 101.

22. Martin Buber, p. 87.

23. Gustavo Gutierrez, p. 155.

24. Michael Walzer, p. 50.

25. Eric Voegelin, *Order and History*, Vol.I: *Israel and Revelation* (Baton Rouge: Louisiana State University Press, 1956), p. 113:
The flight leads nowhere, until we stop in order to find our bearings beyond the world. When the world has become the Desert, man is at ast in the solitude in which he can hear thundering the voice of the spirit that with its urgent whispering has already driven and rescued him from Sheol [Egypt]. In the Desert, God spoke to the leader and his tribes; in the Desert, by listening to the voice, by accepting its offer, and by submitting to its command, [the Hebrews] at last reached life and became the people chosen by God.

26. Michael Walser, p. 84.

27. See Walzer, pp. 102-104 and Gutierrez, pp. 165-168.

28. For an interesting new book on this subject, see Eliot Deutsch, *Creative Being: The Crafting of Person and World* (Honolulu: The University of Hawaii Press, 1992.

29. Martin Buber, p. 186.

30. Cecil Eubanks, "The Homeless Spirit," Unpublished paper.

31. Louis Ginzberg, II, pp. 472-473.

The Ritual of Reading and Reading a Text as a Ritual

Observations on Mieke Bal's Death & Dissymmetry

VERNON K. ROBBINS

R obert Detweiler has contributed to the lives of many people in abundantly different ways. He has contributed to my life in a special way by initiating a graduate seminar which we have taught together three times under the title "Biblical and Secular Modes of Interpretation." In the context of this cooperative venture, he initiated a co-authored essay entitled "From New Criticism and the New Hermeneutic to Poststructuralism: Twentieth Century Hermeneutics" (Detweiler and Robbins 1991). It is a special pleasure to offer this essay in his honor as a small way of showing my appreciation for these and other activities that are so characteristic of his commitment to an intellectual environment of collegiality, nurture, and interchange.

The seminars with Robert Detweiler have created an environment in which it has been natural to entwine the excitement of unrestricted exploration with the satisfaction of detailed, precise analysis. In them, my own practice of "socio-rhetorical criticism" (Robbins 1984) has developed into an interdisciplinary method informed by postmodern modes of interpretation (Robbins 1992a; 1992b). The terminology of "rhetoric revalued," borrowed from the work of Brian Vickers by Wilhelm Wuellner (Wuellner 1987: 453; Vickers 1982; Robbins 1993), describes well the practice of multiple readings of a text in which I engage, and this essay uses this approach as it returns to a chapter of Mieke Bal's work which Robert Detweiler and I discussed in the seminar during Fall 1992.

In *Death & Dissymmetry*, a chapter entitled "Virginity Scattered" presents one step in Mieke Bal's analysis and interpretation of the Book of Judges in the Hebrew Bible (Bal 1988b: 69-93). The present essay approaches this chapter from the perspective of a socio-rhetorical poetics that investigates four aspects of texture in a text: (a) inner texture; (b) intertexture; (c) social and cultural texture; and (d) ideological texture (Robbins 1992a: xxvii-xxxviii; 1992c; 1992d).

There are three basic ways this poetics could be used in the context of Bal's analysis and interpretation. First, it could guide an independent analysis and interpretation of the passages in Judges which Bal analyzes. This investigation would evaluate and reconfigure Bal's statements by putting biblical passages in the foreground and Bal's statements in the background. This is the favored approach in biblical interpretation. With this strategy, analysis of the biblical passages themselves would overspeak her speech, and the pretense would be that the new analysis presents a better interpretation than hers. Here the interpreter functions as judge, and judicial rhetoric pronounces a verdict of guilty where Bal went wrong and acquittal where she went right.

Second, it could guide a programmatic display of Bal's interpretation of the texture of the biblical passages she interprets. In this instance the parts of Bal's commentary that speak specifically about the biblical passages would be in the foreground. The biblical passages would hover near at hand, and statements in her book that do not refer directly to the passages would be in the background. This approach would emphasize exegetical method, and it would identify and display those parts of the biblical passages Bal's method did pursue and it would call attention to aspects of the text she did not investigate. This approach would produce something more like epideictic rhetoric, praising what Bal did well and censuring what she did not do well.

Third, a socio-rhetorical poetics could guide an analysis of Bal's book as a twentieth century text designed to make a cultural and ideological statement about biblical interpretation itself. In this instance the texture of Bal's entire book would be in the foreground, Bal herself would hover closely behind the text, and the biblical passages she interprets would be fully in the background. Biblical interpreters use this last approach only for the giants in the field. This approach implies a near canonical status for the interpretation alongside the biblical text itself. Only with great care, then, does one take fully seriously the text an interpreter has produced. The usual approach is to fragment another interpreter's text in one way or another while producing one's own text, just as one regularly fragments comparative ancient texts that stand alongside the ancient text one is interpreting. This last approach puts the interpreter in the most venturesome position. One functions alternately as philosopher, politician, and priest, engaging partly in philosophical inquiry that negotiates truth claims, partly in deliberative rhetoric that calls for action, and partly in radical rhetoric that calls for belief without argumentation (Kennedy: 6-8, 93, 96, 104-106, 113).

This essay emphasizes the last approach: Bal's text as a cultural and ideological statement about biblical interpretation. Only briefly at the beginning does the essay comment about the biblical text itself, the first approach, and never does it programmatically analyze her commentary on a particular biblical passage, the second approach. The reason is simple. Bal's book is a late twentieth century challenge to biblical interpreters about how they go about the business of reading a text. The degree to which she is judged to be right or wrong in her interpretation of particular passages, therefore, may be less important than the way she approaches the task of biblical interpretation itself. Rather than serve as judge and jury on this occasion, I will serve partly as public orator and partly as philosopher, politician, and priest who will don a robe and concelebrate the ritual of biblical interpretation.

Inner Texture and Intertexture in "Virginity Scattered"

Let us start with some praise. While there are many ways Mieke Bal's book *Death & Dissymmetry* has been, can and will be criticized, it has achieved something that interpreters henceforth, in my opinion, should not attempt to reverse. Interpreters should admit that the story in Judges presents women getting caught, raped, murdered, and mangled in the context of men's games with one another. To approach the issue like this is to start with a mixture of public oratory and sacred pronouncement. But the evidence seems to me to be undeniable. In the path of men's (and God's) conquest of the land of Canaan in the Book of Judges lies the brutalized bodies of women. I do not see how we (meaning "we" traditional biblical interpreters) have any choice but to accept the indictment of the male interests that the text achieves at the expense of women's bodies and voices. And implicitly, at least, this is an indictment of the way we interpret the Bible. We find ways of siding with this and that victimized and marginalized group, but we achieve these interpretations by locating ourselves one way or another in the major plot of the biblical story. Bal's interpretation, therefore, raises serious questions about the manner in which we interpret biblical texts, as well as other texts. To align oneself with the story line and to celebrate God's victory and the victory of the Israelites over the Canaanites is to take a political, ideological, and theological position that must be carefully, thoughtfully, and deeply examined.

Bal achieves this *tour de force* by analyzing the Book of Judges with a series of modern theories that help her win the interpretive results. In chapter one she introduces modern feminist theory of interpretation; in chapter two she exposes the male point of view that guides Freud's definition of virginity; in chapter three she assaults the bulwark of philological definition; in chapter four she uses René Girard's theory of sacrifice and the surrogate victim to explain how the women become female victims caught between men; in chapter five she applies speech-act theory to interpret speech that produces fragmented female flesh and turns it into word to the tribes of Israel; in chapter six she uses the politics of geography and the ideology of space to examine how the houses of husbands become houses of horror for women; and in chapter seven she uses the modern theory of displacement to describe the discrediting of the mothers in the Book of Judges. Near the end, the book calls for a poetics of displacement that re(dis)places the women in the Book of Judges "in order to retrieve sight of how the men and women lived in the era represented in Judges, how their space in the land was organized, and which subjects had power in which spaces" (Bal 1988b: 230). Whether right or wrong in small details or larger vision, the book is a modern assault on much holy ground in biblical interpretation. One would presume, would one not, that the major plot of the story is the one to which one's faith must assent? This is a difficult issue, and it is difficult for men as well as for women, for authorized interpreters as well as marginalized interpreters. And I fear that I will not be able to bring any satisfying resolution to this issue in this essay. But perhaps the essay can at least suggest a way to take the issue seriously in biblical interpretation.

In order to pursue the issue somewhat programmatically, let us turn first to the inner texture of chapter 3 in Bal's book entitled "Virginity Scattered," which is the special focus of this essay. The first sentence in chapter 3 asserts that the Book of Judges is "full of virgins," and the second sentence refers to "collective virginity": "sons. . . exchanging virgins with other, pagan tribes" (Bal 1988b: 69). Throughout Bal's chapter, by my count, the words "virgin(s) or (non)virginal" occur forty-one times and the word "virginity" occurs nineteen times. Six of these occurrences are on the first page (69) and six more occur on the last two pages (92-93). The first seven pages, in which this terminology is repeated thirty two times, introduces the spectrum of Hebrew vocabulary that concerns virginity and formulates an opposing relation between a male and a female concept of virginity (69-75). As the chapter continues, it refers to segments of three stories in the Book of Judges: (a) the daughters of Shiloh in chapter 21; (b) the conception of Samson in chapter 13; and (c) the Levite and his concubine in chapter 19. The last five pages, in which the terminology concerning virgins and virginity is repeated thirteen times, bring the chapter to a conclusion with a dramatically new interpretation of the story about the Levite and his concubine in Judges 19 (89-93). The new interpretation emerges from a new understanding of customary marriage arrangements during the time of the settlement of Israelite tribes in the land of Canaan.

There is a span of text almost seven pages long in the middle of the chapter where no terminology about virgins or virginity occurs (81-87). This section begins with reference to "the limits of philology" (81), which implies the absence from interpretation of something very important; then it refers to the presence in traditional interpretation of "ideology" and "a recognizable ideologeme" (82-83), which implies that something is there which should not be. The traditional ideology, Bal asserts, underlies a "rhetoric of certainty" that replaces argumentation in traditional interpretation and a "rhetoric of philology" that "allows the critics to signal problems without solving them in the light of the story as a whole" (82). From a male perspective, according to Bal, "virgin" means "exclusive property of a father," while a female perspective defines her as a nubile woman concerned about her future and the complete cycle of her life (Bal 1988b:72). This discussion prepares the way for three pages that introduce systematic terminology concerning marriage—nomad(ic) or *beena* marriage, duolocal, uxorilocal, and matrilineal marriage—and proposes new definitions of patrilocal and virilocal marriage (84-86). She secures a firm point for her interpretation with the observation that Samson's first wife remained in her father's house and Samson periodically visited her there (88). Her dramatic challenge to traditional interpretation occurs when she draws the conclusion that the Levite's "concubine" is really a "patrilocal wife": "a wife living in the house of the father, a wife who remains a daughter" (89). When the Levite's wife returned to her father's house, in accord with *her* local customs, the Levite visits her there with anger because she had not submitted to the marriage residence conventions of *his* people (90-93). In other words, the woman in the Levite's house is caught in a male battle over the appropriate place in which a wife should reside. In this context, Bal challenges the traditional philological definition of *pilegesh* as "concubine," which implies prostitution—adultery. Instead of referring to an "unmarried woman," it is the term for a wife whose people think she should remain in her father's house. At this point Bal reaches the conclusion that she may have found "a linguistic development that parallels an ideological one, which is in turn related to an ethnographic one" (87).

Our interest lies in Bal's interpretational procedure. How does her interpretation lead the reader to her conclusions? Once she has introduced terminology concerning virgins and virginity, why does that terminology disappear for a span of text seven pages long? We can begin to answer these questions by turning from the inner texture of her argument to its intertexture.

Bal creates rich intertexture in her chapter by including two block quotations from the Hebrew Bible (69, 78), a block quotation from J. Alberto Soggin's commentary on Judges (82), another block quotation from Phyllis Trible's *Texts of Terror* (83), three art works by Rembrandt numerous bibliographical references in the text itself, and twenty nine end notes. In the midst of all of these references, I as a traditionally trained biblical interpreter began to be haunted by the absence of reference to a kind of resource I will discuss below in some detail. But at this point let us look more closely at the intertextuality Bal explicitly establishes in the chapter.

In her twenty-nine footnotes to the chapter (265-268), Bal refers three times to her own work, eight times to published works other than her own, and three times to museums that own the three art works by Rembrandt. In addition, she refers to "Mary Douglas's pathbreaking work," and to suggestions made to her in conversations with Margaretha Alexiou and Fokkelien van Dijk. The remaining notes contain comments without reference to published works. By including the first name of every woman who is a source of information or comment, the chapter communicates a distinction between male and female authors and colleagues. References to male authors, in contrast, omit the first name.

Bal includes approximately twenty bibliographical references in the text of the chapter itself (depending on how one counts them). Approximately half of these are to male biblical critics whose interpretation she criticizes and another three are to interpretations of Phyllis Trible which she criticizes. The remaining references include Jacques Derrida (72), Claude Lévi-Strauss (77), Kenneth Clark's interpretation of aspects of Rembrandt's art works (79), and a few other people.

The notable omission, for this biblical interpreter, occurs in the seven pages of text that propose an ethnographic interpretation that should displace the traditional philological interpretation presupposed by male biblical scholars and perpetuated by Phyllis Trible's interpretation (81-93) In this span of text, which contains multiple references to biblical scholars here is no reference to any published work by a cultural anthropologist, social anthropologist, ethnographer, or symbolic psychologist—even though there are narratorial comments about "anthropological terminology" (84), an "ethnographic" development (87), and "symbolic-psychological" and "anthropological" levels of the story (88, 90). At this point, I began to look around for the sources of the unvoiced intertextuality in her interpretation. What is the nature of the underlying resources for her analysis and interpretation of the residential patterns of husbands and wives in ancient Israel? Are the resources simply textual, in the manner in which most biblical interpretation is textual rather than pictorial? She includes art work of Rembrandt, and that art work plays an especially strong role in her interpretation. Do her special strategies of interpretation come primarily from the discipline of art interpretation, or do they come from some other disciplinary arena? With these questions in mind, let us turn first to an anthropological text.

Turner's The Ritual Process *As An Intertext For Bal's* "Virginity Scattered"

Bal refers to Victor Turner's *The Ritual Process* both in the bibliography at the end of her book (Bal 1988b: 296) and in note twenty- two for Chapter (264), but she does not refer to Turner's book in chapter 3 or in other chapters of her book. If the reader looks at Turner's book, however, a discussion of residential patterns for husbands and wives appears in a context of great interest for *Death & Dissymmetry*:

> The Ndembu, who practice matrilineal descent combined with virilocal marriage, live in small, mobile villages. The effect of this arrangement is that women, through whom children derive their primary lineage and residential affiliation, spend much of their reproductive cycle in the villages of their husbands and not of their matrilineal kin. . . . One consequence of this is that every fruitful marriage becomes an arena of covert struggle between a woman's husband and her brothers and mother's brothers over the residential affiliation of her children. . . .
>
> Interestingly, it is the shades of direct matrilineal kinswomen—own mothers or own mothers' mothers—that are held to afflict women with reproductive disorders, resulting in temporary barrenness. . . . They have been caught [with infertility], so Ndembu regularly say, because they have "forgotten" those shades who are not only their direct ascendants but also the immediate progenetrices of their matrikin—who form the core membership of villages different from those of their husbands. The curative rites, including Isoma, have as one social function that of "causing them to remember" these shades, who are structural modes of a locally residing matrilineage. The

condition of barrenness these shades bring about is considered to be a temporary one, to be removed by performance of the appropriate rites. Once a woman remembers the afflicting shade, and thus her primary allegiance to matrikin, the interdiction on her fertility will cease; she can go on living with her husband but with a sharpened awareness of where her and her children's ultimate loyalties lie (Turner 1969: 12-13).

This span of text in Turner's *The Ritual Process* has a deep intertextua relationship with Bal's entire book, *Death and Dissymmetry*. But it intertextuality is nowhere more evident than in the chapter on "Virginit Scattered." The following quotations from Bal's chapter will secure thi point:

> In Kallah's story, the opposition between patrilocal and virilocal marriage is the conflict that generates the narrative line. . . . The Levite took a woman, who was. . . a "nomad-wife". . . . He married a woman who, according to the institution valid in Bethlehem, remained in her father's house. (Bal 1988b: 86)
>
> Both the rival males as well as the memory of them has to be "utterly destroyed." So great is, in this male (*zachar*) view, the importance of the history of the people, as distinct from any other people, that the marriageable women have to be "pure" of memory, perpetuating only the sons of Benjamin.
>
> . . . these terrified girls, stripped of their identity, are subsequently captured by the murderers and "brought" to the camp where they will be forced to "know man by lying with a male/memory." (Bal 1988b: 70)

Bal's chapter is a "masterful" reinterpretation of the Book of Judges b means of a spectrum of techniques and practices that are second nature to cultural anthropologist like Victor Turner. Observing that the Israelite during the period of the Judges were constituted by nomadic clans, Ba analyzes the relation of lineal descent to the residential patterns tha accompany marriage. In contrast to the Ndembu, who practice matrilinea descent, the Israelites and Canaanites practice patrilineal descent. Like th nomadic Ndembu, however, the Israelites practice virilocal marriage, tha is, the wife resides in the village of her husband and his kin. In the midst o the conflict that arises as a result of various actions by the men, "barre women" play a special role and "memory" is central to rituals that th people perform either to restore or maintain peace within their villag and/or throughout the region.

But there is more. A careful look at Turner's *The Ritual Process* reveal the presence of photographs interspersed throughout the text in a manne similar to the display of Rembrandt's art work in Bal's chapter. Further, a examination of the text that accompanies the photographs in Turner' chapter entitled "Planes of Classification in a Ritual of Life and Death eveals analysis of holes dug in the earth that represent "tomb" and "womb." "The woman with *lufwisha* [i.e., who has lost three or four children by stillbirth or infant mortality] must go into the hole of life and pass through the tunnel to the hole of death" (Turner 1969: 28). The seven photographs on the following pages exhibit moments in the *Isoma* ritual. First, the man and woman enter the hole together. Second, the woman:

> is given the young white pullet to hold; during the rites she clasps it against her left breast, where a child is held. . . . The mature red cock is laid, trussed up by the feet. . . on the men's side, ready to be sacrificed by beheading at the end of the rites. . . . The white pullet, according to one informant. . . stands for. . . procreative capacity (Turner 1969: 31-32).

After men standing outside the hole pour medicine and beer on the couple, behead the rooster and scatter its blood on them, and pour water on them, the man and the woman go to a newly-made hut and squat beside each other just inside the round opening in the front (Turner 1969: 33-37).

The sequence in Turner's book has a fascinating relation to Bal's display of Rembrandt's art work in the chapter under discussion (Bal 1988b:76-80). Bal's interpretation of "Angel Announcing the Birth of Samson to Manoah" includes the following:

> In the background, the little gate, right in the middle, can be taken to represent the womb whose entrance the messenger heads to, while the husband turns his back to it (Bal 1988b: 75).

Then the following interpretation of "Manoah's Offering" occurs:

> While the man closes his eyes in fright, his head facing toward the woman, she, in turn, closes her eyes in intense communication with the deity, the father of her child. She is, at this very moment, conceiving (Bal 1988b: 75-76).

Bal gives a similar interpretation of "Samson's Wedding Feast" in which one immediately notices the technique of displaying "moments in the ritual" through the art of photography. Her first act of interpretation is to take us to "the left side" of the painting, then, to focus on individual moments: "a woman who attempts to loosen the grip of the man who holds her"; who can only "close her eyes and bend her head." Or she focuses on the concerns of procreation and death. In addition, one notices the interpretation of men and women in relation to holes, doorways, and gateways that symbolize wombs and tombs. In Rembrandt's art work, Bal discovered a display of moments in the ritual of the conception, birth, and marriage of Samson that is analogous to Turner's photographic display o moments in the *Isoma* ritual among the Ndembu (Bal 1988b: 79).

Art interpretation and cultural anthropological interpretation of ritua are related, yet they are distinctive. Is Bal functioning as an interpreter o art or as a cultural anthropologist interpreting a story as a ritual? On th one hand, the emphasis on "a moment" in the story appears to b intensified by the inclusion of interpretation of art. Artistic pieces that focu on historical episodes must feature a moment in the story. For Bal, an ar work features a moment. Focus on the moment as seen in her interest i Rembrandt's art work has also nurtured her approach to stories in the Boo of Judges. But in Bal's interpretation "moments" expand into a "sequence o actions" and "the accompanying positions":

> *First* the men hide and watch. *Then* the girls come out and dance. See and behold: catch. The order to capture the women comes as the consequence of the girls' dancing, rather than of the men's watching without being seen. The girls, like all victims of rape, seem to provoke their abduction. They dance, they are to be watched, and: behold. The memory of the military slogan *veni, vidi, vici* imposes itself nicely (Bal 1988b: 71).

Extending a moment into a sequence of actions makes it a ritual. It is no accidental that Turner's book is entitled *The Ritual Process* and that Bal' book contains an interpretation of sequences of moments in the stories tha make them rituals in the lives of the Israelites. Her use of Rembrandt's ar work helps her to emphasize particular moments in those rituals:

> (a) Manoah's Offering: "While the man closes his eyes in fright, she, in turn, closes her eyes in intense communication with the deity, the father of her child. She is, *at this very moment*, conceiving. (Bal 1988b: 75-76; my italics)
> (b) Samson's Wedding Feast: "The only figure that turns toward her, also a woman, is powerless: in the grip of a sexually aroused man, she can only close her eyes and bend her head. Her hand attempts to loosen the grip of the man who holds her (Bal 1988b: 79).

In each instance, Bal places the moment in the painting in the context o "the ritual of the story" in the Book of Judges. In contrast, art interprete usually interpret "the moment itself" without reference to the sequence c which it is a part:

> (a) Manoah's Offering: "The kneeling figure of his wife is here given the erect stance she has in the painting, and which reminded Kenneth Clark of a Leonardesque Madonna. In the Stockholm drawing the woman's pose is much

the same, but Manoah is seen from the front and shown wholly prostrate." (Bruyn: 530)

(b) Samson's Wedding Feast: "Behind the table, slightly to the right of centre and in the full light, sits the bride dressed in white, with a garland and a bridal crown on her head. Her hands, clasped one over the other, rest on her waist and she looks straight ahead.

To the right of her Samson—distinguished from the other men by his long hair crowned by a circlet—turns round on the bench on which he is sprawling. He is putting his riddle to six of the Philistines, who lean forward toward him, listening, as he grasps the middle finger of his left hand in the thumb and forefinger of the other. The man at the back of this group holds a flute, while the one at the front leans over a harp.

Behind the table, to the left of the bride, a woman turns way from a drinking cup her neighbour is urging on her, his arm round her shoulders. A woman at the front of the table is being embraced by a man; she lies with her legs on a wide bench covered with cushions and a red cloth draped in folds. Both these figures are seen from behind, and in shadow" (Bruyn: 248).

The difference in interpretation is noticeable. The interpreter of art describes the minute details of the moment which stands frozen in time. One who interprets story as ritual places each moment in the context of a sequence of moments which enact or desire: rape, a sacrifice, or a fight.

Social and Cultural Texture in Bal's Interpretation

A context of social ritual, then, embraces all of Bal's interpretation of the Book of Judges. When she turns to the interpretation of the story about the Levite and his concubine (Judges 19) immediately after her interpretation of the Samson ritual, she deepens the analysis with anthropological terminology concerning residential marriage patterns:

The term patrilocal, if used at all, is traditionally synonymous with virilocal marriage, thus conflating husband and father again (Bal 1988b: 85).

The irony here, as mentioned above, is that Bal makes no bibliographical reference to anthropological sources in this section. It is informative for people who are not specialists in anthropology to peruse some of the standard literature on the subject. Robert Pehrson's entry on "Bilateral Kin Groupings as a Structural Type" contains the following statement:

By the time a Lapp is ready to marry, band and family leadership may reside in the person of a sibling or cousin rather than in a member of the parental generation. In other words, a Lapp's relation to his siblings may be as important as his relation to his parents in determining local group membership. Therefore, the terms "matrilocalism" and "patrilocalism" do not correctly characterize the whole situation. The terms "virilocal" and "uxorilocal" are more useful here. Virilocalism means that the married couple lives at the locality of the husband's kinsmen, uxorilocalism that the married couple lives at the locality of the wife's kinsmen. . . . Thus, when dealing with a bilaterally organized society which emphasizes sibling solidarity it seems apropos to use the terms "virilocal" and "uxorilocal" in place of the terms "matrilocal" and "patrilocal" with their implications of unilaterality (Pehrson 1954: 194-195).

Compare this statement with a segment from Bal's chapter:

Anthropological terminology does not escape the sort of rhetoric we are discussing. Both terms—nomadic and duolocal—focus on the husband's situation, not on the locus of the marital union itself. A third and fourth term *uxorilocal* and *matrilineal*, displace the issue in another way . . .

In order to disentangle some of the confusions attached to the current terminology, I will propose to call this *patrilocal marriage*, thus stressing that it is the power of the father, over and against that of the husband, which characterizes this type of marriage and that the place where this power is rooted, the *house*, is the shifter where residence and descendance meet (Bal 1988b: 85).

On the one hand, the quotation from a standard anthropological entry i 1954 exhibits the manner in which anthropologists rework thei terminology to make it function appropriately in an interpretation of th data they have uncovered. On the other hand, a statement in a more recer anthropological publication suggests Bal is approaching the text from a untraditional anthropological stance:

Anthropologists have traditionally analyzed residence in relation to marriage, based on the kin group with which the newly married couple resides. This approach yields a few basic patterns: uxorilocal residence (Lat. *uxor*-wife), where the couple resides with the wife's kin group; virilocal residence (Lat. *vir*-man, husband), where they reside with the husband's kin; and neolocal residence, where a new and independent household is established. Where residence reflects the dominance of a unilineal decent system, an older terminology can be used: patrilocal, describing residence with the husband's father, in a patrilineal system; matrilocal, describing residence with the wife's mother, in a matrilineal system (see Pehrson 1954: 194-195). However, such classifications can be misleading, and several alternative approaches to the analysis of family and residence have been proposed (Winthrop 1991: 116-117).

This entry in 1991 reveals that Bal is using standard anthropologic terminology. About whom is Bal talking when she refers to "tradition usage"? Is Bal in dialogue with "several alternative approaches" (Winthro 1991: 117) of which she does not inform the reader? She does not tell us. *

is point, the fourth arena of socio-rhetorical criticism comes into play: ideological texture. Bal announces the ideological texture of her study on the second page of her book. Thus, it is a rich arena to explore in her interpretation. We will not be able to explore it at any great length, but we do need to turn to it at least for a moment in our ritual of interpretation.

Ideological Texture in Bal's Interpretation

Ideological texture resides in the text under investigation, in the history of interpretation of the text, and in the interpreter's current interpretation. Bal's interpretation makes a strong case for a patriarchal, patrilineal ideology in the text of the Book of Judges. Disagreements about this must surely focus on details, since the basic observation is well grounded. Her particular readings of the stories will undergo careful scrutiny and be mildly or significantly reconstrued—this is the nature of interpretive activity. There should be little doubt that Bal has exhibited deep ideological problems in traditional interpretations and in the understanding of certain key words in the Book of Judges. These call for significant revision of certain lexical entries, of exegesis of particular verses, and of interpretation of the interplay of meanings in various stories. Bal's own interpretation, of course, is ideologically grounded, and here we must pause for a moment.

On the second page of her book, Bal announces her ideological position:

This study is about women's lives and deaths. It is about the complex and fascinating relations between text and social reality. And it is about method. The development of a feminist method of interpretation of ancient texts as sources for our understanding of the history of gender-ideology and as connected to present-day culture is the underlying purpose of this voyage through the Book of Judges (Bal 1988b: 2).

Can I, as a man, say anything about this ideology (Robbins 1992d)? Or am I forced to be silent? Bal's own approach is instructive for me. She looks at that which is absent and that which is present in male interpretations, and she tries to understand both.

To deal with the absence of bibliographical reference to current anthropological literature, I solicited some help from a female colleague and found two respected sources, both written by males, that describe the terminology anthropologists use to describe residential patterns within marriage. The two documents describe the current meaning of the terminology in the manner in which Bal uses it, and they introduce a complexity and flexibility that prepares the way for Bal's use of the terms.

Bal, in turn, simply says that current use of the terminology by most anthropologists is insensitive to the male and female aspects of the residential patterns she describes.

I see two choices before me. On the one hand, I can call upon Harold Bloom's discussion of "the anxiety of influence" (Bloom 1973). Here I can point to the extensive manner in which Bal's method of interpretation uses procedures like Victor Turner, a male author, in *The Ritual Process*, which Bal does not cite in this chapter even though there is ample evidence in her writings that she knows the book well. From this observation, I can reiterate what we have uncovered about the use of anthropological terminology concerning residential patterns within marriage and her assertion that she using the terminology differently from most anthropologists. From the perspective of "the anxiety of influence," it would be especially natural for Bal to omit references to these sources. First, she is so deeply influenced by an anthropological approach like Turner's that citing him and others could blunt the edge of her individual achievement. Second, the critical creativity of these males is so evident that it might compete with her incisive feminist interpretation.

On the other hand, I could use the terminology "the politics of omission," which appeared in an article in the field of biblical studies in 1989 (Martin 1989: 120-126). One of the strengths of this approach would be that the source for the terminology is an article by an African American woman, published initially in a volume entitled "Interpretation for Liberation" and subsequently republished in a volume entitled *The Bible and Liberation: Political and Social Hermeneutics* (Martin 1989). In this article, Clarice J. Martin, Professor of New Testament at Colgate Rochester Divinity School, expresses her bewilderment at the omission of Ethiopia from maps of the New Testament world in the standard Biblical Atlases. I could describe the absence of references in Bal's chapter as a politics of omission of positive reference to male authors and plead for a more inclusive approach. If I were to use this approach, however, I would run the risk of using the authority of one woman interpreter to confront the authority of another woman interpreter, which could have negative implications for me as a man.

Since I am implicated in the first approach and endangered by the second approach, what should I do? Obviously I have already introduced both ideas, even though I have not developed them at any length. But the procedure has been worth it, has it not? A strong interpretation like Bal's *Death & Dissymmetry* deserves detailed scrutiny and pressure, because it offers so much to men and women alike.

But now I must deal with my own "anxiety of influence" or "politics of omission," though it is difficult for me to do so. Who have provided the formative influences on the development of socio-rhetorical criticism? Norman Perrin was a creative interpreter with whom I studied; Charles H. Talbert welcomed me into the Luke-Acts Seminar in the Society of Biblical Literature; Robert C. Tannehill was a close colleague in the Pronouncement Story Work Group from 1975 through 1987; and Burton L. Mack was a co-author of a book with me that appeared in 1989. There is also Robert Detweiler. I notice that he introduces an eight-step procedure for interpreting a text with a combination of strategies from phenomenology and structuralism in his *Story, Sign, and Self* (Detweiler 1978: 204-207). One of the copies of this book (I have two) in my library has my signature in it with a date that reads 1979. And it does have some underlined and circled words in it, in the manner in which I marked books during the 70s. But, honestly, I am quite sure that I never read those pages on the eight-step procedure until today (March 16, 1993). Any influence Detweiler's book may have had on me had to come incidentally as we have talked with each other and taught together during the last few years.

In any case, I shouldn't concern myself with influences of us males on one another, should I? The topic is Mieke Bal, and the male influences on her. In the words of Mieke Bal, the male view considers a virgin to be "exclusive property": "metonymically, the daughter is bound to the father as an ontological property: she is part of him, his synecdoche" (Bal 1988b: 72). For this reason, the virgin daughter has no name. The "female view" of virginity, in contrast, is "oriented toward the future and toward integrating the nubile life stage within the whole life cycle" (Bal 1988b: 72).

Mieke Bal, obviously, has been concerned not to be nameless. So her voice has come, unknowingly perhaps but really, into a conversation between Robert Detweiler and some of the rest of us. Detweiler has things well in hand, applying phenomenological and structuralist strategies of interpretation on a "hermeneutical scene" that he describes "not only as post-New Critical but also as the era of post-formalism, post-structuralism, deconstruction, post-representation, post-modern and even post-hermeneutic" (Detweiler 1989: xii). Detweiler has, in the past, had significant public conversations with Bal, and Bal, in turn, is publishing a paper in this volume. Again, Mieke Bal keeps coming into our conversations. A good colleague, like Robert Detweiler, is like wisdom:

> She is more precious than jewels,
> and nothing you desire can compare with her. . . .
> She is a tree of life to those who lay hold of her;

those who hold her fast are called happy (Proverbs 3:15, 18).

Will I be misunderstood? Even oral presentation cannot assure that an auditor will distinguish tongue in cheek from serious tongue. But what is the difference? To quote Robert Detweiler at the end of *Breaking the Fall*:

> A *communitas* of readers, joined at first merely by the fact that they read, can learn to confess their need of a shared narrative and encourage the creation and interpretation of a literature that holds in useful tension the doubleness we feel: that we live at once both liminally and in conclusion (Detweiler 1989: 190).

This quotation, taken seriously out of context, signals the fruitfulness not only of exposing the vulnerabilities of others but also of exposing our own, not only to ourselves but to others as well. Moreover, this brings us back to the issue with which we began, namely the ways in which our interpretations submit to the major plot of the story, on the one hand, and submit to the liminal, marginal voices in the text, on the other hand. As we make our decisions in this regard, we expose our ideologies, our self interests. We confess the major plots—the beginnings, middles, and ends— in which we participate, as well as the liminal, marginal voices we embrace. Does this introduce a new climate of interpretation? The intensity of certain responses in the academic community to this kind of ideological exposure of our own work and the work of others suggests that a new environment of interpretation truly has been launched during the last two decades. Mieke Bal has contributed decisively to this new environment, and Robert Detweiler has nurtured it for many years. It is a pleasure to show gratitude to Robert Detweiler through dialogue with a colleague with whom he himself has engaged in significant exchange.

WORKS CITED

Bal, Mieke. *Murder and Difference: Gender, Genre, and Scholarship on Sisera's Death*. Bloomington & Indianapolis: Indiana University Press, 1988a.

Bal, Mieke. *Death & Dissymmetry: The Politics of Coherence in the Book of Judges*. Chicago and London: University of Chicago Press,1988b.

Bloom, Harold. *The Anxiety of Influence: A Theory of Poetry*. Oxford: Oxford University Press,1973.

Detweiler, Robert. *Story, Sign, and Self: Phenomenology and Structuralism as Literary-Critical Methods*. SBL Semeia Supplements. Philadelphia: Fortress Press and Missoula: Scholars Press,1979.

Detweiler, Robert. *Breaking the Fall: Religious Readings of Contemporary Fiction.* San Francisco: Harper & Row, 1989.

Detweiler, Robert and Vernon K. Robbins. "From New Criticism and the New Hermeneutic to Poststructuralism: Twentieth Century Hermeneutics." Pp. 225-280 in *Reading the Text: Biblical Criticism and Literary Theory.* Stephen Prickett, ed. Oxford: Basil Blackwell,1991.

Kennedy, George A. *New Testament Interpretation through Rhetorical Criticism.* Chapel Hill and London: University of North Carolina Press,1984.

Martin, Clarice J. "A Chamberlain's Journey and the Challenge of Interpretation for Liberation." *Semeia* 47: 105-35. Reprinted in *The Bible and Liberation: Political and Social Hermeneutics.* Norman K. Gottward and Richard A. Horsley, eds. Revised edition. Maryknoll, NY: Orbis Books ,1989/93.

Pehrson, Robert N. "Bilateral Kin Groupings as a Structural Type: A Preliminary Statement." Pp. 192-195 in Nelson Graburn, ed., *Readings in Kinship and Social Structure.* New York: Harper & Row,1954/71.

Robbins, Vernon K. *Jesus the Teacher: A Socio-Rhetorical Interpretation of Mark.* Philadelphia: Fortress Press,1984.

Robbins, Vernon K. Paperback edition of *Jesus the Teacher* with a new introduction and additional indexes. Minneapolis: Fortress Press,1992a.

Robbins, Vernon K. "The Reversed Contextualization of Psalm 22 in the Markan Crucifixion: A Socio-Rhetorical Analysis," Pp. 1161-1183 in *The Four Gospels* 1992. Festschrift Frans Neirynck. F. Van Segbroeck, C.M. Tuckett, G. Van Belle, J. Verheyden, eds. Vol. 2. BETL 100. Leuven: Leuven University Press,1992b.

Robbins, Vernon K. "Using a Socio-Rhetorical Poetics to Develop a Unified Method: The Woman who Anointed Jesus as a Test Case." Pp. 302-319 in 1992 *SBL Seminar Papers.* Eugene H. Lovering, Jr., ed. Atlanta: Scholars Press,1992c.

Robbins, Vernon K. "A Male Reads a Feminist Reading: The Dialogical Nature of Pippin's Power. A Response to Tina Pippin, 'Eros and the End.'" *Semeia* 59: 211-217,1992d.

Robbins, Vernon K. "Rhetoric and Culture: Exploring Types of Cultural Rhetoric in a Text." Pp. 447-467 in *Rhetoric and the New Testament: Essays from the 1992 Heidelberg Conference.* Stanley E. Porter and Thomas H. Olbricht, eds. Sheffield: Sheffield Academic Press,1993.

Turner, Victor. *The Ritual Process: Structure and Anti-Structure.* Ithaca, NY: Cornell University Press,1969.

Vickers, Brian. "Introduction." Pp. 13-39 in *Rhetoric Revalued. Medieval & Renaissance Texts and Studies 19.* B. Vickers, ed. Binghamton, NY: Center for Medieval & Renaissance Studies,1982.

Winthrop, Robert H. *Dictionary of Concepts in Cultural Anthropology. References for the Social Sciences and Humanities, 11.* New York: Greenwood Press,1991.

Wuellner, Wilhelm. "Where is Rhetorical Criticism Taking Us?" *Catholic Biblical Quarterly* 49: 448-463,1987.

Drawing The Other

The Postmodern and Reading The Bible Imaginatively

GARY A. PHILLIPS

> To my mind the Infinite comes in the signifyingness of the face. The Face signifies the Infinite.
>
> Emmanuel Levinas, Ethics and Infinity

> Here on the pulse of this new day
> You may have the grace to look up and out
> And into your sister's eyes and into
> Your brother's face, your country
> And say simply
> Very simply
> With hope
> "Good Morning"
>
> Maya Angelou, On the Occasion of Bill Clinton's Inauguration

> But the saying is the fact that before the face I do not simply remain there contemplating it, I respond to it. The saying is a way of greeting the Other, but to greet the Other is already to answer for him.
>
> Emmanuel Levinas, Ethics and Infinity

In *Crossing the Postmodern Divide* Albert Borgmann paints the following bleak picture of modern American life:

> We live in self-imposed exile from communal conversation and action. The public square is naked. American politics has lost its soul. The republic has become procedural, and we have become unencumbered selves. Individualism has become cancerous. We live in an age of narcissism and pure loneliness (3).

The flatness, emptiness and sullenness of modern life characterizes not only our shared public existence but permeates every corner of our day-to-day private lives as well. Modern day work life, family life, intellectual and social life, even religious life, has the pedestrian quality of that dreary futuristic American city depicted in *Bladerunner*. Technology reigns, and so does the weather, incessantly. George Steiner's lament for a cultural reaffirmation of "real presences" in its own way both confirms the severity of the modern crisis and serves as an indictment of modernity's incapacity to redeem itself by means of its own resources. The rupture, erosion and leveling of intellectual, familial, civic, ethnic, environmental, intellectual and religious life has proven to be the unanticipated downside of Enlightenment progress, which can be directly equated with the loss of transcendence. It would not be a stretch to read the longing for change and affirmation of shared hopes and dreams in the 1992 American Presidential campaign as a reaction to this loss and a longing to find a way back from our collective exile.[1]

The picture is not entirely without hope. By virtue of its critical and imaginative power, the postmodern, Borgmann suggest, offers a salutary response to the "crisis of modernity." The postmodern names, on the one hand, an epochal shift in the conditions by which we are coming to know ourselves and the world we inhabit differently. And, on the other hand, the postmodern announces a reimagining of forgotten and ignored faces lived out now according to different aesthetics and indigenous politics.[2] Critique and imagination, the epistemic and aesthetic, the ethical and political, narrative and hermeneutic are configured according to a multitude of logics, in different voices for different faces.[3] In these postmodern voices we hear a new expression of what it means to be intellectuals, citizens and believers for today's many communities. We hear in those voices and see in those faces different possibilities of culture and history, the social and personal dimensions of that awareness, and the ethical and political implications that flow from it. Against the backdrop of a dispirited and spiritless modernity, postmodernity enables "us to take up again the pursuit of the good and the beautiful in practical and life-enhancing ways" (Merrill, xii). The hopefulness of Maya Angelou's Inaugural words in celebration of community, local histories and nature *is* just such a postmodern sound. Her words, very simply, anticipate a new morning in political, ethical, and spiritual terms. In the face of modern loneliness the postmodern signals not only alternative epistemic positions and critical voices, but, Borgmann avers, an aesthetic revisioning of the heavenly city and of the earth where celebration of community makes it possible once again to recognize divinity.[4]

Yet, largely absent from the growing chorus of critiques of modernity and the positive revisioning offered in certain postmodern circles is precisely reflection on "divinity," or the religious, or the Other in Levinas' terms, at this epochal moment.[5] Apart from a handful of critics writing explicitly out of a theological framework (for example, Griffin, Smith, Taylor, Beardslee, Lindbeck, Schneiders and Holland) or a literary/cultural critical context (for example, Aichele, Burnett, Castelli, Fowler, Jobling, Moore, Pippin, Phillips, Schwartz, Wuellner) there is little widespread effort to wrestle with the problems of situating the Bible and religious reading on this postmodernism landscape. As a field biblical scholarship finds itself very much on the periphery of these discussions both in terms of the conceptual, theoretical discussions and their religious implications for culture. What traditional, modern biblical critics are apt to recognize in the postmodern is that it represents an alarming transformation and transgression of modern reading strategies and attitudes; what they may not be so ready to admit, however, is the degree to which biblical studies' dominant disciplinary practices embody the very features of individualism, narcissism and isolation endemic to the modern crisis.[6] From a postmodern perspective, the sense of the biblical text and of reading religiously stand on very different epistemic, aesthetic and political grounds. But if what Borgmann says is true, namely, that the postmodern inaugurates a revisioning of divinity and humanity, it is far from clear what that means concretely, for example, to the biblical critic whose engagement with the Bible has been dulled by the modern routines of analytico-referential thinking (Reiss). For much modern criticism the communal and ethical has seemingly disappeared.[7]

What *is* a postmodern read? How does postmodern attention help us to rediscover and recover the Bible critically, religiously, ethically for a new age? How does the postmodern imagination enhance the prospects for seeing the face of the Other for reassessing and becoming community? Robert Detweiler's recent work addresses these issues directly. His engagement with postmodern narrative is of particular value to biblical scholars who struggle to orient themselves to this strange postmodern landscape and to understand what it means to talk about the religious and reading religiously. By focusing attention specifically on postmodern and postformalist narrative and the liminal community as the locus of the religious in the postmodern age, he suggests ways we can read the Bible religiously and make sense of postmodern transformations. If a general feature of the modern crisis could be said to be the loss of transcendence reading religiously will mean something like finding strategies and resources to promote and signify encounter with the Other. Biblical critics will have to develop unexplored resources beyond the biblical narrative and traditional modern reading strategies in order to reenvision what is Other about the Bible and one another. This means more than recalibrating the methodological critical sights; it is rather, as Levinas suggests, a matter of rediscovering the Bible's "ethical plenitude and its mysterious possibilities of exegesis" which signify transcendence (1985:23). As Detweiler shows, the postmodern can be salutary toward this end. Not just as a general *means* for developing critical strategies but as a particular moment for renewal of the critical imagination which once again discovers "ethical plenitude and its mysterious possibilities of exegesis" as a possibility for a community of readers. It is in celebration of Bob Detweiler's contribution to the broad effort to read the Bible critically, ethically, and religiously, then, that this essay is offered.

Mapping the Postmodern Divide for Biblical Readers

Although critics differ as to the cartography of the postmodern, we might think of this strange terrain in Borgmann's terms as a newly formed mountain range. This postmodern divide erupts from out of the modern plains and cuts across geographic, ethnic, national, linguistic, disciplinary, aesthetic and cultural boundaries. Because the modern crisis is a chronic condition of the West in general, the crisis in its American expression must be seen as tectonically linked to European soil. It is there that the pressures of deconstruction, poststructuralism and the postmetaphysical and postindustrial critiques of culture have had their greatest seismic effect. These critical energies have been responsible for shaking the modern ground loose to expose beneath its surface indigenous desires and aspirations, local ways of knowing, revamped economic structures, rediscovered political and ethnic identities, reinvigorated communal relationships, restructured fields of knowledge, alternative representations of truth and the good, and destabilized master narratives. The postmodern terrain is ground still very much in motion. It is also very dangerous ground, as Bosnia and the former Soviet Union attest.

Jean-François Lyotard's ground-breaking efforts to articulate the aesthetic, epistemological and socio-political character of the emergent "postmodern condition" have struck a wide, responsive cord among critics of Western Enlightenment culture. Lyotard claims that the postmodern condition signals a crisis of legitimation at the heart of modern life, which is to say scientific knowledge itself; the relationship of science, language and validating reason, which empowers modern critical thought, has become problematic. And with the "demise" of the two central, grand metanarratives of emancipation and speculative knowledge, the conditions for the legitimation of knowledge have been forcefully altered.[8] Not surprisingly, his analysis has sparked a spirited counter-defense of modernity from defenders on the left and on the right (see Eagleton; Steiner; Jameson; Habermas 1981; 1990). The fallout from this debate has served to catalyze the critical discourse (theoretical and practical) in many cultural quarters: in aesthetics, music, art, philosophy, literary theory, narrative study, architecture, film, law, fashion, physics, anthropology, sociology, philosophy, geography, history, political science, religious studies and health science, to name a few.[9]

Notable by virtue of its absence in the modern/postmodern debate on both sides of the Atlantic, however, is a broad critical engagement with religion (Berry and Wernicke and Smith are the recent exceptions that prove the rule). While the engagement with the postmodern in the field of religious studies has concentrated largely on literature and theology, the broad questions of the place of religion *per se* in the trembling postmodern condition have barely been formulated. What are the implication of the postmodern condition for understanding the religious? religious community? religious discourse? religious readings? With respect to biblical criticism, what is the significance of the postmodern for reading the Bible religiously, critically, and ethically, and what is its impact upon the development of community? The paucity of engagement within biblical studies stands in marked contrast to the often heated, energized debates over postmodernity in literary studies, philosophy, and history. With some few exceptions little disciplinary attention is paid to the nature, role and implications of the postmodern divide for reading/writing the Bible.[10]

One reason for the lack, I would argue, is modern biblical studies' myopic understanding of its own disciplinary accountability. At heart it is an ethical and an institutional power issue. Historically, biblical criticism has served two masters—theological and academy establishments—and the competition for loyalty and obedience between the two has contributed to the isolation and bifurcation modern exegetes often feel. The result is that ethical accountability has been narrowly channeled and divided. From an ideological and political perspective the constricting has contributed to the powerful isolation and disintegration of religious as well as intellectual community. The overwhelming *cultural* character of the postmodern transformation means questioning the "given" organization of the discipline and the nature of its ethical responsibilities and accountability to the field, community and culture.

A second, related reason is biblical studies' deference to and defense of scientific reasoning at the expense of the imagination. Disdain for the imagination is nothing new; it has long been a feature of Western metaphysical thinking tracing its way back to Plato. The more recent conflict over alleged anti-historical (i.e., anti-rational) impulses radiating out of the anti-foundational criticism owing to Nietzsche and Heidegger has made biblical critics untrusting of much feminist, deconstructive and poststructuralist criticism on historical grounds. The counter-response continues to be a kind of arid, methodological fundamentalism and socio-political conservatism. Biblical scholars are reluctant to abandon the Enlightenment speculative myth and the discipline's hard-won critical autonomy and freedom (the loss of the critical "I" and "eye") for fear of becoming blind subjects once again to some discipline, dogma or tradition. Ironically, the effort to keep hold of the "I"/"eye" has come at the cost of losing sight of the transcendent Other. Biblical critics, it seems, cannot relax their grip on the Bible or modern critical method long enough to recognize that one of the costs of modern reading has been to limit the possibilities of reading religiously, of encountering transcendence in the reading of the text and in community.[11] Except for a handful of exegetes, the postmodern divide is a landmark event which modern biblical scholarship by and large has ignored. Most persist in keeping their I's/eyes and no's/nose in the Book.[12]

This pattern of avoidance is a defensive reaction to the pressure postmodern critique has brought to bear on questions about modern representational strategies, the nature of ethical accountability, the cartesian understanding of subjectivity and the defining role of the speculative and liberating master narratives which have shaped contemporary reading/writing and biblical studies as a community of readers. It is not surprising that a common reaction to postmodern criticism is, then, to reduce it to an epistemic issue which can be relegated to the margins with other methodological pretenders.[13] But if Lyotard, Borgmann and Detweiler are correct, the tremulous, postmodern question has less to do with the edges and more with the ground in the sense of a critique of modern foundationalism and the recognition of alternative ways to encounter the Other.

The postmodern gives every indication it will condition future possibilities for reading/writing because the transformation under way is a widespread cultural—not merely disciplinary event. As an academic community that concerns itself with religious texts and experience biblical studies must face the fact that the postmodern change amounts to much more than the speculative choice of a new and improved critical method—the threadbare modern response to any critique. Rather, it entails a transformation in the aesthetic, the socio-political, the ethical spheres; it means a reorientation to the face of the other, to transcendence. This is why the postmodern must be seen, following Detweiler, as a response to the modern crisis of *imagination, ethical action* and *faith* as much as it is to the limitations of *rational critique*. The loss of imagination in particular contributes to the erosion of the community of biblical scholars and constricts its capacity to account for itself as a field, the religious texts that it reads, and the nature of its ethical responsibilities in the face of the brother and sister.

The Postmodern (Con)Tribulation

On the level of critique, the postmodern shift disrupts much of what modern biblical studies identifies as normative for reading/writing the Bible.[14] For one thing the quake has loosened the grip (although not the gaze) of historical and formalist methods upon reader and biblical text alike. As a consequence the operational principle of mimetic realism, epitomized so clearly in Auerbach's now famous description of Abraham and Odysseus in *Mimesis*, which has been determinative for the modern *wissenschaftliche* era of biblical scholarship, has come under severe pressure (Rorty). The critical interventions in art history, architecture, anthropology, philosophy, feminist criticism, deconstruction, and other poststructural criticisms (Moore, 1992; Phillips, 1992) have problematized modern representational strategies on the one hand through critical engagement with theory, and on the other through the imaginative use of parody and paradox. Standing on postmodern terrain, modern biblical exegetes who once oriented themselves by way of the standard methodological sign posts that naturalized mimetic realism, correspondence theory of truth, and linguistic nominalism are understandably disoriented when confronted by poststructural and deconstructive maps.[15] The familiar modern landmarks—the opposition between margin and center, secular and religious, public and private, canonical and non-canonical, self and other, text and context, humanistic and social science, history and fiction, exegesis and interpretation, etc.—are defamiliarized. In practical terms the critical project of modern biblical studies proves inadequate in accounting for the changing order of things. To find your way in Postmodern Country you need a different eye, ear, compass and map.

Specifically, the postmodern condition has fostered (some would say "foisted") a redefinition of the notion of text, reader and reading by situating the Bible rudely in relation to a range of inscriptions drawn, for example, from literature, theory, film, architecture, philosophy, and other cultural sources. Furthermore, a generous understanding of "intertextuality" has emerged in response to the poststructural critique of texts and textuality (see Barthes, 1975; Phillips, 1991). Similarly the notion of authorship and readership is being reshaped, both in theory and praxis. Collective authorship, once associated with the social and natural science disciplines, has become an important means for biblical scholars to reflect a different critical and ideological posture in their exegetical work.[16] And thanks to the new technologies of knowledge production, information management and dissemination, the ways readers interact and communicate with each another have an unreal—Baudrillard would say "hyperreal"—texture. E-mail and information bulletin boards (even their "communicable diseases") are forcing a different orientation toward text and reader. The unauthorized computer-assisted "reconstruction" of the Qumran "text," for example, illustrates the extent to which standard views of what a "text" is, who "authors" and "readers" are, and how the politics of ownership, access and control figure dramatically into the interpretation process have become public issues. These critical conditions and changes were unimaginable just a generation ago.

The postmodern condition also compels a rethinking of Biblical Studies as a distinctive discursive community. The twin modern discursive contexts of faith community and academy and their underlying narratives have determined the shape and telos of modern exegetical reading/writing practices. The legislation of theological and positivist scientific reading strategies, however, has often served to mask issues of disciplinary authority, truth construction, power allocation, and ethical responsibility. What is true? Who can read and how? Who exercises regulative authority over the discourse and by what strategies? The discursive silence surrounding these questions has been broken in large measure due to the pressure of feminist critique and the effort to force an accounting of our ethical responsibilities as scholars (Schüssler-Fiorenza). And from outside the discursive community the expropriation of religious texts in literary and socio-anthropological circles, the indigenous readings arising from religious and non-religious communities, and the variety of critical approaches taken to the Bible has amounted to a challenge to the hegemony of analytico-referential discourse and the institutional power of the Church-Academy as the sole legitimating source of "expert" readers. By raising the question of power and control in this way, one of the effects of the postmodern transformation has been to reframe the ethical and institutional control questions.

But even though the postmodern shaking has been effective in some quarters in generating a level of robust critical activity, the effort to think the place of the ethical and the community (religious or not) within postmodern culture has not been nearly as widespread. Why is it right or good to embrace the postmodern in the first place? Why should we continue to promote the good life in community? Why should we care about the face of the other? Postmodern critics who, like Hassan, want to preserve a special place for the moral life in the context of postmodern living have little to offer us that explains *why* the ethical life should be maintained either inside or outside of community, much less in religious community, which they are even less willing to discuss. On what basis, for example, can the *Utne Reader* announce with such confidence that it is "Time to Return to the Good, the True and the Beautiful"? Bernstein is right to insist that "we need to question this [postmodern] ideal of living well and why it should be affirmed."[17] For all of Borgmann's desire to affirm the importance of renewing and building religious community, he can not adequately explain using Lyotard's epistemic, aesthetic or political grounds why in the final analysis it is *better* to live with the other in community than alone. Detweiler makes a similar point in critique of Lyotard from another direction: if narrative is now to be undervalued from Lyotard's postmodern perspective, how can community and ethics be legitimated?

The difficulty lies in making the case for ethics, community or the religious on the basis of aesthetic, epistemological and political *grounds*. I regard this as one of the major deficiencies of postmodern criticism to date which has not adequately worked through Levinas' critique of the metaphysical tradition (although compare Kearney). Detweiler's insistence upon imagination and transcendence is an important corrective. Until we are prepared to address transcendence as Detweiler and Levinas insist, the fundamental question: "Why should I *live* much less *read*?" will continue to be answered on the basis of the "I" and not the other's face, notwithstanding the postmodern transformation. The postmodern turn does not guarantee the return to community and ethical accountability. As Levinas says, "Religion in fact is not identical to philosophy" (1985:118); so too the postmodern condition is not to be taken as another name for the religious or the ethical. To do so would be to make the postmodern the latest foundational master narrative that seeks to replace its speculative and liberative precursors. Under postmodern conditions the status of the ethical and religious is no less unsettling, no less dispossessing than it was under modernity.[18] What this means is that the hopefulness of the postmodern condition, the reason for community, the necessity of ethics is not self-grounding. The ethical and the community derive their reason to be non-foundationally from the face of the other, the brother and sister in Maya Angelou's words, who call me to responsibility. So long as we equate the religious or the ethical or community with a particular historical givenness of experience or ground, we risk confusing the ethical call with aesthetic, epistemic or socio-political imperatives. It is for this reason that the imagination plays such a strategic role in the postmodern effort to signify the presence of the other and to point to alternative ways of thinking and living. The postmodern imagination is the pro-vision we have for dealing with the con-dition of modernity. Imagination is a propadeutic that helps us to see and hear the ethical call to live in community. The imagination, postmodern critique announces, aids in drawing out transcendence and the other in the encounter with the biblical text.[19]

The Postmodern Draw: Ziggy's Other

Typical of most postmodern critics, Borgmann's view of the current crisis is dependent upon reading an array of cultural "inscriptions" or "texts": literature, political discourse, the physical space of a city and its surrounding environs, the economic activities of a region, recreational activities of a community, the artistic infrastructure of a community, and so forth; these are all signs to be read.[20] As ideological critics tell us, reading different "cultural texts" enables us to discover the ways a people represent to themselves their deepest, most abiding values and aspirations, including, especially, what is religious to them. Reading for the transcendent in postmodern terms, I contend, means learning how to recognize and read an array of cultural signs.

What are the "powerful signs" of postmodern American culture, especially those that can serve to evoke the transcendent? Scouring the modern terrain for the "religious" (although he prefers to say "divinity") Borgmann ends up identifying the simplistically Church as the physical sign of religious experience and faith. Detweiler, however, proposes to send us elsewhere. He turns to difficult postmodern and postformalist narratives which openly traffic in play, indeterminacy and ambiguity of meaning and an affirmation of the Other as an experience of transcendence. Biblical critics are therefore directed to postmodern narrative as one imaginative source that can enable them to return to the Bible once again and read for openness, indeterminacy, ambiguity and transcendent qualities that modern criticism seeks methodically to resolve out of existence. But postmodern narrative, I would argue, is but one of several places for biblical critics to turn. I would suggest another type of cultural inscription that can serve as a gateway to many of the same questions of openness, indeterminacy and transcendence, reading, community and the religious that may prove more accessible. One way to rouse biblical scholars from their modern critical deep slumber is to treat them to an enchanting postmodern kiss.[21] To get in tune with the Bible as a text of transcendence, biblical critics need to hone their skill for reading cartoons with a postmodern eye.

In his nationally syndicated drawing "Ziggy," Tom Wilson regularly features signs, maps, mirrors, faces and eyes as vehicles for commenting upon the ambiguity and confusion of modern life and the complexities associated with its representation. In these drawings Ziggy, his main character, struggles to make sense of the world represented on signposts or reflected in mirrors in various ways. In one memorable drawing Ziggy stands before a large signpost which displays a road map. On the map four arrows point to four different "x's" located on a maze-like path. Inscribed in large block letters across the top of the map are the words "You are either here, here, here, or here." Ziggy stares intently at the map and its confusing topographical message. From a modern reader's perspective, Wilson's representation of Ziggy's mundane experience of temporal and spatial dislocation and dispossession is one with which we can readily identify. The

Ziggy text is a carto(ono)graphy of the modern crisis that Borgmann describes.

At the same time, Wilson's illustration of modern bifurcation and dislocation invites another look, a postmodern read. This time we take an imaginative turn and orient ourselves as readers in a different way to Ziggy before the signpost. We follow along a different path that leads us *into* as well as *across* the surface of the text: call it a three- rather two-dimensional reading. The play of border lines, multiple and multivalent words and signs, perspective, subject identity and the relation between inner and outer textual space opens up an ironic, self-reflexive space in which Ziggy's and the reader's shared modern world are together defamiliarized. From this postmodern perspective we bracket our immediate mimetic impulse to identify our world with Ziggy's toon reality in order to peer through the representational surface to see what lies "behind" the text, to bring into focus the mechanics and rules which make modern reading possible. When we take this imaginative step, Wilson's drawing is transformed into a self-reflexive sign, a sign about signs, a representation of representation. The posted map of Ziggy's modern life now becomes a postmodern map that represents something important about our lives.

Reading the Ziggy drawing this way renders it a cartoon version of an Escheresque *mis-en-abyme*. Wilson's "map en abyme" reads like a palimpsest: the familiar representation of Ziggy's modern world is overwritten/overread by a strange defamiliarization and deconstruction of the representation of the modern world.[22] Along side/over top of/beneath (which is it— one or all?) the surface of the modern map is inscribed a postmodern map in which the self-reflexive character of the reading/writing experience is foregrounded. Ziggy, signpost and map fade out as awareness of sign, representation, self-reference, subjectivity, self-identity and perspective come into focus. Like a Pirandello play with its mutually exclusive views of reality represented at once on stage, Wilson stages a double reading in which two utterly different constructions of the world are co-read in/out of the same text (Gaggi:25).

If modern representational strategy depends upon a "natural" correspondence between signs and reality in the reader's and Ziggy's modern reading, the postmodern reading strategy works intentionally to disrupt such correspondence and identification. It leaves us with a touch of vertigo, uncertain about the sufficiency of our grasp of the "real" and the effort to name or draw it in depth. Through the use of parody, irony, exaggeration and anti-logic, the postmodern read amplifies the indeterminacy and inexhaustibility of the signifying processes *already at work under the surface of* the modern representational strategies, strategies which deconstruction has shown posit the full presence and immediacy of meaning behind each and every sign (Derrida, 1978). In the postmodern draw we imagine ourselves reading these representations otherwise, however, with a kind of parodic double vision: it is a parasitic reading in which we see the modern world from a different place (*para*) as both artifact and artifice, as a *given* and a *constructed* reality of signs, texts, and subjects that invites our active imagination, energy and engagement to be produced. Postmodern carto(ono)graphy succeeds when it draws our imaginative attention to the semiotic complexity, productivity and excessiveness entailed in every signifying act of representation of the world (ancient or modern) around us; it defamiliarizes the ordering and the orderliness of the ordinary from the inside so as to make another kind of imaginative and ethical response possible. It prods us to see otherwise than what we might normally see. We are invited to face ourselves in the mirror, to look ourselves in the eye and see what is other than it appears.

What makes a postmodern reading of Ziggy's encounter with map, signpost and face instructive for biblical critics is that it provides us with an occasion to imagine the text and our position as readers of the Bible differently; it presses us to read otherwise than in mimetic modern ways. In this respect the postmodern read reminds us of the "metaparable" that Crossan describes which narrates the parabolic production process in and through the form of a parabolic narrative itself (Crossan; Phillips, 1985). In strong parodic style, Wilson draws attention—both Ziggy's and our own— to the play upon signs, especially the signs of reading, space and subjectivity.

On a double-footed signpost a dotted-line road representing Ziggy's path zig-zags its way across the map. With no start or finish marked, the maze-like route is strikingly open-ended—like Ziggy's cartoon life itself— delimited only by the borders of the map which coincide with the edges of the signpost itself. The map and signpost offer a mixed perception of space: the right side and legs of the signpost are drawn with perspective while the remainder of the map is represented in flat two-dimensional terms. Ziggy texts are always a mixture of representational perspectives and ethical dilemmas. The character Ziggy, too, is drawn in conflicting dimensions: a three-dimensional torso and a flat, one-eyed, two-dimensional face. Mirroring the flat-faced and stubby-legged Ziggy, the signpost returns the distorted image as if he were standing before a fun house mirror. Semiotic distortion is the hallmark of postmodern reflection; it is an aniconic distortion made famous in Jesus' parabolic narratives.

With defamiliarizing eyes we read Ziggy and his world as an interplay of signs mirroring signs. The signpost serves as an indexical sign (a pointer in the ground) bearing an iconic sign (the roadmap) that mirrors the space of Ziggy's world and marks the multiple places where Ziggy stands (indicated by the symbol "x").[23] Overwritten on the map is the syntactically ill-formed sentence, "You are either here, here, here or here," word-signs with their own indexical or pointing function. We can only imagine Ziggy saying in response "Here, Here, Here, Here I stand". As deictics, the pronouns "you" and "here" point to their referents in the same way as the four arrows point to the four "x's" on the road. One deictic flows into another as the words "here" descend into arrows pointing downward to the four "x's" which mark the spots, like Ziggy's four fingers pointing downward to the ground where he stands. The redundancy of the signs (four different pairs of "here's" and arrows) intensifies all the more the uncertainty about where Ziggy actually stands. It is this uncertainty in knowing where he stands that marks Ziggy's constant moral dilemma: Who am I? Why am I here? What am I to do?[24] As for the "x's" themselves, they are not drawn with simple strokes but in a style that recalls the familiar secret treasure map "x" that marks the spot. This intertextual allusion draws attention to the one-to-one correspondence of the sign-meaning-referent mirror complex necessary for modern representation to work. Modern maps are meaningful so long as they presuppose isomorphic representation. The moment we encounter anisomorphic representation, which emphasizes ambiguity and multivalent signs, the read and road trip cease being "easy" or obvious. Regular followers of Ziggy recognize and resonance with this dilemma.

The postmodern roadmap pictures Ziggy a distorted, disseminated and split subjectivity. Identified discursively within the drawing by the personal pronoun "you," an "empty" sign that requires a specific referent and context to be meaningful, Ziggy stands nameless and, lacking a mouth, voiceless, although he still has his one good eye. He stands in the empty, impersonal subject x-spots distributed along the path, like the non-enunciative third-person discursive positions Benveniste theoretically describes. Given the rich semantic and syntactic ambiguity of these markers, neither Ziggy nor we can specify precisely where Ziggy "is," or for that matter who Ziggy "is," when he began the journey which brings him to the signpost, or when he will be through the trip. The maps give us only vague temporal, spatial and subject clues at best. In a world where signs of time, location, and subjectivity are multiple, multivalent and distorted, the given, natural categories and coordinates of sense no longer work as assured anchor points either for Ziggy's travel or our reading. Like Ziggy, we find ourselves staring into a strange world; we have the experience of looking into the postmodern house of mirrors like John Barth's postmodern readers who find themselves *Lost in the Funhouse.*

As Ziggy's postmodern readers we "enjoy" two very different vantage points from which to regard Ziggy and the map. First, from the outside, we observe that Ziggy's wandering motion mimics the movement of the cartoon text itself winding its intertextual way from newspaper to newspaper in different extratextual times and places. Ziggy the character "circulates" *en route* as a bifurcated and dislocated subject; "Ziggy the cartoon" circulates as an ambiguous text reproduced countless times over for many thousands of nameless readers ("I's/eyes") in as many unnamed places. And second, from inside Ziggy's world we see a time and space set apart from ours. A not-so-solid line frames the entire drawing separating Ziggy's textual time and space from the encompassing intertextual time and space of the newspaper's and our reading contexts. The overwriting of a map within a map creates the vertiginous effect of looking into an infinite series of pictures within a picture that brings to mind Escher's dizzying *Print Gallery.*

We regain our balance momentarily with the help of the proper name. Inscribed at the top left hand side of the drawing outside the frame line is the word "Ziggy," which serves as both proper name for the character inside the text and outside as title for the drawing itself. Outside on the top right edge of the frame are the words "By Tom Wilson," which name the absent drawer but also duplicate the Wilson signature found inside the drawing.[25] Ziggy's world is differentiated, but not in a semiotic airtight fashion, from the external world of the reader: Ziggy is, after all, "present" outside the drawing in the form of his proper name and inside as a drawn character, just as "Tom Wilson" is located outside by name and inside by "drawn" signature. (Could the "x" be Ziggy's signature?) Both names serve an important stabilizing function: "Ziggy" and "Tom Wilson" function as the inverted feet of the drawing anchoring the postmodern signpost and map onto shifting intertextual terrain.[26] The borders separating textual and intertextual worlds are transgressed by signs, sense, subjects and signatures which leech through from one time and space into another. The experience of transgression is acute.

At the near center of the cartoon our eye is drawn to the grammatically ill-formed sentence, "You are either here, here, here or here." It is an enunciation, a saying, whose speaker remains unnamed. The reader does not know if this is the voice of "Tom Wilson" inside the text, the voice of the implied, omniscient drawer of the text located outside the drawing, or a subjectless other voice whose identity remains unspecified. Moreover, the binary logic of this statement self-destructs with too many subjects and too many places on the map. We stumble over the syntactically awkward either/or construction with its two too many "here's". As for the "you" and "here", they serve to locate Ziggy in multiple places at one and the same time and to point to the multiple subject reading positions that transcend the borders circumscribing Ziggy's textual world inverted through the postmodern lens. We readers, too, occupy "multiple, split positions" at once inside and outside of the drawing. We, too, transcend the text and its representations of modern life. We are left with visual, linguistic, textual and logical excess not unlike the visual excess Moses experiences before the burning bush that is not consumed (Ex 3:4), the linguistic excess of a Yahweh who identifies by way of "I am who I am" (Ex 3:14), or the parabolic excess of the Hidden Treasure parable (Mt 13:44) that announces the abandonment of abandoning (Crossan): signs, frames, subjects and syntax are so porous that the text cannot easily contain or control its subject matter and reader. Certainly the reader cannot readily control this process.

If the modern reading of Ziggy's posted map recognizes it as a representation of the bifurcated modern experience—multiple space, multiple identities—the parasitic postmodern reading *re*-cognizes, or in Lyotard's terms *re*-reads (*ana*-lyzes), the drawing as a self-referential representation of the experience of excessiveness, transgression, ambiguity and leakiness of signs, subjects and sense (1989a:7). It is a representation of what is Other inscribed within the text. The postmodern read makes the text other than it seems; it captures fleetingly in Ziggy's face that otherness only to see it quickly disappear behind and inside the text. A postmodern attention to a text like this calls for us to regard the text as a reading for what is other than. Postmodern reading by this definition means active involvement with the modern world read in a defamiliarizing, deconstructive way as a strange representation of a world where solid borders separating worlds, places, times, subjects, readers, experiences and realities are dotted and constantly leak through. I am reminded of the experience of watching toon and human worlds ebb and flow in the movie *Who Framed Roger Rabbit?*.

The challenge to represent representation is indicative of a struggle over perspectival change. Wilson's drawing of Ziggy's two-footed gaze brings to mind another well-known deconstructive portrait: Velázquez's classic effort in *Las Meninas* to signify "representation in its pure form", "the representation ...of Classical representation" in the painter's full gaze made famous in Foucault's *Order of Things* (1973:16). In dealing with the problems of classical representation Velázquez's painting offers a paradoxical image of the impossibility of including within the representation the individual doing the representing (Dreyfus and Rabinow:25; Gaggi:6-8). The complex play of viewer and viewed, frame and framed, perspective and sign focuses the spectator's speculative attention on a figure mirrored on a wall inside the painting. This figure reflects that "ideal," inaccessible point outside of the painting where artist, spectator and subject gather. Wilson, too, is concerned with representing modern representation but with one important difference. Unlike the full-faced painter who gazes outward toward the viewer standing outside of the representation looking inward, Ziggy's profiled gaze looks inward toward a spot within the text in search of the reader, the Other, represented only in the voice of the one who says "You are either here, here, here or here."

Ziggy's averted inward gaze searches intently for the eye if not the face of his readers amidst all the signs. His one eye scours the textual surface of the signpost and map struggling to make sense of what is represented on the surface and what other meanings possibly stand behind it. The modern distinction between *outside* viewing position and *inside* represented position is problematized then in an acute way. The *difference* between viewing from the outside and from the inside gives way under a postmodern pressure to read parasitically both from the inside and from the outside like the two-dimensional character Mr. Square in Edwin Abbott's amazing *Flatland* whose vantage point is both two- and three-dimensional. The binary difference between outside and inside, subject and other, "I" and "you" upon which the representational strategy of *Las Meninas* ultimately depends becomes the object of this deconstructive gaze; the binary difference between outside and inside the text, as Derrida points out, is rendered problematic. Whereas *Las Meninas* represents the double-edge of classical/baroque representational strategies, Ziggy represents the difference between modern and postmodern representation. Velázquez represents representation, Wilson represents difference with a twist.[27]

Our eyes never meet Ziggy's; he does not see our face peering back through the text. There is a gap, a difference, between his eye ("I") and our eyes ("I's"). Ziggy looks intently for any trace of the viewer, but to no avail. The return gaze, in sharp contrast to Velázquez's painter, is not represented by a pair of eyes looking from beyond the modern map. We are represented only in that nameless, faceless, "eye/I"-less enunciation, the voice of the Other that announces "You are here . . . ." Because the postmodern map is parasitic upon the modern drawing, postmodern readers enjoy double vision, "para-sight" you could say. From this split perspective, Ziggy's modern mirror/map turns out also to be a postmodern one-way (one-eye) mirror. We peer back at Ziggy out of the reading place in the depth of the text unseen by Ziggy by dint of our defamiliarizing, self-reflexive effort that he can never quite match; we know he constantly comes up short from other Wilson drawings. Ziggy, who is ever self-absorbed with mirrors, signs and his doubts about the modern quest for self-knowledge, self-presentation and self-satisfaction, never proves quite capable of getting beyond or beneath the limits of the modern cartesian representation, "I see, therefore I am." He never engages that Other on any grounds except the cartesian "egoismes à deux". The ethical response to the Other constantly comes up short. The failure here is not just one of perspective, it is one of relationship, responsibility, and ethical accountability.

In this sense the postmodern reader enjoys a significant perspectival and ethical advantage over Ziggy at his expense: only we are in a position to see the difference between, across and inside borders, to stand in different times and places, both deep inside, far outside and alongside the text, to read differently across and into the map, to see the difference between the face, the reflection and the taine of Ziggy's mirror/signpost/map. The only way to see that illusive difference is to avert the "eye," which means to dispense with the "I" at the center, as Wilson does with one of Ziggy's "eyes" and with the speaking subject in favor of what is Other, what transcends, what is not named by the description. Instead of the modern constative, "I read, therefore I am," we have instead the postmodern imperative, " ...read, therefore..." in which the subject "I" and verb to be "is" are displaced from their grammatical and ontological subject position in the face of the "you" of the text. The "I" is dis-posited toward this presupposed "you" in a way that always precedes the "being" question. Ethics is other than being as Levinas says (1969). This is the different sense of the text, of reading and of ethical subject that a postmodern reading invites.

Averting the eye/I from the look, from the text, we step back out of the drawing and readjust our other eye one last time. As we steady our modern legs we once again see Ziggy standing before the signpost and map. Looking at him staring up at this perplexing sign we not only recognize the truth of that ambiguous modern representation—that the modern experience is indeed one of bifurcation and dislocation—but we also see in the text another truth, another read, an Other, an Other that we hear in the nameless voice that a postmodern perspective encourages us to listen, for we enter a zone where sight and sound relate to each other differently. We discover in this inverted postmodern terrain of reference, textuality, ignification and subjectivity overlaying and distorting the modern one the other side of the modern/postmodern divide. We see an Other side to the text and in the text calling out to us. It is this Other side that our modern representational strategies deliberately hide from sight because the demands associated with an "I"/"eye"-centered reading constantly override/overread all else. An "ear"-centered alternative calls for us to h/ear the text as readers, to become its "read-ears." That is when it becomes possible to hear the voice that places us, albeit ambiguously, in the world in relation to "oth/ears."

Paradoxically, our para-sight enables us to hear a word that makes Ziggy's *Twilight Zone* world simultaneously stable and unstable, right side up and upside down, solid and porous, immanent and transcendent. It is apparently a world where history and life do not progress along a straight line but meander through a textual wilderness; a world that resists iconic mapping but which we struggle nonetheless to make sense with an imaginative look and listen that goes beyond parody and paradox to discover a new ethical imagination (Kearney:345). In the postmodern draw, we have to work hard to make sense of the representation represented on the textual surface and behind it, to make sense of our modern representational strategies while at the same time discovering the power of imaginative perspectives that can deepen and disturb the world we live in. The postmodern read opens up even the most ordinary of texts and enables us to see the face and hear the voice of the other that transcends the text, the reading, the context. He who has ears to imagine.

The Postmodern Imagination and Recovering the Bible

While some biblical critics have conceded the impossibility of locating religious meaning under either modern or postmodern conditions, Robert Detweiler has made a telling case for the possibility of, indeed the necessity for, religious reading/writing and religious community in the postmodern context. He has shown how by embracing the theoretical and practical challenges posed by complex post-modern and post-formalist literature and social and literary theory that religious interpretations of contemporary literature are indeed possible. *Breaking the Fall. Religious Readings of Contemporary Literature* is one example of one way to frame the ethical and religious question from the perspective of an imaginative postmodern *communitas* of readers willing to engage rather than run from post-formalist theory and narrative replete with ambiguity and perplexity.

Unlike Borgmann and others, Detweiler demonstrates both how and why to read religiously and for community. He does so with what Richard

Kearney calls a "postmodern imagination." It is an imagination that "rejects "the nostalgia for a return to the paradigms of onto-theology or humanism" by "proposing the possibility of a postmodern imagination capable of preserving, through reinterpretation, the functions of narrative identity and creativity—or what we call a *poetics of the possible*" (33). Detweiler's affirmation of a postmodern imagination is important to biblical exegetes for at least two reasons. First, biblical critics must draw upon postmodern literary theory and post-formalist narratives as *essential* critical resources for religious reading in a world experienced today as profoundly decentered and marginalized; biblical exegetes must embrace the postmodern critique as a constructive response to a destabilized modern world in crisis in so far as it enables a return and a rereading of the Bible in ways that reaffirm transcendence. Postmodern reading of the Bible means reading that is prepared to take on the complicated challenge of critique of self, text and culture that lies at the heart of postmodern criticism. Biblical exegetes can ill-afford to turn their backs on any tool that can help them make an imaginative recovery from a sullen and empty modernity.

Second, as religious readers biblical exegetes must by necessity be aggressive, persistent and resourceful in the struggle to speak from the margins and to envision the Other that transcends the text. Contemporary postmodern theory and practice is bricolage and the religious reader is a bricoleur who must draw in a canny way upon methodological, literary, linguistic, and existential sources wherever they may be found to engage the uncanny (*Unheimlich*), the Other of the Bible. The modern drive to interpret, to structure life, to master experience, to locate the human "I" at the center of history, and to transcend remains as powerful as ever in the postmodern era; however postmodern critique and imagination underscore the need for a different orientation to interpretation that embraces ambiguity (Madison), allows for the lack of structure in life, and affirms that the cartesian eye is not at center but that the face of the Other is what ultimate calls me to responsible critical thinking and community life. It is a letting be (*Gelassenheit*), a relaxing of authorial self-centeredness and control, that permits the text to become other than it is. That is when it is possible to hear the voice of the other most clearly and when it is possible then to respond.

Attention to the other of the text was what we focused upon in reading the Ziggy drawing. Detweiler invites biblical exegetes to do the same with postmodern and postformalist narrative, with the Bible. The aim is to get critics to imagine their thinking activity in relation to the labyrinth of parody and play in post-modern narrative where issues of self and society are defamiliarized through the narrative process of "inventing alternative modes of existence." Detweiler shows how the religiously reading subject is constructed in and through the process within a communal context. It is here, then, that the locus of the questions "Why should I act ethically?"; "Why should I read religiously?"; or "Why should I be in community?" can finally be answered. As Levinas would argue, the ethical is done face-to-face with the Other because I am obliged or "dis-posed" toward that other person before all else. In a modern epoch characterized by the fractured, aggregate self, where distinctions between religious/secular, self/other (Levinas' expression is *egoismes à deux* where self stands in a relationship of reciprocity with the other face) define the landscape, Detweiler helps problematize these very distinctions by shedding light on the responsibility readers have to *discover* the sense of that which is Other than. This response is not an overdetermination of the text but an allowing the biblical text to speak and be heard. This "letting be" is how biblical scholars can respond to the Greeting of the Other as Levinas put it in the epigram above—by reading in a postmodern way.

Detweiler wants to celebrate the creative possibilities of postmodern critique by reimagining the distinctions between self, community and Other that can be showcased in postmodern narratives and locating them in community—a "religious" community—that reads from a liminal position. What makes it "religious," then, is a stance of openness to experiencing the uncanny (*Unheimlich*). In Ziggy's case the *Unheimlich* was evoked in the ambiguity of the representational strategies, in the voice with no name, and more. But Ziggy found no way to respond. Bible critics can learn to read for the uncanny rather than to homogenize the difference within a world needful of the transcendent but finally afraid to let go of the "I".

One important way they can do this is to read postmodern and postformalist narrative, cartoons, a full range of cultural inscriptions. Reading other cultural texts does not amount to an abandoning of the Bible but rather a refusal to reduce the Bible without remainder to whatever our methods say it means or our legitimating institutions authorize us to say it means. Reading in a postmodern way, imaginatively, encourages biblical critics to imagine much more how to read a text (narrowly defined). It empowers us to imagine what else a text (the Bible) could be saying; to imagine transcendence, for example, once again as a constitutive feature of the intellectual, social, religious, political and national life; to image an ethics of imagination that discovers resources for addressing the Other as brother and sister; to reconfigure community. Imagine what a reading community biblical studies would foster were we to produce commentary series on Ziggy and Farside texts and discuss them at sessions at the AAR/SBL meetings as a way to reimagine, rediscover and recover the Bible. It might mean that instead of holding those frequently dull and sullen national meetings in Chicago, New York or Kansas City we would be more at home in postmodern Orlando or Los Angeles.

NOTES

1. See Robert Bellah's assessment of the tension between individualism and community and its root causes in *Habits of the Heart*. The prospects for repairing the rupture in American life are not good given the degree to which American cultural identity in some fashion needs to perpetuate that split. However, Richard Kearney takes a far more optimistic position. He finds that the "postmodern imagination" makes for the possibility of affirming self and community on entirely different ethical grounds. So Rorty, but for other reasons.

2. The difficulty in defining the "postmodern" to everyone's satisfaction is compounded by the fact that there is no ready consensus as to what the "modern" means. Hebdige puts it best: "... different factions seek to make it [the postmodern] their own, using it to designate a plethora of incommensurable objects, tendencies, emergencies (pp. 181ff.).

3. As such it is a greatly discomforting moment because it represents a struggle "with, in and against *modernism*," (Flax, p. 189), namely, against modern aesthetic assumptions, values and principles, which have been instrumental in shaping the modern understanding of representation, language, subjectivity, textuality, reference, history and discourse prevailing at the heart of western culture and criticism since the Enlightenment.

4. Borgmann acknowledges that "the great majority of people in this country seek orientation in religion. They must be acting from a real need, for whatever charges one may bring against the late modern era, it does not coerce or cajole people to go to church, synagogue, mosque, or temple" (p. 144).

5. The major writers seem to avoid mentioning the religious question entirely. For example, Jameson, Lyotard, Hassan, hardly mention it. But see Berry and Wernicke. If the "seeking of religion" is of such wide-spread significance as Borgmann claims, it is striking that he gives so little space to its description. Although see Wyschogrod's interesting work on hagiographic ethics.

6. Wink anticipated this present crisis two decades ago. Other disciplinary leaders have in recent years attempted to press for a greater awareness of the crisis. Schüssler Fiorenza in her 1987 SBL Presidential address called for a fundamental rethinking of the nature of biblical criticism's ethical accountability; James Robinson in his Presidential address has called for a "deconstruction" of the field.

7. Even Habermas, one of the harsher critics of postmodernism, is prepared to acknowledge the excesses of "instrumental reason."

8. Since the nineteenth century legitimation of truth was assured by the grand narratives symbolized by Hegel and Kant on the philosophical side hand and Marx on the socio-political side; today, however, a logic of practicality and efficiency preside. The speculative hierarchy of knowledge has collapsed as a result of the expansion of capitalism and technological progress, compounded by the disappearance of disciplines and the overlapping of scientific boundaries. A principle of "performativity" has replaced that of speculative knowing. Science now competes along with other "language games," no longer capable of legitimating itself much less to account for emerging new forms of knowledge. Legitimation does not come from the former grand narratives but from locally determined norms for understanding, (as paralogy);—the little narrative. (Smart, p. 173). The *petit récit*, according to Lyotard, grounds not only the domains of science and truth but also the autonomy of interlocutors involved in ethical, social and political praxis. Delegitimation of the metanarratives and the proliferation of performativity criteria characterize the postmodern condition.

9. Hassan's description ranks as one of the most encompassing around. For different treatments of the relationship of postmodernity to modernity see Foster, Hyussen, Jameson, Kroker and Cook, Lyotard, Ross, Smart, and Wakefield.

10. Following Derrida, I prefer to think of reading as reading/writing to reinforce the point that while we may wish to think of them as two distinct operations they are in fact the inseparable other side to each other. For Derrida written signs are never exhausted in the moment of their inscription which means they potentially generate a multitude of meanings (Derrida, 1972, pp. 317). Also see Phillips, 1992.

11. Levinas says, "The Holy Scriptures do not signify through the dogmatic tale of their supernatural or sacred origin, but through the expression of the face of the other man that they illuminate, before he gives himself a countenance or a pose" (1985, p. 117).

12. To the limited extent biblical scholars have engaged directly in the modern/postmodern debate, they have tended to view it from the perspective of the reader and reading (Fowler, 1989; McKnight, 1988; Breech), textuality (Aichele, 1989; Moore, 1989; 1992), or less frequently institutional and social structures (Burnett, 1990; Castelli, 1991; Phillips, 1990). In part it is this social disconnectedness that prompted Elisabeth Schüssler-Fiorenza in her 1987 Presidential address that challenges the Society of Biblical Literature to assess the nature of ethical accountability.

13. This is essentially Alter and Kermode's strategy in the *Literary Guide to the Bible*. Speaking about "Formalism, Structuralism, and their descendents," they find it unnecessary to specify these methods [in their book]; what they have in common are a skeptical attitude to the referential qualities of texts and an intense concern for their internal relationships" (p. 6); also omitted are "critics who use the text as a springboard for cultural or metaphysical ruminations, nor those like the Deconstructionist and some feminist critics who seek to demonstrate that the text is necessarily divided against itself" (p. 7).

14. See Robert Bellah's reflection on the nature and praxis of the religious community in an age that "takes the measure of the limitations of modern consciousness," or we could substitute the postmodern age (1989, p. 79).

15. For example, "Poststructuralism as Exegesis," *Semeia* 54.

16. For example, the *Postmodern Bible* (Yale: forthcoming Spring 1994) is coauthored by ten women and men who have adopted the pseudonym "The Bible and Culture Collective" as a political and ideological statement about what it means to write and read collectively in this age.

17. Quoting Richard Bernstein, in Smith, p. 43. Bernstein has in a mind a statement made by Ihab Hassan: "To think well, to feel well, to act well, to read well, according to the *episteme* of unmasking, is to refuse the tyranny of wholes," cited in Smith, p. 43.

18. Levinas speaks about the original sense of ethos as "dis-position" rather than "position." The face-to-face is not reducible to a relation of two self-constituted subjects present to each other but is irreducible "to my relation to it, or my representation of it." To be dis-possessed is to be decentered and to be dis-posed to the other self even before I think. Ethics precedes thinking; it is otherwise than being (Levinas, p. 1969).

19. The one major exception, of course, would be Kearney. Kearney's assessment is that across the structuralist, poststructuralist and deconstructive spectrum especially there is a common interest to "dismantle the very notion of imagination" (p. 251). However, within the circles of cultural criticism Kearney recognizes "a new modality of relation between imagination and reason" that "pushes postmodernism beyond its present aporias of parody and pastiche to another kind of cultural experience" (p. 345). He describes this as the time of "the ethical imagination" and "the poetic imagination" where a reconfiguration of the historical, narrative and hermeneutic tasks can be envisioned.

20. This resonates with Foucault's (1988) way of doing "intellectual" or "social" history. It looks for the structuring and systemic relationships at a certain moment of time and the flow of power that is distributed across the grid that makes for particular understandings of truth, evidence, and meaning.

21. I am indebted to Stephen Moore for the wonderful image of the "kiss." Moore uses the image to characterize the biblical text as asleep and modern critical effort to awaken it from its original innocence and slumber (see 1989, p. 174). I reverse the positions: it is the critics who need to be awakened. The intertextual linkages are rich. All the way from the tale of Prince Charming to Judas' identification of Jesus. The image of awakening from dogmatic slumbers I have borrowed from Fred Burnett (1991).

22. See Brooke-Rose's adaptation of Salman Rushdie's notion of "palimpsest history," namely that "all stories are haunted by the ghosts of the stories they might have been" (p. 125). Brooke-Rose uses this concept to describe the way realism mingles with the supernatural (p. 137).

23. I have in mind here Charles Sanders Peirce's triadic taxonomy of signs (index, icon and symbol) as an important alternative to the diadic model promoted by Ferdinand de Saussure. For application of Peirce to biblical studies see Phillips, 1985, p. 191.

24. Levinas' characterization of the relation to the Infinite is not revelation or disclosure but "standing. " "When in the presence of the Other, I say 'Here I am!', this 'Here am!' is the place through which the Infinite enters into language without giving itself to be seen" (p. 106).

25. ". . . . the author's name, unlike other proper names, does not pass from the interior of a discourse to the real and exterior individual who produced it; instead, the name

eems always to be present, marking off the edges of the text, revealing, or at least haracterizing, its mode of being" (Foucault, 1979, p. 147).

6. For Foucault, the "author function" is one way to "map" the boundaries of the text nd of meaning and is a fundamental part of the western humanist/critical thought: Those aspects of an individual that we designate as an author (or which comprise an ndividual as author) are projections, in terms always more or less psychological, of our ay of handling texts: in the comparisons we make, the traits we extract as pertinent, the onditions we assign, or the exclusions we practice." (Foucault, 1979, p. 150).

7. Wilson's drawing illustrates what Derrida calls "arche-writing," namely that code hich entails a rupture between signified and signifier. Reversing Saussure's privileging f speech over writing, Derrida's logic shows how speech depends upon writing, and that oth are derived from a generalized notion of "arche-writing." The difference between eech and writing derives from a fundamental difference, which Wilson indirectly ttempts to represent (Derrida, 1976, p. 56).

WORKS CITED

ichele, George. "On Postmodern Biblical Criticism and Exegesis." *Forum* 5/3: 31-35, 1989.

lter, Robert and Frank Kermode, eds. *The Literary Guide to the Bible*. Cambridge, MA: Harvard University Press, 1987.

rac, Jonathan, ed. *Postmodernism and Politics*. Theory and History of Literature 28. Minneapolis: University of Minnesota Press, 1986.

arthes, Roland. The *Pleasure of the Text*. trans. Richard Miller. New York, 1975.

arthes, Roland. "The Death of the Author." pp. 142-48 in *Image—Music— Text*. New York: Hill and Wang, 1977.

arthes, Roland. "Theory of the Text." ed. Robert Young. In *Untying the Text. A Post-Structuralist Reader*. Boston: Routledge & Kegan Paul, 1981.

audrillard, Jean. *The Mirror of Production*. trans. Mark Poster. St. Louis: Telos Press, 1976.

auman, Zygmunt. "Is There a Postmodern Sociology?" *Theory, Culture and Society*. 5/2-3: 217-237, 1988.

auman, Zygmunt. *Modernity and Ambivalence*. Ithaca: Cornell University Press, 1991.

ell, Daniel. *The Cultural Contradictions of Capitalism*. New York: Basic Books, 1976.

ellah, Robert. "Christian Faithfulness in a Pluralistic World." pp. 70-94 in *Postmodern Theology. Christian Faith in a Pluralist World*. ed. Frederic Burnham. San Francisco: Harper, 1989.

ernasconi, R. "Deconstruction and the Possibility of Ethics." pp. 122-39 in *Deconstruction and Philosophy*. ed. J. Sallis. Chicago: University of Chicago Press, 1987.

Bernstein, Richard. "Metaphysics, Critique, Utopia." *Review of Metaphysics*. XLII/2: 250-62, 1989.

Berry, Philippa and Andrew Wernicke, eds. *Shadow of Spirit. Postmodernism and Religion*. London: Routledge, 1993.

Bible and Postmodern Collective. *The Postmodern Bible*. New Haven: Yale University Press. Forthcoming, 1994.

Borgmann, Albert. *Crossing the Postmodern Divide*. Chicago: University of Chicago Press, 1992.

Brooke-Rose, Christine. "Palimpsest History." pp. 125-138 in Umberto Eco et al, *Interpretation and Overinterpretation*. ed. Stefan Collini. Cambridge: Cambridge University Press, 1992.

Burnham, Frederic, ed. *Postmodern Theology. Christian Faith in a Pluralist World*. San Francisco: Harper, 1989.

Burnett, Fred. "Postmodern Biblical Exegesis: The Eve of Historical Criticism." *Semeia* 51:51-80, 1990.

Castelli, Elizabeth. *Body Politics. Interpretations of Power and Discourses of the Body in Early Christianity*. Louisville, KY: Westminster/John Knox Press, 1991.

Connor, Steven. *Postmodernist Culture: An Introduction to Theories of the Contemporary*. Oxford: Blackwell, 1989.

Crossan, John Dominic. *Finding is the First Act. Trove Tales and Jesus' Parable of the Hidden Treasure*. Philadelphia: Fortress, 1979.

Culler, Jonathan. *On Deconstruction: Theory and Criticism after Structuralism*. Ithaca: Cornell University Press, 1982.

Derrida, Jacques. *Of Grammatology*. trans. Gayatri C. Spivak. Baltimore: Johns Hopkins University Press, 1976.

Derrida, Jacques. *Writing and Difference*. Chicago: University of Chicago Press, 1978.

Derrida, Jacques. *Dissemination*. Chicago: University of Chicago Press, 1981.

Derrida, Jacques. *Margins of Philosophy*. Chicago: University of Chicago Press, 1982.

Detweiler, Robert. *Breaking the Fall: Religious Readings of Contemporary Literature*. Studies in Literature and Religion. London: Macmillan, 1989.

Dreyfus, Hubert L. and Paul Rabinow. *Michel Foucault: Beyond Structuralism and Hermeneutics*. 2nd ed. Chicago: University of Chicago Press, 1983.

Eagleton, Terry. "Capitalism, Modernism and Postmodernism." *New Left Review* 152: 60-73, 1985.

Featherstone, M. "In Pursuit of the Postmodern." *Theory, Culture and Society* 5/2-3: 195-215, 1988.

Flax, Jane. *Thinking Fragments: Psychoanalysis, Feminism and Postmodernism in the Contemporary West*. Los Angeles: University of California Press, 1990.

Foster, Hal, ed. "Postmodernism: A Preface." pp. ix-xvi in *The Anti-Aesthetic. Essays on Postmodern Culture*. ed. Hal Foster. Port Townsend, WA.: Bay Press, 1983.

Foster, Hal. ed. *Postmodern Culture*. London: Pluto Press, 1985.

oucault, Michel. *The Order of Things. An Archeology of the Human Sciences.* New York: Vintage Books, 1970.

oucault, Michel. "What is an Author?" pp. 141-160 in *Textual Strategies. Perspectives in Post-Structuralist Criticism.* ed. Josué Harari. Ithaca: Cornell University Press, 1979.

oucault, Michel. *Politics, Philosophy, Culture: Interviews and Other Writings.* ed. and trans. Lawrence Kritzman. London: Routledge, 1988.

owler, Robert M. "Post-Modern Biblical Criticism: The Criticism of Pre-Modern Texts in a Post-Critical, Post-Modern, Post-Literate Era." *Forum* 5/3: 3-30, 1989.

aggi, Silvio. *Modern/Postmodern. A Study in Twentieth Century Arts and Ideas.* Penn Studies in Contemporary American Fiction. Philadelphia: University of Pennsylvania Press, 1989.

itlin, Todd. "Postmodernism Defined, at Last!" *Utne Reader* 34: 52-61, 1989.

riffin, David Ray and Houston Smith. *Primordial Truth and Postmodern Theology.* SUNY Series in Constructive Postmodern Thought. Albany: State University of New York, 1989.

abermas, Jürgen. *Legitimation Crisis.* trans. Thomas McCarthy. London: Heinemann, 1976.

abermas, Jürgen. "Modernity versus Postmodernity." *New German Critique* 22: 3-18, 1981.

abermas, Jürgen. "Modernity—An Incomplete Project." trans. Seyla Ben-Habib. pp. 3-15 in *The Anti-Aesthetic: Essays on Postmodern Culture.* ed. Hal Foster. Port Townsend, WA.: Bay Press, 1983.

abermas, Jürgen. *The Philosophical Discourse of Modernity.* trans. Frederick Lawrence. Cambridge: MIT Press, 1990.

andy, Bruce. "A Guide to Postmodern Everything." *Utne Reader* 34: 53-69, 1989.

artin, P.J. and J.H. Petzer, eds. *Text and Interpretation: New Approaches in the Criticism of the New Testament.* Leiden: E.J. Brill, 1991.

assan, Ihab. *The Dismemberment of Orpheus: Toward a Postmodern Literature.* New York: Oxford University Press, 1971.

assan, Ihab. "The Question of Postmodernism." In *Romanticism, Modernism, Postmodernism,* pp. 117-26. ed. Harry R. Garvin. Lewisburg, PA: Bucknell University Press, 1980.

ebdige, Dick. *Hiding in the Light: on Images and Things.* London: , 1988.

uyssen, Andreas. *After the Great Divide: Modernism, Mass Culture, Postmodernism.* Bloomington: Indiana University Press,1986.

meson, Fredric. "The Politics of Theory: Ideological Positions in the Postmodernism Debate." *New German Critique* 53: 53-65, 1984.

meson, Fredric. "Postmodernism and Consumer Society." pp. 111-125 in Hal Foster, ed. *Postmodern Culture.* London: Pluto Press, 1985.

Jobling, David. "Writing the Wrongs of the World: The Deconstruction of the Biblic Text in the Context of Liberation Theologies." *Semeia* 51: 81-118, 1990.

Jones, Ann Rosalind. "Writing the Body: Toward an Understanding of *l'Ecritu feminine*. pp. 361-78 in *The New Feminist Criticism: Essays on Women, Literatur and Theory*. ed. by Elaine Showalter. New York: Pantheon Books, 1985.

Kearney, Richard. *The Postmodern Imagination: Toward a Postmodern Cultur* Minneapolis: University of Minnesota Press, 1988.

Kolb, David. *Postmodern Sophistications: Philosophy, Architecture, and Tradition* Chicag University of Chicago Press, 1990.

Kroker, Arthur and David Cook. *The Postmodern Scene: Excremental Culture an Hyperaesthetics*. New York: St. Martin's Press, 1986.

Levinas, Emmanuel. *Totality and Infinity. An Essay on Exteriority*. Alphonso Lingis, tran Duquesnes Studies. Philosophical Seris. Vol. 24. Pittsburgh: Duquesn University. Press, 1969.

Levinas, Emmanuel. *Ethics and Infinity*. trans. Richard Cohen. Pittsburgh: Duquesn University Press, 1985.

Lyotard, Jean-François. *The Postmodern Condition: A Report on Knowledge*. Minneapoli University of Minnesota Press, 1984.

Lyotard, Jean-François. "Defining the Postmodern." pp. 7-10 in *Postmodernism. IC. Documents*. ed. Lisa Appignanesi. London: Free Association Books, 1989.

McKnight, Edgar. *The Bible and the Reader: An Introduction to Literary Criticism* Philadelphia: Fortress, 1985.

McKnight, Edgar. *Postmodern Use of the Bible: The Emergence of Reader-Oriented Criticis* Nashville: Abingdon Press, 1988.

Merrill, Robert, ed. *Ethics/Aesthetics: Post-Modern Positions*. Washington, D.C Maisonneuve Press, 1988.

Messmer, Michael. "Making Sense of/with Postmodernism." *Soundings* 68: 404-2 1985.

Moore, Stephen D. "Postmodernism and Biblical Studies." *Forum* 5/3: 36-41, 1989.

Moore, Stephen D. *Literary Criticism and the Gospels: The Theoretical Challenge*. Ne Haven, CT: Yale University Press, 1989.

Moore, Stephen D. *Mark and Luke in Poststructuralist Perspectives. Jesus Begins to Writ* New Haven: Yale University Press, 1992.

Phillips, Gary. "History and Text: The Reader in Context in Matthew's Parabl Discourse." *Semeia*. 32: 111-138, 1985.

Phillips, Gary. "Post-face: Responding to the Postmodern Biblical Exegesis Queries Paper presented at the SBL New England Regional Meeting, College of tł Holy Cross, Worcester, MA, 1989.

Phillips, Gary. "Exegesis as Critical Praxis: Reclaiming History and Text from Postmodern Perspective." *Semeia* 51: 7-49, 1990.

Phillips, Gary. "Toward a Philosophical Biblical Criticism: Cutting the Umbi(b)lic Cord. A Review of Stephen Moore's *Literary Criticism and the Gospels: Tł*

Theoretical Challenge." Paper presented to the Literary Aspects of the Gospels and Acts Group, Annual Meeting of the Society of Biblical Literature/American Academy of Religion, New Orleans, LA, November 13-16, 1990.

Phillips, Gary. "Rethinking the Place of Biblical Studies. Some Questions." pp. 29-48 in *Rethinking the Place of Biblical Studies in the Academy.* ed. Burke Long. Brunswick: Bowdoin College Press, 1990.

Phillips, Gary. "Sign/Text/Difference: The Contribution of Intertextual Theory for Biblical Criticism." pp. 78-87 in *Intertextuality: Research in Text Theory.* Vol. 15. Heinrich Plett, ed. Berlin: Walter de Gruyter, 1991.

Phillipson, Michael. *In Modernity's Wake. The Ameurunculus Letters.* London: Rutledge, 1989.

Prickett, Stephen. *Words and the Word. Language, Poetics and Biblical Interpretation.* Cambridge: Cambridge University Press, 1986.

Rajchman, John."Postmodernism in a Nominalist Frame: The Emergence and Diffusion of a Cultural Category." *Flash Art* 137: 49-51, 1987.

Reiss, Timothy. *The Discourse of Modernism.* Ithaca, NY: Cornell University Press, 1982.

Rorty, Richard. *Philosophy and the Mirror of Nature.* Princeton: Princeton University Press, 1979.

Ross, Margaret. *The Post-Modern and the Post-Industrial.* Cambridge: Cambridge University Press, 1991.

Schüssler-Fiorenza, Elisabeth. "The Ethics of Interpretation: De-Centering Biblical Scholarship." *Journal of Biblical Literature* 107: 3-17, 1988.

Schwartz, Regina, ed. *The Book and the Text: The Bible and Literary Theory.* Oxford: Basil Blackwell, 1990.

Smart, Barry. *Modern Conditions, Postmodern Controversies.* Routledge Social Futures Series. London: Routledge, 1992.

Smith, Huston. *Beyond the Post-modern Mind.* rev. ed. Wheaton, Ill.: Theosophical Publishing House, 1989.

Steiner, George. *Real Presences.* Chicago: University of Chicago Press, 1989.

Taylor, Mark C. "The Eventuality of Texts." *Semeia.* 51: 215-240, 1990.

Tracy, David. *Plurality and Ambiguity.* New York: Harper and Row, 1987.

Ulmer, Gregory. *Applied Grammatology.* Baltimore: Johns Hopkins University Press, 1985.

Wakefield, Neville. *Postmodernism: The Twilight of the Real.* London: Pluto Press, 1990.

Walhout, Clarence and Leland Ryken, eds. *Contemporary Literary Theory. A Christian Appraisal.* Grand Rapids, MI: Eerdmans, 1992.

Wicke, Jennifer. "Postmodernism: The Perfume of Information." *The Yale Journal of Criticism* 1: 145-60, 1988.

Wink, Walter. *The Bible in Human Transformation. Toward a New Paradigm for Biblical Study.* Philadelphia: Fortress Press, 1973.

Wyschogrod, Edith. *Saints and Postmodernism. Revisioning Moral Philosophy.* Chicago: University of Chicago Press, 1990.

A Conversation With Robert Detweiler

SHARON E. GREENE

Q.   Well, an obvious first question is, what do you think of a volume of essays in your honor?

A.   There's an old story in which somebody—I think it was Winston Churchill—has a Member of Parliament pointed out to him, with the comment, "There goes a modest man." To which Churchill is supposed to have replied, "Yes, and he has much to be modest about." I feel like that—having much to be modest about, to the extent that such a volume seems totally unearned to me. At the same time, I take it as a gesture of community as many of my contributing friends and I myself try to define community: a gracious space where we can think/play/play out interpretive possibilities.

Q.   You just started out with story and finished up with interpretation. Isn't that what your writing is about?

A.   Indeed it is, and I'd like to think that my teaching embodies that pattern as well. But yes, I have been deeply interested in story, in narrative, throughout my career, and in the interplay between narrative and interpretation. The truth is that I am far more fascinated by story, any kind of story, than by its formal articulations in "serious" literature. Story has an elemental quality for me; it's virtually a primal mode of expression that can, certainly, be interpreted but not improved upon. The older I get, the less concerned I am with interpreting narrative and the more with nurturing it, celebrating it, and letting it be itself. This is, of course, my preparation for becoming an ancient mariner, when I'll latch on to people at all sorts of august gatherings and make them listen to my tales.

Q.   Heaven forbid; I'll muzzle you. What is the history of this fascination with story?

A.   What a question. I think it has to do with two—three—moments (probably more) in my past. The first occurred in my childhood, when I had to sit through endless sermons in Mennonite churches in eastern Pennsylvania, terribly bored, and would become alert only when the preachers would tell a story—usually some sort of bathetic tale in which the wayward son would accept Jesus, kneeling and weeping beside his mother's deathbed (I think this is where I got my taste for soap opera), but a story nonetheless. In other words, these stories were the high points in the midst of dreary verbiage, and so I came to value, probably overvalue, story. The second was in my young adulthood, when I was a refugee relief worker in the 1950s in what was then West Germany and listened over a number of years literally to thousands of war-and-suffering stories told by the many kinds of survivors. These had a profound effect on me; in some ways I have never recovered from them. They are a part of my identity, although I was not the sufferer. They taught me that narrative and survival are intertwined, indeed that story finally is always, one way or another, about survival. The third has to do with you, specifically the precious experience (the story) of how, over many years, our narratives have become intertwined, to the extent that I can't think my story without thinking yours. In this context I've learned how story is erotic in the deepest and fullest sense. So there you have it: boredom, survival, and eros are behind my fascination with story.

Q.   You just told a story, one that pleases me. Your comments on survival lead me to another subject: the interest in apocalypse that appears, it seems, more and more in your writing. What's going on here?

A.   You noticed, then? That too, I think, is the result of three impulses—and I promise that after this response I'll stop being trinitarian. First, I grew up in eastern Pennsylvania half-believing that the Last Judgment was around the corner, as it were, because this is what I was taught. And it was not just the millenarian Mennonites who believed this, many other religious groups did as well—encouraged among other things by the signs-of-the-times of the second world war, Hitler as the Antichrist and all that. Second, when I lived and worked in Germany in the 1950s, experienced the results of the Hamburg firebombing, saw what was left of the death camps, I felt sometimes as though the Apocalypse had already happened and that we were living out some sort of bad dream as aftermath. Third, much more recently and like many others, I have become acutely aware of human destruction of the planet and have tried to shape my own protests against this insanity, as a literary critic, via utilizing the sensationalist imagery of apocalypticism. And I should add a fourth impulse—I should have thought of this before—which comes from reading a number of contemporary novelists employing apocalyptic scenarios: Martin Amis, Paul Auster, Maggie Gee, B. Wongar, Günter Grass, J. G.

Ballard, Margaret Atwood, Walker Percy are a few who come to mind. These are artists I read and respect and want to write about, people who want to save us from ourselves and who can get quite shameless in their shock tactics.

Keep in mind, too, that the term "apocalypse" comes from Greek *apocalyptein*, "to reveal." I'm as much interested in the revelatory aspects of apocalyptic writing as in its cataclysmic dimensions, and of course I'm fascinated by the connections between revelation and catastrophe, or cataclysm. One could suggest, without going too far afield, that all narrative one way or another, not just apocalyptic kinds, is involved in revelation and cataclysm. It is in the nature of story that it proceeds via telling itself, unfolding itself to us, and it is also in the nature of story that it has to end. Critics like Walter Benjamin and Peter Brooks have argued that the movement of story toward its inevitable ending emulates the human "unfolding" toward death, so the intertwined fates of story and human life are aligned to death.

Q.   But death isn't necessarily catastrophic or cataclysmic. What are you getting at?

A.   I think that death is often enough catastrophic to have earned the general association, and even a quiet and peaceful death is catastrophic insofar as it brings an end to our existence. And narrative, in formal and folk literature, tends to emphasize catastrophic death, a reflex that one sees in classical tragedy, where the term "catastrophe" means "denouement," ending. By the way, the moment of *anagnorisis* or recognition in classical tragedy (e.g., when Agave in *The Bacchae* comes to her senses and realizes that she's killed Pentheus, her son) is to my mind part of the rhythm—a central and heightened part—of revelation that constitutes all narrative. What I'm getting at, I think—you started this by asking about apocalypse on my mind—is that apocalypse in the sense I've been describing it intrigues me not only because of its sensationalist aspects but also—mainly—because it seems to be foundational to story. One could say that apocalyptic narrative, then, the sort that deals in catastrophe, is a heightening or intensification of the key elements that appear in all narrative.

Q.   I gather from what you just said—that death is catastrophic because it brings an end to our existence—that you don't believe in an afterlife?

A.   In human immortality? No, I don't.

Q.   How does that belief—or non-belief—square with your identity as a literature and religion critic?

A. Well, for one, the fact that I am such a critic doesn't mean that I must confess a certain set of religious beliefs, one of which might be a belief in a personal life after death. But having said that, then, I'd like to comment on the modern history of immortality.

Q. Feel free—just don't take an eternity.

A. I'm not sure that I can think clearly under that kind of pressure. Anyhow, I suppose that by "the modern history of immortality" I mean my personal history of coming to terms with the fact that I, and you, and the other people I dearly love will die, and that's it. I spent about the first two decades of my life believing that we Christians, and maybe a very few lucky others, would experience eternal life, then the next two decades getting gradually used to the idea that this wouldn't happen, and the next two occasionally contemplating what the concept of immortality can be made to mean, valuably, for humans who cannot believe in the traditional Christian projection of eternal life. I remember specifically, when I was studying theology in the mid-1950s at the University of Hamburg and encountering the heady thinking of European existentialism—a thinking that has profoundly marked me, more than anything else other than my Anabaptist heritage—how I slowly became aware that discussion of an afterlife, of human immortality, was, if not an outright taboo subject, at least one that was a sort of embarrassment for liberal European theologians. Probably it was part of the embarrassment about discussions of corporeality that continue to be extremely difficult for Christian and other theologies—more on that later, if you like. My guess is that theologians then, as many now, didn't talk much about eternal life because they recognized its impossibility but didn't know what to say about it, or what to put in its place.

Q. Wait! Are you saying that it is possible to be a Christian, or some other sort of religious believer, without believing in a personal immortality?

A. That is exactly what I'm saying. I realize, of course, that millions of people still hold on to the vision of a heaven that they will inhabit forever, and I respect that faith; it has, among other things, tremendous therapeutic value for times of adversity and grief. But it is not a vision that I myself can draw on, and a challenge for me as a literary critic interested in the religious imagination is to discover what "existential" meaning the concept of eternal life might have.

Q. Give us the truth.

A. It's not easy to lay these things out to skeptics like you, but as I used to say during my scuba diving years in Florida, there are no atheists in sinkholes.

Q. I think we'll strike that in the final version.

A.   I thought this was the final version—which returns us to the subject at hand. Reflecting on eternal life these days for me means the usual things: we'll live on through our children, through the species, through our accomplishments, and so on, which are not circumstances of great solace for someone who would want heaven to be a consciously-experienced, idealized extension of our comfortable First World existences. Woody Allen (are we allowed to talk about him?) once asked something along the lines of, where will you get your laundry done in heaven? It is not an insignificant question. My reflection also leads me to realize that eternal life would not necessarily be a good thing. Julian Barnes in the final (appropriately) chapter of *The History of the World in 10 1/2 Chapters* devises a narrative that suggests some of the complexities of immortality; among other things, it could get extremely boring, so boring that you might eventually choose nothingness instead.

Q.   Don't look at me; it's not my argument.

A.   How they abandon us in our time of need. But above all, reflecting on eternal life and immortality leads me to think that what we know of the cosmos, of time and space, is so limited that it is hubristic for us to conjecture—as I have been doing—on the possibility or impossibility of human, personal immortality. Stephen Hawking (who is assuredly no Christian), according to the news magazines, has been thinking thoughts about the nature of temporality and spatiality that are more radical than those he expressed in *A Brief History of Time*—for example, that our memories via the laws of entropy create the "myth" that time runs forward, whereas in fact it might run the other way, or that the "information" that disappears into black holes actually finds its way into another universe.

I wish I had the basis for understanding more of this—you're talking to someone who failed ninth-grade algebra. The point, though, is that Hawking is developing narratives consonant with our contemporary world picture to imagine reality—a late-twentieth century version of what visionaries of any and every age have done to explain themselves and their universe—and I find that his fictions fire my own imagination. The short version (you'll be relieved to learn) of what I'm fumbling to say is that my thoughts, such as they are, of a possible immortality are much more attuned to the speculations that Hawking projects than to attempts to rehabilitate the traditional Christian concept of an eternal life. And notice that I did not say "the New Testament" concept. I am not at all sure that the "original" gospel message had much to say about eternal life. The Gospel of Mark ending with the crucifixion rather than the resurrection is deeply important to me. It enables me to think of Jesus' death as a crucial (a pun there?) end, the consequences of which have not yet been explored, other than by courageous folks like Tom Altizer, and which open up to late-century mythologizing such as Hawking is attempting.

Q.   I think I'd better ask another question, or this could go on forever. What about the embarrassment over corporeality that you mentioned awhile ago?

A.   Once again we begin with my heritage, and I hope this is not getting too tedious. In my childhood and youth, the unclothed body and often the clothed one, virtually all expressions of sexuality, indeed the whole world of eros were considered to be if not outright sinful at least very dangerous to the state of one's soul. Thus appreciation of the body, above all the sexual body, was repressed, with the result that the body became a locus of a special repressed attention, a kind of sacred taboo. We all know about this. The taboo may have been stronger in my religious context and generation, but in significant ways it's still with us. We've now commodified the body and sexuality, as the Marxists like to put it. The result has not been a genuine liberation toward enjoying our corporeality, including our sexuality—I doubt that we'd recognize such a liberation if it were offered to us; rather, I think, we've substituted prurience for a sense of shame—Freud's return of the repressed with a vengeance. One could say that whereas a few decades ago we were secret voyeurs, now we're overt watchers of each other's erotic displays.

Q.   Isn't voyeurism by its very nature secret?

A.   One would think so, but we seem to have managed to maintain a kind of prurience, as I just called it, in our watching that has overtones of secrecy even though it is public. The ultimate commodification of the body and of sexuality these days takes place, of course, in the pornography industry, a multimillion dollar annual business in the United States, and this is also the ultimate prurient public voyeurism. Whatever one may think of porn—whether it is harmful or not—its popularity through, for example, videos for private, "home" use, is hardly, to my mind, a healthy expression of liberated eros. It is, rather, still an obsession with a sacred taboo, an attempt to see others in their most intimate, "secret" moments, even though the secrecy has been put on display. I think that much of what fascinates us in the extreme violence in cinema and television these days—which to me is far more pornographic than sexual displays—also has to do with our prurient curiosity—watching others in intimate postures of injuring and killing, being hurt and killed.

In a way my own career has been involved in such commodification. This would almost have to be the case with anyone who focuses on modern, specifically late-twentieth-century fiction in teaching and writing as I have done, since much of this literature is sex-obsessed. Who knows, since I just evoked Freud: maybe I turned to this literature as my academic focus because unconsciously I wanted to explore my way through the repressions of eros. At any rate, I can remember fairly precisely the moment when I discovered the nexus of fiction and commodification of sexuality. It was when I read John Updike's first Rabbit novel, *Rabbit, Run*, in 1960. Here was a narrative that was graphic in its sexuality (although minimally violent), very well written, and clearly destined to sell because it made private moments public. The fact that the plot itself deals with matters of shame, prurience, and commodification of sex (the protagonist has a typical mid-century convoluted, juvenile male attitude toward sex) makes that novel still more a major example of sex going public in the arts. And as you know, the next three Rabbit novels continued and expanded the prurient sexuality theme without portraying much, if any, sense of maturation about sex in the characters. Thus the quartet stands as a literary expression of our paradoxical relationship to sex and the body: we remain simultaneously fascinated and frustrated by them, relating to them mainly as a force and an object to possess and control.

In any case, since a dominant theme of late-century literature is sex and sexuality, it is something I have addressed often in my teaching and writing, and sometime—before I get too old to remember why it interested me—I'd like to write a substantial study on eros in modern (and so-called postmodern) fiction.

Q.　Who are other writers who interest you, other than Updike, who address sexuality and the body?

A.　The question might well be, which writers *don't*, since the theme is so ubiquitous. But I think of, at random, Martin Amis, Graham Swift, Margaret Atwood, Patrick White (now long gone), Peter Carey, Toni Morrison, Harry Crews, Cecile Pineda (a wonderfully funny West Coast novelist, author of *The Love Queen of the Amazon*), Edna O'Brien (one of the best), our friend Betsy Vaughn, Gabriel Garcia-Marquez—where does one stop? Garcia-Marquez, not incidentally, in *Love in the Time of Cholera* has one of the most moving depictions of obsessive love and senior-citizen eros I have ever read. Of course, we don't have all that many depictions of senior-citizen eros, do we?

Q.　Speak for yourself. Do you want to talk about John Updike, since people who don't know you through your work on literature and religion probably know your writing on Updike?

A.   Not particularly, or at least not very much. I've pretty well had my say on Updike. He was important to me in my own growth as an interpreter of literature, and I think he has written some of the better English-language fiction of the twentieth century, particularly in some short stories. He is also an excellent essayist, and I see him in some ways as a scholar-manqué, someone who really wanted to write academic prose and found himself a successful novelist instead—the reverse of many literature professors. We should all be such "failures." But I am disappointed by the fact that his characters remain remarkably childish in their attitudes toward and expressions of sexuality. Here is a major chronicler of American sexuality whose fictional characters seem to have learned nothing about sex and the body other than how complicated and tricky they can be. One could argue, of course, that he portrays things this way as a realist, because we Americans persist in juvenile attitudes about sex ourselves. But I would have liked to find some maturation emerging as Updike himself ages. Nevertheless, the fact that I just taught a seminar on the Rabbit novels to Danish students in Copenhagen should suggest that I'm not all that disillusioned.

Q.   You hinted at literature professors wishing to write fiction. Do you want to talk about your novel?

A.   Must we?

Q.   I'm afraid so.

A.   Well, they say that every literature professor has a novel in him or her. Mine got out recently, as you know, but I doubt very much that it will ever see publication. As you also know, it's an entertainment, an indulgence, at best a candidate for one of the "airport trade" presses.

Q.   Tell us what it's about.

A.   It's full of sensational goodies: kidnapping, international terrorism, blowing up oil wells, ancient Nazis raising hell. It's terribly violent, which probably has some connection to my pacifist past (and present).

Q.   No sex? And it is violent, although you just said that you find violence in film and television to be pornographic?

A.   Not much sex. I had enough trouble controlling the terrorists, without trying to deal with sexual tensions. As to the violence, I don't think that I glorified it. In a few places, at any rate, I have some of the violent characters condemning the very violence they promulgate.

Q.   So why did you write the novel, if you don't think it's going anywhere?

A.   For a number of reasons, and I really am not making these up after the fact. For one, I fly fairly frequently, and it's been my habit for years to buy and read espionage novels in airports and on planes—I'm one of the reasons such fiction is referred to as "airport trade." Some of these novels are pretty awful, and I'd tell myself while reading them that I could do better, and so eventually I tried it. A second reason is that I had long wanted to view the modern fiction that I teach from the other side, from the perspective of a creator of it. Now, 600 pages later, no matter how inept the result may be, I've gone through that experience, and it has been immensely helpful—to the extent that I cannot teach fiction the way I did before undertaking this fairly large project myself. I learned above all something about the constant choices a novelist has to make—choices that cause a behavior or an action to go this way rather than that—and then live with them. I've also become more alert to the nuances of presenting dialogue, of suggesting as much as possible with as few words as possible, of developing metaphoric patterns throughout a whole text, things like that. All of which is to say that I've gained even more respect for the writer's craft and try to convey that respect when I teach fiction. A third reason is that I've been intrigued for many years by the nature of terrorism—yet another result of living off and on in western Europe during the Seventies and Eighties—and in my novel I gave myself the chance to speculate, from the inside, what might go on in a terrorist's mind.

Q. Isn't another reason that in your heart of hearts you hope that you *will* get it published?

A. Absolutely, although I do think that the chances are not good. Nevertheless, I am about to try to find an enterprising agent somewhere who will agree to market it.

Q. Will you use a pseudonym?

A. Yes indeed. I'm thinking that something like "John LeCarré" might help to sell it to a publisher. Let's change the subject.

Q. All right; you pick one.

A. Let's get back to apocalypticism.

Q. I should have known better. Do you want to discuss the rapture?

A. Not really. I wanted to report on a discovery, something that people like Bill Doty have known about for a long time and that I am just encountering. I'm at work on a book on American literature, religion, and the public sphere, which has led me to look for moments in American history that represent critical junctures of religion and public life which have been treated in fiction. In the process of searching I started looking into Native American history and writing—Ann-Janine Morey started this a few years back by insisting that I read Louise Erdrich. One thing led to another, and I stumbled upon Native American apocalypticism in the form of the events leading up to the Lakota (Sioux) ghost dance that in part provoked the massacre at Wounded Knee in 1890. We have no space to dwell on this here, but I'm referring to the combination of Indian sacred tradition and Christian influence that led some of the Lakotas, in their desperation and distress, to anticipate an apocalypse inspired by a ghost dance that would bring back the ancestors (who were the "ghosts" of the ghost dance), the buffalo, the pristine plains, and rid them of the murderous whites. That in turn led me to further reading, much of it by Native Americans such as James Welch and Frank Fools Crow, on the continuing tragedy of Native American existence in the United States.

It's situations such as this that cause me to remark that for some the Apocalypse has already occurred in the most literal sense. Many American Indian nations have been the target of attempted genocide or left to die a slow death on the reservations or both, and their oral narratives as well as their writing reveal an apocalyptic awareness far more acute than the playing-around with so-called biblical prophecy and speculation that occupies a few million other Americans. In other words, if you're interested in an update on the Apocalypse, bracket the Book of Revelation for a bit and observe what Native Americans have been suffering for generations.

My own revelation in this context is simply, and so late, to be learning some of the dimensions of this national tragedy. Now that I am, I am stunned, appalled, and ashamed. I know, of course, that Native Americans have been "discovered" at last and have become a somewhat fashionable cause, but I doubt that this kind of attention will make much difference. It will not because the implications are so overwhelming and are, finally, theological. One aspect of the tragedy, which is also a deep irony, affects the whites as much as the Indians: it is that we have not merely stolen the land but have ruined it. Our colonial ancestors, had they not been so intent in imposing their own economies (in the broadest sense) on the "new world," might have learned something from the native dwellers about honoring the land rather than subjugating it. They might, in other words, have learned something of the Indian regard for the earth as sacred space and of living in harmony with the land instead of exploiting and destroying it.

Q. Aren't you romanticizing the Native American past?

A. Possibly. But I don't think that American Indians were fundamentally any better or worse than anyone else; they had merely evolved an ecology that was superior to that practiced by your and my industrializing forebears. We missed our chance to adopt it or at least adapt it. Now we live in a blighted landscape and with a perverted attitude toward the natural world. Somewhere, years ago, I read in a Faulkner text about the curse on our land resulting not only from our enslavement of black Africans but also from our treatment of the Indians, and I didn't altogether comprehend what he meant. Now I understand more of it. We are condemned to an environment of congested roads, the spreading cancer of strip malls, dying cities, polluted waters, and all the rest. And our sacred space—another irony—is concentrated in our churches, temples, mosques: buildings that are actually mainly tributes to the spirit of exploitation and control.

Q. That's pretty strong language from someone who explores cathedrals as an avocation.

A. I am fascinated by the old cathedrals, as you know. They awe me. But they also represent to me an aggressive, hegemonic attitude that uses an aspect of religion, the vision of a better spiritual world elsewhere, to exploit the natural world—what's left of it nowadays.

Q. What's the connection to apocalypticism?

A. Well, for one, the tragedy of Native Americans leads me to see how a world can end for a whole group of people without the planet itself disappearing. But for another, the death of our planet does not strike me as a fanciful projection, although the end will not, I think, take place via the nuclear apocalypse that Jonathan Schell describes in *The Fate of the Earth*. I believe the chances are far better that we will eventually destroy ourselves through the continuing destruction of our resources, the accompanying accumulation of waste, and the effects of pollution. We are now seriously contaminating Antarctica, according to the media, the last pristine place on earth, and American scientists are among the worst offenders. Is it necessary that *every* place become a site of investigation? Can't a few spots simply be left alone? Anyhow, this projection of a world ending via waste doesn't have the sensational attraction of a fiery cataclysm, but it's more realistic. It also has a kind of aptness: the civilizations, and the US foremost among them, built on waste may finally be overwhelmed by it.

Q. May we leave the Apocalypse now?

A. I think it's high time.

Q. And now, as they say, for something quite different: you recently wrote an autobiographical essay for a forthcoming collection.

A. Yes. Mine is one of about fourteen such essays by academicians, edited by John Lee at Calvin College. He asked us to tell our stories in any way we wanted, and then briefly reflect on why we chose the strategies we did.

Q. That last is what I'm getting at. You organized your personal story in terms of the classical four elements—earth, air, fire, and water—

commented at the end that these are also Jungian archetypes, but then went on to state some skepticism about the use of Jungian materials. Do we detect some ambivalence about Jung here in someone who has written a fair amount of myth-oriented literary criticism?

A.   I did say that about Jung, didn't I? Actually, I said something to the effect that I am no great friend of Jungian thought, but that doesn't deflect your comment about ambivalence. Yes, I'm of two (or more) minds about Jung and about myth criticism as a whole. They can be easily abused and turned into reinforcing materials for all sorts of enthusiasms such as the current New Age fads. As a result I tend to be cautious about my involvement with Jung and myth studies. Having said that, though, I must add that I have found much of great value in Jung—aspects of the theory of archetypes, for example—and that I find myth criticism, undertaken in a disciplined way, to be invigorating. The way David Miller uses it, for instance, is exemplary.

Q.   I gather then that you are not much impressed with channeling.

A.   The only channeling I've ever experienced was crossing the English one, and every time I've done that I've got seasick. That should tell you something.

Q.   Let's talk about something fairly obvious that we haven't yet addressed. What do you think about the future of the literature-and-religion enterprise?

A.   That's very complicated. At the moment, as an academic discipline, or interdiscipline, it doesn't seem to have much of a future, at least not in terms of the job market. Very few colleges or universities or seminaries are advertising positions in literature and religion. That doesn't strike me, though, as necessarily a bad thing, although it obviously isn't happy news for young PhDs on the job market who identify themselves as literature-and-religion specialists. I myself never had formal training in the interdiscipline but rather was educated, in separate programs, in literature (English and German) and in theology and was prepared to compete for a position in an English department. I landed in one (actually in a number) of those, where I developed my own "expertise" in the relationships of literature to theology and religion over the years. I still think that such an education is the most practical, in terms of the academic job market. Whether one's base is literature or religion, one needs to gain a PhD level competence in that field and then attempt to develop a secondary expertise in the other field and in the interrelations of the two. We try to offer that kind of education at Emory, even though it takes place for the most part in our interdisciplinary institute.

What I have just said, though, merely reacts to the present situation in American higher education. I think that the fortunes of fields such as literature-and-religion will change radically as higher education itself undergoes necessary change.

Q. What kind of changes do you have in mind?

A. I foresee at least three. First, it's become a cliché to say that the academic disciplines are breaking down and that reconfigurations are taking place, because we've been saying this at least since the Sixties. Some folks doubt the truth of this, especially in these recent years of conservatism and economic distress that have led many schools to stress the old disciplinary boundaries and identities. I think, though, that the reconfigurations are inevitable and that some of them will surprise us. They will consist not only of intellectual fields or subject areas but also of amalgams of subject areas (e.g., English literature, cultural anthropology) with computer technology, geopolitical forces, education outside the classroom and library, and so on. In fact, I would guess that certain institutions will emerge to compete with colleges and universities (maybe even with the primary and secondary schools) for the education of the citizenry, not least because the colleges and universities are pricing themselves beyond the reach of so many and, in some instances, are not delivering what one might expect for the price. Too many, I fear, are selling prestige—or trying to—rather than a substantive education.

What does any of this mean for a relatively insignificant endeavor like the combined study of literature and religion? Who knows? It surely means that unless those of us who work in this field stay alert to the changes, not only anticipate them but envision and implement them, the field itself will become increasingly marginalized and eventually disappear. I catch a glimmer of what an invigorated study of literature-and-religion could be like in David Jasper's Centre for the Study of Literature and Theology at the University of Glasgow. David's program functions within the conservative confines of British higher education (a situation remarkable in itself), and that's not where I see the promise. I see it rather in the manner in which he and his colleagues manage to bring together an array of students and visiting professors from a variety of countries, disciplines, and even socio-cultural backgrounds. The mix is a great stimulus and no doubt will generate more problems than resolutions, but that's all right. Such situations teach one to learn to ask the important questions. I wish we could create such an environment in North America; flying to Glasgow gets expensive.

A second change I foresee is in the rehabilitation of the craft of teaching. Some of the signs are here at last. In this effort I suspect that the liberal arts colleges, where effective teaching has never wholly lost its status, will be the leaders rather than the so-called research universities. I believe that the reconfiguration of what we teach will be joined by an examination of how we teach and learn. It's hard to overcome the prejudices that one brings to this matter; we reflect on the nature of teaching, recall various ed-psych disasters we have encountered, and identify these with projects of pedagogy. But there are other ways of teaching and practicing good teaching, and we need to engage them: committed team-teaching, interactive education, workplace education are a few of the challenges. Of course, little will change until we rethink the suppositions and reward systems connected to PhD educations for college and university level "teaching" that are in reality training in specialized research and publication—educations that not only do not prepare one to teach but that can hinder the possibility of learning how to teach.

And that is the third change I foresee, although this may be wishful thinking. What we in academe tend not to talk about is the research and publication apparatus we've set in motion that has tens of thousands trying to publish in thousands of journals and with hundreds of presses and really having little of any importance to say. A main reason for this effort, as everyone knows, is that it serves as a ritual for establishing and promoting careers: publication leads to tenure, promotion, status, higher salary, power (such as it is in academe). I do not mean to denigrate academic research and publication, but I do think that we have lost perspective on them and have allowed them to dominate our educational efforts in harmful, wasteful ways.

Q.   Aren't you a part of what you're criticizing here?

A.   Of course I am, as complicit as anybody. In fact, since I studied for some years at the University of Hamburg in the mid-Fifties, just at a time when the German universities (which supplied the model of research as the foundation of higher education) were becoming democratized, I subscribed without question to the assumption, then taking shape, that one had to be a prolific researcher/publisher in order to be a respectable university professor. I don't mean to say, having enjoyed most of a career that profited from this assumption, that we should now abruptly change the rules for the next generation. On the other hand, the present rules based on that assumption are not doing the next generation, or the one between them and me, much good, so that something *has* to happen.

I believe devoutly that a vital connection exists between research and good teaching, that all good teachers need to keep up with "research in their field," etc., but this doesn't mean that all, or most, college and university professors should be under pressure to write books and articles that only a few specialists, at best, will read, in order that the tenure and promotion committees have some evidence on which to base their decisions. In fact, I think that many of these research projects allow us to narrow our focus to something manageable, something that can be theoretically resolved, and divert us from dealing with the really critical problems of education.

Q. Like what?

A. Like the fact that the humanities do not humanize, or that the sciences do not teach wisdom, or that we socialize our students toward becoming upper-middle replicas of ourselves, or that our society is becoming less and less morally and socially responsible. The modern university has taken itself off the hook by maintaining a stance of "objectivity": we just teach the so-called facts that we generate from our research, and somebody else should apply these toward societal improvement. Needless to say, I consider this a farce. I think that universities and colleges have above all an obligation toward moral education and that, indeed, if it doesn't raise moral questions it isn't education. If we spent some of the energy we put into our research for publication on developing ways of moral teaching—and gave this effort the kind of prestige that we now give to research and publication—we might have the start of a responsible higher education system.

Q. That's quite a tirade.

A. There's one more aspect of it. The "knowledge explosion" is happening—maybe it's more like a big bang—and that has, obviously, the greatest of implications for research and teaching. How can any of us keep up with the new information and opinion that flood our lives, or absorb and interpret them? We can't, of course, but we do an ever poorer job of it under the present habits of specialized, narrowly-focused research (that often tend to ignore the flood of knowledge) and publication. We need to balance such efforts with much more collegial collaboration: team-taught seminars, regularly scheduled informal discussions, computer correspondence, some of which (but not necessarily very much) might lead to formal publication. I need to mention Bill Doty one more time in this connection. I've learned a tremendous amount from Bill through his habit of sending to me, and surely a number of others, bibliographies, clippings, writing in progress, syllabi. This kind of networking will, I hope, become more and more common.

Q. You mentioned earlier your view that "the humanities don't humanize" and the failure, in essence, of contemporary education to educate. What do you have to say about the current trend of "politically correct" education?

A. I suppose I asked for that by running on about moral education. One question about political correctness is, of course, correct according to whose politics? Insofar as political correctness deals with labeling (an aspect of it that the media have overemphasized), it seems to me to focus on effects rather than causes. It is moderately helpful to call attention to demeaning terms for groups of persons, but changing the terms won't do much ultimately for these groups. Changing the terms may be a start, but it can also get in the way of more significant change. Beyond that, I'd like to see less confrontation and more dialogue, and I'd like the dialogue to be moderated by those very persons and groups who are said to be unfairly treated.

Insofar as political correctness in academe has to do with things such as changing the canon, I don't understand the polarization that has evolved on some campuses. You know: teach either the "patriarchal" Western tradition or teach "minority" texts. It seems to me that both sides need each other, or that all sides need the others, and that a group of rationally-minded faculty (is that an oxymoron?) ought to be able to work its way through to a balanced approach. Let me change that: I do understand the polarization, at least in part. It has to do with the fact that too many of us in higher education have not found the vision of an educational community. We may be collegial, but we tend not to commit ourselves to each other and to the institution. Is it too much to expect that we do that? Or shouldn't we ask, at least, why we don't value and practice such commitment?

Q. We need to bring this to a close. Let me ask you finally what you are least and most happy about in your career.

A. I'm least happy about the fact that after my three decades in higher education our society appears to be in worse shape than ever. I take this personally. I am most happy about the connections and friendships that have evolved over the years.

Q. Not about your writing?

A. Not really, although some of these friendships have developed through my writing, and although it's good to learn that people read some of what I have written and are influenced by it. But much more important is the personal dimension, and it's a pleasure to cast this too in the context of education. As you know, over twenty years of my career have been spent largely in graduate level education at Emory, which means working with, for the most part, doctoral students. Along the way I have encountered a number of remarkable, deeply interesting people, including some who are studying with me right now. And studying *with* me is exactly the right way to put it, since I have, over the years, in sum learned as much from them as they have from me. I have been blessed through this context that has allowed me to work so many years in an atmosphere of what I would have to describe as intense academic excitement.

Some of these people have become valuable friends. Others whom I've met through the academic network have become equally dear to me, and some of them, but by no means all, are in this volume. Folks like these make it worth-while and, more often than one has right to expect, outright joyful. I'm grateful.

TRANSCRIBER'S NOTES

When first approached by Mark Ledbetter and David Jasper about contributing to this collection of essays in honor of Robert Detweiler, my first reaction was to decline, not because I did not wish to participate, but because I did not believe I could do justice to the intent of the volume, never mind the honoree. What I proposed instead of a formal essay was an "interview" that would allow Robert Detweiler to voice some of his concerns, many of which have been expressed in his lectures over the past couple of years, some of which will yet find their way into print.

Although structured as a interview, the preceding is representative of many conversations (some might say "lively debates") I have had with Robert over dinner and a bottle of wine, joined on many occasions by some of the contributors to this volume. (Those of you who know him will not be surprised to learn that the first version of this "conversation" was entitled by Robert as "Interview with the VamBob.")

The puns and quick humor in which Robert Detweiler delights should not blind us, however, to the deep seriousness with which he addresses his diverse subjects. To illustrate only one of his concerns, that of the increasing voyeurism that pervades/invades our society: through Robert's work, one confronts head-on the uncomfortable shift from a (more or less) sacred to a secular, yes, even profane, society—from a society in which "His eye is on the sparrow" to that in which the stranger's/strangler's eye may be on you.

What relieves, for the moment at least, the tension inherent in that shift is the recognition that we are not alone in our anxiety. Whether his topic be narrative, religion and literature, visions of Apocalypse or the contemporary university, Robert returns to the concept of a community in which every member is given space for his or her voice to be heard, for each story to be shared. The coming-together of these voices seems particularly appropriate for a collection in honor of Robert Detweiler. After all, in this, as in other such celebrations, the sharing of stories is how we define and make our remembrance of each other.

NOTES ON CONTRIBUTORS

DAVID JASPER is Senior Lecturer and Director of the Centre for the Study of Literature and Theology in the University of Glasgow, Scotland. He was previously Principal of St. Chad's College, Durham University. His books include *The New Testament and the Literary Imagination* (1987), *The Study of Literature and Religion* (Second Ed, 1993), and *Rhetoric, Power, and Community* (1993).

MARK LEDBETTER is an Associate Professor of Religion at Millsaps College, Jackson, Mississippi. He is the author of *Virtuous Intentions* (1989, Scholars Press) and *Doing Violence to the Body: An Ethic of Reading and Writing*, (forthcoming, Macmillan, Fall 1994).

PETER MEINKE is a poet and short story writer who just retired after 27 years directing the Writing Workshop at Eckerd College (formerly Florida Presbyterian College, where he taught with Bob Detweiler). Currently the Visiting Distinguished Writer at the University of Hawaii, Mr. Meinke's most recent book is *Liquid Paper: New & Selected Poems*. His collection of stories, *The Piano Tuner*, won the 1986 Flannery O'Connor Award.

MIEKE BAL is Professor of the Theory of Literature at the University of Amsterdam and Adjunct Visiting Professor of Visual and Cultural Studies at the University of Rochester. Her most recent books are *Reading Rembrandt: Beyond the Word-Image Opposition* and *On Meaning Making:Essays in Semiotics*.

DAVID L, MILLER, Ph.D., is Watson-Ledden Professor of Religions at Syracuse University. He is a member of the Eranos Circle and lectures widely in the United States, Canada, Europe, and Japan. His writings include a fifteen-year, multivolume project demonstrating the mythic background and the literary foreground of Christian theological doctrines

(*Christs; Three Faces of God: Traces of the Trinity in Literature and Life*; *Hell and Holy Ghosts*), and his book, *The New Polytheism* has been translated into French, Italian, and Japanese.

CHRISTOPHER NORRIS was, until last year, a Professor of English and is now Professor of the History of Ideas at the University of Wales in Cardiff. His publications include *William Empson and the Philosophy of Literary Criticism* (1978) and a number of volumes on phiolosophical aspects of deconstruction; also - more recently- *Spinoza and the Origins of Modern Literary Theory* (1990), *Uncritical Theory: Postmodernism, Intellectuals and the Gulf War* (1992), and *The Truth About Postmodernism* (1993). His latest book, to be published in 1994, is entitled *Staying for an Answer Criticism, Truth and the Ethics of Enquiry.*

MARY GERHART is a Professor of Religious Studies at Hobart and William Smith Colleges. She is the author of *The Question of Belief in Literary Criticism: An Introduction to the Hermeneutical Theory of Paul Ricoeur* coauthor of *Metaphoric Process: The Creation of Scientific and Religious Understanding*, and coeditor of *Morphologies of Faith: Essays in Religion and Culture in Honor of Nathan A. Scott, Jr.*

GREGORY C. BRUCE is currently living and working on a farm in Marietta, Georgia. His dissertation, *Bakhtin on Self and Other*, is forthcoming in the Academy Series of The Amercian Academy of Religion. His first novel, near completion, considers "Southern views on sacred spaces, old and new."

DAVID S. PACINI teaches 19th Century Studies at the Candler School of Theology and in the Graduate Division of Religion, Emory University where he also serves as Chair of the Department of Historical Studies in Theology and Religion.

ROBERT L. BLAKELY is an associate professor of anthropology at Georgia State University in Atlanta. He received the Ph. D. degree in anthropology from Indiana University. Blakely's research focuses o the skeletal biology, paleoepidemiology, paleodemography, paleonutrition of prehistoric and historic Native Americans and African-Americans. He edited *Biocultural Adaptation in Prehistoric America* (1977) and *The King Site Continuity and Contact in Sixteenth-Century Georgia* (1988).

BETTINA DETWEILLER-BLAKELY has a unique relationship with Robert Detweiler: She is his daughter. Detweiler-Blakely holds a B.A. degree with honors in anthropology, and serves as a librarian for Georgia State University while preparing for graduate studies. In collaboration with Robert Blakely, she has explored the wellness of prehistoric and historic Native Americans and nineteenth-century African-Americans. Her interests in anthropolgy include skeletal biology, odontolgy, paleopathology, paleoepidemiology, and biomedicine.

GREGORY SALYER is currently Assistant Professor of Religion and Philosophy at Huntingdon College in Montgomery, Alabama. In 1992-93 he served as Assistant Director of the Graduate Institute of the Liberal Arts at Emory University. He has published in *The Journal of Literature and Theology* and *Semeia*.

ANN-JANINE MOREY is the director of General Education and Professor of English at Southern Illinois University at Carbondale, where she teaches American literature, Religion and Literature, and Women's Fiction. She is the author of *Apples and Ashes: Culture, Metaphor and Morality in the American Dream* (Scholars Press 1982), *Religion and Sexuality in American Literature* (Cambridge UP 1992), and numerous articles on religion and literature.

BARBARA DECONCINI is Executive Director of the American Academy of Religion and Professor of Religion and Culture at Emory University. The author of Narrative Remembering (University Press of America, 1990), she completed the PhD in Religion and Literature in Emory's Graduate Institute of the Liberal Arts in 1980, where she discovered -- under Robert Detweiler's tutelage--that graduate work in the humanities can be a humanizing activity.

DAVIS PERKINS (Ph.D.-Vanderbilt) has worked for Scholars Press, Fortress Press, Abingdon Press, and he is currently Director of Westminster/John Knox Press in Louisville, KY. His goal in life is to acquire one-half of Robert Detweiler's wisdom by the time he is twice Detweiler's current age.

WILLIAM G. DOTY is a professor of interdisciplinary humanities at the University of Alabama/ Tuscaloosa. He serves as the National Coordinator for the annual American Academy of Religion competition for the best book in the field. In addition to his work in religious studies, Doty has edited two volumes on interdisciplinary education and a volume of essays on a short story by MArgaret Atwood entitled The Daemonic Imagination: Biblical Text and Secular Story. Both The Mythical Trickster Figure: Contours, Context, and Criticisms and Myths of Masculinity were published in 1993. Picturing Cultural Values in Postmodern America will appear in 1994.

JAMES CHAMPION is a native of Canada. He completed his BA and MA degrees in English at Simon Fraser University in British Columbia and received his PhD in Religion and Literature at the Graduate Institute of the Liberal Arts at Emory University. His dissertation is called *Doubts and Intuitions, Suspicion and Trust: the Hermeneutics of Modern Literature and Religion*. Jim has published articles in the *Journal of Literature and Theology*, *Religion and Intellectual Life*, and *Soundings* and is currently a Lilly Fellow in Humanities and the Arts at Valparaiso University.

DAVID E. KLEMM is Associate Professor of Theology and Ethics at the School of Religion, University of Iowa.

IRENA MAKARUSHKA is an Associate Professor of Religion at Bowdoin College in Brunswick, Maine. She is the author of *Religious Imagination in Emerson and Nietzsche*. She has also written articles on religion and culture. She is currently working on a book on gender, film, and violence.

DANIEL C. NOEL is Professor of Liberal Studies in Religion and Culture at Vermont College of Norwich University. He is the editor of *Paths to the Power of Myth: Joseph Campbell and the Study of Religion* (1990) and the author of *Approaching Earth: A Search for the Mythic Significance of the Space Age* (1986) as well as numerous articles at the intersections of religion, the arts, psychology, and myth studies.

CAROLYN JONES is an Assistant Professor of Religious Studies in English at Louisiana State University. She received her PhD from the University of Virginia in 1991. She has published several articles in journals like African American Review and Callaloo.

VERNON K. ROBBINS is Professor of Religion at Emory University, Atlanta, Georgia. He is author of *Jesus the Teacher* (1984); *Patterns of Persuasion in the Gospels* (with Burton L. Mack, 1989); *Ancient Quotes and*

Anecdotes (1989); and *New Boundaries in Old Territory* (1993). Robbins is currently developing socio-rhetorical criticism into a programmatic method of interdisciplinary interpretation.

GARY A. PHILLIPS is an Associate Professor of Religious Studies at the College of the Holy Cross in Worcester, Massachusetts. His doctoral training in Biblical Studies, Linguistics and theology was at Vanderbilt University and the Sorbonne. Working in the area of gsspel studies, literary and cultural criticism, he is the co-author of the collaboratively written *The Postmodern Bible* and the forthcoming *Scribes and Texts: Making Parables, Making Readers in Matthew's Gospel*. At Holy Cross he serves as the Dirctor of the College's First Year Program and is orgnizer of the campus group Mean Against Violence Toward Women.

SHARON E. GREENE is the Director of Institutional Advancement and of the Work-Study Program at Ben Franklin Academy, a private, alternative high school in Atlanta. She holds a doctorate from the Institute of Liberal Arts at Emory University and wrote her dissertation on French feminist theory and literary criticism.